Short Stories for Mice.

This is mine please return

Handbook of
Memory Disorders

Handbook of Memory Disorders

Edited by

Alan D. Baddeley
Barbara A. Wilson
Fraser N. Watts

MRC Applied Psychology Unit,
Cambridge, UK

JOHN WILEY & SONS

Chichester · New York · Brisbane · Toronto · Singapore

Copyright © 1995 by John Wiley & Sons Ltd.
Baffins Lane, Chichester,
West Sussex PO19 1UD, England
National 01243 779777
International (+44) 1243 779777

Reprinted August 1995

Other Wiley Editorial Offices

John Wiley & Sons, Inc., 605 Third Avenue,
New York, NY 10158-0012, USA

Jacaranda Wiley Ltd, 33 Park Road, Milton,
Queensland 4064, Australia

John Wiley & Sons (Canada) Ltd, 22 Worcester Road,
Rexdale, Ontario M9W 1L1, Canada

John Wiley & Sons (SEA) Pte Ltd, 37 Jalan Pemimpin #05-04,
Block B, Union Industrial Building, Singapore 2057

Library of Congress Cataloging-in-Publication Data

Handbook of memory disorders / edited by Alan D. Baddeley, Barbara A.
Wilson, and Fraser N. Watts.
     p.   cm.
    Includes bibliographical references and index.
    ISBN 0-471-95078-5 (cased.)
    1. Memory disorders.   I. Baddeley, Alan D., *1934–*
II. Wilson, Barbara A.   III. Watts, Fraser N.
    [DNLM: 1. Memory Disorders.   WM 173.7 H2365 1995]
RC394.M46H38 1995
616.8'4—dc20
DNLM/DLC
for Library of Congress   94–28317
                                                               CIP

British Library Cataloguing-in-Publication Data

A catalogue record for this book is available from the British Library

ISBN 0-471-95078-5

Typeset in 10/12pt Times by Compuscript Ltd., Shannon, Co. Clare, Ireland.
Printed and bound in Great Britain by Bookcraft (Bath) Ltd.

Contents

About the Editors

Alan D. Baddeley, *MRC Applied Psychology Unit, 15 Chaucer Road, Cambridge CB2 2EF, England.*

Alan Baddeley is Director of the Medical Research Council Applied Psychology Unit in Cambridge, UK, and Professor of Cognitive Psychology at Cambridge University. He is a cognitive psychologist with broad interests in the functioning of human memory under both normal conditions and conditions of brain damage and stress.

Barbara A. Wilson, *MRC Applied Psychology Unit, 15 Chaucer Road, Cambridge CB2 2EF, England.*

Barbara Wilson is a senior scientist at the MRC Applied Psychology Unit. A clinical psychologist with particular interest in both the impact of neuropsychological memory deficits on everyday functioning and improving methods of neuro-rehabilitation, she was the founding editor of the journal *Neuropsychological Rehabilitation.*

Fraser N. Watts, *MRC Applied Psychology Unit, 15 Chaucer Road, Cambridge CB2 2EF, England.*

Fraser Watts is a clinical psychologist by training, with research interests in the influence of emotion on cognitive processes, including memory. The founding editor of the journal *Cognition and Emotion*, he recently moved from the Applied Psychology Unit to become the first holder of the Starbridge Lectureship in Science and Religion at Cambridge University, UK.

Contributors

Nicole D. Anderson, *Department of Psychology, University of Toronto, Toronto, Ontario M5S 1A1, Canada*

Alan D. Baddeley, *MRC Applied Psychology Unit, 15 Chaucer Road, Cambridge CB2 2EF, England*

George A. Bonanno, *Department of Psychology, The Catholic University of America, 620 Michigan Avenue NE, Washington, DC 20064, USA*

Jason Brandt, *Department of Psychiatry and Behavioral Sciences, Meyer 218, The Johns Hopkins Hospital, 600 N Wolfe Street, Baltimore, MD 21287-7218, USA*

Connie Cahill, *MRC Cyclotron Unit, Hammersmith Hospital, DuCane Road, London W12 0HS, England*

Laird S. Cermak, *Memory Disorders Research Center, Boston University School of Medicine, and Department of Veterans Affairs Medical Center, 150 South Huntington Avenue, Boston, MA 02130, USA*

Linda Clare, *Department of Psychology, University College London, 26 Bedford Way, London WCIE 6BT, England; and North-West Thames Regional Health Authority*

Fergus I.M. Craik, *Department of Psychology, University of Toronto, Toronto, Ontario M5S 1A1, Canada*

Antonio R. Damasio, *Department of Neurology, Division of Behavioral Neurology and Cognitive Neuroscience, University of Iowa College of Medicine, Iowa City, IA 52242, USA*

Chris Frith, *MRC Cyclotron Unit, Hammersmith Hospital, DuCane Road, London W12 0HS, England; and Department of Psychology, University College London, 26 Bedford Way, London WC1E 6BT, England*

Elizabeth L. Glisky, *Amnesia and Cognition Unit, Department of Psychology, University of Arizona, Tucson, AZ 85721, USA*

Hamish P.D. Godfrey, *Clinical Psychology Research and Training Centre, Department of Psychology, University of Otago, PO Box 56, Dunedin, New Zealand*

Georg Goldenberg, *Neurologisches Krankenhaus Rosenhügel, Riedelgasse 5, A- 1130 Vienna, Austria*

Felicia C. Goldstein, *Neurobehavioral Program, Department of Neurology, Emory University School of Medicine and Wesley Woods Center, 1841 Clifton Road NE, Atlanta, GA 30329, USA*

John R. Hodges, *Neurology unit, University of Cambridge, Addenbrooke's Hospital, Hills Road, Cambridge CB2 2QQ, England*

Diane B. Howieson, *Psychology Service (116B), Oregon Health Sciences University, VA Medical Center, PO Box 1034, Portland, OR 97207, USA*

Narinder Kapur, *Department of Clinical Neuropsychology, Wessex Neurological Centre, Southampton General Hospital, Southampton SO16 6YD, England*

Sheila A. Kerr, *Department of Psychology, University of Toronto, Toronto, Ontario M5S 1A1, Canada*

John F. Kihlstrom, *Department of Psychology, PO Box 208205, Yale University, New Haven, CT 06520-8205, USA*

Robert G. Knight, *Clinical Psychology Research and Training Centre, Department of Psychology, University of Otago, PO Box 56, Dunedin, New Zealand*

Michael D. Kopelman, *Division of Psychiatry and Psychology, United Medical and Dental Schools of Guy's and St Thomas's Hospitals, St Thomas's Hospital, Lambeth Palace Road, London SE1 7EH, England*

Harvey S. Levin, *Division of Neurological Surgery, University of Maryland School of Medicine, 22 South Greene Street, Baltimore, MD 21201, USA*

Muriel D. Lezak, *Department of Neurology (L226), Oregon Health Sciences University, 3181 SW Sam Jackson Park Road, Portland, OR 97201, USA*

Karen Z.H. Li, *Department of Psychology, University of Toronto, Toronto, Ontario M5S 1A1, Canada*

Wendy J. Lombardi, *Cognitive Neurosciences Section, Laboratory of Clinical Studies, National Institute on Alcohol Abuse and Alcoholism, Building 10, Room 3B19, Bethesda, MD 20892, USA*

Andrew R. Mayes, *University of Sheffield, Department of Clinical Neurology, 'N' Floor, Royal Hallamshire Hospital, Glossop Road, Sheffield S10 2JF, England*

Peter McKenna, *Mental Health Sciences, Addenbrooke's NHS Trust, Fulbourn Hospital, Cambridge CB1 5EF, England*

Margaret O'Connor, *Memory Disorders Research Center, Boston University School of Medicine, and Department of Veterans Affairs Medical Center, 150 South Huntington Avenue, Boston, MA 02130, USA*

Costanza Papagno, *Clinica Neurologica, Università di Milano, Via Festa del Perdono 7, 20122 Milan, Italy*

Karalyn Patterson, *MRC Applied Psychology Unit, 15 Chaucer Road, Cambridge CB2 2EF, England*

George P. Prigatano, *Barrow Neurological Institute, St Joseph's Hospital and Medical Center, 350 West Thomas Road, Phoenix, AZ 85013-4496, USA*

Jill B. Rich, *Department of Psychiatry and Behavioral Sciences, Meyer 218, The Johns Hopkins Hospital, 600 N Wolfe Street, Baltimore, MD 21287-7218, USA*

Byron P. Rourke, *Department of Psychology, University of Windsor, Windsor, Ontario N9B 3P4, Canada; and Yale University, Box 11 A Yale Station, New Haven CT 06520-7447, USA*

Daniel L. Schacter, *Department of Psychology, William James Hall, Harvard University, Cambridge, MA 02138, USA*

Daniel Tranel, *Department of Psychology, Division of Behavioral Neurology and Cognitive Neuroscience, University of Iowa College of Medicine, Iowa City, IA 52242, USA*

Katherine D. Tsatsanis, *Department of Psychology, University of Windsor, Windsor, Ontario N9B 3P4, Canada*

Giuseppe Vallar, *Dipartimento di Psicologia, Universitá Statale di Roma "La Sapienza", Via dei Marsi 78, 00185, Roma, Italy; and Clinica S. Lucia, Roma, Italy*

Mieke Verfaellie, *Memory Disorders Research Center, Boston University School of Medicine, and Department of Veterans Affairs Medical Center, 150 South Huntington Avenue, Boston, MA 02130, USA*

Fraser N. Watts, *MRC Applied Psychology Unit, 15 Chaucer Road, Cambridge CB2 2EF, England*

Herbert Weingartner, *Cognitive Neurosciences Section, Laboratory of Clinical Studies, National Institute on Alcohol Abuse and Alcoholism, Building 10, Room 3B19, Bethesda, MD 20892, USA*

Robin Lea West, *Department of Psychology, PO Box 112250, University of Florida, Gainesville, FL 32611-2250, USA*

Barbara A. Wilson, *MRC Applied Psychology Unit, 15 Chaucer Road, Cambridge CB2 2EF, England*

Preface

One of the most striking features of the study of memory in recent years has been the extent to which work on clinical populations of subjects has contributed to the understanding of normal function. This has led to a large number of books and conference papers by and for memory research workers. While this material is beginning to filter through to clinicians and practitioners, the process has so far been a relatively slow one. The primary purpose of the present handbook is to speed up this process by encouraging our colleagues with expertise in specific areas of memory deficit to summarise recent work in a way that will make it accessible to the practising clinician.

The book has four components. It begins with a section containing two brief review chapters concerned with the psychology and neurobiological basis of memory. This is followed by three more specialised sections. The first of these describes a range of different types of memory deficit, the second is concerned with issues of assessment of memory performance, while the third is concerned with the clinical management of memory problems.

We attempted to bring together as strong an international team as we could, and were delighted that our colleagues appeared to share our enthusiasm for the project and, almost without exception, agreed to participate. In editing the book we have learned a great deal, and in the process have become convinced that our research colleagues are likely to find it just as useful as our more clinically orientated colleagues, in providing an up-to-date account of the current state of knowledge in the area of memory disorders, a field that has become so extensive that even the most diligent reader is unlikely to be able to keep fully up to date outside his or her area of particular expertise.

We are grateful to Michael Coombs of John Wiley & Sons for convincing us of the potential value of such an enterprise and to Mrs Julia Darling without whose efficient administrative and secretarial help the book would not have been possible. Finally we would like to thank our contributors for finding time in their busy writing schedules to share their expertise with a wider audience.

The psychology of memory has gained immeasurably from the study of patients; we would like to think that this handbook, by summarising what has been learned and feeding it back to our clinical colleagues may represent a small step in the direction of repaying that help.

ADB
BAW
FNW

Section I

Theoretical Background

Chapter 1

The Psychology of Memory

Alan D. Baddeley
MRC Applied Psychology Unit, Cambridge, UK

INTRODUCTION

The psychology of memory has been an area of constant and productive activity over the last 30 years. During that time, it has drawn heavily on neuropsychological evidence derived from patients with memory disorders, and has in turn enriched and influenced our understanding of memory deficits, as I trust the remainder of this book will illustrate. Because of this, analysis of the deficit, and appreciation of potential rehabilitative strategies, will both depend to some extent on an understanding of the functioning of normal memory.

The present chapter attempts to provide an overview of recent developments in memory which should be read in conjunction with Chapter 2, Tranel and Damasio's overview of the neurobiological underpinning of human memory. The reader who is already familiar with research on memory will find little or nothing new here; but if you are unfamiliar with work in this area, or have been out of the field for a few years, then it should help you in reading the more specialised chapters that follow. More detailed overviews of human memory are provided in *Your Memory: A User's Guide* (Baddeley, 1994a), an account for the general reader, and in *Human Memory: Theory and Practice* (Baddeley, 1990), a more specialist text.

SOME HISTORICAL BACKGROUND

The scientific study of memory began with the work of Hermann Ebbinghaus, who first demonstrated that by rigidly controlling experimental conditions, it was possible to ask and answer questions about the characteristics of human me-

Handbook of Memory Disorders. Edited by A.D. Baddeley, B.A. Wilson and F.N. Watts.
© 1995 John Wiley & Sons Ltd.

mory. This lesson was learned, indeed some would say overlearned, by the generations that followed, who continued to be more preoccupied with the need for experimental control than with the need to check the validity of their findings outside the psychological laboratory. Consequently, up to and including the 1960s, the psychology of memory typically meant the psychology of people learning lists of unrelated words or pseudowords. Many of the classic clinical tests such as paired associate learning and digit span stem from this era, and have served well as indicators of the capacity of the memory system of the patient, while being rather less successful in providing information that is readily applicable to rehabilitation, or to advising the patient on how to cope with the memory deficit. We shall return to this issue later.

In the 1960s, memory became one of the more active areas of a new approach which became known as cognitive psychology. It was much more concerned with theory than the earlier memory research, and attempted to use models or theories inspired by the analogy between the human brain and the operation of the computer, both of which were regarded as devices for processing and storing information. Memory began to be fragmented into subsystems—long-term and short-term memory, for example—while models of the systems themselves were proposed, typically comprising different stages.

STAGES OF MEMORY PROCESSING: ENCODING, STORAGE AND RETRIEVAL

While many of the earlier models have now been discarded, some of the assumptions about stages remain useful. For example, any system for storing information, whether biological or artificial, will need (1) to be able to encode, or register information; (2) to store it, preferably without too much loss or forgetting; and subsequently (3) to access or retrieve that information. While these three stages are closely linked, making it difficult to pin down any phenomenon as exclusively occurring at a single stage, nevertheless this division into processing stages continues to be useful in helping understand the working of memory systems.

Encoding

The term "encoding" refers to the initial processing of the information that is to be learned or memorised. Immediate memory for arbitrary sequences of verbal material, such as occurs in digit span, typically relies on encoding in terms of the phonological or sound characteristics of the material. This can be shown by comparing memory span for items that are similar in sound (e.g. *mad, map, can, man, cap*) with dissimilar sequences (e.g. *pit, day, cow, pen, bar*). The similar items are much less likely to be recalled correctly because the system encodes them in terms of sound, a dimension on which they have fewer distinguishing features; hence they are liable to be harder to retrieve accurately. Similarity of meaning (e.g. *large, big, huge, long, tall*) has no such effect, indicating that for this immediate memory task, coding is phonological and not in terms of meaning (Baddeley, 1966a). On the other hand, if long-term learning is demanded, using sequences of 10 items and delayed recall, then the opposite occurs, with similarity of meaning being much more disruptive than phonological similarity (Baddeley, 1966b).

Craik & Lockhart (1972) generalised these and related findings to produce the *levels of processing* hypothesis. This suggests that the more deeply an item is encoded, then the better it is remembered. They showed that when subjects were required to process words superficially, simply in terms of their visual appearance (*Is the word in upper or lower case?—DOG*) subjects subsequently were poor at recalling or recognising the word. Retention was somewhat better when a slightly deeper phonological encoding was required (*Does the word rhyme with hat?—BAT*). The best subsequent performance, however, came from semantic coding (*Does the word PET fit in with the following sentence?—"Many people like to keep cats as a ---"*).

The levels of processing hypothesis proved to be applicable to a wide range of tasks, from memorising cartoons to learning passages of prose, and there is no doubt that it provides a useful rule of thumb. Opinions remain divided as to how useful it has been as a theoretical framework, since it has proved difficult to measure depth of processing independent of the outcome (Baddeley, 1978). As an empirical finding, however, there is no doubt that *elaborative rehearsal*, encoding material richly in terms of existing knowledge, is likely to lead to better recall than is found with *maintenance rehearsal*, the simple process of repetitive rehearsal. This probably occurs because deep or elaborative rehearsal involves the creation of richer semantic codes that allow material to be encoded along more dimensions than occur with phonological or simple visual codes, hence building in redundancy that will aid retrieval and minimise loss through forgetting.

Storage

Forgetting can be regarded as reflecting the loss of information over time. During the middle years of the century, a good deal of attention was devoted to attempting to explain forgetting, and more particularly to deciding whether it resulted from the spontaneous fading of a memory trace over time, or as the active result of interference from other learning.

Disruption of memory by subsequent learning is termed *retroactive interference*, while interference from prior learning is termed *proactive interference*.

A strong test of the trace decay hypothesis would require the demonstration that, in the absence of interpolated or prior learning, no forgetting occurs. In practice, such conditions are of course difficult if not impossible to produce. It is, on the other hand, quite possible to vary the nature of prior or subsequent learning, and when this done, there is no doubt that both proactive interference (PI) and retroactive interference (RI) do occur. Furthermore, interference increases with greater amounts of prior or subsequent interfering material, and with greater similarity between the interfering and the learned material (see Baddeley, 1990, and Crowder, 1976, for a more detailed account).

However, although interference effects certainly occur, their study was tied very closely to a stimulus–response associationist approach to learning that fell from favour during the 1970s when it tried, unsuccessfully, to adapt to the rise of cognitive psychology. There is, however, no doubt that the question of interference, and how new learning interacts with old, is a fundamental issue for any adequate theory of learning and remembering. New learning models using parallel distributed processing (PDP) or connectionist architectures that are assumed to simulate more closely the parallel processing of the neural networks of the brain, have once again begun to raise the issue of interference effects and how the brain deals with interference (Ratcliffe, 1990; Rumelhart & McClelland, 1986). It has proved difficult to demonstrate differential rates of forgetting as a function of different types of brain damage (Kopelman, 1985), and hence the study of forgetting has tended not to play a prominent role in the analysis of memory disorders. The one recent exception to this is provided by the growing interest in retrograde amnesia (see Hodges, Chapter 4), where the impaired capacity of the patient to recollect events from before the onset of brain damage clearly demands a more detailed model of forgetting than is at present available.

Retrieval

The fact that a patient who has received a blow on the head may remember nothing from the weeks or indeed months preceding the accident does not, of course, necessarily imply that the memory trace has been destroyed. Failure to recall may just as well represent difficulty in accessing or retrieving the memory trace. Evidence for this interpretation comes from the observation that retrograde amnesia often tends to "shrink", with memory of more distant events coming back, followed by events closer and closer to the point of insult, although characteristically the last few moments before the head injury are never recovered. This pattern of results suggests that more remote memories are made inaccessible by some form of retrieval problem, while the events just preceding the accident may have been lost because the memory trace never consolidated, and hence was never adequately stored (see Chapter 4).

The importance of retrieval in normal memory has been documented most fully by Tulving and his colleagues. In one study, Tulving (1966) presented subjects with a list of unrelated words, with the instruction to recall as many as possible in any order they wished, the technique known as *free recall*. For one group, the list was presented (P) and tested (T) several times ($PTPTPTPT$), a conventional learning and test procedure. A second group was presented with

the words, tested, then retested, then retested again, before a second presentation and three more tests (*PTTTPTTT*). Two striking findings emerged. First of
all, the two learning procedures led to virtually equivalent speed of acquisition,
despite the fact that the second approach had substantially fewer presentations
of the list to be learned. It appears to be the case that the process of retrieval
itself facilitates learning. Secondly, although subjects in the second group
recalled about the same number of words on each of the groups of three
successive tests (*TTT*), the specific words recalled varied substantially; new
words popped up, but earlier ones were lost, indicating that more words had
been learned than could be reliably recalled on any given trial. In short, more
words had been learned than could be retrieved.

Another source of evidence for the importance of retrieval comes from the
observation that recognition typically leads to a much higher rate of correct
responses than does recall. The reason is that presenting the word that has been
learned facilitates access to its memory trace. Consequently, the contrast between
recall and recognition is sometimes used in order to collect evidence as to
whether a particular memory deficit seems likely to be one of retrieval or
encoding, since retrieval deficits are likely to be reduced with recognition testing
—as for example occurs in patients suffering from Huntington's disease (see
Brandt & Rich, Chapter 10).

It is, however, important to bear in mind that presenting a word that has just
been learned does not guarantee access to the relevant memory trace; recognition facilitates but does not totally dispense with the need for retrieval, as
Tulving & Thomson (1973) elegantly demonstrated. The demonstration depends
on the use of what are termed *retrieval cues*; that is words that are presented
along with the target word, with the instruction to the subject that they might
subsequently be helpful. Typically retrieval cues are low-frequency associates of
the target word—for example *CITY* might have either *dirty* or *village* as a
retrieval cue. A subject who is subsequently cued with the word presented at
learning will show a very high probability of recall when compared with either
free recall, or to cueing with the other, non-presented low-frequency associate.
Retrieval cues can be very powerful, so much so that they can override the
advantage typically enjoyed by recognition over recall (Tulving & Thomson,
1973), a finding that Tulving explains in terms of the *encoding specificity*
principle. This states that a retrieval cue will be effective only when that specific
cue has been encoded with the target word during learning. The theory assumes
that when a fragment of a memory trace is presented, then it will tend to evoke
the rest of the trace, a process that is captured very effectively by the previously
mentioned connectionist PDP models (e.g. Rumelhart & McClelland, 1986).

The role of context has of course been appreciated for centuries (Locke,
1690), and is illustrated particularly clearly by the phenomenon of *context
dependent memory*, where material learned in one environment is better recalled
in that environment than in another. For example, Godden and Baddeley (1975)
showed that divers who learned lists of words while underwater recalled about
40% more when they were tested underwater than when they were tested on the

beach. The effect disappeared when recognition rather than recall was used, suggesting that context has its influence via the retrieval stage (Godden & Baddeley, 1980). Equivalent effects occur when the subject's internal environment is changed by drugs, so-called *state-dependency*; experiments by Eich (1980) using alcohol again implicated retrieval by demonstrating that the effect occurs for recall, but not when performance is tested by recognition. Finally, there is evidence for an equivalent influence of mood on recall, although the pattern here is somewhat more complex; the effect of learning and recall mood on neutral material appears to be unreliable, but there does appear to be a *mood-congruency* effect, whereby depressed mood makes it easier to recall sad memories, and a happy mood the opposite (Williams, Watts, MacLeod & Mathews, 1988).

The role of environmental context is important in rehabilitation, since it is of course crucial to ensure that any new skills the patient develops, or old skills that are recovered, can and will generalise to the home environment and beyond. Performance in the clinic is no guarantee of this, and there is therefore little alternative to training explicitly for generalisation, and then checking that generalisation has indeed occurred.

Organisation

As we have seen, it is conceptually useful to distinguish between encoding, storage and retrieval, and to bear these distinctions in mind when attempting to understand neuropsychological deficits in memory functioning. It is, however, equally important to bear in mind the extent to which the three stages interact.

This is illustrated rather clearly in the case of the role of *organisation* in learning and memory. During the 1960s, the importance of organising material was one of the major themes of the study of learning and memory. Mandler (1967), for example, showed that subjects who were given a list of words and asked to organise them into categories, with no mention of a subsequent test, were later able to recall just as many as subjects who had explicitly tried to memorise them. Many of the mnemonics that have evolved over the centuries are also based on organisation. Consider, for example, visual imagery mnemonics in which subjects are instructed to take the words in a paired-associate task and form an image of them interacting. For example, if the words were *dog* and *hat*, the subject might imagine a German Shepherd dog wearing a top hat. When subsequently given the stimulus word *dog*, the integrated image tends to spring to mind, evoking the response *hat*.

The effectiveness of organisation depends on the way in which the material is encoded, in terms of an interactive visual image for example, or by verbal association, or simply by rote rehearsal. A well-encoded item appears to lead to a stable level of recall over time, suggesting good storage, and is readily retrievable given the appropriate cue. Is such an interactive visual imagery mnemonic an example of encoding, storage or retrieval? It clearly reflects all three. The rich encoding leads to a well-integrated trace that stores the information in more than one dimension, hence making it resistant to forgetting. Furthermore the presence of several dimensions will increase the number of retrieval routes. The fact that encoding, storage and retrieval factors interact does not of course militate against the usefulness of distinguishing the different stages of memory; a patient who has difficulty encoding in terms of imagery because of a visual memory deficit could, for example, be encouraged to use nonvisual semantic encoding in terms of word associations. Similarly, a patient with frontal lobe damage may well have problems in retrieval, in which case structuring the environment or encouragement to use external aids such as diaries may circumvent that problem. It is important to bear in mind that an apparently general memory deficit might, if carefully analysed, prove to be attributable to disruption of one stage, which in turn influences other stages.

THE FRACTIONATION OF MEMORY

We have so far considered memory as if it were a single unitary system, a position that was widely held until the mid-1960s. However, largely but by no means exclusively as a result of neuropsychological evidence, it has become increasingly clear that memory comprises not a single system, but rather an alliance of interrelated subsystems. As early as the 1940s, Hebb (1949) was advocating a distinction between long-term memory which he argued was based on the strengthening of links between assemblies of cells within the brain, and short-term memory, which he regarded as being based on the temporary electrical activation of the relevant neurones.

Empirical evidence for the distinction between long- and short-term memory began to emerge in the 1960s. One source came from the previously described evidence that immediate memory for verbal material appears to rely on phonological coding, while long-term memory appears to be semantically based. A second source of evidence came from the observation that certain tasks appear to have two components. If a subject is presented with a list of words for immediate free recall, there will typically be extremely good recall of the last few items presented, the so-called *recency effect*. If recall is delayed by a few seconds of interpolated counting, then the recency effect disappears, while recall of earlier items is unchanged (Glanzer & Cunitz, 1966). One interpretation of this result is to suggest that the last few items are held in a labile short-term store, whereas earlier items reside in long-term memory. Evidence consistent with this interpretation comes from the observation that virtually any measure that influences long-term learning, including slower presentation, the use of high-frequency words or the presence of distraction during learning, will influence the earlier part of the curve, but have no effect on recency (Glanzer, 1972).

Perhaps the most powerful evidence for a dichotomy, however, comes from neuropsychological studies. Patients suffering from the classic amnesic syndrome show a dramatically impaired capacity for learning new material, or for recollecting events that have recently happened to them (see O'Connor, Ver-faellie & Cermak, Chapter 3), but nevertheless have preserved performance on digit span, and preserved recency in free recall (Baddeley & Warrington, 1970). This syndrome, as Tranel and Damasio illustrate in Chapter 2, is typically associated with damage to the temporal lobes or hippocampal areas, associated with a wide range of aetiologies. The converse pattern of deficits was demonstrated by Shallice and Warrington (1970) in a patient with damage to the perisylvian region of the left hemisphere. This patient had a digit span of only two items, together with a much reduced recency effect in free recall, but nevertheless showed evidence of normal long-term learning. In the face of this and other evidence, theorists began to abandon the idea of a unitary memory system, adopting instead the assumption of two or more memories. The most characteristic and influential of these approaches was that developed by Atkinson and Shiffrin (1968), which because of its representative nature has been termed the *modal model*. It is illustrated in Figure 1.1.

Information from the environment is assumed to enter a series of brief sensory registers, which then pass on information to a *short-term store*. This system plays a crucial role in the model, since without it, information cannot be transferred into or out of the third component, the *long-term store*. Long-term learning is assumed to occur when information is transferred in this way, with the probability of transfer being a direct function of the time that an item resides in the short-term store.

Despite its attractions, the modal model rapidly began to run into problems. The assumption that merely holding an item in the short-term system would guarantee learning proved difficult to sustain (Craik & Watkins, 1973), with levels of processing seeming to give a better account of learning than the modal model. Even more problematic was the evidence for normal learning in patients with a deficit in the short-term store (Shallice & Warrington, 1970). Such patients also appeared to have remarkably few problems in coping with their everyday life, apparently arguing against the importance of the short-term store as a crucial control centre for cognition, as proposed by the modal model. Baddeley and Hitch (1974), however, demonstrated that these problems could be solved by abandoning the assumption of a unitary short-term store, and accepting instead a multi-component *working memory*.

WORKING MEMORY

Baddeley and Hitch proposed a division into at least three subsystems, as illustrated in Figure 1.2. Part of the system is an attentional controller, the *central executive*, which forms an interface between long-term memory and two or possibly more slave systems. These systems combine the capacity for the temporary storage of information with an active set of control processes that allow information to be intentionally registered and maintained within the

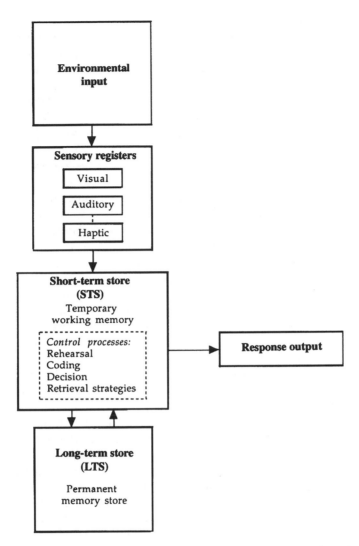

Figure 1.1   The structure of memory proposed by Atkinson & Shiffrin (1968)

subsystem. One of these, the *visuo-spatial scratchpad* or *sketchpad*, is specialised for maintaining visuo-spatial information, while verbal information is held using the *phonological* or *articulatory loop*. These subsystems correspond to the visual and verbal short-term memory systems described in more detail by Vallar and Papagno (Chapter 6).

The central executive is assumed to be responsible for the selection and operation of strategies, and for maintaining and switching attention as the need arises. It is assumed to be associated with the operation of the frontal lobes, and to be sensitive to frontal damage, producing what has been termed the *dysexecutive syndrome* (Baddeley, 1986; Baddeley & Wilson, 1988), a term that is

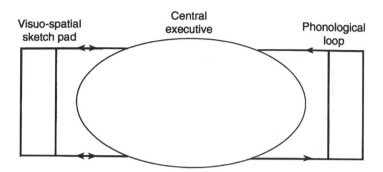

Figure 1.2   The working memory model proposed by Baddeley & Hitch (1974)

preferred to the more commonly used *frontal lobe syndrome* since it separates the functional deficit from questions of its anatomical localisation. Both functional and anatomical questions are highly pertinent, but are better tackled in parallel, since it is entirely possible that executive deficits may result from damage in parts of the brain other than the frontal lobes, while it is certainly the case that the frontal lobes are sufficiently extensive and complex that they may be damaged without producing the dysexecutive syndrome. Baddeley (1986) proposed adopting the concept of a *supervisory attentional system* (SAS) as formulated by Norman and Shallice (1986) as the basis for the central executive. In this model, routine behaviour is assumed to be controlled by well-learned habit structures or *schemata*. When novel action is required, for example in order to cope with an unexpected problem, or to override an old habit in an emergency, the SAS overrides the schemata. It is also responsible for planning and coordinating activities, and is assumed by Shallice (1982) to be the system that is disrupted by extensive bilateral frontal lobe damage.

A range of studies in normal subjects have investigated individual differences in working memory, typically defining working memory as the capacity to perform tasks that involve simultaneously storing and manipulating information. Daneman and Carpenter (1980, 1983) have related such a measure to the capacity for reading and comprehending prose, showing that subjects with small working memory spans show less capacity to draw inferences, particularly when these involve crossing sentence boundaries. A similar conclusion has been reached by Oakhill and her colleagues in studying children who show a good capacity for reading in the sense of pronouncing printed words, coupled with poor comprehension ability, a pattern which she attributes to impaired central executive capacity (Oakhill, Yuill & Parkin, 1988). Kyllonen and Christal (1990) have argued that working memory capacity is central to the concept of intelligence, demonstrating that a range of working memory tasks give scores that correlate highly with more traditional measures of intelligence, based on reasoning tests. Subsequent studies (e.g. Christal, 1991) have shown that such working memory measures provide a better prediction of the subsequent performance of subjects learning computer programing, than more traditional scholastically-based measures of intelligence.

Finally, the central executive is assumed to be responsible for coordinating information from a range of sources. This capacity has been shown to be impaired in patients suffering from Alzheimer's disease (Baddeley et al., 1991) when subjects were required simultaneously to perform a visuo-spatial tracking task and retain sequences of digits. Despite the fact that the level of the individual tasks was matched between Alzheimer patients and controls, nonetheless the requirement to combine the tasks caused a dramatic impairment in the patients, but not in normal elderly subjects. The combined task also proved to be a very sensitive measure of subsequent decline in AD patients (see Brandt & Rich, Chapter 10).

The phonological loop and visuo-spatial sketchpad will be described in more detail in Chapter 6, but briefly, the sketchpad is assumed to be a system that can hold and manipulate material of a visual or spatial nature. It appears to be associated with a number of structures in the right hemisphere (Farah, 1988; Jonides et al., 1993). It is necessary for the manipulation of visuo-spatial images, but does not appear to be responsible for the fact that concrete words are more readily remembered than abstract. This effect appears to be based on the richer representation of concrete words in long-term memory (Baddeley & Lieberman, 1980; Jones, 1988).

The phonological loop is a system that comprises a brief acoustic store, coupled with an articulatory rehearsal process. The articulatory process is capable of both maintaining information in the store, by continued rehearsal, and also of transferring visually presented material to the store, by means of subvocal naming. The characteristics of the store have been explored using the previously-described *phonological similarity effect* (Baddeley, 1966a), while the articulatory rehearsal process is reflected in the *word-length effect*, the tendency for memory span to be inversely related to the length of the words being remembered (Baddeley, Thomson & Buchanan, 1975). Long words take a long time to rehearse or recall, which gives more time for the trace of other words in the store to decay before being refreshed by rehearsal.

LONG-TERM MEMORY

The Implicit–Explicit Distinction

Once again, a system that was initially asssumed to be unitary has proved to be based on a number of interconnected subsystems, and once again, the principal source of evidence for this fractionation came from neuropsychology. More specifically, classic amnesic patients prove to show a preserved form of learning which has become known as *implicit learning*. In a classic observation, Claparède

(1911) secreted a pin in his hand when he shook hands with one of his densely amnesic Korsakoff patients one morning. The next day she refused to shake hands, but appeared to have no recollection of the source of her anxiety.

Later studies observed preserved motor skill acquisition in amnesic patients (Brooks & Baddeley, 1976; Corkin, 1968), while Warrington and Weiskrantz (1982) showed that, although their amnesic patients performed very badly on verbal recall or recognition, they showed clear evidence of having encountered a word if it were tested by *stem completion* (a process whereby a word such as *metal* might be tested by presenting the subject with *me-* and the request to think of a word that begins with those letters). Alternatively, memory can be tested by obscuring the word with noise, and requiring the subject to identify it, a procedure that can also be used to test memory for pictures (Warrington & Weiskrantz, 1968).

By the late 1970s, it had become clear that amnesic patients were capable of demonstrating learning on a wide range of different tasks. The tasks seemed to have in common the fact that learning could be demonstrated by enhanced performance without the need to recollect the experience of learning; hence the term implicit learning. Indeed, at the same time as they were demonstrating preserved learning, the patients would typically deny ever having encountered the task before. The tasks that were preserved in amnesic patients also proved to be distinguishable in normal subjects from the more typical form of *explicit* learning and memory. More specifically, implicit learning proved to be much more dependent upon the physical characteristics of the stimulus and test environment, and much less influenced than explicit learning by depth of processing or amount of attention devoted during learning (Jacoby & Dallas, 1981).

By the mid-1980s this apparently new and strange type of learning was coming to dominate the journals, creating considerable controversy as to exactly how it should be conceptualised, and indeed labelled. An early distinction was that made between *procedural* and *declarative* learning, with procedural learning representing the acquisition of skills, "learning how", while declarative learning involves the acquisition of facts, "learning that" (Squire, 1992). However, while many of the preserved learning capacities could be regarded as skills, it seemed to be stretching the term to regard conditioning, or indeed stem completion, as genuinely procedural. Some theorists have denied the need to assume separate learning systems, preferring other conceptualisations, such as the proposal that the preserved tasks are essentially *data driven*, whereas the impaired tasks are conceptually based (Roediger, 1990). However, this approach has never had much success in dealing with the data from amnesic patients, and for that reason will not be further considered.

Probably the most innovative and thought-provoking work on implicit learning in normal subjects has been carried out by Jacoby and his colleagues (Jacoby & Kelley, 1992). Much of Jacoby's recent work has been concerned with demonstrating that most memory tasks comprise both implicit and explicit components, and devising ingenious ways to separate the two (e.g. Jacoby, 1991). While

Jacoby's own work has principally been concerned with normal subjects, his methods are now being applied extensively to the analysis of implicit and explicit memory in patient populations, with results that are broadly consistent with the hypothesis that implicit memory is spared and explicit memory disrupted in the classic amnesic syndrome (Verfaellie & Treadwell, 1993).

The structure of long-term memory remains an area of controversy, but it is probably true to say that areas of disagreement are becoming less, and in my own view the evidence is pointing increasingly in the direction of a structure somewhat like Figure 1.3, which represents the views of Squire (1992). This view distinguishes between *declarative* and *nondeclarative* memory, terms which more or less map onto the earlier terms of explicit and implicit. While I find the terms slightly clumsy, I do not have a suitable alternative, and so will use them for the purpose of this review.

Declarative Memory

This constitutes the two subsystems originally defined by Tulving (1972) as *episodic* and *semantic* memory. Episodic memory refers to the system involved in recollecting particular experiences or episodes; remembering what you had for breakfast, or setting off for a holiday last year are examples of episodic memory. Semantic memory, on the other hand, refers to knowledge of the world; knowing the chemical formula for salt, or the name of the French capital, or how many inches there are in a foot are all examples of semantic memory.

Episodic Memory

This is the system that is associated most closely with traditional approaches to learning and memory; virtually all of the first section of the paper is thus concerned with episodic memory. It is characteristically accompanied by an

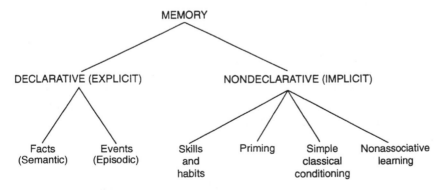

Figure 1.3 Components of long-term memory proposed by Squire (1992)

awareness of the learning experience and is sensitive to depth of processing. Episodic memory is strongly influenced by degree of attention and organisation, which reflects the importance of these processes for setting up memory structures that are accessible to retrieval. It is the episodic memory system that is readily disrupted by brain damage, and whose impairment forms the basis of the classic amnesic syndrome (see Chapter 3). While it is crucially dependent upon the circuit linking the temporal lobes, hippocampus and frontal lobes (see Chapter 2), virtually anything that comprises the functioning of the brain will impact on rate of learning and speed of retrieval, suggesting the operation of a massively parallel system capable of graceful degradation when brain tissue is lost, with the hippocampal region playing a crucial role in learning but not itself being the seat of memory.

Semantic Memory

The process of education could be regarded as the gradual building up of semantic memory, starting with our perceptual knowledge of the physical world around us, and going on to include language, our knowledge of society, and all the detailed specialist information that we acquire as part of our individual trade or profession. Despite its importance, semantic memory was virtually ignored until the 1970s, when attention was drawn to it by the attempt to develop computer programs that could understand language (e.g. Collins & Quillian, 1972). It rapidly became clear that such programs were crucially dependent on built-in knowledge of the world, which in turn raised difficult questions as to how such knowledge should be incorporated, stored and retrieved. This stimulated a flurry of research that all too rapidly burned out when it became apparent just how difficult the problem was (see Baddeley, 1990, Chapter 13).

However, although we clearly do not have entirely satisfactory computer models of semantic memory, this earlier work has at least provided a framework for further investigation of some of the fascinating deficits in semantic memory that have begun to emerge from the study of neuropsychological patients (see Patterson & Hodges, Chapter 7). These have been observed in a range of conditions, but are particularly likely to occur in the later stages of Alzheimer's disease, when the semantic memory system begins to deteriorate, sometimes fractionating along lines that offer intriguing clues as to the underlying structure of the system. In general, the neuropsychological evidence, by linking semantic memory with perceptual as well as language impairments, is beginning to provide the basis for a more adequate theoretical conceptualisation of semantic memory, as well as highlighting an important clinical problem.

The Relation Between Episodic and Semantic Memory

Tulving's initial conceptualisation proposed that semantic and episodic memory are based on quite separate memory systems, but the evidence now seems to point to their reflecting the same system operating under different circumstances. Semantic memory stores information that may have originated in many separate experiences which are no longer individually retrievable. While access to semantic memory may be preserved in the amnesic syndrome, the evidence suggests that without episodic memory, subjects have great difficulty adding *new* information to semantic memory. Amnesic patients fail to update their ongoing knowledge of politics or sport or indeed of any area of specialist skill, although they are likely to be able to access information that is already in semantic memory (see Chapter 3).

My own view is that semantic memory consists of the accumulation of many episodes. A useful analogy is to think of a series of individual episodes being piled one on the other; episodic memory represents the capacity to pull out one episode from the pile, whereas semantic memory reflects our capacity to look at the pile from above, and draw out those features that are common to many of the constituent episodes. This view probably approximates more or less closely the current modal interpretation, although it probably does not reflect the view held by the originator of the distinction, Endel Tulving, who currently seems to regard the phenomenological experience of a past event as being crucial to labelling a memory as episodic. This is certainly a relevant feature of episodic memory, and the simple expedient of asking subjects to make a judgement of material retained as something that is "remembered" or "known" has proved an interesting and promising manipulation (Gardiner, 1988; Tulving, 1985).

Nondeclarative Memory

As mentioned earlier, views currently differ as to whether nondeclarative should genuinely be regarded as a separate kind of memory, and if so whether it represents one or many memory systems. My own view is that nondeclarative memory is best considered as a cluster of learning systems that have in common the fact that they are independent of episodic memory. This means that they are capable of accumulating information, but not of pulling out and identifying specific episodes. The episodic memory system has the remarkable capacity to associate previously unrelated events in a single trial. Because of this, it can associate an event with a context, and hence locate it in time and place. It is this, I suggest, that lies at the heart of the capacity to recollect specific episodes (Baddeley, 1994b). In contrast, nondeclarative systems are specialised for accumulating information from the world, but incapable of keeping separate the individual episodes.

A number of very different kinds of nondeclarative phenomena have been identified. They will be considered in turn:

Priming

As we saw earlier, where a word has been presented, subjects are subsequently more likely to identify a noisy re-presentation of the word, or to produce that word when faced with either its stem or a fragment. Hence, if the subject has just seen the word *crocodile*, then he or she is more likely to respond "crocodile" to the stem *cro-*, and to identify *c-o-o-i-e* as fitting the word *crocodile* than if they had not just encountered the word. As Tulving and Schacter (1990) have pointed out, priming effects occur across a wide range of modalities, and are typically dependent upon the repetition of the physical characteristics of the original stimulus; priming is typically much less sensitive to semantic or conceptual aspects of the primed material. Priming presumably reflects the fact that once a neural structure has been used, there will be some form of neural residue that will either enhance its subsequent speed of use (positive priming), or may have an inhibitory effect (negative priming).

Procedural Learning

This refers to the acquisition of skills, whether perceptual-motor, such as those of riding a bicycle or driving a car, or cognitive, such as in skilled reading or problem solving. They clearly comprise an important area of learning, and do of course represent the archetypal example of procedural learning—learning *how* rather than learning *that*. While skill acquisition is typically preserved in the classic amnesic syndrome, there is evidence to suggest that it is impaired in some conditions, including Huntington's disease (see Chapter 10).

Skills can be divided into two types: *continuous*, in which each component of the skill serves as a cue to the next, as in cycling or steering a car; and *discontinuous*, in which a series of discrete stimulus–response links are involved, as in typing. In general, continuous skills seem to show little or no forgetting, whereas forgetting clearly occurs with discontinuous tasks (see Baddeley, 1990, Chapter 10). There is no evidence to suggest that either of these types of skill is impaired in pure amnesia. Preserved learning includes continuous skills such as performance on the pursuit rotor (Brooks & Baddeley, 1976), perceptual skills such as the reading of transformed script (Cohen & Squire, 1980), and key-pressing tasks involving the learning of sequential dependencies among stimuli (see Chapter 3).

Associative Conditioning

As the Claparède pin incident demonstrates, amnesic patients are capable of learning an avoidance response, a finding that was replicated by Weiskrantz and Warrington (1979) in a classical conditioning study in which subjects were conditioned to blink in response to a tone that consistently preceded a puff of air to the eye. As is typical, the patients showed no capacity to recollect the experience of learning, when subsequently questioned.

Evaluative Conditioning

This refers to the influence of experience on the affective value of a stimulus. In one study, for example, Johnson, Kim and Risse (1985) showed that when normal subjects were asked to judge the pleasantness of Korean musical melodies, they responded negatively to the unaccustomed experience. However, when the same melody had been presented several times, its pleasantness rating gradually improved. This phenomenon was just as marked in amnesic patients who, despite clear evidence of a change in rated pleasantness, denied ever having encountered the melodies before.

EVERYDAY MEMORY

We began by referring to Ebbinghaus and his determination to simplify in order to study the functioning of human memory. There has, however, always existed a parallel tradition that argues against the narrowness of laboratory-based studies, suggesting that they rule out all that is most rich and characteristic of human memory. The work of Galton on visual imagery, and on autobiographical memory, carried out at the same time as Ebbinghaus was performing his classic studies, is a case in point. A more explicit stance was taken by Bartlett (1932) who rejected the use of nonsense syllables to study memory, in favour of the recall of stories and pictures. It seemed during the 1950s and 60s as if the Bartlett tradition might have petered out. However, the 1970s saw a revival of interest in the role of memory in real-world situations, together with the development of computer-based techniques that allowed Bartlett's concept of the *schema*, representing organised knowledge of the particular topic, to be incorporated in models that proved able to simulate some important features of story recall (Rumelhart & Norman, 1985; Schank 1982).

In the USA, J.J. Gibson's ecological approach to perception encouraged researchers such as Neisser to attempt to develop an ecological psychology of memory. While the rhetoric of Neisser's claim that "If X is an interesting or socially significant aspect of memory, then psychologists have hardly ever studied X" (Neisser, 1978) did have the positive effect of stimulating interest and activity, it also had the unfortunate negative effect of polarising opinion, resulting in the controversy surrounding Banaji and Crowder's (1989) paper on "The bankruptcy of everyday memory". There is, of course, no necessary conflict between carrying out research in the laboratory and in the world outside. The laboratory provides the simplification and experimental control that allows the rigorous testing of hypotheses, while more naturalistic studies are essential if we are to evaluate the generality of our theories.

There is also a danger that important aspects of memory that happen to be difficult to test in the laboratory may be ignored. A good example of this is provided by *prospective memory*, the capacity to remember to do things. When someone complains of a bad memory it is much more likely to be because of prospective memory lapses than because of a problem in learning lists of nonsense syllables or recalling complex geometric figures, and yet until quite recently psychology had nothing to say on the topic. While we are still not well endowed with either study paradigms or models, this is an area of growing interest, and it is becoming clear that prospective memory does rely upon some of the same structures as episodic memory, and hence is drastically impaired in the amnesic syndrome (Wilson, Cockburn, Baddeley & Hiorns, 1989). Prospective memory is also much more determined by its social context than by motivational variables.

Consequently, although the elderly are shown to perform particularly poorly on measures of prospective memory under controlled conditions (Cockburn & Smith, 1988), nevertheless under naturalistic conditions in which the task involved remembering to make a telephone call at a particular time, the elderly performed better than the young (Moscovitch, 1982), simply because they are more likely to make better use of external aids such as diaries and reminders.

Clinical Measures of Everyday Memory

Clinical assessment typically tries to do two things: first of all to quantify a patient's cognitive capacities as precisely as possible; and secondly to obtain measures that will allow the clinician to estimate the capacity of the patient to cope in the world outside the clinic (see Mayes, Chapter 15). Traditional measures based on the psychometric approach have typically been concerned with the first of these aims, but have often simply assumed that a test that is sensitive will also be valid as a predictor of everyday functioning. Sunderland, Harris and Baddeley (1983) carried out a study that attempted to assess the validity of this assumption, testing the performance of a group of patients who had suffered a moderate-to-severe head injury, on a range of standard tests, and relating this to estimates of their everyday memory problems, based on questionnaires and interviews with the patients and a close relative. It became clear that some tests were extremely sensitive to the effects of head injury, but were quite unrelated to everyday memory complaints; indeed the only measure that looked at all promising was the recall of a short story.

Stimulated by this need, Barbara Wilson in Oxford developed a new test of everyday memory that attempted to simulate, in scorable form, a whole range of everyday memory lapses. The resulting Rivermead Behavioural Memory Test (RBMT) assesses such factors as remembering a name, learning a new route, recognising faces, orientation in time and place, and prospective memory. It also incorporated the recall of a short story. It has proved to be both sensitive and to correlate very highly with lapses of everyday memory, as measured by many hours of observation of patients by therapists (Wilson et al., 1989). In a subsequent follow-up study, it proved to be the best predictor of whether a patient would or would not be capable of living independently (Wilson, 1991). However, while the RBMT is an excellent predictor of everyday memory problems, it does not aim to provide an analytic estimate of memory performance. We are therefore developing tests that we hope will combine the ecological validity of the RBMT with a more analytic approach, one example being the "Doors and People" test, which uses realistic material to assess visual and verbal recall and recognition, providing in addition measures of learning and forgetting (Baddeley, Emslie and Nimmo-Smith, 1994).

Autobiographical Memory

Our capacity to recollect events of our early life was initially studied by Galton in the 1880s, but then neglected for virtually a century. It is now a thriving area of psychological research which impinges on a range of other topics, including the role of memory in the concept of self, confabulation and the question of how we evaluate the veracity of our memories (Rubin, 1986; in press), the pattern of autobiographical memory across the life-span (Rubin, Wetzler & Nebes, 1986), and the characteristics of vivid and flashbulb memories (Neisser, 1988). In a clinical context, autobiographical memory offers a way of approaching retrograde amnesia that avoids some of the problems of tests based on public knowledge, which suffer from the problem of large individual differences in knowledge about the events probed, and from the need to be repeatedly updated by adding new public events, and re-evaluating the memorability of earlier events (see Hodges, Chapter 4).

The Autobiographical Memory Interview (Kopelman, Wilson & Baddeley, 1990) and the equivalent Italian measure by Borrini, Dall'Orra, Della Sala, Marinelli and Spinnler (1989) provide tools for investigating the deterioration of autobiographical memory in patients. While the test is a relatively new one, it is already becoming clear that some interesting distinctions occur among otherwise similar patients as to whether they show a particularly marked deficit in their retention of autobiographical facts such as the names of school teachers and friends, and the addresses of earlier homes, or of episodes that occurred at a particular time of life (see Chapter 4). It seems likely that the availability of more precise measures will provide yet another example of the value of studying clinical memory deficits for the understanding of normal memory.

CONCLUSION

Our knowledge of normal memory is continually evolving, and being enriched by the attempt to apply basic theory to the neuropsychological study of memory deficits in brain-damaged patients. It is therefore inevitable, and indeed highly desirable, that as the years pass this account will become increasingly outdated. However, experience over the last 20 years strongly suggests that our new conceptions are likely to be developments of the old, and to reflect the continuing and productive dialogue between cognitive theory and neuropsychological practice.

REFERENCES

Atkinson, R.C. & Shiffrin, R.M. (1968). Human memory: A proposed system and its control processes. In K.W. Spence (ed), *The Psychology of Learning and Motivation: Advances in Research and Theory*, vol. 2. Academic Press, New York, pp. 89–195.

Baddeley, A.D. (1966a). Short-term memory for word sequences as a function of acoustic, semantic and formal similarity. *Quarterly Journal of Experimental Psychology*, **18**, 362–365.

Baddeley, A.D. (1966b). The influence of acoustic and semantic similarity on long-term memory for word sequences. *Quarterly Journal of Experimental Psychology*, **18**, 302–309.

Baddeley, A.D. (1978). The trouble with levels: a re-examination of Craik and Lockhart's framework for memory research. *Psychological Review*, **85**, 139–152.

Baddeley, A.D. (1986). *Working Memory*. Clarendon Press, Oxford.

Baddeley, A.D. (1990). *Human Memory: Theory and Practice*. Lawrence Erlbaum Associates, Hove, Sussex.

Baddeley, A.D. (1994a). *Your Memory: A User's Guide*, 2nd edn. Penguin Books, Harmondsworth, Middlesex.

Baddeley, A.D. (1994b). Working memory and conscious awareness. In A. Collins, S. Gathercole, M. Conway & P. Morris (eds), *Theories of Memory*. Lawrence Erlbaum Associates, Hove, pp. 11–28.

Baddeley, A.D., Bressi, S., Della Sala, S., Logie, R. & Spinnler, H. (1991). The decline of working memory in Alzheimer's disease: a longitudinal study. *Brain*, **114**, 2521–2542.

Baddeley, A.D., Emslie, H & Nimmo-Smith, I. (1994). *Doors and People: A Test of Visual and Verbal Recall and Recognition*. Thames Valley Test Company, Flempton, Bury St Edmunds, Suffolk.

Baddeley, A.D. & Hitch, G. (1974). Working memory. In G.A. Bower (ed), *The Psychology of Learning and Motivation*, vol. 8. Academic Press, New York, pp. 47–89.

Baddeley, A.D. & Lieberman, K. (1980). Spatial working memory. In R.S. Nickerson (ed), *Attention and Performance*, vol. 8. Lawrence Erlbaum Associates, Hillsdale, NJ, pp. 521–539.

Baddeley, A.D., Thomson, N. & Buchanan, M. (1975). Word length and the structure of short-term memory. *Journal of Verbal Learning and Verbal Behavior*, **14**, 575–589.

Baddeley, A.D. & Warrington, E.K. (1970). Amnesia and the distinction between long- and short-term memory. *Journal of Verbal Learning and Verbal Behavior*, **9**, 176–189.

Baddeley, A.D. & Wilson, B.A. (1988). Frontal amnesia and the dysexecutive syndrome. *Brain and Cognition*, **7**, 212–230.

Banaji, M.R. & Crowder, R.G. (1989). The bankruptcy of everyday memory. *American Psychologist*, **44**, 1185–1193.

Bartlett, F.C. (1932). *Remembering*. Cambridge University Press, Cambridge.

Borrini, G., Dall'Orra, P., Della Sala, S., Marinelli, L. & Spinnler, H. (1989). Autobiographical memory: sensitivity to age and education of a standardized inquiry. *Psychological Medicine*, **19**, 215–224.

Brooks, D.N. & Baddeley, A.D. (1976). What can amnesic patients learn? *Neuropsychologia*, **14**, 111–122.

Christal, R.E. (1991). *Comparative Validities of ASVAB and Lamp Tests for Logic Gates Learning*. Armstrong Laboratory Human Resources Directorate Technical Report AL-TP-1991-0031 (Brooks Airforce Base, Texas 78235-5000).

Claparède, E. (1911). Récognition et moïite. *Archives Psychologiques Genève*, **11**, 79–90.

Cockburn, J. & Smith, P.T. (1988). Effects of age and intelligence on everyday memory tasks. In M.M. Gruneberg, P. Morris & R.N. Sykes (eds), *Practical Aspects of Memory: Current Research and Issues. Vol. 2: Clinical and Educational Implications*. Wiley, Chichester, pp. 132–136.

Cohen, N.J. & Squire, L.R. (1980). Preserved learning and retention of pattern analyzing skill in amnesia: dissociation of knowing how and knowing that. *Science*, **210**, 207–210.

Collins, A.M. & Quillian, M.R. (1972). Experiments in semantic memory and language comprehension. In L.W. Gregg (ed), *Cognition in Learning and Memory*. Wiley, New York.

Corkin, S. (1968). Acquisition of motor skill after bilateral medial temporal-lobe excision. *Neuropsychologia*, **6**, 255.

Craik, F.I.M. & Lockhart, R.S. (1972). Levels of processing: a framework for memory research. *Journal of Verbal Learning and Verbal Behavior*, **11**, 671–684.

Craik, F.I.M. & Watkins, M.J. (1973). The role of rehearsal in short-term memory. *Journal of Verbal Learning and Verbal Behavior*, **12**, 599–607.

Crowder, R.G. (1976). *Principles of Learning and Memory*. Lawrence Erlbaum Associates, Hillsdale, NJ.

Daneman, M. & Carpenter, P.A. (1980). Individual differences in working memory and reading. *Journal of Verbal Learning and Verbal Behavior*, **19**, 450–466.

Daneman, M. & Carpenter, P.A. (1983). Individual differences in integrating information between and within sentences. *Journal of Experimental Psychology: Learning, Memory and Cognition*, **9**, 561–584.

Eich, J.E. (1980). The cue-dependent nature of state-dependent retrieval. *Memory and Cognition*, **8**, 157–173.

Farah, M. J. (1988). Is visual memory really visual? Overlooked evidence from neuropsychology. *Psychological Review*, **95**, 307–317.

Gardiner, J.M. (1988). Functional aspects of recollective experience. *Memory and Cognition*, **16**, 309–313.

Glanzer, M. (1972). Storage mechanisms in recall. In G. H. Bower (ed), *The Psychology of Learning and Motivation: Advances in Research and Theory*, vol. 5. Academic Press, New York.

Glanzer, M. & Cunitz, A.R. (1966). Two storage mechanisms in free recall. *Journal of Verbal Learning and Verbal Behavior*, **5**, 351–360.

Godden, D. & Baddeley, A.D. (1975). Context-dependent memory in two natural environments: on land and under water. *British Journal of Psychology*, **66**, 325–331.

Godden, D. & Baddeley, A.D. (1980). When does context influence recognition memory? *British Journal of Psychology*, **71**, 99–104.

Hebb, D.O. (1949). *Organization of Behavior*. Wiley, New York.

Jacoby, L.L. (1991). A process dissociation framework: separating automatic from intentional uses of memory. *Journal of Memory and Language*, **30**, 513–541.

Jacoby, L.L. & Dallas, M. (1981). On the relationship between autobiographical memory and perceptual learning. *Journal of Experimental Psychology: General*, **110**, 306–340.

Jacoby, L.L. & Kelley, C. (1992). Unconscious influences of memory: dissociations and automaticity. In A. Milner & M. Rugg (eds), *The Neuropsychology of Consciousness*. Academic Press, London, pp. 201–233.

Johnson, M.K., Kim, J.K. & Risse, G. (1985). Do alcoholic Korsakoff's syndrome patients acquire affective reactions? *Journal of Experimental Psychology: Learning, Memory and Cognition*, **11**, 22–36.

Jones, G.V. (1988). Images, predicates, and retrieval cues. In M. Denis, J. Engelkamp & J.T.E. Richardson (ed), *Cognitive and Neuropsychological Approaches to Mental Imagery*. Martinus Nijhoff, Dordrecht, pp. 89–98.

Jonides, J., Smith, E.E., Koeppe, R.A., Awh, E., Minoshima, S. & Mintun, M.A. (1993). Spatial working memory in humans as revealed by PET. *Nature*, **363**, 623–625.

Kopelman, M.D. (1985). Rates of forgetting in Alzheimer-type dementia and Korsakoff's syndrome. *Neuropsychologia*, **23**, 623–638.

Kopelman, M., Wilson, B.A. & Baddeley, A.D. (1990). *The Autobiographical Memory Interview*. Thames Valley Test Company, Bury St Edmunds, Suffolk.

Kyllonen, P.C. & Christal, R.E. (1990). Reasoning ability is (little more than) working-memory capacity. *Intelligence*, **14**, 389–433.

Locke, J. (1690). *An Essay Concerning Human Understanding*. Everyman's Library Edition 1961, Dent, London.

Mandler, G. (1967). Organization in memory. In K.W. Spence & J.T. Spence (eds), *The Psychology of Learning and Motivation*, vol 1. Academic Press, New York, pp. 327–372.

Moscovitch, M. (1982). A neuropsychological approach to memory and perception in normal and pathological aging. In F.I.M. Craik & S. Trehub (eds), *Aging and Cognitive Processes*. Plenum Press, New York, pp. 55–78.

Neisser, U. (1978). Memory: What are the important questions? In M.M. Gruneberg, P.E. Morris & R.N. Sykes (eds), *Practical Aspects of Memory*. Academic Press, London.

Neisser, U. (1988). Time present and time past. In M.M. Gruneberg, P.E. Morris & R.N. Sykes (eds), *Practical Aspects of Memory: Current Research and Issues. Vol. 2: Clinical and Educational Implications*. Wiley, Chichester, pp. 545–560.

Norman, D.A. & Shallice, T. (1986). Attention to action: willed and automatic control of behavior. In R.J. Davidson, G.E. Schwarts & D. Shapiro (eds), *Consciousness and Self-Regulation. Advances in Research and Theory*. Plenum Press, New York, pp. 1–18.

Oakhill, J.V., Yuill, N. & Parkin, A.J. (1988). Memory and inference in skilled and less-skilled comprehenders. In M.M. Gruneberg, P.E. Morris & R.N. Sykes (eds), *Practical Aspects of Memory: Current Research and Issues. Vol. 2: Clinical and Educational Implications*. Wiley, Chichester, pp. 315–320.

Ratcliffe, R. (1990). Connectionist models of recognition memory: constraints imposed by learning and forgetting functions. *Psychological Review*, **97**, 285–308.

Roediger, H.L. (1990). Implicit memory: retention without remembering. *American Psychologist*, **45**, 1043–1056.

Rubin, D.C. (1986). *Autobiographical Memory*. Cambridge University Press, New York.

Rubin, D.C. (in press). *The Construction of Autobiographical Memory*. Cambridge University Press, New York.

Rubin, D.C., Wetzler, S.E. & Nebes, R.D. (1986). Autobiographical memory across the lifespan. In D.C. Rubin (ed), *Autobiographical Memory*. Cambridge University Press, New York, pp. 202–221.

Rumelhart, D.E. & McClelland, J.L. (eds) (1986). *Parallel Distributed Processing: Explorations in the Microstructures of Cognition. Vol. 1: Foundations*. MIT Press, Cambridge, Mass.

Rumelhart, D.E. & Norman, D.A. (1985). Representation of knowledge. In A.M. Aitkenhead and J.M. Slack (eds), *Issues in Cognitive Modelling*. Lawrence Erlbaum Associates, London, pp. 15–62.

Schank, R.C. (1982). *Dynamic Memory*. Cambridge University Press, New York.

Shallice, T. (1982). Specific impairments of planning. *Philosophical Transactions of the Royal Society London B*, **298**, 199–209.

Shallice, T. & Warrington, E.K. (1970). Independent functioning of verbal memory stores: a neuropsychological study. *Quarterly Journal of Experimental Psychology*, **22**, 261–273.

Squire, L.R. (1992). Declarative and nondeclarative memory: multiple brain systems supporting learning and memory. *Journal of Cognitive Neuroscience*, **4**, 232–243.

Sunderland, A., Harris, J.E. & Baddeley, A.D. (1983). Assessing everyday memory after severe head injury. In J.E. Harris and P.E. Morris (eds), *Everyday Memory, Actions and Absentmindedness*. Academic Press, London, pp. 191–206.

Tulving, E. (1966). Subjective organization and effects of repetition in multi-trial free-recall learning. *Journal of Verbal Learning and Verbal Behavior*, **5**, 193–197.

Tulving, E. (1985). How many memory systems are there? *American Psychologist*, **40**, 385–398.

Tulving, E. & Schacter, D.L. (1990). Priming and human memory systems. *Science*, **247**, 301–306.

Tulving, E. & Thomson, D.M. (1973). Encoding specificity and retrieval processes in episodic memory. *Psychological Review*, **80**, 352–373.

Verfaellie, M. & Treadwell, J.R. (1993). Status of recognition memory in amnesia. *Neuropsychology*, **7**, 5–13.

Warrington, E.K. & Weiskrantz, L. (1968). New methods of testing long-term retention with special reference to amnesic patients. *Nature*, **217**, 972–974.

Warrington, E.K. & Weiskrantz, L. (1982). Amnesia: a disconnection syndrome. *Neuropsychologia*, **20**, 233–238.

Weiskrantz, L. & Warrington, E.K. (1979). Conditioning in amnesic patients. *Neuropsychologia*, **17**, 187–194.

Williams, J.M.G., Watts, F.N., MacLeod, C. & Mathews, A. (1988). *Cognitive Psychology and Emotional Disorders*. Wiley, Chichester.

Wilson, B.A. (1991). Long-term prognosis of patients with severe memory disorders. *Neuropsychological Rehabilitation*, **1**, 117–134.

Wilson, B., Cockburn, J., Baddeley, A.D. & Hiorns, R. (1989). The development and validation of a test battery for detecting and monitoring everyday memory problems. *Journal of Clinical and Experimental Neuropsychology*, **11**, 855–870.

Chapter 2

Neurobiological Foundations of Human Memory

Daniel Tranel
and
Antonio R. Damasio
University of Iowa College of Medicine, Iowa City, USA

INTRODUCTION

The role of memory in the human mind and behavior cannot be overemphasized, since very few aspects of higher nervous function could operate successfully without some memory contribution. Perception, recognition, language, planning, problem-solving and decision-making all rely on memory.

What biological machinery subserves memory? What are the brain mechanisms that allow us to learn the names of several continents, the visual patterns in human faces and in landscapes, a musical place, or the ability to skate or ski? Investigation of these questions has begun to provide preliminary answers. For example, it is now known that a neural structure called the hippocampus, buried deep in the medial part of the temporal lobes, is critical for acquiring new knowledge of factual type. We know that there are neural systems in the lateral parts of the temporal lobes that are critical for retrieving such factual knowledge. And structures such as the basal ganglia and cerebellum are known to play an important role in the acquisition of motor skills. In fact, it is becoming apparent that many brain structures have a role in memory, and it could be argued that in a broad sense, virtually the entire brain is concerned with the operation of memory in some form.

Handbook of Memory Disorders. Edited by A.D. Baddeley, B.A. Wilson and F.N. Watts.
© 1995 John Wiley & Sons Ltd.

Levels of Scientific Inquiry into the Biology of Memory

The objective of this chapter is to provide an overview of the neurobiological substrates of human memory, complementing the treatment of memory from a psychological perspective in Chapter 1. It should be noted that the neural basis of memory has been investigated from the perspective of different levels within neuroscience. For example, some scientists study the molecular basis of memory, and others study memory at a cellular level. Others study neural systems, that is, articulated groups of neuroanatomical units as cortical regions or subcortical nuclei, thousands of neurons which operate in concert. The emphasis in our chapter is on this level, neural systems, and how they subserve different aspects of memory in the adult human. A complete discussion of molecular and cellular mechanisms of memory is beyond the scope of this chapter (see the *Cold Spring Harbor Symposia on Quantitative Biology*, Vol. LV, for recent reviews; and Kandel, Schwartz & Jessell, *Principles of Neural Science*, for textbook treatment of these topics). However, before we approach the main topic of neural systems, a few words regarding the molecular and cellular basis of memory are in order.

Molecular and Cellular Basis of Memory

Investigation at this level has focused on the issue of what happens in the brain when something is learned. Is there some kind of modification in neurons, or in connections between neurons, that takes place as a result of something being learned? For example, when we learn to associate two stimuli (e.g. an unconditioned stimulus and conditioned stimulus, as in classical conditioning), what exactly happens in the brain to support this process?

Early attempts to answer this question can be traced back to Donald Hebb, who in 1949 proposed that the coactivation of connected cells would result in a modification of weights so that when the presynaptic cell fires, the probability of the postsynaptic cell firing is increased. In Hebb's words: "When an axon of a cell A is near enough to excite cell B or repeatedly or persistently takes part in firing it, some growth or metabolic change takes place in both cells such that A's efficiency, as one of the cells firing B, is increased." (1949, p. 62). This learning principle did not specify exactly what was meant by "growths" or "metabolic changes", but it served as a useful starting point, and it has become the widely cited heuristic for neurobiological investigations of learning and memory.

Another major advance took place about two decades ago, when it was discovered that a postsynaptic cell's excitability was increased for hours, or even days or weeks, after a related presynaptic cell had been stimulated with a high-frequency volley of pulses, known as a tetanus (Bliss & Lomo, 1973). Specifically, when the primary afferents of dentate granule cells in hippocampus were stimulated with a tetanic stimulus, the depolarization potential of the postsynaptic cell was enhanced, and this potentiation lasted for a considerable period of time. At the time of this discovery, it was already known that the hippocampus probably played a central role in memory (e.g. from the classic studies of H.M.; see below), and the fact that the potentiation effect occurred in hippocampal cells lent further support to the notion that the effect had something to do with memory. The effect came to be known as *long-term potentiation* (LTP), and it has become a pivotal construct in modern conceptualizations of the cellular basis of learning and memory.

The notion that LTP was an important factor in learning received additional support from a series of experiments by Richard Morris and colleagues (e.g. Morris, Davis & Butcher, 1990). Previously, most experiments investigating LTP were done *in vitro*, i.e. in a slice of hippocampal tissue kept alive in a nutrient bath. Morris' experiments were conducted in awake, behaving animals. It had already been shown that the hippocampus is important for the learning of spatial information (Morris, Garrud, Rawlins & O'Keefe, 1982). Specifically, in order for a rat to learn successfully to swim to a submerged platform through an opaque water solution (what is known as the "water maze test"), the rat must have an intact hippocampus. Morris et al. applied various doses of a substance known as AP5 (or APV), which blocks induction of LTP in slice preparations, to rats performing the water maze test. This application blocked the learning curve at the behavioral level; i.e. the rats failed to acquire spatial knowledge about the location of the submerged platform. Furthermore, the relationship was dose-dependent, meaning that the more AP5 reached the hippocampus, the more retarded was the learning curve. Morris et al. also demonstrated that the retardation of the behavioral learning curve in the water maze task was directly congruent with the extent to which LTP was blocked in the hippocampus. In other words, less LTP was correlated with poorer learning, and more LTP was correlated with better learning. These results provided strong behavioral evidence supporting the role of LTP in the cellular basis of learning.

Important advances in the understanding of learning and memory at the molecular level have come from the work of Eric Kandel and his colleagues (e.g. Kandel & Schwartz, 1982; Hawkins, Abrams, Carew & Kandel, 1983). Much of this work has been done in the marine mollusc *Aplysia californica*, chosen because it has a simple nervous system composed of approximately 10 000 neurons. The neurons are unusually large and easily identifiable, making *Aplysia* far more amenable to cellular-level studies than are vertebrates with infinitely more complex systems. Detailed investigations in *Aplysia* have elucidated several important findings regarding the cellular basis of learning. At the same time, genetic studies in *Drosophila melanogaster* (a fruit fly) have yielded complementary data (e.g. Dudai, 1988; Tully, 1991). This simple organism has several important advantages which have greatly facilitated the genetic dissection of learning and memory. It is easy to culture, it is prolific, it has a short generation cycle, and it makes hundreds of single-gene mutations affecting varied traits such as enzyme kinetics and neuronal ion channel function, which are already known from previous work.

Work in *Aplysia* by Kandel and colleagues furnished some of the first direct evidence that alterations of synaptic efficacy play a causal role in learning. In a general sense, this supported the principle articulated by Hebb. Specifically, they discovered that behavioral habituation of the gill and siphon withdrawal reflex, a staple behavioral preparation in *Aplysia*, was mediated by a reduction in transmitter release at a defined synaptic locus (Pinsker, Kupfermann, Castellucci, & Kandel, 1970; Castellucci & Kandel, 1974). Subsequently, Bailey and Chen (1983) showed that habituation was accompanied by alterations in the morphology of electrophysiologically identified synapses.

Work along these lines has led to three general principles. First, the findings suggest that information storage is intrinsic to sensorimotor pathways mediating a particular learned behavior. Second, information storage is an alteration in the efficacy of existing neural pathways. A corollary of this second principle is that overall synaptic throughput can be enhanced by having more presynaptic terminals available to release transmitter. A third principle is that the detection of contiguity in classical conditioning is a biological property of neurons. This property arises out of a capacity for dual activation of adenylate cyclase, by a G-protein, which is believed to represent the unconditioned stimulus in classical conditioning paradigms, and by calcium-calmodulin, which is believed to represent the conditioned stimulus. The consequence of the "allosteric" modification of the adenylate cyclase is that its subsequent activation by unconditioned stimuli will result in greater production of cAMP and in turn, enhanced phosphorylation of presynaptic K^+ channels. Later conditioned stimuli will then cause even greater transmitter release than occurs after presynaptic facilitation on its own.

Other important discoveries at the molecular level include the finding that the substance glutamate is an important neurotransmitter released by hippocampal afferents. It is an excitatory neurotransmitter for most pyramidal neurons, and it binds to three different receptor types on the postsynaptic cell. One of them is known as the NMDA receptor because it is activated by the glutamate analog, *N*-methyl-D-aspartate. The NMDA receptor is a protein that has binding sites for both glutamate and glycine, and also has a channel that opens to extracellular ions only when the cell is depolarized from its resting level by about 30 mV or more. This property (i.e. a dual requirement for both receptor-site binding and previous depolarization of the cell) implies that the NMDA receptor may act as a sort of conjunction detector. In other words, the NMDA receptor might be one important cellular mechanism for LTP and associative learning. Convergent evidence comes from molecular studies showing that AP5, which was alluded to earlier, blocks LTP in CA1 pyramidal cells by acting as an antagonist for glutamate, competing for specific receptor sites on the NMDA receptor.

There are varied opinions regarding specific interpretations of the studies of *Aplysia* (cf. Morris, 1990), but there is no question that these investigations have provided direct evidence for forms of synaptic plasticity that could provide the cellular and molecular basis for at least some forms of learning and memory.

GLOSSARY AND RESEARCH PARADIGMS

We begin our discussion on memory at systems level by reviewing a number of terms and paradigms.

"Memory" refers to knowledge that is stored in the brain and to the processes of acquiring and retrieving such knowledge.

The process of forming memory involves three basic steps: (1) acquisition, (2) consolidation, and (3) storage. *Acquisition* refers to the process of bringing knowledge into the brain and into a first-stage memory "buffer", via sensory organs and primary sensory cortices. *Consolidation* is the process of rehearsing knowledge and building a robust representation of it in the brain. *Storage* refers to the creation of a relatively stable "memory trace" or "record" of knowledge in the brain. In learning a new face, for example, you would consolidate information concerning the visual pattern, and create a relatively permanent record of this pattern, a record which would then be connected to other pertinent knowledge (e.g. facts about the situation in which you met the person, the person's name, and so on). Our brains use *dynamic* records, rather than static, immutable memory traces. For examples, the "record" of the face you learned in the example above is a set of neuron circuit changes which can be reactivated, rather than a "picture" that is stored somewhere in the brain. Dynamic records can be modified to reflect your evolving experience (cf. Damasio, 1989, 1994). There is good reason to believe that, depending on the type of memory under consideration, the storage may be *selectional* or *instructional*; i.e. it may depend more or less on selection from a pre-existing repertoire of neuron circuit states (cf. Edelman, 1987; Shenoy, Kaufman, McGrann & Shaw, 1993).

"Retrieval" is the process of reactivating knowledge in such a way that it can become an image in consciousness (as in recall and recognition) or translated into a motor output (movement in a limb or in the vocal apparatus, autonomic activity).

Research Paradigms

Investigation of the neural basis of human memory at systems level has utilized several paradigms. Foremost among these is the *lesion method*, which refers to the study of cognitive functions in individuals with focal brain injuries (Damasio & Damasio, 1989). In fact, detailed investigations of a few subjects with rare patterns of brain damage have provided much of the current information regarding the neural substrates of human memory. One is a patient known as "H.M.", a man who developed a severe inability to acquire new factual knowledge following bilateral resection of the mesial temporal lobes to control seizures (Corkin, 1984; Milner, 1972; Scoville & Milner, 1957). Another is the patient known as "Boswell", a man who suffered extensive damage to both temporal lobes following herpes simplex encephalitis. Boswell lost his capacity to acquire new factual knowledge, and also to retrieve previously learned knowledge of varied types (Damasio, Eslinger et al., 1985; Damasio, Tranel & Damasio, 1989). Both subjects are remarkable for the fact that their profound memory disturbance occurs in the setting of otherwise well-preserved cognitive functioning—for example, they have normal language, basic intellectual abilities, perception, and attention. The two provide an ideal contrast, because in H.M. the memory impairment is confined to new learning (anterograde memory), whereas in Boswell, both new learning and previously acquired knowledge (retrograde memory) are affected.

The lesion method is a time-honored tradition of investigating the neural basis of mental functions, and in fact, the initial studies of H.M. began nearly four decades ago. However, recent advances in neuroimaging have increased the power of the method. First was the arrival of computed tomography (CT) in the mid-1970s; this was followed by magnetic resonance imaging (MRI) about a decade later. These techniques have permitted *in vivo* visualization of brain structures with a degree of detail many orders of magnitude greater than that available previously. Coupled with advances in experimental neuropsychology, which provided well-controlled, standardized methods of measuring memory and other cognitive functions (cf. Benton, 1988), the neuroimaging techniques have facilitated a fine-grained analysis of neural correlations of complex human functions.

Other methods are currently being used. *Positron emission tomography*, known as PET, involves the measurement of brain cell activity, such as glucose metabolism and local blood flow. In the PET paradigm, it is possible to study which brain regions are "active" during particular cognitive tasks (and which ones are not), allowing inferences about how certain neural units are related to certain mental functions. Another new technique is *functional magnetic resonance imaging* (fMRI). Similar to PET, functional MRI can be used to measure levels of activity in various brain regions during cognitive tasks, permitting inferences about how neural units relate to mental activity.

MEMORY SYSTEMS IN THE HUMAN BRAIN

The principal systems which subserve memory are constituted by cortical regions and nuclei located in various sectors of the cerebral cortex and subcortical gray matter. Accordingly, we have chosen to arrange the presentation according to a neuroanatomical criterion. Some of the subdivisions in each section are arranged around psychological constructs, and the reader is referred to Chapter 1 for complementary information regarding those constructs.

The framework for our presentation on the neural foundations of memory has been discussed elsewhere (see Damasio & Damasio, 1994; Damasio, 1989). Briefly, this framework specifies that there is a relative functional compartmentalization in the brain. One large set of systems in early sensory cortices and motor cortices explicitly represents "sense" and "action" knowledge. Another set of systems in higher-order cortices and subcortical structures such as the basal ganglia orchestrates the construction of those explicit representations in sensory-motor cortices; that is, promotes and establishes temporal correspondences among the activities of separate areas. Yet another set of systems ensures the attentional enhancement required for the concerted operation of the others. All of these systems operate under the influence of internal preferences and biases, as expressed in brain core networks concerned with enacting survival-related biological drives and instincts.

The reconstruction of explicit representations is accomplished in separate "early sensory" regions, by means of long-range cortico-cortical feedback projections which mediate relatively synchronous excitatory activation. The time scale of the large-scale synchronization from higher-order cortices is of the order of several thousand milliseconds, the scale required for meaningful cognition. At more local levels, the scale is smaller, of the order of tens of milliseconds. In this framework, the neural device from which reconstructions are conducted is known as a *convergence zone* (Damasio, 1989).

A convergence zone is an ensemble of neurons within which many feedforward/feedback loops make contact. A convergence zone:

- Receives feedforward projections from cortical regions located in the connectional level immediately below;
- Sends reciprocal feedback projections to the originating cortices;
- Sends feedforward projections to cortical regions in the next connectional level;
- Receives projections from heterarchically placed cortices and from subcortical nuclei in thalamus, basal forebrain, and brain stem.

Knowledge retrieval is based on relatively simultaneous, attended activity in many early cortical regions, engendered over several recurrences in such a system. The result is a *topographically organized* representation. The level at which knowledge is retrieved (e.g. superordinate, subordinate) depends on the scope of multiregional activation, which in turn depends on the level of convergence zone that is activated. Low-level convergence zones bind signals relative to entity categories (e.g. color, shape), and are placed in association cortices located immediately beyond ("downstream" from) the cortices whose activity defines featural representations. Higher-level convergence zones bind signals relative to more complex combinations, and are placed at a higher level in the cortico-cortical hierarchy. The convergence zones capable of binding entities into events and describing their categorization are located at the "top" of the hierarchical streams, in anterior temporal and frontal regions.

The *dispositional* representation embodied in a convergence zone is the result of previous learning, during which feedforward projections and reciprocating feedback projections were simultaneously active. During both learning and retrieval, the neurons in a convergence zone are under the control of a variety of cortical and non-cortical projections. These include projections from thalamus, non-specific neurotransmitter nuclei, and other cortical projections from convergence zones in prefrontal cortices; cortices located higher up in the feedforward hierarchy; homologous cortices of the opposite hemisphere; and heterarchical cortices of parallel hierarchical streams.

In short, the structures and processes required to store and access dispositional representations must be distinguished from the structures and processes needed for on-line topographically organized representations. Activation of neuron assemblies in anterior temporal region does *not* produce, within the assembly itself, a topographically organized representation, and as a consequence, we cannot be made conscious of the activity within the anterior temporal cortex itself. Instead, when the neuron assemblies which hold dispositional representations are activated, and lead in turn to the activation of early sensory cortices, they cause topographically organized representations to be formed in those cortices. Eventually, we experience the latter as images, their quality being less vivid than those that are produced during perception but their essential nature being no different.

We turn now to a discussion of specific neural systems dedicated to varied aspects of memory. We begin with the temporal lobes, which contain a large proportion of the neural systems critical for memory.

Temporal Lobes

The Hippocampus and Related Structures

Anatomy. The mesial temporal lobe contains several structures that are critical for memory, including the hippocampus, the amygdala, the entorhinal and perirhinal cortices, and the portion of parahippocampal gyrus not occupied by the entorhinal cortex (Figures 2.1 and 2.2). The hippocampus is the key component in this set of structures, which can be conveniently referred to as the *hippocampal complex.*

The components of the hippocampal complex are highly interconnected by means of recurrent neuroanatomical circuits. In turn, the hippocampal complex is extensively interconnected with higher-order association cortices located in the temporal lobe. Those cortices receive signals from the association cortices of all sensory modalities, and also receive back projections from the hippocampus. Their relationships are shown in Figure 2.3. Structures in the hippocampal complex have access to, and influence over, signals from virtually the entire brain. The system is thus in a position to create records that bind together various aspects of memory experiences, including visual, auditory, and somatosensory information.

In a general sense, it is reasonable to describe the principal function of the

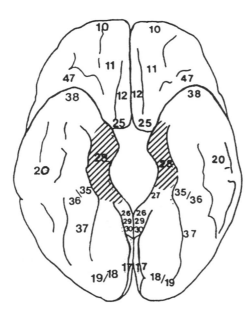

Figure 2.1 The inferior (ventral) aspect of the cerebral hemispheres (the left hemisphere is on the right side, and vice versa). The mesial location of the hippocampal complex is stippled. The parahippocampal gyrus (area 28) shows in this view; the hippocampus is buried deep within the region

hippocampal complex as the acquisition of new factual knowledge. The system is certainly essential to create records of the interactions between organisms and the world outside, as well as records of thought processes such as those engaged in planning. The precise computational operations performed by the hippocampus, however, have not been fully clarified (cf. Mishkin, 1978; Squire, 1992).

The ability of the brain to acquire new knowledge is of obvious importance in numerous aspects of everyday life, and disruption of this function, such as occurs frequently in Alzheimer's disease, head injury, certain types of brain infection, and anoxia and ischemia, can have devastating consequences.

There are two hippocampal complexes, one in the left hemisphere and one in the right. Anatomically, the two are roughly equivalent, but there are major differences in their functional roles. The two hippocampal complexes are specialized for different types of knowledge in a manner that parallels the usual functional arrangement of the brain, in which most individuals develop left-hemisphere specialization for language, and right-hemisphere specialization for spatial and nonlinguistic abilities. The left-sided complex seems to have greater involvement in verbal material. The hippocampal complex on the right seems mostly specialized for nonverbal material, such as faces, geographical routes, melodies, spatial information. When one of the hippocampal complexes is damaged, the capacity to acquire the aspect of knowledge which relies upon the damaged system is lost or relatively reduced. After damage to the *left* hippocam-

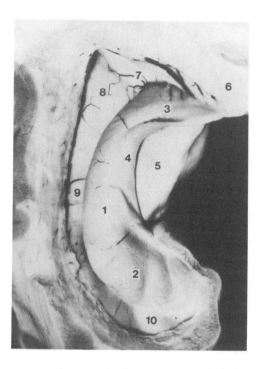

Figure 2.2   The hippocampus (1–3) and related structures (4–10). Adapted from Duvernoy (1988) by permission of the author and publisher

pus, for example, a patient may lose the ability to learn new names, but remain capable of learning new faces and spatial arrangements (e.g. Tranel, 1991).

Involvement in declarative memory. Another feature of the hippocampal complex is that it is dedicated primarily to *declarative* forms of memory; i.e. the learning of new facts, words, names, faces, and other material that can be "declared" and "brought to mind" (see Chapter 1). There are several types of *nondeclarative* learning and retrieval that appear to be entirely independent of hippocampal function. Thus, the learning of motor skills, habits, and other nondeclarative knowledge is not linked to the hippocampal complex (e.g Gabrieli, Corkin, Mickel & Growden, 1993; Squire, 1992; Tranel & Damasio, 1993; Tranel et al., 1994).

Involvement in anterograde memory. As noted above, the key function of the hippocampal complex is the acquisition of new factual knowledge (anterograde memory). By contrast, the system does not seem to have a crucial role in retrieval of previously learned knowledge (retrograde memory). Extensive bilateral damage to the hippocampus spares the capacity to retrieve knowledge from the past, even when new learning has been rendered virtually impossible. This is illustrated in compelling fashion by patient H.M., who despite complete bilateral

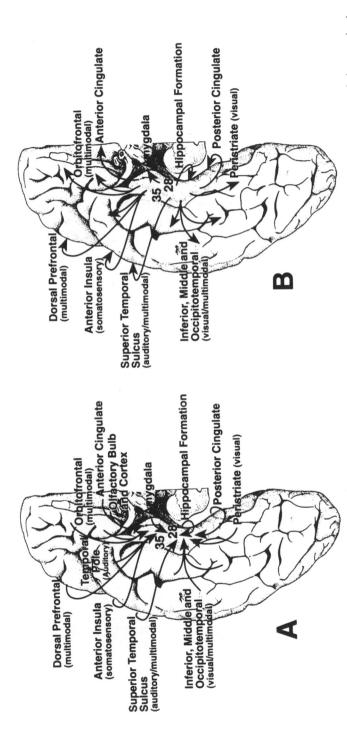

Figure 2.3 Drawings depicting neuroanatomical connectivity between the hippocampal complex and various parts of the cerebral cortices. The system has extensive bidirectional connections with unimodal and polymodal association cortices throughout the brain. The figure shows ventral views of the human brain depicting likely input (A) and output (B) relationships of the entorhinal (area 28) and perirhinal (area 35) cortices as gleaned from nonhuman primate neuroanatomical research (see Van Hoesen, 1982; also Hyman et al., 1988). These areas probably receive extensive direct or indirect sensory-specific (unimodal) association input (olfactory, auditory, somatosensory, and visual) as well as multimodal sensory input from the prefrontal, superior temporal and occipitotemporal regions of the cortex. Limbic system input from the amygdala, hippocampal formation, temporal polar and cingulate areas is also a probable neuroanatomical feature. In all instances, the input structures receive direct or indirect feedback from areas 28 and 35. The powerful interconnections between the entorhinal/perirhinal cortices and the hippocampal formation assure widespread cortical and hippocampal interactions in a multitude of neural systems

removal of the hippocampus, can remember information that he had acquired prior to his surgery. Also, in patients with moderate or even advanced Alzheimer's disease, in whom hippocampal pathology is extensive and learning of new factual knowledge has been reduced virtually to zero, there may remain a surprising degree of accurate recall of information from the past; in fact, it is often the case that the farther back in time one goes, the better the patient's recall is.

Other Temporal Lobe Structures

We turn now to memory-related regions of the temporal lobe that are outside the medial hippocampal complex. These structures comprise anatomical units in anterior, inferior, and lateral portions of the temporal lobe (Figure 2.4), which can be referred to collectively as the nonmedial temporal region. Included are cortices in the temporal pole (Brodmann area 38), the inferotemporal region (Brodmann areas 20/21, 36, part of 37), and the region of transition between the posterior temporal lobe and the inferior occipital lobe (Brodmann area 37). Details of brain–behavior relationships regarding this region are less well understood than those of the medial hippocampal complex. Some of the better known findings are reviewed below.

Role in retrograde memory. In a general sense, structures in the nonmedial temporal region are important for the retrieval of previously learned knowledge;

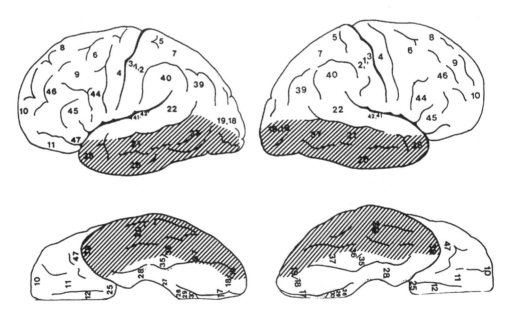

Figure 2.4 Lateral (upper) and inferior (lower) views of the left (left side of figure) and right (right side of figure) cerebral hemispheres. The regions formed by areas 38, 20/21, 36, 37, and ventral 18/19 (stippling) are important for long-term memory

i.e. *retrograde memory*. Damage to the nonmedial system can impair significantly the capacity to retrieve previously learned information. When the damage is bilateral, in fact, retrograde memory may be severely compromised for a wide array of knowledge. Patient Boswell, one of the few well-studied cases with extensive bilateral nonmedial temporal destruction, has lost nearly all capacity to retrieve knowledge about his past. Outside of a few shreds of general information regarding his hometown, and his former occupation, he can recall virtually nothing regarding important events of his past life—for example, he cannot remember details about his spouse, his children, places he has lived, or his educational history. Even the few pieces of information that he does retrieve cannot be placed correctly in the context of his autobiography (Jones & Tranel, 1993).

The left- and right-sided systems. In general, the nonmedial temporal region follows the same organizational principles as other parts of the brain; i.e. the left side is specialized for verbal material, and the right for nonverbal material. For example, the left nonmedial structures play a key role in the retrieval of lexical knowledge, particularly common and proper nouns that denote nonunique and unique entities, respectively. The right-sided structures, on the other hand, are specialized for knowledge such as faces and geographical routes.

Unique and nonunique knowledge. There is considerable subspecialization within the nonmedial temporal region for unique and nonunique types of knowledge (Damasio & Damasio, 1994; Damasio, Damasio, Tranel & Brandt, 1990). Knowledge which belongs to conceptual categories in which there are many members (e.g. "tools") is referred to as nonunique, while knowledge that belongs to categories of one (e.g. Clint Eastwood) is referred to as unique. The units which compose the knowledge systems are arranged in hierarchical fashion, so that structures located more posteriorly are concerned with nonunique forms of knowledge, while structures located more anteriorly are dedicated to unique forms of knowledge.

Consider a subunit in the nonmedial temporal system known as the inferotemporal region (IT), whose role in higher-order visually-related memory processes has been well established from neuroanatomical and neurophysiological studies in nonhuman primates (Felleman & Van Essen, 1991; Rockland & Van Hoesen, 1994; Ungerleider & Mishkin, 1982; Kaas, 1988; Gross, 1972; Perrett, Mistlin & Chitty, 1987; Tanaka, Saito, Fukada & Moriya, 1991; Miyashita, 1993; Fujita, Tanaka, Ito & Cheng, 1992), and from lesion studies in humans (Damasio, Damasio, Tranel & Brandt, 1990; Damasio & Damasio, 1994). This region is formed primarily by the lateral and inferior aspects of areas 20/21, 36, and 37 (Figure 2.4). The IT region has a role in the retrieval of conceptual knowledge related to *nonunique* entities (e.g. animals, fruits and vegetables) and other items that are normally recognized at a basic object level (e.g. a "raccoon" or an "eggplant"), but not more specifically (not as individual members of the class). Thus, recognition of various nonunique entities depends on retrieval of conceptual information supported by neural systems in IT (Damasio et al., 1990; see also Warrington & McCarthy, 1987).

The anterior parts of the nonmedial temporal region are involved in the retrieval of *unique* conceptual information. To recognize a familiar person, for example, we call on information that is supported by structures in the anterior nonmedial temporal region (e.g. Tranel & Damasio, 1985). Bilateral damage that precludes modality-specific access to this region can produce a condition in which affected individuals lose their ability to recognize familiar faces (*prosopagnosia*) and other visual stimuli that are normally recognized at unique level (e.g. the White House, Buckingham Palace).

There is some degree of left–right specialization of nonmedial temporal systems, although much of this remains to be explored. With regard to face recognition, for example, units in the right hemisphere part of the system seem to use a more holistic, gestalt-based method of analysis, while units in the left hemisphere systems seem to operate with a more sequential, feature-based method. Damage restricted to units in one of the two systems (confined to the left or right side) usually does not produce full-blown defects in face recognition, and patients with bilateral damage manifest the most profound forms of prosopagnosia.

There is strong left-sided specialization for the retrieval of lexical items (words) that denote various entities. Thus, retrieval of the names that go with nonunique and unique entities depends on neural structures in the left nonmedial temporal region. Following the principle of hierarchical arrangement mentioned earlier, the retrieval of common nouns, which denote nonunique concrete entities (animals, fruits/vegetables, tools/utensils, etc.), depends on more posterior structures, including part of the IT complex. By contrast, retrieval of proper nouns, which denote unique entities such as faces and landmarks, depends on the anterior-most part of the nonmedial temporal region, including area 38 located in the pole of the temporal lobe.

The right nonmedial temporal system does not appear to play a role in lexical retrieval; however, the anterior part of this system may be important for the retrieval of unique personal knowledge—information about various entities and events that comprise the autobiography of an individual. For instance, if you were asked to remember your graduation from high school, your wedding, the birth of your first child, and so on, you would utilize factual knowledge that is supported by neural systems in the right anterolateral temporal region.

Modality-Specific "Early" Sensory Cortices

Each of the primary sensory modalities (visual, auditory, somatosensory) has associated with it a band of adjacent cortex that is termed a *primary association area*, and these association cortices have important roles in memory.

In the visual modality, for example, the cortex in the lingual gyrus, immediately adjacent to primary visual cortex in the inferior mesial occipital lobe, contains important neural units for the processing of color. Other visual association cortices in this region (in the lingual and fusiform gyri) are important for the processing of form (shape). In an intriguing functional design that is only recently beginning to be understood, it appears that the same association cortices that are called into play when we *perceive* various information, are used when we *recall* that information.

For example, consider a well-known place, such as your bedroom. In the many times that you have looked at your bedroom, information regarding color, shape and texture was perceptually processed by visual association cortices. If you now attempt to imagine your bedroom (without being there to look at it), to bring it into your mind's eye, you can conjure up details about the place, including aspects of color and form. Recent studies suggest that the color and form information generated in recall is based on the same neural structures that were used to perceive the information in the first place; i.e. visual association regions in the inferior occipital lobes (Damasio, Grabowski, et al., 1993; Kosslyn et al., 1993).

This design is probably repeated in other sensory modalities, so that association regions for each modality process basic information related to the sensory modality, and support the retrieval of that knowledge in recall. For audition, this includes knowledge about various auditory features of a stimulus or event, such as the blend of sounds, the pitches, melodies, acoustic word-forms, and other aural patterns. The association cortices connected to the somatosensory modality contain neural units used in the perception and recall of knowledge regarding texture, weight, smoothness, and other tactile percepts.

Frontal Lobes

There are several memory-related neural systems in the frontal lobes, including those in the ventromedial and dorsolateral frontal regions. There is some controversy regarding whether these systems actually play primary roles in memory (cf. Shimamura, Janowsky & Squire, 1991). Some investigators have maintained that the role of frontal lobe systems in memory is indirect, secondary to their involvement in processes such as attention, encoding and problem-solving. In any event, there is no question that the memory disorders associated with lesions to frontal systems are quite distinct from those that occur with medial temporal damage. We review here some of the main findings in this area.

Ventromedial Frontal Region

The ventromedial frontal region is comprised by (1) the orbital cortices in the ventral and lower mesial part of the frontal lobe, including Brodmann areas 11 and 12, and (2) parts of areas 32 and 10 in the lower mesial aspect of the frontal lobe. Related nearby neural units include the posterior aspect of the orbital region (area 25) and the anterior cignulate gyrus (area 24). This region has interesting anatomical connections with other parts of the brain. It receives projections from all sensory modalities, either directly or indirectly, including vision, audition and touch (Chavis & Pandya, 1976; Jones & Powell, 1970; Pandya & Kuypers, 1969; Potter & Nauta, 1979). It is also a source of projections from frontal regions to central autonomic control structures (Nauta, 1971). In addition, the ventromedial cortices have extensive bidirectional connections with the hippocampus and amygdala. Thus, the ventromedial region has direct influence over basic autonomic functions including various patterns of visceral and musculoskeletal activity that are involved in emotional processing (e.g feelings of fear, anger, happiness, surprise). At the same time, the region is privy to information hailing from all major sensory modalities.

In keeping with the anatomical arrangement, the ventromedial frontal region has an important memory function that pertains to the relationship between memory and emotion. The region contains circuits which help link categorized factual knowledge to pertinent emotions and feelings, or what have been termed "somatic markers" (Damasio, Tranel & Damasio, 1991). For example, many learning experiences take place in the context of particular emotions, and a certain feeling may be an important part of the overall memory episode. Consider an example in which a child learns the relationship between the size of flame in the woodstove and the temperature of the chimney pipe (onto which the child puts her hand). Learning that a large flame predicts a red-hot stovepipe will be accompanied by a strong somatic marker, namely, the feeling of pain (burned hand); in fact, the feeling may be sufficiently strong that one learning trial will establish the association firmly and permanently in the child's brain.

Learning experiments of this type, in which a distinct somatic marker is part of the set of memorial information, are important in the socialization process. We learn that certain stimulus configurations are associated with certain feeling states, and this information helps us guide our behavior in our overall best interest, in both the short and long term.

Circuits in the ventromedial frontal lobe provide the support for linking various stimuli with various feeling states, thus helping us make advantageous decisions. Following damage to those circuits, individuals develop patterns of maladaptive social behavior and decision-making (Damasio, 1994; Damasio, Tranel & Damasio, 1991). They behave as if they have no regard for potential punishment (Bechara et al., 1994). Such persons, in fact, may behave sociopathically. Moreover, improper early development of critical neural units in the ventromedial frontal region, which would deprive the individual of the opportunity to establish links between various stimulus configurations and various feeling states, could lead to a lifelong pattern of psychopathy (antisocial personality disorder; see Tranel, 1994).

The ventromedial frontal region may also play a role in prospective memory, the capacity of "remembering in the future" (e.g. Wilkins & Baddeley, 1978; see Chapter 1). Take as an example the following scenario. You are supposed to remember to call your spouse at around mid-day, to arrange plans for picking up children from school. You can appose a "somatic marker" to this stimulus configuration, so that when noon-time arrives, you are "reminded" by your brain to call your spouse (via a signal from the ventromedial frontal region, which may come as the feeling that "something needs to be done").

Dorsolateral Frontal Region

A curious form of memory capacity has been linked to the dorsolateral sector of the frontal lobes (Anderson, Damasio & Tranel, 1993; Milner, 1971; Milner, Corsi & Leonard, 1991; Smith & Milner, 1988), that is, the expanse of cortex and attendant white matter that comprises the prefrontal region on the convexity of the hemispheres. This is a type of memory in which we are called upon to estimate the number of times that a particular event has occurred (frequency judgment), or how long ago something took place (recency judgment).

For example, if you were asked, "How many times did you look at your watch yesterday?", you would form an estimate by searching back through your memories of yesterday, bringing to mind the events of the day, what you were doing, and so on. Answering the question requires a judgment or estimate of *frequency*. A similar capacity is called for when you are asked a question such as, "When was the last time your talked to your mother on the phone?" The answer may be anywhere from minutes to years. Estimating the *recency* of a behavior such as this is another capacity that requires a type of memory that has been linked to the dorsolateral sector of the frontal lobes.

In general, there may be some degree of hemispheric specialization for recency/frequency judgments, whereby the left dorsolateral region is dominant for verbally-coded information, while the right is dominant for nonverbal, visuospatial information (in keeping with the overall hemispheric specialization of the brain). It should be noted, though, that there are very few studies of this topic, and the neuroanatomical basis of recency/frequency judgments must be considered tentative.

One other type of memory, known as working memory, should be mentioned. Working memory refers to a transient type of memory processing, of the order of seconds, in which we can hold "online" the relevant stimuli, rules and mental representations that are needed to execute a particular task (Baddeley, 1992; Goldman-Rakic, 1987; see Chapter 1). In particular, working memory is used to bridge temporal gaps—that is, to hold representations in a mental workspace long enough so that we can make appropriate responses to stimulus configurations or contingencies in which some, or even all, of the basic ingredients are no longer extant in perceptual space (Fuster, 1989; Goldman-Rakic, 1987). The concept of working memory has some overlap with short-term memory, as both are considered relatively transient and of limited capacity (see Chapter 11).

A reason for mentioning working memory in the current section is because this memory function has been linked to the prefrontal region of the brain, i.e. part of the dorsolateral frontal lobe that comprises the anterior convexity of the cerebral hemispheres (Goldman-Rakic & Friedman, 1991; Fuster, 1991). However, most of the studies of working memory have been done in nonhuman primates, making it difficult to draw direct neuroanatomical comparisons with humans. Nonetheless, there is strong evidence in nonhuman primates that the prefrontal region plays a crucial role in working memory, and it is likely that this relationship will apply to humans as well, at least to some extent (see Baddeley, 1986, Chapter 10).

Basal Forebrain

The basal forebrain is formed by a set of bilateral paramidline gray nuclei that includes the septal nuclei, the diagonal band of Broca, and the substantia innominata. It is not part of the frontal lobe technically, but it may be involved in cases of damage to ventromedial frontal cortices, and it is thus important to know about its functions.

One of the principal functions of this region is to deliver the critical neurotransmitter acetylcholine to the hippocampus and many regions of the cerebral cortex. The basal forebrain also delivers to various parts of the cerebral cortex other important neurotransmitters such as dopamine, norepinephrine, and serotonin. When the delivery of these neurotransmitters is disrupted by damage in basal forebrain, defects in memory can result (Damasio, Graff-Radford et al., 1985). The memory impairment, however, is much different from that produced by lesions in the medial temporal hippocampal complex.

The basal forebrain appears to contribute to the *binding together of different modal components of a particular memory*. That is, different pieces of modal information that belong together in a memory "set" are linked together in a coherent fashion by the influence of neuronal units in the basal forebrain. Consider the following example: We are watching a program on television about a small-country dictator who has gone on a rampage to destroy all persons of a certain ethnic origin. During the program, we learn (1) the face and general appearance of the dictator; (2) his name; (3) the accent he has when speaking English; and (4) various facts about his regime. The basic learning of these pieces of information is dependent upon the medial temporal system, as discussed previously. However, the basal forebrain plays a key role in the *binding together* of these pieces of information, so that they form a set in recall. For example, when we recall the name of the dictator, we will also recall the nature of his speech accent and specific information about his activities.

When the basal forebrain is functioning improperly or not at all, the capacity to keep various components of memorial episodes linked together in coherent sets is lost. In the example above, the face of the dictator may be recalled, but it will be put together with an incorrect name, an incorrect speech accent, or incorrect factual information about his activities. This modal mismatching of information can affect retrograde as well as the anterograde recall. For example, a patient may remember various facts about an occupation from ten years previously, but link these facts with the wrong business name and wrong geographical location. The following quote from a patient illustrates this problem: "I used to work on an assembly line (correct) putting metal rings on the legs of frozen turkeys (correct), at the Hawkeye Packing Plant (incorrect) in the southwest part of town (incorrect)."

Basal Ganglia and Cerebellum

The basal ganglia are a set of gray-matter nuclei buried deep at the base of the cerebral hemispheres. They include the caudate nucleus, the putamen, the globus pallidus, and the subthalamic nucleus. Although the principal function of these structures is motor control, recent evidence suggests that they also have some important memory functions. Specifically, the basal ganglia have been linked to various forms of nondeclarative memory, particularly those types of memory that are dependent upon a motor act for their realization, or what has been termed *procedural memory* (e.g. riding a bicycle, skating). The cerebellum, another motor-related structure situated behind the brainstem at the base of the brain, participates along with the basal ganglia in many types of procedural learning and memory (e.g. Glickstein, 1993; Thompson, 1986, 1990).

The roles of the basal ganglia and cerebellum in procedural memory, on the one hand, and the medial temporal region (hippocampal complex) in declarative memory, on the other, are quite independent. Damage to one system may have little or no effect on the capacities of the other (e.g. Cohen & Squire, 1980; Gabrieli et al., 1993; Tranel et al., 1994). For example, the severe neuropathology in the medial temporal region caused by Alzheimer's disease may spare entirely the integrity of the basal ganglia and cerebellum; as a consequence, many patients with Alzheimer's disease remain fully capable of performing complex motor activities such as dancing or playing golf, and such patients may even be able to acquire new motor skills (Eslinger & Damasio, 1986). In fact, patients with virtually complete destruction of the medial temporal region, such as H.M. and Boswell, are capable of learning new motor skills, even when they cannot remember where, when, or any other factual (declarative) information about the context in which those skills were acquired (Gabrieli et al., 1993; Damasio et al., 1989; Tranel et al., 1994). The reverse situation occurs when disease strikes the basal ganglia, but spares the hippocampal complex. For example, in patients with Parkinson's or Huntington's disease, in whom neuropathology affects the basal ganglia but not the medial temporal region, the retrieval and learning of motor skills may be severely impaired, while memory for declarative knowledge is spared (e.g. Heindel et al., 1989). Damage to the cerebellum can also produce motor learning defects while sparing declarative memory.

The caudate nucleus, which together with the putamen forms the *striatal* component of the basal ganglia, may have nondeclarative memory functions that have to do with the development of habits and other "nonconscious" response tendencies. The tendencies we develop to respond to certain situations in certain ways, behaviors such as following the same route home each day, or repeatedly seeking out a particular person for moral support and encouragement, are examples of habits and response tendencies that we engage on a fairly automatic basis, with little or no conscious deliberation. These types of "memory" behavior have been linked to the striatum, and in particular, the caudate nucleus (e.g Tranel & Damasio, 1993).

Thalamus

Similar to the basal ganglia, the principal functions of the thalamus are outside the domain of memory. However, parts of the thalamus and related diencephalic structures do have important roles to play in it. Structures that have been consistently linked to memory include the dorsomedial and anterior nuclei of the thalamus, the mammillary bodies, and two related fiber tracts—the mammillothalamic tract, which connects the medial hippocampal complex to the anterior nuclei of the thalamus, and the ventroamygdalofugal pathway, which connects the amygdala to the dorsomedial nuclei.

The precise roles of these diencephalic structures in memory are not well specified, but in general, they support memory capacities in a manner that supplements the support of the medial temporal system (Butters & Stuss, 1989). In particular, structures in the diencephalon contribute to the acquisition of factual knowledge. They are less involved in retrieval of previously learned knowledge, and they do not appear to support nondeclarative memory. Anterior parts of the thalamus may make an important contribution to the temporal sequencing of memories; i.e. situating memories in correct temporal context. Also, the thalamus appears to have material-specific functions that parallel those of the medial temporal memory system: left-sided thalamic nuclei are specialized for verbal information, while right-sided nuclei are specialized for nonverbal, visuospatial material.

The diencephalon gives rises to a number of important neurochemical systems that innervate widespread regions of cerebral cortex. Thus, structures such as the mammillary bodies and certain thalamic nuclei may provide to the cortex important neurotransmitters that are needed for normal memory function. It follows that damage to the diencephalon may not only disrupt important neuroanatomical connections between limbic regions (including the hippocampal complex) and the neocortex, but it might also interfere with memory-related neurochemical influences on cortex.

CLOSING COMMENT

To provide a reasonable summary of the neural substrates of human memory, it is necessary to review a large number and variety of neural structures. In fact, it could be argued that virtually the entire human brain is concerned with memory, of one kind or another, at one level or another. From a scientific perspective, understanding the manner in which neural structures subserve memory remains a central question in neuroscience. Much progress has been realized since the days when notable researchers threw up their hands in despair and declared that memory "traces" could not be found in the brain. However, much remains to be discovered. We have barely begun to unravel some of the mysteries of how our brains subserve memory.

ACKNOWLEDGEMENT

The work reported here is supported by NINDS Program Project Grant NS 19632, ONR Grant N00014-91-J-1240, and the Mathers Foundation.

REFERENCES

Anderson, S.W., Damasio, H. & Tranel, D. (1993). Impaired memory for temporal order (recency) following ventromedial frontal lobe damage. *Society for Neuroscience Abstracts*, **19**, 791.

Baddeley, A.D. (1986). *Working Memory*. Oxford University Press. Oxford.

Bailey, C.H. & Chen, M.C. (1983). Morphological basis of long-term habituation and sensitization in *Aplysia*. *Science*, **220**, 91–93.

Bechara, A., Damasio, A.R., Damasio, H. & Anderson, S.W. (1994) Insensitivity to future consequences following damage to human prefrontal cortex. *Cognition*, **50**, 7–15.

Benton, A. (1988). Neuropsychology: Past, present, and future. In F. Boller & J. Grafman (eds), *Handbook of Neuropsychology*, vol. 1. Elsevier, Amsterdam, pp. 3–27.

Bliss, T.V. & Lomo, T. (1973). Long-lasting potentiation of synaptic transmission in the dentate area of the anaesthetized rabbit following stimulation of the perforant path. *Journal of Physiology* (*London*), **232**, 331–356.

Butters, N. & Stuss, D.T. (1989). Diencephalic amnesia. In F. Boller & J. Grafman (eds), *Handbook of Neuropsychology*, vol. 3. Elsevier, Amsterdam, pp. 107–148.

Castellucci, V.F. & Kandel, E.R. (1974). A quantal analysis of the synaptic depression underlying habituation of the gill-withdrawal reflex in *Aplysia*. *Proceedings of the National Academy of Sciences*, **71**, 5004–5008.

Chavis, D.A. & Pandya, D.N. (1976). Further observations on corticofrontal connections in the rhesus monkey. *Brain Research*, **117**, 369–386.

Cohen, N.J. & Squire, L.R. (1980). Preserved learning and retention of pattern-analyzing skill in amnesia: dissociation of knowing how and knowing that. *Science*, **210**, 207–210.

Cold Spring Harbor Symposia on Quantitative Biology (1990). *vol. LV: The Brain*. Cold Spring Harbor Laboratory Press, Plainview, NY.

Corkin, S. (1984). Lasting consequences of bilateral medial temporal lobectomy: clinical course and experimental findings in H.M. *Seminars in Neurology*, **4**, 249–259.

Damasio, A.R. (1989). Time-locked multiregional retroactivation: a systems-level proposal for the neural substrates of recall and recognition. *Cognition*, **33**, 25–62.

Damasio, A.R. (1994). *Descartes' Error: Emotion, Reason, and the Human Brain*. Grosset/Putnam, New York.

Damasio, H. & Damasio, A.R. (1989). *Lesion Analysis in Neuropsychology*. Oxford University Press, New York.

Damasio, A.R. & Damasio, H. (1994). Cortical systems for retrieval of concrete knowledge: the convergence zone framework. In C. Koch & J.L. Davis (eds), *Large-Scale Neuronal Theories of the Brain*. MIT Press, Cambridge, MA, pp. 61–74.

Damasio, A.R., Damasio, H., Tranel, D. & Brandt, J.P. (1990). The neural regionalization of knowledge access: preliminary evidence. *Quantitative Biology*, **55**, 1039–1047.

Damasio, A.R., Eslinger, P.J., Damasio, H., Van Hoesen, G.W. & Cornell, S. (1985). Multimodal amnesic syndrome following bilateral temporal and basal forebrain damage. *Archives of Neurology*, **42**, 252–259.

Damasio, A.R., Graff-Radford, N.R., Eslinger, P.J., Damasio, H. & Kassell, N. (1985). Amnesia following basal forebrain lesions. *Archives of Neurology*, **42**, 263–271.

Damasio, A.R., Tranel, D. & Damasio, H. (1989). Amnesia caused by herpes simplex encephalitis, infarctions in basal forebrain, Alzheimer's disease, and anoxia. In F. Boller & J. Grafman (eds), *Handbook of Neuropsychology* vol. 3. Elsevier, Amsterdam, pp. 149–166.

Damasio, A.R., Tranel, D. & Damasio, H. (1991). Somatic markers and the guidance of behavior: theory and preliminary testing. In H.S. Levin, H.M. Eisenberg & A.L. Benton (eds), *Frontal Lobe Function and Dysfunction*. Oxford University Press, New York, pp. 217–229.

Damasio, H., Grabowski, T.J., Damasio, A.R., Tranel, D., Boles-Ponto, L., Watkins, L.G. & Hichwa, R.D. (1993). Visual recall with eyes closed and covered activates early visual cortices. *Society for Neuroscience Abstracts*, **19**, 1603.

Dudai, Y. (1988). Neurogenetic dissection of learning and short-term memory in *Drosophila*. *Annual Review of Neuroscience*, **11**, 537–563.

Duvernoy, H.M. (1988). *The Human Hippocampus: An Atlas of Applied Anatomy*. J.F. Bergmann Verlag, Munich, Germany.

Edelman, G. (1987). *Neural Darwinism*. Basic Books, New York.

Eslinger, P.J. & Damasio, A.R. (1986). Preserved motor learning in Alzheimer's disease: implications for anatomy and behavior. *Journal of Neuroscience*, **6**, 3006–3009.

Felleman, D.J. & Van Essen, D.C. (1991). Distributed hierarchical processing in the primate cerebral cortex. *Cerebral Cortex*, **1**, 1–47.

Fujita, I., Tanaka, K., Ito, M, & Cheng, K. (1992). Columns for visual features of objects in monkey inferotemporal cortex. *Nature*, **360**, 343–346.

Fuster, J.M. (1989). *The Prefrontal Cortex*, 2nd edn. Raven Press, New York.

Fuster, J.M. (1991). Role of prefrontal cortex in delay tasks: evidence from reversible lesion and unit recording in the monkey. In H.S. Levin, H.M. Eisenberg & A.L. Benton (eds), *Frontal Lobe Function and Dysfunction*. Oxford University Press, New York, pp. 59–71.

Gabrieli, J.D.E., Corkin, S., Mickel, S.F. & Growden, J.H. (1993). Intact acquisition and long-term retention of mirror-tracing skill in Alzheimer's disease and in global amnesia. *Behavioral Neuroscience*, **107**, 899–910.

Glickstein, M. (1993). Cerebellar function in normal movement and in motor learning. In P. Andersen, O. Hvalby, O. Paulsen & B. Hokfelt (eds), *Memory Concepts—1993*. Elsevier, Amsterdam, pp. 127–135.

Goldman-Rakic, P.S. (1987). Circuitry of primate prefrontal cortex and regulation of behavior by representational memory. In F. Plum (ed.), *Handbook of Physiology: The Nervous System*, vol. 3. American Physiological Society, Bethesda, MD, pp. 373–417.

Goldman-Rakic, P.S. & Friedman, H.R. (1991). The circuitry of working memory revealed by anatomy and metabolic imaging. In H.S. Levin, H.M. Eisenberg & A.L. Benton (eds), *Frontal Lobe Function and Dysfunction*, Oxford University Press, New York, pp. 72–91.

Gross, C.G. (1972). Visual functions of inferotemporal cortex. In R. Jung (ed.), *Handbook of Sensory Physiology*, vol. 8, part 3B. Springer, Berlin, pp. 451–482.

Hawkins, R.D., Abrams, T.W., Carew, T.J. & Kandel, E.R. (1983). A cellular mechanism of classical conditioning in *Aplysia*: activity-dependent amplification of presynaptic facilitation. *Science*, **219**, 400–405.

Hebb, D.O. (1949). *Organization of Behavior*. Wiley, New York.

Heindel, W.C., Salmon, D.P. Shults, C.W., Walicke, P.A. & Butters, N. (1989). Neuropsychological evidence for multiple implicit memory systems: a comparison of Alzheimer's, Huntington's and Parkinson's disease patients. *Journal of Neuroscience*, **9**, 582–587.

Hyman, B.T., Kromer, L.J. & Van Hoesen, G.W. (1988). A direct demonstration of the perforant pathway terminal zone in Alzheimer's disease using the monoclonal antibody Alz-50. *Brain Research*, **450**, 392–397.

Jones, E.G. & Powell, T.P.S. (1970). An anatomical study of converging sensory pathways within the cerebral cortex of the monkey. *Brain*, **93**, 793–820.

Jones, R.D. & Tranel, D. (1993). Autobiographical memory in patients with focal brain lesions. *The Clinical Neuropsychologist*, **7**, 340.

Kass, J.H. (1988). Why does the brain have so many visual areas? *Journal of Cognitive Neuroscience*, **1**, 121–135.

Kandel, E.R. & Schwartz, J.H. (1982). Molecular biology of learning: modulation of transmitter release. *Science*, **218**, 433–443.

Kandel, E.R., Schwartz, J.H. & Jessell, T.M. (1991). *Principles of Neural Science*, 3rd edn. Elsevier, New York.

Kosslyn, S.M., Alpert, N.M., Thompson, W.L., Maljkovic, V., Weise, S.B., Chabris, C.F., Hamilton, S.E., Rauch, S.L. & Buonanno, F.S. (1993). Visual mental imagery activates topographically organized visual cortex: PET investigations. *Journal of Cognitive Neuroscience*, **5**, 263–287.

Milner, B. (1971). Interhemispheric differences in the localisation of psychological processes in man. *British Medical Bulletin*, **27**, 272–277.

Milner, B. (1972). Disorders of learning and memory after temporal lobe lesions in man. *Clinical Neurosurgery*, **19**, 421–446.

Milner, B., Corsi, P. & Leonard, G. (1991). Frontal-lobe contribution to recency judgments. *Neuropsychologia*, **29**, 601–618.

Mishkin, M. (1978). Memory in monkeys severely impaired by combined but not separate removal of amygdala and hippocampus. *Nature*, **273**, 297–298.

Miyashita, Y. (1993). Inferior temporal cortex: where visual perception meets memory. *Annual Review of Neuroscience*, **16**, 245–263.

Morris, R.G.M. (1990). Synaptic plasticity, neural architecture, and forms of memory. In J.L. McGaugh, N.M. Weinberger & G. Lynch (eds), *Brain Organization and Memory: Cells, Systems and Circuits*. Oxford University Press, New York, pp. 52–77.

Morris, R.G.M., Davis, S. & Butcher, S.P. (1990). Hippocampal synaptic plasticity and NMDA receptors: a role in information storage? *Philosophical Transactions of the Royal Society of London B*, **329**, 187–204.

Morris, R.G.M., Garrud, P., Rawlins, J.N.P. & O'Keefe, J. (1982). Place navigation impaired in rats with hippocampal lesions. *Nature*, **297**, 681–683.

Nauta, W.J.H. (1971). The problem of the frontal lobe: a reinterpretation. *Journal of Psychiatric Research*, **8**, 167–187.

Pandya, D.N. & Kuypers, H.G.J.M. (1969). Cortico-cortical connections in the rhesus monkey. *Brain Research*, **13**, 13–36.

Perrett, D.I., Mistlin, A.J. & Chitty, A.J. (1987). Visual neurons responsive to faces. *Trends in Neurosciences*, **10**, 358–364.

Pinsker, H., Kupfermann, I., Castellucci, V.F. & Kandel, E.R. (1970). Habituation and dishabituation of the gill-withdrawal reflex in *Aplysia*. *Science*, **167**, 1740–1742.

Potter, H. & Nauta W.J.H. (1979). A note on the problem of olfactory associations of the orbitofrontal cortex in the monkey. *Neuroscience*, **4**, 316–367.

Rockland, K.S. & Van Hoesen, G.W. (1994). Direct temporal–occipital feedback connections to striate cortex (V1) in the macaque monkey. *Cerebral Cortex*, **4**, 300–313.

Schimamura, A.P., Janowsky, J.S. & Squire, L.R. (1991). What is the role of frontal lobe damage in memory disorders? In H.S. Levin, H.M. Eisenberg & A.L. Benton (eds), *Frontal Lobe Function and Dysfunction*. Oxford University Press, New York, pp. 173–195.

Scoville, W.B. & Milner, B. (1957). Loss of recent memory after bilateral hippocampal lesions. *Journal of Neurology, Neurosurgery and Psychiatry*, **20**, 11–21.

Shenoy, K.V., Kaufman, J., McGrann, J.V. & Shaw, G.L. (1993). Learning by selection in the trion model of cortical organization. *Cerebral Cortex*, **3**, 239–248.

Smith, M.L. & Milner, B. (1988). Estimation of frequency of occurrence of abstract designs after frontal or temporal lobectomy. *Neuropsychologia*, **26**, 297–306.

Squire, L.R. (1992). Memory and the hippocampus: a synthesis from findings with rats, monkeys and humans. *Psychological Review*, **99**, 195–231.

Tanaka, K., Saito, H., Fukada, Y. & Moriya, M. (1991). Coding of visual images of objects in the inferotemporal cortex of the macaque monkey. *Journal of Neurophysiology*, **66**, 170–189.

Thompson, R.F. (1986). The neurobiology of learning and memory. *Science*, **233**, 941–947.

Thompson, R.F. (1990). Neural mechanisms of classical conditioning in mammals. *Philosophical Transactions of the Royal Society of London B*, **329**, 161–170.

Tranel, D. (1991). Dissociated verbal and nonverbal retrieval and learning following left anterior temporal damage. *Brain and Cognition*, **15**, 187–200.

Tranel, D. (1994). "Acquired sociopathy": the development of sociopathic behavior following focal brain damage. In D.C. Fowles, P. Sutker & S.H. Goodman (eds), *Progress in Experimental Personality and Psychopathology Research*, vol. 17. Springer, New York, pp. 285–311.

Tranel, D. and Damasio, A.R. (1985). Knowledge without awareness: an autonomic index of facial recognition by prosopagnosics. *Science*, **228**, 1453–1454.

Tranel, D. and Damasio, A.R. (1993). The covert learning of affective valence does not require structures in hippocampal system or amygdala. *Journal of Cognitive Neuroscience*, **5**, 79–88.

Tranel, D., Damasio, A.R., Damasio, H. & Brandt, J.P. (1994). Sensorimotor skill learning in amnesia: Additional evidence for the neural basis of nondeclarative memory. *Learning and Memory*, **1**, (in press).

Tully, T. (1991). Genetic dissection of learning and memory in *Drosophila melanogaster*. In J. Madden IV (ed.), *Neurobiology of Learning, Emotion and Affect*. Raven Press, New York, pp. 29–66.

Ungerleider, L.G. & Mishkin, M. (1982). Two cortical visual systems. In D.J. Ingle, M.A. Goodale & R.J.W. Mansfield (eds), *Analysis of visual behavior*. MIT Press, Cambridge, MA, pp. 549–586.

Van Hoesen, G.W. (1982). The parahippocampal gyrus. *Trends in Neurosciences*, **5**, 345–350.

Warrington, E.K. and McCarthy, R.A. (1987). Categories of knowledge: further fractionations and an attempted integration. *Brain*, **110**, 1273–1296.

Wilkins, A. & Baddeley, A. (1978). Remembering to recall in everyday life: an approach to absentmindedness. In M.M. Gruneberg, P.E. Morris & R.N. Sykes (eds), *Practical Aspects of Memory*. Academic Press, New York, pp. 27–34.

Section II

Varieties of Memory Disorder

Chapter 3

Clinical Differentiation of Amnesic Subtypes

Margaret O'Connor
Mieke Verfaellie
and
Laird S. Cermak
*Memory Disorders Research Center, and
Department of Veterans Affairs Medical Center, Boston, USA*

INTRODUCTION

Amnesic patients are individuals who demonstrate severe memory deficits yet retain perfectly normal intelligence. In this context, it would seem that the task of delineating core features of the amnesic syndrome would be straightforward. However, the complexities of arriving at a consensual definition of amnesia emerge as one contemplates precisely what is meant by amnesia. Further consideration underscores the need for clarity regarding both quantitative and qualitative aspects of the amnesic syndrome.

Consensus regarding the definition of amnesia has important implications for clinical diagnosis because the presence of amnesia suggests bilateral neuropathology in specific brain regions including medial temporal areas (Scoville & Milner, 1957; Milner, 1966) and diencephalic areas (Cramon, Hebel & Schuri, 1985; Mair, 1979). Such information is relevant to the formulation of medical diagnoses and is often suggestive of a specific disease process. Diagnostic clarity is also important because global amnesia is typically associated with a persistent and severe memory deficit whereas other types of memory problems, such as those secondary to attentional compromise, are not. Another clinical issue that depends upon the accurate classification of amnesic disorders is the identifica-

Handbook of Memory Disorders. Edited by A.D. Baddeley, B.A. Wilson and F.N. Watts.
© 1995 John Wiley & Sons Ltd.

tion of appropriate treatment strategies. A valid diagnosis of amnesia may even predict the extent to which pharmacological or psychological interventions are warranted.

The need for a mutually agreed definition of amnesia is also of paramount importance for research studies of amnesia. These studies generally address a broad spectrum of issues ranging from the neural substrates of memory and amnesia to cognitive aspects of these phenomena. Many investigators examine related issues in a dialectical manner; a specific question is pursued by several research teams utilizing very different experimental procedures. The validity of their respective findings and the extent to which cross-study comparisons can be made depend upon relative homogeneity of classification criteria. Consequently, the use of vague and ill-defined criteria confounds the research enterprise.

Amnesia occurs in conjunction with many neurologic or psychiatric disorders. In some instances, it is a transient phenomenon secondary to seizure activity or temporary vascular abnormalities (Kapur, 1993). In others, amnesia is of a more permanent nature. The neurologic conditions that give rise to amnesia include: herpes simplex encephalitis (Cermak, 1976; Cermak & O'Connor, 1983; Damasio et al., 1985a), cerebrovascular accidents (Katz, Alexander & Mandell, 1987; Stuss, Guberman, Nelson & Larochelle, 1988; Winocur et al., 1984), rupture and surgical repair of anterior communicating artery aneurysms (Alexander & Freedman, 1984; Vilkki, 1985), anoxia secondary to cardiac arrest or atherosclerosis (Volpe & Hirst, 1983; Zola-Morgan, Squire & Amaral, 1986), Wernicke Korsakoff syndrome (WKS) (Butters & Cermak, 1980; Victor, Adams & Collins, 1989), degenerative disorders (Weintraub & Mesulam, 1993), paraneoplastic limbic encephalitis (Ahern et al., 1994) and surgical ablation of limbic brain areas (Milner, 1966; Scovill & Milner, 1957).

In order to present this wide spectrum of disorders and to bring some clarity to a definition of amnesia, we have divided this chapter into two sections. In the first section, we present a framework for deriving a valid definition of amnesia and delineate some of the difficulties inherent in this task. In the second section, neuropsychological heterogeneity within the amnesic syndrome will be explored and patients will be described who present with amnesia based on a variety of etiological conditions. The neuropsychological features common to each of these conditions will be analyzed, as will the characteristics that distinguish them.

DEFINING AMNESIA

The most commonly agreed features of the amnesic syndrome include the following:

- Normal intelligence
- Normal attention span
- A severe and permanent learning deficit (i.e. anterograde amnesia)

- Loss of memory for information predating the onset of the brain damage (i.e. retrograde amnesia)
- Preserved skill acquisition (Parkin & Leng, 1993)

Despite the widespread acceptance of these criteria as core features of the amnesic syndrome, a precise clinical definition of amnesia has never been clearly demarcated. Most neuropsychologists use standardized tests of memory in their assessment of amnesia. The clinical diagnosis of amnesia becomes operationalized through test performance. However, there is no consensus concerning cut-off scores that are diagnostic of amnesia.

Some investigators have proposed quantitative criteria as indices of amnesia (Butters & Cermak, 1980). Traditionally, a 20-point disparity between performance on a test of general intelligence (WAIS-R IQ; Wechsler, 1981) and a standardized test of memory (WMS MQ; Wechsler, 1987) was considered evidence of amnesia. More recently, Butters and colleagues (Butters et al., 1988) reported that amnesic patients can be distinguished from normal control subjects and Alzheimer patients using difference scores between the Attention and General Memory Indices of the WMS-R.

While difference scores provide some information regarding the extent of memory impairment, there are problems with the use of this method in estimation of amnesia. For instance, an individual with a high IQ and a normal MQ can have the same difference score as someone of average intelligence and below-average memory abilities. If both individuals are to be considered amnesic, a very heterogeneous group of "amnesics" will result, with some demonstrating MQs well within the normal range. The use of difference scores between the Attention and General Memory Indices of the WMS-R (Butters et al., 1988) carries the same problem because a significant difference between these two indices does not guarantee that an individual has intact attention and impaired memory.

At the Memory Disorders Research Center the diagnosis of amnesia includes a comprehensive neuropsychological examination in order to describe a patient's neuropsychological profile. The evaluation of memory is the central focus of this assessment, but a wide range of other cognitive functions is sampled using standardized tests of intelligence, reasoning, judgment, attention span, vigilance, mental flexibility, language, perception, and personality. The need for such a comprehensive neuropsychological examination in the assessment of amnesia cannot be overemphasized. There are many factors that influence memory (e.g. aphasia, agnosia, depression, etc.), but not all are primary features of the amnesic syndrome. These need to be identified in order to understand the impact of such problems on the memory deficit. Only patients with pure amnesias, uncontaminated by extraneous factors, ought to be entered into group studies of the amnesic syndrome. Other patients may be interesting and could be evaluated in the form of single-case investigations, but they should not be placed into amnesic groups as their memory impairment may be influenced by other deficits.

VARIATIONS WITHIN THE AMNESIC SYNDROME

A great deal of heterogeneity exists within the amnesic syndrome simply because amnesic patients present with a wide variety of medical, neuropsychological and psychosocial conditions that influence the pattern of memory loss and residual learning abilities. Despite this heterogeneity, there have been several attempts to group amnesics according to etiological and/or neuroanatomical factors. Researchers have proposed different classification systems of amnesia, each with distinct neuropsychological profiles. The most accepted system contrasts amnesics with diencephalic pathology (e.g. WKS, thalamic infarcts, and tumors of the third ventricle) with amnesics with damage in medial temporal brain areas (e.g. surgical ablation, herpes simplex encephalitis, and anoxic brain injury). Patients with damage in the diencephalon are depicted as having confabulatory tendencies, diminished insight, extensive and temporally graded retrograde amnesias, while patients with medial temporal lobe damage are described as having preserved insight, no confabulation, limited retrograde amnesias and tendencies towards rapid forgetting (Lhermitte & Signoret, 1972; Parkin, 1984; Zangwill, 1966).

Recently, a third group of memory impaired patients with damage in frontal network systems has been described (Janowsky, Shimamura & Squire, 1989). Many of these patients might not be deemed amnesic by strict research criteria because they exhibit attentional problems that could account for their memory deficit. Nonetheless, they demonstrate day-to-day memory deficits that conform to a predictable pattern: relative preservation of recognition (versus deficient free recall), deficits on tasks of contextual memory, and impaired semantic categorization.

Despite the acceptance of this classification system, the issue of amnesic subtypes is still a highly controversial topic. Weiskrantz (1985), in particular, underscored the problems in this area by arguing that the neuroanatomical distinctions between medial temporal and diencephalic groups are not clear-cut and that common neuropathology (i.e. mammillary body damage) underlies all forms of amnesia (Weiskrantz, 1985). Recent MRI evidence that many Korsakoff patients sustain damage in medial temporal areas is consistent with the possibility that various etiologies of amnesia share common sites of neural damage (Jernigan, Schafer, Butters & Cermak, 1991).

Another approach to classifying patients focuses on distinctions in the behavioral presentations of different patient groups. Weiskrantz questioned the validity of behavioral subtypes, however, noting that nonobligatory factors such as attentional deficits confound the analysis of amnesia in certain groups such as those with frontal systems damage. Other problems complicating the investigation of behavioral subtypes include failure to control for intelligence and density of amnesia. For instance, patients H.M. and S.S., both of superior intelligence, have been compared with Korsakoff patients who are often of somewhat lower intelligence (Butters & Cermak, 1980).

In the following section on Case Studies, patients with various forms of amnesia are presented in order to illustrate features common to all etiological groups and to highlight differences among them. These patients have all had comprehensive neuropsychological evaluations. Because presentation of all the test results would be too cumbersome, only scores regarding intelligence, attention and memory are displayed. Performance on tests of language, perception, problem-solving and reasoning were normal unless otherwise noted. In most cases, patients of equal intelligence have been chosen for comparison, but in some instances this was not possible because a small number of patients represented a particular neurological condition.

The core tests administered to evaluate anterograde memory are: WMS-R (Wechsler, 1987), Brown–Peterson Test (Brown, 1958; Peterson & Peterson, 1959), Rey Auditory Verbal Learning Test (Rey, 1964), Warrington Recognition Memory Test (Warrington, 1984), and the Rey–Osterreith Complex Figure (Rey, 1941).

- In addition to providing a quantitative index of amnesia, the WMS-R yields data about verbal and nonverbal memory on tasks of recall and recognition in both immediate and delayed memory conditions.
- The Brown–Peterson Test is used to examine recall of aurally presented stimuli over brief delay intervals (0 to 18 seconds) during which time interfering stimuli are presented. Performance on this test provides information regarding immediate memory and sensitivity to interference.
- The Rey Auditory Verbal Learning Test is used to measure free recall of a random word list. It provides data relevant to organizational strategies as well as primacy and recency effects. In addition it allows for a comparison of immediate and delayed memory as well as free recall and recognition.
- The Warrington Recognition Memory Test is used to assess recognition of words and faces displayed in the visual modality, allowing for the study of material-specific (i.e. verbal or nonverbal) aspects of memory.
- Additional information regarding nonverbal memory for complex information is obtained by examining incidental and delayed recall of the Rey–Osterreith Complex Figure.

Retrograde memory is assessed with a variety of experimental test procedures. First, an autobiographical interview is conducted to determine memories for specific life events from the recent and remote past. Second, a modified version of the Crovitz paradigm (Crovitz & Schiffman, 1974) is administered to assess recall of experientially-based memories in response to verbal cues. Each memory is scored on a scale of 0 to 2, with highest scores indicating responses containing specific details. Third, several tests of memory for public events are utilized. These include the Famous Faces Test (Albert, Butters & Levin, 1979), which requires the identification of photographs of famous individuals from the 1920s to the 1980s, and the Transient Events Test (O'Connor, Kaplan &

Cermak, 1990) which assesses recall and recognition of events of transient notoriety from the 1950s to 1990.

CASE STUDIES

Amnesia Associated with Herpes Simplex Encephalitis

Amnesia associated with herpes simplex encephalitis (HSE) has been described in a number of case reports (Cermak, 1976; Cermak & O'Connor, 1983; Warrington & McCarthy, 1988). In the acute phase, aphasia, agnosia and confusion have been noted, problems that may persist to varying degrees in the chronic phase of the illness and which obviously affect the assessment of amnesia. In general, postencephalitic patients exhibit global impairment on tasks of new learning and remote recall, although the specific pattern of memory loss may vary. Generally, the behavioral sequelae of HSE have been attributed to damage in lateral and medial temporal cortices (Damasio et al., 1985a); however, these lesions may be distributed asymmetrically (Eslinger, Damasio, Damasio & Butters, 1993).

Patient S.S.

Over the past decade we have reported numerous studies involving patient S.S. who became amnesic at age 44 as a result of HSE (Cermak, 1976; Cermak & O'Connor, 1983). S.S. was a successful physicist who owned and managed a private company dedicated to the development of laser technology. He was in his normal state of health until 17 August 1971 when he developed lethargy accompanied by a headache and fever. A left temporal biopsy was performed and the culture was positive for HSE. S.S. was comatose for approximately one month. Upon regaining consciousness he was described as aphasic, amnesic and mildly hemiparetic. Over time, speech and motor problems subsided but a severe memory disorder persisted. To this day, S.S. demonstrates severe memory problems characterized by an inability to learn new information and deficient recollection of events preceding the episode of encephalitis.

CT scan studies from March 1988 revealed bilateral lesions in anterior and medial portions of the temporal lobes. Bilateral lesions were also noted in the insula and putamen. There is further evidence of a lesion in the left frontal lobe secondary to shunt placement.

A recent neuropsychological evaluation of S.S. revealed the following results (Table 3.1). S.S. demonstrated superior intellectual abilities with above-average performance on tests measuring fund of verbal knowledge, vocabulary, arithmetic skills, deductive reasoning, perception and problem-solving. Simple attention span was intact, as were other aspects of attention including vigilance, selective

Table 3.1 Neuropsychological profile for patient S.S.

Test or procedure	Results
General intelligence	
Wechsler Adult Intelligence Scale–Revised	
Verbal IQ	126
Performance IQ	126
Full scale IQ	130
Attention	
Digits forward	7
Digits backward	8
Stroop Color-Word Test (50 item)	
Color interference	40 seconds, 1 errors (within normal limits)
Trail-Making Test, Part B	65 seconds, 0 errors (within normal limits)
Wisconsin Card Sorting Test	6/6 sorts in 128 cards
Word List Generation	
Phonemic (FAS)	95 + %ile
Semantic (grocery items)	28 items (within normal limits)
Anterograde memory	
Brown–Peterson Task	
letters (immed. recall; 3″, 9″, 18″ delay)	15/15, 15/15, 15/15, 12/15
words (immed. recall; 3″, 9″, 18″ delay)	15/15, 15/15, 14/15, 13/15
Rey Auditory Verbal Learning Test	
Immediate free recall trials	6, 6, 8, 7, and 7 (impaired)
20-minute delayed recall	4/15 (impaired)
20-minute delayed recognition	12/15 (2 false positive errors)
Warrington Recognition Memory Test	
Verbal recognition	35/50 (< 5th percentile)
Facial recognition	37/50 (< 5th percentile)
Wechsler Memory Scale–Revised	
Attention/Concentration Index	114
General Memory Index	102
Verbal Memory Index	104
Visual Memory Index	100
Delayed Memory Index	< 50
Rey–Osterreith Complex Figure	Accurate, well organized
Copy	36/36
Incidental recall	5/36
Delayed recall	0/36

Retrograde memory

Crovitz   1/18 (impaired)

Famous Faces	20s	30s	40s	50s	60s	70s	80s	
Uncued/8	2	4	7	3	2	1	0	
Cued/8	7	7	8	6	8	3	2	

Transient Events Test	50–54	55–59	60–64	65–69	70–74	75–79	80–84	85–90
Recall/10	0	0	0	1	0	0	0	0
Recognition/10	4	6	7	7	4	7	5	3

attention and mental flexibility. Speech was fluent and articulate. There was no evidence of word-finding difficulties or paraphasic errors. Comprehension of simple and complex commands was normal. Visuospatial examination revealed that S.S. scanned a random array of letters in a systematic manner; there was no evidence of hemispatial inattention or other perceptual problems. Visuo-constructive skills were normal.

Memory evaluation revealed that S.S. performed normally on the Brown–Peterson Test. This suggests that he was able to retain information over very short time intervals despite interfering stimuli. It is noteworthy that this is not a core feature of the amnesic syndrome and that other amnesics (e.g. Korsakoff patients) perform poorly on this task (Butters and Cermak, 1980). S.S.'s performance on all other tasks of anterograde memory was impaired. On the RAVLT, he demonstrated a flat learning curve and was unable to encode information that exceeded attention span limitations. Performance on delayed recall and recognition conditions of this test was impaired, indicating a tendency to lose information over long (20-minute) time intervals. Performance on the WMS-R revealed intact attention (Attention Index = 114) alongside deficient mnemonic functions. S.S.'s General Memory Index of 102 was below the score expected of someone with an IQ of 130. Furthermore, there was evidence of dramatically accelerated forgetting as indicated by his Delayed Memory Index of < 50. Finally, S.S.'s memory for faces and words was impaired on the Warrington Recognition Memory Test, underscoring the global nature of his amnesia.

S.S. demonstrated a profound loss of memory for personal and public events preceding the onset of encephalitis. His recollection of autobiographical material, including his wedding in 1951, lacked detail. Performance on the Crovitz procedure, a test requiring recall of autobiographical episodes in response to verbal cues, was impaired. Recall of famous faces and public events was uniformly poor. In general, S.S.'s retrograde amnesia would be characterized as temporally-extended because it encompasses information preceding his illness by decades. It is also noteworthy that serial testing revealed inconsistency in his retrieval of remote information. On some occasions he was able to access memories that were not available to him at other times. This inconsistency suggests that S.S. was impaired in the retrieval process itself (Cermak & O'Connor, 1983), in addition to a possible loss of mnemonic information.

S.S. represents a pure case of amnesia as a consequence of HSE. It should be noted, however, that many HSE patients suffer from other cognitive and perceptual problems as noted above. These deficits may be a result of the neuropathological variations; while HSE shows a proclivity for damaging lateral and medial temporal cortices, damage can also occur in other brain areas. The heterogeneity in the HSE population is best exemplified by several case reports of unusual memory problems in this patient population. Eslinger and colleagues described a material-specific (nonverbal) amnesia in a postencephalitic patient (Eslinger, Damasio, Damasio & Butters, 1993). O'Connor and associates had described an idiosyncratic pattern of retrograde amnesia in the same patient (O'Connor et al., 1992), and McCarthy and Warrington (1988) emphasized atypical features of the retrograde amnesia of a postencephalitic patient. These cases underline the considerable heterogeneity in the HSE population, emphasizing the need for comprehensive evaluations of these patients.

Amnesia Associated with Paraneoplastic Temporal Lobe Epilepsy

Limbic encephalitis caused by the remote effects of cancer has been referred to as paraneoplastic limbic encephalitis (Corsellis, Goldberg & Norton, 1969). This is not caused by tumors or any direct invasion of the nervous system (Adams & Victor, 1993). Instead, it probably involves abnormal autoimmune, viral or endocrine responses. The clinical manifestations of paraneoplastic limbic encephalitis include memory loss and emotional problems (Newman, Bell & McKee, 1990). Associated damage in limbic brain areas has been indicated by radiological and autopsy studies (Bakheit, Kennedy & Behan, 1990; Kohler et al., 1988; Newman, Bell & McKee, 1990; Lacomis, Khoshbin & Schick, 1990). In most cases, paraneoplastic limbic encephalitis is caused by primary carcinomas of the lung (Henson & Urich, 1982), although its association with other forms of cancer has been noted (Ahern et al., 1994; Burton, Bullard, Walther & Burger, 1988).

Patient J.T.

We recently studied a patient (J.T.) with paraneoplastic limbic encephalitis secondary to testicular malignancy (Ahern et al., 1994). J.T.'s clinical presentation was unusual for several reasons. First, he developed temporal lobe seizures three years before the discovery of his tumor. Second, J.T. presented with a very unusual memory problem characterized by adequate retention of information over periods up to 24 hours, but rapid forgetting thereafter. Third, serological studies demonstrated an unusual antibody reactivity pattern. The latter studies and details of J.T.'s clinical evaluation have been reviewed elsewhere (Ahern et al., 1994). In this chapter, the unique features of his cognitive profile will be emphasized.

J.T.'s neurobehavioral problems began in September of 1986 when forgetfulness, depression, apathy, and lethargy were noted. Temporal lobe seizures were reported in February of the following year. Initial neurobehavioral evaluations were puzzling. J.T. demonstrated normal performance on laboratory tests of memory, but claimed amnesia for events that preceded the test session by more than a day. Aside from abnormal left-sided slowing on EEG, a variety of neurodiagnostic procedures (including CT scan) were reported as normal. In light of J.T.'s depression, his relatively normal neurological examination, and the unusual nature of his memory deficit, a psychiatric etiology was considered. The persistence of his amnesia and an increase in seizure activity suggested otherwise, however. Follow-up MRI studies (1987, 1989, 1990) indicated pathological changes in medial temporal regions bilaterally and in the anterior medial temporal lobe on the left. EEG studies (including depth electrode recordings) were consistent with bitemporal epileptic foci, with a tendency for the right side to be more active.

J.T.'s severe memory deficit caused him to leave his work as a computer engineer early in the course of his illness. He could not drive due to his seizures. He did not socialize with former friends because he could not remember many of their shared activities. Most of his time was spent at home. Well versed in computer programming, he wrote programs to keep track of seizure activity. Three years following the onset of J.T.'s symptoms, he complained of testicular pain and a mass lesion was identified in the right testicle. Two months later, he underwent a radical right orchiectomy and chemotherapy was initiated. Since that time, J.T. has been in remission.

Neuropsychological testing took place over many test sessions spanning several years. There was some variability on tasks of anterograde memory, but other cognitive abilities were relatively stable. J.T. demonstrated above-average performance on tests of general reasoning abilities, abstract thinking and fund of acquired knowledge. Performance was intact on measures of attention span as well as measures of higher-order attention. Speech was fluent, articulate and prosodic with no evidence of word-finding difficulties. Spatial skills were variable. On some occasions, J.T. performed in the normal to high average range on measures of visuoconstructive abilities. On others, his performance was low average. This variability appeared to be linked to the frequency of seizure activity and probably reflected greater right hemisphere dysfunction. Motor examination was unremarkable with adequate performance on tasks of strength and dexterity.

The most unusual feature of J.T.'s clinical presentation was his performance on tests of memory which varied across test sessions, but which usually indicated normal performance on conventional measures of anterograde memory (Table 3.2). In contrast, J.T.'s recall of personal and public events from the past was abysmal. He did not remember any information about a two-week trip to Disney World he had taken two months earlier. Nor did he recall his father-in-law's open heart surgery one year earlier, the recent death of a close friend, or any major family events from the years before his illness. He did not recall that President Johnson or John Lennon had died. He also did not recognize the names of individuals prominent in the news in the years antedating his illness (e.g. Claus von Bulow, Geraldine Ferraro, and John Hinckley).

Initially, the discrepancy between relatively normal performance on tasks of new learning and impaired recall of remote events suggested that J.T. had an isolated retrograde amnesia. Further study indicated that anterograde memory was also impaired. When memory was tested over week-long intervals of time, with J.T.'s brother as a control subject, J.T. was invariably amnesic for new information the third day after its presentation. J.T.'s brother retained the same information over week-long intervals of time.

Despite evidence of a static brain lesion, J.T.'s unusual memory problem led us to suspect that seizures contributed to his memory deficit by interfering with

Table 3.2 Neuropsychological profile for patient J.T.

Test or procedure	Results
General intelligence	
Wechsler Adult Intelligence Scale–Revised	
Verbal IQ	127
Performance IQ	90
Attention	
Digits forward	8
Digits backward	4
Stroop Color-Word Test (50 item)	
Color interference	77 seconds, 0 errors (within normal limits)
Trail-Making Test, Part B	53 seconds, 0 errors (within normal limits)
Wisconsin Card Sorting Test	6/6 sorts in 128 cards
Word List Generation	
Phenomic (FAS)	95+%ile
Semantic (grocery items)	28 items (within normal limits)
Anterograde Memory	
Brown–Peterson Task	
letters (immed. recall; 3″, 9″, 18″ delay)	15/15, 15/15, 15/15, 12/15
words (immed. recall; 3″, 9″, 18″ delay)	15/15, 15/15, 14/15, 13/15
Rey Auditory Verbal Learning Test	
Immediate free recall trials	7, 11, 12, 14, a 13
20-minute delayed recall	9/15
20-minute delayed recognition	13/15 (0 false positive errors)
Warrington recognition Memory Test	
Verbal recognition	50th percentile
Facial recognition	25th percentile
Wechsler Memory Scale–Revised	
Attention/Concentration Index	112
General Memory Index	120
Verbal Memory Index	117
Visual Memory Index	111
Delayed Memory Index	111

Retrograde Memory								
Crovitz				4/18				
Famous Faces	20s	30s	40s	50s	60s	70s	80s	
Uncued/8	2	1	2	3	3	5	0	
Cued/8	5	2	3	4	8	5	2	
Transient Events Test	50–54	55–59	60–64	65–69	70–74	75–79	80–84	85–90
Recall/10	0	0	0	0	2	1	1	0

consolidation. Although not all patients with paraneoplastic limbic encephalitis have seizures, it is clear that these patients, like those with HSE, exhibit a variety of memory problems. For instance, in one patient we observed a material-specific pattern of memory loss. In contrast, Parkin and Leng (1993) described a case with global anterograde memory deficits accompanied by a dense retrograde amnesia of approximately 25 years. Their patient also showed confabulatory tendencies. Clearly further studies of paraneoplastic limbic encephalitis are needed in order to understand this syndrome more fully.

Amnesia Secondary to Anoxic Encephalopathy

Anoxic encephalopathy results from reduced cerebral perfusion or deficient circulating arterial oxygen. It can be caused by a number of factors including cardiac arrest, respiratory distress, strangulation, and carbon monoxide poisoning (Adams & Victor, 1993). When oxygen saturation is totally depleted for five minutes or more, permanent brain damage occurs. At one end of the spectrum is the syndrome of brain death accompanied by widespread pathology in cerebral and cerebellar cortices. In less serious cases of hypoxia, an initial loss of consciousness may still occur and this may be followed by a variety of cognitive, perceptual and motor abnormalities that may abate or that may become permanent. Similar to HSE, anoxia can result in extensive brain damage and in cognitive deficits beyond amnesia. However, because the temporal lobes are particularly susceptible to oxygen deprivation, it is possible to incur selective damage to temporal areas and, consequently, to develop a circumscribed amnesia as a result of an anoxic event, as described in a number of investigations (Volpe & Hirst, 1983; Zola-Morgan, Squire & Amaral, 1986). Putative agents of destruction include the pathological accumulation of excitatory neurotransmitters (such as glutamate) and/or lactic acid (Adams & Victor, 1993). Area CA1 of the hippocampus has been identified as particularly sensitive to the effects of ischemia and an isolated lesion in this area can result in a moderately severe amnesia (Zola-Morgan et al., 1986).

Patient P.S.

P.S. is a 35-year-old right-handed woman who suffered an episode of anoxia within the context of a severe asthmatic attack and pneumonia in 1981. She was comatose for several days. Upon regaining consciousness, a profound amnesia was noted. Initial records were not available, but more recent MRI findings were interpreted as negative. Neuropsychological examination revealed average intellectual abilities with adequate performance on tasks of simple and complex attention (Table 3.3). P.S.'s most salient deficit was her amnesia. Although she retained new information across short time intervals (e.g. the Brown–Peterson task), this did not result in retention over longer periods of time. P.S. demonstrated a severe learning deficit accompanied by diminished recollection of autobiographical and public events predating the anoxic episode.

Prior to the onset of her illness, P.S. owned and managed a small business. She was described as an extrovert who had a wide range of interests and many friends. Her comportment in social situations was invariably gracious. In the

Table 3.3 Neuropsychological profile for patient P.S.

Test or procedure	Results
General intelligence	
Wechsler Adult Intelligence Scale–Revised	
Verbal IQ	104
Performance IQ	95
Full scale IQ	100

Attention	
Digits forward	8
Digits backward	7
Stroop Color-Word Test (50 item)	
Color interference	45 seconds, 0 errors (within normal limits)
Trail-Making Test, Part B	82 seconds, 0 errors (within normal limits)
Wisconsin Card Sorting Test	6/6 sorts in 128 cards; 8/ perseverations
Word List Generation	
Phonemic (FAS)	69th percentile
Semantic (grocery items)	18 items (within normal limits)

Anterograde Memory	
Brown–Peterson Task	
letters (immed. recall; 3″, 9″, 18″ delay)	15/15, 14/15, 12/15, 15/15
words (immed. recall; 3″, 9″, 18″ delay)	15/15, 12/15, 15/15, 14/15
Rey Auditory Verbal Learning Test	
Imediate free recall trials	8, 7, 10, 10, 7 (impaired)
20-minute delayed recall	0/15 (impaired)
20-minute delayed recognition	7/15 (4 false positive errors)
Warrington Recognition Memory Test	
Verbal recognition	29/50 (< 5th percentile)
Facial recognition	33/50 (< 5th percentile)
Wechsler Memory Scale–Revised	
Attention/Concentration Index	115
General Memory Index	90
Verbal Memory Index	89
Visual Memory Index	95
Delayed Memory Index	< 50
Rey–Osterreith Complex Figure	Accurate, well organized
Copy	35/36
Incidental recall	9/36
Delayed recall	8/36

Retrograde memory

Crovits				1/18 (impaired)				
Famous Faces	20s	30s	40s	50s	60s	70s	80s	
Uncued/8	0	0	0	0	1	0	0	
Cued/8	4	2	1	3	4	5	5	
Transient Events Test	50–54	55–59	60–64	65–69	70–74	75–79	80–84	85–90
Recall/10	0	0	0	0	0	4	2	0
Recognition/10	1	6	7	4	4	7	8	8

aftermath of her illness, P.S. underwent intensive rehabilitation geared towards mitigating the impact of amnesia. Through rote repetition, she was taught excellent organizational strategies including the habitual use of external memory aids. The early implementation of these strategies and P.S.'s personal resilience resulted in greater social independence than most amnesic patients are privy to. P.S. drove a car, lived in a semi-independent situation (with daily visits from her mother and neighbors) and worked in a number of high-level, but supervised, situations. Amazingly, she also managed to complete an associated degree at a local college, although P.S. did not retain any information regarding her studies. Nonetheless, she completed class assignments in a timely fashion and was granted special privileges (e.g. writing papers in lieu of taking examinations) that allowed her to maintain adequate academic standing.

P.S.'s seemingly good adaptation to chronic amnesia was remarkable. However, over time, the social ramifications of her disability became more apparent. Despite her intelligence and enthusiasm for work, she had difficulties completing job assignments and, consequently, lost several jobs. In addition, her rehabilitation program was discontinued. Unemployed and socially isolated, P.S. became increasingly moody and despondent. Furthermore, she developed paranoid suspicions that family members had stolen her personal belongings and that other individuals had caused her harm, beliefs that had no basis in reality. P.S.'s delusional propensities were exacerbated by her tendency to incorporate these erroneous ideas into her daily diary, thereby making them seem as real as other autobiographical events.

Aside from illustrating the neuropsychological impact of anoxic brain injury, P.S.'s story is instructive for several reasons. For many years she was considered an example of successful adaptation to amnesia. In this context, she demonstrated that patients with profound memory problems are capable of living rich, activity-filled lives as long as there is family and social support for these endeavors. Her more recent problems reflect the reversal of fortune; in the absence of this support, P.S.'s amnesia has become a powerful barrier to her happiness as well as to her capacity for independent living.

Amnesia Secondary to Damage in Diencephalic Brain Structures

Diencephalic forms of amnesia arise as a result of a number of neurological disorders, including infarction of the paramedian artery (Cramon, Hebel & Schuri, 1985; Katz, Alexander & Mandell, 1987; Speedie & Heilman, 1982; Winocur et al., 1984), trauma (Squire & Moore, 1979), diencephalic tumors (Delay, Brion, & Derouesne, 1964; Sporfkin & Sciarra, 1952; Ziegler, Kaufman & Marshall, 1977), and Wernicke–Korsakoff syndrome (Butters & Cermak, 1980; Victor, Adams & Collins, 1989). The latter condition will be considered separately due to the fact that it is associated with a distinct constellation of psychological and social factors (Butters & Stuss, 1989).

Research investigations of diencephalic amnesia highlight severe learning deficits that have been attributed to damage in medial thalamic structures, the mammillary bodies, or both regions (Markowitsch, 1982). In the latter instances, amnesia is a result of a disruption of neural networks that normally connect limbic areas involved in memory. Qualitative descriptions of patients with thalamic amnesias emphasize deficits in the initial processing stages of memory (Winocur et al., 1984) and deficient recall of information over longer time intervals (Katz, Alexander & Mandell, 1987; Speedie & Heilman, 1982; Winocur et al., 1984). Further evidence for the notion that thalamic amnesia reflects primarily a deficit in the initial stages of encoding comes from a number of studies demonstrating that, once initial acquisition has been achieved, these patients forget information at a normal rate (Huppert & Piercy, 1978; Squire, 1981; but see Winocur et al., 1984, for different results). Also noteworthy, material-specific memory deficits occur as a result of unilateral thalamic lesions (Speedie & Heilman, 1982; Squire & Moore, 1979). The status of retrograde memory is less clear. Some researchers have found that thalamic damage is accompanied by minimal effects on remote memory, while others have described severe problems in the retrieval of events predating the onset of amnesia (Butters & Stuss, 1989).

Patient C.W.

Patient C.W. is a 49-year-old, right-handed man who suffered bilateral anterior thalamic infarcts following a cardiac catheterization procedure. Prior to his illness he was employed as an independent sign painter and was described as an outgoing person who led an active social life. Even four years after the illness, major cognitive and personality changes continue to affect his life. Most noticeable are severe impairments in memory for which C.W. has only limited insight, as well as general lack of motivation and initiative. His family describes him as withdrawn and isolated at times, boisterous and socially inappropriate at other times. C.W. spends most of his time at home watching television, and even under the close supervision of his son, he has been unable to resume any work-related activities.

Neuropsychological testing in the acute phase of the illness and over the last year have revealed essentially the same profile. Assessment of C.W.'s intellectual functioning revealed it to be in the low average range, with poorest performance on tests of general knowledge and abstract reasoning. This likely represents a decline from his premorbid level of functioning, which was estimated to be in the high average range. Language functioning, reading, spelling and perceptual abilities were intact. In contrast, attention span was impaired as was performance on tasks of cognitive flexibility.

Most significant were C.W.'s problems on all tasks of memory and new learning (Table 3.4), deficits that were more severe on verbal than on nonverbal tasks. On list learning tasks, he demonstrated very slow learning across trials, with most of his performance accounted for by memory for the last item on the

Table 3.4 Neuropsychological profile for patient C.W.

Test or procedure	Results
General intelligence	
Wechsler Adult Intelligence Scale–Revised	
Verbal IQ	87
Performance IQ	96
Full scale IQ	90
Attention	
Digits forward	5
Digits backward	4
Corsi Blocks forward	6
Corsi Block backward	4
Stroop Color-Word Test (50 Item)	
Color interference	100 seconds, 0 errors (impaired)
Trail-Making Test, Part B	72 seconds, 0 errors (within normal limits)
Wisconsin Card Sorting Test	1/6 sorts in 128 cards; 29% perseverations
Word List Generation	
Phonemic (FAS)	95+percentile
Semantic (grocery items)	17 items (within normal limits)
Anterograde memory	
Brown–Peterson Task	
letters (immed. recall; 3″, 9″, 18″ delay)	14/15, 13/15, 9/15, 8/15
words (immed. recall; 3″, 9″, 18″delay)	15/15, 6/15, 5/15, 2/15
Rey Auditory Verbal Learning Test	
Immediate free recall trials	1, 4, 4, 5, 8 (impaired)
20-minute delayed recall	1/15 (impaired)
20-minute delayed recognition	10/15 (10 false positive errors)
Warrington Recognition Memory Test	
Verbal recognition	30/50 (< 5th percentile)
Facial recognition	28/50 (< 5th percentile)
Wechsler Memory Scale–Revised	
Attention/Concentration Index	89
General Memory Index	79
Verbal Memory Index	76
Visual Memory Index	92
Delayed Memory Index	76
Rey–Osterreith Complex Figure	Accurate, well organized
Copy	36/36
Incidental recall	14/36
Delayed recall	14/36

Retrograde memory

Crovitz   N/A

Famous faces	20s	30s	40s	50s	60s	70s	80s	
Uncued/8	3	3	5	7	6	5	4	
Cued/8	7	6	5	7	8	8	7	

Transient Events Test	50–54	55–59	60–64	65–69	70–74	75–79	80–84	85–90
Recall/10	0	0	0	1	0	0	0	0
Recognition/10	6	7	2	6	6	8	7	10

list. The presence of internal list structure and categorical cues did not improve his performance, suggesting impoverished encoding of the information. This was also evident on the Brown–Peterson Test: he was able to repeat three words perfectly when no interfering activity was imposed, but his performance declined rapidly when he was asked to count backwards for variable amounts of time. Of interest is the fact that C.W. also suffered a significant deficit in recognition memory for both verbal and nonverbal information. This suggests that his memory impairments are not due only to defective retrieval strategies, as is often seen in patients with frontal lobe lesions.

C.W. demonstrates several of the features of memory impairment that have previously been described in patients with thalamic lesions, such as impaired encoding and increased sensitivity to interference. However, his case also highlights the fact that thalamic lesions rarely affect memory in isolation. His attention and concentration are quite impaired, and a general decline in intellectual functioning is of note. These features are reminiscent of the patients described by Katz and colleagues (1987) who suggested that dementia may be a common occurrence following infarction of the paramedian artery. In the case of C.W., however, the decline on tests of intelligence is mild relative to his severe impairment in memory functioning.

Wernicke–Korsakoff Syndrome

Patients with Wernicke–Korsakoff syndrome (WKS), amnesia secondary to chronic alcohol abuse and thiamine deficiency, have received considerable attention in the amnesia literature (Victor, Adams & Collins, 1989; Butters & Cermak, 1980). In the acute (Wernicke) phase of WKS, patients exhibit a classic triad of deficits including oculomotor palsies, ataxia and confusion. These symptoms persist in 60% of patients diagnosed with WKS (Adams & Victor, 1993). Confabulation may also be present at this time. The chronic (Korsakoff) phase of the illness is accompanied by severe memory deficits and personality changes with increased irritability and apathy (Butters & Cermak, 1980; Butters & Stuss, 1989). Neuroanatomical studies of patients with WKS have highlighted damage in thalamic nuclei, the mammillary bodies and frontal systems (Cramon, Hebel & Schuri, 1985; Mair, 1979; Victor et al., 1989). Other studies have indicated additional damage in medial temporal areas beyond that seen in conjunction with chronic alcohol abuse (Jernigan, et al., 1991; Mayes, Meudell, Mann & Pickering, 1988). The extent to which these latter areas separately or convergently result in amnesia remains controversial.

The neuropsychological profile of patients with WKS has been reviewed in numerous articles and books devoted to this topic (Butters & Cermak, 1980; Butters & Stuss, 1989). Amnesia in this patient group has been attributed to superficial and deficient encoding strategies (Cermak, 1973; Cermak, Naus & Reale, 1976), or the faulty analysis and retrieval of contextual features of new information (Winocur & Kinsbourne, 1978). Some researchers have noted additional cognitive problems on tasks of frontal lobe functions (Squire, 1982; Shimamura, Jernigan & Squire, 1988) and visuospatial skills (Oscar-Berman, Shahakian & Wilmark, 1976). Whether these problems are central features of the syndrome or whether they represent additive neurotoxic effects of alcohol is still not certain. It is clear, however, that these problems exert detrimental effects on specific memory tests (Butters & Stuss, 1989). Of additional significance, it has been noted that patients with WKS are prone to emotional problems such as apathy and low motivation and such problems could undermine performance on tasks of new learning (Oscar–Berman, 1980). Finally, it is important to note that chronic alcohol abuse is often accompanied by social isolation and a lack of interest in world events. These tendencies probably put WKS patients at a disadvantage on tests of remote memory.

Patient G.P.

Patient G.P. is a 71-year-old right-handed retired salesman with a 25 + year history of alcohol abuse who was hospitalized for withdrawal seizures and alcohol treatment in January of 1981 (age 59). Prior to this admission, G.P. was hospitalized several times for alcohol-related seizures and one episode of status epilepticus. Social history revealed that G.P. was educated through several years of college and that he served as a First Lieutenant in the Navy during World War II. He married shortly thereafter and worked as a greeting cards salesman from 1946 to 1972. G.P.'s alcohol consumption increased between the years 1972 to 1980 during which time he separated from his wife, lived in a rooming house and worked sporadically. It is significant that his wife did not notice personality change or memory problems during a visit with G.P. one month prior to hospitalization, indicating an acute onset to his amnesia.

Initial neurological examination (1981) revealed cerebellar dysfunction, peripheral neuropathy, and amnesia. Mild abnormalities on tasks of frontal lobe functions were noted. There was no evidence of confabulation. G.P. demonstrated concern about his memory problem and, in fact, was described as dysphoric. A premorbid history of dysphoric tendencies was mentioned, but G.P.'s wife denied a history of depression. Family history was positive for alcoholism and negative for other psychiatric problems. Past medical history, aside from the above, was noncontributory. In light of G.P.'s marked memory deficit and history of chronic alcohol abuse, he was diagnosed with WKS even though a clear episode of Wernicke's encephalopathy had not been documented. CT scan findings indicated mild to moderate cerebral atrophy and enlargement of the third ventricle.

Since the onset of WKS, G.P. has remained abstinent. He resides in a nursing home and spends most of his time watching television. He leads a rather isolated existence and has little interest in structured social activities. G.P. continues to express sadness about his amnesia. However, he has not attempted to utilize remedial techniques to circumvent his problems despite constant encouragement to do so.

Serial neuropsychological evaluations were conducted over the last decade and these revealed a consistent pattern of deficits. The most recent examination (Table 3.5) demonstrated high average to superior performance on tests of general intelligence. Performance on tasks of simple attention was intact, but performance on tasks of complex attention was variable. G.P. was able to maintain vigilance over long periods of time. However, he demonstrated slowed performance on timed tasks of attention. Basic language skills were preserved, as were perceptual abilities.

In contrast with the above, G.P.'s anterograde amnesia was extremely dense. Unlike most WKS patients, he performed normally on the Brown Peterson Test, indicating adequate analysis of incoming information. He was unable to retain new information over longer time intervals, however, and performance on all other measures of new learning was deficient. His retrograde amnesia was also severe. G.P. had difficulty recalling autobiographical events in response to verbal cues (i.e. the Crovitz procedure). His recall of famous individuals (i.e. the Famous Faces test) conformed to the classic WKS pattern: there was a temporal gradient with better recall of remote (i.e. the 20s) versus recent (i.e. the 80s) individuals. Free recall of news items from the Transient Events Test was uniformly poor, although recognition of the same items was normal.

Patient G.P. is one of a group of patients with WKS studied at the Memory Disorders Research Center over the last two decades. In some ways, he embodies classic features of WKS: his amnesia is dense for new information and information predating the onset of WKS, there is evidence of frontal systems deficits (although this was not as severe as seen in other WKS patients), and he appears totally apathetic with regard to daily activities. He differs from other WKS patients in a number of ways, however. First of all, he is far more intelligent than most WKS patients. Second, there was no evidence of confabulation at any time during his illness. Third, G.P. demonstrated insight into his medical condition. Finally, his social and educational accomplishments exceed those of most patients with WKS.

Amnesia Associated with Rupture and Repair of Anterior Communicating Artery Aneurysms

Anterior communicating artery (ACoA) aneurysms cause brain damage and associated neurobehavioral deficits as a result of subarachnoid hemorrhage, vasospasm, hematoma formation, herniation of the medial temporal lobes, hydrocephalus, and surgical intervention. Although many studies are biased by selection factors (i.e. patients with established memory deficits are referred for evaluation), even nonbiased studies demonstrate a high proportion of cognitive difficulties in this patient population (Stenhouse, Knight, Longmore & Bishara, 1991). Brain lesions are seen in the basal forebrain, striatum and frontal areas. The assumption has been that the basal forebrain lesion is the critical underpinning of the mnemonic deficits in this patient group (Alexander & Freedman, 1984; Damasio et al., 1985b; Gade, 1982). Presumably, damage in this area would result in a disconnection syndrome, separating cortical systems from the

Table 3.5 Neuropsychological profile for patient G.P.

Test or procedure	Results
General intelligence	
Wechsler Adult Intelligence Scale–Revised	
Verbal IQ	123
Performance IQ	118
Full scale IQ	122
Attention	
Digits forwards	7
Digits backward	8
Stroop Color-Word Test (50 item)	
Color interference	97 seconds, 2 errors (mild impairment)
Trail-Making Test, Part B	135 seconds, 0 errors (low normal)
Wisconsin Card Sorting Test	6/6 sorts in 128 cards; 12% perseveration
Word List Generation	
Phonemic (FAS)	44th percentile
Semantic (grocery items)	21 items (within normal limits)
Anterograde memory	
Brown–Peterson Task	
letters (immed. recall; 3″, 9″, 18″ delay)	15/15, 15/15, 11/15, 13/15
words (immed. recall; 3″, 9″, 18″ delay)	15/15, 14/15, 14/15, 12/15
Rey Auditory Verbal Learning Test	
Immediate free recall trials	5, 7, 7, 7, 7, (impaired)
20-minute delayed recall	0/15 (impaired)
20-minute delayed recognition	11/15 (7 false positive errors)
Warrington Recognition Memory Test	
Verbal recognition	28/50 (< 5th percentile)
Facial recognition	26/50 (< 5th percentile)
Wechsler Memory Scale1Revised	
Attention/Concentration Index	116
General Memory Indes	104
Verbal Memory Index	105
Visual Memory Index	100
Delayed Memory Index	56
Rey–Osterreith Complex Figure	Accurate, well organized
Copy	31/36
Incidental recall	9/36
Delayed recall	5/36

Retrogade Memory								
Crovitz				3/18 (impaired)				
Famous Faces	20s	30s	40s	50s	60s	70s	80s	
Uncued/8	7	7	6	6	5	3	2	
Cued/8	8	8	7	8	7	5	3	
Transient Events Test	50–54	55–59	60–64	65–69	70–74	75–79	80–84	85–90
Recall/10	0	2	4	1	2	2	1	1
Recognition/10	7	7	8	6	9	8	8	8

hippocampus. Based on a large sample of patients with ACoA aneurysms, Irle and colleagues concluded that discrete damage to basal forebrain or striatal structures did not cause amnesia. Combined basal forebrain and striatal lesions were seen as necessary for the occurrence of mnemonic deficits (Irle et al., 1992).

Psychological descriptions of an ACoA syndrome emphasize memory deficits, confabulation, and personality change (Alexander & Freedman, 1984). Further scrutiny of the memory profile of this patient group reveals disproportionate difficulties on tasks of "short-term" memory (Laiacona et al., 1989). ACoA patients are described as showing increased benefit from recognition cues, perhaps due to problems in the strategic search of memory (Damasio et al., 1985b; Moscovitch, 1989). Other researchers have compared the memory problems of patients with ACoA aneurysms to the memory deficits of WKS patients (Gade & Mortensen, 1990; Parkin, Leng, Stanhope & Smith, 1988; Talland & Ballantine, 1976). Shared problems include sensitivity to proactive interference, impaired temporal discrimination, source forgetting, and failure on tasks of semantic clustering. Gade and colleagues (1990) reported that ACoA aneurysm patients had extensive and temporally graded retrograde amnesias reminiscent of the remote memory problems exhibited by patients with WKS. Despite these comparisons, other researchers argue that patients with ACoA aneurysms do not exhibit a consistent pattern of neuropsychological deficits (Laiacona et al., 1989).

Patient F.M.

Patient F.M. is a 64-year-old right-handed retired electrical engineer who was in his normal state of health until August 1990 at which time he complained of a severe headache and visual changes. He was brought to an ophthalmologist who noted bilateral retinal hemorrhages and elevated blood pressure. F.M. was brought to an emergency room where a CT scan revealed a large left frontal aneurysm with subarachnoid hemorrhage. Subsequent angiography revealed a large ACoA aneurysm. Initial neurological examination revealed confusion and disorientation. A left frontotemporal craniotomy and clipping of the aneurysm took place the following week. Following surgical intervention, F.M. was described as disoriented. There was evidence of frontal deficits with confabulation, perseveration, stimulus-bound behaviors, and distractibility. Memory was severely impaired on tasks of new learning and remote recall.

F.M. was subsequently transferred for continued rehabilitative care. Over the course of the following months, memory improvement was noted. However, he continued to demonstrate confabulation and temporal disorientation. Specifically, he believed that his wife, who had died six years earlier, was still living. F.M. related details of recent visits and telephone conversations with his wife. On each occasion, he was gently reminded that she was no longer living. Neither these reminders, nor even visits to her grave site, dissuaded F.M. from the belief that his wife was alive. His typical response to such information was "I see my wife's name on this grave, but I just saw her in the garden yesterday". F.M.'s other confabulation concerned the VA Hospital. Each time he was scheduled for neuropsychological examination he became markedly anxious and reported that he feared he was being inducted into active service during the Desert Storm crisis.

Neuropsychological examination of F.M. was conducted on several occasions. The most recent evaluation (Table 3.6) was one and a half years following surgery, at which time confabulations were prominent. Inspection of the test findings revealed salient deficits on tasks of memory within the context of diminished attention and, otherwise, normal cognitive abilities.

F.M.'s memory profile was characterized by deficient encoding of new information regardless of the nature of the material, although he showed slightly worse recall of verbal material consistent with the site of lesion in the left frontal region. Also noteworthy, his forgetting was less severe than that of most amnesic patients. F.M. showed adequate recall of everyday events although he was consistently confused regarding the temporal order of these events. F.M. demonstrated a limited retrograde memory impairment; there was temporal gradient on the Famous Faces Test, however. Performance on the Transient Events Test indicated a dissociation between poor spontaneous retrieval and intact recognition consistent with the notion that ACoA patients benefit from recognition cues to a greater extent than most amnesics. Further investigation of temporal orientation abilities revealed impairment on tasks of temporal sequence and perception of time duration. The relationship between F.M.'s temporal discrimination difficulties and his confabulatory tendencies was considered and it was theorized that confusion about the timing of real life events (e.g. interactions with his wife, induction into the service) contributed to this confabulation (Talland, 1965).

F.M. was examined within the context of a larger study of the effects of rupture and surgical repair of ACoA aneurysms which included 19 patients referred from local rehabilitation facilities. Like F.M., many of these patients exhibited confabulation accompanied by diminished insight. Most patients did not confabulate one year after ACoA rupture; however, many of them continued to demonstrate a superficial grasp of their memory problems. Although the group was heterogeneous with respect to the density of amnesia and extent of attentional impairment, the majority of patients were sensitive to proactive interference and benefited significantly from recognition cues. Patients varied greatly in their ability to profit from semantic categorization. Performance on tasks of retrograde amnesia provided mixed support for the idea that ACoA patients are similar to WKS patients. On the Famous Faces Test they demonstrated a temporal gradient like that seen in patients with WKS. However, their performance on the Transient Events Test was like that of normal control subjects.

A subgroup of seven patients was examined serially and there was evidence of attenuation of frontal deficits and concomitant improvement in retrograde memory. However, the anterograde memory impairment remained stable over time (D'Esposito et al., 1993).

Table 3.6 Neuropsychological profile for patient F.M.

Test or Procedure	Results
General intelligence	
Wechsler Adult Intelligence Scale–Revised	
Verbal IQ	125
Performance IQ	108
Full scale IQ	120
Attention	
Digits forward	7
Digits backward	9
Stroop Color-Word Test (50 Item)	
Color interference	113 seconds, 3 errors (impaired)
Trail-Making Test, Part B	76 seconds, 2 errors (impaired)
Wisconsin Card Sorting Test	4/6 sorts in 128 cards
Word List Generation	
Phonemic (FAS)	29th percentile
Semantic (grocery items)	16 items
Anterograde memory	
Brown–Peterson Task	
letters (immed. recall; 3″, 9″, 18″ delay)	15/15, 11/15, 5/15, 10/15
words (immed. recall; 3″, 9″, 18″ delay)	15/15, 9/15, 10/15, 15/15
Rey Auditory Verbal Learning Test	
Immediate free recall trials	5, 5, 7, 6, a 6 (impaired)
20-minute delayed recall	0/15 (impaired)
20-minute delayed recognition	10/15 (7 false positive errors)
Warrington Recognition Memory Test	
Verbal recognition	39/50 (20th percentile)
Facial recognition	30/50 (< 5th percentile)
Wechsler Memory Scale–Revised	
Attention/Concentration Index	103
General Memory Index	99
Verbal Memory Index	91
Visual Memory Index	116
Delayed Memory Index	75
Rey–Osterreith Complex Figure	Accurate, well organized
Copy	33/36
Incidental recall	16/36
Delayed recall	12/36

Retrograde memory

Crovitz				6/18 (impaired)				
Famous Faces	20s	30s	40s	50s	60s	70s	80s	
Uncued/8	8	6	8	6	8	6	5	
Cued/8	NA							
Transient Events Test	50–54	55–59	60–64	65–69	70–74	75–79	80–84	85–90
Recall/10	1	6	3	4	5	5	5	4
Recognition/10	6	10	10	10	9	9	9	10

CONCLUSIONS

This review illustrates the diversity in presentations of patients with amnesia. On the one hand, this diversity has complicated attempts to arrive at a generally accepted definition of the amnesic syndrome. On the other hand, it has served as an impetus to the development of various classification systems. In the present chapter, six patients with bitemporal, diencephalic and frontal forms of amnesia were described. An attempt was made to equate patients for overall intelligence in order to study specific features of their memory problems without the confounds of differing intellectual abilities.

The three patients (S.S., J.T. and P.S.) who had memory problems secondary to damage in medial temporal brain areas all demonstrated preserved insight, absence of confabulation, normal immediate memory, and normal performance on tasks of complex attention. However, these patients differed from one another on tasks of forgetting. J.T. demonstrated little forgetting on standard memory tests, even though he was profoundly amnesic for new information after day-long delays. In contrast, S.S. and P.S. demonstrated severe forgetting even over short time intervals. However, their forgetting rate was no more severe than that observed for the diencephalic patient, G.P.

Thus, the notion that all amnesics with medial temporal pathology forget new information faster than do diencephalic amnesics is not supported by these individual cases. This clinical observation is consistent with the results of an experimental investigation of H.M. that also demonstrated a normal rate of forgetting (Freed, Corkin & Cohen, 1987). These three medial temporal amnesics also exhibited extended retrograde amnesias; a finding that runs counter to some prevailing opinions that medial temporal damage is associated with a relatively brief retrograde amnesia. Thus, it is apparent that group generalizations concerning these two populations of amnesics do not prove highly diagnostic in these three well-documented single cases.

G.P.'s clinical history and behavioral presentation were consistent with Wernicke–Korsakoff syndrome in that there is evidence of reduced motivation and slowed speed of processing alongside severe global memory problems. In addition, he demonstrated a complete inability to learn new information and a temporally graded retrograde amnesia characterized by better recall of remote relative to recent public events. However, G.P. differed from most other WKS patients in that his insight was preserved and there was no evidence of confabulation. His clinical presentation also illustrated that not all WKS patients are impaired on tests of attention and immediate memory, as exemplified by his normal performance on the Brown–Peterson Test. Differences between G.P. and other WKS patients may well be due to his superior intelligence; but alternatively, it may also be the case that he has sustained less brain damage than most patients with Korsakoff's syndrome. The other diencephalic patient, C.W., presents a neuropsychological profile quite similar to the classic Korsakoff's profile. Testing revealed that C.W.'s amnesia was primarily due to an inability to encode new information and he had an extensive retrograde amnesia.

Finally, patient F.M. clearly exemplified memory problems characteristic of frontal systems damage. There was evidence of confabulation, lack of insight, attention deficits and less severe forgetting. F.M.'s retrograde amnesia was limited and was ameliorated under conditions where recognition cues were provided.

Although, to date, classification systems have focused heavily on differences in information-processing deficits between subgroups of amnesics, the results of our survey of six cases suggests that these differences may be subtle at best. Overriding the possible differences in how patients organize and encode new material is the appearance of a core inability to reconstruct past experience from fragments of the initial episode. Beyond this core amnesia, salient group differences arise in the areas of attention, insight and confabulation; domains that impact on memory, but that are not invariably affected in the amnesic syndrome. The importance of conducting a comprehensive neuropsychological examination before making a diagnosis of amnesia cannot be overemphasized. Otherwise, other neuropsychological deficiencies could easily add to the overall cognitive presentation, independently of the overriding primary memory disturbance.

ACKNOWLEDGEMENTS

The work reported here is funded in part by NINCDS program project grant NS 26985, funds from the Department of Veterans Affairs Medical Research Service, and by NIAAA grant AA-00187. The authors express their appreciation to Dr Marie Walbridge for editorial comments.

REFERENCES

Adams, R.D. & Victor, M. (1993). *Principles of Neurology*, 5th edn. McGraw-Hill, New York.

Ahern, G.L., O'Connor, M.G., Dalmau, J., Coleman, A., Posner, J.B., Schomer, D.L., Herzog, A.G., Kolb, D.A. & Mesulam, M.M. (1994). Paraneoplastic temporal lobe epilepsy with testicular neoplasm and atypical amnesia. *Neurology*, **44**, 1270–1274.

Albert, M.S., Butters, N. & Levin, J. (1979). Temporal gradients in retrograde amnesia of patients with alcoholic Korsakoff's disease, *Archives of Neurology*, **36**, 211–216.

Alexander, M.P. & Freedman, M. (1984). Amnesia after anterior communicating artery rupture. *Neurology*, **34**, 752–759.

Brown, J. (1958). Some tests of the decay theory of immediate memory. *Quarterly Journal of Experimental Psychology*, **10**, 12–21.

Burton, G.V., Bullard, D.E., Walther, P.J. & Burger, P.C. (1988). Paraneoplastic limbic encephalopathy with testicular carcinoma. *Cancer*, **62**, 2248–2251.

Butters, N. & Cermak, L.S. (1980). *Alcoholic Korsakoff's Syndrome: An Information Processing Approach*. Academic Press, New York.

Butters, N., Salmon, D.P., Cullum, C.M., Cairns, P., Troster, A., Jacobs, D., Moss, M. &

Cermak, L.S. (1988). Differentiation of amnesic and demented patients with the Wechsler Memory Scale—Revised. *Clinical Neuropsychologist*, **2**, 133–148.

Butters, N. & Stuss, D.T. (1989). Diencephalic amnesia. In F. Boller & J. Grafman (eds), *Handbook of Neuropsychology*. Elsevier Science Publishers, Amsterdam.

Cermak, L.S. (1973). Information processing deficits of alcoholic Korsakoff patients. *Quarterly Journal of Studies of Alcohol*, **34**, 1110–1132.

Cermak, L.S. (1976). The encoding capacity of a patient with amnesia due to encephalitis. *Neuropsychologia*, **14**, 311–326.

Cermak, L.S., Naus, M. & Reale, L. (1976). Rehearsal and organizational strategies of alcoholic Korsakoff patients. *Brain and Language*, **3**, 375–385.

Cermak, L.S. & O'Connor, M.G. (1983). The anterograde and retrograde retrieval ability of a patient with amnesia due to encephalitis. *Neuropsychologia*, **21**, 213–234.

Corsellis, J., Goldberg, G.J. & Norton, A.R. (1969). Limbic encephalitis and its association with carcinoma. *Brain*, **91**, 481.

Cramon, D.Y.V., Hebel, N. & Schuri, U. (1985). A contribution to the anatomical basis of thalamic amnesia. *Brain*, **108**, 993–1008.

Crovitz, H.F. & Schiffman, H. (1974). Frequency of episodic memories as a function of their age. *Bulletin of the Psychonomic Society*, **4**, 517–518.

D'Esposito, M., McGlinchey-Berroth, R., Alexander, M.P., Fischer, R.S., O'Connor, M.G. & Walbridge, M. (1993). Cognitive recovery following anterior communicating artery rupture. In *International Neuropsychological Society, Twenty-Second Annual Meeting*. INS, Cincinnati, Ohio.

Damasio, A., Eslinger, P.J., Damasio, H., Van Hoesen, G.W. & Cornell, S. (1985a). Multi-modal amnesic syndrome following bilateral temporal and basal forebrain lesions. *Archives of Neurology*, **42**, 252–259.

Damasio, A.R., Graff-Radford, N.R., Eslinger, P.J., Damasio, H. & Kassell, N. (1985b). Amnesia following basal forebrain lesions. *Archives of Neurology*, **42**, 263–271.

Delay, J., Brion, S. & Derouesne, C. (1964). Memoires originaux–Syndrome de Korsakoff et etiologie tumorale: Etude anatomo-clinique de trois observations. *Revue Neurologie*, **111**, 97–133.

Eslinger, P.J., Damasio, H., Damasio, A.R. & Butters, N. (1993). Nonverbal amnesia and asymmetric cerebral lesions following encephalitis. *Brain and Cognition*, **21**, 140–152.

Freed, D.M., Corkin, S. & Cohen, N.J. (1987). Forgetting in H.M.: A second look. *Neuropsychologia*, **25**(3), 461–471.

Gade, A. (1982). Amnesia after operations on aneurysms on the anterior communicating artery. *Surgical Neurology*, **18**, 46–49.

Gade, A. & Mortensen, E.L. (1990). Temporal gradient in the remote memory impairment of amnesic patients with lesions in the basal forebrain. *Neuropsychologia*, **28**, 985–1001.

Henson, R. A. & Urich, H. (1982). *Cancer and the Nervous System*. Oxford, Blackwell.

Huppert, F.A. & Piercy, M. (1978). Dissociation between learning and remembering in organic amnesia. *Nature*, **275**, 317–318.

Irle, E., Wowra, B., Kunert, H.J., Hampl, J. & Kunze, S. (1992). Memory disturbance following anterior communicating artery rupture. *Annals of Neurology*, **31**, 473–480.

Janowsky, J.S., Shimamura, A.P. & Squire, L.R. (1989). Source memory impairment in patients with frontal lobe lesions. *Neuropsychologia*, **27**(8), 1043–1056.

Jernigan, T.L., Schafer, K., Butters, N. & Cermak, L.S. (1991). Magnetic resonance imaging of alcoholic Korsakoff patients. *Neuropsychopharmacology*, **4**(3), 175–186.

Kapur, N. (1993). Focal retrograde amnesia in neurological disease: a critical review. *Cortex*, **29**, 217–234.

Katz, D.I., Alexander, M.P. & Mandell, A.M. (1987). Dementia following strokes in the mesencephalon and diencephalon. *Archives of Neurology*, **44**, 127–1133.

Kohler, J., Hufschmidt, A., Hermle, L., Volk, B. & Lucking, C.H. (1988). Limbic encephalitis: Two cases. *Neuroimmunology*, **20**, 177–178.

Lacomis, D., Khoshbin, S. & Schick, R.M. (1990). MR imaging of paraneoplastic limbic encephalitis. *Journal of Computer Assisted Tomography*, **14**, 115–117.

Laiacona, M., DeSantis, A., Barbarotto, R., Basso, A., Spagnoli, D. & Caiptani, E. (1989). Neuropsychological follow-up of patients operated for aneurysms of anterior communicating artery. *Cortex*, **25**, 261–273.

Lhermitte, F. & Signoret, J.L. (1972). Analyse neuropsychologique et differentiation des syndromes amnesiques. *Revue Neurologique*, **126**, 161–178.

Mair, W.G.P., Warrington, E.K. and Weiskrantz, L. (1979). Memory disorders in Korsakoff's psychosis: a neuropathological and neuropsychological investigation of two cases. *Brain*, **102**, 749–783.

Markowitsch, H.J. (1982). Thalamic mediodorsal nucleus and memory: a critical evaluation of studies in animals and man. *Neuroscience and Biobehavioral Reviews*, **6**, 351–380.

Mayes, A.R., Meudell, P.R., Mann, D. & Pickering, A. (1988). Location of lesions in Korsakoff's syndrome: neuropsychological and neuropathological data on two patients. *Cortex*, **24**, 367–388.

Milner, B. (1966). Amnesia following operation on the temporal lobes. In C.W.M. Whitte & O.L. Zangwill (eds), *Amnesia*. Butterworths, London, pp. 109–133.

Moscovitch, M. (1989). Confabulation and the frontal systems: Strategic versus associative retrieval in neuropsychological theories of memory. In H.L. Roediger III & F.I.M. Criak (eds), *Varieties of memory and consciousness: Essays in honour of Endel Tulving* (pp. 133–160). Hillsdale, NJ: Erlbaum.

Newman, N.J., Bell, I.R. & McKee, A.C. (1990). Paraneoplastic limbic encephalitis: neuropsychiatric presentation. *Biological Psychiatry*, **27**, 529–542.

O'Connor, M.G., Butters, N., Miliotis, P., Eslinger, P.J. & Cermak, L. (1992). The dissociation of anterograde and retrograde amnesia in a patient with herpes encephalitis. *Journal of Clinical and Experimental Neuropsychology*, **14**(2), 159–178.

O'Connor, M.G., Kaplan, B. & Cermak, L.S. (1990). *Transient Events Test*. Unpublished manuscript.

Oscar-Berman, M. (1980). Neuropsychological consequences of long-term chronic alcoholism. *American Scientist*, **68**, 410–419.

Oscar-Berman, M., Shahakian, B.J. & Wilmark, G. (1976). Spatial probability learning by alcoholic Korsakoff patients. *Journal of Experimental Psychology: Learning, Memory and Cognition*, **2**, 215–222.

Parkin, A. (1984). Amnesic syndrome: a lesion specific disorder? *Cortex*, **20**, 479–508.

Parkin, A., Leng, N.R., Stanhope, N. & Smith, M.P. (1988). Memory impairment following ruptured aneurysm of the anterior communicating artery. *Brain and Cognition*, **7**, 231–243.

Parkin, A.J. & Leng, R.C. (1993). *Neuropsychology of the Amnesic Syndrome*. Lawrence Erlbaum Associates, Hillsdale.

Peterson, L.R. & Peterson, M.J. (1959). Short-term retention of individual verbal items. *Journal of Experimental Psychology*, **58**, 193–198.

Rey, A. (1941). L'examen psychologique dans les cas d'encepalopathie traumatique. *Archives de Psychologie*, **28**, 286–340.

Rey, A. (1964). *L'examen clinique en psychologie*. Presses Universitaires de France, Paris.

Scoville, W.B. & Milner, B. (1957). Loss of recent memory after bilateral hippocampal lesions. *Journal of Neurology, Neurosurgery and Psychiatry*, **20**, 11–12.

Shimamura, A., Jernigan, T. & Squire, L.R. (1988). Korsakoff's syndrome: radiological (CT) findings and neuropsychological correlates. *Journal of Neurosciences*, **8**, 4400–4410.

Speedie, L.J. & Heilman, K.M. (1982). Amnesic disturbance following infarction of the left dorsomedial nucleus of the thalamus. *Neuropsychologia*, **20**, 597–604.

Sporfkin, B.E. & Sciarra, D. (1952). Korsakoff's psychosis associated with cerebral tumors. *Neurology*, **2**, 427–434.

Squire, L.R. (1981). Two forms of human amnesia: an analysis of forgetting. *Journal of Neuroscience*, **6**, 635–640.

Squire, L.R. & Moore, R.Y. (1979). Dorsal thalamic lesion in a noted case of human memory dysfunction. *Annals of Neurology*, **6**, 503–506.

Squire, L.R. & Shimamura, A.P. (1986). Characterizing amnesic patients for neurobehavioral study. *Behavioral Neuroscience*, **100**, 866–877.

Stenhouse, L.M., Knight, R.G., Longmore, B.E. & Bishara, S.M. (1991). Long-term cognitive deficits in patients after surgery on aneurysms of the anterior communicating artery. *Journal of Neurology, Neurosurgery and Psychiatry*, **54**, 909–914.

Talland, G.A. (1965). *Deranged Memory*. Academic Press, New York.

Talland, G.A. & Ballantine, H.T. (1967). Amnesic syndrome with anterior communicating artery aneurysm. *Journal of Nervous and Mental Diseases*, **145**, 179–192.

Victor, M., Adams, R.D. & Collings, G.H. (1989). *The Wernicke–Korsakoff Syndrome and Related Neurologic Disorders due to Alcoholism and Malnutrition*, 2nd ed. Davis, Philadelphia.

Vilkki, J. (1985). Amnesic syndromes after surgery of anterior communicating artery aneurysms. *Cortex*, **21**, 431–444.

Volpe, B.T. & Hirst, W. (1983). The characterization of an amnesic syndrome following hypoxic ischemic injury. *Archives of Neurology*, **40**, 436–440.

Warrington, E.K. (1984). *Recognition Memory Test*. NFER-Nelson, London.

Warrington, E.K. & McCarthy, R.A. (1988). The fractionation of retrograde amnesia. *Brain and Cognition*, **7**, 184–200.

Wechsler, D. (1981). *WAIS–R Manual*. Psychological Corporation, New York.

Wechsler, D. (1987). *WMS–R Manual*. Psychological Corporation, New York.

Weintraub, S. & Mesulam, M.M. (1993). Four neuropsychological profiles in dementia. In F. Boller & H. Spinnler (eds), *Handbook of Neuropsychology*, Elsevier Science Publishers, Amsterdam.

Weiskrantz. K. (1985). Issues and theories in the study of the amnesic syndrome. In N.M. Weinberger, K.F. Berham & G. Lynch (eds), *Memory Systems of the Brain*. Guilford Press, New York.

Winocur, G. & Kinsbourne, M. (1978). Contextual cueing as an aid to Korsakoff amnesics. *Neuropsychologia*, **14**, 97–110.

Winocur, G., Oxbury, S., Roberts, R., Agnetti, V. & Davis, C. (1984). Amnesia in a patient with bilateral lesions to the thalamus. *Neuropsychologia*, **22**, 123–143.

Zangwill, O.L. (1966). The amnesic syndrome. In C.W.M. Whitty & O.L. Zangwill (eds), *Amnesia*. Butterworths, London.

Ziegler, D.K., Kaufman, A. & Marshall, H.E. (1977). Abrupt memory loss associated with thalamic tumor. *Archives of Neurology*, **34**, 545–548.

Zola-Morgan, S., Squire, L.R. & Amaral, D.G. (1986). Human amnesia and the medial temporal region: enduring memory impairment following a bilateral lesion limited to field CA1 of the hippocampus. *Journal of Neuroscience*, **6**, 2950–2967.

Chapter 4

Retrograde Amnesia

John R. Hodges
University of Cambridge Neurology unit, Cambridge, UK

INTRODUCTION

Retrograde amnesia (RA), the phenomenon of loss of memory for events that occurred before the onset of brain trauma or other damage, has been extremely important for theories of amnesia and in attempts to understand normal memory functioning. Four basic patterns of remote memory impairment have been reported:

1. RA may be short, affecting months or at most a few years before the insult. This pattern has been extensively demonstrated, largely by Squire and his co-workers, after electroconvulsive therapy (Squire, Slater & Chace, 1975; Squire, Chace & Slater, 1976; Cohen & Squire, 1981). A similar pattern of temporally limited RA was initially described in the celebrated patient H.M., who underwent bilateral medial temporal lobectomy for the relief of intractable epilepsy before the role of the hippocampus and related medial temporal structures was fully appreciated (Scoville & Milner, 1957; Milner, Corkin & Teuber, 1968; Marslen-Wilson & Teuber, 1975). It should be noted, however, that subsequent investigations suggest that H.M.'s RA may be more extensive than was originally recognised (Corkin, 1984). The more recently documented patient R.B., who sustained hypoxic damage limited to the CA1 zone of the hippocampus, is also an example of a patient with a very limited RA in the presence of a moderately severe anterograde amnesia (Zola-Morgan, Squire & Amaral, 1986).

Handbook of Memory Disorders. Edited by A.D. Baddeley, B.A. Wilson and F.N. Watts.
© 1995 John Wiley & Sons Ltd.

2. An extensive RA, affecting recall of events from the preceding decades equally without evidence of a temporal gradient (i.e. a "flat" profile on remote memory tests), has been shown in a variety of conditions including chronic progressive multiple sclerosis (Beatty et al., 1988a), Huntington's disease (Albert, Butters & Levin, 1981; Beatty et al., 1988b), Parkinson's disease (Sagar et al., 1988), frontal lobe dementia (Hodges & Gurd, 1994), herpes simplex encephalitis (Cermak & O'Connor, 1983; Damasio et al., 1985a; Warrington & McCarthy, 1988), and in some studies of patients with dementia of Alzheimer's type (DAT, see below).

3. Some amnesic patients have an extensive RA which is temporally graded with sparing of memory from more distant time-periods. This pattern has been consistently demonstrated in the alcoholic Korsakoff's syndrome (Seltzer & Benson, 1974; Marslen-Wilson & Teuber, 1975; Albert, Butters & Levin, 1979; Meudell, Northern, Snowden & Neary, 1980; Cohen and Squire, 1981; Butters & Cermak, 1986; Kopelman, 1989; Squire, Haist & Shimamura, 1989; but for counter example see Sanders & Warrington, 1971); and in some patients with acute diencephalic damage as a result of bilateral thalamic infarction (for a review, see Butters & Stuss, 1989; Hodges & McCarthy, 1993) or basal forebrain lesions following surgical treatment of ruptured anterior communicating aneurysms (see Gade & Mortensen, 1990). A similar pattern has been observed in patients during transient global amnesia (Hodges & Ward, 1989; Kritchevsky, Squire & Zouzounis, 1988; Kritchevsky & Squire, 1989; Evans, Wilson, Wraight & Hodges, 1993).

4. Very occasionally patients may have extensive RA with minimal anterograde memory impairment. This pattern of so-called "isolated RA" is well-recognised in the context of functional or psychogenic amnesia (see Schacter, Wang, Tulving & Freedman, 1982; Hodges, 1991), but over the past decade an increasing number of convincing cases with radiologically documented brain damage resulting in relatively isolated RA have been reported (e.g., Goldberg et al., 1981; Kapur, Young, Bateman & Kennedy, 1989; Kapur et al., 1992; O'Connor et al., 1992; Markowitsch et al., 1993a). In these cases there is converging evidence to implicate damage to anterior temporal structures (the pole, entorhinal and parahippocampal cortices).

All theories of normal memory organisation and of the amnesic syndrome need to take into account these patterns of RA. Unfortunately there is, as yet, no wholly satisfactory theory which adequately explains these findings. For this reason, and because this is primarily a practical handbook, I have dedicated most of the remainder of this chapter to describing the pattern of RA in the most commonly encountered clinical disorders, and to emphasising the areas of uncertainty. Each section attempts to integrate the empirical findings and the implications for theories of amnesia. At the end of the chapter there is a brief overview with suggestions for further research in the area.

ASSESSMENT OF REMOTE MEMORY

A clinical impression of RA can be gained at bedside examination by using a semistructured interview technique in which the patient is asked to relate their life history with details of schools attended, past addresses, jobs, recent family events and holidays etc. Particular attention should be paid to the months preceding the onset of brain injury since memory of this period is always the most vulnerable. Details can then be checked with a spouse, other family member or friend. The clinical examination should also include an enquiry about news events from the recent and more distant past, but bearing in mind the background and interests of the patient; many people are more interested in, and hence better informed about, sporting events than they are about politics!

It is difficult to undertake formal tests of remote public memory outside the setting of specific experimental studies as there are virtually no commercially available tests (the exception is the Autobiographical Memory Interview which is described below). Investigators in this field have either adapted tests borrowed from other groups, or developed their own instruments. The major problem in test development in this domain is the enormous variability in normal subjects' performance on all such tests. For instance, the identification of famous faces or events depends upon gender, age, IQ, cultural background, and probably other factors as well, which make it practically impossible to design a universally applicable famous faces/events test.

In an experimental setting, a wide variety of tasks have been employed. Perhaps the most commonly used is a variation on the "famous faces test" first used by Sanders and Warrington (1971) and subsequently adapted by a number of workers (e.g. Marslen-Wilson & Teuber, 1975; Albert, Butters & Levin, 1979; Hodges & Ward, 1989). Such tests are constructed in the following way. A number of portrait photographs (say around 100) are chosen of people who came to prominence in a certain decade (e.g. 1940s, 1950s, 1960s etc.) and remained in the public eye for a relatively limited time. The photographs are then piloted on normal controls. Based on these data, a final selection—on which the controls attain a consistent 50–70% correct across the decades—is chosen. However, there has been considerable debate about the intrinsic biases introduced by this selection method; the faces chosen to represent the 1940s are likely to be much more famous, and hence to have been seen on many subsequent occasions, compared with faces selected from the 1980s (see Weiskrantz, 1985; Butters & Stuss, 1989; Hodges, 1991). In an attempt to overcome these criticisms, other workers have used pictorial news scenes which are perhaps less likely to have been seen repeatedly (Sagar et al., 1988; Kopelman, 1989), voices of famous personalities (Meudell, Northern, Snowden & Neary, 1980) or TV programmes aired for a single season (Cohen & Squire, 1981). Another approach has been to use tests based upon the identification of the names of famous people or events from among non-famous foils (Hodges & Ward, 1989; Kapur et al., 1992), or the recall and recognition of famous events (e.g. "What was the name of the first satellite to be launched?" ... and later in a four-choice alternative: "Was it Discover, Explorer, Sputnik or Telstar?" from Squire et al., 1989; also see Albert et al., 1979; Gade & Mortensen, 1990).

Autobiographical memory is clearly of considerable practical importance but until recently has been relatively neglected owing to difficulties in designing tasks with sufficient reliability and to problems with the quantification of personal memories. Initial attempts to assess autobiographical memory used a modification of the cueing method devised by Crovitz and Schiffman (1974). In this, subjects are asked to relate specific, personally experienced events evoked by a series of 10 to 20 common nouns (e.g. *boy, car, tree, bird* etc.) and then to estimate when that event occurred. The exact technique for test administration has been described in a number of publications (Zola-Morgan, Cohen & Squire, 1983; Baddeley & Wilson, 1986; Sagar et al., 1988; Hodges & Ward, 1989) which also include the methods used for scoring memories in terms of their descriptive richness and for specificity to time and place. With appropriate pre-test instruction, normal subjects have no difficulty performing this task and usually produce memories which are rich in detail and specific to time and place. It has also been shown that there is a consistent recency effect; that is to say, normal subjects produce a high proportion of memories from the most recent past. For instance, in one study 25% of approximately 500 memories produced by a group of 40 controls were from the last five years (Hodges, 1991). As will be discussed below, this test has been used to look at the temporal distribution of memories in amnesic patients.

A difficulty with the Crovitz–Schiffman technique is that subjects are not constrained to produce memories from specified time-periods. There is also considerable inter-individual variation in the time profile of the memories produced, which may be ironed out in group studies but produces difficulties when assessing single cases. It is impossible to know whether failure to recollect recent memories reflects a true inability or a test artefact. Also this technique samples only personal episodic memory and not knowledge of personal semantic facts. In an attempt to overcome these problems, Kopelman, Wilson and Baddeley (1989a) designed the Autobiographical Memory Interview in which subjects are questioned to elicit personal semantic information (e.g. addresses where lived, names of school friends/teachers/colleagues at work etc.) and autobiographical incidents from three life periods (childhood, early adult life and recent adult life). In this way scores for both types of memory (i.e., episodic and semantic) from the three periods can be derived using a specified scoring system. This test has since been marketed by the Thames Valley Test Company (Kopelman et al., 1989b) and remains the only commercially available test of remote memory. Results from its administration in Korsakoff's syndrome, dementia of Alzheimer type and other conditions will be described below. Interestingly, a standardised autobiographical enquiry very similar to that devised by Kopelman et al. was reported simultaneously by Italian workers (Borrini et al.,

1989), although this test is not yet available commercially.

HIPPOCAMPAL AMNESIA

Until quite recently the situation regarding RA in patients with medial temporal pathology was quite straightforward; it was generally believed that damage to this region resulted in severe anterograde amnesia with only very limited RA. Unfortunately, this simple view can no longer be regarded as correct. Since the former belief was based, very largely, on assessments of patient H.M., it seems appropriate to begin this section with a discussion of the findings in this most famous of all amnesic patients.

In 1953, at the age of 27, H.M. underwent a bilateral medial temporal lobe resection for the relief of intractable epilepsy (Scoville & Milner, 1957). The removal extended posteriorly along the medial surface of the temporal lobe for a distance of 8 cm from the anterior poles, probably destroying the anterior two-thirds of the hippocampus, and parahippocampal gyrus bilaterally together with the amygdala and the peri-amygdaloid cortex. This resulted in a devastating amnesic syndrome. In 1968, Milner and colleagues reported that H.M.'s RA was restricted to about two years preceding the operation. This conclusion was based on postoperative interviews with H.M. and his mother. The first formal investigation of H.M.'s remote memory, using a famous faces test, supported the earlier conclusion by showing essentially normal identification of faces from the 1930s and 40s, but severe impairment for faces that had become famous during the 1950s and 60s (Marslen-Wilson & Teuber, 1975). However, subsequent investigation in the early 1980s using a verbal recognition test of public events, a pictorial famous scenes test and a modified version of Crovitz and Schiffman's (1974) personal remote memory test indicated a more extensive RA. As stated by Corkin (1984): "These experiments, taken together, provide clear evidence that H.M.'s remote memory impairment extends back to the age of 16, 11 years before the operation." The explanation of these contradictory findings remains unclear. It may be that earlier findings were fallacious, and that ever since his operation he has, in fact, suffered a more extensive RA than was previously realised. Moreover, it is possible that the RA may be, at least in part, a result of the frequent preoperative seizures or the toxic doses of anticonvulsants prescribed to control these, as suggested by Corkin (1984). Another intriguing possibility is that, over the 30 or so years since the surgery, his RA has actually worsened due to impoverished rehearsal of remote memories.

The situation is further confused by a number of reports of patients with bilateral or unilateral hippocampal damage, resulting from herpes simplex encephalitis (Cermak & O'Connor, 1983; Damasio et al., 1985b; Warrington & McCarthy, 1988), posterior cerebral artery occlusion (Benson, Marsden & Meadows, 1974; Woods, Schoene & Kneisley, 1982; DeRenzi, Zamboli & Crisi, 1987), hypoxic damage (Beatty, Salmon, Bernstein & Butters, 1987) or as a nonmetastatic complication of neoplasia (Duyckaerts et al., 1985), some of whom appear to have limited RA while others have had a more extensive deficit. But in many of these, assessment of RA has been based on informal observations. The more recent application of quantitative tests to series of cases with damage to radiologically or pathologically defined structures is, however, now producing a more coherent picture (see Squire, 1992).

One of the most important observations comes from the study of a patient (case R.B.) who developed an amnesic syndrome in 1978 following complications of cardiac bypass surgery. Despite a moderately severe anterograde amnesia, a battery of remote memory tests showed that R.B. had little, if any, loss of information about premorbid public or personal events. Five years later, R.B. suffered a fatal cardiac arrest. Post-mortem examination revealed ischaemic damage involving the entire CA1 zone of the hippocampus but sparing all other limbic structures (Zola-Morgan et al., 1986). In contrast, a group of four other patients with anoxic damage, studied by the same group of investigators using identical tests of remote memory, exhibited extensive and temporally graded RA (Squire et al., 1989). These cases had more severe anterograde amnesia than patient R.B., suggesting perhaps more extensive damage. Support for this assumption comes from neuroimaging studies: two of the four have undergone quantitative MRI scans using a state-of-the-art method for identifying and measuring the hippocampus and related structures (Press, Amaral & Quire, 1989). In contrast to patient R.B. these patients had a marked reduction in the overall size of the hippocampus, affecting all zones of the hippocampus together with the dentate gyrus and the subicular complex. Based on these findings, Squire (1992) has postulated that pathology confined to the hippocampus *per se* can produce moderately severe anterograde amnesia with temporally limited RA, but more widespread damage—involving parahippocampal structures—produces a profound anterograde amnesia with a severe but temporally graded RA. The theoretical counterpart of this hypothesis is that the hippocampus is involved in the establishment of new memories and their temporary storage, but over time these memories become independent of the hippocampus due to a process of reorganisation or consolidation. Hence RA would result from either damage to the storage sites of remote memories or problems with retrieval or reconstruction of remote memory. The former may account for the extensive RA seen after herpes simplex encephalitis which destroys areas of temporal neocortex, whereas the latter is a more plausible explanation for the extensive RA seen in patients with focal damage to the diencephalon (for instance after thalamic infarction, as will be discussed below).

Extensive loss of remote memory for both autobiographical and public events is a well-recognised consequence of herpes simplex encephalitis. One of the best illustrations of this devastating complication comes from Cermak and O'Connor (1983) who reported a patient (case S.S.) who appeared on informal and formal testing to have "no episodic memory for any events in his life past or present". He was also severely impaired on a famous faces test without sparing of more distant memories. Similar observations were made by Damasio et al. (1985a) on their patient D.R.B.; they suggested, in keeping with the hypothesis proposed by

Squire (see above), that the devastating RA for both episodic and semantic memory resulted from the combination of medial temporal damage (accounting for the anterograde amnesia) and bilateral temporal neocortical damage (accounting for the dense and non-temporally graded RA). Warrington and McCarthy (1988; McCarthy & Warrington, 1992) have also reported a post-encephalitic patient (case R.F.R.) who has a profound amnesic syndrome with a RA, affecting both personal and public memory stretching back into the remote past, who is "unable to give a detailed or coherent account of any episode from either domain". For instance, he failed to recognise photographs of his own children and only hesitantly recognised his mother. Experimental investigation documented his inability to recall, recognise, and place in temporal order the names and faces of famous people for all time periods. By constrast, his recall of famous faces and names was facilitated by the verbal cue of the person's first name and initial of the surname (e.g. Margaret T...). In addition, he retained the ability to select the famous name or face from amongst two distracters. These observations, together with other detailed single-case studies (e.g. Hodges & McCarthy, 1992, discussed below), are important because they are beginning to show that RA is not an "all or none phenomenon" which is present to an equal degree independent of the nature of the test material (faces versus scenes; autobiographical versus general knowledge etc.) and mode of testing (recall versus recognition etc.) It seems likely that further fractionations of this type will be discovered which, if combined with detailed neuroanatomical investigation, should reveal important insights about the cognitive organisation and neural basis of remote memory.

In summary, damage restricted purely to the hippocampus appears to result in a moderately severe anterograde amnesia with a temporally limited and mild RA, although this is based, at present, on a study of a single patient. When the structures closely connected with the hippocampus (the parahippocampal gyrus, subiculum etc.) are also involved, the anterograde amnesia is more severe and accompanied by an extensive RA which can be temporally graded. Following herpes simplex encephalitis there is often a severe amnesic syndrome; in such cases the RA does not show a temporally graded pattern, being equally severe for all periods of past life. The application of detailed single-case methodology is beginning to show interesting patterns of preservations and loss within the general domain of remote memory.

DIENCEPHALIC AMNESIA

Alcoholic Korsakoff's Syndrome

It has been known for many years that RA is a consistent clinical feature in patients with alcoholic Korsakoff's syndrome (for a review, see Talland, 1965;

Butters, 1984; Butters & Stuss, 1989). A typical Korsakoff patient has marked difficulty in retrieving information about their own life and about public events that occurred prior to the onset of amnesia. This difficulty is, in general, most pronounced for events that occurred in the past decade or two. Very remote memories are relatively preserved. In the acute stages of the illness, often referred to as the Wernicke–Korsakoff confusional state, confabulation is common. This may take the form of fantastic and highly implausible false responses, or more often the fusing together or temporal misplacing of true past events. Beyond the acute stages of the illness fantastic confabulation is, however, unusual. As stated by Butters (1984): "The notion that confabulation is a cardinal symptom of Korsakoff's disorder is not consistent with most experiences with such patients."

Despite the clinical impression that patients with Korsakoff's syndrome show sparing of more distant memories, initial quantitative assessment produced conflicting results. Sanders and Warrington (1971), in the first formal investigation of RA in amnesic patients, using a famous events questionnaire and a famous faces test, failed to demonstrate a temporal gradient. In contrast, other early investigators did find a temporally graded pattern on a variety of measures including a multiple-choice public events questionnaire (Seltzer & Benson, 1974), a famous face test (Marslen-Wilson & Teuber, 1975) and a famous voices test (Meudell et al., 1980), or a combination of these tasks (Albert et al., 1979). This conflict created considerable debate about the validity of the test measures (see Butters, 1985; Weiskrantz, 1985; Butters & Stuss, 1989; Hodges, 1991). It was suggested that most tests demonstrating a sparing of remote memories may have failed to control for the relative difficulty and degree of exposure of the faces and events under study. More specifically, faces or events selected to achieve a supposedly equivalent ("flat") level of performance across the decades in the normal control subjects may not, in fact, be equivalent: for example, faces selected from the 1940s (e.g. Winston Churchill) have been exposed to the public repeatedly since then, whereas many of the faces of equivalent difficulty from the 1980s (e.g. Michael Heseltine) are likely to fade rapidly from public view. Various attempts have been made to address these criticisms. For instance, Butters and Albert (1982) re-examined the data from their earlier study (Albert et al., 1979) making use of the fact that their famous faces tests contained items that were judged as "easy" for controls and items that were generally graded as "hard". Reanalysis showed that the amnesic Korsakoff patients were impaired on both subsets and, more importantly, identified more hard faces from the remote past (e.g. the 1930s and 40s) than easy faces from the recent past (e.g. the 1970s). Squire and his colleagues tried to avoid the problem of equivalence of test items by selecting TV programmes that had been aired for a single season to construct their recall and recognition test (Cohen & Squire, 1981). Using this technique, they demonstrated that a group of patients with Korsakoff's syndrome had an extensive and temporally graded loss of remote memory which contrasted with that present in patients tested after receiving bilateral ECT.

The finding that Korsakoff patients show selective impairment when asked to recall autobiographical memories from the recent past is also difficult to explain on the basis of test artefact. Zola-Morgan, Cohen and Squire (1983) used a cueing technique modified from the work of Crovitz and Schiffman (1974). The results showed that although the Korsakoff patients and control subjects did not differ in their overall ability to retrieve detailed and personal episodic memories, they differed significantly in terms of the life-periods from which the memories emanated. As in other studies (Sagar et al., 1988; Hodges & Ward, 1989), the controls drew particularly from the recent past, whereas the Korsakoff patients recalled episodes almost exclusively from their childhood and early adulthood. Similar conclusions were reached by Kopelman (1989) who administered the Autobiographical Memory Interview to a large group of Korsakoff patients. Compared with controls, the patients were markedly impaired on both the personal semantic and episodic parts of the schedule with a strong correlation between their performance on the two parts.

Given that it is now established fairly conclusively that patients with Korsakoff's syndrome do indeed have an extensive and temporally graded RA, it is necessary to explain this pattern. In the early 1980s two groups of investigators simultaneously advanced the hypothesis that the loss of remote memories may be secondary to a primary defect in laying down (or encoding) new memories during the 20 or more years of alcohol abuse that typically precede the onset of the amnesic syndrome (see Squire & Cohen, 1982; Butters & Albert, 1982). According to this hypothesis, the pattern of extensive and temporally graded loss is regarded as a consequence of the chronic alcoholism and *not* as an intrinsic part of the amnesia. However, experimental testing of this hypothesis produced only weak support; chronic detoxified alcoholics without Korsakoff's syndrome were shown to be only very mildly impaired on measures of remote memory, and only for the recent time periods (Albert et al., 1980; Cohen & Squire, 1981).

As is so often the case in cognitive neuropsychology, a significant contribution to this area came from the detailed investigation of a single case (Butters & Cermak, 1986). This patient, an eminent scientist (case P.Z.), developed alcoholic Korsakoff's syndrome at the age of 65. He had written several hundred research papers, and, most importantly, had completed an extensive autobiography just three years prior to the onset of his amnesic syndrome. In a series of ingenious experiments, in which they designed test materials with the aid of his autobiography and used as controls other similarly aged scientists from the same research field, Butters and Cermak were able to demonstrate that P.Z. had lost knowledge of technical facts and names of scientists that were previously familiar to him, as well as autobiographical material. Furthermore, there was clear-cut evidence of a temporal gradient in all areas tested. The hypothesis that the extensive and graded RA seen in alcoholic Korsakoff's syndrome results from increasingly deleterious effects of chronic alcohol abuse is clearly implausible as a total explanation of these findings. Butters and Cermak were forced to adopt a two-factor model; in this, one factor is the effect of long-term alcohol, so that alcoholics retain somewhat less information each year, due to their well documented chronic learning deficit. The second factor is a loss, or lack of access to, old memories that appears acutely as a result of diencephalic damage. The latter results in a selective deficit in recalling episodic memories. Butters and Cermak built on the earlier suggestion by Cermak (1984) that newly acquired knowledge may be episodic in nature, but with time and continued rehearsal the memories become independent of specific temporal and spatial contexts, and thus acquire the characteristics of semantic memories. They noted, however, that P.Z.—and by analogy other patients with alcoholic Korsakoff's syndrome—do not have complete sparing of semantic memory, it is merely less vulnerable to diencephalic damage. A possible explanation for this selective vulnerability is discussed further below in the context of acute diencephalic infarction.

A similar multiple-factor hypothesis has been advanced by Kopelman (1989) who compared the performance of patients with alcoholic Korsakoff's syndrome and dementia of Alzheimer's type on a battery of tasks designed to test remote personal and public memory. In the Korsakoff group, there was evidence of partial independence between memory for personal events/facts and memory for public events/facts. Performance on the latter, but not the former, correlated with current IQ measures. These findings suggest that different subdivisions within remote memory are differentially vulnerable in alcoholic Korsakoff's syndrome.

A number of authors have drawn attention to the consistent "frontal" dysfunction found in Korsakoff patients, and have speculated that the extensive RA reflects the combined effects of alcohol-mediated frontal and acute diencephalic damage (see Squire, 1986). However, more recent studies have found only a very weak correlation between performance on tests of frontal function and extent of RA (Kopelman, 1989, 1991). Furthermore, it is now well established that some patients without frontal system damage may exhibit an extensive RA (e.g. Beatty, Salmon, Berstein & Butters, 1987; Salmon, Lasker, Butters & Beatty, 1988; Squire et al., 1989). It is also clear, from the work of Shimamura and Squire (1986) and Kopelman (1989), that within a group of Korsakoff patients there is no significant correlation between the severity of anterograde amnesia and RA. This finding concurs with observations during transient global amnesia which produces in all patients a profound anterograde amnesia, but a very variable RA.

The fact that non-alcoholic diencephalic damage, such as following acute bilateral thalamic infarction (see Hodges & McCarthy, 1993), can cause an extensive and temporally graded RA is also evidence against long-term alcohol abuse being the major cause of the extensive RA in Korsakoff's syndrome.

In summary, extensive study of RA in alcoholic Korsakoff's syndrome over the past two decades has established, beyond all reasonable doubt, that there is a consistent pattern of extensive and temporally graded loss of memory for both public events/faces and autobiographical memories. It is no longer plausible to explain this pattern entirely as a failure of new learning prior to the onset of the amnesic syndrome. Interpretations of the relative role of diencephalic and other cortical (frontal) damage in the genesis of the extensive RA differ, but in view of the evidence from patients with thalamic infarction it seems likely that diencephalic damage *per se* is the most important factor.

Diencephalic Amnesia of Vascular and Neoplastic Aetiology

In view of the controversy (discussed above) regarding the cause of the extensive RA found in patients with alcoholic Korsakoff's syndrome, the pattern of remote memory impairment in patients with non-alcohol-related causes of acute diencephalic damage is clearly of considerable theoretical importance. Unfortunately, however, in contrast to the multitude of studies of Korsakoff's syndrome, there have been relatively few detailed studies of such patients. But it is clear that bilateral thalamic infarction (e.g. Stuss, Gubermann, Nelson & Larochelle, 1988; Hodges & McCarthy, 1993) or tumours in the region of the diencephalon (e.g. Ziegler, Kaufman & Marshall, 1977; Butters, 1984) can produce an extensive RA.

Of these various disorders, the neuropsychology of acute bilateral infarction of paramedian thalamic structures, has been best studied. Immediately following the stroke there is often impaired consciousness. Patients who remain conscious invariably have a marked acute confusional state with diminished attention and severe disorientation. As this resolves, after days or weeks, the patient exhibits a severe anterograde amnesia. Other neuropsychological deficits may be present (e.g. aphasia, perceptual deficits etc.) depending upon the anatomical locus of the damage. A disorder of voluntary eye movements, affecting particularly upwards gaze, is also common in such patients. Although considerable numbers of patients with thalamic infarction resulting in persistent amnesia have now been reported (e.g. Guberman & Stuss, 1983; Graff-Radford et al., 1984; 1985; 1990; Winocur et al., 1984; von Crammon, Hebel & Schuri, 1985; Stuss et al., 1988; Markowitsch, von Crammon & Schuri, 1993b; Hodges and McCarthy, 1993), the overwhelming emphasis in these studies has been on the anterograde aspects of memory. Only eight reports, totalling eleven patients, have included any quantitative assessment of remote memory. Analysis of the data on these cases, summarised in Table 4.1, shows that ten patients had evidence of extensive retrograde memory impairment. Thus, there is little doubt that RA occurs in this situation, but its characteristics are less well established. In most instances only one or two tests of remote memory were employed, and there have been only three attempts to assess autobiographical memory (Stuss et al., 1988; Markowitsch et al., 1993b; Hodges & McCarthy, 1993).

Stuss et al. (1988) reported on the RA of a well-educated patient (case R.C.) with isolated bilateral paramedian thalamic infarction resulting in a fairly pure amnesic syndrome. On a test of public events, R.C. was severely impaired on both recall and recognition measures with apparent equivalence across all time periods (i.e. without evidence of a temporal gradient). When R.C.'s memory for

Table 4.1 Summary of all reported cases of diencephalic amnesia resulting from acute bilateral thalamic strokes in whom quantitative tests of remote memory have been applied

Authors	Number of cases	Retrograde amnesia	Remote memory tests used	Data given
Graff-Radford et al., 1984	1	Yes 1/1	FFT	Yes
Winocur et al., 1984	1	No 1/1	FFT and FNT	Yes
Graff-Radford et al., 1985	1*	Yes 1/1	FFT	Yes
von Crammon et al., 1985	3	Yes 2/3	FFT and Life Events	No
Stuss et al., 1988	1	Yes 1/1	Famous Events and Autobiographical	Yes
Graff-Radford et al., 1990	2†	Yes 2/2	FFT and Events tests	Yes
Markowitsch et al., 1993b	1	Yes	FFT, FNT Autobiographical	Yes
Hodges & McCarthy, 1993	1	Yes	FFT, FNT, FET Autobiographical	Yes

FFT = Famous Faces Test; FNT = Famous Names Test; FET = Famous Events Test.
*Although three cases reported, only one underwent formal testing.
†Paper reports four cases, but only two were considered to show amnesia.

autobiographical events was evaluated, his severe inability to recall past episodes was again very apparent, and although the period immediately prior to the stroke was most affected, there was patchy loss for most of his life.

A similar patient (case A.B.) with a dense amnesic syndrome after bilateral thalamic infarction has been studied in considerable detail over a 10-year period by Markowitsch and colleagues (1993b). Of the 50 memory and other cognitive tasks reported, unfortunately only three concern remote memory: on a test of autobiographical memory, A.B. was unable to produce any memories from the recent past; a famous faces test showed a severe deficit with evidence of relative sparing for earlier decades; and a famous names test also revealed a profound RA.

The most comprehensive study to date of RA in this situation concerned an almost identical patient to those described above (case P.S.) who likewise suffered symmetrical bilateral paramedian infarction in the territory of the paramedian artery (Hodges & McCarthy, 1993). The lesions involved the dorso-medial nuclei as well as the internal medullary lamina and the mammillo-thalamic tract bilaterally; in addition the parafasicular nuclei and the retroflex fascicle may also have been damaged. Following the stroke, P.S. had a classic amnesic syndrome with preservation of general intellectual abilities and short-term (immediate) memory. His severe anterograde amnesia was accompanied by a profound loss of personal memory encompassing virtually the whole of his adult life since. The persistence of a paramnesic state of delusional proportions, in which he believed that he was still on active service in the navy, was the most striking clinical observation. Formal tests of autobiographical memory indicated a profound deficit in recalling specific life events whether using a clinical interview technique, a modification of the Crovitz–Schiffman personal remote memory test, the Autobiographical Memory Interview (Kopelman, Wilson & Baddeley, 1989a,b), or cueing with family photographs. P.S. showed some preservation of semantic information about his early life, but even salient facts about his own life after 1940 were related inconsistently. In contrast to his performance on tests of autobiographical memory, P.S. showed striking preservation of knowledge about famous people from all eras. Although poor at naming famous faces, he could generate specific identifying semantic information in the majority of instances, whether tested using faces or names. His ability to distinguish famous faces and names from non-famous foils was extremely good. Even more remarkable was his ability to place triplets of faces and names in their correct sequence, although his ability to date individual names was severely impaired. P.S.'s preservation of specific semantic information about famous people appeared not to generalise to other domains of public knowledge since his performance on tests of famous event identification (from name and photograph) was extremely poor.

The results of these three studies confirm that an extensive RA may result from non-alcoholic damage to thalamic structures, although anterograde amnesia without significant RA has also been reported (Winocur et al., 1984). This implies that damage to certain structures within the diencephalon is critical for the production of RA. Clearly further combined neuropsychological and radiological studies are required to address this issue. Regarding the psychological explanations for RA in thalamic infarction, it is implausible to propose that there has been a loss of memory store. *A priori*, there is insufficient neuronal space in the medial thalamus for a store of one's adult life memories!

It seems more plausible to attribute such dense impairments to a form of retrieval deficit, perhaps secondary to loss of a critical link within a closely integrated but spatially distributed memory system. This is similar to the disconnection hypothesis of diencephalic amnesia advanced by Warrington and Weiskrantz (1982). Hodges and McCarthy (1993) extended this hypothesis, drawing on contemporary cognitive theories of autobiographical memory which emphasise the view of memory as a complex integrated retrieval and storage system (e.g. Baddeley, 1990); the overall process of retrieval and remembering is viewed as a dynamic cognitive operation involving problem-solving, cross-checking, verification and inference (e.g. Norman & Bobrow, 1979). At the lowest level are the elements of autobiographical records which may be relatively fragmentary and cognitively unstructured (Morton, Hammersley & Bekerian, 1985). Memories may *become* structured and coherent by virtue of operations that are carried out in the processes of retrieval. At the highest level of the program are retrieval "frameworks" (Conway, 1992). The major role of the retrieval frameworks is in providing pointers, and a basic organisational structure, for guiding retrieval and integration of the lower-level records. The relationship between the higher and lower levels of the hierarchy can be thought of as being much like the card index system of a library which guides the reader towards books. The RA in thalamic damage is viewed, in this model, as a failure at the higher level of organisation (the higher-level retrieval frameworks) with preservation of basic lower-order memories. The latter are, however, inaccessible because of a disconnection between frontal (retrieval and initiation) and posterior (storage) components of the memory system.

Traumatic and Surgical Damage to Other Diencephalic and Limbic Structures Including the Fornix

Traumatic damage to the medial diencephalon and/or mammillary bodies has been reported in two remarkable cases (N.A. and B.J.). Patient N.A.'s amnesia resulted from an accident in 1960 when a miniature foil entered his brain through the right nostril. He was originally unable to recall any significant personal or public events for at least two years preceding the accident (Teuber, Milner & Vaughan, 1968). His RA diminished over time, leaving N.A. with minimal, if any, remote memory loss despite an enduring anterograde amnesia of moderate severity (Cohen & Squire, 1981). The location of the damage in N.A. has been a topic of controversy (see Weiskrantz, 1985), but a recent MRI has revealed that N.A.'s lesion involves the left medial thalamic region, left mammillo-thalamic tract, the hypothalamus and the mammillary bodies bilaterally (Squire et al., 1989b). A strangely identical patient (case B.J.), who developed severe amnesia following a penetrating brain injury by a snooker cue which entered through the left nostril, was reported by Dusoir et al. (1990). As with N.A., there was considerable improvement post-injury, but the patient was left with a severe anterograde amnesia for verbal material with an RA for the six months before the injury. MRI showed a lesion in the hypothalamus in the region of the mammillary bodies.

Fornix damage, which most commonly results from attempts to remove colloid cysts or other lesions from the IIIrd ventricle, may be associated with an amnesia syndrome (see Gaffan & Gaffan, 1991). Two recently reported cases, who sustained MRI documented fornical transection, developed a moderate anterograde amnesia which was selective for verbal material. But in neither case was there a significant RA, as assessed by both a famous faces test and a test of autobiographical memory (Hodges & Carpenter, 1991).

Damage to the posterior section of the fornix is one of the mechanisms postulated to account for the amnesia found in patients with lesions of the splenium (so called "retrospenial amnesia"). Rudge and Warrington (1991) reported eight cases with severe anterograde amnesia associated with tumours of the posterior corpus callosum which involved the splenium. There was circumstantial clinical evidence to suggest extensive RA in some cases, but formal tests of remote memory were not reported. Valenstein et al. (1987) documented a similar patient who became amnesic following haemorrhage from an anteriovenous malformation in the region of the splenium. His RA was initially judged to be around 4 years, but later shrunk to 12 months or less, which was in keeping with his normal performance on a famous faces test.

Severe amnesia may arise as a complication of surgery for ruptured anterior communicating artery aneurysms. Damage to basal forebrain structures including the septal nucleus and subcallosal area appears responsible (Damasio et al., 1985; Philips, Sangalang & Sterns, 1987). In the acute stages, marked spontaneous confabulation has been reported (Damasio et al., 1985). Recently, a formal study of a large group of such patients, tested two years post-onset, has documented the presence of marked RA with a temporally-graded pattern identical to that observed in patients with chronic Korsakoff's syndrome (Gade & Mortensen, 1990).

ISOLATED RETROGRADE AMNESIA

Although some patients with moderately severe anterograde amnesia have only mild temporally limited RA (Zola-Morgan, Squire & Amaral, 1986; Hodges & Ward, 1989), the reverse situation—namely severe RA in combination with relatively mild or no anterograde amnesia—appears to be exceedingly rare. Indeed, until fairly recently the existence of this syndrome—which is potentially of great theoretical importance—has been in considerable doubt. Severe loss of remote memory, is a cardinal feature of hysterical or psychogenic amnesia (Schacter, Wang, Tulving & Freedman, 1982; Kopelman, 1987; Hodges 1991). In many of the cases of so called "isolated RA" it is, therefore, difficult to be sure that functional amnesia has been excluded (e.g. Roman-Campos, Poser & Wood, 1980; Andrews, Posner & Kessler, 1982). This is illustrated by the case reported by Stuss and Guzman (1988) of a 50-year old man who presented with an insidious onset of personality change, seizures, features of the Kluver–Bucy syndrome and apparently isolated RA; MRI scanning showed damage to the anterior pole of the left temporal lobe and neuropsychological assessment confirmed the presence of a mild to moderate degree of anterograde amnesia, but a profound RA encompassing virtually the whole of the patient's life. The aetiology of his amnesic problems was not determined precisely, although in a footnote the authors added an interesting comment about his performance during a subsequent sodium amytal study: "During this investigation, questioning readily elicited detailed descriptions of many specific events from all stages of his life." Clearly this finding casts some doubt upon the organic nature of the patient's RA.

Over the past decade, however, a number of convincing cases with organic brain damage resulting in relatively isolated RA have been reported. The first clearly documented case was, perhaps, that of Goldberg et al. (1981) who studied a 36-year-old male patient who developed amnesia following an open head injury. Initially this patient's anterograde amnesia and RA were of equivalent severity, but over several years his anterograde amnesia resolved, and he was left with a dense 20-year RA for both public and autobiographical events. CT scanning revealed extensive damage to the right middle and posterior temporal areas and a smaller area of damage in the left mid-temporal region. There was evidence also of infarction of the paramedian region of the upper mid-brain involving particularly the ventral tegmental area. The authors speculated that the extensive isolated RA resulted from the latter damage although, as we shall see, subsequent evidence strongly suggests that this interpretation was in fact incorrect, and that the critically damaged area was the temporal lobe.

Kapur and coworkers (1989) described a 74-year-old man who presented with recurrent episodes of acute memory loss thought initially to be due to transient global amnesia, but eventually diagnosed as temporal lobe epilepsy. Over a number of years, they documented a progressive loss of remote memory on a variety of quantitative measures without an accompanying anterograde amnesia.

Three more recent studies, which have combined detailed neuroanatomical examination by MRI with quantitative assessment of remote memory, have implicated the temporal neocortex as the critical structure for storing or maintaining remote memories. O'Connor et al. (1992) described a 26-year-old patient, who following herpes simplex encephalitis, was left with a mild to moderate anterograde amnesia, more marked for nonverbal than verbal material, and a profound RA; she was virtually unable to recall any events from her past life and had a severely impoverished fund of more general semantic knowledge. MRI showed complete destruction of the right temporal lobe involving the hippocampus, the parahippocampal gyrus and ventromedial portion of the frontal lobe. Interestingly, the patient also had a degree of "visual agnosia" for objects, implying a loss of general semantic memory as well. The other two recently reported cases also sustained asymmetric damage to temporal lobe structures, interestingly in both instances as a result of riding accidents (Kapur et al., 1992; Markowitsch et al., 1993a). Kapur et al.'s patient, a 28-year old woman, had minimal anterograde amnesia but severe RA documented on tests of both autobiographical and remote memory for scenes, faces and names. The locus of damage on MRI was the anterior right temporal pole, medial temporal cortex and anterior parahippocampus. The patient reported by Markowitsch et al. had a mild anterograde amnesia but a profound RA which affected personal–episodic rather than personal–semantic memories. An MRI showed prefrontal and temporal neocortical damage which was much more marked on the right.

In conclusion, this review of the literature suggests that isolated RA may arise as a consequence of brain disease, although it appears to be rare in comparison to more conventional amnesic syndromes. The recent neuroradiological evidence points to anterior temporal structures (the pole, entorhinal and parahippocampal cortices) as the areas most consistently damaged in such cases. The two main interpretations of these data are either that these areas are the storage sites for remote memory, or alternatively, in the words of O'Connor et al. (1992), they can be "viewed as the regions that contain combinatory codes necessary for the retrieval of remote information". Circumstantial evidence derived from the study of patients with loss of general semantic memory, causing anomia, impaired word comprehension and visual agnosia, suggests that the former explanation is likely to be correct; semantic memory impairment has been consistently associated with damage to the temporal neocortex following herpes simplex encephalitis (Warrington & Shallice, 1984; Damasio et al., 1985), or in the context of progressive focal lobar atrophy (Warrington, 1975; Hodges, Patterson, Oxbury & Funnell, 1992).

TRANSIENT GLOBAL AMNESIA

The clinical features and neuropsychology of transient global amnesia (TGA) are dealt with in detail elsewhere in this book. In brief, this syndrome, first described fully by Fisher and Adams (1964), is characterised by a sudden onset of severe amnesia and confusion, often with repetitive questioning. The attack lasts for a number of hours then gradually resolves, leaving the patient with a dense amnesic gap, which covers the whole period of the attack and often a few hours preceding it (Hodges, 1991).

There is still relatively limited information on the characteristics of the memory deficit during TGA. This is not surprising as recurrence of TGA is unusual and it is clearly very difficult to test patients while they are amnesic. However, the data obtained to date are of considerable theoretical importance. Taken together, the studies by Hodges and colleagues (Hodges & Ward, 1989; Evans et al., 1993; Hodges, 1994) and by Kritchevsky and colleagues (Kritchevsky, Squire & Zouzounis, 1988; Kritchevsky & Squire, 1989) have demonstrated that in TGA there may be a temporally extensive and graded RA affecting memory for both personal and public events. The time immediately preceding the attack is invariably most affected. However, by comparison with the universally profound anterograde amnesia, the RA is much more variable in extent. In the most detailed study to date, there was considerable heterogeneity amongst five patients studied; while some patients had an extensive retrograde memory loss encompassing several decades, others had a very limited RA for the past few months only (Hodges & Ward, 1989). Several studies have suggested that autobiographical memory may be particularly affected. For instance, Evans et al. (1993) recently tested one patient during TGA using the Autobiographical Memory Interview and demonstrated a marked impairment on the personal episodic component of the test (e.g. first day of school, wedding day, holidays etc.) which contrasted with her normal performance on the personal semantic component (e.g. names of school friends, teachers, past addresses etc.). This finding is in keeping with two earlier reports using the Crovitz and Schiffman technique of cued autobiographical recall (Hodges & Ward, 1989; Kritchevsky et al., 1989); both studies demonstrated that during TGA patients had great difficulty in recalling specific events. The episodes that were produced lacked the richness and detail with which the same memories were related after the attack. It appears, therefore, that during TGA there is difficulty building up the normal contextual richness of autobiographical memories. There is also impairment, at least in some cases, on more traditional tests of remote public memory involving the identification and naming of famous faces and events (Hodges & Ward, 1989).

One aspect of the findings during TGA, which has largely been ignored by memory theorists, is their contribution to the debate on temporally graded memory loss. Much of the controversy regarding the pattern of RA in chronic amnesic patients results from the fact that it is seldom possible to distinguish between deficits in acquisition and retrieval of old memories. In other words, evaluation of the content of memory prior to the onset of amnesia can hardly ever be made. One exception to this is the elegant series of studies performed on patient P.Z. by Butters and Cermak (1986), which was discussed above. Furthermore, to measure remote memory, comparisons must usually be made between—rather than within—subjects. This poses major problems due to the great inter-individual variation in knowledge of public people and events. TGA provides the opportunity to compare patients' performance during an episode of dense amnesia with their own performance after the attack. The studies discussed above have demonstrated that during TGA some cases demonstrate a temporally extensive and graded RA. This cannot possibly be explained on the basis of an encoding, or even a storage deficit, and must result from disruption of the processes involved in memory retrieval.

The other important theoretical implication of the findings during TGA concerns the relationship between anterograde amnesia and RA. The fact that all patients have a profound anterograde amnesia yet some patients have only a very limited RA adds to the growing evidence that anterograde amnesia and RA are functionally separable, and therefore depend presumably upon anatomically distinct structures.

There are a number of possible explanations for the observed variability in RA during TGA. The simplest is that it reflects variation in the brain structures affected during attacks. Evidence in support of this position comes from studies of cerebral blood flow using single photon emission computed tomography or SPECT; a number of investigators have demonstrated bilateral temporal lobe hypoperfusion during TGA (Stillhard et al., 1990; Tanabe et al., 1991; Evans et al., 1993), whereas Goldenberg et al. (1991) found reduction in regional blood flow in the left thalamus, as well as more diffuse hypoperfusion of the cerebral cortex, including frontal areas. It is tempting to associate these findings with the observed differences in RA, but further studies combining functional brain imaging and neuropsychological assessment are clearly required.

In conclusion, TGA is a relatively unusual condition, but one which is encountered by practically all clinical neurologists and neuropsychologists. Observations on memory function during TGA are clearly of wider relevance and can teach a great deal about normal memory function and amnesia.

RETROGRADE AMNESIA IN THE DEMENTIAS

Alzheimer's Disease

Impairment of memory is the cardinal feature of dementia of Alzheimer type (DAT) and is present to a marked degree in the vast majority of cases from early in the course of the disease. The nature of the anterograde memory deficit has now been extensively investigated using theoretically based tests borrowed from cognitive psychology. Although the profound deficit in episodic memory has been attributed principally to defective encoding and storage of new information, there is also evidence of increased sensitivity to proactive interference and accelerated rates of forgetting (see Chapter 10).

Although it appears that DAT affects remote memory as well as the ability to establish new memories, the nature of the RA has received relatively little attention. In assessing patients' ability to identify photographs of famous persons or events, investigators have focused mainly on the overall temporal pattern of performance rather than the nature of the underlying deficit.

Three studies have examined the ability of patients with DAT to identify and name photographs of famous personalities (Wilson, Kasniak & Fox, 1981; Beatty et al., 1988b; Hodges, Salmon & Butters, 1993). All three used versions of the original Boston Famous Faces Test (Albert, Butters & Levin, 1979). There is no controversy concerning the principal finding that DAT patients show substantial impairment at naming famous faces. However, whilst Wilson et al. (1981) reported no difference in their patients' performance across the decades, the other studies found a significant temporal gradient with better performance on items from more distant decades. Hodges et al. (1993) extended these observations by exploring the nature of the cognitive deficit underlying the deficit in naming famous faces, and the effects of disease severity. The test was modified to include recognition (in arrays consisting of famous and non-famous faces), naming, identification (i.e. the ability to provide person-specific details about un-named faces), and cued naming using semantic and first-name cues. The DAT patients were impaired in all test conditions. Performance in all five conditions declined with disease severity, but this effect did not reach significance in the recognition and naming with phonological (first name) cues. A number of lines of converging evidence suggested that the primary deficit was not in name access, but instead represented a loss of stored semantic knowledge about the person represented. First, the patients named and identified a significantly smaller proportion of faces that they recognised as famous than did controls; second, at no stage was identification superior to spontaneous naming; and third, semantic cueing did not aid performance.

Pictorial famous scenes tests have been used in two studies (Sagar et al., 1988; Kopelman, 1989). Sagar et al. (1988) demonstrated a marked impairment in the recall of information specific to the famous event with evidence of a temporal gradient. They also found impairments in patients' ability to derive nonspecific information about the events depicted, of the type deducible using general semantic or world knowledge. Recognition of the events' names in a multiple-choice format form amongst several foils was also impaired, but there was *no* evidence of a temporal gradient for recognition, suggesting that different memory processes are involved in recall and recognition. Kopelman (1989) confirmed the presence of a temporal gradient in the recall condition. He observed, in addition, that the DAT patients were remarkably better at recognition than recall, and hypothesised that defective information retrieval contributed very largely to the impaired recall. Gade and Mortensen (1990) compared the performance of patients with DAT and amnesia of various aetiologies on a famous events questionnaire test with free recall and forced choice conditions. The DAT group were severely impaired in both conditions, without evidence of a temporal gradient. Furthermore, in contrast to the findings of Kopelman, the dementia of Alzheimer's type patients did *not* benefit relatively more than controls in the recognition condition.

Despite its obvious importance in everyday life, autobiographical memory has been investigated very little in DAT. Sagar et al. (1988) gave the cued autobiographical test (modified from Crovitz & Schiffman, 1974) and showed poor recall of specific life-events with a tendency to produce vague generic responses. There was also shift in the temporal pattern of responses; normal subjects produced a high proportion of memories from the recent past but the DAT group recalled episodes preferentially from more remote time periods. Using the Autobiographical Memory Interview, Kopelman (1989) showed that patients with relatively mild DAT were significantly impaired on both the personal semantic (e.g. names of school friends, teachers, past addresses etc.) and episodic (personal recollections of specific events such as first day at school) components of the schedule with evidence of a modest temporal gradient. Using a very similar standardised autobiographical assessment interview, Dall'Ora, Della Sala & Spinnler (1989) also found marked impairment in recall of specific episodes from all life periods but, in contrast to Kopelman (1989), they did not find a significant temporal gradient.

In summary, it is clear that patients with DAT show marked impairment on tests of remote memory. Whether or not they show a temporal gradient remains controversial, but the recent results suggest that this depends on both the way in which remote memory is tested and the stage of the disease. As to the cause of the remote memory deficit, this might well be attributed to the known deficits in both episodic and semantic memory. There is emerging evidence that in the very earliest stages episodic memory alone may be affected, as a result of selective involvement of parahippocampal structures, most notably the transentorhinal area (Damasio, Van Hoesen & Hyman, 1990; Braak and Braak, 1991). It might, therefore, be predicted that at this early stage, remote memory impairment should be limited to the most recent few years, and should affect episodic aspects preferentially. As the disease progresses, there is breakdown in semantic memory (see Hodges, Salmon & Butters, 1990, 1991, 1992) which should result in an extensive and ungraded impairment on famous faces and event-based tests. This hypothesis awaits confirmation by longitudinal study of patients with initially mild disease, using a battery of different remote memory tests.

Other Forms of Dementia

Compared with DAT there have been very few investigations of remote memory in other forms of dementia. In Huntington's disease, remote memory is also impaired, but with a different pattern from that found in dementia of Alzheimer's type. Albert, Butters & Brandt (1981a,b), employing the same battery as they had used in Korsakoff patients, found patients with Huntington's disease are equally impaired across all life periods without a temporal gradient. This finding was confirmed in a later study by Beatty et al. (1988b) who contrasted groups of patients with DAT and Huntington's disease using a famous faces and public events recall questionnaire. The latter group showed milder impairment, without a temporal gradient, in both the free recall and cued conditions. This global impairment was postulated to result from a general deficit in retrieval, secondary to interruption of frontostriatal circuits (see Hodges et al., 1990).

Although it has been estimated that up to 20% of younger patients with dementia may have one of the forms of focal lobar atrophy—which would previously have been included within the rubric of dementia of Alzheimer's type —very little is known about the remote memory in these cases (see Gustafson, 1987; Neary, Snowden, Northern & Goulding, 1988; Gregory & Hodges, 1993). One exception is a recently reported case study of a patient (F.Z.), who presented with features of frontal-lobe type dementia and was subsequently shown to have Pick's disease at post-mortem (Hodges & Gurd, 1994). Longitudinal neuropsychological assessment showed an initial dissociation between anterograde memory, which was severely impaired, and relatively spared remote memory. Within retrograde memory, there was also evidence of selective difficulty in retrieving personal memories, and in dating personal and public memories. In contrast, retrieval of names of famous persons and recognition of famous events were relatively normal. As the disease progressed, performance on all remote memory tests worsened but without a temporally graded pattern. The findings in this case were very similar to those in Huntington's disease, and lend support to the hypothesis that frontal retrieval deficit results in a RA without temporal gradient.

CONCLUSIONS

The past decade has seen a rapid growth of interest in RA. Much has been learnt, but uncertainty remains in many areas. There is a particular need for further detailed case studies employing a range of remote memory measures with parallel radiological and/or neuropathological data. The investigation of autobiographical memory and its relationship to knowledge of more public events/faces is in its infancy. In addition, the study of patients with dementia has been relatively neglected and there is a particular dearth of longitudinal studies in this area.

At present, it appears that damage restricted purely to the hippocampus results in a moderately severe anterograde amnesia with a temporally limited RA. When the structures closely connected with the hippocampus (the parahippocampal gyrus, subiculum, etc.) are also involved, the anterograde amnesia is more severe and accompanied by an extensive RA which can be temporally graded. Damage confined to the anterolateral temporal neocortical structures can cause "isolated RA", in which case it is likely that other more general aspects of semantic memory are also impaired. A theoretical interpretation of these findings is as follows. The hippocampus is essential for the encoding and retrieval of new memories, but after a period of weeks or months, their retrieval becomes independent of the hippocampus due to a process of consolidation. The area critical for the storage or maintenance of very long-term memories appears to be the anterior temporal lobe.

Extensive and temporally graded RA occurs in alcoholic Korsakoff's syndrome. It is no longer plausible to explain this pattern entirely as a failure of new learning prior to the onset of the amnesic syndrome. Interpretations of the relative role of diencephalic and other cortical (frontal) damage in the genesis of the extensive RA differ, but in view of the evidence from patients with thalamic infarction it seems likely that diencephalic damage *per se* is the most important factor. Regarding psychological explanations for the RA in diencephalic amnesia, it seems most likely that this represents a retrieval deficit. The process of recollection and remembering is a dynamic cognitive operation involving problem-solving, cross-checking, verification and inference for which the frontal lobes are critical. By this account, RA in diencephalic damage arises because of a disconnection between frontal (retrieval and verification) and temporal (storage) components of the memory system.

In patients with Alzheimer-type dementia, the underlying cause of the RA is likely to be complex and to depend upon the stage of the disease. In the early stage, hippocampal pathology predominates, but as the disease progresses semantic memory is severely affected. In Huntington's disease and dementia of frontal type, RA reflects a general retrieval deficit secondary to disruption of frontostriatal circuits.

REFERENCES

Albert, M.S., Butters, N. & Brandt, J. (1980). Memory for remote events in alcoholics. *Journal of Studies in Alcoholism*, **41**, 1071–1081.

Albert, M.S., Butters, N. & Brandt, J. (1981a). Patterns of remote memory loss in amnesic and demented patients. *Archives of Neurology*, **38**, 495–500.

Albert, M.S., Butters, N. & Brandt, J. (1981b). Development of remote memory loss in Huntington's disease. *Journal of Clinical Neuropsychology*, **3**, 1–12.

Albert, M.S., Butters, N. & Levin, J. (1979). Temporal gradients in the retrograde amnesia of patients with alcoholic Korsakoff's disease. *Archives of Neurology*, **36**, 211–216.

Andrews, E., Posner, C.M. & Kessler, M. (1982). Retrograde amnesia for forty years. *Cortex*, **18**, 441–458.

Baddeley, A.D. (1990). *Human Memory: Theory and Practice*. Lawrence Erlbaum Associates, Hove and London.

Baddeley, A.D. & Wilson, B. (1986). Amnesia, autobiographical memory and confabulation. In D.C. Rubin (ed.), *Autobiographical Memory*, Cambridge University Press, Cambridge, pp. 225–252.

Beatty, W.W., Salmon, D., Bernstein, N. & Butters, N. (1987). Remote memory in a patient with amnesia due to hypoxia. *Psychological Medicine*, **17**, 657–665.

Beatty, W.W., Goodkin, D.E., Monson, N., Beatty, P.A. & Hertsgaard, D. (1988a). Anterograde and retrograde amnesia with chronic progressive multiple sclerosis. *Archives of Neurology*, **45**, 611–619.

Beatty, W.W., Salmon, D.P., Butters, N., Heindel, W.C. & Granholm, E. (1988b). Retrograde amnesia in patients with Alzheimer's and Huntington's disease. *Neurobiology of Ageing*, **9**, 181–186.

Benson, D.F., Marsden, C.D. & Meadows, J. (1974). The amnesic syndrome of posterior cerebral artery occlusion. *Acta Neurologica Scandinavica*, **50**, 133–145.

Borrini, G., Dall'Ora, P., Della Sala, S., Marinelli, L. & Spinnler, H. (1989). Autobiographical memory: sensitivity to age and education of a standardised enquiry. *Psychological Medicine*, **19**, 215–224.

Braak, H. & Braak, E. (1991). Neuropathological stageing of Alzheimer-related changes. *Acta Neuropathologica*, **82**, 239–259.

Butters, N. (1984). Alcoholic Korsakoff's syndrome: an update. *Seminars in Neurology*, **4**, 226–244.

Butters, N. (1985). Alcoholic Korsakoff's syndrome: some unresolved issues concerning aetiology, neuropathology and cognitive deficits. *Journal of Clinical and Experimental Neuropsychology*, **7**, 181–210.

Butters, N. & Albert, M.S. (1982). Processes underlying failures to recall remote memory events. In L.S. Cermak (ed.), *Human Memory and Amnesia*. Lawrence Erlbaum, New Jersey, pp. 257–274.

Butters, N. & Cermak, L.S. (1986). A case study of the forgetting of autobiographical knowledge: implications for the study of retrograde amnesia. In D.C. Rubin (ed.), *Autobiographical Memory*. Cambridge University Press, Cambridge, pp. 253–272.

Butters, N. & Stuss, D.T. (1989). Diencephalic amnesia. In F. Boller & J. Grafman (eds), *Handbook of Neuropsychology*, vol. 3. Elsevier Publishers, Amsterdam, pp. 107–148.

Cermak, L.S. (1984). The episodic–semantic distinction in amnesia. In L.R. Squire & N. Butters (eds), *Neuropsychology of Memory*. Guilford Press, New York, pp. 55–62.

Cermak, L.S. & O'Connor, M. (1983). The anterograde and retrograde retrieval ability of a patient with amnesia due to encephalitis. *Neuropsychologia*, **21**, 213–233.

Cohen, N.J. & Squire, L.R. (1981). Retrograde amnesia and remote memory impairment. *Neuropsychologia*, **19**, 337–356.

Conway, M.A. (1992). A structural model of autobiographical memory. In M.A. Conway, D.C. Rubin, H. Spinnler & W. Wagenaar (eds), *Theoretical Perspectives on Autobiographical Memory*. Kluwer Academic Publishers, Amsterdam, pp. 167–193.

Corkin, S. (1984). Lasting consequences of bilateral medial lobectomy: clinical course and experimental findings in H.M. *Seminars in Neurology*, **4**, 249–259.

Crovitz, H.F. & Schiffman, H. (1974). Frequency of episodic memories as a function of their age. *Bulletin of the Psychonomic Society*, **4**, 517–518.

Dall'Ora, P., Della Sala, S. & Spinnler, H. (1989). Autobiographical memory: its impairment in amnesic syndromes. *Cortex*, **25**, 197–217.

Damasio, A.R., Eslinger, P.G., Damasio, H., Van Hoesen, G.W. & Cornell, S. (1985a). Multimodal amnesic syndrome following bilateral temporal and basal forebrain damage. *Archives of Neurology*, **42**, 252–259.

Damasio, A.R., Graff-Radford, N.R., Eslinger, P.G., Damasio, H. & Kassell, N. (1985b). Amnesia following basal forebrain lesions. *Archives of Neurology*, **42**, 263–271.

Damasio, A.R., Van Hoesen, G.W. & Hyman, B.T. (1990). Reflections on the selectivity of neuropathological changes in Alzheimer's disease. In M.F. Schwartz (ed.), *Modular deficits in Alzheimer's-type dementia*. MIT Press, Cambridge, Mass, pp. 83–101.

DeRenzi, E., Zamboli, A. & Crisi, G. (1987). The pattern of neuropsychological impairment associated with left posterior cerebral artery infarcts. *Brain*, **110**, 1099–1116.

Dusoir, H., Kapur, N., Byrnes, D.P., McKinstry, S. & Hoare, R.D. (1990). The role of diencephalic pathology in human memory disorder. *Brain*, **113**, 1695–1706.

Duyckaerts, C., Derouesne, C., Signoret, J.L., Gray, F., Escourelle, R. & Castaigne, P. (1985). Bilateral and limited amygdalohippocampal lesions causing a pure amnesia syndrome. *Annals of Neurology*, **18**, 314–319.

Evans, J., Wilson, B., Wraight, E.P. & Hodges,OB J.R. (1993). Neuropsychological and SPECT scan findings during and after transient global amnesia: evidence for the differential impairment of remote episodic memory. *Journal of Neurology, Neurosurgery and Psychiatry*, **56**, 1227–1230.

Fisher, C.M. & Adams, R.B. (1964). Transient global amnesia. *Acta Neurologica Scandinavica*, **40**, 1–83.

Gade, A. & Mortensen, E.L. (1990). Temporal gradient in the remote memory impairment of amnesic patients with lesions in the basal forebrain. *Neuropsychologia*, **28**, 985–1001.

Gaffan, D. & Gaffan, E.A. (1991). Amnesia in man following transection of the fornix: a review. *Brain*, **114**, 2611–2619.

Goldberg, E., Antin, S.P., Bilder, R.M., Gerstman, L.J., Hughes, J.E.O. & Mattis, S. (1981). Retrograde amnesia: possible role of mesencephalic reticular activation in long-term memory. *Science*, **213**, 1392–1394.

Goldenberg, G., Podreka, I., Pfafflmeyer, N., Wessely, P. & Deecke, L. (1991). Thalamic ischemia in transient global amnesia: a SPECT study. *Neurology*, **41**, 1748–1752.

Graff-Radford, N.R., Eslinger, P.J., Damasio, A.R. & Yamada, T. (1984). Nonhemorrhagic infarction of the thalamus: behavioural, anatomic, and physiological correlates. *Neurology*, **34**, 14–23.

Graff-Radford, N.R., Damasio, H., Yamada, T., Eslinger, P.G. & Damasio, A.R. (1985). Non-haemorrhagic thalamic infarction. *Brain*, **108**, 485–516.

Graff-Radford, N.R., Tranel, D., Van Hoesen, G.W. & Brandt, J.P. (1990). Diencephalic amnesia. *Brain*, **113**, 1–25.

Gregory, C.A. & Hodges, J.R. (1993). Dementia of frontal lobe type and the focal lobar atrophies. *International Review of Psychiatry*, **5**, 397–409.

Guberman, A. & Stuss, D. (1983). The syndrome of bilateral paramedian thalamic infarction. *Neurology*, **33**, 540–546.

Gustafson, L. (1987). Frontal lobe degeneration of non-Alzheimer type. II: Clinical picture and differential diagnosis. *Archives of Gerontology and Geriatrics*, **6**, 209–223.

Hodges, J.R. (1991). *Transient Amnesia: Clinical and Neuropsychological Aspects*, WB Saunders, London.

Hodges, J.R. (1994). Semantic memory and frontal executive function during transient global amnesia. *Journal of Neurology, Neurosurgery and Psychiatry*, **57**, 605–608.

Hodges, J.R. & Carpenter, C. (1991). Anterograde amnesia with fornix damage following removal of IIIrd ventricle colloid cyst. *Journal of Neurology, Neurosurgery and Psychiatry*, **54**, 633–638.

Hodges, J.R. & Gurd, J. (1994). Remote memory and lexical retrieval in a case of frontal Pick's disease. *Archives of Neurology*, **51**, 821–827.

Hodges, J.R. & McCarthy, R.A. (1993). Autobiographical amnesia resulting from bilateral paramedian thalamic infarction: a case study in cognitive neurobiology. *Brain*, **116**, 921–940.

Hodges, J.R., Patterson, K., Oxbury, S. & Funnell, E. (1992). Semantic dementia: progressive fluent aphasia with temporal lobe atrophy. *Brain*, **115**, 1783–1806.

Hodges, J.R., Salmon, D.P. & Butters, N. (1990). Differential impairment of semantic and episodic memory in Alzheimer's and Huntington's disease: a controlled prospective study. *Journal of Neurology, Neurosurgery and Psychiatry*, **53**, 1089–1095.

Hodges, J.R., Salmon, D.P. & Butters, N. (1991). The nature of the naming deficit in Alzheimer's and Huntington's disease. *Brain*, **114**, 1547–1558.

Hodges, J.R., Salmon, D.P. & Butters, N. (1992). Semantic memory impairment in Alzheimer's disease: failure of access or degraded knowledge? *Neuropsychologia*, **30**, 301–314.

Hodges, J.R., Salmon, D.P. & Butters, N. (1993). Recognition and naming of famous faces in Alzheimer's disease: a cognitive analysis. *Neuropsychologia*.

Hodges, J.R. & Ward, C.D. (1989). Observations during transient global amnesia. *Brain*, **112**, 595–620.

Kapur, N., Ellison, D., Smith, M.P., McLellen, D.L. & Burrows, E.H., (1992). Focal retrograde amnesia following bilateral temporal lobe pathology. *Brain*, **115**, 73–85.

Kapur, N., Young, A., Bateman, D. & Kennedy, P. (1989). Focal retrograde amnesia: a long term clinical and neuropsychological follow-up. *Cortex*, **25**, 387–402.

Kopelman, M.D. (1987). Amnesia: organic and psychogenic. *British Journal of Psychiatry*, **150**, 428–442.

Kopelman, M.D. (1989). Remote and autobiographical memory, temporal context memory and frontal atrophy in Korsakoff and Alzheimer patients. *Neuropsychologia*, **27**, 437–460.

Kopelman, M.D. (1991). Frontal dysfunction and memory deficits in alcoholic Korsakoff syndrome and Alzheimer-type dementia. *Brain*, **114**, 117–137.

Kopelman, M.D., Wilson, B. & Baddeley, A. (1989a). The Autobiographical Interview — a new assessment of autobiographical and personal semantic memory in amnesic patients. *Journal of Clinical and Experimental Neuropsychology*, **11**, 724–744.

Kopelman, M.D., Wilson, B. & Baddeley, A. (1989b). *The Autobiographical Memory Interview*. Thames Valley Test Company, Bury St Edmunds.

Kritchevsky, M., Squire, L.R. & Zouzounis, J.A. (1988). Transient global amnesia: characterisation of anterograde and retrograde amnesia. *Neurology*, **38**, 213–219.

Kritchevsky, M. & Squire, L.R. (1989). Transient global amnesia: evidence for extensive, temporally graded retrograde amnesia. *Neurology*, **39**, 213–218.

Marslen-Wilson, W.D. & Teuber, H.L. (1975). Memory for remote events in anterograde amnesia: recognition of public figures from news photographs. *Neuropsychologia*, **13**, 353–364.

Markowitsch, H.J., Calabrese, P., Liess, J., Haupt, M., Durwen, H.F. & Gehlen. (1993a). Retrograde amnesia after traumatic injury of the fronto-temporal cortex. *Journal of Neurology, Neurosurgery and Psychiatry*, **56**, 988–992.

Markowitsch, H.J., von Crammon, D.Y. & Schuri, U. (1993b). Mnestic performance profile of a bilateral diencephalic infarct patient with preserved intelligence and severe amnesia disturbances. *Journal of Clinical and Experimental Neuropsychology*, **15**, 625–652.

McCarthy, R.A. & Warrington, E.K. (1992). Actors but not scripts: the dissociation of people and events in retrograde amnesia. *Neuropsychologia*, **30**, 633–644.

Meudell, P.R., Northern, B., Snowden, J.S. & Neary, D. (1980). Long-term memory for famous voices in amnesic and normal subjects. *Neuropsychologia*, **18**, 133–139.

Milner, B., Corkin, S. & Teuber, H.L. (1968). Further analysis of hippocampal amnesia — 14-year follow-up of H.M. *Neuropsychologia*, **6**, 215–234.

Morton, J., Hammersley, R.H. & Bekerian, D.A. (1985). Headed records: a model for memory and its failures. *Cognition*, **20**, 1–23.

Neary, D., Snowden, J.S., Northern, P. & Goulding, P. (1988). Dementia of frontal lobe type. *Journal of Neurology, Neurosurgery and Psychiatry*, **51**, 353–361.

Norman, D.A. & Bobrow, D.G. (1979). Descriptions and intermediate stages in memory retrieval. *Cognitive Psychology*, **11**, 107–123.

O'Connor, M., Butters, N., Miliotis, P., Eslinger, P. & Cermak, L.S. (1992). The dissociation of anterograde and retrograde amnesia in a patient with herpes encephalitis. *Journal of Clinical and Experimental Neuropsychology*, **14**, 159–178.

Philips, S., Sangalang, V. & Sterns, G. (1987). Basal forebrain infarction: a clinicopathological correlation. *Archives of Neurology*, **44**, 1134–1138.

Press, G.A., Amaral, D.G. & Squire, L.R. (1989). Hippocampal abnormalities in amnesic patients revealed by high-resolution magnetic resonance imaging. *Nature*, **341**, 54–57.

Roman-Campos, G., Poser, C.M. & Wood, F.B. (1980). Persistent retrograde amnesia after transient global amnesia. *Cortex*, **16**, 509–519.

Rudge, P. & Warrington, E.K. (1991). Selective impairment of memory and visual perception in splenial tumours. *Brain*, **114**, 349–360.

Sagar, H.J., Cohen, N.J., Sullivan, E.V., Corkin, S. & Growden, J.H. (1988). Remote memory function in Alzheimer's disease and Parkinson's disease. *Brain*, **111**, 185–206.

Salmon, D., Lasker, B.R., Butters, N. & Beatty, W.W. (1988). Remote memory in a patient with circumscribed amnesia. *Brain and Cognition*, **7**, 201–211.

Sanders, H.I. & Warrington, E.K. (1971). Memory for remote events in amnesia patients. *Brain*, **94**, 661–668.

Schacter, D.L., Wang, P.L., Tulving, E. & Freedman, M. (1982). Functional retrograde amnesia: a quantitative case study. *Neuropsychologia*, **20**, 523–532.

Scoville, W.B. & Milner, B. (1957). Loss of recent memory after bilateral hippocampal lesions. *Journal of Neurology, Neurosurgery and Psychiatry*, **20**, 11–21.

Seltzer, B. & Benson, D.F. (1974). The temporal gradient of retrograde amnesia in Korsakoff's disease. *Neurology*, **24**, 527–530.

Shimamura, A. & Squire, L.R. (1986). Korsakoff's syndrome: a study of the relationship between anterograde and remote memory. *Behavioural Neuroscience*, **100**, 165–170.

Squire, L.R. (1986). Mechanisms of memory. *Science*, **232**, 1612–1619.

Squire, L.R. (1992). Memory and the hippocampus: a synthesis from findings with rats, monkeys and humans. *Psychological Review*, **99**, 195–231.

Squire, L.R., Amaral, D.G., Zola-Morgan, S., Kritchevsky, M. & Press, M. (1989). Description of brain injury in the amnesic patient N.A. based on magnetic resonance imaging. *Experimental Neurology*, **105**, 23–25.

Squire, L.R., Chace, P.M. & Slater, P.C. (1976). Retrograde amnesia following electroconvulsive therapy. *Nature*, **260**, 775–777.

Squire, L.R. & Cohen, N.J. (1982). Remote memory, retrograde amnesia, and the neuropsychology of memory. In L.S. Cermak (ed.), *Human Memory and Amnesia*. Lawrence Erlbaum, New Jersey, pp. 275–303.

Squire, L.R., Haist, F. & Shimamura, A.P. (1989). The neurology of memory: quantitative assessment of retrograde amnesia in two groups of amnesic patients. *Journal of Neuroscience*, **9**, 828–839.

Squire, L.R., Slater, P.C. & Chace, P.M. (1975). Retrograde amnesia: temporal gradient in very long-term memory following electroconvulsive therapy. *Science*, **187**, 77–79.

Stillhard, G., Landis, T., Schiess, R., Regard, M. & Sialer, G. (1990). Bitemporal hypoperfusion in transient global amnesia: a 99m-Tc-HM-PAO SPECT and neuropsychological findings during and after an attack. *Journal of Neurology, Neurosurgery and Psychiatry*, **53**, 339–342.

Stuss, D.T., Gubermann, A., Nelson, R. & Larochelle, S. (1988). The neuropsychology of paramedian thalamic infarction. *Brain and Cognition*, **8**, 348–378.

Stuss, D.T. & Guzman, D.A. (1988). Severe memory loss with minimal anterograde amnesia: a clinical note. *Brain and Cognition*, **8**, 21–30.

Talland, G.A. (1965). *Deranged Memory*, Academic Press, New York.

Tanabe, H., Hashikawa, T.H., Nakagawa, K., et al. (1991). Memory loss due to transient hypoperfusion in the medial temporal lobes including the hippocampus. *Acta Neurologica Scandinavica*, **84**, 22–27.

Teuber, H.L., Milner, B. & Vaughan, H.G. (1968). Persistent anterograde amnesia after stab wound of the basal forebrain. *Neuropsychologia*, **6**, 267–282.

Valenstein, E., Bowers, D., Verfaille, M., Heilman, K.M., Day, A. & Watson, R.T. (1987). Retrosplenial amnesia. *Brain*, **110**, 1631–1646.

Von Cramon, D.Y., Hebel, N. & Schuri, U. (1985). A contribution to the anatomical basis of thalamic amnesia. *Brain*, **108**, 993–1008.

Warrington, E.K. (1975). The selective impairment of semantic memory. *Quarterly Journal of Experimental Psychology*, **27**, 187–199.

Warrington, E.K. & McCarthy, R.A. (1988). The fractionation of retrograde amnesia. *Brain and Cognition*, **7**, 184–200.

Warrington, E.K. & Shallice, T. (1984). Category-specific semantic impairments. *Brain*, **107**, 829–854.

Warrington, E.K. & Weiskrantz, L. (1982). Amnesia: a disconnection syndrome. *Neuropsychologia*, **20**, 233–249.

Weiskrantz, L. (1985). On issues and theories of the human amnesic syndrome. In N.M. Weinberger, K.L. McGaugh & G. Lynch (eds), *Memory Systems and the Brain*. Guilford Press, New York, pp. 380–415.

Wilson, R.S., Kasniak, A.W. & Fox, J.H. (1981). Remote memory in senile dementia. *Cortex*, **17**, 41–48.

Winocur, G., Oxbury, S., Roberts, R., Agnetti, V. & Davis, C.J.F. (1984). Amnesia in a patient with bilateral lesions to the thalamus. *Neuropsychologia*, **22**, 123–143.

Woods, B.T., Schoene, W. & Kneisley, L. (1982). Are hippocampal lesions sufficient to cause lasting amnesia? *Journal of Neurology, Neurosurgery and Psychiatry*, **45**, 243–247.

Ziegler, K., Kaufman, A. & Marshall, H.E. (1977). Abrupt memory loss associated with thalamic tumor. *Archives of Neurology*, **34**, 545–548.

Zola-Morgan, S., Cohen, N.J. & Squire, L.R. (1983). Recall of remote episodic memory in amnesia. *Neuropsychologia*, **21**, 487–500.

Zola-Morgan, S., Squire, L.R. & Amaral, D.G. (1986). Human amnesia and the medial temporal region: enduring memory impairment following bilateral lesions limited to field CA1 of the hippocampus. *Journal of Neuroscience*, **6**, 2950–2967.

Chapter 5

Transient Global Amnesia

Georg Goldenberg
Neurologisches Krankenhaus Rosenhügel, Vienna, Austria

INTRODUCTION

Transient loss of memory has been recognized as a distinct neurological disorder for nearly 40 years (Bender, 1956; Guyotat & Courjon, 1956). The term "transient global amnesia" (TGA) was introduced by Fisher and Adams in 1964. Some 1000 cases have been described (see Caplan, 1985; Caplan, 1990; Hodges, 1991, for reviews) and several large studies have investigated the epidemiology and prognosis of TGA. It has emerged as a coherent clinical entity and, although its aetiology and pathogenesis are still controversial, the collected clinical and laboratory findings do at least put constraints on theorizing about its cause.

Starting from two typical case reports, this chapter outlines the clinical features, differential diagnosis and definition of TGA. Neuropsychological, laboratory and epidemiological findings are then reviewed. There follows a discussion of how these findings can be reconciled with what is known about the anatomy of brain structures responsible for memory and how they constrain the possibilities of aetiology and pathogenesis.

TWO CASES OF TGA

Case 1 (Goldenberg et al., 1991)

The patient was a 55-year-old female teacher whose medical history was uneventful. She was a moderate smoker whose blood pressure was low. At Christmas 1989 she stayed with her husband in their weekend house. One evening, when preparing for bed, her husband asked her to take away a packet

Handbook of Memory Disorders. Edited by A.D. Baddeley, B.A. Wilson and F.N. Watts.
© 1995 John Wiley & Sons Ltd.

of cigarettes she had left on the table. She responded that she did not remember having left these cigarettes, and asked for how long she had been in the weekend house and whether Christmas was already over. She then repeatedly asked these questions and complained that she did not remember when and how she had come to the house. Apart from her loss of memory and her bewilderment, the husband did not note any physical changes. She recognized the house, him and other relatives who soon came to help. Her blood pressure was found to be elevated to 200/120 mmHg. She was brought to the Neurological University Clinic.

On arrival at about midnight, her blood pressure was 120/80 and cardiac action rhythmic. Neurological examination was completely normal. She was alert and friendly. Spontaneous speech was normal. She knew that she was in hospital but asked repeatedly how she had come there, and, when given the response, invariably commented that she was sorry to cause trouble for her family. Every few minutes she asked the examiner whether he happened to know her daughter who was a psychiatrist. She was unable to retain new information and did not recognize the examiner when he had been absent for a few minutes. She did not remember public or personal events of the last one and a half years, and gave the age and occupation of her children as they had been before that time. Recall of remote events appeared to be fairly normal but was not tested extensively.

On neuropsychological examination, spontaneous speech was normal but confrontation naming was not tested. In her copy of the Rey complex figure she omitted one detail. Immediate recall of the figure was restricted to its gross structure, and delayed recall after 5 minutes impossible. She did not recognize any of 30 concrete pictures and scored at chance on a multiple-choice recognition trial. The number of words repeated from a 12-word list did not improve at all across five learning trials. When recall was tested after 5 minutes she denied having heard any words before, and she scored at chance on a multiple-choice recognition trial. In contrast, she markedly improved across three trials of a procedural memory test probing the reading of fragmented digits.

Single photon emission tomography (SPECT) was performed the same night. When it was finished at about 4 o'clock in the morning, she was still wide awake. Asked about her estimation of the present time she answered that it must be "fairly late, about 8 or 9 in the evening".

She then slept quietly, and the next morning her mental status appeared to be normal again. There was a complete amnesia for the TGA and for half an hour preceding the attack. Some patchy recollections started during SPECT data collection, but she did not remember at all the injection of the isotope. (The distribution of the isotope which is measured by SPECT is accomplished within about two minutes after injection.)

She was re-examined in the afternoon. Confrontation naming was normal, and a copy of the Rey figure perfect. Immediate and delayed recall of the figure was mildly defective, as were memory for concrete pictures and learning of a 15-word list. The patient did not remember having seen the stimuli of the procedural learning test before, but her performance betrayed complete preservation of the procedural knowledge acquired during TGA. She found 5 out of 6 possible criteria on a card-sorting task. Design fluency was good. When tested for verbal fluency she produced a sufficient number of words but also numerous repetitions.

On a follow-up examination after 10 days the patient reported that the night after the incident she had slept much longer than normal. On neuropsychological testing, recognition memory for pictures was still slightly impaired, but learning of a 15-word list and recall of a complex figure were normal. On both, verbal and design fluency tasks, the number of items produced was well within the normal range but the number of repetitions elevated.

After one month she reported that 2 weeks after TGA she had experienced for 15 minutes a blurring of the whole visual field as if it were "covered by lace". All memory tests were now normal. Design fluency was unremarkable too, but the number of repetitions was still elevated in the word-fluency task.

CT, EEG and sonography of the carotid and vertebral arteries were done on the first day after TGA, and NMR 10 days later. All of them were normal. SPECT was performed in the night of the TGA, 12 days later, and 40 days later. During TGA there was a diffuse reduction of cerebral HMPAO uptake. Over and above the global reduction, local flow was severely reduced in the left thalamus, and less severely in the right thalamus. At follow-up, global isotope uptake normalized as well as local flow in the thalami, but there was a persistent hypoperfusion of left frontal areas (Goldenberg et al., 1991; Figure 5.1).

Case 2

The second patient was a 75-year-old female retired tailor. Mild hypertension had been treated for 10 years. She had suffered from frequent headaches and occasional attacks of migraine since youth. 30 years earlier she had been admitted to a Neurological Hospital with a suspicion of meningitis because of severe headache. 10 years ago she had been hospitalized with a confusional state lasting two days. In April 1990, in the morning after returning by bus from an exhausting sight-seeing trip to Budapest, she rose and breakfasted as usual. Her husband then left home to go shopping and when he came back he found her sitting on a chair and complaining. "What's the matter with me, it's starting again, it's like last time." She repeatedly asked where she had been the last days and when she had returned home. When the answer was given she said "Oh yes, I remember", but asked the same questions again shortly afterwards.

She was brought to the Neurological Department. When seen there two hours after her arrival she knew that she was in hospital and that her relatives had brought her there. She knew the month but neither the year nor the day. She had no recollection at all of the time already spent in hospital and did not recognize persons whom she had encountered during that time.

The patient knew that she had returned from a journey one day ago, but she was not sure whether she had been in Budapest or in Tyrol where she actually had spent her last winter holiday. When asked about both of these stays she

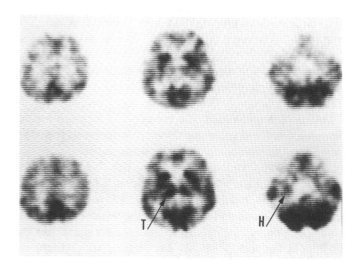

Figure 5.1 99-Tc-HMPAO SPECT studies of Case 1. Upper row: during attack; lower row: at follow-up 12 days later. The left side of the slices corresponds to the left side of the brain. The arrows indicate the location of the left thalamus (T) and of the left hippocampus formation (H). The SPECT images show the distribution of blood flow but not its absolute value. Each row of images is scaled to its own maximum and no correction is made for differences in global blood flow between both studies. A reduction of global blood flow can be deduced from the apparent reduction of brain volume in the study made during the attack and was confirmed by an analysis of absolute HMPAO uptake. During the attack there was a reduction of HMPAO uptake in the thalami over and above the global reduction of cerebral blood flow which was more marked on the left side. Compared with controls, left frontal flow values were reduced at follow-up (Goldenberg et al., 1991)

confounded their circumstances and details. She could neither enumerate a single specific sight seen in Budapest nor recall the name of her hotel there. Her recall of previous hospitalizations and of recent and remote political events was similar in that she confounded their circumstances, and in that she was unable to enumerate specific details. A clear-cut temporal limit of this retrograde memory impairment could not be established, but recall of events up to 1950 appeared unimpaired and was not different from that given at follow-up.

During the examination she would remark with a frequency of up to twice a minute that she was now "starting to have a little headache". Application of analgesics had no influence on the frequency of this complaint. When unable to answer a question she would invariably respond: "I don't know what was yesterday, but I do know what happened twenty years ago."

The neurological examination was normal. On neuropsychological examination spontaneous speech was normal, and there was no apraxia. A copy of the Rey figure was turned by 90 degrees, and the position of details was distorted. She did not recognize any of 30 concrete pictures and scored at chance on a multiple-choice recognition trial. Across five trials she could never repeat more than 5 words of a 12-word list. 15 minutes later she did not remember having heard a word list at all and was at chance level when identifying the words in the multiple choice task. Immediate recall of the Rey figure was restricted to its gross outlines, and delayed recall impossible. On the procedural learning task probing reading of fragmented digits, her score improved across three trials, but after the last trial she thought that she had seen the digits only once or twice. Both verbal and design fluency were reduced and she produced multiple perseverations. On a card-sorting task she found only one out of six possible criteria and repeated sorting to this criterion three times. In addition, she attempted two illogical sortings.

SPECT was performed immediately after the neuropsychological examination.

On the next day her memory appeared to be normal again. She had a complete amnesia for the first three to four hours of the attack and for the morning before. She had some vague recollections of the SPECT examinations and of the neuropsychological tests preceding it. Recall of previous events was richer and more orderly than during TGA, but details were still lacking and she was insecure with respect to the distinction between events. She still repeatedly commented that "the headache is starting now" and that she did not know what was yesterday but did know what had happened twenty years ago; but the frequency of these repetitive comments was much lower than during the attack. Recognition memory for concrete pictures was at the lower margin of the normal range. Learning and delayed recall of a 15-word list betrayed some storage in secondary memory but was still markedly reduced. When copying the Rey figure she duplicated one detail and omitted another, but preserved the main topological relationships and the orientation, and her score was in the normal range, while reproduction from memory was impoverished. Both verbal and design fluency were in the low normal range. On the procedural learning task her initial performance was below the final performance of the previous day, which was reached only on the second trial.

At follow-up 2 weeks later, she claimed to have regained a recollection of the morning before the spell. Asked about her headache she said that she used to have headaches frequently but did not remember a particular aggravation during or after the attack. Her recall of previous events was chronologically correct without confusions, and she recalled without hesitation details she had been unable to remember during TGA. On neuropsychological examination, recognition memory for concrete pictures was perfect and she scored in the normal range on word-list learning and recall of a complex figure. Word fluency had improved while design fluency had remained the same. On the sorting task she now found two criteria and produced neither perseverations nor illogical sortings. On the procedural learning task she started at the final level of the last examination and improved further across three trials.

CT on the day of TGA was normal. SPECT done during the attack demonstrated hypoperfusion of both thalami and the left frontal and left temporal lobe (Figure 5.2). The temporal hypoperfusion affected the mesial temporal region,

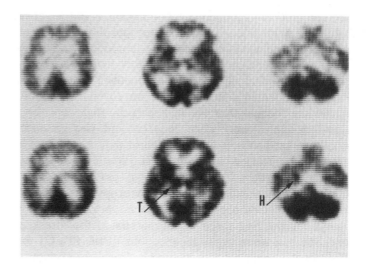

Figure 5.2 99-Tc-HMPAO SPECT studies of Case 2. Upper row: during attack; lower row: at follow-up 2 weeks later. Orientation of the slices and anatomical designations are as in Figure 5.1. Compared with the follow-up study, the study during the attack shows a marked reduction of the volume of both thalami which presumably indicates local hypoperfusion. There is a diminution of local HMPAO uptake in the left temporal lobe which extends into the mesial temporal region, in the left frontal lobe, and possibly also in the right mesial temporal region

and there was some reduction of local HMPAO uptake also in the right mesial temporal region. A follow-up SPECT 2 weeks later was normal.

CLINICAL FEATURES OF TGA

Complete anterograde amnesia is the most impressive symptom of TGA. As patients are incapable of retaining any record of what is going on, they may be disoriented to time and place. They are, however, able to use contextual clues and general world knowledge for making inferences about their situation. When confronted with a failure of memory, patients may try to guess what they should remember, but frank confabulations have never been reported in TGA. Many patients notice that something is wrong with their mental capacities and are worried about this.

Anterograde amnesia is not the only behavioural abnormality in TGA. A further impressive symptom which is observed in nearly all of the cases is repetitive questioning and comments. Not only do patients ask the same questions over and over, they frequently use exactly the same wording in each round of questions and give exactly the same comments to the answer. The simple explanation that patients repeat the questions because they forget the answers does not hold as patients repeat the same questions regardless of changing circumstances, and may repeat questions which are only loosely related to the worry brought forward by the experience of not knowing what is happening to them. Indeed, there are patients who repeat questions over and over in spite of being apparently little concerned or even anosognosic about their disorder (Stillhard et al., 1990; Hodges & Ward, 1989). Repetitive behaviour is not necessarily confined to questions or comments but may also concern senseless motor actions like washing hands (Caplan, 1990) or going up and down stairs (Mazzuchi, Moretti, Caffarra & Parma, 1980). A further behavioural abnormality observed in a significant proportion of patients is either agitation or apathy (Caplan, 1990; Kritchevsky, Squire & Zouzounis, 1988; Hodges & Ward, 1989; Kritchevsky & Squire, 1989), and Case 1 described above would suggest disturbances of sleep–wake rhythm as another possible concomitant of TGA. Some patients complain of headache either during or after the attack, and there may occur vegetative symptoms like vomiting, diarrhoea, or transient elevations of blood pressure (Caplan, 1985; Stillhard et al., 1990; Hodges, 1991).

In about one-third of patients, TGA appears to be triggered by precipitating events. Most frequent is physical exertion, less frequent is exposure to cold or heat, sexual intercourse or a long drive in a motor vehicle (Caplan, 1990; Miller et al., 1987; Hodges & Warlow, 1990a). The importance of emotional stress is more difficult to assess as there may be a tendency to overestimate the emotional significance of any event which is followed by a complete amnesia. It has been estimated to be nearly as high as that of physical stress (Caplan, 1990; Hodges & Warlow, 1990a).

Differential Diagnosis of TGA

The other main conditions to be considered in the differential diagnosis of TGA are head trauma, epilepsy and stroke.

Head Trauma

Concussion can lead to a transient confusional state whose clinical appearance is very similar to that of TGA, although repetitive questioning is rarely as impressive as in TGA. In any case, a preceding head trauma must be reliably excluded before a diagnosis of TGA can be made.

Epilepsy

Epilepsy has once been considered as a possible cause of TGA (Fisher & Adams, 1964). The low recurrence rate of TGA and the absence of epileptic discharges in EEG recordings made during the attack (Miller et al., 1990) speak definitely against this hypothesis. Rather than as the cause of TGA, epilepsy has to be considered as a differential diagnosis. Transient amnesia can follow grand mal seizures, or it can be the most conspicuous if not the only manifestation of nonconvulsive epilepsy resulting from a focus in the temporal lobe. Epileptic amnesia can be associated with repetitive questioning and may thus mimic almost completely the clinical presentation of TGA (Kapur, 1990; Gallassi & Morreale, 1990). A suspicion of epileptic origin should be raised if episodes of TGA are shorter than half an hour and if they recur within a few weeks. If both of these features apply, the chance of proving an epileptic origin of the spells is said to be 100% (Hodges & Warlow, 1990a). Unnoticed epileptic convulsions preceding the amnesia should be suspected if amnesia is manifest immediately after awakening from sleep.

Amnesic Stroke

Stroke affecting memory-relevant brain structures can cause a permanent amnesic syndrome. The term "amnesic stroke" has been applied to infarctions of the left posterior cerebral artery which cause other conspicuous cognitive deficits and visual field defects in addition to memory problems (Geschwind & Fusillo, 1966; Caplan & Hedley-White, 1974; Benson, Marsden & Meadows, 1974), but amnesia can be the single most prominent symptom of infarctions restricted to the inferior polar portion of the thalamus (Castaigne et al. 1981; von Cramon, Hebel & Schuri, 1985; Signoret & Goldenberg, 1986). There have been patients in whom a typical episode of TGA was followed by chronic memory problems, suggesting that TGA was the initial symptom of an amnesic stroke (Gorelick, Amico, Ganellen & Benevento, 1988; Jensen & Olivarius, 1981; Goldenberg, Wimmer & Maly, 1983).

DEFINITION OF TGA

Criteria have been proposed which should permit a diagnosis of TGA and facilitate the exclusion of other possible causes of transient memory dysfunction (Caplan, 1985):

1. *Information about the beginning of the attack should be available from a capable observer who witnessed the onset.* This criterion is intended to exclude epileptic seizures and head trauma as causes of transient amnesia. In practice, cases with typical symptoms in whom most of the episode has been witnessed and in whom there is no circumstantial evidence for seizures or head trauma, are usually accepted as TGA (Hodges, 1991).
2. *The patient should have been examined during the attack to be certain that other neurological symptoms and signs did not accompany the amnesia.*
3. *There should be no important accompanying neurological signs.*
   These criteria are not unequivocal. As will be outlined in the following sections, additional neuropsychological abnormalities are the rule rather than

the exception in TGA. As far as the neurological examination is concerned, it must be said that the estimation of, for example, a positive Babinsky sign or a side difference of tendon reflexes is not terribly reliable and may heavily depend on the scrutiny of the examination if not on the expectations of the examiner (Frederiks, 1990). On the other hand there is evidence, reviewed in a later section of this chapter, that accompanying neurological symptoms do have implications for the prognosis and management of TGA. In practice, it seems appropriate to distinguish between "pure TGA" and TGA accompanied by overt neurological symptoms like clouding of consciousness, hemiparesis, ataxia, disturbed oculomotor motility, visual field loss, or aphasia.

4. *The memory loss should be transient.* To be applicable, this criterion should be restricted to the behavioural manifestation of severe amnesia. On neuropsychological testing, restoration of memory proceeds much slower than the rapid restoration of normal behaviour would lead us to assume, and there may even be permanent subtle memory deficits in patients with typical TGA (see below). In the majority of patients the length of the spell is in the range of several hours, but no limits have been set as to the possible duration of TGA.

NEUROPSYCHOLOGY OF TGA

During the Attack

The clinical impression that patients are completely unable to lay down new permanent memories is confirmed by neuropsychological assessment during the attack. While immediate memory is preserved or only slightly reduced (Hodges & Ward, 1989), the acquisition of information into secondary memory is impossible. Amnesia affects not only verbal and visual, but also olfactory, tactile, and kinaesthetic information and environmental sounds (Shuttleworth & Wise, 1973), and no significant sparing has as yet been observed for any kind of material.

In addition to the complete incapacity to lay down new memories, patients are unable to recall memories which have been at their disposition before the attack. The degree of retrograde amnesia is variable and is more difficult to assess than that of anterograde amnesia, because the patient's recall has to be compared with their own premorbid memories in order to estimate the severity of memory loss. From clinical case reports and formal studies of retrograde amnesia during TGA (Caffarra, Moretti, Mazucchi & Parma, 1981; Regard & Landis, 1984; Stracciari, Revucci & Gallasi, 1987; Kritchevsky, Squire & Zouzounis, 1988; Hodges & Ward, 1989; Kritchevsky & Squire, 1989), it appears that there are two types of impaired access to previously acquired memories which are not mutually exclusive.

On the one hand, there may be a loss of any recollection for a limited period of time preceding the attack. Personal and public circumstances are believed to be as they had been before this period, which may span up to several years

(Case 1; Caffarra et al., 1981; Kritchevsky & Squire, 1989). On the other hand, and apparently more frequently, there can be a patchy memory loss which has no clear-cut temporal limit but may stretch back as far as some decades or even to childhood (Case 2; Caffarra et al., 1981; Hodges & Ward, 1989; Kritchevsky et al., 1988; Stracciari et al., 1987). Patients are able to recollect main public and personal events but their reports are "curiously empty and lacking in colour, as if reduced to the bare bones of memory" (Hodges & Ward, 1989). A peculiar feature of this type of retrograde amnesia are difficulties with the dating and chronological ordering of recalled events (Case 2; Caffarra et al., 1981; Regard & Landis, 1984; Kritchevsky et al., 1988; Stracciari et al., 1987; Hodges & Ward, 1989).

Semantic memory—that is, general knowledge whose recall is not bound to the recollection of specific events or personal experiences—appears to be spared insofar as patients do recognize objects, can use language meaningfully and know how to behave in a civilized way. More demanding tests requiring recall of less easily accessible detailed or domain-specific knowledge (e.g. Warrington & McCarthy, 1987; Goldenberg & Artner, 1991) have not yet been applied to patients during TGA. The idea that the dissociation between pre-served recall of general knowledge and impaired recall of temporally bound events is not simply an artefact of different ways of testing found support in a study of the recognition of famous events (Hodges & Ward, 1989). Patients examined during TGA could normally distinguish real from fictitious events, but made more errors than after the TGA when trying to date the events. However, the same patients did have a deficit in the naming of famous faces even if they were not asked to date the period during which they had been famous nor to relate any personal experience connected to them. Semantic memory in TGA is surely a topic in need of further research.

A further aspect of memory that has not yet been adequately tested during TGA is *procedural* or *implicit memory*. Implicit or procedural memory enables acquisition or modifications of skills and habits in the absence of any conscious recollection of the modifying experience (Squire, 1982). The two patients pre-sented in the introduction of this chapter both showed normal procedural learning of a perceptual skill during the attack; but whereas in one of them the learning effect was preserved after the attack, it appeared to be partially lost in the other. What makes the study of implicit memory in TGA particularly interesting is the fact that different aspects of it seem to be preserved or affected in various diseases which give rise to chronic amnesia (Soliveri, Brown, Jahanashahi & Marsden, 1992). If similar fractionations of implicit memory were detected in TGA they might provide clues as to the nature of brain damage underlying it.

At least in a significant proportion of patients with typical TGA, careful neuropsychological examination can reveal mild but definite impairments of cognitive functions other than memory. Reduced fluency of production of words or designs has been noted in some patients (Stillhard et al., 1990; Cases 1 and 2) but not in others (Regard & Landis, 1984). Digit span backwards can be slightly reduced during TGA (Hodges, 1991; Hodges & Ward, 1989). Patients may have difficulties with the copy of a complex figure (Case 2; Kritchevsky et al., 1988; Kritchevsky & Squire, 1989). Finally, one study found a slight but statistically significant reduction of correct naming on the Boston Naming Test during TGA as compared with the same patient's performance after TGA (Kritchevsky & Squire, 1989). The prevalence of mild additional cognitive deficits in TGA might be higher than appears from the reported cases, as the memory impairment prevents patients from tackling cognitively demanding tasks anyhow, and as many examiners do not probe them.

Follow-up

TGA leaves a dense amnesic gap for the time of complete amnesia which may extend backwards for up to one hour preceding the attack.

Clinically, TGA is assumed to be over when behaviour and everyday memory are inconspicuous again. Neuropsychological follow-up examinations have established that restoration of memory proceeds much slower than subjectively experienced and that normal performance on memory tests is achieved only after several days or even weeks (Cases 1 and 2; Regard & Landis, 1984; Stillhard et al., 1990; Hodges & Ward, 1989). Although most patients then reach test results which fall into the range of normality and do not complain about memory loss or other cognitive problems in daily life, comparisons of groups of TGA patients with carefully matched controls suggest some persistent memory impairments even after a single typical TGA (Mazzuchi et al., 1980; Hodges & Oxbury, 1990). A consistent finding has been impaired recall of short stories as used in the logical memory subtest of the Wechsler Memory Scale. Impaired recall of a complex geometrical figure has been found in one study (Mazzuchi et al., 1980) but not in another (Hodges & Oxbury, 1990). One study (Hodges & Oxbury, 1990) looked for remote memory after TGA and found impaired naming of famous faces, impaired dating of famous events, and impoverished recall of autobiographical episodes. These deficits of retrograde memory were not temporally graded.

NEURORADIOLOGY OF TGA

Since the advent of computerized tomography, many patients with TGA have undergone CT after the attack. In some 10% of them CT shows cerebral infarctions without relationship to anatomical structures relevant to memory (Miller et al., 1987; Hodges & Warlow, 1990a; Colombo & Scarpa, 1988; Matias-Guiu, Colomer, Segura & Codina, 1986). There are, however, cases in whom CT after TGA demonstrated ischaemic lesions in either the thalamus (Puel et al., 1982; Kushner & Hauser, 1985; Colombo & Scarpa, 1988; Bogous-slavsky & Regli, 1988) or the medial temporal lobe (Kushner & Hauser, 1985; Ladurner et al., 1982; Bogousslavsky & Regli, 1988; Tanabe et al., 1991) of one side which was the left more often than the right. The interpretation of these lesions as indicating the cause of TGA is made problematic by the fact that TGA is transient and the lesions are permanent. As the lesions were present when memory was normalized they may have existed already before it became abnormal at all.

More compelling evidence for the location of lesions underlying TGA is provided if TGA is followed by a persistent memory deficit and CT shows lesions in memory-relevant structures. The occurrence of a permanent memory deficit which correlates with the lesion's location makes it unlikely that the lesion has silently been present before the TGA. Goldenberg, Wimmer & Maly (1983) found a left polar thalamic lesion in a 40-year-old patient whose TGA was followed by a predominantly verbal memory deficit and an impairment of autobiographical memory which reached back into school days. Gorelik, Amico, Ganallen & Benevento, (1988) reported a patient who suffered three typical TGAs. Memory recovered completely after the first and second attacks, and a CT after the second attack was normal. After the third attack there remained a persistent, predominantly verbal, memory deficit and CT showed a left polar thalamic infarction.

Cerebral angiography in several patients after TGA revealed a considerable incidence of atherosclerotic plaques, stenoses, occlusions and hypoplasias of arteries particularly in the vertebrobasilar territory (Frederiks, 1990; Jensen & Olivarius, 1980). Again, the causal relationship to TGA is questionable, as the pathogenetic relationship between arterial narrowing and cerebral symptoms is far from being straightforward, and as clinically silent stenoses or occlusions of cerebral arteries are a common finding in elderly patients undergoing angiography (e.g. Goldenberg & Reisner, 1983).

As TGA is caused by a reversible cerebral dysfunction, the most promising way for finding its anatomical substrate is to acquire measures of brain function during the attack and afterwards. Until now, mainly regional cerebral flow (rCBF) has been assessed (Volpe et al., 1983; Trillet et al., 1987; Stillhard et al., 1990; Goldenberg et al., 1991; Tanabe et al., 1991; Evans et al., 1993). Flow reductions which are present during the attack and not at follow-up are likely to be causally related to the transient memory loss, although even this apparently obvious correlation can be doubted. TGA starts abruptly but ends gradually. The first patchy recollections may be acquired when the patient's behaviour is still much the same as in fully fledged TGA (see case reports above). As rCBF measurement is rarely achieved immediately after the start of the attack, there is the possibility that the measurement reflects the distribution of CBF during recovery rather than during complete amnesia. A further problem in the interpretation of blood flow studies is that alterations of local flow can be either the cause or the sequel of neuronal dysfunction. Reduction of blood flow due to vascular disease can cause neuronal dysfunction, but, conversely, reduced neuronal activity due to other causes can manifest itself by a reduction of local cerebral blood flow. Of the different methods used for CBF measurement, only positron emission tomography (PET) allows a distinction between these possibilities.

Volpe et al. (1983) performed PET in one patient during TGA and afterwards. During the attack, there was a diffuse reduction of CBF which was particularly marked in the mesial temporal lobes. In the mesial temporal lobe, oxygen uptake was reduced beyond the reduction of rCBF. This constellation would indicate neuronal dysfunction rather than ischaemia. Thalamic rCBF values were not reported. Trillet et al. (1987) used surface measurement of 133-xenon washout for assessment of rCBF in two patients during TGA, and found a diffuse reduction of cortical rCBF. This method does not allow the visualization of flow in deep structures like the mesial temporal lobes or the thalamus. Stillhard et al. (1990) and Evans et al. (1993) each made HMPAO-SPECT in one patient during TGA and afterwards. The images of Stillhard et al. show diffuse hypoperfusion of the temporal and frontal lobes, and those of Evans et al. hypoperfusion of the temporal lobes which was more marked on the left side than on the right. In both patients, SPECT was normal after the TGA. However, in both of these studies SPECT was done without attenuation correction, and therefore neither the mesial temporal lobes nor the thalamus can be evaluated. Lin et al. (1993) made SPECT in one patient during TGA and twice afterwards. During TGA there was hypoperfusion of the left thalamus in addition to perfusion deficits in left temporal and bilateral occipital regions. Two SPECT studies during TGA performed by the author have already been reported in the introduction. While one (Case 2) showed a reduction of isotope uptake affecting the left frontal and temporal lobes and both thalami, the other (Goldenberg et al., 1991; Case 1) demonstrated a diminution of regional flow in the thalami over and above a general reduction of isotope uptake. Thalamic ischaemia was more marked on the left than on the right side.

Tanabe et al. (1991) performed SPECT in a patient one and a half hours after the end of TGA. At this time, behaviour had normalized, but memory was still deficient on formal testing. Compared with a follow-up SPECT there was hypoperfusion of both medial temporal lobes and hyperaemia of both thalami. Sakashita, Sugimoto, Taki & Matsudo, (1993) examined two patients about two hours after the end of TGA and at follow-up. In one patient they found hypoperfusion of both thalami and of the left hippocampus which did not recover at follow-up. In the other patient, significant hypoperfusion was restricted to the right inferior temporal region and normalized at follow-up. Baron et al. (1994) studied one patient with PET in the early recovery phase and again three months later. They found a matched reduction of CBF and oxygen consumption over the entire right frontal cortex and in the right thalamus in the first study. The reduction of oxygen consumption suggests neuronal dysfunction as the cause of CBF reduction.

EPIDEMIOLOGY AND PROGNOSIS OF TGA

Two district based studies found the annual incidence of TGA to be 3 per 100 thousand (Hodges, 1991) and 5.2 per 100 thousand respectively (Miller et al., 1987). For most patients TGA remains a unique event, as the annual recurrence rate across several years of follow-up is only between 2 and 5% (Mumenthaler & Treig, 1984; Kushner & Hauser, 1985; Hinge et al., 1986; Miller et al., 1987; Colombo & Scarpa, 1988; Guidotti, Anzalone, Morabito & Landi, 1989; Hinge & Jensen, 1990).

The vast majority of patients are aged between 50 and 70 years and the mean age of representative samples of TGA patients tends to be very close to 60 years (Hodges, 1991; Hinge et al., 1986; Crowell et al., 1984; Guidotti et al., 1989; Hodges & Warlow, 1990b; Mumenthaler & Treig, 1984; Miller et al., 1987; Colombo & Scarpa, 1988; Frederiks, 1990). The incidence of TGA is as high in the sixth decade as it is in the seventh and falls sharply in the eighth. Patients older than 80 are as rare as patients younger than 40 (Hodges, 1991; Caplan, 1985). This contrasts with the incidence of cerebrovascular disease which shows a continuous increase with advancing age (Kurtzke & Kurland, 1983). The age distribution is also very different from that of migraine. Migraine usually starts in adolescence or young adulthood and the frequency of attacks tends to diminish in advanced age (Poeck, 1990).

In a search for the aetiology of TGA, several studies have investigated the prevalence of risk factors for atherosclerosis in patients with TGA. In different samples of TGA patients the frequency of arterial hypertension varies from 13% (Hinge et al., 1986) to 50% (Colombo & Scarpa, 1988; Kushner & Hauser, 1985; Crowell et al., 1984; Guidotti et al., 1989), and is between 25 and 35% in a majority of studies (Mumenthaler & Treig, 1984; Matias-Guiu et al., 1986; Miller et al., 1987; Frederiks, 1990; Hodges & Warlow, 1990b). A history of coronary heart disease was found with frequencies between about 5% (Mumenthaler & Treig, 1984; Hodges & Warlow, 1990b; Hinge et al., 1986) and 25% (Guidotti et al., 1989; Hinge et al., 1986, Frederiks, 1990, Miller et al., 1987). The frequency of previous cerebrovascular events was reported to be as high as 67% in one study (Kushner & Hauser, 1985), but only 10% or lower in the remainder (Hodges & Warlow, 1990b; Matias-Guiu et al., 1986; Frederiks, 1990; Miller et al., 1987; Colombo & Scarpa, 1988). Studies comparing the prevalence of vascular risk factors in TGA with their prevalence in age-matched healthy controls and in patients with transient ischaemic attacks yielded conflicting results. While some of them estimated the frequency of risk factors in TGA patients to be higher than in controls and similar to that in patients with transient ischaemic attacks (Guidotti et al., 1989; Kushner & Hauser, 1985), others found it not higher than in controls (Hodges & Warlow, 1990b; Hinge et al., 1986; Miller et al., 1987; Matias-Guiu et al., 1986) and definitely lower than in patients with transient ischaemic attacks (Matias-Guiu et al., 1986; Hodges & Warlow, 1990b).

Whereas there is disagreement as to the frequency of vascular risk factors in patients with TGA, there is near unanimity that for mean follow-up periods of about three to four years the risk for transient ischaemic attacks, stroke, or myocardial infarction is not elevated (Hinge et al., 1986; Hinge & Jensen, 1990; Kushner & Hauser, 1985; Guidotti et al., 1989; Hodges & Warlow, 1990b; Mumenthaler & Treig, 1984; Frederiks, 1990; Miller et al., 1987; Colombo & Scarpa, 1988). A large study which included careful clinical assessment of all

TGAs found that the prognosis for subsequent coronary or cerebrovascular ischaemic events was definitely worse in patients in whom TGA was accompanied by other neurological symptoms (Hodges & Warlow, 1990a). These patients also had a higher prevalence of vascular risk factors than those with pure TGA. Another study which did not differentiate between TGA with and without associated neurological symptoms found the prognosis for subsequent cerebrovascular disease to be worse in TGA patients with vascular risk factors than in those without (Jensen & Olivarius, 1981).

A further topic of particular interest of epidemiological studies has been the association of TGA with migraine. As the diagnosis of migraine rests nearly entirely on the patient's and the doctor's scrutiny in history-taking, estimates of its prevalence are notoriously unreliable and prone to being influenced by the doctor's expectations. Accordingly, the given frequency of a history of migraine in patients with TGA varies from 3.6% (Colombo & Scarpa, 1988) to 40% (Crowell et al., 1984). However, some 20% appears to be a reasonable estimate on which several studies accord (Matias-Guiu et al., 1986, Hinge et al., 1986, Hodges & Warlow, 1990b). The estimate for the prevalence of migraine in an unselected population is about 10–20% (Poeck, 1990). A study which used the same diagnostic procedure for assessing migraine in TGA patients and in age-matched controls found a history of classical migraine in 22.8% of TGA patients and in 11.0% of controls (Hodges & Warlow, 1990b). This difference was statistically significant. It is not very impressive and implies that about eight out of ten TGA patients do *not* have a history of migraine. The coincidence of migraine and TGA becomes even less convincing when viewed the other way round: from the prevalence or, respectively, incidence rates and age-distribution of both diseases it can be calculated that out of 10 000 patients with a history of migraine only one will suffer TGA.

Tentatively, the following conclusions can be drawn from these epidemiological studies. TGA can occur in patients without significant risk factors for atherosclerosis and the occurrence of TGA does not indicate the presence of advanced atherosclerosis. There are cases in whom TGA appears in a context of symptomatic atherosclerosis, but it may be that most of them suffer TGA with associated neurological symptoms rather than pure TGA. The majority of patients with TGA do not have a history of migraine, and the vast majority of patients with migraine never suffer TGA. The age distribution of TGA is definitely different from that of migraine but does also differ from that of atherosclerotic cerebrovascular disease. As it appears, TGA is a fairly unique disorder which cannot easily be referred to as being a manifestation of other, more common, diseases.

THE ANATOMY OF TGA

From the study of chronic amnesic syndromes, three main locations have emerged where lesions can cause amnesia: the hippocampal formation, the diencephalon, and the basal forebrain-septal region. With respect to the diencephalon, the crucial site for lesions causing amnesia appears to be the inferior polar thalamic region (von Cramon, Hebel & Schuri, 1985; Markowitsch, 1988). The basal forebrain has not yet been considered as being a possible locus of pathology in TGA. It is typically damaged in amnesia caused by bleeding from anterior cerebral artery aneurysms (e.g. de Luca & Cicerone, 1991; Parkin, Leng, Stanhope & Smith, 1988) and may play a crucial role for memory impairment in degenerative dementia (Kesner, 1988), but the anatomy of its vascular supply does not permit for selective ischaemia, nor have other mechanisms been suggested which might cause transient dysfunction of the basal forebrain. For both thalamic and hippocampal damage it has been demonstrated that unilateral lesions can cause memory problems but are not sufficient for an amnesia as global and as severe as in TGA (Milner, 1968a; Milner, 1971; Squire & Moore, 1979; Speedie & Heilman 1982, 1983; Goldenberg et al., 1983; Bogousslavsky, Regli & Uske, 1988).

It is a matter of debate whether the neuropsychological features of diencephalic amnesia are distinct from those of hippocampal amnesia (Lhermitte & Signoret, 1972; Squire, 1982). Diencephalic amnesia has been said to be characterized by a more severe and not temporally limited retrograde amnesia and by particular difficulties with the evocation of temporal order, context, and details of retrieved information (Goldenberg et al., 1983; Signoret & Goldenberg, 1986; Stuss et al., 1988; Graff-Radford et al., 1990), whereas hippocampal damage produces a more "pure" amnesic syndrome which is predominated by the inability to acquire new information (Milner, 1968b; Zola-Morgan et al., 1986; Wilson & Baddeley, 1988). However, most of the evidence concerning diencephalic amnesia is derived from patients with alcoholic Korsakoff syndrome who frequently have diffuse cortical brain damage in addition to the diencephalic lesions. Moreover, even if diencephalic amnesia is caused by circumscribed (e.g. ischaemic) thalamic lesions, these are not necessarily restricted to the small portion of the thalamus which is relevant for memory function. The thalamus has long been recognized as "the key to the cortex", and thalamic lesions can cause widespread cortical dysfunction which may predominate in the frontal cortex when the thalamic lesions are situated in the polar region (Baron et al., 1986, 1992; Markowitsch, 1988; Levasseur et al., 1992). The peculiarities of diencephalic amnesia could be caused by the addition of diffuse and particularly frontal cortical dysfunction to a "pure" amnesic syndrome.

The thalamus and hippocampal formations differ in important aspects of their vascular supply (see Figure 5.3). The hippocampal formation receives blood via the temporal branches of the posterior cerebral artery. These branches originate bilaterally from the posterior cerebral arteries. They are situated distally from the circle of Willis, and proximally to the branches supplying the temporooccipital and occipital regions of the brain. As occlusion of the stem of the posterior cerebral artery proximal to the origin of the temporal branches would invariably cause temporo-occipital and occipital ischaemia with consecutive neurological symptoms, pure amnesia could result only from occlusion of one or several of the temporal branches themselves. Bilateral damage causing amnesia would afford two simultaneous lesions, one in a temporal branch of the left side, and one on the right. Memory disorders can also be brought forward by occlusions of the temporo-occipital posterior cerebral artery branches, as brain damage in this location interrupts limbic circuits which connect the hippocampus formation to the diencephalon, the septum and the basal forebrain (von Cramon et al., 1988). In this case, simultaneous bilateral lesions are more likely, as emboli from the common origin of the posterior cerebral arteries can travel straightforwardly into these major branches which continue the direction of the main stem (see Figure 5.3). However, amnesic disturbances caused by temporo-occipital lesions are associated with upper visual field defects and other visual perceptual disturbances which would hardly escape detection in TGA (Geschwind & Fusillo, 1966; Benson, Marsden & Meadows, 1974; Caplan & Hedley-White, 1974; de Renzi, Zambolini & Crisi, 1987; Goldenberg, 1992).

Blood supply for the polar thalamic region is provided by the polar and by the paramedian thalamic arteries (Percheron, 1976a,b; Castaigne et al., 1981; von Cramon et al., 1985). The respective importance of their vascular territories varies greatly. Both originate directly from the circle of Willis. The polar arteries issue from the posterior communicating arteries which on each side link the carotid artery and the posterior cerebral artery. The paramedian arteries arise from the basilar communicating arteries which connect the tip of the unique basilar artery with both posterior cerebral arteries (Percheron, 1976b). The paramedian thalamic arteries are the only vessels originating from this part of the circle of Willis. As a frequent variation, both paramedian arteries can arise from a common stem on either the left or the right side (see Figure 5.3). Consequently, symmetric paramedian thalamic infarctions are not at all rare (Percheron, 1976a; Castaigne et al., 1981; von Cramon et al., 1985; Bogousslavsky & Regli, 1988).

THE AETIOLOGY AND PATHOGENESIS OF TGA

It may be useful to re-emphasize a few facts which have emerged from the preceding considerations and which need to be accommodated by a valid explanation of TGA.

- TGA is a distinct disorder which cannot easily be referred to as being a manifestation of other diseases. The age range of patients has both a lower and an upper limit. TGA has a low recurrence rate and remains a unique event in most of the patients.
- There is an extraordinarily dense and global anterograde amnesia which to all neuropsychological experience would point to bilateral dysfunction of memory-relevant brain structures.
- Behavioural observation, neuropsychological examination and CBF studies during the attack concur to suggest that in addition to the severe amnesic

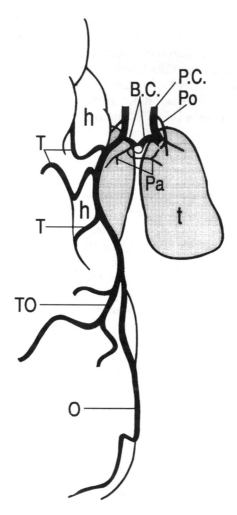

Figure 5.3 Vessels supplying the hippocampus formation (h) and the thalamus (t). The brain is seen from below. Structures lying between the temporal lobes and the thalamus are omitted to allow a synoptic view of both vascular territories. B.C.=basilar communicating artery; P.C.=posterior communicating artery; Po=polar thalamic artery; Pa= paramedian thalamic artery; T=temporal branches of posterior cerebral artery; TO= temporo-occipital branches of posterior cerebral artery; O=occipital branches of posterior cerebral artery. The image shows an anatomical variant: there is only one paramedian thalamic artery which supplies vascular territories in both thalami

syndrome there is mild diffuse cortical dysfunction which might be particularly prominent for frontal lobe functions.

- The restoration of memory is much slower than it would appear to be from the rapid restoration of normal behaviour, and possibly there are lasting deficits in a significant number of patients.
- The anatomy of the vascular supply does not allow for selective ischaemia of

the basal forebrain and makes simultaneous bilateral ischaemia of the hippocampus improbable, but does provide a possibility for bilateral ischaemia of the polar thalamic region.

Currently, there are two main opinions concerning the aetiology and pathogenesis of TGA. One holds that vascular occlusive disease causes transient ischaemia in either the hippocampus formation or the thalamus (Frederiks, 1990), and the other that spreading depression causes transient dysfunction of the hippocampus (Olesen & Jorgensen, 1986). How does each of these ideas cope with the constraints outlined above?

Transient Ischaemia due to Occlusive Vascular Disease

Because of the anatomy of the vascular supply and the presumed bilaterality of the deficit, the hypothesis of transient ischaemia of vascular origin would imply that TGA is caused by bilateral thalamic dysfunction. As thalamic injury can cause diffuse and particularly frontal cortical dysfunction, no additional mechanisms must be invoked to accommodate the accompanying behavioural abnormalities and cognitive disturbances in TGA. A possible explanation for the slowness of neuropsychological recovery and for remaining deficits would be that ischaemia does cause small structural lesions whose symptoms subside slowly and not always completely, and that the dramatic initial symptoms which recover rapidly are expressions of oedema and diaschisis in the immediate neighbourhood of the permanent lesions. Completed infarction as the substrate of TGA would also account for the low recurrence rate. If the compromised tissue is destroyed, there is nothing left for further ischaemic damage in the same location. The paucity of reported adequate neuroradiological findings at follow-up could be referred to the insensitivity of computed tomography and might change with refinement and increasing use of NMR imaging in the follow-up of TGA.

The hypothesis of bilateral thalamic ischaemia provides a plausible pathogenesis of TGA but faces difficulties with aetiology, as it has to be reconciled with the apparent independence of TGA from general atherosclerosis and with the fact that the incidence of TGA declines at an age when that of other cerebrovascular accidents increases. One may speculate on an anatomical explanation for these facts. Being exposed to the high-pressure blood stream from the basilar artery, the bifurcation of the basilar communicating arteries and the origin of the paramedian arteries are loci of predilection for atherosclerotic plaques (Robinson & Toole, 1989). The diameters of the paramedian artery and of the basilar communicating artery vary greatly between individuals (Alpers, Berry & Paddison, 1959; Percheron, 1976b). One might easily conceive of anatomical constellations in which mild atherosclerotic changes at or near to the tip of the basilar artery suffice to severely compromise blood flow in a thin paramedian artery at a time when general atherosclerosis is not yet sufficiently advanced to manifest itself by other vascular symptoms. If there is only one paramedian artery supplying both thalami, and if its vascular territories are very small, ischaemia would lead to transient bilateral thalamic dysfunction, but would leave little if any permanent symptoms. TGA becomes rare when atherosclerosis advances, as patients who have the anatomical predisposition for TGA will have suffered the insult early in the course of atherosclerotic disease. Presumably, paramedian arteries which are thick enough to resist mild atherosclerotic changes supply larger vascular territories. If they happen to be occluded by advanced atherosclerosis, this would lead to amnesic stroke or TGA with associated neurological symptoms rather than to pure TGA.

Spreading Depression

Spreading depression (SD) is a phenomenon which has been demonstrated in experimental animals. Local physical or chemical stimuli can induce a depolarization of neurons which spreads to surrounding tissue and temporarily abolishes the functioning of the affected nerve cells (Bures, Koroleva & Vinogradova, 1992). In human pathology, SD is thought to play a role in the pathogenesis of lasting neuronal damage after ischaemia or head trauma (Somjen, Herreras & Jing, 1992).

Although primarily a neuronal event, SD is accompanied by changes of rCBF. The spreading wave of SD manifests itself by a short-lasting elevation of blood flow which is followed by a longer lasting period of decreased rCBF. Within this period the regional metabolic rates of oxygen and of glucose are normal, and there are no focal neurological symptoms corresponding to the depression of rCBF (Lauritzen, 1992). Studies of rCBF during the aura symptoms of migraine attacks showed areas of reduced blood flow which travelled across the cortex with the same speed as the waves of SD in experimental animals, and whose location did not correspond to that of the focal symptoms of the aura. Because of the similarity of this flow depression to the wandering fields of flow reductions following SD, SD has been invoked as being part of the pathogenesis of migraine (Lauritzen, Olsen, Lassen & Paulson, 1983; Lauritzen, 1992). Although no similar travelling waves of flow reduction have yet been demonstrated in TGA, the findings of diffusely depressed cortical blood flow in TGA have been estimated to be similar enough to justify the assumption that SD is at work in TGA. The hypothesis has been put forward that stressful stimuli lead to an overstimulation of the hippocampus which provokes local SD, inactivating the hippocampus and spreading from there to the cerebral cortex (Olesen & Jorgensen, 1986; Hodges, 1991). This hypothesis emphasizes a link between migraine and TGA and the importance of precipitating factors in triggering TGA (Crowell et al., 1984; Caplan, Chedru, Lhermitte & Mayman, 1981; Hodges & Warlow, 1990b).

However, these two pieces of the argument do not fit together very convincingly. Physical exertion, which appears to be the most frequent precipitating factor of TGA, is not very common as a trigger of migraine, attacks of which may even be aborted by physical exercise (Poeck, 1990; Ziegler & Murrow,

1988). On the other hand, fasting, dietary irregularities, sleep deprivation and excessive sleep which are known as precipitating factors of migraine have not been documented to trigger TGA. As the existence of SD in migraine is hypothetical anyway, the lack of a profound similarity between migraine and TGA does not necessarily invalidate the hypothesis that SD is at work in TGA.

The lack of experience with clinical presentation of SD in humans makes it difficult to discuss how the SD hypothesis copes with the constraints put forward in the preceding section. It does appear to do well in explaining the combination of dense amnesia with symptoms of diffuse cortical dysfunction, and it certainly does not have problems with vascular anatomy. In the absence of knowledge about the course of SD in humans, the hypothesis is indecisive as to the slow recovery, and possibly lasting deficits, of memory in TGA. It does, however, have problems with the age distribution and recurrence rate of TGA. If subjects are prone to react to stressful stimuli with SD of the hippocampus, it is hard to see why they do so only at a certain age and only once or twice in their life.

CONCLUSIONS

In spite of the considerable accumulation of data on the epidemiology, clinical features, neuropsychology, course, and prognosis of TGA, its aetiology and pathogenesis are still a matter of speculation. Possibly, refinement and increasing use of functional neuroimaging techniques during TGA will help to elucidate the cause of this impressive but elusive disorder.

REFERENCES

Alpers, B.J., Berry, R.G. & Paddison, R.M. (1959). Anatomical studies of the circle of Willis in normal brain. *Archives of Neurology*, **81**, 409–418.

Baron, J.C., D'Antona, R.D., Pantano, P., Serdaru, M., Samson, Y. & Bousser, M.G. (1986). Effects of thalamic stroke on energy metabolism of the cerebral cortex. *Brain*, **109**, 1243–1259.

Baron, J.C., Levasseur, M., Mazoyer, B., Legault-Demare, F., Maugière, F., Pappata, S., Jednyak, P., Derome, P., Cambier, J., Tran-Dinh, S. & Cambon, H. (1992). Thalamocortical diaschisis: positron emission tomography in humans. *Journal of Neurology, Neurosurgery and Psychiatry*, **55**, 935–942.

Baron, J.C., Petit-Taboué, M.C., Le Doze, F., Desgranges, B., Ravenel, N. & Marchal, G. (1994). Right frontal cortex hypometabolism in transient global amnesia: A PET study. *Brain*, **117**, 545–552.

Bender, M.B. (1956). Syndrome of isolated episode of confusion with amnesia. *Journal of Hillside Hospital*, **5**, 212–215.

Benson, D.F., Marsden, C.D. & Meadows, J.C. (1974). The amnesic syndrome of posterior cerebral artery occlusion. *Acta Neurologica Scandinavica*, **50**, 133–145.

Bogousslavsky, J. & Regli, F. (1988). Transient global amnesia and stroke. *European Neurology*, **28**, 106–110.

Bogousslavsky, J., Regli, F. & Uske, A. (1988). Thalamic infarcts: clinical syndromes, etiology, and prognosis. *Neurology*, **38**, 837–848.

Brown, G.G., Kieran, S. & Patel, S. (1989). Memory functioning following a left medial thalamic hematoma. *Journal of Clinical and Experimental Neuropsychology*, **11**, 206–218.

Bures, J., Koroleva, V.I. & Vinogradova, L.V. (1992). Synergetics of spreading depression: re-entry waves and reverberators in the rat brain. In R.J. Do Carmo, (ed.), *Spreading Depression*. Springer, New York, pp. 35–48.

Caffarra, P., Moretti, G., Mazucchi, A. & Parma, M. (1981). Neuropsychological testing during a transient global amnesia period and its follow-up. *Acta Neurologica Scandinavica*, **63**, 44–50.

Caplan, L., Chedru, F., Lhermitte, F. & Mayman, C. (1981). Transient global amnesia and migraine. *Neurology*, **31**, 1167–1170.

Caplan, L.B. (1985). Transient global amnesia. In J.A.M. Frederiks (ed.), *Handbook of Clinical Neurology*, vol. 1. Elsevier Science Publishers, Amsterdam, pp. 205–218.

Caplan, L.R. (1990). Transient global amnesia: characteristic features and overview. In H.J. Markowitsch (ed.), *Transient Global Amnesia and Related Disorders*. Hogrefe & Huber, New York, pp. 15–27.

Caplan, L.R. & Hedley-White, T. (1974). Cuing and memory dysfunction in alexia without agraphia. *Brain*, **97**, 251–262.

Castaigne, P., Lhermitte, F., Buge, A., Escourolle, R., Hauw, J.J. & Lyon-Caen, O. (1981). Paramedian and midbrain infarcts: clinical and neuropathological study. *Annals of Neurology*, **10**, 128–148.

Colombo, A. & Scarpa, M. (1988). Transient global amnesia: pathogenesis and prognosis. *European Neurology*, **28**, 111–114.

Crowell, G.F., Stump, D.A., Biller, J., McHenry, L.C. & Toole, J.F. (1984). The transient global amnesia–migraine connection. *Archives of Neurology*, **41**, 75–79.

de Luca, J. & Cicerone, K.D. (1991). Confabulation following aneurysm of the anterior communicating artery. *Cortex*, **23**, 417–424.

de Renzi, E., Zambolini, A. & Crisi, G. (1987). The pattern of neuropsychological impairment associated with left posterior cerebral artery infarcts. *Brain*, **110**, 1099–1116.

Evans, J., Wilson, B.A., Wraight, E.P. & Hodges, J.R. (1993). Neuropsychological and SPECT scan findings during and after transient global amnesia: evidence for the differential impairment of remote episodic memory. *Journal of Neurology, Neurosurgery and Psychiatry*, **56**, 1227–1230.

Fisher, C.M. & Adams, R.D. (1964). Transient global amnesia. *Acta Neurologica Scandinavica*, **40**, 1–83.

Frederiks, J.A.M. (1990). Transient global amnesia: an amnesic TIA. In H.J. Markowitsch (ed.), *Transient Global Amnesia and Related Disorders*. Hogrefe & Huber, New York, pp. 28–47.

Gallassi, R. & Morreale, A. (1990). Transient global amnesia and epilepsy. In H.J. Markowitsch (ed.), *Transient Global Amnesia and Related Disorders*. Hogrefe & Huber, New York, pp. 58–65.

Geschwind, N. & Fusillo, M. (1966). Color naming deficits in association with alexia. *Archives of Neurology*, **15**, 137–146.

Goldenberg, G. (1992). Loss of visual imagery and loss of visual knowledge–a case study. *Neuropsychologia*, **30**, 1081–1099.

Goldenberg, G. & Artner, C. (1991). Visual imagery and knowledge about the visual appearance of objects in patients with posterior cerebral artery lesions. *Brain and Cognition*, **15**, 160–186.

Goldenberg, G., Podreka, I., Pfaffelmeyer, N., Wessely, P. & Deecke, L. (1991). Thalamic ischemia in transient global amnesia: a SPECT study. *Neurology*, **41**, 1748–1752.

Goldenberg, G. & Reisner, T. (1983). Angiographic findings in relation to clinical course and results of computed tomography in cerebrovascular disease. *European Neurology*, **22**, 124–130.

Goldenberg, G., Wimmer, A. & Maly, J. (1983). Amnesic syndrome with a unilateral thalamic lesion: a case report. *Journal of Neurology*, **229**, 79–86.

Gorelick, P.B., Amico, L.A., Ganellen, R. & Benevento, L.A. (1988). Transient global amnesia and thalamic infarction. *Neurology*, **38**, 496–499.

Graff-Radford, N.R., Tranel, D., van Hoesen, G.W. & Brandt, J.B. (1990). Diencephalic amnesia. *Brain*, **113**, 1–25.

Guidotti, M., Anzalone, N., Morabito, A. & Landi, G. (1989). A case–control study of transient global amnesia. *Journal of Neurology, Neurosurgery and Psychiatry*, **52**, 321–323.

Guyotat, J. & Courjon, J. (1956). Les ictus amnésiques. *Journal de Medicine de Lyon*, **37**, 697–701.

Hinge, H.H. & Jensen, T.S. (1990). The prognosis of transient global amnesia. In H.J. Markowitsch (ed.), *Transient Global Amnesia and Related Disorders*. Hogrefe & Huber, New York, pp. 172–180.

Hinge, H.H., Jensen, T.S., Kjaer, M., Marquardsen, J. & Olivarius, B.D.F. (1986). The prognosis of transient global amnesia: results of a multicenter study. *Archives of Neurology*, **43**, 673–676.

Hodges, J.R. (1991). *Transient Amnesia—Clinical and Neuropsychological Aspects*. W.B. Saunders, London.

Hodges, J.R. & Oxbury, S.M. (1990). Persistent memory impairment following transient global amnesia. *Journal of Clinical and Experimental Neuropsychology*, **12**, 904–920.

Hodges, J.R. & Ward, C.D. (1989). Observations during transient global amnesia. *Brain*, **112**, 595–620.

Hodges, J.R. & Warlow, C.P. (1990a). Syndromes of transient amnesia: towards a classification. A study of 153 cases. *Journal of Neurology, Neurosurgery and Psychiatry*, **53**, 834–843.

Hodges, J.R. & Warlow, C.P. (1990b). The aetiology of transient global amnesia. *Brain*, **113**, 639–657.

Jensen, T.S. & Olivarius, B.D.F. (1980). Transient global amnesia as a manifestation of transient cerebral ischemia. *Acta Neurologica Scandinavica*, **61**, 115–124.

Jensen, T.S. & Olivarius, B.D.F. (1981). Transient global amnesia—its clinical and pathophysiological basis and prognosis. *Acta Neurologica Scandinavica*, **63**, 220–230.

Kapur, N. (1990). Transient epileptic amnesia: a clinically distinct form of neurological memory disorder. In H.J. Markowitsch (ed.), *Transient Global Amnesia and Related Disorders*. Hogrefe & Huber, New York, pp. 140–151.

Kesner, R.P. (1988). Re-evaluation of the contribution of the basal forebrain cholinergic system to memory. *Neurobiology of Aging*, **9**, 609–616.

Kritchevsky, M. & Squire, L.R. (1989). Transient global amnesia: evidence for extensive, temporally graded retrograde amnesia. *Neurology*, **39**, 213–218.

Kritchevsky, M., Squire, L.R. & Zouzounis, J.A. (1988). Transient global amnesia: characterization of anterograde and retrograde amnesia. *Neurology*, **38**, 213–219.

Kurtzke, J.F. & Kurland, L.T. (1983). The epidemiology of neurologic disease. In R.J. Joynt, A.B. Baker and L.H. Baker (eds.), *Clinical Neurology*. J.B. Lippincott, Philadelphia, chap. 65.

Kushner, M.J. & Hauser, W.A. (1985). Transient global amnesia: a case–control study. *Annals of Neurology*, **18**, 684–691.

Ladurner, G., Skvarc, A. & Sager, W.D. (1982). Computer tomography in transient global amnesia. *European Neurology*, **21**, 34–40.

Lauritzen, M. (1992). Cortical spreading depression as a migraine mechanism: clinical and experimental aspects. In R.J. Do Carmo (ed.), *Spreading Depression*. Springer, New York, pp. 7–16.

Lauritzen, M., Olsen, T.S., Lassen, N.A. & Paulson, O.B. (1983). Changes in regional cerebral blood flow during the course of classic migraine attacks. *Annals of Neurology*, **13**, 633–641.

Levasseur, M., Baron, J.C., Sette, G., Legault-Demare, F., Pappata, S., Maguière, F., Benoit, N., Dinh, S.T., Degos, J.D., Laplane, D. & Mazoyer, B. (1992). Brain energy metabolism in bilateral paramedian thalamic infarcts. *Brain*, **115**, 795–807.

Lhermitte, F. & Signoret, J.L. (1972). Analyse neuropsychologique et differenciation des syndromes amnesiques. *Revue Neurologique*, **126**, 161–178.

Lin, K.-N., Liu, R.-S., Yeh, T.-P., Wang, S.-J. & Liu, H.-C. (1993). Posterior ischemia during an attack of transient global amnesia. *Stroke*, **24**, 1093–1095.

Markowitsch, H.J. (1988). Diencephalic amnesia: a reorientation towards tracts? *Brain Research Reviews*, **13**, 351–370.

Matias-Guiu, J., Colomer, R., Segura, A. & Codina, A. (1986). Cranial CT scan in transient global amnesia. *Acta Neurologica Scandinavica*, **73**, 298–301.

Mazzuchi, A., Moretti, G., Caffarra, P. & Parma, M. (1980). Neuropsychological functions in the follow-up of transient global amnesia. *Brain*, **103**, 161–178.

Miller, J.W., Petersen, R.C., Metter, E.J., Millikan, C.H. & Yanagihara, T. (1987). Transient global amnesia: clinical characteristics and prognosis. *Neurology*, **37**, 733–737.

Miller, J.W., Yanagihara, T., Petersen, R.C. & Klass, D.W. (1990). Transient global amnesia and epilepsy—electroencephalographic distinction. *Archives of Neurology*, **44**, 629–633.

Milner, B. (1968a). Visual recognition and recall after right temporal lobe excision in man. *Neuropsychologia*, **6**, 191–209.

Milner, B. (1968b). Further analysis of the hippocampal amnesic syndrome: 14-year follow-up study of H.M. *Neuropsychologia*, **6**, 215–234.

Milner, B. (1971). Interhemispheric differences in the localization of psychological processes in man. *British Medical Bulletin*, **27**, 272–277.

Mumenthaler, M. & Treig, T. (1984). Amnestische Episoden—Analyse von 111 eignenen Beobachtungen. *Schweizer medizinische Wochenschrift*, **114**, 1163–1170.

Olesen, J. & Jorgensen, M.B. (1986). Leao's spreading depression in the hippo-campus explains transient global amnesia—a hypothesis. *Acta Neurologica Scandinavica*, **73**, 219–220.

Parkin, A.J., Leng, N.R.C., Stanhope, N. & Smith, A.P. (1988). Memory impairment following ruptured aneurysm of the anterior communicating artery. *Brain and Cognition*, **7**, 231–243.

Percheron, G. (1976a). Les artères du thalamus humain. I: Artères et territoires thalamiques polaires de l'artère communicante postérieure. *Revue Neurologique*, **132**, 297–307.

Percheron, G. (1976b). Les artères du thalamus humain. II: Artères et territoires thalamiques paramédians de l'artère basilaire communicante. *Revue Neurologique*, **132**, 309–324.

Poeck, K. (1990). *Neurologie*. Springer, Heidelberg, New York.

Puel, M., Joanette, Y., Levrat, M., Nespoulous, J.L., Viala, M.F., Roch-Lecours, A. & Rascol, A. (1982). Aphasie croisée chez les droitiers. II: Étude neurolinguistique et neuropsychologique d'un cas. Évolution sur deux ans. *Revue Neurologique*, **138**, 587–600.

Regard, M. & Landis, T. (1984). Transient global amnesia: neuropsychological dysfunction during attack and recovery in two "pure" cases. *Journal of Neurology, Neurosurgery and Psychiatry*, **47**, 668–672.

Robinson, M.K. & Toole, J.F. (1989). Ischemic cerebrovascular disease. In R.J. Joynt (ed.), *Clinical Neurology*. J.B. Lippincott, Philadelphia, chap. 15.

Sakashita, Y., Sugimoto, T., Taki, S. & Matsudo, H. (1993). Abnormal blood flow following transient global amnesia. *Journal of Neurology, Neurosurgery and Psychiatry*, **56**, 1327–1329.

Shuttleworth, E.C. & Wise, G.R. (1973). Transient global amnesia due to arterial embolism. *Archives of Neurology*, **29**, 340–342.

Signoret, J.L. & Goldenberg, G. (1986). Troubles de memoire lors des lesions du thalamus chez l'homme. *Revue Neurologique*, **142**, 445–448.

Soliveri, P., Brown, R.G., Jahanashahi, M. & Marsden, C.D. (1992). Procedural memory and neurological disease. *European Journal of Cognitive Psychology*, **4**, 161–194.

Somjen, G.G., Herreras, O. & Jing, J. (1992). Spreading depression and neuron damage: a brief review. In R.J. Do Carmo, (ed.), *Spreading Depression*. Springer, New York, pp. 27–34.

Speedie, L. & Heilman, K. (1982). Amnesic disturbance following infarction of the left dorsomedial nucleus of the thalamus. *Neuropsychologia*, **20**, 597–604.

Speedie, L. & Heilman, K. (1983). Anterograde memory deficits for visuospatial material after infarction of the right thalamus. *Archives of Neurology*, **49**, 183–204.

Squire, L.R. (1982). The neuropsychology of human memory. *Annual Review of Neuroscience*, **5**, 241–273.

Squire, L.R. & Moore, R.Y. (1979). Dorsal thalamic lesion in a noted case of human memory dysfunction. *Annals of Neurology*, **6**, 503–506.

Stillhard, G., Landis, T., Schiess, R., Regard, M. & Sialer, G. (1990). Bitemporal hypoperfusion in transient global amnesia: 99m-Tc-HM-PAO SPECT and neuropsychological findings during and after an attack. *Journal of Neurology, Neurosurgery and Psychiatry*, **53**, 339–342.

Stracciari, A., Rebucci, G.G. & Gallasi, R. (1987). Transient global amnesia: neuropsychological study of a "pure" case. *Journal of Neurology*, **234**, 126–127.

Stuss, D.T., Guberman, A., Nelson R. & Larochelle, S. (1988). The neuropsychology of paramedian thalamic infarction. *Brain and Cognition*, **8**, 348–378.

Tanabe, H., Hashiwaka, K., Nakagawa, Y., Ikeda, M., Yamamoto, H., Harada, K., Tsumoto, T., Nishimura, T., Shiraishi, J. & Kimura, K. (1991). Memory loss due to transient hypoperfusion in the medial temporal lobe including hippocampus. *Acta Neurologica Scandinavica*, **84**, 22–27.

Trillet, M., Croisile, B., Phillipon, B., Vial, C., Laurent, B. & Guillot, M. (1987). Ictus amnésique et débits sanguins cérébraux. *Revue Neurologique*, **143**, 536–539.

Volpe, B.T., Herscovitch, P., Raichle, M.E., Hirst, W. & Gazzaniga, M.S. (1983). Cerebral blood flow and metabolism in human amnesia. *Journal of Cerebral Blood Flow and Metabolism*, **3**, (suppl. 1), S5–6.

von Cramon, D.Y., Hebel, N. & Schuri, U. (1985). A contribution to the anatomical basis of thalamic amnesia. *Brain*, **108**, 993–1008.

von Cramon, D.Y., Hebel, N. & Schuri, U. (1988). Verbal memory and learning in unilateral posterior cerebral infarction. *Brain*, **111**, 1061–1077.

Warrington, E.K. & McCarthy, R.A. (1987). Categories of knowledge–further fractionations and an attempted integration. *Brain*, **110**, 1273–1296.

Wilson, B.A. & Baddeley, A.D. (1988). Semantic, episodic, and autobiographical memory in a postmeningitis amnesic patient. *Brain and Cognition*, **8**, 31–46.

Ziegler, D.K. & Murrow, R.W. (1988). Headache. In R.J. Joynt (ed.), *Clinical Neurology*. J.B. Lippincott, Philadelphia, chap. 13.

Zola-Morgan, S., Squire, L.R. & Amaral, D.G. (1986). Human amnesia and the medial temporal region: enduring memory impairment following a bilateral lesion limited to field CA1 of the hippocampus. *Journal of Neuroscience*, **6**, 2950–2967.

Chapter 6

Neuropsychological Impairments of Short-Term Memory

Giuseppe Vallar
*Università Statale di Roma "La Sapienza", and
IRCCS Clinica S. Lucia, Rome*
and
Costanza Papagno
Università di Milano, Milan, Italy

Studies in normal subjects and in patients with brain damage suggest that the system subserving retention over short periods of time (of the order of seconds) is not unitary, but comprises a number of independent components, which have discrete anatomical correlates. Two such components, which have been investigated in patients with brain lesions, are considered in this chapter: a verbal (phonological) system and a visuospatial system.

FUNCTIONAL ARCHITECTURE OF SHORT-TERM MEMORY SYSTEMS

Phonological Short-Term Memory

Since the late 1960s, the psychological features of the system involved in the short-term retention of verbal information have been extensively investigated (see reviews by Crowder, 1976; Baddeley, 1990; Shallice & Vallar, 1990).

Handbook of Memory Disorders. Edited by A.D. Baddeley, B.A. Wilson and F.N. Watts.
© 1995 John Wiley & Sons Ltd.

Short-term retention of verbal material involves the activity of a number of inter-related components. Figure 6.1 shows a model which distinguishes a component devoted to the *storage* of verbal information (*phonological short-term store*; STS) and a *process* (*articulatory rehearsal*) which revives the memory trace held in the phonological STS, preventing its decay. The rehearsal process involves the recirculation of information between the phonological STS and a component (phonological output buffer, or assembly system) involved in speech production. This system contributes to the articulatory programming of speech output, storing phonological segments prior to the application of various output processes, such as planning and editing of articulatory procedures (Burani, Vallar & Bottini, 1991). Auditory-verbal information has a direct access to the phonological STS, after phonological analysis. Visual information, by contrast, requires a number of steps, before gaining access to the phonological STS: visual

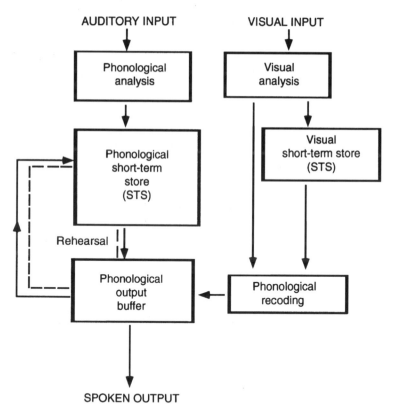

Figure 6.1   A functional model (based on Vallar & Cappa, 1987) of phonological and visual short-term memory. The dashed lines denote the components involved in the rehearsal process, which recirculates information between the phonological short-term store and the phonological output buffer. Visual information may enter the phonological store, after recoding, through rehearsal. Neuropsychological evidence indicates left hemisphere networks as anatomical correlates of these storage and rehearsal systems

analysis, phonological recoding (grapheme-to-phoneme conversion), and articulatory rehearsal. Visual information may be temporarily held in a visual STS system.

Investigation of three variables affecting immediate memory span (phonological similarity, word length, and articulatory suppression) has been the main source of empirical data, which constrain the structure of this memory system. The data from normal subjects relevant to the interpretation of the pattern of impairment of brain-damaged patients are briefly summarised here (see also Baddeley, Chapter 1).

The phonological similarity effect. (Conrad, 1964; Conrad & Hull, 1964; Wickelgren, 1965; Baddeley, 1966). In immediate serial recall, performance level is greatest for lists of phonologically dissimilar stimuli. This suggests that verbal information held in the STS is coded phonologically. The presence of the effect with both auditory and visual input indicates that written material also gains access to the phonological STS, when immediate retention is required.

The word-length effect. (Baddeley, Thomson & Buchanan, 1975; Baddeley, Lewis & Vallar, 1984). In immediate serial recall, memory span for short words is greater than span for long, with both auditory and visual presentation.

Articulatory suppression. (Murray, 1968; Peterson & Johnson, 1971; Levy, 1971; Baddeley, Thomson & Buchanan, 1975; Baddeley, Lewis & Vallar, 1984). The continuous uttering of an irrelevant speech sound (e.g. "the, the, the...") has three main effects on immediate memory span:

- It produces a slight but significant reduction of performance level.
- It eliminates the effect of phonological similarity when the material has been presented visually, but not with auditory presentation.
- It abolishes the effect of word length with both auditory and visual presentation.

According to the model in Figure 6.1, the phonological similarity effect is not removed by suppression when the stimuli are auditorily presented, because information has a direct access to the phonological STS, without any involvement of the rehearsal process. The persistence of the effect during suppression, when input is auditory, indicates also that information in this system is coded in a phonological nonarticulatory format. By contrast, the disappearance of the effect with visual presentation suggests that written input requires the intermediate step of articulatory rehearsal, before gaining access to the phonological STS.

The absence of any significant effect of word length during suppression with both auditory and visual presentation argues for an interpretation in terms of the activity of the articulatory rehearsal system. This may be metaphorically described as a time-based tape of fixed length which recirculates more short words than long.

Finally, the model distinguished between articulatory rehearsal and phonological recoding, or grapheme-to-phoneme conversion: written material, before entering the rehearsal process, needs to be recoded phonologically. This distinction is based on the observation that in normal subjects phonological tasks, such as homophone judgements on written pairs of letter strings (i.e. deciding whether or not two items, when pronounced, have the same sound), are not interfered with by articulatory suppression. As judgements of this sort involve operations on phonological representations, the absence of interfering effects by suppression implies the existence of nonarticulatory phonological codes, available to written material. By contrast, phonological judgements requiring segmentation and deletion (e.g. rhyme and initial sound) are interfered with by suppression, suggesting the involvement of the rehearsal system (see reviews by Besner, 1987; Burani, Vallar & Bottini, 1991).

Visual and Spatial Short-Term Memory

The system devoted to immediate retention of visuospatial information has been explored less than its verbal counterpart. The precise nature of the coding of this short-term memory system and its putative fractionation into subcomponents are much less clear. By analogy with phonological short-term memory, the visuospatial system might comprise storage and rehearsal subcomponents. Furthermore, separate visual, spatial and visuospatial subsystems might exist. The data from normal subjects will not be reviewed in more detail because the patterns of neuropsychological impairment, the topic of this chapter, have been explored less than the deficits of phonological memory (see reviews by Baddeley, 1990; issue 4 of *European Journal of Cognitive Psychology*, 1989, and specifically the review by Logie, 1989).

Working Memory and Short-Term Memory

The various storage components and rehearsal processes may be conceived as *working memory spaces*, in which information is held temporarily prior to and during the application of procedures, strategies and analyses.

For example, planning and editing of the articulatory procedures needed for the smooth production of speech may be applied to the phonological segments stored in the output buffer (see Burani, Vallar & Bottini, 1991). The segmentation and deletion procedures required for some phonological judgements are applied to the material held in the output buffer (see Besner, 1987; Burani, Vallar & Bottini, 1991). In sentence comprehension, syntactic and lexical-semantic processes may be applied to material held in the phonological input STS (see Vallar, Basso & Bottini, 1990).

The contribution of the phonological STS to vocabulary acquisition in native and foreign languages (Baddeley, Papagno & Vallar, 1988; Gathercole & Baddeley, 1989) may also be seen in this perspective: new words are temporarily stored, to allow the building up of new phonological representations in the long-term memory. This again involves application of the appropriate procedures to the content of a specific storage system. In the case of visuospatial short-term memory, the mental manipulation of images may illustrate the use of this system as a working memory space (e.g. Baddeley & Lieberman, 1980; Hanley, Young & Pearson, 1991).

In the patients discussed in this chapter, impairment concerns the storage systems themselves, rather than the procedures and strategies which may be applied to stored information. An illustrative example of this is the performance of patient P.V. in recall tasks, which in normal subjects produce a recency effect —that is, a better recall of the final items of the list. P.V.'s defective recency is confined to lists of spoken words (e.g. Basso, Spinnler, Vallar & Zanobio, 1982). P.V. shows normal recency effects both with visual presentation (Vallar & Papagno, 1986) and in delayed-recall tasks (Vallar, Papagno & Baddeley, 1991). P.V. is also able to recall auditory and visual information in the order suggested by the examiner, from the beginning or from the end of the list (Vallar & Papagno, 1986). These data suggest that P.V.'s defective recency does not reflect impairment of the ordinal and temporally-based retrieval strategies, which underlie the normal advantage of the final items of a list (Baddeley & Hitch, 1993). These preserved procedures, however, cannot be applied to the content of a specific working memory space (the phonological STS), which is selectively damaged in the patient. This brings about a selective deficit of recency in immediate recall of spoken material.

NEUROANATOMICAL STUDIES

Phonological Short-Term Memory

Our knowledge of the neural correlates of phonological short-term memory comes from three main sources of evidence:

- Traditional anatomical–clinical correlations (Vallar, 1991) in brain-damaged patients with a selective deficit of this system
- Measurement of regional cerebral activity by PET in normal subjects engaged in short-term memory tasks
- Correlations between span performance and regional cerebral activity, as assessed by PET, in patients with Alzheimer's disease.

In most anatomical correlation studies, phonological short-term memory was assessed by auditory–verbal span.

Lesion localisation in patients with a selective deficit of auditory–verbal span, and a superior performance level with visual input, is summarised in Table 6.1.

Table 6.1 Lesion localisation in patients with defective auditory–verbal span

Patient	Aetiology	Source	Lesion site			
			Frontal	Temporal	Parietal	Occipital
K.F.	Head injury	Post-mortem		×	Inferior	×
J.B.	Meningioma	Surgery		Superior/ middle	Inferior	
W.H.	CVA?	Brain scan		×	Inferior	
L.S.	Head injury	Angiography			×	×
I.L.	CVA?	Brain scan?			Posterior	
M.C.	CVA	CT scan		Posterior/ superior	Inferior	
P.V.	CVA	CT scan	×	×	×	
E.A.	CVA	CT scan		Posterior	×	
R.A.N.	CVA	CT scan			×	
E.R.	CVA	CT scan		×	×	
R.R.	CVA	CT scan		×	×	
S.C.	CVA	CT scan		×	×	
J.O.	CVA?	Brain scan	×	×		

Sources: K.F.: Shallice & Warrington, 1980; J.B. and W.H.: Warrington, Logue & Pratt, 1971; L.S.: Strub & Gardner, 1974; I.L.: Saffran & Marin, 1975; M.C.: Caramazza, Basili, Koller & Berndt, 1981; P.V.: Basso, Spinnler, Vallar & Zanobio, 1982; E.A.: Friedrich, Glenn & Marin, 1984; R.A.N.,: McCarthy & Warrington, 1987; E.R.: Vallar, Basso & Bottini, 1990; R.R.: Bisiacchi, Cipolotti & Denes, 1989, S.C.: Trojano, Stanzione & Grossi, 1992; J.O.: Kinsbourne, 1972

It is apparent that, although patients differ in the aetiology of their cerebral disease and in the method of assessment of the lesion, the left parietal region is involved in most cases. More specifically, the lesion data implicate the supramarginal gyrus of the inferior parietal lobule as the crucial region for the function of the phonological STS (Warrington, 1979). It is worth noting that in patient J.O. (Kinsbourne, 1972), whose defective span performance may be at least in part traced back to output deficits (see Shallice & Warrington, 1977), the lesion is mainly frontal. This anterior damage is also suggested by the neurological examination, which revealed a right hemiparesis, without any sensory deficit. This major frontal involvement, which differs from the predominantly parietal damage found in most patients, may represent the anatomical correlate of J.O.'s output difficulties. These data from individual patients are in line with the results of a group study by Risse, Rubens & Jordan (1984). In a series of 20 left-brain-damaged patients with anterior-basal ganglia, or postrolandic damage, defective auditory–verbal span was associated with lesions clustering in the inferior parietal lobule. A PET study in normal subjects has recently investigated the anatomical localisation of the phonological STS, and the rehearsal process (Paulesu, Frith & Frackowiak, 1993). A comparison of the patterns of regional cerebral blood flow during a task engaging both components (immediate memory for letter sequences) and during a task which involves only the rehearsal process (rhyme judgement for letters: see Burani, Vallar & Bottini, 1991) suggests a localisation of the phonological STS in the left supramarginal gyrus (area 40), and of the rehearsal process in premotor frontal area 44 (Broca's area). This anatomical localisation of the rehearsal process is compatible with the view that the recirculation and refreshment of the memory trace held in the phonological STS makes use of systems, such as the phonological output buffer, primarily involved in the programming of speech output, rather than requiring actual articulation (Shallice & Vallar, 1990; Burani, Vallar & Bottini, 1991).

A recent PET study in a series of 18 patients with Alzheimer's disease of recent onset provides converging evidence, showing a significant correlation of auditory digit span with metabolic activity in the left associative and basal frontal, parietal and superior temporal cortices (Perani et al., 1993).

To summarise, two discrete regions in the left hemisphere are the anatomical correlates of the phonological STS, and of the rehearsal process: the inferior parietal lobule (supramarginal gyrus), and premotor area 44.

Visual and Spatial Short–Term Memory

In the 1960s, Kimura (1963) and Warrington and James (1967) investigated the neural correlates of the impairment of number estimation. A variable number of scattered dots was tachistoscopically presented in each trial, and patients reported how many dots they had seen. This span-of-apprehension task may involve some form of immediate visuospatial memory, in addition to perceptual processing. Both studies showed a more severe impairment after right- than after left-brain damage. While Kimura's series was confined to patients who had undergone a unilateral temporal lobe excision, Warrington and James' patients in addition had lesions involving other cerebral lobes. Patients with right parietal damage showed the more severe deficit, in both the ipsilateral and the contralateral half-field. Right-brain-damaged patients, however, were more impaired also in the detection of single dots, suggesting a contribution from defective perceptual processing to the deficit of number estimation.

In more recent studies in groups of brain-damaged patients with unilateral lesions, short-term memory for visuospatial locations has been investigated by a nonverbal analogue of auditory–verbal span. In this test, devised by Corsi (see Milner, 1971), subjects are required to reproduce, immediately after presentation, sequences of increasing length of blocks tapped by the examiner. The association between defective visuospatial span and visual half-field deficits suggests that the posterior (parieto-occipital) regions of both the left and the right hemisphere disrupt visuospatial short-term memory. The role of right-brain damage, however, seems to be much more relevant (De Renzi & Nichelli, 1975; De Renzi, Faglioni & Previdi, 1977). This hemispheric asymmetry is further confirmed by reports of individual patients with selective deficits of visuospatial span. In two patients reported by De Renzi and Nichelli (1975), the only neurological deficit was a left hemianopia. One such patient had undergone a right occipital lobectomy and coagulation of the right amygdala and right fornix. In patient E.L.D. (Hanley, Pearson & Young, 1990), the rupture of a right middle cerebral artery aneurysm produced a haematoma in the Sylvian Fissure, and an extensive area of infarction in the right frontotemporal region.

Two more recent PET studies have investigated the anatomical correlates of visuospatial short-term memory. Perani et al. (1993) have found, in patients with Alzheimer's disease, significant correlations between visuospatial span performance and metabolic activity in the right frontal and parietal associative areas. Jonides et al. (1993) compared, in normal humans, the patterns of regional cerebral blood flow in a perceptual task (to decide whether or not a probe encircles a dot) and in a memory task (to decide whether or not a probe encircles the position of a previously presented dot, with a retention interval of 3 seconds). The memory task was associated with right hemisphere activation in the occipital visual association cortex (Brodmann's area 19), in the posterior inferior parietal lobule (area 40), and in the prefrontal cortex (area 47). It is suggested that these areas provide different contributions to the retention of visuospatial information: the occipital regions would be involved in image generation, the parietal cortex in computing the coordinates of the stimulus, the prefrontal cortex mainly in the retention process proper.

Kinsbourne and Warrington (1962) described four patients with brain lesions who were able to identify single meaningful forms visually (letters, numbers, geometric figures). If two stimuli were presented, however, one was frequently misidentified (deficit of simultaneous form perception). The deficit was present with both horizontal and vertical pairs of stimuli, ruling out an interpretation in terms of hemineglect. Number estimation (see above: Warrington & James, 1967) was preserved. The deterioration of identification performance when more than a single stimulus was presented may reflect a limitation of the capacity of a visual STS (see McCarthy & Warrington, 1990, pp. 280–285). All four patients had lesions in the left hemisphere, involving the posterior regions. In one patient, a post-mortem showed left occipital and (small) superior temporal lesions (Kinsbourne & Warrington, 1963).

Finally, lesions in the parieto-occipital regions of the left hemisphere impair the immediate reproduction of sequences of visual verbal and nonverbal (straight or curved lines) stimuli (Warrington & Rabin, 1971).

To summarise, the anatomical correlates of the impairment of visual and spatial short-term memory suggest a distinction between two main components. A *visuospatial system* in the posterior–inferior parietal and frontal association regions of the right hemisphere ((visuo)-spatial STS; the visuospatial "sketchpad" of Baddeley, 1990) may play a major role in the retention of location information (a "where" system: see Wilson, O'Scalaidhe & Goldman-Rakic, 1993). The frontal component may code location in terms of programming of movements towards relevant targets. A *visual system* (visual STS; see Figure 6.1) in the posterior regions of the left hemisphere (association parietal and occipital cortex) may retain verbal and nonverbal patterns.

CLINICAL PRESENTATIONS OF IMPAIRMENT

Deficits of Phonological Memory

Patients with defective phonological memory have lesions in the posterior regions of the left hemisphere. They may then show, in addition to the specific disorder of immediate retention, neurological deficits and dysphasia, which are a major problem for everyday life.

A few patients have been reported, however, who suffered from a selective impairment of auditory–verbal span, without any major associated disorders. The main disability reported by one such patient, J.B. (Warrington, Logue & Pratt, 1971, p. 379), was "an impaired memory for spoken names or telephone numbers even if she attempted to write them down immediately". P.V.'s main subjective report was the inability to "understand" (this was the term she used) even short sequences of digits (prices of goods, telephone numbers) spoken to her. The difficulty was considerably less, however, when she read similar sequences. P.V. also complained about her inability to perform mental arithmetic. For instance, when shopping she had problems in checking that she was paying the right amount of money, due to a difficulty in computing change. P.V. also mentioned a difficulty in the acquisition of a foreign language: after the onset of her disease she attempted to study French, but gave up because it was too difficult (Basso, Spinnler, Vallar & Zanobio, 1982; Papagno & Vallar, in press).

In patients of this sort the auditory–verbal short-term memory deficit is highly selective and spares episodic memory, visuospatial processes, and general intelligence. These patients may therefore live on their own, without any specific assistance. J.B. was able to resume her job. P.V. set up as a dealer in pottery painted by herself and took care of her two sons.

Deficits of Visual and Spatial Memory

The clinical disabilities specifically related to impairment of visuospatial short-term memory systems are less clear. The two patients of De Renzi and Nichelli (1975), with a selective deficit of visuospatial span on the block tapping test, were identified retrospectively, on examination of the protocols of a series of brain-damaged patients with a poor performance on spatial span. De Renzi and Nichelli did not mention any specific complaint by these patients, related to the deficit of span, and neither of them suffered topographical disorientation or impairment in learning new visuospatial information, such as the path of a visual maze.

Patient E.L.D. (Hanley, Pearson & Young, 1990; Hanley, Young & Pearson, 1991), who had defective span on the block tapping test and for unfamiliar faces, reported an inability to recognise the faces of people she had met since the time of her illness, and problems in finding her way home. E.L.D.'s visual and spatial memory problems occurred only with information with which she was unfamiliar before her illness. In the light of De Renzi and Nichelli's (1975) observation, it is unclear whether E.L.D's complaints were specifically related to the impairment of visuospatial short-term memory systems, or reflected a more general impairment of nonverbal memory. E.L.D.'s memory deficit, for instance, extended to unfamiliar voices (Hanley, Pearson & Young, 1990).

Selective Deficits of Phonological Short-Term Memory

The association between defective auditory–verbal span, left hemisphere damage and dysphasia has long been known (e.g. Zangwill, 1946). Selective patterns of impairment were reported only in the late 1960s, however. Luria, Sokolov and Klimkowski (1967) described two patients (B and K), who had both suffered a traumatic injury in the left temporal lobe. B and K showed defective repetition of auditory sequences of verbal stimuli (phonemes, words, digits), but their performance level was higher with visual presentation. Luria et al. explained this deficit in terms of modality-specific disturbances of auditory–verbal memory traces. Warrington and Shallice (1969) reported a selective deficit of auditory–verbal span in patient K.F., and suggested an impairment of auditory–verbal short-term memory. A number of similar patients were subsequently reported. Their patterns of impairment shared these main features (see also Shallice & Vallar, 1990):

- A selective deficit of span, impairing immediate serial recall of all strings of unconnected auditory–verbal material (digits, letters, words).
- A higher level of performance with visual presentation than with auditory input.
- The deficit arising neither from defective speech perception nor from impaired speech production.

Table 6.2 shows the results of a meta-analysis of the immediate memory span performance of 22 patients. When input is auditory, performance level is defective for all stimulus materials. In the series of 1355 Italian normal adult subjects of Orsini et al. (1987), the cut-off score for auditory digit span (adjusted for age and educational level) was 3.75, and no patient included in Table 6.2 had a span above 3.6. In the 13 patients in whom digit, letter and word spans were assessed, digit span was higher. This advantage of digits may reflect the reduced number of alternatives in the memory set (9 digits), as compared with both letters and words.

A further aspect illustrated by Table 6.2 is the superior span performance when the material is presented visually. Normal subjects, by contrast, have a better performance level with auditory input (e.g. Levy, 1971). This dissociation indicates that the defective system is not a supra-modal store (see Waugh &

Table 6.2 Average verbal span (range in brackets) in 22 patients with defective phonological short-term memory, by input modality and stimulus material*

Auditory span			Visual digit span
Digits (N=22)	Letters (N=13)	Words (n=16)	(N=19)
2.30 (1–3.6)	1.85 (1–2.5)	2.03 (1.05–2.5)	3.16 (2–6)

* The measure of span is the summed probabilities for all lengths of lists, where possible. For patients for whom precise information is unavailable, approximations have been used
Auditory versus visual digit span: Paired *t*-test ($t=4.64$; $d.f.=17$; $p=0.0002$)
Auditory span: One-factor analysis of variance: $d.f.=2, 24$; $F=15.28$; $p<0.001$
Scheffé F-test: Digit versus letter, and digit versus word span, $p<0.05$
Sources: K.F.: Warrington & Shallice, 1969; J.B. and W.H.: Warrington, Logue & Pratt, 1971; J.T. and J.O.: Kinsbourne, 1972; CA1, CA2 and CA3: Tzortis & Albert, 1974; L.S.: Strub & Gardner, 1974; I.L.: Saffran & Marin, 1975; M.C.: Caramazza, Basili, Koller & Berndt, 1981; P.V.: Basso, Spinnler, Vallar & Zanobio, 1982; E.A.: Friedrich, Glenn & Marin, 1984; R.A.N. and N.H.A: McCarthy & Warrington, 1987; T.B.: Baddeley & Wilson, 1988; R.R.: Bisiacchi, Cipolotti & Denes, 1989; T.I. and C.N.: Saffran & Martin, 1990; E.D.E.: Berndt & Mitchum, 1990; E.R.: Vallar, Basso & Bottini, 1990; S.C.: Trojano, Stanzione & Grossi, 1992

Norman, 1965; Atkinson & Schiffrin, 1971), suggesting instead the existence of discrete auditory (phonological) and visual STSs as in Figure 6.1. The former system is selectively damaged in these patients, thus accounting for the auditory–visual dissociation in span. Coding in the visual STS may be in terms of shape. Warrington and Shallice (1972) showed in patient K.F. a high incidence of visual errors in visual span (i.e. confusions between visually similar letters, such as O and Q, or P and R). Unlike K.F., normal subjects show acoustic confusions also in visual span; this indicates phonological recoding and storage in the phonological STS (see Figure 6.1).

This deficit of auditory–verbal span cannot be attributed to impaired phonological analysis. In a number of patients, immediate repetition of single stimuli was over 90% correct or errorless (K.F., J.B., W.H.: Warrington, Logue & Pratt, 1971; I.L.: Saffran & Marin, 1975; M.C.: Caramazza, Basili, Koller & Berndt, 1981; P.V.: Basso et al., 1982; R.R.: Bisiacchi, Cipolotti & Denes, 1989). Furthermore, a few such patients also showed normal performance in tasks requiring phonological analysis and posing minimal demands on immediate retention, such as discrimination between consonant–vowel pairs differing in single distinctive features (P.V.: Vallar & Baddeley, 1984a; T.B.: Baddeley, Vallar & Wilson, 1987; Baddeley and Wilson, 1988; E.D.E.: Berndt & Mitchum, 1990), or phonemic categorisation (R.R.: Bisiacchi, Cipolotti & Denes, 1989). In patients of this sort, the immediate retention deficit is *primary*; that is, it is not produced by processing disorders, but reflects the reduced capacity of the phonological STS (see Figure 6.1).

In other patients with defective auditory–verbal span, phonological analysis is also impaired (E.R.: Vallar, Basso & Bottini, 1990; E.A.: Friedrich, Glenn & Marin, 1984; S.C.: Trojano, Stanzione & Grossi, 1992). In such patients, the memory disorder may be *secondary*, wholly or in part, to the processing deficit. The pattern of immediate memory impairment in these cases is similar to that of patients with a primary disorder, and it may be difficult to tease apart the relative contributions of the processing and storage deficits (see a discussion in Vallar, Basso & Bottini, 1990).

The distinction between storage and processing components outlined in Figure 6.1 is further supported by the observation that *mild* deficits of phonological processing may not impair auditory digit span (case M.P.: Martin & Breedin, 1992). Martin and Breedin account for this dissociation, which contrasts with the case of secondary deficits of auditory span, by suggesting that it reflects a contribution to immediate retention from unimpaired lexical phonological representations. This interpretation predicts that such patients will show some impairment of immediate retention of stimuli such as nonwords, that are not represented in the lexicon (see related data in Bisiacchi, Cipolotti & Denes, 1989).

The patients' defective auditory–verbal span does not result from speech production problems, since it does not improve when a non-speech response is required, such as pointing to the items to be recalled in a multiple choice display (e.g. K.F.: Warrington & Shallice, 1969; P.V.: Basso et al., 1982). Similarly, the patients' performance remains defective when immediate memory is assessed by matching (e.g. K.F., J.B., W.H.: Warrington et al., 1971; E.D.E.: Berndt & Mitchum, 1990) or probing techniques (K.F.: Shallice & Warrington, 1970). In line with the individual case studies, the 24 left-brain-damaged patients investigated by Vallar, Corno & Basso (1992) did not improve their span performance when response was by pointing among alternatives, as compared with oral repetition. The use of these methods, which do not involve any oral response, has revealed in a few patients a definite improvement in immediate memory performance (e.g. Kinsbourne, 1972; Romani, 1992). In these cases the deficit in repetition span is not due to a reduced capacity of the phonological STS, but reflects, at least in part, the impairment of processes involved in the production of speech.

The conclusion that the selective impairment of auditory–verbal span cannot be explained in terms of dysfunction of systems participating in speech production, such as the phonological output buffer (e.g. Ellis, 1979), is further supported by the observation that in such patients oral speech may be entirely spared. A quantitative analysis of pauses, rate of speech, and errors in spontaneous speech did not show any abnormality in case J.B. (Shallice & Butterworth, 1977). P.V. had a normal articulation rate (Vallar & Baddeley, 1984b). Other patients (I.L.: Saffran & Marin, 1975; T.B.: Baddeley, Vallar & Wilson, 1987; Baddeley & Wilson, 1988) had normal spontaneous speech on a clinical assessment.

The existence of an auditory–visual dissociation in most patients with defective auditory–verbal span (see Table 6.2) is readily compatible with the hypothesis that the deficit involves an input system, such as the phonological STS. In a few patients (T.B.: Baddeley, Vallar & Wilson, 1987; Baddeley & Wilson, 1988;

T.I.: Saffran & Martin, 1990) span performances were similar, with visual and auditory presentation. In the case of T.B., this may be explained by an associated impairment of the visual STS. This interpretation is also anatomically plausible: the neural correlates of the two storage systems putatively impaired in T.B. (phonological and visual STSs) are contiguous, including the posterior regions of the left hemisphere, and may then be disrupted jointly by brain damage. T.I. had a mild impairment of auditory digit span (3.5) and his visual digit span (about 3 items) was comparable to the putative capacity of the visual STS, as computed by Zhang and Simon (1985).

Interpretation of the deficit of auditory–verbal span in terms of a defective phonological STS is supported by the finding that these patients are also impaired in two other tasks, which reflect the operation of this system. First, when engaged in the verbal interfering activity of counting backwards (Peterson & Peterson, 1959) these patients show an abnormally steep rate of forgetting of auditorily presented verbal stimuli, such as a single letter; by contrast, forgetting rate is minor with visual presentation (e.g. K.F., J.B., W.H.: Warrington, Logue & Pratt, 1971; P.V.: Basso et al., 1982; R.A.N., N.H.A.: McCarthy & Warrington, 1987). A discussion of the use of the Peterson task in patients with defective auditory–verbal span may be found in Shallice and Vallar (1990).

Second, in immediate free recall of a list of auditorily presented words the final positions show an advantage, the recency effect. Patients with reduced auditory–verbal span show a reduced or absent recency effect (e.g. K.F., J.B., W.H.: Warrington, Logue & Pratt, 1971; P.V.: Basso et al., 1982; Vallar & Papagno, 1986; S.C.: Trojano, Stanzione & Grossi, 1992). P.V.'s recency remained defective, even when she was specifically instructed to recall the final items first (Vallar & Papagno, 1986). The recency effect in immediate recall may, however, be normal when presentation is visual (P.V.: Vallar & Papagno, 1986). Long-term recency effects may also be normal: in the delayed recall of a list of solutions of anagrams, P.V., as normal controls, showed a better performance for the final items (Vallar, Papagno & Baddeley, 1991). Taken together, these findings support the view that recency effects reflect the application of temporally-based retrieval strategies to specific components of memory, which implicates, in the case of immediate recall of auditory–verbal stimuli, the content of the phonological STS. The deficit of this system, therefore, selectively disrupts recency in immediate recall of auditory–verbal material. For a general discussion of recency phenomena, see Baddeley and Hitch (1993).

The effects of *phonological similarity, word length* and *articulatory suppression* on immediate serial recall have been investigated in a limited number of patients with defective auditory–verbal span. As shown in Table 6.3, most patients showed the effect of phonological similarity with auditory input. Unlike with normal subjects, however, the effect was absent with visual presentation. The effect of word length was absent with both auditory and visual presentation. These observations in individual patients are in line with the results of Vallar, Corno and Basso (1992), who in 24 aphasic patients found the effect of phonological similarity with auditory, but not with visual, presentation.

Table 6.3 Phonological similarity and word-length effects in brain-damaged patients, and a developmental case (R.E.) with defective auditory–verbal span, by input modality (auditory and visual); n.a.: not assessed

Patient	Phonological similarity effect		Word length effect	
	Auditory	Visual	Auditory	Visual
K.F.	+	–	n.a.	n.a.
P.V.	+	–	–	n.a.
R.E.	+	–	–	–
T.B.	–	–	–	n.a.
E.A.	+	–	–	n.a.
R.R.	+	–	–	–
E.R.	+	–	–	–
E.D.E.	+	–	–	n.a.

Sources: K.F.: Warrington & Shallice, 1972; P.V.: Vallar & Baddeley, 1984b; R.E.: Campbell & Butterworth, 1985; T.B.: Baddeley & Wilson, 1988; E.A.: Martin, 1987; R.R.: Bisiacchi, Cipolotti & Denes, 1989; E.R.: Vallar, Basso & Bottini, 1990; E.D.E.: Berndt & Mitchum, 1990

This pattern is similar to that found in normal subjects during articulatory suppression, which disrupts the operation of the rehearsal process. An impairment of the rehearsal system might then be the core disorder underlying the deficit of auditory–verbal span. This interpretation would account for the persistence of the phonological similarity effect with auditory input, since auditory stimuli would have a direct access to an unimpaired phonological STS. By contrast, the phonological similarity effect with visual input and the effect of word length with both input modalities would be abolished by the rehearsal deficit, since they require the integrity of this system (see Figure 6.1). However, if rehearsal, as discussed above, makes use of a phonological output buffer involved in speech production, then this hypothesis can account neither for the normal speech of some patients with reduced auditory–verbal span, nor for the auditory–visual dissociation in span. The latter finding specifically suggests the impairment of an input, modality-specific system. Alternatively, rehearsal may be an independent process, specifically supporting the phonological STS, but not involved in speech production. (See a discussion of these two hypotheses in Shallice & Vallar, 1990; Burani, Vallar & Bottini, 1991.) This interpretation also runs into difficulties, however. In normal subjects, suppression has significant but minor detrimental effects: in the study of Baddeley and Lewis (1984) auditory span dropped from 7.96 to 5.79 digits during concurrent articulation. By contrast, the average span of patients with defective phonological short-term memory is 2.3 (see Table 6.2). Furthermore, patients with defective auditory–verbal span also show a reduced or absent auditory recency effect in immediate free recall, despite the fact that recency involves only a minor contribution from rehearsal (Vallar & Papagno, 1986). Finally, patient P.V. showed a normal performance on rhyme and stress assignment tasks (Vallar & Baddeley, 1984a), which involve the activity of the rehearsal process (Burani, Vallar & Bottini, 1991). A selective deficit of rehearsal is therefore unable to explain the patients' pathologically low auditory–verbal span.

Vallar and Baddeley (1984a,b), who took the view that rehearsal of information held in the phonological STS makes use of phonological processes involved in speech production, suggested that P.V.'s failure to rehearse was a *strategy choice*. They reasoned that it is likely to be of little use to convey written material to a damaged phonological STS, and to rehearse traces stored in this system. This hypothesis predicts that articulatory suppression, which has detrimental effects on the recall performance of normal subjects, should not impair immediate memory for written material in patients with a defective auditory–verbal span. Such patients would not make use of the phonological STS, but instead would store visuo-verbal information in a nonphonological system, such as the visual STS (see, e.g., K.F.: Warrington & Shallice, 1972). The absence of detectable effects of suppression on visual span of patients P.V. (Vallar & Baddeley, 1984b) and R.R. (Bisiacchi, Cipolotti & Denes, 1989) confirms this prediction. The unimpaired rehearsal system, however, can be used in order to produce normal speech output (e.g. J.B.: Shallice & Butterworth, 1977; P.V.: Vallar & Baddeley, 1984b).

The precise articulatory nature of the rehearsal process has been elucidated by the investigation of anarthric patients, who are unable to articulate any detectable speech sound. A number of such cases have been reported, made anarthric by brainstem (G.F.: Vallar & Cappa, 1987; C.M.: Cubelli & Nichelli, 1992) and cortical (E.C.: Nebes, 1975; M.D.C.: Vallar & Cappa, 1987; F.C.: Cubelli & Nichelli, 1992) focal lesions, and by diffuse brain damage, such as closed head injury (G.B.: Baddeley & Wilson, 1985). All these patients have an auditory–verbal span within the normal range, even though response production may be very slow and effortful, due to the motor deficit, which may be extremely severe. In patient E.C., Nebes (1975) found a normal effect of phonological similarity with written presentation. Similarly, in case G.B. and in the patients with brainstem lesions (G.F. and C.M.), the effect of phonological similarity was present with both visual and auditory input. The effect of word length was found in patient G.B. with auditory input, but not in patients G.F. and C.M. (see data and discussion in Vallar and Cappa, 1987; Cubelli & Nichelli, 1992). Bishop and Robson (1989), using visual stimuli (line drawings), found that congenitally anarthric children have preserved memory span and show the normal effects of phonological similarity and word length. Taken together, these findings show that rehearsal does not necessarily require the peripheral (muscular) implementation of the articulatory code (Baddeley & Wilson, 1985; Vallar & Cappa, 1987), but occurs at the more central level of premotor planning of speech output (the phonological output buffer).

In line with this conclusion, and with Vallar and Baddeley's interpretation of P.V.'s deficit, Paulesu, Frith and Frackowiak's (1992) localisation by PET of the rehearsal process is in a premotor area (Broca's area 44), which participates in the programming of speech output, and not in the motor cortex. This localisation of rehearsal by PET corroborates the view that the affected component in patients with a selective impairment of auditory–verbal span is the phonological STS. In such patients (see Table 6.1) the left hemisphere lesions tend to cluster in the inferior–posterior parietal areas, sparing the frontal cortex.

Cortical lesions involving the frontal (pre-rolandic) regions, which produce anarthria, may however selectively impair the phonological recoding process, sparing the phonological STS-rehearsal process. Two patients have been described (M.D.C.: Vallar & Cappa, 1987; F.C.: Cubelli & Nichelli, 1992) who have a normal auditory–verbal span and similarity and word length effects, with auditory presentation. Such effects are, however, absent with visual input. This modality-dependent dissociation suggests that visual material cannot enter an unimpaired rehearsal process. This access failure may be due to a dysfunction of the phonological recoding process, as suggested by M.D.C.'s impairment in phonological judgements on written material (Vallar & Cappa, 1987).

The defective immediate retention of auditory–verbal material cannot be attributed to the impairment of memory systems different from phonological short-term memory. A number of such patients have preserved long-term episodic memory for verbal material (K.F., J.B., W.H.: Shallice & Warrington, 1970; Warrington, Logue & Pratt, 1971; P.V.: Basso et al., 1982; Vallar & Papagno, 1986; R.R.: Bisiacchi, Cipolotti & Denes, 1992) and visuospatial material (P.V.: Basso et al., 1982). Short-term memory may also be spared for auditory nonverbal (J.B.: Shallice & Warrington, 1974) and visuospatial material (P.V.: Basso et al., 1982; S.C.: Trojano, Stanzione & Grossi, 1992).

Finally, patients with severe deficits of general intelligence (Vallar & Papagno, 1993) or episodic long-term memory (e.g. Baddeley & Warrington, 1970) may have a preserved auditory–verbal span. These components of the cognitive system, therefore, do not provide a crucial contribution to immediate retention. A review of the role of the lexical–semantic system in immediate memory performance may be found in Saffran (1990).

Selective Deficits of Visuospatial Short-Term Memory

As discussed in the anatomical section of this chapter, lesions in the right parieto-occipital regions disproportionately impair number estimation of visual dots (Warrington & James, 1967) and span for sequences of visuospatial positions (De Renzi & Nichelli, 1975; De Renzi, Faglioni & Previdi, 1977).

De Renzi and Nichelli (1975) reported two patients with right posterior lesions and a selective deficit of spatial span: both auditory digit span and spatial learning, assessed by a visual stepping stone maze, were preserved. This pattern of impairment is the visuospatial counterpart of the auditory–verbal short-term memory disorder discussed in the previous section. The observation that, both in the verbal and in the non-verbal domain, deficits of short-term retention do not need to interfere with long-term learning suggests a parallel organisation of short- and long-term memory systems.

De Renzi and Nichelli's original findings have been confirmed recently by Hanley, Young and Pearson (1991). Right-brain-damaged patient E.L.D. had a defective visuospatial span on Corsi's block tapping test and on an immediate memory task for unfamiliar faces. She was also impaired in a task which requires the recall of sentences of increasing length, describing the relative spatial location of numbers in a 4×4 matrix (see Baddeley & Lieberman, 1980; Brooks, 1967). By contrast, her auditory–verbal span was normal and she showed the effect of phonological similarity with both visual and auditory presentation. Furthermore, her visuoverbal span when articulation was suppressed was comparable to control performance. In this condition, written material may have been stored in a visual STS which differs from the visuospatial system impaired in the patient. Another possibility is that she relied on the temporary activation of lexical representations (see also Zhang & Simon, 1985). E.L.D. was also impaired in the use of imagery mnemonics and on mental rotation tasks. This suggests that the spatial manipulation of mental images may require temporary retention in a visuospatial storage system. E.L.D.'s performance was, however, normal in tasks involving the retrieval of visual information from long-term memory (e.g. stating the characteristic colour of an object, or making a size comparison), but not spatial manipulation. Finally, E.L.D.'s visual recognition memory for unfamiliar faces and objects was defective; her deficit, however, was not confined to visual nonverbal memory, since her recognition of unfamiliar voices was also impaired (Hanley, Pearson & Young, 1990).

Farah, Hammond, Levine and Calvanio (1988) described a patient with a pattern of impairment, which in some respects was opposite to that found in E.L.D. by Hanley et al. (1990). Patient L.H. was defective on tasks assessing visual imagery, but not involving spatial manipulation, whereas his performance was normal in spatial imagery tasks (form and letter rotation, matrix memory). The bilateral lesion of L.H. involved the temporo-occipital regions and the right inferior frontal areas, sparing the parietal lobes, which, as discussed above, play a relevant role in the retention of spatial (location) information.

The distinction between visual and visuospatial storage systems is supported by the observation of Warrington and Rabin (1971) that left-brain-damaged patients were impaired in span for sequences of line stimuli (straight or curved), with a more severe deficit in the group with posterior lesions; right-brain-damaged patients had a performance level comparable to the control group. Lesions in the right hemisphere, by contrast, disrupt span for sequences of visuospatial locations, as assessed by the block tapping test (De Renzi & Nichelli, 1975; De Renzi, Faglioni & Previdi, 1977; Hanley, Young & Pearson, 1991).

As in many other areas of cognitive neuroscience and neurology (Vallar, 1994), nonverbal short-term memory systems are found to fractionate into additional subcomponents, and selective patterns of impairment. Davidoff and Ostergaard (1984) have suggested the existence of a visual STS specific for colours, which is involved in the activation of a colour lexicon, for instance in colour-naming. The main deficit of Davidoff and Ostergaard's patient P.L., who had a left temporo-occipital lesion, was colour anomia, associated with preserved pointing to named colours. P.L.'s immediate recognition memory for colours was defective, whereas his performance was within the normal range in the case of meaningless shapes. Finally, the existence of selective deficits of tactile (spatial-kinesthetic?) memory has been suggested (Ross, 1980).

Deficits of Phonological and Visuospatial Short-Term Memory in Dementia

Patients suffering from dementia of the Alzheimer-type, considered as a group, show a mild-to-moderate reduction of auditory digit span and a somewhat more severe impairment of visuospatial span, as assessed by Corsi's blocks. The recency effect in immediate free recall of verbal material is normal or mildly defective, while performance in the Peterson task is more severely impaired (Cantone, Orsini, Grossi & De Michele, 1978; see reviews by Morris & Baddeley, 1988; Spinnler, Della Sala, Bandera & Baddeley, 1988). This moderate impairment of immediate retention may be contrasted with the severe deficit in long-term memory, which is the hallmark of Alzheimer's disease. There is, however, a considerable amount of variability across patients (see, e.g., Becker, 1988; Baddeley, Della Sala & Spinnler, 1991).

In Alzheimer's disease the deficit of span tends to be minor, as compared with the severe reduction found in the patients with focal hemispheric lesions, discussed earlier. For instance, Martin, Brouwers, Cox and Fedio (1985) found an average span of 5.9 digits in their 14 patients with 3.8 years of reported duration of symptoms. In Spinnler et al.'s (1988) 29 patients, auditory span for bi-syllabic words was 3.35, Corsi's visuospatial span 3.66. In another series of 18 patients with probable Alzheimer's disease of recent onset (mean length of illness 16 months), auditory digit span was 4.9 and Corsi's spatial span 3.7 (Perani et al., 1993). With reference to cut-off scores, in this series two patients (11%) had a defective digit span, five (28%) an impaired spatial span; long-term episodic memory, by contrast, was impaired in all 18 cases. In patients with dementia of the Alzheimer-type, Morris (1984) found normal effects of phonological similarity, word length and articulatory suppression. This indicates a qualitatively preserved function of both the phonological STS and the rehearsal process. Rate of articulation, however, was slower in patients with Alzheimer's disease, as compared with control subjects (Morris, 1986, 1987), suggesting a reduced efficiency of the rehearsal process.

The mild deficit of span in patients suffering from dementia of the Alzheimer-type has been interpreted in terms of impairment of an attentional control system supporting phonological and visuospatial short-term memory, such as the "central executive" (Morris & Baddeley, 1988). One possible role of this system is to coordinate and schedule concurrent tasks. In patients with dementia of the Alzheimer-type, the deficit of this component may therefore account for the severe impairment in the Peterson task (Morris, 1986) and in other dual-task conditions (Baddeley et al., 1986; Baddeley et al., 1991), and the relatively preserved recency effect in immediate free recall of auditory material, which involves a minimal contribution from control processes (Baddeley & Hitch, 1977; Hitch, 1980; Vallar & Papagno, 1986).

The moderately defective span of patients with dementia of the Alzheimer-type could be produced by the disordered function of short-term storage systems, in addition to the impairment of more central processes. In the patients of Perani et al. (1993), auditory–verbal span performance was significantly correlated with metabolic values in the left superior temporal, parietal, basal and associative frontal regions, and visuospatial span was correlated with values in the right parietal and frontal associative regions. These cerebral areas include both the left posterior–inferior parietal region (which is the well-known anatomical correlate of the phonological STS) and the posterior regions of the right hemisphere, which are involved in the immediate retention of visuospatial information. The frontal involvement, by contrast, may reflect the contribution to the span deficit of the impairments of both rehearsal and control processes.

Finally, the relatively minor span disorder in demented patients, as compared with the severity of the selective impairments described in the previous sections, may be related to differences in the aetiology, pathology and course of the underlying diseases. In dementia this involves a progressive neuronal dysfunction and loss, whereas in patients with selective and severe deficits of span it reflects the more or less complete destruction of specifically committed brain regions, produced by cerebrovascular, neoplastic or traumatic lesions (see Shallice & Vallar, 1990).

ASSOCIATED DEFICITS: THE USES OF SHORT-TERM MEMORY

Phonological Short-Term Memory and Sentence Comprehension

Patients with a selective disorder of auditory–verbal span show an associated deficit of sentence comprehension. This cannot be attributed to the defective processing of individual words, which is typically spared (see, e.g., Warrington, Logue & Pratt, 1971; Saffran & Marin, 1975; Shallice, 1979). The hypothesis of a role of the phonological STS in sentence comprehension is by and large in line with the view that the system has an "input locus", and is not involved in output processes such as the programming of oral speech. Most patients show defective sentence comprehension in tasks in which word order is crucial. For instance, they are impaired in the Token Test (De Renzi & Faglioni, 1978), which includes items such as "Touch the small green square and the large black circle", and may fail to understand semantically reversible sentences (e.g. "The cat that the dog chased was white"). By contrast, when lexical information constrains sentence interpretation, patients' performance is preserved (see reviews by Caplan & Waters, 1990; Saffran, 1990; Vallar, Basso & Bottini, 1990).

A possible interpretation of this pattern of impairment is that phonological memory is the working space of syntactic parsing processes (Clark & Clark, 1977; Caramazza & Berndt, 1985). A pathological reduction of the capacity of this system, produced by brain damage, would interfere with the patients' ability to process syntactic information. Sentence comprehension would then be defective when the linear arrangement of words provides crucial information, and lexical–semantic analyses do not constrain meaning, such as in the examples mentioned above. These patients, however, may be successful in deciding whether or not long sentences, exceeding their defective auditory–verbal span, are grammatically correct (P.V.: Vallar & Baddeley, 1987; T.I.: Saffran & Martin, 1990; J.B.: Butterworth, Shallice & Watson, 1990). This makes unlikely the hypothesis that phonological memory is an intrinsic part of syntactic processing systems.

According to a number of alternative suggestions, phonological memory may be conceived as an independent system, providing temporary storage of phonological information, which may, under specific circumstances, contribute to sentence comprehension. Proposed functions include the following:

- A backup store which allows repeated attempts to understand "complex" sentences (Saffran & Marin, 1975; Shallice, 1979).
- A "mnemonic window", which preserves word order by a verbatim phonological record, and hence allows the interpretation of sentences where order is crucial (Vallar & Baddeley, 1984a; Baddeley & Wilson, 1988).
- A system which, in a post-interpretative stage, adjudicates between conflicting interpretations of a given sentence (Caplan & Waters, 1990).
- A system which may allow the appropriate mapping of syntactic descriptions of sentences onto their representations, based on lexical–semantic processes, when this is not specified by lexical–semantic information (Vallar, Basso & Bottini, 1990; see also Saffran & Martin, 1990; Saffran, 1990).

While these views attempt to elucidate the contribution of phonological memory to sentence comprehension, its precise role remains controversial and a matter of debate.

The hypothesis that phonological memory is involved in sentence comprehension has been supported by a follow-up study in patient T.B. (Baddeley, Vallar & Wilson, 1987; Baddeley & Wilson, 1988), which shows a correlation between memory span and sentence comprehension. Several years after initial testing, which had shown defective auditory–verbal span and sentence comprehension, T.B.'s digit span recovered from 1 to 9 digits and his performance on a series of sentence comprehension tasks became normal. By contrast, his performance in two tasks requiring phonological judgements remained defective, making unlikely an interpretation in terms of general and nonspecific recovery (Wilson & Baddeley, 1993).

The Role of Short-Term Memory in the Acquisition of New Information

Phonological Short-Term Memory and Vocabulary Acquisition

Patients with defective phonological short-term memory may have preserved performance on standard episodic memory tasks, requiring the acquisition of verbal material. Learning and retention of new words (that is, pronounceable letter strings without any pre-existing lexical–semantic representations) is, however, grossly defective.

In 1988, Baddeley, Papagno and Vallar showed that patient P.V. was unable to learn new words (Russian words transliterated into Italian) by a paired-associate paradigm, whereas her learning of pairs of Italian words was entirely preserved. With auditory presentation her learning deficit was complete, with P.V. unable to acquire a single new word. With visual input, some learning was possible, but performance was grossly defective. A similar disproportionate difficulty in learning new words has been recently found by Baddeley (1993) in a 23-year-old graduate student, S.R., who had a span performance (4 digits) lower than that of matched controls (fellow students). As with P.V., S.R. was able to learn pairs of words at a normal rate and had a normal level of general intelligence (full-scale IQ, WAIS-R: 128). At variance with P.V., however, S.R. was not a brain-damaged patient, and showed the effects of phonological similarity and word length, suggesting that the operation of the phonological STS and the rehearsal process was qualitatively normal. Patient S.C. (Trojano, Stanzione & Grossi, 1992), who had a defective auditory–verbal span, was able to learn concrete and abstract nouns, reaching after seven trials the performance level of control subjects, even though his initial learning rate was slower. By contrast, S.C.'s learning of function words was slightly defective. Function words are likely to have a less rich semantic representation, as compared with content words. In this respect, functors may be similar to nonwords: both items receive relatively minor support from semantic long-term memory systems (see Caramazza, Basili, Koller & Berndt, 1981), placing more emphasis on the role of phonological short-term memory in learning. Finally, S.C.'s slower rate of learning in the initial trials, even when the stimuli were concrete nouns, may reflect the contribution of phonological short-term memory to the early phase of word learning (see converging evidence from normal subjects in Papagno & Vallar, 1992).

Baddeley, Papagno and Vallar's (1988) conclusion that phonological short-term memory is involved in the acquisition of vocabulary has been supported by studies in normal subjects and children. Phonological similarity, item length, and articulatory suppression, which, as discussed earlier, affect memory span, also interfere with the learning of new words, while their effects on word learning are minimal or absent (Papagno, Valentine & Baddeley, 1991; Papagno & Vallar, 1992). In children, performance on immediate memory tasks, such as repetition of nonwords, predicts subsequent acquisition of vocabulary both in the native language (Gathercole & Baddeley, 1989) and in a foreign language (Service, 1992). The predictive value of immediate memory performance is higher than that of other factors such as general intelligence (Gathercole & Baddeley, 1989), syntactic–semantic skills, or the ability to copy nonwords (Service, 1992).

A neuropsychological study by Vallar and Papagno (1993) provides further support for the hypothesis that phonological short-term memory plays a crucial role in the acquisition of new vocabulary. F.F., a 23-year-old subject suffering from Down's syndrome, was able to learn three languages (Italian, English and French), in spite of defective general intelligence, visuospatial skills, and episodic long-term memory. F.F. had an entirely preserved auditory–verbal span and showed the normal effects of phonological similarity and word length. In contrast to the case of P.V., F.F. was able to learn new words at a normal rate, but her learning of real words was defective. These data not only corroborate the view, based on data from patients or subjects with a low auditory–verbal span, that phonological short-term memory plays an important role in vocabulary acquisition; they also indicate that learning of new vocabulary may occur in the presence of severe cognitive deficits, including a dysfunction of episodic memory.

Visuospatial Short-Term Memory and the Long-Term Acquisition of Visuospatial Information

Patient E.L.D. (Hanley, Pearson & Young, 1990; Hanley, Young & Pearson, 1991), who had a defective immediate memory span for spatial positions and unfamiliar faces, was also impaired on tasks assessing the acquisition of new visual information, such as recognition memory for unfamiliar faces and objects. By contrast, E.L.D.'s recognition memory was preserved when the material was familiar to her. In line with these findings, E.L.D.'s defective recognition of famous faces was confined to people who had achieved prominence after the onset of her disease (1985). These experimental observations are in line with E.L.D.'s complaints (an inability to recognise the faces of people that she has met since the onset of her illness, to remember her way around new houses she visited, etc.).

This pattern of impairment parallels in the visuospatial domain Baddeley et al.'s (1988) observations in patient P.V.: defective auditory–verbal span, associated with a selective inability to acquire new verbal information, such as vocabulary in foreign languages. Taken together, these findings suggest that the long-term acquisition of new unfamiliar information requires temporary storage in short-term memory systems. As discussed in the previous section, in the case of phonological memory and vocabulary acquisition evidence from both patients and normal subjects provides strong support to this view. Less definite conclusions can, however, be drawn for visuospatial memory. The two patients of De Renzi and Nichelli (1975), who had a defective visuospatial span (2.5 blocks), did not suffer from topographical disorientation, and were able to learn the path of a visual maze, unknown to them, with a number of trials to criterion comparable to the performance of normal subjects. These findings indicate that some new visuo-spatial material may be successfully learned, despite a defective visuospatial short-term memory.

THE ASSESSMENT OF SHORT-TERM MEMORY FUNCTION

Phonological Short-Term Memory

Immediate memory span is the most popular and widely used test to assess short-term memory function. In the serial span technique subjects are presented with a sequence of verbal items, which they attempt to recall in the presentation order. Simple and highly familiar stimuli such as auditorily presented digits have been used most often. Digit span, which typically ranges between 5 and 9 digits, shows slight but significant age decrements, is affected by educational level, but not by sex (Orsini et al., 1987).

With the WAIS technique (see Orsini et al., 1987), the examiner recites lists of digits of increasing length, starting with a 2-digit sequence, at the rate of one item per second. If the subject does not repeat the first sequence correctly, a second string of equal length is presented. When a string is repeated correctly, the examiner reads the next longer sequence, continuing until the subject fails both sequences of a given length, or repeats a 9-digit sequence correctly. The digit span score is the length of the longest correctly recalled sequence. Stimuli different from digits, such as words or letters, can also be used (e.g. Spinnler & Tognoni, 1987; Vallar & Baddeley, 1984b) and span should be also tested with visual presentation (e.g. Vallar, Basso & Corno, 1992). Perception and production may be assessed by requiring the repetition of individual items: normal performance suggests that a defective span cannot be traced back to impaired analysis or output processes.

Auditory–verbal span examines short-term memory performance, without distinguishing phonological STS and articulatory rehearsal. The operation of these two components is assessed by testing the effects of phonological similarity (phonological STS) and word length (rehearsal) on span.

Sequences of increasing length (two, three, four, five and six similar letters, or words) are presented to the subject, who has to repeat the items of each sequence in the correct order, immediately after presentation. The same procedure is used for sequences of dissimilar letters or words. Stimulus sets which produce reliable effects of phonological similarity are the following: letters (similar: *B, C, D, V, P, T*; dissimilar: *F, K, Q, R, X, Z*; see Vallar & Baddeley, 1984b), words (similar, *mad, man, map, can, cad, cap*; dissimilar: *pen, rig, day, bar, cow, sup*; see Baddeley, 1966). The effect, which should be tested with both visual and auditory presentation, is typically present at span or above-span length of the presented sequence. Two scores are usually noted, the number of correctly recalled *sequences*, and the number of *items* recalled in the appropriate serial position. The presence of the phonological similarity effect with both auditory and visual input indicates that both auditory and visual information have gained access to the phonological STS. The phonological similarity effect with visual input also suggests that the articulatory rehearsal process is qualitatively functioning normally.

The effect of word length is assessed by a span paradigm similar to that used in the case of the phonological similarity effect. In order to obtain a clear-cut effect in the individual case, sets of items that are clearly different in length should be used (e.g. two- versus four- or five-syllable words; see Vallar & Baddeley, 1984b). The presence of the word length effect indicates the qualitatively normal functioning of the rehearsal process.

A few additional tests should be performed to assess whether other deficits are present (phonological processing and speech production disorders), which may produce a defective span performance.

Phonological processing may be assessed by using pairs of consonant–vowel nonsense syllables, which can be identical (e.g. *pa–pa*) or differ in voicing, in place, or in both distinctive features (e.g. *pa–ba, pa–ta, pa–ga*). In this discrimination task the subject has to judge whether the two members of the pair are same or different in sound. The diagnosis of a selective and primary deficit of phonological short-term memory (Vallar, Basso & Bottini, 1990) requires performance on phonological discrimination tasks within the normal range (Vallar & Baddeley, 1984a). Other phonological tasks such as phonemic categorisation, may be also used (see Bisiacchi, Cipolotti & Denes, 1989).

The possibility that covert deficits of speech *production* might impair span performance may be assessed by a recognition paradigm. Patients provide their response by pointing to the correct alternatives in a multiple-choice display, using a response modality which does not require overt articulation (e.g. Vallar, Corno & Basso, 1992). If a pointing response is also impossible (e.g. due to motor deficits), matching (Warrington & Shallice, 1972) or probing (Shallice & Warrington, 1970) techniques may be used.

The span tests mentioned above may be regarded as the minimal battery which provides a complete assessment of the function of phonological short-term memory. Additional tests, which, as discussed earlier, may offer converging evidence include immediate free recall (recency effect), the Peterson and Peterson (1959) paradigm, and learning of new words.

Visuospatial Short-Term Memory

A widely used visuospatial version of the span task is Corsi's block-tapping test (Milner, 1971). Visuospatial span, which in the normal subject is about 4–5 items, declines after the late sixties and is affected by educational level. A sex difference has been found, with male subjects scoring better (Orsini et al., 1987). In this test, nine cubes are arranged over a wooden board. On any given trial, the examiner taps some of the blocks in a particular sequence, the subject being required to tap out exactly the same sequence immediately afterwards. Sequences of increasing length are presented. A maximum of five sequences is tapped out by the examiner for each length: if the subject correctly recalls three out of five sequences, the examiner moves up to the next length. The spatial span score is the length of the longest sequence correctly recalled in three out of five trials.

Defective performance on visuospatial span may also be produced by perceptual deficits, unilateral neglect, or difficulties in providing the required pointing response. The unimpaired immediate capacity to point to individual blocks tapped by the examiner rules out the possibility that a pathological reduction of span may be attributed to severe visuoperceptual or pointing disorders (see De Renzi & Nichelli, 1975). Visuoperceptual deficits and neglect may be assessed in more detail by specific batteries (e.g. Benton, Hamsher, Varney & Spreen, 1983; Bisiach & Vallar, 1988).

Visual short-term memory for nonverbal material may be assessed by Warrington and Rabin's (1971) span task for sequences of line stimuli, which does not involve memory for spatial position. Span tasks may also be devised for other types of visual nonverbal material such as familiar and unfamiliar faces or objects (see Hanley, Young & Pearson, 1991). Suggestions for further assessments concerning visual and spatial imagery may be found in Farah, Hammond, Levine and Calvanio (1988).

CONCLUSIONS

A number of different and independent systems are involved in the immediate retention of information, and may be selectively impaired by brain damage. A main distinction can be drawn between systems concerned with verbal information (*phonological STS and rehearsal process*) and systems dealing with nonverbal information. The nonverbal systems are likely to include *visuospatial and visual subcomponents*. In addition to immediate retention *per se*, a main general role of these short-term storage systems may concern the acquisition of new information, such as words in a foreign unknown language or new visual material (e.g. unfamiliar faces). Phonological memory is also specifically involved in some aspects of speech comprehension.

These short-term storage systems differ not only in their functional properties, but also in their neural correlates. Parietofrontal neural networks in the left hemisphere are the anatomical correlate of the phonological component. The parieto-occipital regions in the left hemisphere are the neural basis of the visual storage system. Parietofrontal neural networks in the right hemisphere are the correlate of the visuospatial storage system.

ACKNOWLEDGEMENT

The work reported here was supported in part by CNR and MURST grants to one author (G.V.).

REFERENCES

Atkinson, R.C. & Shiffrin, R.M. (1971). The control of short-term memory. *Scientific American*, **225**, 82–90.

Baddeley, A.D. (1966). Short-term memory for word sequences as a function of acoustic, semantic and formal similarity. *Quarterly Journal of Experimental Psychology*, **18**, 362–365.

Baddeley, A.D. (1990). *Human Memory: Theory and Practice*. Lawrence Erlbaum, London.

Baddeley, A.D. (1993). Short-term phonological memory and long-term learning: a single case study. *European Journal of Cognitive Psychology*, **5**, 129–148.

Baddeley, A.D., Bressi, S., Della Sala, S., Logie, R.H. & Spinnler, H. (1991). The decline of working memory in Alzheimer's disease: a longitudinal study. *Brain*, **114**, 2521–2542.

Baddeley, A.D., Della Sala, S. & Spinnler, H. (1991). The two-component hypothesis of memory deficit in Alzheimer's disease. *Journal of Clinical and Experimental Neuropsychology*, **13**, 372–380.

Baddeley, A.D. & Hitch, G.J. (1977). Recency re-examined. In S. Dornic (ed.), *Attention and Performance*, vol. 6. Lawrence Erlbaum, Hillsdale, NJ, pp. 647–677.

Baddeley, A.D. & Hitch, G.J. (1993). The recency effect: implicit learning with explicit retrieval? *Memory and Cognition*, **21**, 146–155.

Baddeley, A.D. & Lewis, V. (1984). When does rapid presentation enhance digit span? *Bulletin of the Psychonomic Society*, **22**, 403–405.

Baddeley, A.D., Lewis, V. & Vallar, G. (1984). Exploring the articulatory loop. *Quarterly Journal of Experimental Psychology*, **36A**, 233–252.

Baddeley, A.D. & Lieberman, K. (1980). Spatial working memory. In R.S. Nickerson (ed.), *Attention and Performance*, vol. 8. Lawrence Erlbaum, Hillsdale, NJ, pp. 521–539.

Baddeley, A.D., Logie, R.H., Bressi, S., Della Sala, S. & Spinnler, H. (1986). Dementia and working memory. *Quarterly Journal of Experimental Psychology*, **38A**, 603–618.

Baddeley, A.D., Papagno, C. & Vallar, G. (1988). When long-term learning depends on short-term storage. *Journal of Memory and Language*, **27**, 586–595.

Baddeley, A.D., Thomson, N. & Buchanan, M. (1975). Word length and the structure of short-term memory. *Journal of Verbal Learning and Verbal Behavior*, **14**, 575–589.

Baddeley, A., Vallar, G. & Wilson, B. (1987). Sentence comprehension and phonological memory: some neuropsychological evidence. In M. Coltheart (ed.), *Attention and Performance*, vol. 12. Lawrence Erlbaum, London, pp. 509–529.

Baddeley, A.D. & Warrington, E.K. (1970). Amnesia and the distinction between long- and short-term memory. *Journal of Verbal Learning and Verbal Behavior*, **9**, 176–189.

Baddeley, A. & Wilson, B. (1985). Phonological coding and short-term memory in patients without speech. *Journal of Memory and Language*, **24**, 490–502.

Baddeley, A. & Wilson, B. (1988). Comprehension and working memory: a single-case neuropsychological study. *Journal of Memory and Language*, **27**, 479–498.

Basso, A., Spinnler, H., Vallar, G. & Zanobio, M.E. (1982). Left hemisphere damage and selective impairment of auditory–verbal short-term memory. *Neuropsychologia*, **20**, 263–274.

Becker, J.T. (1988). Working memory and secondary memory deficits in Alzheimer's disease. *Journal of Clinical and Experimental Neuropsychology*, **10**, 739–753.

Benton, A.L., de S. Hamsher, K., Varney, N.R. & Spreen, O. (1983). *Contributions to Neuropsychological Assessment*. Oxford University Press, New York.

Berndt, R.S. & Mitchum, C.C. (1990). Auditory and lexical information sources in immediate recall: evidence from a patient with deficit to the phonological short-term store. In G. Vallar & T. Shallice (eds), *Neuropsychological Impairments of Short-Term Memory*. Cambridge University Press, Cambridge, pp. 115–144.

Besner, D. (1987). Phonology, lexical access in reading, and articulatory suppression: a critical review. *Quarterly Journal of Experimental Psychology*, **39A**, 467–478.

Bishop, D.V.M. & Robson, J. (1989). Unimpaired short-term memory and rhyme judgement in congenitally speechless individuals: implications for the notion of articulatory coding. *Quarterly Journal of Experimental Psychology*, **41A**, 123–140.

Bisiach, E. & Vallar, G. (1988). Hemineglect in humans. In F. Boller & J. Grafman (eds), *Handbook of Neuropsychology*, vol. 1. Elsevier Science Publishers, Amsterdam, pp. 195–222.

Bisiacchi, P.S., Cipolotti, L. & Denes, G. (1989). Impairment in processing meaningless verbal material in several modalities: the relationship between short-term memory and phonological skills. *Quarterly Journal of Experimental Psychology*, **41A**, 293–319.

Brooks, L.R. (1967). The suppression of visualisation by reading. *Quarterly Journal of Experimental Psychology*, **19**, 289–299.

Burani, C., Vallar, G., Bottini, G. (1991). Articulatory coding and phonological judgements on written words and pictures: the role of the phonological output buffer. *European Journal of Cognitive Psychology*, **3**, 379–398.

Butterworth, B., Shallice, T. & Watson, F.L. (1990). Short-term retention without short-term memory. In G. Vallar & T. Shallice (eds), *Neuropsychological Impairments of Short-Term Memory*. Cambridge University Press, Cambridge, pp. 187–213.

Campbell, R. & Butterworth, B. (1985). Phonological dyslexia and dysgraphia in a highly literate subject: a developmental case with associated deficits of phonemic processing and awareness. *Quarterly Journal of Experimental Psychology*, **37A**, 435–475.

Cantone, G., Orsini, A., Grossi, D. & De Michele, G. (1978). Verbal and spatial memory span in dementia. *Acta Neurologica*, **33**, 175–183.

Caplan, D. & Waters, G. (1990). Short-term memory and language comprehension: a critical review of the neuropsychological literature. In G. Vallar & T. Shallice (eds), *Neuropsychological Impairments of Short-Term Memory*. Cambridge University Press, Cambridge, pp. 337–389.

Caramazza, A., Basili, A.G., Koller, J.J. & Berndt, R.S. (1981). An investigation of repetition and language processing in a case of conduction aphasia. *Brain and Language*, **14**, 235–271.

Caramazza, A. & Berndt, R.S. (1985). A multicomponent deficit view of agrammatic Broca's aphasia. In M.-L. Kean (ed.), *Agrammatism*. Academic Press, Orlando, pp. 27–63.

Clark, H.H. & Clark. E.V. (1977). *Psychology and Language*. Harcourt Brace, New York.

Conrad, R. (1964). Acoustic confusions in immediate memory. *British Journal of Psychology*, **55**, 75–84.

Conrad, R. & Hull, A.J. (1964). Information, acoustic confusion and memory span. *British Journal of Psychology*, **55**, 429–432.

Crowder, R.G. (1976). *Principles of Learning and Memory*. Lawrence Erlbaum, Hillsdale, NJ.

Cubelli, R. & Nichelli, P. (1992). Inner speech in anarthria: neuropsychological evidence of differential effects of cerebral lesions on subvocal articulation. *Journal of Clinical and Experimental Neuropsychology*, **14**, 499–517.

Davidoff, J.B. & Ostergaard, A.L. (1984). Colour anomia resulting from weakened short-term colour memory. *Brain*, **107**, 415–431.

De Renzi, E. & Faglioni, P. (1978). Normative data and screening power of a shortened version of the token test. *Cortex*, **14**, 41–49.

De Renzi, E., Faglioni, P. & Previdi, P. (1977). Spatial memory and hemispheric locus of lesion. *Cortex*, **13**, 424–433.

De Renzi, E. & Nichelli, P. (1975). Verbal and nonverbal short-term memory impairment following hemispheric damage. *Cortex*, **11**, 341–354.

Ellis, A.W. (1979). Speech production and short-term memory. In J. Morton & J.C. Marshall (eds), *Psycholinguistics Series. Vol. 2: Structures and Processes*. Paul Elek, London, pp. 157–187.

Farah, M.J., Hammond, K.M., Levine, D.N. & Calvanio, R. (1988). Visual and spatial imagery: dissociable systems of representations. *Cognitive Psychology*, **20**, 439–462.

Friedrich, F.J., Glenn, C.G. & Marin, O.S.M. (1984). Interruption of phonological coding in conduction aphasia. *Brain and Language*, **22**, 266–291.

Gathercole, S.E. & Baddeley, A.D. (1989). Evaluation of the role of phonological short-term memory in the development of vocabulary in children: a longitudinal study. *Journal of Memory and Language*, **28**, 200–213.

Hanley, J.R., Pearson, N.A. & Young, A.W. (1990). Impaired memory for new visual forms. *Brain*, **113**, 1131–1148.

Hanley, J.R., Young, A.W. & Pearson, N.A. (1991). Impairment of the visuo-spatial sketch pad. *Quarterly Journal of Experimental Psychology*, **43A**, 101–125.

Hitch, G.J. (1980). Developing the concept of working memory. In G. Claxton (ed.), *Cognitive Psychology: New Directions*. Routledge & Kegan Paul, London, pp. 154–196.

Jonides, J., Smith, E.E., Koeppe, R.A., Awh, E., Minoshima, S. & Mintun, M.A. (1993). Spatial working memory in humans as revealed by PET. *Nature*, **363**, 623–625.

Kimura, D. (1963). Right temporal-lobe damage. *Archives of Neurology*, **8**, 48–55.

Kinsbourne, M. (1972). Behavioral analysis of the repetition deficit in conduction aphasia. *Neurology*, **22**, 1126–1132.

Kinsbourne, M. & Warrington, E.K. (1962). A disorder of simultaneous form perception. *Brain*, **85**, 461–486.

Kinsbourne, M. & Warrington, E.K. (1963). The localizing significance of limited simultaneous visual form perception. *Brain*, **86**, 697–702.

Levy, B.A. (1971). Role of articulation in auditory and visual short-term memory. *Journal of Verbal Learning and Verbal Behavior*, **10**, 123–132.

Logie, R. (1989). Characteristics of visual short-term memory. *European Journal of Cognitive Psychology*, **1**, 275–284.

Luria, A.R., Sokolov, E.N. & Klimkowski, M. (1967). Towards a neurodynamic analysis of memory disturbances with lesions of the left temporal lobe. *Neuropsychologia*, **5**, 1–11.

Martin, R.C. (1987). Articulatory and phonological deficits in short-term memory and their relation to syntactic processing. *Brain and Language*, **32**, 159–192.

Martin, R.C. & Breedin, S.D. (1992). Dissociation between speech perception and phonological short-term memory deficits. *Cognitive Neuropsychology*, **9**, 509–534.

Martin, A., Brouwers, P., Cox, C. & Fedio, P. (1985). On the nature of the verbal memory deficit in Alzheimer's disease. *Brain and Language*, **25**, 323–341.

McCarthy, R.A. & Warrington, E.K. (1987). The double dissociation of short-term memory for lists and sentences. *Brain*, **110**, 1545–1563.

McCarthy, R.A. & Warrington, E.K. (1990). *Cognitive Neuropsychology: A Clinical Introduction*. Academic Press, San Diego.

Milner, B. (1971). Interhemispheric differences in the localization of psychological processes in man. *British Medical Bulletin*, **27**, 272–277.

Morris, R.G. (1984). Dementia and the functioning of the articulatory loop. *Cognitive Neuropsychology*, **1**, 143–157.

Morris, R.G. (1986). Short-term forgetting in senile dementia of the Alzheimer's type. *Cognitive Neuropsychology*, **3**, 77–97.

Morris, R.G. (1987). Articulatory rehearsal in Alzheimer type dementia. *Brain and Language*, **30**, 351–362.

Morris, R. & Baddeley, A.D. (1988). Primary and working memory functioning in Alzheimer-type dementia. *Journal of Clinical and Experimental Neuropsychology*, **10**, 279–296.

Murray, D.J. (1968). Articulation and acoustic confusability in short-term memory. *Journal of Experimental Psychology*, **78**, 679–684.

Nebes, R. (1975). The nature of internal speech in anarthria. *Brain and Language*, **2**, 489–497.

Orsini, A., Grossi, D., Capitani, E., Laiacona, M., Papagno, C. & Vallar, G. (1987). Verbal and spatial immediate memory span. *Italian Journal of Neurological Sciences*, **8**, 539–548.

Papagno, C., Valentine, T. & Baddeley, A.D. (1991). Phonological short-term memory and foreign-language vocabulary learning. *Journal of Memory and Language*, **30**, 331–347.

Papagno, C. & Vallar, G. (1992). Phonological short-term memory and the learning of novel words: the effect of phonological similarity and item length. *Quarterly Journal of Experimental Psychology*, **44A**, 47–67.

Papagno, C. & Vallar, G. (in press). To learn or not to learn vocabulary in foreign languages: the problem with phonological memory. In R. Campbell & M. Conway (eds), *Broken Memories*. Basil Blackwell, Oxford.

Paulesu, E., Frith, C.D. & Frackowiak, R.S.J. (1993). The neural correlates of the verbal component of working memory. *Nature*, **362**, 342–345.

Perani, D., Bressi, S., Cappa, S.F., Vallar, G., Alberoni, M., Grassi, F., Caltagirone, C., Cipolotti, L., Franceschi, M., Lenzi, G. & Fazio, F. (1993). Evidence of multiple memory systems in the human brain: a [18F] FDG PET metabolic study. *Brain*, **116**, 903–919.

Peterson, L.R. & Johnson, S.T. (1971). Some effects of minimizing articulation on short-term retention. *Journal of Verbal Learning and Verbal Behavior*, **10**, 346–354.

Peterson, L.R. & Peterson, M.J. (1959). Short-term retention of individual verbal items. *Journal of Experimental Psychology*, **58**, 193–198.

Risse, G.L., Rubens, A.B. & Jordan, L.S. (1984). Disturbances of long-term memory in aphasic patients. *Brain*, **107**, 605–617.

Romani, C. (1992). Are there distinct input and output buffers? Evidence from an aphasic patient with an impaired output buffer. *Language and Cognitive Processes*, **7**, 131–162.

Ross, E.D. (1980). Sensory-specific and fractional disorders of recent memory in man. II: Unilateral loss of tactile recent memory. *Archives of Neurology*, **37**, 267–272.

Saffran, E.M. (1990). Short-term memory impairment and language processing. In A. Caramazza (ed.), *Cognitive Neuropsychology and Neurolinguistics*. Lawrence Erlbaum, Hillsdale, NJ, pp. 137–168.

Saffran, E.M. & Marin, O.S.M. (1975). Immediate memory for word lists and sentences in a patient with deficient auditory short-term memory. *Brain and Language*, **2**, 420–433.

Saffran, E.M. & Martin, N. (1990). Short-term memory impairment and sentence processing: a case study. In G. Vallar & T. Shallice (eds), *Neuropsychological Impairments of Short-Term Memory*. Cambridge University Press, Cambridge, pp. 428–447.

Service, E. (1992). Phonology, working memory, and foreign-language learning. *Quarterly Journal of Experimental Psychology*, **45A**, 21–50.

Shallice, T. (1979). Neuropsychological research and the fractionation of memory systems. In L.G. Nillson (ed.), *Perspectives on Memory Research*. Lawrence Erlbaum, Hillsdale, NJ. pp. 257–277.

Shallice, T. & Butterworth, B. (1977). Short-term memory impairment and spontaneous speech. *Neuropsychologia*, **15**, 729–735.

Shallice, T. & Vallar, G. (1990). The impairment of auditory-verbal short-term storage. In G. Vallar & T. Shallice (eds), *Neuropsychological Impairments of Short-Term Memory*. Cambridge University Press, Cambridge, pp. 11–53.

Shallice, T. & Warrington, E.K. (1970). Independent functioning of verbal memory stores: a neuropsychological study. *Quarterly Journal of Experimental Psychology*, **22**, 261–273.

Shallice, T. & Warrington, E.K. (1974). The dissociation between short-term retention of meaningful sounds and verbal material. *Neuropsychologia*, **12**, 553–555.

Shallice, T. & Warrington, E.K. (1977). Auditory-verbal short-term memory impairment and conduction aphasia. *Brain and Language*, **4**, 479–491.

Shallice, T. & Warrington, E.K. (1980). K.F.: Post-mortem findings. In M. Coltheart, K. Patterson & J.C. Marshall (eds), *Deep Dyslexia*. Routledge & Kegan Paul, London, p. 411.

Spinnler, H., Della Sala, S., Bandera, R. & Baddeley, A.D. (1988). Dementia, ageing and the structure of human memory. *Cognitive Neuropsychology*, **5**, 193–211.

Spinnler, H. & Tognoni, G. (1987). Standardizzazione e taratura italiana di test neuropsicologici. *Italian Journal of Neurological Sciences*, supp. 8.

Strub, R.L. & Gardner, H. (1974). The repetition defect in conduction aphasia: mnestic or linguistic? *Brain and Language*, **1**, 241–255.

Trojano, L., Stanzione, M. & Grossi, D. (1992). Short-term memory and verbal learning with auditory phonological coding defect: a neuropsychological case study. *Brain and Cognition*, **18**, 12–33.

Tzortis, C. & Albert, M.L. (1974). Impairment of memory for sequences in conduction aphasia. *Neuropsychologia*, **12**, 355–366.

Vallar, G. (1991). Current methodological issues in human neuropsychology. In F. Boller & J. Grafman (eds), *Handbook of Neuropsychology*. Elsevier, Amsterdam, pp. 343–378.

Vallar, G. (1994). Left spatial hemineglect: an unmanageable explosion of dissociations? No. *Neuropsychological Rehabilitation*, **4**, 290–212.

Vallar, G. & Baddeley, A.D. (1984a). Phonological short-term store, phonological processing and sentence comprehension. *Cognitive Neuropsychology*, **1**, 121–141.

Vallar, G. & Baddeley, A.D. (1984b). Fractionation of working memory: neuropsychological evidence for a phonological short-term store. *Journal of Verbal Learning and Verbal Behavior*, **23**, 151–161.

Vallar, G. & Baddeley, A.D. (1987). Phonological short-term store and sentence processing. *Cognitive Neuropsychology*, **4**, 417–438.

Vallar, G., Basso, A. & Bottini, G. (1990). Phonological processing and sentence comprehension: a neuropsychological case study. In G. Vallar & T. Shallice (eds), *Neuropsychological Impairments of Short-Term Memory*. Cambridge University Press, Cambridge, pp. 448–476.

Vallar, G. & Cappa, S.F. (1987). Articulation and verbal short-term memory: evidence from anarthria. *Cognitive Neuropsychology*, **4**, 55–78.

Vallar, G., Corno, M. & Basso, A. (1992). Auditory and visual verbal short-term memory in aphasia. *Cortex*, **28**, 383–389.

Vallar, G. & Papagno, C. (1986). Phonological short-term store and the nature of the recency effect: evidence from neuropsychology. *Brain and Cognition*, **5**, 428–442.

Vallar, G. & Papagno, C. (1993). Preserved vocabulary acquisition in Down's syndrome: the role of phonological short-term memory. *Cortex*, **29**, 467–483.

Vallar, G., Papagno, C. & Baddeley, A.D. (1991). Long-term recency effects and phonological short-term memory: a neuropsychological case study. *Cortex*, **27**, 323–326.

Warrington, E.K. (1979). Neuropsychological evidence for multiple memory systems. In *Brain and Mind: Ciba Foundation Symposium 69 (new series)*. Excerpta Medica, Amsterdam, pp. 153–166.

Warrington, E.K. & James, M. (1967). Tachistoscopic number estimation in patients with unilateral cerebral lesions. *Journal of Neurology, Neurosurgery and Psychiatry*, **30**, 468–474.

Warrington, E.K., Logue, V. & Pratt, R.T.C. (1971). The anatomical localisation of selective impairment of auditory–verbal short-term memory. *Neuropsychologia*, **9**, 377–387.

Warrington, E.K. & Rabin, P. (1971). Visual span of apprehension in patients with unilateral cerebral lesions. *Quarterly Journal of Experimental Psychology*, **23**, 423–431.

Warrington, E.K. & Shallice, T. (1969). The selective impairment of auditory–verbal short-term memory. *Brain*, **92**, 885–896.

Warrington, E.K. & Shallice, T. (1972). Neuropsychological evidence of visual storage in short-term memory tasks. *Quarterly Journal of Experimental Psychology*, **24**, 30–40.

Waugh, N.C. & Norman, D.A. (1965). Primary memory. *Psychological Review*, **72**, 89–104.

Wickelgren, W.A. (1965). Short-term memory for phonemically similar lists. *American Journal of Psychology*, **78**, 567–574.

Wilson, B.A. & Baddeley, A. (1993). Spontaneous recovery of impaired memory span: does comprehension recover? *Cortex*, **29**, 153–159.

Wilson, F.A. W., O'Scalaidhe, S.P. & Goldman-Rakic, P.S. (1993). Dissociation of object and spatial processing domains in primate prefrontal cortex. *Science*, **260**, 1955–1958.

Zangwill, O.L. (1946). Some qualitative observations on verbal memory in cases of cerebral lesion. *British Journal of Psychology*, **37**, 8–19.

Zhang, G. & Simon, H.A. (1985). STM capacity for Chinese words and idioms: chunking and acoustical loop hypotheses. *Memory and Cognition*, **13**, 193–201.

Chapter 7

Disorders of Semantic Memory

Karalyn Patterson
MRC Applied Psychology Unit, Cambridge, UK
and
John R. Hodges
University of Cambridge Neurology unit, Cambridge, UK

INTRODUCTION

We were interviewing P.P., a 69-year old patient with a progressive disorder of semantic memory. "Is a cat an animal?" we asked her. "Is a cat an animal?" she repeated; "I wish I could remember what an animal was". This striking example illustrates several ways in which semantic memory is separable from other aspects of human cognitive ability, indeed from other aspects of memory discussed in this book. The fact that P.P. effortlessly repeated the question suggests that there is nothing wrong with her speech perception, nor with her auditory–verbal working memory. Her comment on the question ("I wish I could remember...") suggests that there is no impairment in her ability to produce a grammatically acceptable sentence composed of correctly articulated words, and also that she has considerable insight into her deficit. The fact that she could not give the correct answer to this trivially easy question indicates, however, that something is severely amiss with P.P.'s semantic memory. Every normal person, even a 2-year-old child, knows what animals are; it seems that P.P. no longer does.

Revealing though it might be, this example would immediately provoke a number of queries from any experimental neuropsychologist confronted with P.P.'s behaviour. For example:

1. Is it just a language impairment? Perhaps P.P. knows conceptually about cats and other animals, and would respond appropriately to real animals or even to pictures of them, but no longer comprehends their verbal labels.

Handbook of Memory Disorders. Edited by A.D. Baddeley, B.A. Wilson and F.N. Watts.

2. Does her problem reflect actual loss of knowledge, or is there instead a difficulty in gaining access to this information? Perhaps on another occasion, or with the question put differently, or in a different kind of task involving comprehension of the words "cat" and "animal", she would be able to demonstrate retained comprehension.
3. Is there something special about animals that makes knowledge of them vulnerable to the sort of brain disease from which P.P. is suffering? Perhaps she would be able to answer questions about other kinds of things, such as inanimate objects like cars or non-object concepts like love.

These are some of the issues that are currently guiding investigations of the nature of semantic memory and its breakdown in patients like P.P.

In this chapter on disorders of semantic memory, we first describe how the field of psychology and neuropsychology conceives of semantic memory and how to assess it. Second, we discuss briefly what is known about the brain regions which seem to be most critical to the maintenance of semantic memory and the types of brain diseases to which it seems to be most vulnerable. Finally (and at greatest length) we review evidence germane to theoretical issues that are prominent in research on semantic memory.

SEMANTIC MEMORY, AND HOW IT CAN BEST BE ASSESSED

In 1972, Tulving published an influential paper in which he distinguished between two different systems, or types, of long-term human memory. Episodic memory, in Tulving's description, represents what most non-psychologists would think of as memory: remembering that you ate Szechuan chicken in yellow-bean sauce for dinner two nights ago, that you were at the Peking Restaurant with your friend Mark when you ate this, that the last time you ordered this dish at this restaurant, they brought the diced chicken with almonds instead, etc. The critical feature of information in episodic memory is that it refers to a specific episode which you experienced and which can be identified, more or less accurately, as having happened at a particular time. The contrasting type of memory in Tulving's framework, semantic memory, is your knowledge about the meanings of words, objects and concepts: what Szechuan means, what almonds taste like, how to find the Peking Restaurant. All of this information must have been learned from specific experiences; but the claim is that, in semantic memory, knowledge is no longer defined by, and indeed may no longer yield any information regarding, particular episodes. You know that it was a couple of nights ago that you were at the Peking Restaurant eating Szechuan chicken; you probably have no idea when or where you learned the meaning of the term Szechuan or the taste of almonds, and no amount of memory search could produce such information.

Now, the fact that you can readily retrieve a specific episode for your most recent ingestion of Szechuan chicken but none for the semantics of Szechuan is not sufficient reason to consider these genuinely separate memory systems in the brain. Indeed, some memory theorists (Baddeley, 1976; Cermak, 1984) have argued that Tulving's dichotomy is better captured by a continuum, based on degree of abstraction, in which information to which you are exposed repeatedly, over a long time scale and in many different contexts, gradually loses its distinctive episodic components and becomes general knowledge. What might constitute evidence that these two types of memory do differ in kind rather than degree? Perhaps the most widely accepted criterion is the double dissociation: if brain damage can selectively disrupt episodic memory, leaving semantic memory relatively intact, *and* vice versa, then it seems likely that they are different subsystems of memory. Double dissociation can also be operationalised with respect to experimental manipulations with normal subjects—i.e., where one type of manipulation influences performance on task A but not B and another type of manipulation has the reverse effect (see Tulving, 1983, for a review). For present purposes, however, we shall restrict our considerations to the neuropsychological variety of double dissociation.

So, do episodic and semantic memory doubly dissociate? In our view, with two caveats, the answer is yes. The first caveat is a rather general one: since the experimental study of memory disorders is in its infancy for semantic memory and no older than adolescence for episodic memory, it is perhaps premature to draw firm conclusions. All we can say is that the evidence currently available seems most compatible with a real distinction between these types of memory. The second caveat is more specific. The fact that two cognitive subsystems are separable does not mean that they are functionally independent, and it seems likely that there is considerable functional interdependence between episodic and semantic memory. In the amnesic syndrome (see Chapters 3–5) the ability to establish new memories on the basis of current experience is disrupted; this disruption may have relatively little impact on semantic knowledge previously built up over a lifetime's experience but will obviously interfere with the acquisition of new knowledge. Furthermore, things that are difficult to understand are difficult to remember, because the understanding of events as they occur determines how they are represented in memory. Thus, P.P. appeared to have a considerable memory for recent episodes when we first began to study her disorder of semantic memory (e.g. she could correctly report, in her anomic way, that she had been to visit "the little girl" (her granddaughter) the day before, etc.); but, especially with increasing severity of the semantic deficit over the subsequent few years, it would be unrealistic to expect P.P. to remember that she ate Szechuan chicken with her friend Mark two nights ago: since she can no longer identify the taste or appearance of chicken, nor understand the word for it, nor recognise most previously familiar people, her interpretation of the experience at the time would presumably be too impoverished to provide the basis for a memory of the episode. Our summary of the dissociation, then, is that while episodic and semantic memory do appear to be separate subsystems, the extent to which each can function normally is somewhat constrained by the intactness of the other.

If semantic memory represents all of our general knowledge, including the meaning of the term Szechuan, the colour of a carrot, the name of the British prime minister during the second world war, etc., the task of assessing its status seems a formidable one. Subjects can of course be asked questions like "What colour is a carrot?" or "Who was the prime minister during World War II?"; neuropsychologists *do* ask such general knowledge questions, but in the awareness that this is a rather one-sided technique. That is, if the subject answers such questions easily and accurately, one can conclude that his or her semantic memory is intact; but failure to answer correctly is not so readily interpretable. Semantic memory is perhaps the most central of human cognitive abilities, depending on a large number of peripheral systems as sources of both input (all of the sensory/perceptual systems, plus language) and output (language again, plus various forms of action). The key to assessing this complex central system, therefore, is to use a multiplicity of types of both input and output, to build up a picture of the status of semantic knowledge that is independent of any one modality of access to or from it.

A semantic test battery based on this key principle has been designed by Hodges, and is currently being used to study various forms of semantic memory disorder (Hodges, Salmon & Butters, 1991, 1992; Hodges, Patterson, Funnell & Oxbury, 1992; Hodges, Patterson & Tyler, 1994). The identical set of 48 stimulus items (half animals, half man-made objects) is presented in a variety of combinations of different modalities of input and output, including pictures to be named (pictorial input, verbal output), words to be defined (verbal input and output), pictures to be sorted into categories (pictorial input, action as output), pointing to the picture amongst a set of alternatives that matches a spoken or written word (pictorial *and* verbal input, action as output), and so on.

If we want to determine what a patient like P.P. knows about colours and/or vegetables, as well as asking her verbally what colour a carrot is, we can, for example, (a) give her an outline drawing of a carrot and ask her to colour it in with her choice of coloured pencils, (b) show her pictures of an orange carrot and a blue carrot and ask her to choose the correct one, (c) show her a picture of a carrot and ask her whether it "goes with" a picture of a donkey or a lion, and so on. Howard and Patterson (1992) designed a test of associative semantics comprised of items like the last one; the test is called Pyramids and Palm trees because in one of the items the target is an Egyptian pyramid and the two choices are a palm tree and a pine tree. The underlying principle is that a wide variety of semantic knowledge is required to judge that pyramids are found with palm trees rather than pine trees, that carrots are eaten by donkeys rather than lions, and so on. Also, once again on the principle regarding different modalities of input to semantic memory, this test can be administered with either pictures or words as stimuli.

Even if the patient fails on all of the tests just described, this does not necessarily license the conclusion that she has lost all semantic knowledge of carrots. All of the tasks listed above are ones requiring so-called "declarative" knowledge (Schacter, 1987; Squire, 1987; Tyler, 1992), where the subject is asked not only to retrieve some aspect of knowledge but also to "declare" the knowledge explicitly. Psychologists have recently been employing an alternative type of test, where fully or partially retained knowledge can be expressed in a more implicit way. Thus, for example, we might ask the patient to perform some simple classification task on pictures or words, and measure her response time to each item. If she is faster to classify an orange-coloured carrot than a blue one, or faster to respond to the spoken word "carrot" when it is preceded by the related word "onion" than by the unrelated word "union", this suggests that she has automatic access to some semantic knowledge about carrots, even if she cannot express this knowledge when asked an explicit question. (See Tyler (1992) for detailed discussion of the implicit/explicit distinction with regard to spoken word comprehension.)

A fuller picture of the types of tests used to assess semantic memory will emerge when we review the evidence on varieties of disorder in this domain; assessment is also discussed in Chapter 15. The important message of this section is that no single form of testing will be adequate to evaluate something as complex and multi-faceted as semantic memory.

THE NEUROANATOMY OF SEMANTIC MEMORY, AND BRAIN DISEASES/INJURIES MOST LIKELY TO DISRUPT IT

There are probably substantial differences between various cognitive subsystems in their degree of focal representation and, as a general principle, central, complex functions are probably less focally represented than peripheral, specific functions. For example, recognition of spoken words appears to rely on a rather specific region in the posterior, superior left temporal lobe (originally identified by Wernicke, 1874, and confirmed by recent functional brain imaging techniques; see Howard et al., 1992; Petersen et al., 1988, 1989). By contrast, we might expect semantic memory to depend on multiple neural networks, distributed over broad areas of bilateral cerebral cortex. The most that can be said at present is that, to the extent that there *are* specific brain regions or structures crucial to the operation of semantic memory, these seem to be in anterolateral areas of temporal neocortex, and perhaps more on the left than the right. What sort of evidence, from what sorts of aetiologies, supports this conjecture?

The four forms of brain disease or injury to which semantic memory seems most vulnerable are (i) Alzheimer's disease, (ii) herpes simplex encephalitis, (iii) severe head injury with relatively localised effects, and (iv) a form of progressive focal atrophy now known as semantic dementia (Hodges, Patterson, Oxbury & Funnell, 1992; Saffran & Schwartz, 1994; Snowden, Goulding & Neary, 1989). Semantic dementia, the condition which appears to have the most selective impact on semantic memory, has only recently been identified as a specific syndrome. (See Schwartz, Martin & Saffran (1979) and Warrington (1975) for the most thorough initial reports of such cases, though not with this sobriquet.) Hodges et al. (1992) defined the core features of semantic dementia as follows:

- Selective impairment of semantic memory, causing severe anomia, impaired single-word comprehension (both spoken and written), reduced generation of exemplars on category fluency tests (where the subject is asked to produce as many items as possible from a specified semantic category, such as animals or vehicles or things you would buy in a supermarket), and an impoverished fund of general knowledge.
- Relative sparing of other components of speech production, notably syntax and phonology.
- Unimpaired perceptual skills and nonverbal problem-solving abilities.
- Relatively preserved day-to-day (episodic) memory.

Of the few identified cases of semantic dementia that have come to post mortem, all have displayed non-Alzheimer pathology, showing either nonspecific neuronal loss with spongiform change (Snowden et al., 1992) or the specific intraneuronal inclusions associated with Pick's disease (Graff-Radford et al., 1990; Hodges, 1993; Hodges, Graham & Patterson, in press). In all cases, the affected areas have been predominantly temporal. There is rather more information from structural (MRI) and functional (PET or SPECT) *in vivo* imaging of patients with semantic dementia, though of course imaging reveals only the location of affected brain regions, and not the underlying pathology. Consonant with the localisation information from post-mortem analysis, however, the structural atrophy and reduced metabolism apparent on brain imaging have been almost exclusively in temporal neocortex, either predominantly in the left hemisphere or sometimes bilaterally (Hodges et al., 1992; Snowden et al., 1992). The identical neuroanatomical pattern has been demonstrated in a series of Japanese patients studied by Tanabe (1992); the disorder in these cases, referred to as "Gogi" (word-meaning) aphasia, is almost certainly the same as semantic dementia.

In dementia of Alzheimer's type (DAT), which is of course a much more common and hence more researched condition, the pathological changes characteristic of the disease are thought to begin typically in the medial temporal structures critical for episodic rather than semantic memory (Braak & Braak, 1991; Damasio, Van Hoesen & Hyman, 1990); thus the earliest and most profound deficit in DAT is one of episodic memory (see Chapter 10). As the disease progresses, however, pathology spreads to bilateral posterior association cortices, including the lateral temporal structures that are more selectively affected in semantic dementia. Disrupted semantic memory—which may be relatively mild, though detectable, in early stages of DAT (Hodges & Patterson, in press)—then becomes a major feature in later stages (Bayles & Tomoeda,

1983; Cherkow & Bub, 1990; Hodges, Salmon & Butters, 1990, 1991, 1992; Martin & Fedio, 1983; Nebes, 1989).

Herpes simplex encephalitis was, until fairly recently, an almost invariably fatal condition. Since the advent of effective antiviral agents, patients with this disease are much more likely to survive, but typically they suffer from profound neuropsychological deficits. In the acute stages, the herpes virus invades the brain via limbic and related medial temporal and frontal lobe structures, causing inflammation and necrosis. The damage is usually bilateral, although a marked asymmetry in the degree of destruction occurs in a substantial minority of cases. A severe impairment of episodic memory with both anterograde and retrograde amnesia is the commonest deficit. In some cases, however, the damage is not confined to medial temporal structures but includes variable degrees of temporal and frontal neocortex. A growing number of cases with impaired semantic memory have been reported, in whom temporal neocortical damage is a common factor (e.g. Damasio et al., 1985; McCarthy & Warrington, 1992; Pietrini et al., 1988; Sartori & Job, 1988; Warrington & Shallice, 1984).

Finally, there have been reports of head injury in which the prominent cognitive impairment is semantic memory; perhaps the most thoroughly studied of these is the case M.P. (Behrmann & Bub, 1992; Bub, Black, Hampson & Kertesz, 1988; Bub, Cancelliere & Kertesz 1985). Consistent with all of the other aetiologies described above, this patient—who suffered a severe head injury when she was struck by a motor vehicle—had predominantly left temporal lobe damage.

It is interesting to note the rarity of reports of selective semantic memory loss resulting from cerebrovascular accident (stroke). This may be because the area that appears to be most crucial for semantic memory is supplied by both the middle and posterior cerebral arteries: dual vascular territory strokes are unusual and are likely to produce multiple cognitive deficits. Furthermore, in many stroke patients with left-hemisphere damage, severe language deficits may complicate the assessment of semantic memory.

It would be premature to draw definitive conclusions about the neuroanatomical basis of semantic memory; most of the critical data have yet to be collected, and a system as central as semantic memory is perhaps not a good candidate for precise focal representation. Nonetheless, it seems clear that anterolateral regions of the temporal lobes, perhaps especially on the left side, must be critically implicated in the representation of semantic knowledge. The role of these regions in the long-term storage of memory is discussed further in Chapter 4.

HOW SEMANTIC MEMORY IS ORGANISED, AND RELATES TO OTHER COGNITIVE SUBSYSTEMS

We turn now to the major section of this chapter, a review of the neuropsychology of semantic memory. We will not attempt to cover all of the detailed theoretical issues, partly because an excellent recent review is already available (Saffran & Schwartz, 1994) and partly because some of these issues may be rather recondite with regard to the broad interests of readers of this handbook. We will also often be forced to conclude that the issues and controversies remain to be resolved; as indicated above, research in this area has scarcely begun.

In an influential book published in 1983, Fodor distinguished between modular and nonmodular cognitive abilities. Modular subsystems, he argued, perform their computations largely without need for other general-purpose capabilities, such as deliberate attention, and also without reference to information from a large number of domains of processing. Other aspects of cognition, especially more central systems like semantic memory, do not constitute independent modules in Fodor's scheme. The ensuing decade has seen considerable debate about the usefulness of this distinction; we will not rehearse this debate here, except to say that we endorse the conclusion of Shallice who argued that, whatever their merits in other contexts, "... for neuropsychological purposes, the criteria he [i.e. Fodor] suggests may well be too specific and the systems to which they are supposed to apply, too limited" (Shallice, 1988, p. 20). Semantic knowledge would certainly not fulfil most of Fodor's criteria for modularity; for example, rather than being selectively geared to a limited domain of information, it takes input from all sensory/perceptual systems (vision, hearing, touch, taste, etc.). Yet, reinforcing Shallice's assessment, semantic memory does seem to have at least a degree of independence from other cognitive processes, since it can apparently be selectively disrupted by brain disease. Our review of what has been learned from research on this topic will be organised around two main issues:

1. What is revealed about the internal organisation of semantic memory by its impairments?
2. What is the impact of these impairments on the status of other cognitive subsystems that are, in normal processing, in constant interaction with semantic memory?

The Internal Organisation of Semantic Memory

In our view, two main questions summarise a large number of rather specific controversies regarding the structure of semantic memory.

Is the "Module" of Semantic Memory an Assemblage of Several Separable Modular Subsystems?

Neuropsychologists have made at least three (not entirely unrelated) proposals about ways in which semantic knowledge might fractionate:

1. Knowledge of the meanings of *words* might be separately represented from

knowledge about *objects*. This hypothesis has been advanced to explain findings on so-called optic aphasia, a form of anomia restricted to visual presentation of objects (see Beauvois, 1982).

2. Knowledge about *concrete* or *imageable* concepts—which are concepts with sensory properties, i.e. things that we can see, hear, touch, taste etc.—might be separately represented from knowledge about more *abstract* concepts (Warrington, 1975, 1981). Note that this has some overlap with (1) but is not identical to it, because concrete words (like "table") and abstract words (like "idea") would be on the same side of a putative cognitive fence in (1) but on separate sides in (2).

3. Knowledge about *sensory properties* of objects might be separately represented from knowledge of their *functional properties* (Warrington & McCarthy, 1987; Warrington & Shallice, 1984). Again note that, whilst this proposal has somewhat the same flavour as (2), it is not identical. In (2), knowledge fractionates along the lines of different types of concepts. In proposal (3), in the limit, even different properties of a single concept may have separable representations. For example, the sensory (mainly visual) things that you know about an elephant, such as its size, shape and colour, might be sufficiently separate from the more functional aspects of your elephant knowledge (what an elephant eats, what countries it lives in, whether it is fierce, etc.) that brain damage could selectively disrupt one but not the other. In fact, this proposal typically takes the form that some classes of objects, mainly living things, are primarily known to us by their visual properties, whereas man-made objects are critically defined by their functions as well as their sensory features. Thus, if one of the putative sensory/functional subsystems were to be independently affected, this should have disproportionate consequences for knowledge about either living things or man-made objects (see Farah & McClelland, 1991, for discussion).

Some data from patients with disorders of semantic memory are, at least on the face of it, compatible with each of these three proposals. The data might, however, be subject to a number of alternative explanations, some of genuine theoretical interest and others due simply to failures to control for other dimensions on which experimental stimuli or conditions might differ. To try to adjudicate between various explanations of these results would, as already indicated, be premature. A more appropriate goal is simply to try to sketch some of the patterns of data which have provoked these proposals about the structure of semantic memory.

Words versus objects? Patient T.O.B. was a senior civil servant and teacher suffering from progressive loss of both receptive and expressive vocabulary associated with left temporal atrophy and hypometabolism (McCarthy & Warrington, 1988, 1990; Parkin, 1993; Patterson & Hodges, 1992; Tyrrell, Warrington, Frackowiak & Rossor, 1990). McCarthy and Warrington (1988) asked T.O.B. to define various concepts from either their spoken names or pictures. Asked to describe, from the word, what a dolphin is, T.O.B. replied: "A fish or a bird"; shown a picture of a dolphin, he responded "Dolphin lives in the water...they are trained to jump up and come out... In America during the war years, they started to train this particular animal to go through to look into ships" (McCarthy & Warrington, 1988, p. 428). Since this apparent dissociation between types of knowledge (for words and objects) involves different modalities of presentation, one must consider the possibility that T.O.B.'s behaviour reflects not a characteristic of the way in which the knowledge itself is centrally represented but rather a disorder of access. That is, even if both the word "dolphin" and a picture of a dolphin produce activation in the same semantic knowledge system, one might observe a pattern like T.O.B.'s if an impairment in language processing has disrupted semantic access from words (Farah & Mc-Clelland, 1991). This explanation cannot be ruled out entirely; however, as argued by Bub, Black, Hampson and Kertesz (1988) with reference to a somewhat similar pattern of performance in patient M.P., the selective access impairment would be a more plausible interpretation if these patients demonstrated relatively preserved knowledge given pictures but understood essentially nothing from the spoken word. Even the meagre comprehension that a "dolphin" is an animal (fish or bird!) suggests that the spoken word must have been processed correctly.

Concrete versus abstract concepts? Abstract concepts like *idea*, *loyalty* or *suspense* are clearly, in some regard, more difficult than concrete or imageable concepts such as *itch*, *avalanche* or *lapel* (we have deliberately chosen some rather uncommon concrete concepts as examples in order to make it clear that the advantage enjoyed by concrete/imageable things is not due to the frequency with which one encounters them). The precise basis for this differential difficulty is not clear, but it has been hypothesised that abstract concepts are represented by fewer semantic features than concrete things, or that abstract things have a more variable meaning as a function of context than concrete things (see Jones, 1985, and Plaut & Shallice, 1993, for discussion). If two aspects of cognitive processing differ substantially in difficulty for normal people, then one is perhaps not surprised to find cases where this premorbid discrepancy is exaggerated as a result of brain damage. Thus, for example, some patients with aphasia due to cerebrovascular accident can still comprehend or produce words with concrete/imageable referents but fail to understand even fairly common abstract words such as *idea*. Indeed, it has been proposed that aphasia entails loss of an "abstract attitude" (Goldstein, 1948), though this is not an idea currently in fashion. Cases where the dissociation goes against the normal grain of difficulty are much more striking.

The abstract/concrete dimension was not explicitly evaluated in patient T.O.B.; however, his severe anomia for common objects (e.g. he correctly named only 54% of the relatively easy Snodgrass & Vanderwart pictures (Parkin, 1993) and failed to score at all on the more difficult Graded Naming Test (McCarthy & Warrington, 1988)) contrasts markedly with the plethora of abstract words used appropriately in his spontaneous speech (words such as *attention*, *discus-*

sion, integration, function, etc.; see Parkin, 1993), suggesting an advantage for his knowledge of abstract concepts. Furthermore, several other patients with disorders similar to T.O.B.'s have demonstrated a convincing abstractness advantage on various formal tests. Patient A.B. (Warrington, 1975) could define abstract spoken words like *supplication* ("Making a serious request for help", he said) and *arbiter* ("He is a man who tries to arbitrate, produce a peaceful solution") but not concrete words like *geese* ("An animal but I've forgotten precisely") or *needle* ("I've forgotten"). Patient D.B. (Breedin, Saffran & Coslett, 1995), given an "odd-man-out" test of word comprehension in which the subject is asked to say which two words of a triad are more similar in meaning, scored 85% on abstract triads like *loyalty–allegiance–obsession* but only 58% on concrete triads like *avalanche–landslide–earthquake*.

Sensory versus functional properties? A number of cases have been described where a patient demonstrates significantly better comprehension (and/or naming) of pictures (and/or words) that refer to man-made objects, such as tools, vehicles, household objects, than to living things (or actually, natural kinds) such as animals, fruit and vegetables. For example, T.O.B. (McCarthy & Warrington, 1988) was asked to define spoken names of man-made objects and living things (48 of each): he adequately identified 89% of the former but only 33% of the living. A smaller number of patients, and typically displaying a less marked discrepancy between categories, have been documented with the reverse dissociation; i.e. better performance on living things. To the extent that these dissociations are accepted as real (rather than artefactually caused by other differences between living and man-made things, such as the frequency with which we encounter them, or the visual complexity of their appearances; see Funnell & Sheridan, 1992, for discussion), the double dissociation has—as indicated earlier—been interpreted mainly as a differential weighting in the importance of sensory (particularly visual) versus functional properties in our semantic knowledge about living versus nonliving things. Farah and McClelland (1991) asked normal subjects to categorise descriptors, from dictionary definitions of living and nonliving things, as either visual or functional; this technique yielded ratios of visual to functional features of 7.7 to 1 for living things and 1.4 to 1 for man-made objects, supporting the conjecture that visual properties play an especially prominent role in what we know about living things. If visual and functional knowledge were represented in relatively separate components of semantic memory, then selective damage to visual knowledge would plausibly have more catastrophic consequences for performance on exemplars of living things—as observed in the data mentioned above.

What might compel the brain to establish separable systems for information about objects and words, abstract and imageable concepts, or sensory and functional features of concepts? Two notions seem germane to speculation on this question. The first involves developmental considerations: for example, the preverbal infant learns a great deal about objects before he or she knows words for them, and probably also learns about the sensory features of those objects before their functional properties become clear. (See Mandler, Bauer & Mc-Donough (1991) for discussion of perceptual distinctions that could lead to very early discrimination between living and nonliving things.) When language enters the picture, the child learns names for concrete concepts before abstract ones (it is even claimed that primitive languages have no abstract words; Gelhorn, 1978; Lyons, 1994). The subdivisions of knowledge apparently implicated by neuropsychological dissociations might, in other words, be understood in terms of differences between early and later learning. The second proposal, discussed by Allport (1985), Saffran and Schwartz (1994) and Warrington and McCarthy (1987), amongst others, is that—at any age—the manner in which you learn information, and particularly the sensory channels through which that information is acquired, will always form a prominent part of the representation of that knowledge.

How is Knowledge in Semantic Memory Represented?

Does our knowledge about a particular concept consist of individual semantic features, both sensory/perceptual and more abstract or functional? How might the collection of features characteristic of that concept be bound together such that, when we see a picture or hear a word referring to the concept, many or all of the pertinent features are activated? How might features characteristic of many concepts be represented—e.g. is *large African animal* represented in semantic memory in such a way that it can be "shared" by elephant, rhinoceros and giraffe? We know from many different experimental techniques, including priming, sorting and category fluency, that subjects' behaviour suggests a kind of similarity space in which the "distance" between elephant and giraffe, for example, may be smaller than that between elephant and tiger, which in turn is smaller than that between elephant and bear (see, e.g., Chan et al., 1993). Does this mean that semantic knowledge about these concepts comprises a sort of hierarchical tree, in which elephant and giraffe diverge into separate branches (or twigs) at a point further down the tree than less similar animals? The relationship between data and theory is even less secure in this domain than it was for the issue of category-specific aspects of knowledge; we will, therefore, restrict ourselves to one example of the kind of research that has been undertaken to address these questions.

Starting with the important observations of Warrington (1975), many investigators have established that, in tasks like sorting pictures or answering questions, patients may succeed at higher levels of a putative hierarchy but fail at lower levels. For example, when we first tested P.P. her sorting of pictures from the semantic battery (described above in the section on assessment) into two categories was perfect at level 1 (animals versus man-made objects), impaired but above chance at level 2 (e.g. land versus water animals) and no better than chance at level 3 (e.g. native versus foreign animals). A few months later, P.P. had declined to chance at level-2 sorting, but she was still flawless at level 1 and remained so for another year, after which this performance also declined steadily to chance (Hodges, Patterson & Tyler, 1994). Thus, both in the relative success on the three levels of the task at initial assessment and in the pattern of subsequent deterioration, there is clear differentiation between levels. There are at least three possible explanations of this pattern.

The first explanation, and perhaps the most intuitively appealing, is that P.P.'s performance actually reflects the hierarchical manner in which knowledge is organised (Collins & Quillan, 1969), with more specific aspects of the hierarchy more vulnerable to brain damage (Shallice, 1988). The second explanation, and perhaps less appealing because it locates the effect in the form of testing rather than in the form of knowledge representation, is that the words used to describe higher levels of the putative tree (e.g. "animal", "water", etc.) are more common vocabulary items than those for more specific distinctions (e.g. "foreign"). P.P., like all patients with a central semantic impairment, was gradually losing her vocabulary, receptive as well as expressive; perhaps her apparently hierarchical loss of knowledge indicates nothing more than the fact that she could only understand the verbal labels applied to more general, "higher" levels (Funnell, 1995). The third explanation, and the one that we favour, is that degraded semantic information is better able to support general than specific distinctions (Rapp & Caramazza, 1993). This view requires no assumptions about hierarchical forms of representation. If one's knowledge about an elephant consists of a network of semantic features, then, even when a substantial number of these have been lost or blurred, it is possible that the remaining information would permit the classification of an elephant as an animal (rather than a man-made object), because almost any "animal" feature distinguished it from a nonliving thing. The distinction between foreign and native animals, on the other hand, which depends on a much more limited and specific set of features would be more vulnerable.

The Impact of Semantic Impairments on Other Cognitive Abilities

In the remaining section of the chapter, we will briefly discuss an even more recent issue concerning disorders of semantic memory: whether cognitive sub-systems that are, in normal processing, in constant interaction with semantic memory can remain intact when semantic knowledge deteriorates. This may seem like a rather odd question: if an impairment of module A has deleterious consequences for the functioning of a different module B, what force is there to the concept of separate modules? The issue harks back to the point that we made, early in the chapter, about the separability but non-independence of semantic and episodic memory. Our hypothesis is that whether any two given subsystems are able to operate independently will depend on the nature of the computations that they perform. With the arrival of good functional brain imaging techniques like PET (positron-emission tomography), it is a rather common observation that, if one compares a patient's PET scan with even the best available structural brain images (from magnetic resonance imaging; MRI), the areas of functional abnormality as indicated by PET may significantly exceed the structural abnormalities measured by MRI (see Tyrrell, Warrington, Frackowiak and Rossor, 1990, for example). This observation indicates that a part of the brain which is itself structurally intact is failing to perform its normal computations because of lack of input from or communication with another, now damaged, region. Neuroanatomical considerations would suggest that such interdependence of regions should be based on physical proximity; but computational considerations would suggest that interdependence will also be determined by the nature of the cognitive processes.

On the basis of such cognitive principles, one might expect that the early stages of processing sensory input would be unaffected by central semantic dysfunction; and evidence from semantic dementia supports this independence. For example, performance on a range of visuoperceptual tasks was entirely within normal limits in five patients with semantic dementia (Hodges et al., 1992). On the other hand, the subsystems that are, in normal processing, in constant interaction with meaning might not be able to perform adequately when semantic representations are degraded. A number of aspects of cognitive processing qualify as subsystems that "talk to" semantic memory in order to perform their jobs; our own research on this topic has, thus far, been concerned mainly with two of these: the representations of phonology (which simply means the sound patterns of any given language) which allow us efficiently to speak familiar words, and the internal representations of object form which allow us rapidly to recognise familiar objects.

Except for the strictly grammatical parts of language (in English, function words like *of*, *by* and *that*, plus affixes such as *-ed* and *-ing*), words for speech production must be activated on the basis of a message from meaning (Levelt, 1992). Not surprisingly, then, a semantic deficit disrupts the patient's ability to produce appropriate words under any conditions where the input to the speech production system must come from semantic memory; these include spontaneous speech, object naming, and various tests used by neuropsychologists such as category fluency. This much is uncontroversial, and would be predicted by all theories concerning the relationship between meaning and speech production. The more controversial question is whether the phonological representations for speech production *themselves* depend for their normal operation on communication with semantic memory. If not, then a patient with a semantic deficit should be able to produce familiar words correctly *provided* that these representations are activated by something other than meaning—for example, in a word repetition task where the patient simply listens to words and repeats them back immediately. If, on the other hand, the structural integrity of phonological representations is partly dependent on communication with meaning, then even repetition performance might be affected by semantic deterioration. Initial research supports the latter view. In experiments with either sentence repetition (McCarthy & Warrington, 1987) or repetition of strings of 3–4 unrelated words (Patterson, Graham & Hodges, 1994), several patients with central semantic impairments have been shown to perform dramatically better on sentences or strings containing words whose meanings they still "know" (as assessed by tests of comprehension) than on sequences composed of previously familiar words whose meanings are now degraded for that patient. Since these patients all had normal short-term verbal memory capacity as assessed by digit span, their difficulty in reproducing "unknown" words cannot be attributed to any deficit in short-term memory *per se*. The errors on sequences with unknown words, consisting mainly of transpositions of sound segments between words (e.g. *mint*, *rug* repeated back as "rint, mug") resemble the errors made by normal subjects when asked to repeat sequences of nonsense words (Treiman & Danis, 1988).

With regard to object recognition, the techniques and logic of the test are somewhat different but the basic underlying principle is the same. Here, instead of determining whether the patients' representations for output might "come apart" as in the speech production task above, the experimenter does the "taking apart" on stimulus materials for input. In an "object decision" task originally designed by Humphreys, Riddoch and Quinlan (1988), pictures of familiar objects such as animals are presented to the subject either in their normal form or in a chimeric form consisting of part of one object combined with part of another—say, the body of a dog with the head of a sheep. Subjects are asked simply to judge whether each of the drawings represents a real object, and normal subjects do so accurately. Patients with prominent semantic memory impairments, however (either semantic dementia: see Hodges et al., 1992; or DAT: see Chertkow, Bub & Caplan, 1992) are reliably impaired on object decision tests. This suggests that the structural description system which enables us to classify objects as familiar depends on semantic knowledge about those objects. When semantic knowledge about dogs and sheep deteriorates, the incorrect conjunction of a dog's body with a sheep's head begins to appear as plausible as a correct conjunction. Many interesting aspects of this line of research remain to be explored, especially in trying to relate an individual patient's retained or impaired knowledge of specific concepts to his or her performance on various input and output tasks involving these concepts.

CONCLUDING COMMENT

In a review paper published in 1982, Kintsch concluded rather gloomily that precious little of real interest had been learned from the preceding decade of studies on semantic memory. In 1994, Sartori, Coltheart, Miozza and Job claimed that the "fortunes" of semantic memory research had substantially improved in the decade following Kintsch's assessment, and they attributed these advances in our understanding of semantic memory primarily to research on its disorders. We concur with the view of Sartori et al., although—as must be apparent from this chapter—in our opinion, major progress is more incipient than tangible. We offer three suggestions for lines of inquiry or approaches that seem likely to assist progress.

1. Semantic dementia is one promising source of pertinent data, firstly because this condition seems to have the most selective impact on semantic memory; and secondly because the progressive nature of the condition means that one can use patients as their own longitudinal controls to chart the deterioration of semantic memory and the specific brain regions affected.

2. An approach that seems promising is to incorporate results from, and techniques developed for, studies of knowledge in normal prelinguistic infants (e.g. Mandler, Bauer & McDonough, 1991). Semantic memory goes far beyond language (Kintsch, 1982); but language skills tend to dominate adult human cognition, and the tasks and instructions typically used in the study of semantic memory have relied heavily on language. New non-language-based methods must be explored if we are to understand the ways in which semantic memory in the adult human is, and is not, inextricably linked to language.

3. Finally, it may be important to develop techniques that eschew not only language but also the rather artificial tasks employed in most studies of semantic memory. We hasten to note that such contrived tasks are used for very good reason: although it might be informative to follow patients around in their daily lives, observing whether their responses to natural situations reflect intact or impaired comprehension, there are formidable difficulties in devising reliable and valid ways to score such behaviour. Nonetheless, the performance of a patient like P.P. on easy-to-score tasks such as naming a knife and fork or selecting a knife in response to its name simply does not tell us enough. In particular, it does not tell us whether P.P. will use a knife and fork appropriately when it is time to eat lunch. She did so on the one occasion on which we observed her in a restaurant, but of course we do not know what she would have done if the implements beside her plate had been a comb and brush instead. Some progress with this sort of approach has been made by Snowden, Griffiths and Neary (1994), who studied the responses of a patient with semantic dementia to objects in her own home that were either familiar (e.g. the patient's own kettle) or not (a kettle brought in by the experimenter) and that were either in their familiar places (a kettle in the kitchen) or not (a kettle in the bathroom). Like P.P., this patient was completely unable to name any of the items; but her descriptive and gestural responses revealed significant sensitivity to familiarity of both specific object and location. In other words, this patient's object recognition was severely impaired, because normal subjects will recognise a kettle (though perhaps more slowly), even in a totally incongruous location; however, given known objects in known places, the patient could still demonstrate some limited semantic knowledge.

REFERENCES

Allport, D. A. (1985). Distributed memory, modular subsystems and dysphasia. In S.K. Newman & R. Epstein (eds), *Current Perspectives in Dysphasia*. Churchill Livingstone, Edinburgh.

Baddeley, A.D. (1976). *The Psychology of Memory*. Basic Books, New York.

Bayles, K.A. & Tomoeda, C.K. (1983). Confrontational naming impairment in dementia. *Brain and Language*, **19**, 98–114.

Beauvois, M.-F. (1982). Optic aphasia: a process of interaction between vision and language. *Philosophical Transactions of the Royal Society of London B*, **298**, 35–47.

Behrmann, M. & Bub, D. (1992). Surface dyslexia and dysgraphia: dual routes, single lexicon. *Cognitive Neuropsychology*, **9**, 209–251.

Braak, H. & Braak, E. (1991). Neuropathological staging of Alzheimer-related changes. *Acta Neuropathologica*, **82**, 239–259.

Breedin, S.D., Saffran, E.M. & Coslett, H.B. (1995). Reversal of the concreteness effect in a patient with semantic dementia. *Cognitive Neuropsychology*, (in press).

Bub, D., Black, S., Hampson, E. & Kertesz, A. (1988). Semantic encoding of pictures and words: some neuropsychological observations. *Cognitive Neuropsychology*, **5**, 27–66.

Bub, D., Cancelliere, A. & Kertesz, A. (1985). Whole-word and analytic translation of spelling to sound in a nonsemantic reader. In K. Patterson, J.C. Marshall & M. Coltheart (eds), *Surface Dyslexia*. Erlbaum, London.

Butters, N., Granholm, E., Salmon, D.P., Grant, I. & Wolfe, J. (1987). Episodic and semantic memory: a comparison of amnesic and demented patients. *Journal of Clinical and Experimental Neuropsychology*, **9**, 479–497.

Cermak, L.S. (1984). The episodic–semantic distinction in amnesia. In L.R. Squire & N. Butters (eds), *Neuropsychology of Memory*. Guilford Press, New York, pp. 55–62.

Chan, A.S., Butters, N., Paulsen, J.S., Salmon, D.P., Swenson, M. & Maloney, L. (1993). An assessment of the semantic network in patients with Alzheimer's disease. *Journal of Cognitive Neuroscience*, **5**, 254–261.

Chertkow, H. & Bub, D. (1990). Semantic memory loss in dementia of Alzheimer's type. *Brain*, **113**, 397–417.

Chertkow, H., Bub, D. & Caplan, D. (1992). Constraining theories of semantic memory processing: evidence from dementia. *Cognitive Neuropsychology*, **9**, 327–365.

Collins, A.M. & Quillian, M.R. (1969). Retrieval time from semantic memory. *Journal of Verbal Learning and Verbal Behavior*, **8**, 240–247.

Damasio, A.R., Enlinger, P.G., Damasio, H., Van Hoesen, G.W. & Cornell, S. (1985). Multimodal amnesic syndrome following bilateral temporal and basal forebrain damage. *Archives of Neurology*, **42**, 252–259.

Damasio, A.R., Van Hoesen, G.W. & Hyman, B.T. (1990). Reflections on the selectivity of neuropathological changes in Alzheimer's disease. In M. Schwartz (ed.), *Modular Deficits in Alzheimer-type Dementia*. MIT Press, Cambridge, Mass.

Farah, M. & McClelland, J.L. (1991). A computational model of semantic memory impairment: modality specificity and emergent category specificity. *Journal of Experimental Psychology: General*, **120**, 339–357.

Fodor, J.A. (1983). *The Modularity of Mind*. MIT Press, Cambridge, Mass.

Funnell, E. (1995). From objects to properties: evidence for spreading activation in a case of semantic dementia. *Memory*, (in press).

Funnell, E. & Sheridan, J. (1992). Categories of knowledge? Unfamiliar aspects of living and nonliving things. *Cognitive Neuropsychology*, **9**, 135–153.

Gelhorn, M. (1978). *Travels with Myself and Another*. Eland Books, London.

Goldstein, K. (1948). *Language and Language Disturbance*. Grune & Stratton, New York.

Graff-Radford, N.R., Damasio, A.R., Hyman, B.T., Hart, M.N., Tranel, D., Damasio, H., Van Hoesen, G.W. & Rezai, K. (1990). Progressive aphasia in a patient with Pick's disease. *Neurology*, **40**, 620–626.

Hodges, J.R. (1993). Pick's disease. In A. Burns & R. Levy (eds), *Dementia*. Chapman & Hall, London.

Hodges, J.R., Graham, N. & Patterson, K. (in press). Charting the progression of semantic dementia: Implications for the organisation of semantic memory. *Memory*.

Hodges, J.R. & Patterson, K. (in press). Is semantic memory consistently impaired early in the course of Alzheimer's disease? Neuroanatomical and diagnostic implications. *Neuropsychologia*.

Hodges, J.R., Patterson, K., Oxbury, S. & Funnell, E. (1992). Semantic dementia: progressive fluent aphasia with temporal lobe atrophy. *Brain*, **115**, 1783–1806.

Hodges, J.R., Patterson, K. & Tyler, L.K. (1994). Loss of semantic memory: Implications for the modularity of mind. *Cognitive Neuropsychology*, **11**, 505–542.

Hodges, J.R., Salmon, D.P. & Butters, N. (1990). Differential impairment of semantic and episodic memory in Alzheimer's and Huntington's disease: a controlled prospective study. *Journal of Neurology, Neurosurgery and Psychiatry*, **53**, 1089–1095.

Hodges, J.R., Salmon, D.P. & Butters, N. (1991). The nature of the naming deficit in Alzheimer's and Huntington's disease. *Brain*, **114**, 1547–1558.

Hodges, J.R., Salmon, D.P. & Butters, N. (1992). Semantic memory impairment in Alzheimer's disease: failure of access or degraded knowledge? *Neuropsychologia*, **30**, 301–314.

Horner, M.D. (1990). Psychobiological evidence for the distinction between episodic and semantic memory. *Neuropsychology Review*, **1**, 281–321.

Howard, D. & Patterson, K. (1992). *Pyramids and Palm Trees: A Test of Semantic Access from Pictures and Words*. Thames Valley Publishing Company, Bury St. Edmunds.

Howard, D., Patterson, K., Wise, R., Brown, W.D., Friston, K., Weiller, C. & Frackowiak, R. (1992). The cortical localisation of the lexicons: positron emission tomography evidence. *Brain*, **115**, 1769–1782.

Humphreys, M.S., Bain, J.D. & Pike, R. (1989). Different ways to cue a coherent memory system: a theory for episodic, semantic and procedural tasks. *Psychological Review*, **96**, 208–233.

Humphreys, G.W., Riddoch, M.J. & Quinlan, P.T. (1988). Cascade processes in picture identification. *Cognitive Neuropsychology*, **5**, 67–104.

Jones, G.V. (1985). Deep dyslexia, imageability, and ease of predication. *Brain and Language*, **24**, 1–19.

Kintsch, W. (1982). Semantic memory: a tutorial. In R.S. Nickerson (ed.), *Attention & Performance*, Vol. 8., Erlbaum, Hillsdale, NJ.

Levelt, W.J.M. (1992). Accessing words in speech production: stages, processes and representations. *Cognition*, **42**, 1–22.

Lyons, J. (1994). Colour in language. In T. Lamb (ed.), *Colour: The 9th Annual Darwin Lecture Series*. Cambridge University Press, Cambridge, UK.

Mandler, J.M., Bauer, P.J. & McDonough, L. (1991). Separating the sheep from the goats: differentiating global categories. *Cognitive Psychology*, **23**, 263–298.

Martin, A. & Fedio, P. (1983). Word production and comprehension in Alzheimer's disease: the breakdown of semantic knowledge. *Brain and Language*, **19**, 124–141.

McCarthy, R. & Warrington, E.K. (1987). The double dissociation of short-term memory for lists and sentences. *Brain*, **110**, 1545–1563.

McCarthy, R. & Warrington, E.K. (1988). Evidence for modality-specific meaning systems in the brain. *Nature*, **334**, 428–430.

McCarthy, R. & Warrington, E.K. (1990). The dissolution of semantics. *Nature*, **343**, 599.

McCarthy, R. & Warrington, E.K. (1992). Actors but not scripts: the dissociation of people and events in retrograde amnesia. *Neuropsychologia*, **30**, 633–644.

Nebes, R.B. (1989). Semantic memory in Alzheimer's disease. *Psychological Bulletin*, **106**, 377–394.

Parkin, A.J. (1993). Progressive aphasia without dementia—a clinical and cognitive neuropsychological analysis. *Brain and Language*, **44**, 201–220.

Patterson, K. & Hodges, J.R. (1992). Loss of word meaning: implications for reading. *Neuropsychologia*, **30**, 1025–1040.

Patterson, K., Graham, N. & Hodges, J.R. (1994). The impact of semantic memory loss on phonological representations. *Journal of Cognitive Neuroscience*, **6**, 57–69.

Petersen, S.E., Fox, P.T., Posner, M.I., Mintun, M. & Raichle, M.E. (1988). Positron emission tomographic studies of the cortical anatomy of single-word processing. *Nature*, **331**, 585–589.

Petersen, S.E., Fox, P.T., Posner, M.I., Mintun, M. & Raichle, M.E. (1989). Positron emission tomographic studies of the processing of single words. *Journal of Cognitive Neuroscience*, **1**, 153–170.

Pietrini, V., Nertempi, P., Vaglia, A., Revello, M.G., Pinna, V. and Ferro-Milone, F. (1988). Recovery from herpes simplex encephalitis: selective impairment of specific semantic categories with neuroradiological correlation. *Journal of Neurology, Neurosurgery and Psychiatry*, **51**, 1284–1293.

Plaut, D.C. & Shallice, T. (1993). Deep dyslexia: a case study of connectionist neuropsychology. *Cognitive Neuropsychology*, **10**, 377–500.

Rapp, B.A. & Caramazza, A. (1993). On the distinction between deficits of access and deficits of storage: a question of theory. *Cognitive Neuropsychology*, **10**, 113–141.

Saffran, E.M. & Schwartz, M.F. (1994). Of cabbages and things: semantic memory from a neuropsychological perspective—a tutorial review. In C. Umilta & M. Moscovitch (eds), *Attention & Performance*, Vol. 15. MIT Press, Cambridge, Mass.

Sartori, G., Coltheart, M., Miozza, M. & Job, R. (1994). Category specificity and informational specificity in neuropsychological impairment of semantic memory. In C. Umilta & M. Moscovitch (eds), *Attention & Performance*, Vol. 15. MIT Press, Cambridge, Mass.

Sartori, G. & Job, R. (1988). The oyster with four legs: a neuropsychological study on the interaction of visual and semantic information. *Cognitive Neuropsychology*, **4**, 105–132.

Schwartz, M.F., Marin, O.S.M. & Saffran, E.M. (1979). Dissociations of language function in dementia: a case study. *Brain and Language*, **7**, 277–306.

Schacter, D.L. (1987). Implicit memory: history and current status. *Journal of Experimental Psychology; Learning, Memory and Cognition*, **13**, 501–518.

Shallice, T. (1988). *From Neuropsychology to Mental Structure*. Cambridge University Press, Cambridge.

Snowden, J.S., Goulding, P.J. & Neary, D. (1989). Semantic dementia: a form of circumscribed cerebral atrophy. *Behavioural Neurology*, **2**, 167–182.

Snowden, J.S., Griffiths & Neary, D. (1994). Semantic dementia: autobiographical contribution to preservation of meaning. *Cognitive Neuropsychology*, **11**, 265–288.

Snowden, J.S., Neary, D., Mann, D.M.A., Goulding, P.J. & Tsta, H.J. (1992). Progressive language disorder due to lobar atrophy. *Annals of Neurology*, **31**, 174–183.

Squire, L.R. (1987). *Memory and the Brain*. Oxford University Press, New York.

Tanabe, H. (1992). Personality of typical Gogi (word-meaning) aphasics. *Japanese Journal of Neuropsychology*, **8**, 34–42.

Treiman, R. & Danis, C. (1988). Short-term memory errors for spoken syllables are affected by the linguistic structure of the syllables. *Journal of Experimental Psychology: Learning, Memory and Cognition*, **14**, 145–152.

Tulving, E. (1972). Episodic and semantic memory. In E. Tulving & W. Donaldson (eds), *Organization of Memory*. Academic Press, New York.

Tulving, E. (1983). *Elements of Episodic Memory*. Oxford University Press, New York.

Tyler, L.K. (1992). *Spoken Language Comprehension: An Experimental Approach to Disordered and Normal Processing*. MIT Press, Cambridge, Mass.

Tyrrell, P.J., Warrington, E.K., Frackowiak, R.S.J. and Rossor, M.N. (1990). Heterogeneity in progressive aphasia due to focal cortical atrophy: a clinical and PET study. *Brain*, **113**, 1321–1336.

Warrington, E.K. (1975). Selective impairment of semantic memory. *Quarterly Journal of Experimental Psychology*, **27**, 635–657.

Warrington, E.K. (1981). Concrete word dyslexia. *British Journal of Psychology*, **72**, 175–196.

Warrington, E.K. & McCarthy, R. (1987). Categories of knowledge: further fractionation and an attempted integration. *Brain*, **110**, 1273–1296.

Warrington, E.K. & Shallice, T. (1984). Category specific semantic impairments. *Brain*, **107**, 829–854.

Wernicke, C. (1874). *Der aphasischer Symptomenkomplex*: *eine psychologische Studie auf anatomischer Basis*: Cohn & Weigert, Breslau. Translated by G.H. Eggert (1977) in *Wernicke's Works on Aphasia*: *A Sourcebook and Review*: Mouton, The Hague, pp. 91–145.

Chapter 8

Post-Traumatic and Anterograde Amnesia Following Closed Head Injury

Felicia C. Goldstein
Emory University School of Medicine and
Wesley Woods Center, Atlanta
and
Harvey S. Levin
University of Maryland School of Medicine, Baltimore, USA

INTRODUCTION

Of all the cognitive abilities affected by closed head injury (CHI), memory functioning has received the most intensive scrutiny from researchers interested in its initial and long-term characteristics, relationship to severity features, and recovery patterns. Findings from the academic arena have relevance to clinicians who provide hands-on treatment and recommendations to patients and significant others. For example, the knowledge that patients in post-traumatic amnesia exhibit learning of new skills (Ewert, Levin, Watson & Kalisky, 1989; Wilson, Baddeley, Shiel & Patton, 1992) implies that occupational and physical therapies can be taught and retained when they are implemented early after emergence from coma. Moreover, evidence for preserved components of memory such as the ability to recognize and to utilize semantic relationships (Levin & Goldstein, 1986; Goldstein, Levin, Boake & Lohrey, 1990; Haut, Petros & Frank, 1991; Haut, Petros, Frank & Haut, 1991) suggests potentially effective rehabilitation strategies including emphasis on the meaning of to-be-learned material and clustering of related information into categories.

Handbook of Memory Disorders. Edited by A.D. Baddeley, B.A. Wilson and F.N. Watts.
© 1995 John Wiley & Sons Ltd.

In this chapter, we review studies concerning memory functioning in the acute and long-term stages of recovery in adult survivors of head injury. First we examine the measurement and clinical features of memory during the early stage of post-traumatic amnesia. Next we discuss anterograde amnesia, delineating the characteristics of mnestic performance in mild injuries and in patients with moderate to severe injuries. Retrograde amnesia is covered in Chapter 4 and thus will not be elaborated here. Management of memory problems is discussed in Section IV of this volume and also will not be addressed in our review.

POST-TRAUMATIC AMNESIA

Post-traumatic amnesia (PTA) refers to the early period following head injury, and emergence from coma in severely injured patients, in which there is difficulty recording and retrieving information concerning daily events (Jennett & Teasdale, 1981; Levin, Benton & Grossman, 1982; Russell, 1971; Russell & Smith, 1961). During PTA, the patient may exhibit agitation, disinhibition, confabulation, disorientation, and impaired attention.

PTA is clinically important to examine because its length provides a measure of injury severity, and the presence of an amnestic period may be the only objective evidence that the patient has sustained brain insult. This applies to cases of mild head injury in which loss of consciousness is momentary or absent, and neurologic and neuroradiologic findings are normal. Assessment of PTA is useful in detecting unappreciated cases of mild head trauma following spinal cord injury and should be routinely performed (Davidoff, Morris, Roth & Bleiberg, 1985; Davidoff et al., 1988). Roth and colleagues (1989) observed PTA in 35 (43%) of their 81 spinal-cord injured patients. PTA should also be evaluated in elderly patients who have fallen, in order to document any occult head injury that could interfere with rehabilitation and discharge placement.

PTA is longer than would be expected on the basis of impaired consciousness in approximately 10–15% of survivors of mild or moderate head injury (Levin & Eisenberg, 1987). Investigators have reported that PTA duration predicts the presence and chronicity of memory impairment. In general, PTA durations greater than two weeks are related to long-term deficits (Brooks et al., 1987; Dikmen et al., 1987). Thus, knowledge of PTA length can help the clinician to anticipate a chronic memory problem and plan for future treatment.

Retrospective Estimation Versus Direct Assessment of PTA

Traditionally, PTA is evaluated subjectively by asking patients to describe their first memory after the accident and to report when they resumed continuous recall. This retrospective method, however, may be inaccurate due to confabulation and difficulty with reality monitoring. Gronwall and Wrightson (1980), in fact, noted that a quarter of their patients with mild head injury changed their original estimates of PTA when re-interviewed three months later. This suggests that their estimates may have been modified by intervening events, including reports of others. Objective methods include serial testing via questionnaires or behavioral observations. Scores at a predesignated level on each scale are used to judge whether a patient is still "in" PTA.

Table 8.1 indicates measures for evaluating PTA and the similarities and differences in the areas they examine. These measures enquire about the patient's orientation to person, place and time as well as their recall of autobiographical information such as birthdate and address. They differ, though, in the other components of memory they assess. The Galveston Orientation and Amnesia Test (GOAT) asks about recall of events immediately preceding and following the accident, with error points assigned on the basis of the completeness and plausibility of the information. Two other instruments assess the patient's capacity for new learning. The Westmead PTA Scale examines the ability to remember three objects and to recall the examiner's face and name over three days. Similarly, the scale developed by Artiolai Fortuny and colleagues includes a picture recall task and recall of the examiner's name. Finally, the Orientation Group Monitoring System (OGMS) is a behavioral rating scale based on observation of the patient in a group setting over an extended time period. The OGMS examines orientation to time and place, knowledge of group members and rehabilitation staff, ability to pay attention to group activities and to respond appropriately, repetition of paired associates, recall of events that happened on a previous day, and use of external aids to report daily activities. These measures will provide differing estimates of PTA length based on the abilities they emphasize. For example, the GOAT is heavily weighted towards assessing orientation as opposed to new learning. It may therefore be useful to include items which tap memory for novel information (e.g. visual recognition memory).

The ability to predict PTA length in acutely injured patients has practical implications for anticipating and planning remediation strategies. Demographic and clinical features have been identified in relation to outcome. Older patients exhibit lengthier PTAs and are more likely to say that the date is earlier than the actual date; i.e. to say "1930" rather than "1970" (High, Levin & Gary, 1990; Katz, Kehs & Alexander, 1990). In addition, High and colleagues found that patients with frontal lobe lesions had longer PTA durations than patients with lesions outside the frontal or temporal lobes or those without lesions. Saneda and Corrigan (1992) studied moderate and severely injured patients who were admitted to a rehabilitation program while still in PTA, and found that patients who had shorter times from acute injury to placement were more likely to show a resolution of their acute confusional state. The associative learning score on the OGMS which tests the patient's retention of five paired associates was also related to outcome. As Saneda and Corrigan noted, however, there was sufficient variation in their sample to create problems for accurate prediction.

Table 8.1   Aspects of memory examined in selected measures of post-traumatic amnesia

	Orienta-tion	Autobio-graphical memory	Recall surrounding accident		New learning	Atten-tion	Use of aids
			Before	*After*			
GOAT*	+	+	+	+			
Westmead PTA Scale†	+	+			+		
Artiola et al. PTA Scale‡	+	+	+	+	+		
Orientation Group Monitoring System§	+				+	+	+

* Galveston Orientation and Amnesia Test — Levin, O'Donnell & Grossman (1979)
†Shores, Marosszeky, Sandanam & Batchelor (1986)
‡Artiolai Fortuny et al. (1980)
§Corrigan, Arnett, Houck & Jackson (1985)

Characteristics of Memory During PTA

Acquisition and retention during PTA have been addressed in a few studies, but attempts to improve memory have not been systematically explored. Patients in PTA exhibit rapid forgetting and a passive approach to learning. Levin, High and Eisenberg (1988) observed that patients in PTA (based upon the GOAT score), compared with those no longer in PTA and normal controls, had more pronounced rates of forgetting when tested on visual recognition memory two hours and 32 hours after the initial slide presentation. In order to equate learning for the three groups, patients in PTA required extended viewing of the material. Gasquoine (1991) examined list learning over five sessions in survivors of severe closed head injury. Patients in PTA, defined by GOAT scores ≤ 75 points, were read a list of 12 words belonging to four categories. Survivors exhibited flat learning curves over the five trials of each session as well as a lack of benefit from repeated presentations over five successive training days. In addition, patients did not cluster the words belonging to the same categories, nor did semantic cueing facilitate their recall as it does in neurologically intact individuals. Gasquoine interpreted these findings as demonstrating inactive encoding and retrieval strategies during PTA.

While these previous studies indicate impaired memory for new information during PTA, there are indications that some components may be relatively preserved. One such area involves procedural memory; i.e. retention of motor or visually based procedures and skills that is not dependent on remembering specific conditions or facts under which this information was learned. Ewert, Levin, Watson & Kalisky (1989) studied patients in PTA over three sessions during which they were given procedural tasks including using a pencil to trace their way out of mazes (Porteus Mazes), and keeping a stylus on a rotating turntable (Pursuit Rotor Task). They were then tested in a fourth session following the resolution of PTA. Table 8.2 summarizes performance for the Porteus Mazes and Pursuit Rotor Tasks. Patients displayed procedural learning over sessions as indicated by their decreased latencies to solve the mazes and their increased time on the rotating target. Moreover, these skills were retained when PTA ended. In contrast, they showed severe declarative memory deficits (e.g. not recalling the examiner or the words on the mirror-reading task).

Wilson et al. (1992) also observed preserved procedural learning in survivors of severe head injury. These investigators compared the pursuit rotor performance of head injured patients in PTA with long-term memory impaired survivors, patients with amnesia due to other etiologies, and normal controls. The PTA group showed an overall increase in their percentage of time on the rotating target. This improvement was primarily attributable to the slowest (15 rpm) compared to the fastest (40 rpm) presentation conditions.

In addition to these studies demonstrating procedural learning, Gasquoine (1991) found that patients in PTA showed relatively intact spatial memory (recalling the location of rooms on a floorplan) over three successive sessions, and they retained this information over two subsequent sessions.

Table 8.2 Performance of severe head injured patients on procedural memory tasks

	CHI patients	Control subjects
Porteus maze performance Mean (SD) time to completion		
*In PTA**		
Session 1	42.3 (21.0)	14.0 (5.2)
Session 2	36.3 (18.5)	12.3 (4.4)
Session 3	30.1 (15.9)	10.7 (3.1)
After PTA		
Session 4	24.4 (10.9)	9.9(3.1)
Pursuit rotor performance Mean (SD) percentage of time on target (45rpm)		
In PTA		
Session 1	15.8 (15.4)	63.4 (12.7)
Session 2	22.7 (19.8)	78.1 (9.2)
Session 3	25.2 (21.1)	80.7 (8.0)
After PTA		
Session 4	39.8 (20.3)	78.2 (10.3)

*PTA defined by a score falling below the normal range on the Galveston Orientation and Amnesia Test (Levin, O'Donnell & Grossman, 1979).
Source: Modified from Ewert, Levin, Watson & Kalisky (1989). Reproduced with permission. Copyright 1989 American Medical Association.

These results suggest that some types of learning are possible during PTA and are encouraging in terms of supporting the feasibility of rehabilitation efforts. Future research should delineate areas of mnestic strengths in survivors in order to help define effective strategies for teaching new information.

Following the emergence from PTA, patients often exhibit an anterograde memory deficit for new information. Over half the survivors of moderate and severe closed head injury display impaired memory as revealed by objective neuropsychological measures and subjective estimates by patients and significant others (Brooks et al., 1986; Levin, Goldstein, High & Eisenberg, 1988; Levin et al., 1990; Wilson, 1992). Memory difficulties are also common during the first month after mild head injury, but generally resolve within three months (Levin et al., 1987b). Although there is a high frequency of memory deficits in this population, there is increasing evidence for preserved abilities as well as heterogeneity in outcome (Ruff et al., 1991; Wilson, 1992). In the following sections we describe findings on memory functioning in mild and then moderately to severely injured patients, emphasizing the salient clinical manifestations and recovery patterns.

ANTEROGRADE AMNESIA

Mild Head Injury

Mild head injury produces brief (i.e. 30 minutes or less) or no loss of consciousness and no neurologic or neurosurgical complications. The Glasgow Coma Scale (GCS; Teasdale & Jennett, 1974) is used to characterize the depth and duration of impaired consciousness. The GCS involves a numerical rating of the patient's best eye, motor and verbal responses. Scores range from 3 points (no eye-opening, no motor response to stimulation, no verbal response) to 15 points (spontaneous eye-opening, able to obey commands, oriented). Scores of 13–15 on hospital admission without deterioration denote a mild injury. Post-concussion sequelae include cognitive complaints of which memory disturbance is the most prominent (McLean et al., 1984; Dikmen, McLean & Temkin, 1986; Levin et al., 1987b).

Dikmen and colleagues (1986) evaluated the subjective complaints of patients with mild head injury at one month after injury. Figure 8.1 shows the cognitive, somatic and affective symptoms reported. The report of memory disturbance occurred significantly more often in patients than in normal controls without head injury. A high frequency of memory problems is also observed on neuropsychological tests administered the first week after injury. Levin et al. (1987b) administered verbal and visual memory measures to mildly injured patients who had no antecedent history of head injury or neuropsychiatric disturbance. When tested within a week of injury, 85% of patients with mild head injury scored below normal control performance on a verbal memory test requiring them to

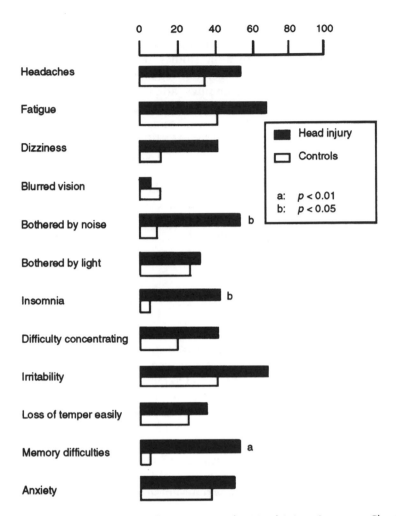

Figure 8.1 Median percentage endorsement on the Head Injury Symptom Checklist at one month. Reproduced from Dikmen, McLean & Temkin (1986) by permission of the authors and the BMJ Publishing Group

learn and to retain words over repeated trials. In addition, 76% of the sample performed more poorly than controls on a test of immediate visual memory.

Neuroradiologic findings have been inconsistent in predicting memory disturbance following head injury. While temporal lobe pathology has been implicated in memory disorders in other populations (e.g. herpes simplex encephalitis, patients undergoing electroconvulsive therapy), Levin et al. (1992) did not observe relationships between the presence and site of temporal lobe lesions and neuropsychological test performance. Four of eight patients with normal MRIs at one month continued to display significant neuropsychological deficits. Humayun et al. (1989) noted the superiority of functional imaging (positron emission tomography or PET) in detecting cerebral dysfunction in patients with mild head injury in whom CT and MRI findings were normal. Humayun and colleagues performed PET activation studies on three right-handed patients with mild head injury within one year following injury. These patients had loss of consciousness not greater than 20 minutes, admission GCS scores of 13–15, and normal neurologic evaluations. Neuropsychological testing indicated impaired verbal and visual memory involving new learning, delayed memory and recognition. Patients and normal controls underwent PET scanning while engaged in a vigilance task requiring them to determine if a visual stimulus was the same or different from a preceding stimulus. Compared with controls without head injury, the patients exhibited glucose metabolic disturbances involving the left and right temporal regions, the left caudate nucleus, and the right frontal cortex. In view of the small sample size, possible selection bias, and the lack of PET and memory studies during an earlier phase of recovery, these findings reported by Humayun and colleagues should be interpreted with caution.

Features of Memory Functioning and Recovery

Memory for new information should be examined in the clinical setting since this is the most frequent type of memory disturbance after mild head injury. Multitrial recall tasks which emphasize delayed recall following a period filled with distraction are especially sensitive. Dikmen, McLean and Temkin (1986) reported that their patients with mild head injury at one month exhibited a selective deficit in remembering words after a 4-hour interval. The impact of an attentional disturbance on memory performance should also be evaluated since impaired concentration is frequently reported after mild head injury. The contribution of attention can be assessed indirectly by considering qualitative features of memory such as consistency in recall over trials, better delayed than immediate recall, and facilitation whenever structure is imposed (e.g. story versus word recall). Direct assessment can be obtained through attentional tasks such as those requiring sustained effort, speed of processing, and freedom from distraction (e.g. Paced Auditory Serial Addition Test: Gronwall & Wrightson, 1974; Stroop Test: Stroop, 1935).

A challenge to clinicians working with patients with mild head injury concerns the prediction of recovery. Controlled, prospective studies that examine all patients, regardless of their subjective complaints, report a return of memory to normal levels within 1–3 months after injury (Dikmen, McLean & Temkin, 1986; Gentilini et al., 1985; Levin et al., 1987b). In contrast, studies of patients who are referred for neuropsychological testing because they are encountering difficulties have noted that problems persist at 3 months and for as long as two years (Leininger et al., 1990; Rimel et al., 1981). Subjectively, patients may continue to report post-concussional symptoms despite a return to "normal" levels on neuropsychological tests. Complications such as depression, adverse effects of medication, and questionable motivation may contribute to poor memory performance at long intervals after a mild head injury. Levin et al.

(1987b) observed that patients' complaints at one month postinjury remained unchanged despite clear improvement on neuropsychological measures. There was a trend for cognitive symptoms to be reported as more pronounced at the follow-up.

Several features are important for the clinician to consider when gauging the temporal course of recovery. First, one should ask whether a patient has ever had a previous injury since the neurobehavioral effects of mild head injury may be cumulative (Gronwall & Wrightson, 1975). Secondly, allegedly mild head injuries may have been more severe, particularly in cases of delayed emergency evacuation, inaccurate assessment of consciousness level in the emergency room caused by a failure to use standardized measures such as the GCS, and lack of an early CT or MRI scan. In addition, the age of the patient can affect recovery, with patients 40 years or over more likely to exhibit a slower course (Fenton et al., 1993; Gronwall, 1989; Rutherford, 1989). Characteristics of the injury such as whether there was an associated brain lesion or severe multiple trauma need to be determined since these events are associated with a poorer neurobehavioral outcome (Dikmen et al., 1986; Williams, Levin & Eisenberg, 1990). Premorbid features, including alcohol and drug use as well as psychiatric disturbance, can alter recovery. Finally, depression and anxiety may complicate the patient's neurobehavioral profile and ability to resume independence.

Persisting complaints that are out of proportion to the severity of the injury suggest that emotional features or malingering are operating. Forced-choice techniques, discussed in greater detail in Chapter 18, have been developed to detect malingering (Binder & Pankratz, 1987; Hiscock & Hiscock, 1989; Pankratz, 1979, 1983). The rationale behind these tests is that a patient who is guessing will be correct at least 50% of the time. Malingering is inferred when the patient's performance is below chance, implying deception. In the Digit Memory Test (Hiscock & Hiscock, 1989), for example, the patient views a 5-digit number written on a card, engages in a distracting task for five seconds, and is then given a recognition memory test consisting of the target plus a distractor series which differs in at least two numbers, including the first or last digit. Following a group of trials, the patient is now told that the procedure will become even more difficult because the interval between seeing the numbers and being tested will increase. The forced-choice technique to detect malingering has recently been criticized because it has been found that simulators perform above chance levels. Baker et al. (1993), therefore, recommend a comparison of memory under conditions of distraction (e.g. counting backwards before recall) versus no distraction. Using this method, they found that simulators were more likely to perform poorly under both conditions compared with patients with head injury who exhibited good recall under the no-distraction manipulation.

To summarize, mild head injury produces memory difficulties that are prominent in the initial months. Memory functioning typically recovers in patients without pre-existing neuropsychiatric disorder and comorbidities. In patients with prolonged symptoms, other factors should be considered including neurologic complications, emotional difficulties such as depression, and, in a subset of individuals, intentional exaggeration for secondary gain.

Moderate and Severe Head Injury

Moderate and severe head injury produce memory difficulties in the early stages of recovery. However, these deficits typically persist beyond the first few months, and they therefore affect long-range plans including return to school or work (Brooks et al., 1987; Ryan et al., 1992). Patients with moderate head injuries obtain GCS scores of 9–12 with or without neuropathologic complications such as focal brain lesions or depressed skull fractures. Patients with GCS scores of 13–15 but with coexisting neuroradiologic findings are best considered as having sustained moderate rather than mild injuries. These patients perform more poorly on memory tests than patients with GCS scores of 13–15 but without neuroradiologic abnormalities (Williams, Levin & Eisenberg, 1990). Thus, the clinician may anticipate prolonged memory deficits and complaints. Severe head injury includes patients who obtain GCS scores ≤ 8, implying the inability to obey commands, no eye opening, and inability to speak intelligible words (i.e. coma).

Recovery of Memory

A number of neurologic indices have been examined with the goal of predicting memory recovery. The depth and duration of impaired consciousness as well as ocular responses frequently emerge as the strongest predictors after moderate and severe CHI (Dikmen et al., 1987; Levin et al., 1990; Vilkki, Poropudas & Servo, 1988; Wilson, 1992). The combination of these two neurologic indices as opposed to a single index is especially prognostic.

Levin et al. (1990) evaluated verbal learning and retrieval in survivors of severe CHI and found a significant correlation between the lowest post-resuscitation GCS score and nonreactive pupils in predicting memory performance at one year. Hypoxia also portends a poor memory outcome (Ruff et al. 1991). Ruff and colleagues found that severely injured patients who exhibited no recovery in memory over one year were more likely to have sustained acute hypoxic brain damage. Attempts to correlate memory outcome with the presence and site of focal brain lesions, in contrast, have been inconsistent using a variety of imaging techniques including CT, MRI and single photon emission computed tomography (SPECT) (Goldenberg, Oder, Spatt & Podreka, 1992; Levin et al., 1990, 1992; Wilson et al., 1988). This most likely reflects the diffuseness of brain damage, the fact that characteristics such as depth of lesion rather than its mere presence may affect memory functioning, and the myriad extra injury features that contribute to outcome, such as age and premorbid history. Raised intracranial pressure (ICP) also inconsistently predicts outcome. Although Uzzell, Obrist, Dolinskas & Langfitt (1986) reported a significant relationship between elevated ICP and memory functioning at one year after severe head injury, Levin et al. (1991) noted minimal relationships at 6 months and nonsignificant findings at one year.

The remarkable heterogeneity in outcome from head injury is becoming appreciated as investigators look at individual recovery curves as opposed to combining all survivors into one group. Approximately one-third to one-half of severely injured patients exhibit improvements in memory abilities (Ruff et al., 1991; Wilson, 1992). Ruff et al. (1991) observed three subtypes of memory recovery after severe head injury. Patients were administered a verbal learning test requiring them to recall 12 words over 12 trials. Figure 8.2 displays their profiles in terms of the ability to recall consistently the same words on each trial without reminding by the examiner. Subtype-1 patients, comprising one-third of the sample, showed an initial improvement from baseline to 6 months but then a performance decline by one year. Subtype-2 patients (17%) displayed a flat profile, whereas subtype-3 patients (50%) continued to display memory gains over the year. These latter patients showed a lessening in depression whereas the other groups increased or continued at the same level, suggesting an association between affective functioning and memory performance. Wilson (1992) also observed heterogeneity in memory recovery after severe CHI. Patients were re-evaluated 5–10 years after they were initially treated for memory disturbance. Fifty-six percent showed no change, 32% improved, and the remaining patients declined. Neither study, however, had a control group that was followed at the same intervals in which to examine normal temporal variations in memory.

Apart from heterogeneity in memory recovery, disassociations from other neurobehavioral areas occur. Memory performance can lag behind the improvement of such abilities as language and visuospatial processing (Levin et al., 1990; Ruff et al., 1991). Levin et al. (1990) observed significant differences in verbal and visual recall between patients with severe head injury at one year compared with normal controls. Patients performed nearly 50% below the median of controls on a word recall task, and they also made more than two times the number of errors in reproducing designs. In contrast, the groups were comparable in visual naming and the ability to put blocks together to match designs. On the other hand, neurobehavioral deficits can coexist and exacerbate memory impairments. Divided attention deficits and slow information processing speed can affect the ability to retain information after a period filled with distraction (Stuss et al., 1985). These findings emphasize the need for comprehensive neuropsychological testing to assess primary and secondary impairments adequately.

In summary, there is variability among individual patients in recovery patterns as well as in the relationship of memory functioning to other neurobehavioral areas. In the following section, we review qualitative features of memory performance.

Features of Memory Performance Following Moderate and Severe CHI

A number of areas of memory functioning and their clinical manifestations have been studied following moderate and severe CHI. These include the ability to

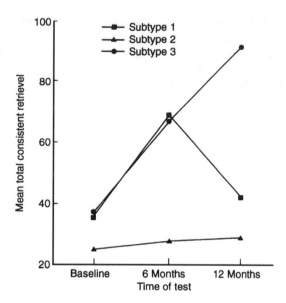

Figure 8.2 Mean total consistent long-term retrieval of words in 59 patients at baseline and at 6 and 12 months post-trauma. Reprinted from Ruff et al. (1991) by permission of the author and the *Journal of Neurosurgery*

reproduce accurately the original material and the conditions in which it was learned, to hold on to information after a delay, to impose executive processing strategies whenever tasks are unorganized, and to process material semantically.

Inaccurate Recall of Information and Context: Intrusions and Source Errors

Normal memory depends on being able to retain as closely as possible the features of original learning, including not only the memorized information but the context in which it was acquired. There is evidence, however, that head injured patients have difficulty with both these aspects, leading to distortions and inaccurate recall. It has been found, for example, that patients make excessive intrusions on verbal recall tasks (Brooks, 1975; Crosson, Novack, Trenerry & Craig, 1988; Crosson et al., 1993; Levin & Goldstein, 1986). This deficit is illustrated by Crosson and colleagues who noted intrusion errors on the California Verbal Learning Test (CVLT; Delis, Kramer, Kaplan & Ober, 1987), a procedure requiring patients to recall 16 words belonging to four semantic categories. Figure 8.3 shows the percentage of intrusions made by patients and normal controls over five trials. As can be seen, the patients were more prone to this type of error. In addition patients with a greater impairment of learning were most likely to exhibit intrusions in other memory conditions including cued and delayed recall.

Intrusions can be clinically manifested as phonemic or semantic distortions of the original material, unrelated words, or confusion of old with new learning

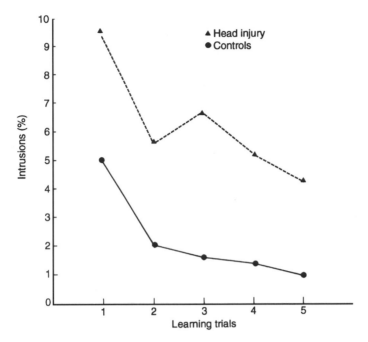

Figure 8.3 Intrusions (i.e. non-List A responses) expressed as a percentage of the total response output. Reproduced from Crosson, Novack, Trenerry & Craig (1988) by permission of the authors and Swets & Zeitlinger

such as recalling words from another list. Thus, in recalling Monday shopping items on the CVLT, patients may incorrectly recall words that were presented on the Tuesday shopping list. Crosson et al. (1993) found that verbal intrusions in head injured patients were associated with dominant temporal lobe damage. Intrusions also occur on visual reproduction or recognition tasks. Patients may adopt a tendency to respond "yes" to a large number of stimuli that have not been previously encountered, resulting in excessive false alarm errors (Hannay, Levin & Grossman, 1979; Levin et al., 1985).

Patients with head injury may also confuse the source of their learning such that when they do recall material, they are impaired in knowing how this information was acquired. Clinically, this is seen as confabulation. Impaired memory for how, when, or where information was learned despite retention of the facts themselves is referred to as source amnesia (Shimamura & Squire, 1987, 1991). Dywan, Segalowitz, Henderson & Jacoby (1993) examined source amnesia in moderately and severely injured patients who were at least one year post-injury. Patients were administered a fame judgment procedure in which they read names of nonfamous people and were told that the experimenter was simply interested in how the names were pronounced. Later, they were given a list of names including some which they had read before, new nonfamous names, and names of famous people. They then rated each name as famous or nonfamous. Dywan and colleagues found that patients, compared with normal controls, made significantly more source errors consisting of calling previously read nonfamous names "famous". This impairment was not attributable to a response bias (i.e. tendency to say "famous"), a general inability to distinguish famous and nonfamous names, or poor recognition memory, but rather by a problem in recreating the initial exposure conditions. Patients with prolonged coma durations made a greater number of source errors. Poorer performance on a measure of face recognition (Benton Facial Recognition Test; Benton, Hamsher, Varney & Spreen, 1983) also predicted source errors. The investigators proposed that the face recognition task requires careful consideration of subtle alternatives and the ability to inhibit impulsive tendencies. Such impairments may have contributed to errors on the judgment procedure.

Long-Term Memory: Impaired Delayed Recall and Susceptibility to Interference

In addition to their distortions of to-be-remembered information, patients with moderate and severe CHI demonstrate a disproportionate impairment of delayed as compared with immediate recall (Baddeley et al., 1987; Brooks, 1975; Dikmen et al., 1987; Stuss et al., 1985), similar to that observed after mild head injury. Thus, patients may perform reasonably well on immediate recall tasks such as repeating digit strings or recalling words after they are read. In addition, they may exhibit a relatively normal recency effect characterized by good retrieval of the words occurring at the terminal portions of a list. However, their recall shows an exaggerated decline following a delay filled with distraction.

An example of this type of impairment was found by Crosson et al. (1988) who asked severely injured patients and normal controls to remember 16 words over five trials. Recall was tested after a short delay filled with learning a new list and then a long delay after 20 minutes of interpolated activity. Patients recalled a significantly lower percentage of the words they initially recalled under both free and cued recall, indicating that they were unable to access or retain these words in long-term memory. During assessment, it is useful to examine memory after a delay since immediate recall tasks may provide an inflated view of performance. In addition, free recall should be supplemented by cued recall and recognition. Normal functioning on these latter measures despite impaired spontaneous recall may reflect a retrieval as opposed to a storage deficit.

Difficulties with delayed recall are commonly attributed to problems in transferring information from working memory (Baddeley, 1986; Baddeley et al., 1987) to a permanent long-term system. Patients may exhibit impaired long-term memory because they rapidly forget the material, resulting in either transfer of less information from temporary storage or loss of this material once it arrives. Evidence concerning faster rates of forgetting in head injured patients is equivocal, however. Baddeley et al. (1987) did not find that chronic survivors of severe head injury were more likely than normal young and elderly controls to lose information over intervals of one and two weeks. Vulnerability to interference may also explain why delayed recall is so affected after head injury. Stuss et al. (1985) found that patients who were employed and did not have neurologic deficits were selectively impaired on a task requiring them to recall three consonants after interference delays of varying durations. The investigators attributed this to problems in maintaining consistent directed attention when faced with interference. Finally, head injury may produce slowness in processing information in working memory.

Organization and Effortful Processing

Clinical assessment typically focuses on quantitative features of memory as reflected by summary indices such as the total number of words or pictures recalled. However, it is also important to evaluate the executive processing strategies that patients apply to learning situations and the way in which the quality of their recall causes mnestic deficiencies. There is evidence that patients with moderate or severe head injury have problems in applying active strategies which, in turn, contributes to their poor memory (Blachstein, Vakil & Hoofien, 1993; Crosson et al., 1988; Levin & Goldstein, 1986; Paniak, Shore & Rourke, 1989).

Passive learning is illustrated by Paniak, Shore and Rourke (1989) who examined survivors of severe CHI at 6 months and one year. Patients were administered the Selective Reminding Test (Buschke, 1973), a list learning procedure in which they were reminded only of those words that were not recalled on the previous trial. Paniak and colleagues found that patients exhibited inefficient and unorganized learning and retrieval strategies characterized by sporadic recall of items from trial to trial. Similarly, Blachstein, Vakil and Hoofien (1993) noted that survivors of moderate and severe head injuries enrolled in rehabilitation used inefficient retrieval patterns on a list learning procedure. Figure 8.4 shows the number of words added and omitted by patients and controls over five trials of a list learning procedure. As can be appreciated, the flatter learning curve by patients was due not only to their adding fewer words on each trial but also to their increased omissions.

The pattern of passive and unorganized retrieval found after head injury is reminiscent of Luria's (1973) observations regarding the impact of frontal lobe lesions on memory performance. Luria noted that subjects with brain lesions outside the frontal lobes improved their recall over repeated trials, but their performance fell off after capacity was reached or fatigue set in. Subjects with frontal lobe lesions, in contrast, retained two to five words on every trial, with no attempt to retrieve additional words from memory. The frontal lobe is the most frequent site of focal lesion after head injury (Adams et al., 1980; Levin et al., 1987a, 1992), thus raising the possibility of its contribution to such deficits in these patients.

Semantic Processing

Survivors of moderate and severe head injury process and utilize semantic relationships to guide their learning in contrast to their difficulties with episodic

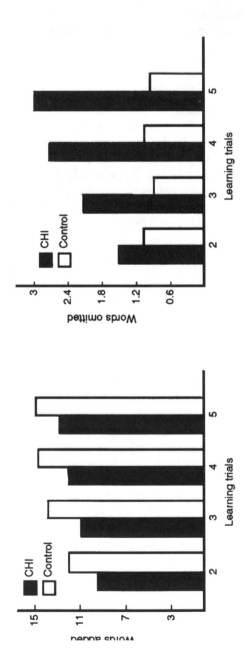

Figure 8.4 Cumulative number of words added or omitted by control and CHI groups. Reproduced by permission from Blachstein, Vakil & Hoofien (1993). Copyright 1993 by the American Psychological Association

memory (Baddeley et al., 1987; Goldstein, Levin & Boake, 1989; Goldstein et al., 1990; Levin & Goldstein, 1986; Haut, Petros & Frank, 1991; Haut, Petros, Frank & Haut, 1991; Schmitter-Edgecombe, Marks & Fahy, 1993). Levin and Goldstein (1986) found that long-term survivors of severe head injury who were enrolled in rehabilitation remembered significantly more words belonging to categories such as fruits or animals as opposed to words that did not share conceptual relationships. In a subsequent study, Goldstein et al. (1990) observed that patients showed a benefit in their recall when they were required to process words semantically by being asked questions about their category membership (e.g. chair: "Is it furniture?") versus questions concerning phonemic ("Does it rhyme with dare?") or physical ("Does it have the letter A?") properties. We have additionally found that patients automatically encode the meaning of to-be-remembered information (Goldstein et al., 1989). Severe CHI patients were given the release from proactive interference paradigm (PI; Wickens, 1970) in which they received repeated trials of recalling words belonging to the same category and then were unexpectedly switched to recalling words from another category. Normal retrieval declines across trials because of the interference caused by being exposed to similar material, followed by an improvement when the category is switched. We noted that patients showed release from PI, indicating that they were sensitive to the semantic properties of the words and that they encoded category membership. Haut, Petros and Frank (1991) also observed intact semantic processing following moderate and severe CHI. Prose passages from the Logical Memory subtest (Wechsler, 1981) were divided into high, medium and low idea units in terms of the importance of the information to the gist of the story. Similar to controls, the patients recalled more of the high idea units, reflecting their sensitivity to the meaning of the passages and the information that was conveyed.

Although survivors process semantic material, there is evidence that they are inefficient at doing so. Consistent with their approach to unrelated material, it has been found that patients employ inactive strategies. For example they are less likely than normal controls to utilize clustering, and they represent fewer categories in their recall (Crosson et al., 1988; Levin & Goldstein, 1986). Furthermore, patients are slower at making semantic decisions. Goldstein et al. (1990) observed that patients were disproportionately slower than normal controls in judging whether a word belonged to a particular category. Haut, Petros & Haut (1991) similarly found a slowness of patients in judging category membership. Severe CHI patients less than one year post-injury were asked to judge whether word pairs were from the same category. Words were either high or low exemplars. During a control task, the examiners subtracted out motor from cognitive response speed by having subjects press the key after an X appeared. The patients were disproportionately slower at making semantic decisions in both the low and high typicality conditions. Moreover, their selective slowness was not attributable to a higher error rate, suggesting that patients could correctly process this information.

These preceding findings indicate that remedial interventions might focus on teaching patients strategies for improving their recall, such as clustering information at both encoding and retrieval, as well as providing them with more time to process the meaning of to-be-learned information.

CONCLUSIONS

This chapter has reviewed the common memory deficits following closed head injury and has highlighted the areas that need to be evaluated. From a clinical perspective, the findings of passive approaches to learning indicate the importance of a process-based neuropsychological approach which focuses on the quality of encoding and retrieval. Such observations during the session can provide insights into the nature of the patient's impairment and also suggest potential remediation strategies such as organization and consistency of recall. In addition, the evidence that the memory disorder following head injury may be part of a larger neurobehavioral syndrome indicates the need for assessment to evaluate other cognitive and affective spheres. Memory dysfunction may be the primary deficit or secondary to other features such as impaired attention, executive functioning, or depression. Neuropsychological assessment can identify the role of primary versus secondary memory dysfunction, guide the focus of rehabilitation, and determine the need for psychological treatment. Finally, the findings by Ruff and colleagues (1991) and Wilson (1992) reveal that a subgroup of patients with devastating injuries do show improvement when examined at advanced post-acute intervals. These results are beginning to provide a more optimistic outlook concerning recovery of memory in certain survivors and will be critical in convincing health care providers of the need for long-term services.

In terms of future research, the area of preserved learning capabilities after CHI is relatively unexplored. This is especially true of patients in PTA who might derive maximum benefit from early intervention. The findings by Ewert and colleagues (1989) of intact procedural memory reveal that learning is possible during this stage. Other modes of learning, such as priming, memory for motor actions, or training through nontraditional modalities including somatosensory functions, may also be intact and provide guidelines for therapists working with patients. Researchers should adopt a qualitative approach to data analysis which examines individual recovery curves and predictors of specific outcomes as opposed to a group oriented strategy. Particular severity indices may predict a positive outcome in a subgroup of these patients. Such findings would direct decision-making processes concerning triage and appropriate use of resources as well as provide patients and family members with early prognostic information about the recovery of memory abilities. Continued efforts towards communicating the results of laboratory-based research in terms of practical implications for clinical management will improve the ability to treat memory disorders effectively and thereby improve patients' quality of life.

ACKNOWLEDGEMENT

Preparation of this chapter was supported in part by NIDRR grant H133G30051 and NS-21889.

REFERENCES

Adams, J.H., Graham, D.I., Scott, G., Parker, L.S. & Doyle, D. (1980). Brain damage in fatal non-missile head injury. *Journal of Clinical Pathology*, **33**, 1132–1145.

Artiolai Fortuny, L., Briggs, M., Newcombe, F., Ratcliff, G. & Thomas, C. (1980). Measuring the duration of post-traumatic amnesia. *Journal of Neurology, Neurosurgery and Psychiatry*, **43**, 377–379.

Baddeley, A. (1986). *Working Memory*. Oxford University Press, Oxford.

Baddeley, A., Harris, J., Sunderland, A., Watts, K.P. & Wilson, B.A. (1987). Closed head injury and memory. In H.S. Levin, J. Grafman & H.M. Eisenberg (eds), *Neurobehavioral Recovery from Head Injury*. Oxford University Press, New York, pp. 295–317.

Baker, G.A., Hanley, J.R., Jackson, H.F., Kimmance, S. & Slade, P. (1993). Detecting the faking of amnesia: performance differences between simulators and patients with memory impairment. *Journal of Clinical and Experimental Neuropsychology*, **15**, 668–684.

Benton, A.L., Hamsher, K. deS., Varney, N.R. & Spreen, O. (1983). *Contributions to Neuropsychological Assessment: A clinical Manual*. Oxford University Press, New York.

Binder, L.M. & Pankratz, L. (1987). Neuropsychological evidence of a factitious memory complaint. *Journal of Clinical and Experimental Neuropsychology*, **9**, 167–171.

Blachstein, H., Vakil, E. & Hoofien, D. (1993). Impaired learning in patients with closed-head injuries: an analysis of components of the acquisition process. *Neuropsychology*, **7**, 530–535.

Brooks, D.N. (1975). Long and short term memory in head injured patients. *Cortex*, **11**, 329–340.

Brooks, N., Campsie, L., Symington, C., Beattie, A. & McKinlay, W. (1986). The five-year outcome of severe blunt head injury: a relative's view. *Journal of Neurology, Neurosurgery, and Psychiatry*, **49**, 764–770.

Brooks, N., McKinlay, W., Symington, C., Beattie, A. & Campsie, L. (1987). Return to work within the first seven years of severe head injury. *Brain Injury*, **1**, 5–19.

Buschke, H. (1973). Selective reminding for analysis of memory and learning. *Journal of Verbal Learning and Behavior*, **12**, 543–550.

Corrigan, J.D., Arnett, J.A., Houck, L.J. & Jackson, R.D. (1985). Reality orientation for brain injured patients: group treatment and monitoring of recovery. *Archives of Physical Medicine and Rehabilitation*, **66**, 626–630.

Crosson, B., Novack, T.A., Trenerry, M.R. & Craig, P.L. (1988). California Verbal Learning Test (CVLT) performance in severely head-injured and neurologically normal adult males. *Journal of Clinical and Experimental Neuropsychology*, **10**, 754–768.

Crosson, B., Sartor, K.J., Jenny, A.F., Nabors, N.A. & Moberg, P.J. (1993). Increased intrusions during verbal recall in traumatic and nontraumatic lesions of the temporal lobe. *Neuropsychology*, **7**, 193–208.

Davidoff, G., Doljanac, R., Berent, S., Johnson, M.B., Thomas, P., Dijkers, M. & Klisz, D. (1988). Galveston Orientation and Amnesia Test: its utility in the determination of closed injury in acute spinal cord injury patients. *Archives of Physical Medicine and Rehabilitation*, **69**, 432–434.

Davidoff, G., Morris, J., Roth, E. & Bleiberg, J. (1985). Cognitive dysfunction and mild closed head injury in traumatic spinal cord injury. *Archives of Physical Medicine and Rehabilitation*, **66**, 489–491.

Delis, D.C., Kramer, J.H., Kaplan, E. & Ober, B.A. (1987). *California Verbal Learning Test*. Psychological Corporation, New York.

Dikmen, S., McLean, A. & Temkin, N. (1986). Neuropsychological and psychosocial consequences of minor head injury. *Journal of Neurology, Neurosurgery and Psychiatry*, **49**, 1227–1232.

Dikmen, S., Temkin, N., McLean, A., Wyler, A. & Machamer, J. (1987). Memory and head injury severity. *Journal of Neurology, Neurosurgery and Psychiatry*, **50**, 1613–1618.

Dywan, J., Segalowitz, S.J., Henderson, D. & Jacoby, L. (1993). Memory for source after traumatic brain injury. *Brain and Cognition*, **21**, 20–43.

Ewert, J., Levin, H.S., Watson, M.G. & Kalisky, Z. (1989). Procedural memory during posttraumatic amnesia in survivors of severe closed head injury: implications for rehabilitation. *Archives of Neurology*, **46**, 911–916.

Fenton, G., McClelland, R., Montgomery, A., MacFlynn, G. & Rutherford, W. (1993). The postconcussional syndrome: social antecedents and psychological sequelae. *British Journal of Psychiatry*, **162**, 493–497.

Gasquoine, P.G. (1991). Learning in post-traumatic amnesia following extremely severe closed head injury. *Brain Injury*, **5**, 169–175.

Gentilini, M., Nichelli, P., Schoenhuber, R., Bortolotti, P., Tonelli, L., Falasca, A. & Merli, G.A. (1985). Neuropsychological evaluation of mild head injury. *Journal of Neurology, Neurosurgery and Psychiatry*, **48**, 137–140.

Goldenberg, G., Oder, W., Spatt, J. & Podreka, I. (1992). Cerebral correlates of disturbed executive function and memory in survivors of severe closed head injury: a SPECT study. *Journal of Neurology, Neurosurgery and Psychiatry*, **55**, 362–368.

Goldstein, F.C., Levin, H.S. & Boake, C. (1989). Conceptual encoding following severe closed head injury. *Cortex*, **25**, 541–554.

Goldstein, F.C., Levin, H.S., Boake, C. & Lohrey, J.H. (1990). Facilitation of memory performance through induced semantic processing in survivors of severe closed head injury. *Journal of Clinical and Experimental Neuropsychology*, **12**, 286–300.

Gronwall, D. (1989). Cumulative and persisting effects of concussion on attention and cognition. In H.S. Levin, H.M. Eisenberg & A.L. Benton (eds), *Mild Head Injury*. Oxford University Press, New York, pp. 153–162.

Gronwall, D. & Wrightson, P. (1974). Delayed recovery of intellectual function after minor head injury. *Lancet*, **2**, 605–609.

Gronwall, D. & Wrightson, P. (1975). Cumulative effect of concussion. *Lancet*, **2**, 995–997.

Gronwall, D. & Wrightson, P. (1980). Duration of post-traumatic amnesia after mild head injury. *Journal of Clinical Neuropsychology*, **2**, 51–60.

Hannay, H.J., Levin, H.S. & Grossman, R.G. (1979). Impaired recognition memory after head injury. *Cortex*, **15**, 269–283.

Haut, M.W., Petros, T.V. & Frank, R.G. (1991a). Semantic sensitivity in the acute phase of recovery from moderate and severe closed head injury. *Neuropsychology*, **5**, 81–88.

Haut, M.W., Petros, T.V., Frank, R.G. & Haut, J.S. (1991b). Speed of processing within semantic memory following severe closed head injury. *Brain and Cognition*, **17**, 31–41.

High, W.M., Levin, H.S. & Gary, H.E. (1990). Recovery of orientation following closed-head injury. *Journal of Clinical and Experimental Neuropsychology*, **12**, 703–714.

Hiscock, M. & Hiscock, C.K. (1989). Refining the forced-choice method for the detection of malingering. *Journal of Clinical and Experimental Neuropsychology*, **11**, 967–974.

Humayun, M.S., Presty, S.K., LaFrance, N.D., Holcomb, H.H., Loats, H., Long, D.M., Wagner, H.N. & Gordon, B. (1989). Local cerebral glucose abnormalities in mild closed head injured patients with cognitive impairments. *Nuclear Medicine Communications*, **10**, 335–344.

Jennett, B. & Teasdale, G. (1981). *Management of Head Injuries*. F.A. Davis, Philadelphia.

Katz, D.I., Kehs, G.J. & Alexander, M.P. (1990). Prognosis and recovery from traumatic head injury: the influence of advancing age. *Neurology*, **40**, (*suppl* 1), 276.

Leininger, B.E., Gramling, S.E., Farrell, A.D., Kreutzer, J.S. & Peck, E.A. (1990). Neuropsychological deficits in symptomatic minor head injury patients after concussion and mild concussion. *Journal of Neurology, Neurosurgery and Psychiatry*, **53**, 293–296.

Levin, H.S., Amparo, E., Eisenberg, H.M., Williams, D.H., High, W.M., McArdle, C.B. & Weiner, R.L. (1987a). Magnetic resonance imaging and computerized tomography in relation to the neurobehavioral sequelae of mild and moderate head injuries. *Journal of Neurosurgery*, **66**, 706–713.

Levin, H.S., Benton, A.L. & Grossman, R.G. (1982). *Neurobehavioral Consequences of Closed Head Injury*. Oxford University Press, New York.

Levin, H.S. & Eisenberg, H.M. (1987). Postconcussional syndrome. In R.T. Johnson (ed.), *Current Therapy in Neurologic Disease*, vol. 2. B.C. Decker, Philadelphia, pp. 193–196.

Levin, H.S., Eisenberg, H.M., Gary, H.E., Marmarou, A., Foulkes, M.A., Jane, J.A., Marshall, L.F. & Portman, S.M. (1991). Intracranial hypertension in relation to memory functioning during the first year after severe head injury. *Neurosurgery*, **28**, 196–200.

Levin, H.S., Gary, H.E., Eisenberg, H.M., Ruff, R.M., Barth, J.T., Kreutzer, J., High, W.M., Portman, S., Foulkes, M.A., Jane, J.A., Marmarou, A. & Marshall, L.F. (1990). Neurobehavioral outcome one year after severe head injury: experience of the Traumatic Coma Data Bank. *Journal of Neurosurgery*, **73**, 699–709.

Levin, H.S. & Goldstein, F.C. (1986). Organization of verbal memory after severe closed-head injury. *Journal of Clinical and Experimental Neuropsychology*, **8**, 643–656.

Levin, H.S., Goldstein, F.C., High, W.M. & Eisenberg, H.M. (1988). Disproportionately severe memory deficit in relation to normal intellectual functioning after closed head injury. *Journal of Neurology, Neurosurgery and Psychiatry*, **51**, 1294–1301.

Levin, H.S., Handel, S.F., Goldman, A.M., Eisenberg, H.M. & Guinto, F.C. (1985). Magnetic resonance imaging after "diffuse" nonmissile head injury. A neurobehavioral study. *Archives of Neurology*, **42**, 963–968.

Levin, H.S., High, W.M. & Eisenberg, H.M. (1988). Learning and forgetting during posttraumatic amnesia in head injured patients. *Journal of Neurology, Neurosurgery and Psychiatry*, **51**, 14–20.

Levin, H.S., Mattis, S., Ruff, R.M., Eisenberg, H.M., Marshall, L.F., Tabaddor, K., High, W.M. & Frankowski, R.F. (1987b). Neurobehavioral outcome following minor head injury: a three-center study. *Journal of Neurosurgery*, **66**, 234–243.

Levin, H.S., O'Donnell, V.M. & Grossman, R.G. (1979). The Galveston Orientation and Amnesia Test: a practical scale to assess cognition after head injury. *Journal of Nervous and Mental Disease*, **167**, 675–684.

Levin, H.S., Williams, D.H., Eisenberg, H.M., High, W.M. & Guinto, F.C. (1992). Serial MRI and neurobehavioural findings after mild to moderate closed head injury. *Journal of Neurology, Neurosurgery and Psychiatry*, **55**, 255–262.

Luria, A.R. (1973). *The Working Brain*. Basic Books, New York.

McLean, A., Dikmen, S., Temkin, N., Wyler, A.R. & Gale, J.L. (1984). Psychosocial functioning at 1 month after head injury. *Neurosurgery*, **14**, 393–399.

Paniak, C.E., Shore, D.L. & Rourke, B.P. (1989). Recovery of memory after severe closed head injury: dissociations in recovery of memory parameters and predictors of outcome. *Journal of Clinical and Experimental Neuropsychology*, **11**, 631–644.

Pankratz, L. (1979). Symptom validity testing and symptom retraining: procedures for the assessment and treatment of functional sensory deficits. *Journal of Consulting and Clinical Psychology*, **47**, 409–410.

Pankratz, L. (1983). A new technique for the assessment and modification of feigned memory deficit. *Perceptual and Motor Skills*, **57**, 367–372.

Rimel, R.W., Giordani, B., Barth, J.T., Boll, T.J. & Jane, J.A. (1981). Disability caused by minor head injury. *Neurosurgery*, **9**, 221–228.

Roth, E., Davidoff, G., Thomas, P., Doljanac, R., Dijkers, M., Berent, S., Morris, J. & Yarkony, G. (1989). A controlled study of neuropsychological deficits in acute spinal cord injury patients. *Paraplegia*, **27**, 480–489.

Ruff, R.M., Young, D., Gautille, T., Marshall, L.F., Barth, J., Jane, J.A., Kreutzer, J., Marmarou, A., Levin, H.S., Eisenberg, H.M. & Foulkes, M.A. (1991). Verbal learning deficits following severe head injury: heterogeneity in recovery over 1 year. *Journal of Neurosurgery*, **75**, S50–S58.

Russell, W.R. (1971). *The Traumatic Amnesias*. Oxford University Press, New York.

Russell, W.R. & Smith, A. (1961). Post-traumatic amnesia in closed head injury. *Archives of Neurology*, **5**, 4–17.

Rutherford, W.H. (1989). Postconcussion symptoms: relationship to acute neurological indices, individual differences, and circumstances of injury. In H.S. Levin, H.M. Eisenberg & A.L. Benton (eds), *Mild Head Injury*. Oxford University Press, New York, pp. 217–228.

Ryan, T.V., Sautter, S.W., Capps, C.F., Meneese, W. & Barth, J.T. (1992). Utilizing neuropsychological measures to predict vocational outcome in a head trauma population. *Brain Injury*, **6**, 175–182.

Saneda, D.L. & Corrigan, J.D. (1992). Predicting clearing of post-traumatic amnesia following closed-head injury. *Brain Injury*, **6**, 167–174.

Schmitter-Edgecombe, M.E., Marks, W. & Fahy, J.F. (1993). Semantic priming after severe closed head trauma: automatic and attentional processes. *Neuropsychology*, **7**, 136–148.

Shimamura, A.P. & Squire, L.R. (1987). A neuropsychological study of fact memory and source amnesia. *Journal of Experimental Psychology: Learning, Memory and Cognition*, **13**, 464–473.

Shimamura, A.P. & Squire, L.R. (1991). The relationship between fact and source memory: findings from amnesic patients and normal subjects. *Psychobiology*, **19**, 1–10.

Shores, E.A., Marosszeky, J.E., Sandanam, J. & Batchelor, J. (1986). Preliminary validation of a clinical scale for measuring the duration of post-traumatic amnesia. *Medical Journal of Australia*, **144**, 569–572.

Stroop, J.R. (1935). Studies of interference in serial verbal reactions. *Journal of Experimental Psychology*, **18**, 643–662.

Stuss, D.T., Ely, P., Hugenholtz, H., Richard, M.T., LaRochelle, S., Poirier, C.A. & Bell, I. (1985). Subtle neuropsychological deficits in patients with good recovery after closed head injury. *Neurosurgery*, **17**, 41–47.

Teasdale, G. & Jennett, B. (1974). Assessment of coma and impaired consciousness: a practical scale. *Lancet*, **2**, 81–84.

Uzzell, B.P., Obrist, W.D., Dolinskas, C.A. & Langfitt, T.W. (1986). Relationship of acute CBF and ICP findings to neuropsychological outcome in severe head injury. *Journal of Neurosurgery*, **65**, 630–635.

Vilkki, J., Poropudas, K. & Servo, A. (1988). Memory disorder related to coma duration after head injury. *Journal of Neurology, Neurosurgery and Psychiatry*, **51**, 1452–1454.

Wechsler, D. (1981). *WAIS-R Manual*. Psychological Corporation, New York.

Wickens, D.D. (1970). Encoding categories of words: an empirical approach to meaning. *Psychological Review*, **77**, 1–15.

Williams, D.H., Levin, H.S. & Eisenberg, H.M. (1990). Mild head injury classification. *Neurosurgery*, **27**, 422–428.

Wilson, B. (1992). Recovery and compensatory strategies in head injured memory impaired people several years after insult. *Journal of Neurology, Neurosurgery and Psychiatry*, **55**, 177–180.

Wilson, B.A., Baddeley, A., Shiel, A. & Patton, G. (1992). How does post-traumatic amnesia differ from the amnesic syndrome and from chronic memory impairment? *Neuropsychological Rehabilitation*, **2**, 231–243.

Wilson, J.T.L., Wiedmann, K.D., Hadley, D.M., Condon, B., Teasdale, G. & Brooks, D.N. (1988). Early and late magnetic resonance imaging and neuropsychological outcome after head injury. *Journal of Neurology, Neurosurgery and Psychiatry*, **51**, 391–396

Chapter 9

Memory Changes in Normal Ageing

Fergus I.M. Craik
Nicole D. Anderson
Sheila A. Kerr
and
Karen Z.H. Li
University of Toronto, Toronto, Canada

INTRODUCTION

A decline in the ability to learn and remember new information is very typically reported as people enter middle age. Older adults in their 60s and 70s complain of forgetfulness and an inability to hold information in mind; even earlier in their 40s and 50s, many people note that their memory is not as good as it used to be, and complain of difficulties in recalling names of acquaintances and of uncommon objects. The purpose of the present chapter is to review the evidence for these beliefs and to pose a set of related questions. Does memory really decline with age? If so, is the decline inevitable or can it be slowed, halted or reversed? Are age-related declines associated with every type of memory, or are certain types more vulnerable than others? To what extent are observed losses a function of ageing as such, and to what extent are they attributable to other factors that may differentiate younger from older adults—for example, differences in educational or job experience, differences in motivation, or differences in health and liability to depression? Finally, is the "benign" memory loss accompanying normal ageing related to the more dramatic losses associated with pathological conditions such as Alzheimer's disease?

Handbook of Memory Disorders. Edited by A.D. Baddeley, B.A. Wilson and F.N. Watts.
© 1995 John Wiley & Sons Ltd.

TYPES OF MEMORY

The literature on laboratory studies of age changes in memory is very clear on one major point—that age-related decrements are obvious and virtually universal in some situations but negligible in others. For example, older subjects typically perform much less well on tasks involving unaided recall of items no longer "in mind"; e.g. free recall of lists of unrelated words, or recall of a descriptive passage. Older people also show losses in source and contextual memory—remembering where and when an event took place—and this decrement is found both for perceived events and for information produced by the older person; the latter failure resulting in the mildly annoying habit of older people to retell the same anecdotes many times to the same audience.

On the other hand, some memory tasks show little or no change as a function of the subject's age. Procedural learning holds up very well; that is, both motor skills (such as driving or playing a musical instrument) and cognitive skills (such as reading and arithmetic) decline very little so long as they are kept in practice. Such skilled procedures may be linked to laboratory demonstrations of "priming" in which, for example, the ability to complete a word fragment like *a__a__in* is greatly increased by the recent study of the complete word (in this case *assassin*). As documented later in the chapter, the amount and persistence of priming changes very little across the adult life-span. Other types of memory that hold up well with age include memory for well-learned facts and knowledge, including vocabulary, recognition memory for events (as opposed to recall), and "primary memory" for information held and rehearsed in mind.

Older people themselves often claim excellent memory for one further category—specific events that happened in their childhood or teenage years. Researchers and clinicians often hear the question from older patients: "Why is it that I have such a poor memory for events that happened yesterday while I have vivid memories of my first day at school over 70 years ago?" We will discuss the topic of remote memory later in the chapter, but it may be pointed out here that such personal memories are (a) highly selective and typically not mundane daily occurrences, (b) frequently rehearsed and recounted, and (c) quite liable to unconscious distortion and embellishment. Such memories must therefore be treated rather cautiously by memory researchers and practitioners.

It seems clear, however, that age-related memory losses are quite variable, and one task of the memory theorist is to provide a coherent account of these strengths and weaknesses. Such accounts typically invoke different types of memory, but unfortunately the terminology used by psychologists is often confusing and inconsistent. In the present chapter we will organise the discussion of age-related changes into the traditional categories of *short-term* and *long-term memory*. By "short-term memory" (STM) we mean cases in which a small amount of material is held in mind over a period of several seconds; such STM tasks are described as involving "primary memory" if the material is held passively and then given back as a response in the same form as it was presented, and as "working memory" if the information must be reorganised while being held, or integrated either with further incoming information or with previously learned material.

The expression "long-term memory" (LTM) is used here to designate tasks in which the material to be remembered is no longer in conscious awareness. By this depiction the material may have been acquired many years ago or only seconds before; the principles of operation appear to be very similar, regardless of the length of time the event has been stored. In this connection the processes of acquisition (or encoding) and retrieval are of central importance since they are obvious sites for possible age-related inefficiencies. The intervening process of storage is of lesser concern since it is silent behaviourally, although it is certainly possible that trace decay occurs more rapidly in older people.

Within LTM, theorists (e.g. Tulving, 1972) have distinguished memory for specific autobiographical events (*episodic memory*) from memory for context-independent knowledge (*semantic memory*), and this distinction is relevant to an understanding of age differences. Another recent distinction is between *implicit* and *explicit memory* (see Schacter, 1987; and Chapter 1 in this volume). As detailed later, age differences are much greater in the case of explicit memory, where the subject must consciously recollect the original event, than in implicit memory, where the original information is simply used (often unconsciously) to facilitate performance on some current task.

Other important topics to be addressed include *prospective memory*—remembering to carry out planned actions at some future time; and *metamemory*—introspective knowledge of one's own memory capabilities and of the factors that modify them. Finally, while the bulk of experimental evidence relates to memory for verbal materials (words, numbers, sentences, and text passages), we will also deal with age changes in memory for pictorial and spatial information.

SHORT-TERM MEMORY

Primary Memory

The term "primary memory" (PM) was revived by Waugh and Norman (1965) following an early descriptive analysis by William James. Items "in PM" may be thought of as those recently perceived events whose representations are still present in conscious awareness, although the usage may be broadened to include items recently retrieved from LTM. Thus defined, the capacity of PM is equivalent to the number of items a person can hold simultaneously in mind, and it may be measured by "memory span"—the longest string of items (e.g. digits, words) that the subject can reproduce accurately immediately after hearing them. It is generally agreed that digit span declines with age (Parkinson, 1982), although the drop between university undergraduates and senior citizens is not very great—an average of 6.6 digits for the students and 5.8 digits for the older group in Parkinson's study. Word span is generally lower than digit span and typically shows a somewhat greater age decrement (Wingfield, Stine, Lahar & Aberdeen, 1988). In general, however, memory span tasks are relatively insensitive to the ageing process, and should therefore not be used clinically as an index of memory impairment in older patients. Other simple tasks (such as free recall of a short string of words) are much more sensitive.

A second measure of PM is the size of the recency effect in the free recall of a list of 12–20 words. Craik (1968) reported that recency remained relatively constant with increasing age, and a more recent study by Delbecq-Derouesné and Beauvois (1989) provided more complete evidence pointing to the same conclusion. In the later study the investigators gave subjects lists of 15 unrelated words, and asked them first to recall as many words as possible from the end of the list, and then as many other words as they could remember. A recalled word was counted as retrieved from PM provided that no more than 7 words (presentations or recalls) intervened between the word's presentation and retrieval. Using this measure, the researchers found that PM capacity ranged only from 4.0 in subjects in their early 20s to 3.7 for subjects aged between 65 and 86. The conclusion is, therefore, that PM capacity declines only slightly with age. This slight deficit is unlikely to be the crucial cause of longer-term memory failures in the elderly, and it would be unwise in clinical practice to base an assessment of a patient's memory status on any primary memory measure.

Working Memory

As outlined previously, working memory (WM) can be considered a cognitive activity involving the simultaneous storage and manipulation of information held in mind. An everyday activity such as mental arithmetic can be considered a WM task, as one must hold the numbers and perhaps some intermediate products in mind while performing further computations. In his classic book *Ageing and Human Skill*, Welford (1958) suggested that age-related decrements in short-term memory functioning underlie age differences in many cognitive and motor tasks. This suggestion does not fit well with the conclusion that primary memory abilities decline rather little with age; however, Welford's suggestion *does* fit well with the emerging evidence on WM and age, which in general points to large age decrements. Various measures of WM performance have been investigated, and most decline with age, although there is no guarantee that the tasks all tap identical underlying abilities.

Craik (1986) proposed a simple variant of the memory span procedure to measure WM. In this variant (termed "alpha span"), a short list of common words is presented and subjects must hold them in mind while they are being presented, rearrange them mentally, and then recall them in correct alphabetical order. Craik reported age-related declines on this task although no age decrements were found in the subjects when forward digit span was measured. A similar contrast was observed by Dobbs and Rule (1989), who used a running memory task with several conditions. Ten digits were presented auditorily in each trial. In the simplest condition, subjects were instructed to repeat each digit that was heard immediately after its presentation (Lag 0). In the next condition, subjects were instructed to repeat item $n - 1$ each time a digit (n) was presented, such that they were shadowing the number series with a one-item delay (Lag 1). At the highest level of WM load, subjects repeated item $n - 2$ after each digit was presented (Lag 2). It was found that task performance dropped substantially at Lags 1 and 2 for subjects in the 50s, 60s and 70 + groups, but that performance at Lag 0 showed only slight age differences. Dobbs and Rule suggested that, because this working memory task is age-sensitive and easy to administer, it may prove useful for the assessment of WM abilities in clinical populations.

Various theoretical approaches have been taken to understand the relation between WM and ageing. Three will be mentioned here: individual differences, processing resources, and disinhibition.

One goal of the *individual differences approach* is to assess subcomponents of WM that may account for age-related variance in WM performance. Timothy Salthouse has been a major proponent of this strategy, and he has produced an abundance of evidence suggesting that cognitive slowing is such a factor (Salthouse, 1991a, 1992a,b). His general procedure is to measure indices of cognitive slowing (typically, the WAIS-R digit–symbol substitution task) as well as indices of WM capacity across the adult age range. Salthouse has found a substantial decrease in age-related variance on WM performance when the variance attributed to cognitive slowing is removed, suggesting that cognitive slowing underlies much of the age-related decline in WM performance.

The *processing resources hypothesis* has also been used to explain age-related decrements in a variety of working memory tasks (Salthouse, 1991b). According to the theory, if older adults have diminished processing resources, one would expect them to be differentially penalised by increases in WM load, or processing resource demands. Craik, Morris and Gick (1990) found that when young and elderly adults were given several memory preload items to study, and then were presented with a sentence verification task prior to recall of the preload items, the elderly group was differentially penalised by increased sentence complexity, but was not penalised more than the young group by an increase in the number of preload items. In contrast, using spatial and numerical WM tasks, Salthouse, Babcock and Shaw (1991) found that, in a series of eight experiments, young and elderly groups were comparably penalised by increases in required storage and processing operations (see also Babcock & Salthouse, 1990). Such mixed results suggest that there may be a subset of WM processes that decline with age, and that the magnitude of age-related performance differences varies depending on the way in which WM load is manipulated.

The mechanism of *disinhibition* has recently been hypothesised to underlie the age-related decline in WM abilities (Hasher & Zacks, 1988). This hypothesis predicts that as we age, it becomes more difficult to inhibit task-irrelevant information, such that the contents of WM become cluttered with superfluous information, thus reducing the functional size of WM. At present, a significant amount of effort has been focused on exploring the parameters of the disinhibition found in elderly adults. However, more research needs to be aimed at demonstrating a link between inhibitory decline and consequent reductions in WM capacity, as Hasher and Zacks predicted. Stoltzfus and Hasher (1992) provided support for the disinhibition hypothesis by presenting young and old adults with sentences in which the last word was left out. After reading a sentence, a word or nonword was presented; the subjects' task was to decide whether the item was a word or not (lexical decision). It was found that both young and older adults' responses were facilitated when the item was an appropriate end-word for the sentence context, suggesting that both young and old adults can activate the appropriate concepts. Interestingly, however, older adults were also facilitated when the item presented was a less appropriate word for the sentence context, suggesting that they hold more irrelevant concepts active in working memory than do young adults.

Ageing and Short-Term Memory

The picture that emerges from this short survey of age-related differences in STM is that age decrements are relatively slight on tasks in which a short string of items is perceived and then reproduced in the same order. The everyday task of looking up a telephone number and then dialling it should therefore hold up well in older people. However, as the task changes to involve simultaneous storage and processing as opposed to passive reproduction (i.e. the task taps WM as opposed to PM processes) the age decrements are exaggerated. Note that it is not necessary to invoke two different memory systems—PM and WM —to account for this pattern of effects; it is sufficient to suggest a continuum of *tasks* running from those involving passive reproduction to tasks involving progressively more complex mental manipulation. In terms of the influential model of WM proposed by Baddeley and Hitch (1974), it seems that ageing has little effect on the relatively passive phonological loop (Craik, Morris & Gick, 1990), but has a markedly deleterious effect on the flexibility and power of the central executive system. In turn, this age-related decline may be speculatively attributed to an age-related deterioration in the effectiveness of frontal systems of the brain (Baddeley, 1986).

Age decrements in WM functioning may present as difficulties with higher-level cognitive functions such as comprehension of difficult text or messages, and the ability to draw inferences (Cohen, 1988; Zacks & Hasher, 1988). Additionally, an inefficiency in the ability to allocate processing resources may result in problems in dealing with two simultaneous streams of information; thus older people are less able to recall two short lists of digits or words presented simultaneously, one list to each ear ("dichotic listening"), although in other dual-task situations the age differences are relatively slight (Hartley, 1992). Also, to the extent that ageing is associated with a decline in the ability to inhibit unwanted information, the older person will be less able to maintain attention and more vulnerable to distraction. As a final practical point, it is evident from comparing the results of various task manipulations that WM tasks do not all emphasise or measure the same component processes. Therefore, it is advisable to assess WM by using several measures rather than one global measure.

LONG-TERM MEMORY

When older adults complain of failing memory they are typically referring to a decline in episodic memory for events that occurred relatively recently—from minutes to days before. In this section we will review a selection of laboratory studies that address this issue and that attempt to specify the reasons for any losses. One general finding is that if initial performance levels are equated across age groups, subsequent forgetting rates are essentially equivalent across the adult age range (see Craik, 1977a, and Craik & Salthouse, 1992, for reviews). The implication is therefore that storage factors are relatively unaffected by ageing and that the sites of age-related losses are likely to be either *encoding* (acquisition) processes, *retrieval* processes, or both.

Encoding Processes

An age-related deficit in encoding implies that older people encode words and other events in a way that is less semantically rich and distinctive than the encodings achieved by their younger counterparts. The evidence for this position is rather mixed, however. Rankin and Collins (1986) presented younger and older subjects with simple sentences and asked the subjects to elaborate their meaning. The elaborations generated by the young subjects were judged to be more precise than those generated by the older group, and more precise elaborations were associated with higher levels of subsequent recall. In this study the elderly adults benefited most from a condition in which the precise elaborations were provided by the experimenter. However, a similar study by Hashtroudi, Parker, Luis and Reisen (1989) found that the older group came closest to matching the recall levels of the young subjects (0.66 and 0.76 respectively) when the subjects generated their own precise elaborators (Table 9.1). The studies agree in finding an empirical benefit for precise (distinctive) elaborations and in finding that younger subjects perform best when they actively generate their own elaborations, as opposed to having them provided passively. The mean age of the older group in the Hashtroudi et al. study was 65.8 years, as opposed to 73.4 years in the Rankin and Collins study, and it seems that the former group behaved more like the young controls. It may be the case that as people age, they first profit from the same active encoding strategies that help their younger counterparts, but later rely more on passively provided aids.

Table 9.1 Proportions of target words recalled with elaborators provided or generated

	Elaborator provided		Elaborator generated	
	Imprecise	Precise	Imprecise	Precise
Rankin &Collins				
Young	0.41	0.65	0.68	0.84
Old	0.21	0.52	0.28	0.41
Hashtroudi et al.				
Young	0.28	0.72	0.69	0.76
Old	0.18	0.35	0.53	0.66

Environmental Support

Craik (1983, 1986) pointed out that, whereas most psychological models of memory (and *all* biological models of memory and learning) deal with mechanisms and processes inside the head, a more appropriate view is that the behavioural characteristics of memory reflect an interaction between such internal processes and external influences. That is, at the time of acquisition, the external context in the form of the task and the surrounding environment interacts with brain processes to modify the encoded record of the initially perceived event in specific ways, and such environmental influences again interact with internal processes at the time of retrieval to facilitate remembering to a greater or lesser extent. These rather abstract ideas boil down to the simple notions that a rich learning context can enrich the encoded trace of an event to be remembered and make it *potentially* more memorable, provided that the same contextual influences at retrieval act to reinstate the same mental processes that occurred during learning. These ideas have been studied (and corroborated) under the labels of *state-dependent learning* (e.g. Eich, 1980) and the *encoding specificity hypothesis* (Tulving & Thomson, 1973).

Craik's point was that older people rely more on external influences such as reminders to perform tasks, and on reinstatement of the original learning context. They are less able to "self-initiate" effective encoding and retrieval operations, but if such operations are guided and supported by the external environment they can perform quite well—almost at the level of young adults, as shown by the Precise Elaborator Generated condition in the experiment by Hashtroudi et al. (1989). Bäckman (1989) has proposed and illustrated the similar concept of *compensation*. He attributes the superior memory performance of younger adults to their ability to spontaneously recode information in order to make it richer and contextually more meaningful, and states that the need for compensation increases with decreases in the ability to recode information.

Why should ageing be associated with a decline in the ability to self-initiate effective encoding and retrieval operations? Presumably the root cause is biological, a decline in the efficiency of cortical processing. At the psychological level it has been suggested that processing resources decline with age (e.g. Rabinowitz, Craik & Ackerman, 1982; Salthouse, 1982) with "processing resources" described alternatively as "mental energy" or "attentional capacity". A decline in processing resources in the elderly is given some credibility by the finding that division of attention in young subjects (by having them perform a second task concurrently with the memory task) results in a pattern of memory performance that is indistinguishable from the pattern seen in older adults (Craik, 1982; Craik & Jennings, 1992; Rabinowitz, Craik & Ackerman, 1982). The idea that processing resources decline with age also fits well with the previously discussed evidence for the reduced efficiency of WM in the elderly—especially perhaps in reduced effectiveness of central executive operations.

Evidence for Environmental Support

The straightforward prediction from the environmental support hypothesis is that the memory performance of older adults should improve differentially relative to a young group, as the support provided by the encoding (or retrieval) task increases. However, Light (1991) pointed out that a review of the literature reveals disparate findings. In some cases the elderly do benefit more than the young (e.g. Rabinowitz, Craik & Ackerman, 1982; Sharps & Gollin, 1988); in other cases the young benefit more (e.g. Perlmutter, 1979; Simon, 1979); and in many cases the young and elderly benefit equally (e.g. Bäckman & Mäntylä, 1988, Nilsson & Craik, 1990; Rabinowitz, Ackerman, Craik & Hinchley, 1982). It seems clear that other factors must play a role in determining the pattern of findings, and one active area of research is concerned with specifying the conditions under which one or another of the patterns is found.

One consistent finding is that age-related differences are reduced substantially when supportive cues are presented with the target items at encoding, and re-presented at the time of retrieval (Craik, Byrd & Swanson, 1987; Shaw & Craik, 1989; Smith, 1977; West & Boatwright, 1983). The results from studies that presented cues at encoding only, or at retrieval only, are mixed, although it appears that as conditions improve, age-related differences in benefit shift from greater benefits for the young, to parallel benefits for young and elderly, to greater benefits for the elderly.

Orienting Tasks and Mnemonic Techniques

Mostly we think of people learning or memorising information by making some deliberate effort to commit it to memory. If the information is particularly important the learner may employ a conscious strategy such as repeating the information mentally, or by associating the information with other well known material. Laboratory studies have shown rather clearly that the crucial aspect of good learning is not whether the person has the conscious intention to learn, but is the qualitative nature of the mental representation achieved—even if the information was acquired "incidentally", without intention to learn. The characteristics of such "good" encodings are that they are semantically rich and elaborate (Craik & Tulving, 1975), well-organised, and linked to previously well-learned information in the person's knowledge base (Bower, Clark, Lesgold & Winzenz, 1969; Kliegl, Smith & Baltes, 1989; Tulving, 1972). One possibility in the case of older learners is that they still possess the ability to encode information in a rich, associative manner, but do not employ such strategies spontaneously. This line of reasoning is similar to the environmental support ideas discussed previously, and suggests that older people may profit differentially from advice on *how* to learn information, or from tasks that orient the individual to attend to useful aspects of the items to be remembered.

A few studies have compared the benefit of instructions to use verbal or imaginal mediation at encoding, relative to instructions to simply "learn" the material. In an early study, Hulicka and Grossman (1967) used a paired associate procedure. Subjects were given no specific instructions, except to learn the pairs for a later retention test, or they were given instructions to form a mental image of the pair members. The results showed a disproportionate benefit from the imagery instructions, favouring the elderly. Similar results were found by Treat and Reese (1976). In a paired associates study, they gave younger and older subjects either no specific instructions, experimenter-provided images to connect the pair of words (their example for *tree—shoe* is 'a tree growing out of a shoe'), or they instructed subjects to generate their own images. Furthermore, the pairs of words were presented either briefly or for a longer time. They found that the young and elderly performed equally poorly when no instructions were provided at the short presentation times, and that the two age groups performed equally well with imagery instructions at the long presentation times. This result replicates and extends that of Hulicka and Grossman (1967): in both studies the elderly showed a larger benefit from imagery instructions, but in addition Treat and Reese demonstrated that longer presentation times were required for this disproportionate benefit to emerge. A recent study (McEvoy, Nelson, Holley & Stelnicki, 1992) equated the overall performance of older and younger adults by providing more supportive study conditions to the elderly (the presentation rate was slower and the lists were shorter for the elderly), and found equal benefits from imagery instructions for young and older adults.

Carrying this idea further, some investigators have taught younger and older people mnemonic techniques—typically training subjects to associate the items to be remembered with a well-known series of facts or locations. A review of earlier work in this area by Poon, Walsh-Sweeney and Fozard (1980) found that older learners clearly benefited from such training. The review also highlighted the importance of giving the older learners sufficient time and practice, and (on the negative side) the difficulty in getting older learners to *use* the technique in their daily lives unless they were reminded to do so.

A more recent series of studies was conducted in Berlin by Kliegl, Smith and Baltes (1989). They trained subjects to associate successive words in a list with a well-known series of local landmarks. The results were spectacular: after some

25 sessions of training, the older people improved their recall from an average of 3.1 words (out of 40) to 23.0 words. However, the investigators also found that younger subjects improved even more (from 4.8 to 37.8 words). The conclusion is that people of all ages can certainly use such techniques to improve memory, but the improvements may not be as dramatic in the elderly as in the young, and the practical usefulness of the techniques is limited by their applicability to real-life situations, and by the willingness of older people in particular to use them when not reminded to do so.

Other laboratory tasks improve memory performance simply by obliging the subject to carry out more extensive processing to complete the task itself. One such paradigm compares remembering a list of instructions (e.g. "point at the ceiling", "pick up the book") with a condition in which the subject actually performs the series of mini-tasks. Memory for the instructions is reliably enhanced in the second case, presumably because the encoded record is enriched by motoric information, and possibly also by deeper semantic processing. The majority of studies using this paradigm have found equal benefits to younger and older adults in the "subject-performed task" or SPT condition (see Craik & Jennings, 1992, for a review), although some have found greater benefits to the elderly (e.g. Bäckman & Nilsson, 1984).

Another experimental manipulation which leads to surprisingly robust improvements in memory is called the *generation effect*. In this paradigm, subjects either read a complete word or are given an incomplete word to generate on their own, usually with the help of cues. Thus, subjects might be given pairs of antonyms presented either as *hot—cold* (read condition) or as *hot–c _ _ _* (generate condition). The generation effect refers to the better recall and recognition of words in the latter condition. Again, equal generation effects have typically been reported for younger and older adults (Mitchell, Hunt & Schmitt, 1986; Rabinowitz, 1989). If the generation effect reflects greater amounts of semantic processing, it is perhaps surprising that the effect is not differentially beneficial to the elderly. Speculatively, techniques that enrich encoding in a passive, automatic fashion (e.g. the generation effect, subject-performed tasks, presenting pictures rather than words) may be associated with equal effects across the age range, provided that performance is neither close to chance nor to perfect levels of performance.

The Effects of Time Restrictions

One early question asked by researchers was whether time restrictions contribute to some age-related differences in memory performance (see Welford, 1958). The question was whether the elderly would perform similarly to the young if they were given more time to encode information; if so, it would suggest that the elderly are able to engage in equally effective encoding processes, but that it just takes them more time to do so. As mentioned earlier, Treat and Reese (1976) conducted a paired associates study in which in one condition they instructed subjects to form an interactive image between pairs of words. When subjects were allowed little time (2 s) to form the image, the young outperformed the elderly in a subsequent memory test; however, when subjects were allowed more time (6 s), there was no difference between younger and older adults in subsequent memory performance. This result suggests that given an effective strategy, and given enough time to exercise that strategy, the young and elderly can perform similarly. It should be emphasised that without the efficient strategy instructions, the longer presentation times did not improve the elderly subjects' performance; thus, the benefit for the elderly can be attributed to the interaction of strategy and presentation time, but not to either one alone.

Murphy, Sanders, Gabriesheski, and Schmitt (1981) allowed subjects unlimited time to learn a set of line drawings. They found that the elderly subjects underestimated the difficulty of the task, studied the drawings for less time and performed less well on the subsequent test. Furthermore, the elderly were less responsive to increases in difficulty: as the set length increased, the younger adults increased their study time more than did the elderly. Rabinowitz (1989) compared the benefit from unlimited study time, relative to a fixed presentation time, and found that, in the unlimited condition, younger and older adults spontaneously spent similar amounts of extra time; nevertheless, the younger adults' memory performance benefited more than the elderly from the extra study time.

In summary, it appears that time restriction by itself will not account for age-related differences. Given unlimited time, but no specific strategy instruction, the elderly still perform substantially less well than their younger counterparts (Murphy et al., 1981; Rabinowitz, 1989). When elderly subjects are given effective strategy instructions, and enough time to employ the strategy, then their performance levels are similar to those of the young.

Retrieval Processes

It is clear that many of our memory failures reflect the inability to retrieve information that we certainly do possess. The temporary forgetting of names is a common example; given that older people frequently complain of this irritating inefficiency, it seems likely that retrieval processes become less effective with age. The literature supports this view (Burke & Light, 1981; Craik & Jennings, 1992). The environmental support hypothesis, discussed earlier, suggests that any such age-related retrieval deficits should be greater when retrieval must be self-initiated by the rememberer, and reduced to the extent that effective cues are provided by the task or by the environment. The contrast between unaided recall and recognition (where the items are re-presented at the time of test) exemplifies this distinction, and the bulk of the evidence suggests that age decrements are greater in recall than in recognition (Schonfield & Robertson, 1966). One possible flaw in the argument is that recognition may simply be the easier task, but Craik and McDowd (1987) addressed this criticism by contrasting performance on a relatively easy recall task with performance on a relatively difficult recognition task. Age-related decrements were still larger in the recall task.

A further common memory failure is to remember a fact or a person's face, but to forget where the fact was learned or where the person was originally encountered. In its extreme form in amnesic patients this failure is termed "source amnesia", and it does appear to increase in normal ageing, although in a much milder form. Following a paradigm devised by Schacter, Harbluk and McLachlan (1984), a study by McIntyre and Craik (1987) presented made-up "facts" to old and younger subjects (e.g. "Bob Hope's father was a fireman") and one week later tested memory for the facts, now mixed with real facts (e.g. What was Pablo Picasso's profession? What did Bob Hope's father do for a living?). The subjects were also asked where they had first learned the information—e.g. in a newspaper, from a book, on TV, or from the study session one week before. The experiment showed substantially more "source amnesia" in the older group. In a follow-up study, Craik, Morris, Morris and Loewen (1990) showed that the degree of source amnesia was significantly related to poorer scores on some behavioural tests of frontal-lobe functioning. This finding gives some speculative backing to the suggestion by Schacter et al. (1984) and by Shimamura and Squire (1987) that one of the functions of the frontal lobes is to integrate contextual detail with focal events, and that this aspect of frontal lobe functioning declines with age. Finally, age-related inefficiencies of source memory can occur for information generated by the older person as well as for information perceived by him or herself. This observation is illustrated by the propensity of older people to "tell the same story twice" (Koriat, Ben-Zur & Sheffer, 1988).

DIFFERENT TYPES OF MEMORY

Nonverbal Memory

Most work on age-related memory problems has concentrated on memory for words, letters and numbers, but some studies have tackled the equally important problems of age differences in memory for pictures, faces and spatial information. Reassuringly, many of the principles that emerge from studies of these more realistic stimulus materials agree well with the principles gleaned from research on verbal memory.

Memory for Pictures and Faces

One such point of agreement concerns the contrast between recognition and recall using pictorial materials. Age differences in the recognition of photographed scenes or drawings are typically slight (e.g. Park, Puglisi & Smith, 1986; Till, Bartlett & Doyle, 1982); but age-related deficits *are* found when free recall or cued recall is the measure (Puglisi & Park, 1987). In the case of faces, Bartlett and Leslie (1986) reported no age differences in face recognition when the studied faces had to be discriminated from new faces and when subjects were shown four different poses of the face at the time of learning. Age-related decrements were found, however, when only one pose was shown at study and the distractors were the same face in a different pose or with a different expression. It seems, then, that age differences in memory for rich pictorial materials are slight—unless the older person must recall details of the stimuli or make subtle distinctions between the original studied materials and similar distractor items.

Spatial Memory

Lipman (1991) showed young and elderly subjects a slide presentation of two routes through an unfamiliar neighbourhood. Afterwards, she asked subjects to tell the experimenter what they saw. The results showed that the elderly recalled fewer landmarks, and that their recall did not follow the routes in a sequential order, whereas the young's did. When subjects were also given photographs of scenes from the presentation, and were told to sort them into two piles, one for each route, the young were better able to sort the photos into the correct route. The older subjects were also less able to select critical scenes for finding their way. The author concluded that the elderly may be worse at coordinating temporal/spatial information about their environment. However, these findings could result from differences in motivation, cognitive resources, or a number of other individual difference variables. Furthermore, does testing subjects' memory for pictures that make a sequence actually tap *spatial* memory, or would these results be expected from a study of *picture* memory? That is, the effects found in this study may not reflect any kind of specific impairment of spatial memory, but may be indistinguishable from age-related decrements found in other tests of episodic memory.

More naturalistic studies of age-related differences in spatial memory have been conducted. Ohta and Kirasic (1983) had younger and older subjects walk a route through a medical centre four times, and then draw a sketch map of the area covered. They found that the younger group's drawings were more accurate on the three dependent measures: estimation of the angle and distance between the starting and ending point, and accuracy in sequencing the turns that were made. One problem with these results is that it is unclear whether the age-related effects reflect differences in the acquisition of environmental/spatial information, or in the short-term memory of such information.

The solution to this problem is to examine spatial memory abilities in younger and older adults when acquisition is roughly equated in the two age groups. Evans, Brennan, Skorpanich and Held (1984) tested younger and older residents of Orange, California. All subjects had lived in Orange for at least a year, with the young averaging 10.5 years of residency, and the elderly 17.9 years. Furthermore, each subject either worked, or attended a meeting in the central area of the city at least once a week. The results showed that the young adults recalled a greater number of buildings, and when given a list of 13 highly familiar building names, the younger adults were better able to recall their locations on a grid matrix map of the city. From the free recall of building names data, the authors also calculated the organisation of recall. Similar to Lipman's (1991) findings from a novel environment, Evans et al. found that the young group's recall followed the actual spatial order of buildings in geographical space. The authors concluded that the elderly have a less complete knowledge of their real-world geographical environments. These results and those of Lipman (1991) suggest that the young and the elderly employ different retrieval strategies. An empirical question that needs to be addressed is whether the elderly would be capable of utilising their knowledge of geographical space to facilitate recall if the appropriate kinds of retrieval support were provided.

A naturalistic experiment which provides a partial answer to this question was conducted by Rabbitt (1989). He asked groups of middle-aged (50–59 years) and older (70–79 years) volunteers to describe each location (e.g. buildings, shops, offices) on two streets in their town by one of two cueing methods. In one cueing condition, subjects were asked to imagine themselves walking along the street and to identify each location in turn. In the second condition, subjects were cued by functions of possible shops and offices (e.g. "Are there any dry cleaners in the street?"), although only half of these cues were valid. Both groups of subjects identified more locations correctly with function cues, and the function cues were especially helpful to the older participants. The "mental walk" condition is quite similar to free recall in verbal memory experiments, and the greater benefit of function cues to the elderly subjects may be considered another example of more beneficial retrieval support to the older age group.

Memory for the Distant Past

Older people often claim that whereas their memory for recent events is poor, their memory for events that occurred 50 or 60 years ago is sharp and vivid. How could this be? There are several factors that must be taken into account when evaluating such claims; one is that the remote events are typically not comparable to the mundane events of last week, but are often emotionally-charged, salient events of childhood and adolescence. A related factor is that these remote events are selected by the subject and not by the researcher; the older person may not remember what she had for dinner yesterday, but she probably cannot remember what she had for dinner on 14 July 1933 either! A third point is that the "memory" is usually not being retrieved from 50 years ago, but from the last time that the memory was rehearsed or recounted; such material is very prone to reconstructive distortions (Bartlett, 1932) so there is no guarantee that the memory, however sincerely believed, accurately reflects the original event.

Scientific investigators have therefore typically used verifiable public events as material. In general, the results show that retrieval of such memories declines from recent events to events that occurred many years ago. A second technique involves giving subjects a series of single words and asking them to produce a personal memory that each word evokes. The subjects then attempt to date each memory as accurately as possible, and their distribution over the past decades may be calculated. Rubin, Wetzler and Nebes (1986) used this method with 20-year olds and 70-year olds. Figure 9.1 shows that their results were very systematic; the likelihood of a memory being evoked again declined from the present to the past, and the decline is well described by a power function. There is no convincing evidence at present that events occurring during childhood are better remembered than comparable events occurring later in life. On the contrary, given that the second event is closer to the present, it has a higher probability of being retrieved. Cermak (1984) made the interesting suggestion that early autobiographical memories may become "crystallised" through repeated acts of retrieval, and so become more like part of our generalised world knowledge (semantic memory) than they are like true episodic memories.

Prospective Memory

Prospective memory has been defined as memory for activities to be performed in the future (Einstein & McDaniel, 1990), remembering to carry out an activity

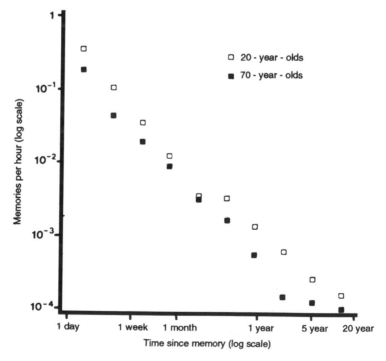

Figure 9.1 Mean number of evoked memories as a function of time since the event occurred. Reproduced by permission from Rubin, Wetzler & Nebes (1986)

(West, 1988), or as memory for planned action (Meacham, 1982). Although these definitions are broadly satisfactory, they do not emphasise the crucial element of prospective memory performance—timeliness. Prospective memory requires not only that people remember to do something; the critical factor is that they must remember to do it at the appropriate time—it is of no use to remember yesterday's medical appointment. Prospective memory is better defined, then, as the timely remembering of a planned action (Winograd, 1988; Kvavilashvili, 1987).

The early studies on prospective memory were naturalistic; that is, they focused on everyday tasks. Subjects were typically asked to phone the experimenter at specific times, or to mail postcards to the experimenter on specific days (Maylor, 1990; Moscovitch, 1982; West, 1988). Older subjects tended to perform better than younger subjects at these tasks. This was an unexpected finding, given the typical age-related declines on standard laboratory retrospective memory tests such as recall and recognition. Moscovitch (1982) asked his subjects how they managed to make their phone calls on time and discovered that the elderly subjects provided themselves with reminders such as notes, alarms, and entries on their calendar. When Moscovitch repeated the study asking the elderly subject not to use external memory aids, their performance decreased to the level of the young people.

This use of memory aids in naturalistic prospective memory tasks was investigated more fully by Maylor (1990). Maylor asked subjects between the ages of 52 and 95 to telephone her laboratory every day for one week. Subjects were required to either telephone at an exact time, or between two times, and were asked to fill out a questionnaire about how they remembered to make their calls. She found that subjects who chose to use internal cues (from their own memory) performed less well than those subjects who used external cues such as notes. Age-related decrements were found for subjects using the internal cues; that is, older subjects tended to forget to call more often than younger subjects when they did not write down their intentions. When subjects chose to use external cues, however, the older subjects performed better than the younger subjects. This age-difference in favour of the elderly subjects is in contrast to other research showing equal performance when young and old subjects use external cues (Einstein & McDaniel, 1990).

Prospective memory has also been studied in the laboratory by means of a paradigm developed by Einstein and McDaniel (1990). They gave subjects a series of short-term memory tasks, but also asked subjects to perform a second task—to press a key whenever a certain target word appeared during the short-term memory trials. Rather against expectation, Einstein and McDaniel found no age-related decrement on this second prospective memory task. The absence of age-related effects in this paradigm is surprising, given that older people themselves often complain of increased everyday forgetfulness in carrying out intended acts. Also, Cockburn and Smith (1991) found large age-related decrements in remembering to carry out future tasks such as asking for the return of a borrowed comb, arranging a future appointment, and delivering a message. Einstein and McDaniel (1990) proposed a possible solution to this paradox. They pointed out that prospective memory tasks can either be time-based (e.g. leaving to go to a meeting at 2:30p.m.), or event-based (e.g. remembering to ask a friend to dinner when you meet him). Further, event-based tasks *are* well supported in the sense that the event acts as a cue. By this argument, time-based tasks should show age-related decrements, and preliminary work by Einstein, McDaniel, Cunfer and Guynn (1991, reported by McDaniel & Einstein, 1992) supports this view.

A further factor in this area is the size of the time-window in which the future action must be performed. Some situations demand that action must be taken within a short time frame (e.g. taking a tea-bag out of your tea) and others have a much longer time frame (e.g. buying a birthday present sometime next week). Short time-window tasks may be associated with more failures of prospective memory than long time-window tasks, in that when people are very involved in a demanding or interesting ongoing task they often show momentary lapses of intention. That is, people can be reminded to carry out some action and then forget to carry it out, even though a period of only 10 seconds has elapsed between the reminder and the target time (Harris & Wilkins, 1982). Older people may be especially vulnerable to such lapses; in a problem-solving experiment conducted by Schonfield and Shooter (cited by Welford, 1958) subjects were asked to press a key before giving each answer. There was an almost tenfold increase in the average number of times that subjects forgot to press the key (0.6 to 5.6) between a group in their teens and a group aged between 50 and 71. Given the importance of prospective remembering to older people (e.g. taking medication, making telephone calls, switching off domestic appliances) it will form an important topic for future study.

Semantic Memory

All of the work described so far has referred to memory for specific events that the subject experienced directly. This type of personal, autobiographical memory was labelled "episodic memory" by Tulving (1972). He distinguished episodic memory from "semantic memory", by which he meant our store of facts and general knowledge of the world. Semantic memories are typically not associated with a specific learning context, whereas time and place are of the essence in episodic memory. Remembering what you had for dinner last night is therefore an episodic memory, and remembering that Sofia is the capital of Bulgaria is a semantic memory. In further work, Tulving (1983) has made a persuasive case for episodic and semantic memory being separate (though interconnected) systems.

The previous work described in this chapter has suggested strongly that episodic memory declines with age over the adult years; what about semantic memory? At first it seems clear that semantic memory performance either does not decline, or declines much less with age than episodic memory. For example, knowledge of vocabulary shows relatively little change with age, and memory for general knowledge, as measured in various IQ tests, also changes rather slightly over the adult years (see Salthouse, 1982, 1991b, for reviews). In several comprehensive reviews of language and ageing, Light (1991, 1992; Light & Burke, 1988) also concluded that semantic knowledge and use show little change across the adult life-span.

More subtle age-related differences may exist, however. For example, Bowles and Poon (Bowles, 1989; Bowles & Poon, 1985) found large age-related decrements when subjects attempted to retrieve words when given their definitions. The retrieval of names certainly gives more problems to older adults (Cohen & Faulkner, 1986; Maylor, 1990) and word-finding failures also increase with age (Burke, MacKay, Worthley & Wade, 1991). It may be the case that well-known and frequently used information is retained and retrieved as well in the elderly, but that difficulties become apparent when retrieval cues are minimal or when the information is infrequently used.

Are such difficulties restricted to retrieval or do older people also have some difficulties in learning new factual information? Most of the contrasts in the literature are between episodic memory for once-presented events and semantic memory for well-learned information. There are relatively few studies of this problem, but in one study McIntyre and Craik (1987) taught new facts about Canada to younger and older Canadians. Memory for the new facts was tested after one week, and no significant age difference was found; recall scores were 0.40 and 0.36 for younger and older subjects respectively. However, the older group had more expertise in this domain of knowledge, and when the age groups were matched on background knowledge, a reliable age difference was found (0.43 and 0.30 for young and old respectively). In a second study, McIntyre and Craik used made-up facts and found a substantial age-related decrement in memory for this new information, both in an immediate test and after a one-week delay. An interim conclusion might therefore be that, while older people show little change in their ability to remember well-learned material in semantic memory, they do show subtle deficits in retrieval when conditions are unfavourable, and also appear to show greater difficulties in learning new factual material. This latter deficit may be offset, however, if the new material is in an area where the older person has substantial background knowledge and expertise.

Implicit Memory

Memory researchers have recently turned their attention to situations in which a prior occurrence (reading a word, say, or looking at a picture) influences later behaviour without the subject consciously recollecting the initial event. For example, the subject may be asked to complete a word fragment (e.g. _u_ge__), to complete a word whose first three letters are given (e.g. mar___), or to identify a word exposed very briefly on a tachistoscope. The finding is that subjects perform these tasks more successfully if they have recently studied appropriate words (e.g. *Surgeon*, *Marble*) although they may fail to consciously recollect having encountered them recently. Just as learning can be intentional or incidental, so retrieval can involve deliberate attempts to recall or recognise a prior event (termed *explicit memory*) so retrieval can be unconsciously evoked by the task (termed *implicit memory*). The distinction between explicit and implicit remembering is thus best viewed as a difference in retrieval orientation.

One striking finding in this area is that amnesic patients, who by definition have very poor explicit memory capabilities, show essentially normal performance on tasks of implicit memory (Schacter, 1987). In general, the same pattern of results has been found when younger and older adults are compared; groups which show substantial age-related deficits in explicit tasks such as free recall, paired-associate learning, or recognition, show negligible age differences in implicit tasks such as word-stem completion or word fragment completion (e.g. Howard & Wiggs, 1993; Light & Singh, 1987; Light, Singh & Capps, 1986).

Three examples may be presented briefly. Howard (1988) had subjects study the less frequently occurring member of homophone pairs (e.g. *reed* as opposed to *read*; *reign* as opposed to *rain*). In a later "spelling test" she asked people to spell words presented auditorily, and found first that the subjects exposed to the prior words had a greater tendency than control subjects to write down the less frequent word, and second that there was no age difference in this respect. As a second example, Light and Singh (1987) presented words to younger and older learners, and later gave them word stems (the first three letters) either "as cues for the words you recently studied" (explicit test) or to another group simply "to complete with the first word that comes to mind" (implicit test). The researchers found a large age-related decrement in the explicit test but no age differences in the likelihood of writing down a list word in the implicit test. A third test of implicit memory involves presenting either a word or a nonword; the subject's task is to decide as rapidly as possible whether each item is or is not a word. The speed of this lexical decision is faster when the target word is preceded by a semantically related word (e.g. doctor—*nurse*); Laver and Burke (1993) have recently noted that the amount of this semantic priming effect is typically *greater* in older people. Thus, although some contrary cases have been reported, the consensus is that implicit memory and learning are generally intact in older people.

This is a positive and encouraging conclusion, but the findings should not be taken as evidence that acquisition of learned materials is unaffected by ageing and that the deficit therefore lies in explicit retrieval processes. There is good evidence that many implicit memory tasks rely on sensory aspects of stimuli for their successful completion (e.g. Roediger, Weldon & Challis, 1989). It may therefore be the case that older and younger people encode such surface or sensory aspects of stimuli equivalently, and therefore show equivalent performance on implicit tasks. However, explicit tasks may demand richer and more complex information which is encoded less fully by the older adult. In addition, there is consistent evidence to show that older adults acquire new cognitive skills more slowly in real-life situations (Charness & Bosman, 1992; Park 1992). For example, in studies of training word-processing skills, older adults took 1.5 to 2.5 times longer to reach given levels of expertise, although it is important to note that they *did* reach these same levels (Elias, Elias, Robbins & Gage, 1987; Zandri & Charness, 1989).

Ageing and Metamemory

The term *metamemory* has taken on several connotations in the ageing and memory literature. Three main categories of inquiry which encompass most prevailing meanings of metamemory are as follows (1) self-evaluations of memory abilities, (2) knowledge about memory and mnemonic strategy use, and (3) monitoring of one's own memory functioning in an online manner. Studying the relation between these three factors and ageing should clarify the contributions of such non-memorial factors to age-related changes in memory performance.

Self-Evaluation of Memory Abilities

Although good measures of self-rated memory abilities and memory complaints have been developed (e.g. Hultsch, Hertzog, Dixon & Davidson, 1988), correlations between those measures and actual memory performance have been consistently low; that is, the self appraisal scores do not predict memory performance reliably (e.g. Hultsch et al., 1988; Taylor, Miller & Tinklenberg, 1992). One exception is a study by Sunderland, Watts, Baddeley and Harris (1986) in which the investigators found a reliable relation between scores on a questionnaire and performance on a story recall test. The correlation was not very high, however (correlation coefficients were 0.37 and 0.31 for immediate and delayed recall, respectively, with 60 subjects), and questionnaire scores did not correlate with other objective memory tests. Sunderland and colleagues discuss the possibility that questions on the *difference* between a person's perceived current memory abilities and his or her abilities as a young adult might prove more sensitive. Two other interesting points made in this article are, first, that whereas the elderly participants believed strongly that their memory abilities had declined with age, very few of them felt that this decline was a handicap. The second point is that one obvious factor restricting the usefulness of questionnaire studies is that people with memory problems will tend to forget instances of memory failure! In general, then, there is little experimental evidence for a causal link between memory self-efficacy and actual performance, although self-rated memory tends to decline with age. It may be that lower self-evaluation scores are a *result* of performance feedback as well as a reflection of social attitudes about ageing and memory (Light, 1991).

Knowledge About Memory and Mnemonic Strategy Use

A well-replicated finding in the ageing and metamemory literature is that there are negligible age differences in knowledge about memory task demands (e.g. Hultsch, Hertzog & Dixon, 1987; Loewen, Shaw & Craik, 1990). Such a result suggests that age differences in memory performance are most likely not attributable to differences in knowledge about aspects of memory. However, age differences in the *spontaneous use* of mnemonic strategies have been observed and implicated in age-related memory differences (see previous section "encoding processes").

Memory Monitoring

Memory monitoring refers to the ability to assess online memory states, or test-readiness. Snyder, Murphy and Sanders (1992) recently examined the effects of monitoring in young and older adults on several memory tasks. They found an improvement in serial recall performance for older adults when they were trained to self-monitor their memory performance by self-testing, although self-testing did not generalise well to other memory tasks following training. There is some evidence for age differences in test-readiness as assessed by estimates of study time necessary for equal performance on a given memory task (Murphy et al., 1981; Zacks & Hasher, 1988). However, even with unlimited study time, young and elderly groups often do not perform at the same levels (e.g. Craik & Rabinowitz, 1985).

Implications

Current research on the link between metamemory and age-related memory differences suggests that, although some group differences in memory monitoring and self-appraisal have been found, these differences have not been shown to cause age differences in actual memory performance. Out of all the aspects of metamemory discussed above, knowledge about memory processes appears to be the most stable across the age span. The main practical implication of this area of research is that measures of self-reported memory abilities should not be used in lieu of measures of actual memory performance.

CONCLUDING COMMENTS

Summary of Findings

The experimental evidence confirms the general view that memory performance does decline as a function of normal ageing, but that it declines more in some situations than in others. We have reviewed the evidence showing that immediate recall of a short sequence of items drops very little with age, but that substantial losses are found in working memory. In this latter case the person must not only hold information in mind, but also manipulate and reorganise it, or combine it with further incoming information. In longer-term memory situations, older people typically do show performance decrements, although here too the size of the effect depends on the task and its conditions. The largest age-related decrements are found in tasks that provide little guidance to encoding operations and little support to retrieval operations. The decrements are reduced, however, to the extent that instructions, or certain orienting tasks (e.g. generating precise elaborators, or performing small motor tasks) are given at the time of acquisition, and combined with supportive conditions (e.g. cued recall, or recognition) at the time of retrieval.

Older people forget new facts and events unless the task is modified in these ways. They are also more likely to forget the source of learned information or the context in which an event occurred. Memory for rich pictorial materials seems to hold up quite well with age, but memory for spatial information declines. Contrary to what many older people believe, memory for childhood events does not appear to grow relatively stronger with age—although it is possible that more time spent in reminiscence would bring such memories to light. Prospective memory—remembering to carry out future actions—holds up well if people are left to their own devices; older people are often *better* at such tasks, but this is likely due to their taking the task more seriously, and therefore making notes and providing themselves with reminders. However, when prospective memory tasks do not involve external cues and therefore involve self-initiation, such as in the case where people must remember to perform an action at a particular time, older people do not perform as well as their younger counterparts.

With regard to different "types" of memory, it is often claimed that age decrements are greater in episodic memory than in semantic memory, but care must be taken to equate learning and expertise in these two systems; when this is done, memory for new facts may be no better than memory for specific events. Retrieval of proper names (a semantic memory task) is clearly poorer in older people. Finally, two areas in which age differences are minimal are implicit memory—the unconscious effect of past experience on present performance—and metamemory, the ability to assess one's own memory capacities.

Are these changes essentially biological and universal, or can they be modified by cultural and other factors? The following sections discuss this question briefly.

Other Relevant Factors

Educational or Job Experience

One of the many difficulties inherent in the study of cognitive ageing stems from the fact that present-day subjects in their teens and 20s have received a richer educational experience than older people received 50 or 60 years ago. It is therefore possible that age-related differences in memory and other cognitive abilities are due to this difference in educational experience rather than to age as such. Researchers have attempted to counter this criticism by matching younger and older samples on their number of years of formal education. When this is done, substantial age differences typically remain (for a review, see Craik & Jennings, 1992). In a discussion of this problem, Salthouse (1991b) concluded that "it does not appear that variation in education can account for more than a small proportion of the age differences observed in certain measures of cognitive functioning" (p. 77).

With respect to job-related skills, Park (1992) suggests that memory for and performance of well-learned procedures are well maintained in the older worker. However, the acquisition of *new* skills—such as learning word processing or other software packages—takes substantially longer in older learners (Park, 1992, p. 480). In a similar vein, Charness (1981) found that older chess players maintained their level of skill in choosing the best move when given the board setting of a game in progress, but that older players were poorer than their younger colleagues when given a later unexpected recall test for the board settings they had studied.

In general, then, it seems unlikely that observed age decrements are artifacts of differential educational experience. Continued practice of motor and cognitive skills will maintain these skills, but memory for new events within such skilled domains may still show age-related declines. On the positive side, memory is typically a function of expertise, and if older people are more expert in some domain than their younger counterparts, the older group may well exhibit higher levels of memory performance (e.g. McIntyre & Craik, 1987).

Motivation

One plausible reason for age-related declines in memory and other laboratory tasks is that older people don't see the point of trying hard to perform tests that are often meaningless and almost always artificial. The arguments against this motivational explanation are rather indirect. First, our own experience and that of other researchers, (e.g. Salthouse, 1991b, p. 183) is that older volunteers are if anything *more* motivated to succeed than their younger counterparts; they have more personal investment in showing that their abilities are intact. Second, most experiments look at interactions rather than main effects of age. That is, experiments are designed to show that age-related performance differences are much greater under one condition (e.g. working memory, free recall) than under another (e.g. primary memory, recognition). If the *same* older subjects do well under one condition but not under another, it is difficult to attribute their weaker performance to an age-related difference in motivation.

Finally, Salthouse (1991a, p. 184) reviews evidence which suggests that the addition of a reward increases performance equally in younger and older subjects. All in all, there is little sound evidence pointing to a decrease in motivation as the underlying cause of poorer memory in the elderly. Whereas older people may often show a reluctance to attempt new tasks, the primary factor may be a reduced capacity to think through the new situation, the apparent decline in motivation being secondary (Hebb, 1978).

Health Status

It is clear that health-related problems increase from early to late adulthood; is it possible that the well-documented changes in memory with age are really attributable to poorer health in the elderly? Unfortunately there is no definitive answer to this question at present, and the conclusions drawn from the literature seem to depend on whether the reviewer is biased towards believing that sociocultural or biological factors play the dominant role in determining cognitive behaviours. In the first category, Siegler and Costa (1985) cite studies showing that health status rather than age is associated with learning and memory performance. In the second category, Salthouse (1991b, p. 65) reports the results of five recent studies, all of which showed little or no decline in the negative correlation between age and memory performance when differences in self-rated health were partialled out statistically. The resolution may depend on obtaining more objective measures of health status; or perhaps the *severity* of the health impairment is crucial. For the moment, it seems to us that, *for normal ageing*, health status may be a contributing factor but is not the prime determinant of age-related memory loss.

Similarity to Other Conditions

It is of great scientific interest that the patterns of memory strengths and weaknesses found in normal elderly adults are also found, partly or completely, in other experimental and clinical conditions. It is striking to realise that when young adults learn material under conditions of divided attention, the resulting pattern is essentially identical to that found in older adults (Craik, 1982, 1983). One implication of this finding is that decreased processing resources may be the factor common to the two situations. The same pattern of results has also been found following sleep deprivation, and with alcoholic intoxication (Craik, 1977b; Nilsson, Bäckman & Karlsson, 1989).

When more clearly pathological conditions are examined, as they are described in other chapters of this volume, further interesting parallels emerge. Unaided recall is often found to be more sensitive than is recognition as an indicator of memory impairment. For example Kaszniak (1990) reviews evidence suggesting that depressed patients show deficits on recall, but not on recognition tests, whereas Alzheimer patients show deficits on both types of test. Kaszniak also discusses the tendency of both older adults and depressed patients to complain of memory deficits more than is warranted by their relatively good performance levels.

A further intriguing point for future research spanning the laboratory and clinic is the particular difficulty for effortful, self-initiated processing found in normal older adults (Craik, 1983), in depression (Kaszniak, 1990), in Parkinson's disease (Massman et al., 1990), and in patients with frontal lobe lesions (Moscovitch, 1989; Stuss & Benson, 1986). The positive complement of this difficulty is that people in these groups may benefit greatly from an increase in "environmental support" in the shape of cues, reminders, or reinstatement of context in other forms.

Finally, does the pattern of memory loss seen in Alzheimer's disease reflect a distinctively different underlying "pathology" from that found in normal ageing, or is it simply an exaggerated version of the normal condition? After a thoughtful review of the evidence, Nebes (1992) states that, whereas there is relatively little evidence at present for qualitative differences between Alzheimer's disease and normal ageing, we require a great deal more information before a definitive pronouncement can be made.

ACKNOWLEDGEMENTS

Preparation of this chapter was supported by a grant from the Natural Sciences and Engineering Research Council of Canada to F.I.M. Craik. We are grateful to Alan Baddeley and Scott Brown for their helpful comments on an earlier draft.

REFERENCES

Babcock, R.L. & Salthouse, T.A. (1990). Effects of increased processing demands on age differences in working memory. *Psychology and Aging*, **5**, 421–428.

Bäckman, L. (1989). Varieties of memory compensation by older adults in episodic remembering. In L.W. Poon, D.C. Rubin & B.A. Wilson (eds), *Everyday Cognition in Adulthood and Late Life*. Cambridge University Press, Cambridge, pp. 509–544.

Bäckman, L. & Mäntylä, T. (1988). Effectiveness of self-generated cues in younger and older adults: the role of retention interval. *International Journal of Aging and Human Development*, **26**, 241–247.

Bäckman, L. & Nilsson, L.-G. (1984). Aging effects in free recall: an exception to the rule. *Human Learning*, **3**, 53–69.

Baddeley, A.D. (1986). *Working Memory*. Oxford University Press, Oxford.

Baddeley, A.D. & Hitch, G. (1974). Working memory. In G. Bower (ed.), *The Psychology of Learning and Motivation*, vol. 8. Academic Press, New York, pp. 47–89.

Bartlett, F.C. (1932). *Remembering*. Cambridge University Press, Cambridge.

Bartlett, J.C. & Leslie, J.E. (1986). Aging and memory for faces versus single views of faces. *Memory and Cognition*, **14**, 371–381.

Bower, G.H., Clark, M.C., Lesgold, A.M. & Winzenz, D. (1969). Hierarchical retrieval schemes in recall of categorized word lists. *Journal of Verbal Learning and Verbal Behavior*, **8**, 323–343.

Bowles, N.L. (1989). Age and semantic inhibition in word retrieval. *Journal of Gerontology*, **44**, 88–90.

Bowles, N.L. & Poon, L.W. (1985). Aging and retrieval of words in semantic memory. *Journal of Gerontology*, **40**, 71–77.

Burke, D.M. & Light, L.L. (1981). Memory and aging: the role of retrieval processes. *Psychological Bulletin*, **90**, 513–546.

Burke, D.M., MacKay, D.G., Worthley, J.S. & Wade, E. (1991). On the tip of the tongue: what causes word finding failures in young and older adults? *Journal of Memory and Language*, **30**, 542–579.

Cermak, L.A. (1984). The episodic/semantic distinction in amnesia. In N. Butters & L.R. Squire (eds), *The Neuropsychology of Memory*. Guilford, New York, pp. 55–62.

Charness, N. (1981). Ageing and skilled problem solving. *Journal of Experimental Psychology: General*, **110**, 21–38.

Charness, N. & Bosman, E.A. (1992). Human factors and age. In F.I.M. Craik & T.A. Salthouse (eds), *The Handbook of Aging and Cognition*. Erlbaum, Hillsdale, NJ.

Cockburn, J. & Smith, P.T. (1991). The relative influence of intelligence and age on everyday memory. *Journal of Gerontology: Psychological Sciences*, **46**, P31–P36.

Cohen, G. (1988). Age differences in memory for texts: production deficiency or processing limitations? In L.L. Light & D.M. Burke (eds), *Language, Memory, and Aging*. Cambridge University Press, Cambridge, pp. 171–190.

Cohen, G. & Faulkner, D. (1986). Memory for proper names: age differences in retrieval. *British Journal of Developmental Psychology*, **4**, 187–197.

Craik, F.I.M. (1968). Short-term memory and the aging process. In G.A. Talland (ed.), *Human Aging and Behavior*. Academic Press, New York, pp. 131–168.

Craik, F.I.M. (1977a). Age differences in human memory. In J.E. Birren & K.W. Schaie (eds), *Handbook of the Psychology of Aging*. Van Nostrand Reinhold, New York, pp. 384–420.

Craik, F.I.M. (1977b). Similarities between the effects of aging and alcoholic intoxication on memory performance, construed within a "levels of processing" framework. In I.M. Birnbaum & E.S. Parker (eds), *Alcohol and Human Memory*. Erlbaum, Hillsdale, NJ.

Craik, F.I.M. (1982). Selective changes in encoding as a function of reduced processing capacity. In F. Klix, J. Hoffman & E. van der Meer (eds), *Cognitive Research in Psychology*, Deutscher Verlag der Wissenschaffen, Berlin, pp. 152–161.

Craik, F.I.M. (1983). On the transfer of information from temporary to permanent memory. *Philosophical Transactions of the Royal Society of London B*, **302**, 341–359.

Craik, F.I.M. (1986). A functional account of age differences in memory. In F. Klix & H. Hagendorf (eds), *Human Memory and Cognitive Capabilities, Mechanisms, and Performance*. Elsevier Science Publishers, Amsterdam, pp. 409–422.

Craik, F.I.M., Byrd, M. & Swanson, J.M. (1987). Patterns of memory loss in three elderly samples. *Psychology and Aging*, **2**, 79–86.

Craik, F.I.M. & Jennings, J.M. (1992). Human memory. In F.I.M. Craik & T.A. Salthouse (eds), *Handbook of Aging and Cognition*. Erlbaum, Hillsdale, pp. 51–100.

Craik, F.I.M. & McDowd, J.M. (1987). Age differences in recall and recognition. *Journal of Experimental Psychology: Learning, Memory and Cognition*, **13**, 474–479.

Craik, F.I.M., Morris, R.G. & Gick, M.L. (1990). Adult age differences in working memory. In G. Vallar & T. Shallice (eds), *Neuropsychological Impairments of Short-Term Memory*. Cambridge University Press, Cambridge, pp. 247–267.

Craik, F.I.M., Morris, L.W., Morris, R.G. & Loewen, E.R. (1990). Relations between source amnesia and frontal lobe functioning in older adults. *Psychology and Aging*, **5**, 148–151.

Craik, F.I.M. & Rabinowitz, J.C. (1985). The effects of presentation rate and encoding task on age-related memory deficits. *Journal of Gerontology*, **40**, 309–315.

Craik, F.I.M. & Salthouse, T.A. (1992). *The Handbook of Aging and Cognition*, Erlbaum, Hillsdale, NJ.

Craik, F.I.M. & Tulving, E. (1975). Depth of processing and the retention of words in episodic memory. *Journal of Experimental Psychology*: *General*, **104**, 268–294.

Delbecq-Derouesné, J. & Beauvois, M.F. (1989). Memory processes and aging: a defect of automatic rather than controlled processes? *Archives of Gerontology and Geriatrics*, Suppl. 1, 121–150.

Dobbs, A.R. & Rule, B.G. (1989). Adult age differences in working memory. *Psychology and Aging*, **4**, 500–503.

Eich, J.E. (1980). The cue-dependent nature of state-dependent retrieval. *Memory and Cognition*, **8**, 157–173.

Einstein, G.O. & McDaniel, M.A. (1990). Normal aging and prospective memory. *Journal of Experimental Psychology*: *Learning, Memory and Cognition*, **16**, 717–726.

Elias, P.K., Elias, F.M., Robbins, M.A. & Gage, P. (1987). Acquisition of word-processing skills by younger, middle-age, and older adults. *Psychology and Aging*, **2**, 340–348.

Evans, G.W., Brennan, P.L., Skorpanich, M.A. & Held, D. (1984). Cognitive mapping and elderly adults: verbal and location memory for urban landmarks. *Journal of Gerontology*, **39**, 452–457.

Harris, J.E. & Wilkins, A.J. (1982). Remembering to do things: a theoretical framework and an illustrative experiment. *Human Learning*, **1**, 123–136.

Hartley, A.A. (1992). Attention. In F.I.M. Craik & T.A. Salthouse (eds), *The Handbook of Aging and Cognition*. Erlbaum, Hillsdale, NJ.

Hasher, L. & Zacks, R.T. (1988). Working memory, comprehension, and aging: a review and a new view. In G. Bower (ed.), *The Psychology of Learning and Motivation*, vol. 22. Academic Press, New York, pp. 193–225.

Hashtroudi, S., Parker, E.S., Luis, J.D. & Reisen, C.A. (1989). Generation and elaboration in older adults. *Experimental Aging Research*, **15**, 73–78.

Hebb, D.O. (1978). On watching myself growing old. *Psychology Today*, **12**, 20–23.

Howard, D.V. (1988). Aging and semantic activation: the priming of semantic and episodic memories. In L.L. Light & D.M. Burke (eds), *Language, Memory and Aging*. Cambridge University Press, New York. pp. 77–100.

Howard, D.V. & Wiggs, C.L. (1993). Aging and learning: insights from implicit and explicit tests. In J. Cerella, W.J. Hoyer, J. Rybash & M. Commons (eds), *Adult Information Processing*: *Limits on Loss*. Academic Press, New York.

Hulicka, I.M. & Grossman, J.L. (1967). Age-group comparisons for the use of mediators in paired-associate learning. *Journal of Gerontology*, **46**, 22–30.

Hultsch, D.F., Hertzog, C. & Dixon, R.A. (1987). Age differences in metamemory: resolving the inconsistencies. *Canadian Journal of Psychology*, **41**, 209–222.

Hultsch, D.F., Hertzog, C., Dixon, R.A. & Davidson, H. (1988). Memory self-knowledge and self-efficacy in the aged. In M.L. Howe & C.J. Brainerd (eds), *Cognitive Development in Adulthood*: *Progress in Cognitive Development Research*. Springer-Verlag, New York, pp. 65–92.

Kaszniak, A.W. (1990). Psychological assessment of the aging individual. In J.E. Birren & K.W. Schaie (eds), *Handbook of the Psychology of Aging*, 3rd edn. Academic Press, New York.

Kliegl, R., Smith, J. & Baltes, P.B. (1989). Testing-the-limits and the study of adult age differences in cognitive plasticity of a mnemonic skill. *Developmental Psychology*, **25**, 247–256.

Koriat, A., Ben-Zur, H. & Sheffer, D. (1988). Telling the same story twice: output monitoring and age. *Journal of Memory and Language*, **27**, 23–39.

Kvavilashvili, L. (1987). Remembering intention as a distinct form of memory. *British Journal of Psychology*, **78**, 507–518.

Laver, G.D. & Burke, D.M. (1993). Why do semantic priming effects increase in old age? A meta-analysis. *Psychology and Aging*, **8**, 34–43.

Light, L.L. (1991). Memory and aging: four hypotheses in search of data. *Annual Review of Psychology*, **42**, 333–376.

Light, L.L. (1992). The organization of memory in old age. In F.I.M. Craik & T.A. Salthouse (eds), *The Handbook of Aging and Cognition*. Erlbaum, Hillsdale, NJ, pp. 111–165.

Light, L.L. & Burke, D.M. (1988). Patterns of language and memory in old age. In D.M. Burke & L.L. Light (eds), *Language, Memory, and Aging*. Cambridge University Press, Cambridge, pp. 244–272.

Light, L.L. & Singh, A. (1987). Implicit and explicit memory in young and older adults. *Journal of Experimental Psychology: Learning, Memory and Cognition*, **13**, 531–541.

Light, L.L, Singh, A. & Capps, J.L. (1986). Dissociation of memory and awareness in young and older adults. *Journal of Experimental Psychology: Learning, Memory and Cognition*, **13**, 531–541.

Lipman, P.D. (1991). Age and exposure differences in acquisition of route information. *Psychology and Aging*, **6**, 128–133.

Loewen, E.R., Shaw, R.J. & Craik, F.I.M. (1990). Age differences in components of metamemory. *Experimental Aging Research*, **16**, 43–48.

Massman, P.J., Delis, D.C., Butters, N., Levin, B.E. & Salmon, D.P. (1990). Are all subcortical dementias alike? Verbal learning in Parkinson's and Huntington's disease patients. *Journal of Clinical and Experimental Neuropsychology*, **12**, 729–744.

Maylor, E.A. (1990). Age and prospective memory. *Quarterly Journal of Experimental Psychology*, **42A**, 471–493.

McDaniel, M.A. & Einstein, G.O. (1992). Aging and prospective memory: basic findings and practical applications. *Advances in Learning and Behavioral Disabilities*, **7**, 87–105.

McEvoy, C.L., Nelson, D.L., Holley, P.E. & Stelnicki, G.S. (1992). Implicit processing in the cued recall of young and old adults. *Psychology and Aging*, **7**, 401–408.

McIntyre, J.S. & Craik, F.I.M. (1987). Age differences in memory for item and source information. *Canadian Journal of Psychology*, **41**, 175–192.

Meacham, J.A. (1982). A note on remembering to execute planned actions. *Journal of Applied Developmental Psychology*, **3**, 121–133.

Mitchell, D.B., Hunt, R.R. & Schmitt, F.A. (1986). The generation effect and reality monitoring: evidence from dementia and normal aging. *Journal of Gerontology*, **41**, 79–84.

Moscovitch, M. (1982). A neuropsychological approach to memory and perception in normal and pathological aging. In F.I.M. Craik & S. Trehub (eds), *Aging and Cognitive Processes*. Plenum Press, New York.

Moscovitch, M. (1989). Confabulation and the frontal systems: strategic versus associative retrieval in neuropsychological theories of memory. In H.L. Roediger & F.I.M. Craik (eds), *Varieties of Memory and Consciousness*. Erlbaum, Hillsdale, NJ.

Murphy, M.D., Sanders, R.E., Gabriesheski, A.S. & Schmitt, F.A. (1981). Metamemory and the aged. *Journal of Gerontology*, **36**, 185–193.

Nilsson, L.G., Bäckman, L. & Karlsson, T. (1989). Priming and cued recall in elderly, alcohol intoxicated and sleep deprived subjects: a case of functionally similar memory deficits. *Psychological Medicine*, **19**, 423–433.

Nilsson, L.-G. & Craik, F.I.M. (1990). Additive and interactive effects in memory for subject-performed tasks. *European Journal of Cognitive Psychology*, **2**, 305–324.

Ohta, R.J. & Kirasic, K.C. (1983). The investigation of environmental learning in the elderly. In G.D. Rowles & R.J. Ohta (eds), *Aging and Milieu: Environmental Perspectives on Growing Old*. Academic Press, New York. pp. 83–95.

Park, D.C. (1992). Applied cognitive aging research. In F.I.M. Craik & T.A. Salthouse (eds), *The Handbook of Aging and Cognition*. Erlbaum, Hillsdale, NJ.

Park, D.C., Puglisi, J.T. & Smith, A.D. (1986). Memory for pictures: does an age-related decline exist? *Psychology and Aging*, **1**, 11–17.

Parkinson, S.R. (1982). Performance deficits in short-term memory tasks: a comparison of amnesic Korsakoff patients and the aged. In L.S. Cermak (ed.), *Human Memory and Amnesia*. Erlbaum, Hillsdale, pp. 77–96.

Perlmutter, M. (1979). Age differences in adults' free recall, cued recall, and recognition. *Journal of Gerontology*, **34**, 533–539.

Poon, L.W., Walsh-Sweeney, L. & Fozard, J.L. (1980). Memory skill training for the elderly: salient issues on the use of imagery mnemonics. In L.W. Poon, J.L. Fozard, L.S. Cermak, D. Arenberg & L.W. Thompson (eds), *New Directions in Memory and Aging*. Erlbaum, Hillsdale, NJ, pp. 461–484.

Puglisi, J.T. & Park, D.C. (1987). Perceptual elaboration and memory in older adults. *Journal of Gerontology*, **42**, 160–162.

Rabbitt, P. (1989). Inner-city decay? Age changes in structure and process in recall of familiar topographical information. In L.W. Poon, D.C. Rubin & B.A. Wilson (eds), *Everyday Cognition in Adulthood and Late Life*. Cambridge University Press, Cambridge.

Rabinowitz, J.C. (1989). Judgments of origin and generation effects: comparisons between young and elderly adults. *Psychology and Aging*, **4**, 259–268.

Rabinowitz, J.C., Ackerman, B.P., Craik, F.I.M. & Hinchley, J.L. (1982). Aging and metamemory: the roles of relatedness and imagery. *Journal of Gerontology*, **37**, 688–695.

Rabinowitz, J.C., Craik, F.I.M. & Ackerman, B.P. (1982). A processing resource account of age differences in recall. *Canadian Journal of Psychology*, **36**, 325–344.

Rankin, J.L. & Collins, M. (1986). The effects of memory elaboration on adult age differences in incidental recall. *Experimental Aging Research*, **12**, 231–234.

Roediger, H.L., Weldon, M.S. & Challis, B.H. (1989). Explaining dissociations between implicit and explicit measures of retention: a processing account. In H.L. Roediger & F.I.M. Craik (eds), *Varieties of Memory and Consciousness: Essays in Honour of Endel Tulving*. Erlbaum, Hillsdale, NJ, pp. 3–42.

Rubin, D.C., Wetzler, S.E. & Nebes, R.D. (1986). Autobiographical memory across the lifespan. In D.C. Rubin (ed.), *Autobiographical Memory*. Cambridge University Press, Cambridge, pp. 202–221.

Salthouse, T.A. (1982). *Adult Cognition: An Experimental Psychology of Human Aging*. Springer Verlag, New York.

Salthouse, T.A. (1991a). Mediation of adult age differences in cognition by reductions in working memory and speed of processing. *Psychological Science*, **2**, 179–183.

Salthouse, T.A. (1991b). *Theoretical Perspectives on Cognitive Aging*. Erlbaum, Hillsdale, NJ.

Salthouse, T.A. (1992a). Influences of processing speed on adult age differences in working memory. *Acta Psychologica*, **79**, 155–170.

Salthouse, T.A. (1992b). Working-memory mediation of adult age differences in integrative reasoning. *Memory and Cognition*, **20**, 413–423.

Salthouse, T.A., Babcock, R.L. & Shaw, R.J. (1991). Effects of adult age on structural and operational capacities in working memory. *Psychology and Aging*, **6**, 118–127.

Schacter, D.L. (1987). Implicit memory: history and current status. *Journal of Experimental Psychology: Learning, Memory and Cognition*, **13**, 368–379.

Schacter, D.L., Harbluk, J.L. & McLachlan, D. (1987). Retrieval without recollection: an experimental analysis of source amnesia. *Journal of Verbal Learning and Verbal Behavior*, **23**, 593–611.

Schonfield, D. & Robertson, B. (1966). Memory storage and aging. *Canadian Journal of Psychology*, **20**, 228–236.

Sharps, M.J. & Gollin, E.S. (1988). Aging and free recall for objects located in space. *Journal of Gerontology*, **43**, 8–11.

Shaw, R.J. & Craik, F.I.M. (1989). Age differences in predictions and performance on a cued recall task. *Psychology and Aging*, **4**, 131–135.

Shimamura, A.P. & Squire, L.R. (1987). A neuropsychological study of fact memory and source amnesia. *Journal of Experimental Psychology: Learning, Memory and Cognition*, **13**, 464–473.

Siegler, I.C. & Costa, P.T. (1985). Health behavior relationships. In J.E. Birren & K.W. Schaie (eds), *Handbook of the Psychology of Aging*, 2nd edn. Van Nostrand Reinhold, New York.

Simon, E. (1979). Depth and elaboration of processing in relation to age. *Journal of Experimental Psychology: Human Learning and Memory*, **5**, 115–124.

Smith, A.D. (1977). Adult age differences in cued recall. *Developmental Psychology*, **13**, 326–331.

Snyder, T.L., Murphy, M.D. & Sanders, R.E. Generalization of memory monitoring. Poster presented at the Fourth Biennial Cognitive Aging Conference, Atlanta, GA, April 1992.

Stoltzfus, E.R. & Hasher, L. Aging and the breadth of availability during language processing. Poster presented at the Fourth Cognitive Aging Conference, Atlanta, GA, April 1992.

Stuss, D.T. & Benson, D.F. (1986). *The Frontal Lobes*. Raven Press, New York.

Sunderland, A., Watts, K., Baddeley, A.D. & Harris, J.E. (1986). Subjective memory assessment and test performance in elderly adults. *Journal of Gerontology*, **41**, 376–384.

Taylor, J.L., Miller, T.P. & Tinklenberg, J.R. (1992). Correlates of memory decline: 4-year longitudinal study of older adults with memory complaints. *Psychology and Aging*, **7**, 185–193.

Till, R.E., Bartlett, J.C. & Doyle, A.H. (1982). Age differences in picture memory with resemblance and discrimination tasks. *Experimental Aging Research*, **8**, 179–184.

Treat, N.J. & Reese, H.W. (1976). Age, pacing and imagery in paired-associate learning. *Developmental Psychology*, **12**, 119–124.

Tulving, E. (1972). Episodic and semantic memory. In E. Tulving & W. Donaldson (eds), *Organization of Memory*. Academic Press, New York, pp. 382–404.

Tulving, E. (1983). *Elements of Episodic Memory*. Oxford University Press, New York.

Tulving, E. & Thomson, D.M. (1973). Encoding specificity and retrieval processes in episodic memory. *Psychological Review*, **80**, 352–373.

Waugh, N.C. & Norman, D.A. (1965). Primary memory. *Psychological Review*, **72**, 89–104.

Welford, A.T. (1958). *Ageing and Human Skill*. Oxford University Press, London.

West, R.L. (1988). Prospective memory and aging. In M.M. Gruneberg, P.E. Morris & R.N. Sykes (eds), *Practical Aspects of Memory. Current Research and Issues, Vol. 2: Clinical and Educational Implications*. Wiley, Chichester, pp. 119–125.

West, R.L. & Boatwright, L.K. (1983). Age differences in cued recall and recognition under varying encoding and retrieval conditions. *Experimental Aging Research*, **9**, 185–189.

Wingfield, A., Stine, A.L., Lahar, C.J. & Aberdeen, J.S. (1988). Does the capacity of working memory change with age? *Experimental Aging Research*, **14**, 103–107.

Winograd, E. (1988). Some observations on prospective remembering. In M.M. Gruneberg, P.E. Morris, & R.N. Sykes (eds), *Practical Aspects of Memory. Current Research and Issues, Vol. 1: Memory in Everyday Life*. Wiley, Chichester, pp. 348–353.

Zacks, R.T. & Hasher, L. (1988). Capacity theory and the processing of inferences. In L.L. Light & D.M. Burke (eds), *Language, Memory and Aging*. Cambridge University Press, Cambridge, pp. 154–170.

Zandri, E. & Charness, N. (1989). Training older and younger adults to use software. *Educational Gerontology*, **15**, 615–631.

Chapter 10

Memory Disorders in the Dementias

Jason Brandt
and
Jill B. Rich
Johns Hopkins University School of Medicine, Baltimore, USA

INTRODUCTION

Dementia is the general term given to neuropsychiatric syndromes characterized by acquired cognitive impairment in multiple spheres but without impaired consciousness (Brandt & Benedict, 1993; McKhann et al., 1984; Rebok & Folstein,1993). Although the cognitive syndromes associated with different dementing illnesses vary somewhat, one thing all dementias have in common is a severe impairment in the ability to learn new information. In fact, the presence of memory impairment is obligatory for the diagnosis of dementia (American Psychiatric Association, 1987; McKhann et al., 1984). The term "dementia" does not by itself imply a progressive or irreversible disorder of the type associated with Alzheimer's disease. Thus, survivors of severe traumatic brain injury, for example, often meet diagnostic criteria for dementia, although their cognitive functioning may actually improve with the passage of time.

This chapter is concerned with dementia as it appears in degenerative brain diseases. These are diseases that affect primarily the elderly. Estimates of the prevalence of dementia vary widely as a function of the particular population sampled, the tests used, and the criteria for diagnosis. Nevertheless, approximately 15% of the population over age 65 is believed to suffer from some form of dementia (Cummings & Benson, 1992). This figure rises dramatically with

Handbook of Memory Disorders. Edited by A.D. Baddeley, B.A. Wilson and F.N. Watts.
© 1995 John Wiley & Sons Ltd.

increasing age, with reports ranging from approximately 25% (Mortimer, 1983) to as many as 47% (Evans et al., 1989) of those over age 85.

MEMORY COMPLAINTS AND THE EPIDEMIOLOGY OF MEMORY IMPAIRMENT IN THE ELDERLY

Not all complaints of memory inefficiencies or even actual performance declines in old age reflect dementing illnesses. Kral (1962) coined the term *benign senescent forgetfulness* to describe the clinical entity of greater than average memory loss in otherwise healthy elderly individuals. However, operational diagnostic criteria for this entity have never been developed. A related (possibly identical) syndrome is that of *age-associated memory impairment* (AAMI). In the USA, a National Institute of Mental Health work group proposed the following diagnostic criteria for AAMI (Crook et al., 1986; Crook & Larrabee, 1988):

1. Age 50 or older.
2. Complaints of memory impairment in everyday life.
3. Objective memory test performance at least one standard deviation below the mean for young adults.
4. Absence of dementia.
5. Average or above-average intelligence.

Lane and Snowdon (1989) reported a prevalence of 35% for AAMI among older adults, a figure that suggests that the diagnostic criteria for this entity may be too liberal. Recently, Youngjohn and Crook (1993, p. 413) reported that persons meeting these criteria do not decline over time on tasks of everyday memory. The authors concluded that "AAMI is essentially equivalent to the effects of normal aging" and that it is the subjective complaint of worsening memory that earns the diagnostic label.

Severe depression is often accompanied by a dementia syndrome that resembles degenerative dementia in several respects but is reversible with successful treatment of the depression. This syndrome, which was formerly called "pseudodementia", can be differentiated from dementia due to frank brain degeneration by the degree of correspondence between complaints of impaired cognition and objective cognitive performance. Among elderly individuals ascertained by community survey, O'Connor et al. (1990) found that those who met criteria for severe depression complained more of indecisiveness, impaired concentration, and mental slowing than did mildly demented patients. However, the depressed patients actually performed significantly better than the demented patients on six of the seven memory tasks administered. In a related study, McGlone et al. (1990) reported that, among elderly persons presenting to a dementia clinic with memory complaints, those judged nondemented by clinical neurologic and neuropsychologic assessments had significantly higher scores on the Geriatric Depression Scale than did those diagnosed with early-stage Alzheimer's disease.

MEMORY ASSESSMENT IN THE EARLY DIAGNOSIS OF DEMENTIA

Whereas most mental status examinations are insufficiently sensitive to detect mild dementia syndromes, simple free recall of a word list is highly effective in distinguishing demented from healthy elderly individuals (Brandt, 1991; Harris & Dowson, 1982). For example, Brandt and Bylsma (1993) reported that Huntington's disease patients who obtained perfect scores on the Mini-Mental State Examination (Folstein, Folstein & McHugh, 1975) nonetheless displayed severe performance deficits on the Hopkins Verbal Learning Test, a word-list memory task that requires only 5 minutes for administration. Similarly, Whelihan, Lesher, Kleban and Granick (1984) reported that adding a brief delayed memory test to a standardized mental status examination improved significantly the ability to distinguish mildly demented patients from nondemented elderly.

Christensen, Hadzi-Pavlovic and Jacomb (1991) performed a meta-analysis of 77 published studies reporting a differentiation of dementia from normal aging. They found that tests of memory, including the Buschke Selective Reminding Test (Buschke, 1973) and the Wechsler Memory Scale (Wechsler, 1945, 1987) were the most discriminating. The memory tests had significantly larger effect sizes (i.e. standardized differences between demented and normal groups) than did measures of language, praxis or perception. However, the memory tests were not superior to mental status examinations for the diagnosis of dementia.

Actually, there is some degree of circularity in all studies that attempt to differentiate dementia from normal aging based solely on cognitive test performances, since cognitive failures are central to making the clinical diagnosis of dementia. A similar problem emerges in comparative studies, where groups of patients with different forms of dementia are matched for severity of dementia. If one group has a more severe memory impairment, the other group must have a more severe impairment in some other sphere (e.g. language, spatial cognition) in order for them to have equivalent levels of overall dementia. In an effort to minimize this dilemma, some investigators have relied on clinical severity ratings or measures of adaptive functioning, rather than psychometric performance, for detecting and grading impairment. The Clinical Dementia Rating (CDR) scale is one such tool (Hughes et al., 1982). Based on clinical assessment of the patient and interview with an informant, ratings are made for memory, orientation, judgment, home and hobbies, community affairs and personal care. Total scores range from CDR 0 (no evidence of dementia) to CDR 3 (severe dementia). CDR ratings during life have been shown to be predictive of neuropathologic changes seen at autopsy (Berg et al., 1993; Morris et al., 1988).

MEMORY IMPAIRMENT IN ALZHEIMER'S DISEASE

Alzheimer's disease (AD) is the most common cause of dementia in the elderly, accounting for more than 50% of all cases of dementia in those over 65 (Evans et al., 1989; Terry & Katzman, 1992). This disease, which is characterized by the presence of amyloid-containing plaques and neurofibrillary tangles in the hippocampal formation and association cortices, can be diagnosed definitively only at autopsy. Therefore, diagnostic criteria based on clinical criteria (including neuropsychological performance) allow one to make only the diagnoses of possible or probable AD.

Although the course of AD varies widely across individuals, the disease usually begins with relatively mild forgetfulness and word-finding difficulties and the slightest impairments in mental efficiency (CDR 0.5). Often, early-stage patients display an increased tendency to misplace objects and forget familiar names. In fact, some investigators have found that AD patients can have isolated memory impairments for several years before they go on to display impairments in abstract reasoning, attention, language, and spatial cognition (Grady et al., 1988). In the early and middle stages, patients may show increased "tip-of-the-tongue" experiences, a sign of the word-finding difficulties that typically emerge on formal testing. Spatial perception and route-finding may be somewhat compromised as well. At first, patients may become lost only in unfamiliar locales, but this may eventually progress to trouble negotiating the aisles of a neighborhood grocery store or the patient's own house.

In midstage disease (CDR 2), patients have moderately severe impairments in memory and language and clearly impaired judgment; typically, they are unable to function independently outside the home and require assistance for their hygiene, dressing, feeding, etc. Late-stage patients (CDR 3) may not recognize spouses, children, or even their mirror reflections. Their language is often deteriorated to the point of muteness or incoherent babbling. Delusions, hallucinations and bizarre behaviors, such as hoarding, may occur. End-stage patients often show clear signs of neurologic dysfunction, such as seizures, myoclonus, incontinence, and the release of infantile reflexes.

Because AD is the most common cause of dementia and memory is the prominent initial symptom, more memory research has been conducted on this illness than on any other dementing illness.

Episodic Memory

Virtually all the well-known memory tests that are used clinically for the evaluation of AD patients are tests of episodic memory. This variety of memory refers to the encoding and storage of information about one's personal experiences in relation to other events (Tulving, 1972). Thus, episodic memory has an autobiographical referent; it can be dated (either absolutely, in terms of clocks or calendars, or relatively, such as before or after some event), and it records the spatial context of the learning experience. Interference has a deleterious effect on episodic memory, as occurs when one forgets a phone number if interrupted between looking it up and actually dialing. Conversely, relating new information in a meaningful way to one's knowledge base (i.e. elaborative encoding) enhances episodic memory performance.

Episodic memory impairments are the hallmark of dementia. Even early-stage AD patients display striking deficits on tests requiring the learning and recall of word lists, such as the Buschke Selective Reminding Test (Masur et al., 1989), Rey Auditory Verbal Learning Test (Zec & Vicari, 1990), California Verbal Learning Test (Delis et al., 1991), and Hopkins Verbal Learning Test (Brandt, 1991).

Knopman and Ryberg (1989) developed a highly sensitive and specific verbal memory test, which they administered to 28 mildly-to-moderately demented AD patients (mean Mini-Mental State Examination score = 23.4) and 55 healthy elderly individuals. The subjects were required to generate a sentence for each of 10 to-be-remembered words in an attempt to force them to engage in elaborative encoding. This procedure was then repeated a second time with the same 10 words. After 5 minutes of other testing, free recall was elicited. Scores on this test correctly identified group membership in 95% of the subjects. Only one normal subject and three AD patients were misclassified.

The Consortium to Establish a Registry for Alzheimer's Disease (CERAD) is a large, multicenter study in the USA that is standardizing methods for diagnosing, evaluating and following AD patients. The assessment contains a standardized battery of neuropsychological tests: the Mini-Mental State Examination, a short form of the Boston Naming Test, Verbal Fluency (orally generating a list of animals), Constructional Praxis (design copying), and a Word List Memory Test (Morris et al., 1989). This last test consists of three trials of free recall of a 10-word list followed by a 5-minute delayed recall and a yes/no recognition task. Welsh et al. (1991) found that of all the neuropsychological measures, delayed recall of the word list was the most successful in differentiating mild AD patients (Mini-Mental State Examination scores of 24 or higher) from healthy elderly subjects. By itself, delayed recall successfully classified 86% of the mild AD patients and 96% of the healthy elderly control subjects. Immediate recall, intrusion (false recall) errors, and recognition memory performances were much less useful for distinguishing the groups.

Welsh et al., (1992) subsequently confirmed their earlier finding for delayed recall, and reported that confrontation naming ability also helped in the identification of early AD. Further, they reported that performances on recognition memory, verbal fluency, and constructional praxis measures were useful for distinguishing among AD groups differing in dementia severity, but delayed recall performance was not. The failure of delayed recall to contribute to this differentiation was attributed to a "floor effect". Earlier, Mohs et al. (1986) also reported that verbal recall was a sensitive measure for detecting early memory impairments in AD, whereas recognition memory measures were better for documenting progression.

On verbal learning tasks, AD patients, even very early in their illness, display a shallow learning curve (Duchek, Cheney, Ferraro & Storandt, 1991) and a dramatic loss of information after only a few minutes (Hart, Kwentus, Harkins & Taylor, 1988; Moss, Albert, Butters & Payne, 1986). However, Becker, Boller, Saxton and McGonigle-Gibson (1987) reported that AD patients did not forget verbal or nonverbal material faster than their nondemented peers. Procedural differences (e.g. how forgetting is measured, variations in difficulty level or types of tasks used) may account for apparent discrepancies among these studies. For example, Moss, Albert, Buttess and Payne (1986) measured the percentage retained, after a 2-minute delay, of items recalled after a 15-second delay interval. The AD patients lost a significantly greater proportion of material that they had originally recalled than did healthy subjects and two other memory-disordered patient groups. In contrast, Becker et al. (1987) computed the absolute difference between initial and delayed recall scores. Because the healthy elderly subjects and AD patients in the Becker et al. study lost similar amounts of material after 30 minutes, the patients were said to show normal forgetting. Kopelman (1985) reported that AD patients displayed increased forgetting from episodic memory, but found that this could be overcome by raising their immediate memory to normal levels with prolonged exposure times during initial learning. Again, procedural differences (here, changing task difficulty so as to equate groups for initial learning) may determine whether normal or abnormally rapid forgetting is found among AD patients. In general, if forgetting is expressed as a percentage of initial learning, AD patients appear to show excessive forgetting; but when raw scores for initial and delayed recall are compared between groups, AD patients and normal elderly have parallel forgetting functions. It should be recognized, however, that the interpretation of differences in forgetting functions (or learning curves) for groups that differ in starting points is a matter of some controversy, and depends on one's theoretical/mathematical model (Loftus, 1985; Slamecka & McElree, 1983).

Many reports have shown that AD patients produce an excessive number of intrusion errors on memory tasks (Fuld, Katzman, Davies & Terry, 1982; Jacobs, Salmon, Tröster & Butters, 1990). When asked to recall a list of words, for example, these patients often report words that have not been presented. The erroneous words reported by AD patients are often semantically related to the target items (e.g. reporting "tiger" for "leopard"), which suggests an erosion of the distinctions between items belonging to particular semantic categories. Intrusive errors are thought to have particular diagnostic significance for AD, as a correlation has been found between these types of errors and low choline acetyltransferase levels and senile plaque counts in the brains of AD patients (Fuld et al., 1982).

Although most studies of episodic memory in AD employ verbal materials, memory for nonverbal materials is also severely impaired. This deficit is observed routinely in the Fuld Object Memory Evaluation (Fuld et al., 1990), in which subjects are instructed to recall objects that they have palpated and then named. AD patients also show poor memory for geometric designs, whether tested by their reproduction of presented figures (Jacobs et al., 1990) or by recognition (Youngjohn, Larrabee & Crook, 1992). Similarly, the ability to recognize faces is compromised in AD, whether tested by forced-choice recognition of "old" and "new" faces (Wilson et al., 1982) or by having patients identify the newest stimulus added to an array of faces (Youngjohn, Larrabee & Crook, 1992).

Primary Memory

Within episodic memory, a distinction has been made between primary memory and secondary memory (Waugh & Norman, 1965). Primary memory is invoked when material is at the focus of conscious attention, such as during rehearsal or active encoding (Craik, 1977; Craik & Levy, 1976). The recency portion of the serial position curve is often used as a crude estimate of primary memory. Using that estimate and related methods (Tulving & Colotla, 1970), some studies have indicated that AD patients have defective primary memory (Miller, 1971; Wilson, Bacon, Fox & Kaszniak, 1983). Nevertheless, any aberration in the recency effect in AD is generally much milder than other indices of memory impairment in this group. Spinnler, Della Sala, Bandera and Baddeley (1988) found a preserved recency effect despite impaired secondary memory in mild to moderately impaired AD patients.

There is some evidence to suggest that the extent of AD patients' impairment on primary memory tasks may be related to dementia severity. For example, Corkin (1982) found a relationship between AD patients' performance on digit span and the Brown–Peterson distractor task (Peterson & Peterson, 1959) and a clinical rating of dementia severity.

Recently, a number of investigators (Baddeley, 1992; Baddeley, Bressi et al., 1991; Morris & Baddeley, 1988; Morris & Kopelman, 1986) have contended that a defect in a specific component of primary or working memory underlies the cognitive deterioration observed in AD. The term *working memory* (Baddeley & Hitch, 1974) refers to a system that can hold and manipulate information temporarily while performing various cognitive tasks. Baddeley (1986, 1992) has formulated a specific model of working memory consisting of a central executive system (CES) responsible for the selection and allocation of attention and other processing resources and several subsidiary "slave" systems. These latter components include an articulatory or phonological "loop" for recording speech-based material and a visuospatial "scratch pad" for creating and maintaining visual images. Baddeley and others (Baddeley, Bressi et al., 1991; Morris, 1986) posit that the CES is defective in AD, resulting in poor performance on tests of divided attention and primary memory, as well as impaired retrieval from semantic memory.

In one experiment, Baddeley et al. (1986) had AD patients and healthy control subjects engage in a pursuit tracking task that was adjusted in difficulty for each subject in order to yield equivalent performance between groups. Simultaneously, subjects engaged in a secondary task: either repetitive articulation, simple auditory reaction time, or digit span. Although the AD patients performed well on the individual tasks, their dual task performance was impaired relative to that of their healthy peers. Moreover, dual-task (but not single-task) performance declined systematically in the AD group over a 6-month period, suggesting that the deterioration of the CES tracks the progression of the disease. Normal elderly subjects, in contrast, showed no evidence of decline on the dual tasks from initial to later test sessions. In a second experiment by the same investigators (Baddeley, Bressi et al., 1991), AD patients did not show progressive deterioration over time when difficulty level was varied within a single task. Thus, one may reasonably conclude that the patients' impairment cannot be attributed simply to task difficulty, but rather to a defect in the CES.

Becker (1988) performed a principal components analysis of memory tests used in a longitudinal study of AD patients and found two factors: one composed of tasks requiring an intact CES (digit span forward, reaction time, and verbal fluency), and the other composed of secondary memory tasks (story recall, design recall, verbal paired-associate learning, and face–name paired-associate learning). Individual patients showed differential impairment in one or the other memory factor, which further supports a differentiation between these two memory deficits in AD. Conversely, the different patterns of performance observed by Becker (1988) may be interpreted as but one of many demonstrations of the heterogeneity of cognitive deficits found in AD (Martin et al., 1986). For example, Baddeley, Della Sala and Spinnler (1991) found AD patients with impaired auditory short-term memory combined with relatively preserved long-term memory; others had isolated visual and verbal memory deficits. Thus, the patterns observed by Becker (1988) may be more a reflection of variability among AD patients than true subtypes, suggesting a two-component memory deficit in this disease.

Semantic Memory

Although there are many definitions of semantic memory, most investigators would agree that the term refers to an organized, highly structured body of knowledge about words, concepts and symbols (e.g. their meanings, properties, associations), as well as general factual knowledge (Tulving 1972). It is also generally accepted that many of the memory and communication deficits found in AD reflect some dysfunction in semantic memory (Butters et al., 1987; Grober, Buschke, Kawas & Fuld, 1985; Huff, Corkin & Growdon, 1986; Martin & Fedio, 1983; Ober et al., 1986).

Much of the evidence for impaired semantic memory in AD comes from tests of naming (either to visual confrontation or to verbal descriptions) and verbal fluency (word-list generation). On naming tasks, AD patients often err by producing superordinate category names (e.g. "animal" for a picture of a camel) or semantic associates (e.g. "hippopotamus" for rhinoceros) (Bayles & Tomoeda, 1983; Hodges, Salmon & Butters, 1991; Martin & Fedio, 1983). These errors have been interpreted as reflecting a deterioration of the fine structure of the semantic network, leaving intact the coarser category distinctions. On fluency tasks, AD patients appear to have greater impairment in producing lists of words belonging to specific semantic categories (e.g. animals, foods, cities) than words beginning with particular letters of the alphabet (e.g. F, A, S) (Butters et al., 1987; Monsch et al., 1992), suggesting an impairment in accessing the lexicon via word meanings. When asked to generate items that can be purchased in a supermarket, AD patients tend to produce superordinate categories (e.g. meat, fruit, vegetables), rather than specific items (e.g. hamburger, apples, carrots). This, too, has been interpreted as reflecting a "bottom-up" deterioration of the semantic network, characterized by degradation of category and especially subcategory exemplars, with relative preservation of the categories themselves.

Further evidence of semantic memory deficits in AD can be found in episodic memory tasks involving free recall. In a study conducted by Weingartner et al. (1982), AD patients did not benefit from the inherent organization provided by categorized word lists. Martin and colleagues (Martin, Brouwers, Cox & Fedio, 1985; Martin & Fedio, 1983) have found that AD patients often give accurate but incomplete responses on tasks such as defining words or describing objects. When probed directly, they judge accurately the categorical relationship of many concepts (e.g. "Is a canary a bird?"), but perform poorly when asked about specific features and attributes of concepts (e.g. "Does a canary have skin?"). Taken together, these studies suggest that AD patients fail to appreciate the full meaning of verbal concepts, which could account in part for their learning and memory failures. When task instructions explicitly require subjects to engage in elaborative encoding, results are mixed. Martin et al. (1985) found that semantic orienting tasks led to improved memory performance in AD. In contrast, others have found that patients fail to benefit from such procedures when memory is assessed by recognition tests (Corkin, 1982; Wilson et al., 1982).

Nebes and coworkers have challenged the assumption of degraded or disorganized semantic representations in AD. They have shown that the same stimulus and task variables that affect the performance of healthy, cognitively normal subjects also affect the performance of AD patients on a wide variety of semantic memory tests (Nebes, 1989; Nebes, Boller & Holland, 1986; Nebes, Martin & Horn, 1984). For example, in the lexical-decision task paradigm, subjects decide whether a letter string constitutes a real word or a nonword. Decision times are faster when words are repeated or are preceded by a semantically related word—phenomena known as "repetition" and "associative priming", respectively. As long as the elapsed time between the "prime" (the initially exposed word) and "target" (the repeated or related word on which the prime exerts an effect) is very short, AD patients exhibit normal priming (Nebes et al., 1984, 1986; Nebes, Brady & Huff, 1989). In addition, when deciding whether a word is a member of a particular semantic category (e.g. "Is a robin a bird?"), AD patients are slower than normal, but they show the same effects of category dominance (i.e. the extent to which the item is prototypical of the category) as do normal subjects (Nebes et al., 1986). These and related observations led Nebes (1989) to conclude that AD patients demonstrate near-normal semantic memory when tested with procedures that make minimal demands on effortful retrieval.

Recently, Chan and colleagues (Chan et al., 1993; Chan, Butters, Salmon & McGuire, 1993) evaluated semantic memory in AD patients with methods that allow the structure of individual patients' semantic networks to be evaluated. These investigators derived similarity ratings of animals from patients and control subjects based on the proximity of reported animal names in a verbal fluency task or from direct comparisons of animal-name triads (e.g. "Which two of these three animals are most alike?"). Using a combination of multidimensional scaling and clustering procedures, Chan and coworkers found that AD patients' mental "maps" of the category *animals* were less clearly organized than were those of neurologically normal subjects or patients with Huntington's disease. Unlike those of healthy subjects, the semantic networks of AD patients were based more on concrete perceptual features (e.g. size) than on abstract conceptual characteristics (e.g. domesticity). The patients also tended to use concept attributes inconsistently when making similarity judgments. These results have been interpreted as further evidence of a breakdown in the semantic network (i.e. the structure of semantic knowledge) in AD.

IMPLICIT MEMORY IN AD

Implicit memory refers to a diverse set of phenomena in which the effects of prior experiences are manifest in behavior even though no reference is made to the prior events and the subject may be unaware of the association between the initial learning and subsequent episodes (Roediger, 1990; Schacter, 1987). Implicit memory is distinguished from explicit memory, which is measured by tasks and instructions that require the intentional retrieval of previously studied material. There are several categories of implicit memory, including skill-learning (motor skills, perceptual analysis skills), priming, nonassociative memory (i.e. sensitization and habituation), and classical conditioning.

In the classical amnestic syndrome, most aspects of implicit memory are spared. Thus, patients with alcoholic Korsakoff's syndrome and those who have sustained mesial temporal lobe lesions generally display normal skill acquisition and perform nearly normally on tests of perceptual and semantic priming (Cohen & Squire, 1980; Martone et al., 1984). A number of implicit memory paradigms involve the processing of fragmented, incomplete or degraded stimuli. Typically, subjects are given a set of stimulus materials (e.g. a list of words) and some type of encoding instruction (e.g. rate the words for likeability). Subsequently, another set of materials, composed of incomplete stimuli, is presented. Among the most commonly used stimuli are word fragments (e.g. *a--a-si-* for *assassin*) or word stems (e.g. *but____* for *butterfly*). When subjects are told to complete the fragments or stems with the first word that comes to mind, they tend to complete the partial stimuli with studied items at a rate that exceeds chance.

The nature of implicit memory performance in AD has received much attention recently. In general, priming paradigms employing response latencies as the dependent variable, which may invoke relatively "automatic" processing, tend to be preserved in AD (Ober, Shenaut, Jagust & Stillman, 1991). As noted earlier, AD patients typically demonstrate normal repetition priming on word-naming, lexical-decision, and category-decision tasks (Nebes et al., 1984, 1986, 1989). AD patients also show preserved implicit memory on tests of motor skill learning. For example, Knopman and Nissen (1987) reported that AD patients learned a repeated sequence of motor responses embedded in a visual reaction-time task at the same rate across blocks of trials as did healthy subjects. Heindel et al. (1989) found nearly identical learning curves for the pursuit-rotor task in AD patients and age-matched normal subjects, once the groups were equated for initial performance. AD patients also display relatively normal patterns of improvement across trials when learning to read mirror-reversed text (Deweer, Pillon, Michon & Dubois, 1993; Moscovitch, 1982).

In contrast, AD patients display significant impairments on several varieties of implicit memory tasks, particularly those involving completion paradigms. For example, they typically show impaired semantic priming, where verbal responses are "primed" by semantically related words (Brandt, Spencer, McSorley & Folstein, 1988; Salmon & Heindel, 1992; Salmon, Shimamura, Butters & Smith, 1988). Lexical priming, as measured by the word-stem completion task, is also consistently impaired in AD (Butters, Salmon, Heindel & Granholm, 1988; Heindel et al., 1989; Salmon, Shimamura, Butters & Smith 1988). It should be noted that in these studies, AD patients do show some lexical and semantic priming, but the magnitude of the effect is reduced relative to that in healthy elderly subjects.

Two recent studies compared lexical priming (using the word-stem completion task) and perceptual priming in AD. Keane et al. (1991) varied word frequency (high or low) and number of presentations (one or three) of stimulus words presented for study. At test, AD patients displayed impaired word-stem completion priming for all four conditions. However, the magnitude of their repetition priming was as large as that of healthy subjects for the identification (i.e. reading) of briefly presented words. In another study (Rich, 1993), AD patients and healthy young and old subjects were exposed to three different orienting conditions: reading words aloud, naming pictures, and generating the best-fit endings to sentence frames (e.g. "He hit the nail with the —" for hammer). Mildly-to-moderately demented AD patients did not show priming on word-stem completion, regardless of study condition. When required to identify visually degraded line drawings, however, AD patients benefited as much as did healthy young and elderly subjects from previous exposure to drawings from the picture-naming study task. Together, these studies reveal a dissociation between impaired lexical/semantic priming and preserved perceptual priming among AD patients. The authors suggest that, whereas priming in word-stem completion requires the activity of the temporal–parietal association areas known to be severely affected in AD, repetition priming reflects primarily the operation of perceptual mechanisms of the occipital cortex, which is relatively spared in AD.

THE "SUBCORTICAL DEMENTIAS"

Although memory impairment is one of the defining features of AD, significant memory impairments are also found in:

- Huntington's disease (Brandt, 1985, 1990; Butters et al., 1985; Butters, Salmon & Heindel, 1990; Folstein, Brandt & Folstein, 1990; Wilson et al., 1987)
- Parkinson's disease (Flowers, Pearce & Pearce, 1984; Hugdahl, Asbjørnsen & Wester, 1993)
- Progressive supranuclear palsy (Albert, Feldman & Willis, 1974; Pillon, Dubois, Lhermitte & Agid, 1986)
- Multiple sclerosis (Beatty et al., 1988; Grafman, Rao, Bernardin & Leo, 1991; Rao et al., 1984)
- Depression (Massman et al., 1992; Wolfe et al., 1987)
- Wilson's disease (Cummings & Benson, 1992)
- HIV infection (Wilkie et al., 1990)
- Thalamic degeneration (McDaniel, 1990)
- Small-vessel cerebrovascular disease (Stuss & Cummings, 1990).

These disorders have all been described as producing "subcortical dementia" syndromes on the basis of their known or suspected neuropathology (Cummings, 1990; Cummings & Benson, 1984). The primary clinical features of subcortical dementia are slowed movement and thinking, memory inefficiencies, poor planning, impaired judgment and reasoning, and affective changes, all of which occur in the absence of frank aphasia, agnosia or apraxia (Cummings, 1990).

The distinction between cortical and subcortical dementias has been criticized on neuroanatomical grounds, as patients with Alzheimer's disease (the prototypic cortical dementia) have clear and possibly primary pathology in subcortical nuclei, while patients with Huntington's disease or Parkinson's disease (prototypes of the subcortical dementias) usually have cortical pathology as well (Cummings & Benson, 1992; Whitehouse, 1986). However, there appear to be sufficient differences in patterns of neuropsychological functioning between these two types of dementia to warrant the use of these terms (Brandt, Folstein & Folstein, 1988; Mayeux, Stern, Rosen & Benson, 1983).

Huntington's disease (HD) is an incurable neurodegenerative disease that is inherited as an autosomal-dominant trait. It has an insidious onset, usually around age 40; it progresses slowly, until the patient succumbs, usually before age 60. The first noticeable motor signs may be involuntary, jerky movements of the extremities or incoordination. Early cognitive complaints include difficulty with attention and concentration, problems with organizing and planning activities, and memory decline. Depression occurs in a large proportion of patients, and may appear several years before the motor abnormalities. Other emotional disturbances, such as irritability, apathy and changes in sexual interest, are also associated with the disease. The symptoms progress relentlessly, and patients eventually become severely demented, motorically dilapidated, and completely dependent on others for their care.

Parkinson's disease (PD) is a well-studied, neurodegenerative disease whose most notable feature is a movement disorder. The most prominent motor abnormalities include: tremor, which occurs primarily at rest and is characterized by a "pill-rolling" motion of involuntary finger oscillation; limb rigidity; bradykinesia; stooped posture; a "masked" or expressionless face; dysarthric speech; festinating gait (involuntary quickening and shortening of steps); and micrographia (small handwriting). In idiopathic PD, these symptoms are produced by a loss of neurons in the substantia nigra, typically beginning after age 50. Dementia and depression each occur, either singly or together, in approximately 30% of PD patients.

COMPARISON OF MEMORY IN THE CORTICAL AND SUBCORTICAL DEMENTIAS

Explicit Memory

In general, the episodic memory impairment in the subcortical dementias is less pervasive than that found in AD. In spite of poor immediate recall of supraspan material, patients with subcortical dementia often display relatively intact primary memory (Hugdahl, Asbjørnsen & Wester, 1993), near-normal recognition of to-be-learned material (Flowers, Pearce & Pearce, 1984), and normal rates of forgetting (Butters, Salmon, Cullum et al., 1988; Moss, Albert, Butters & Payne, 1986) on episodic memory tasks. They also make many fewer intrusion errors (Kramer, Levin, Brandt & Delis, 1989; Jacobs, Salmon et al., 1990; Jacobs, Tröster et al., 1990) than do AD patients.

Results from verbal learning studies suggest that the episodic memory performance of subcortical dementia patients is hampered most by inefficient strategies for retrieving information. HD patients, for example, often show very impaired free recall, but near-normal multiple-choice recognition performance (Butters et al., 1985; Butters Wolfe, Granholm & Martone, 1986). PD patients also appear to have a retrieval deficit, as suggested by their poor performance on measures of verbal fluency (Raskin, Sliwinski & Borod, 1992). Direct comparison of the performance of HD and PD patients on the California Verbal Learning Test (Delis, Kramer, Kaplan & Ober, 1987) has revealed a very similar deficit pattern (Massman et al., 1990). Both groups display much poorer free recall than recognition. The results have been attributed to a combination of generally intact memory storage, mild encoding inefficiencies, and impaired use of retrieval strategies.

Recently, Pillon, Deweer, Agid and Dubois (1993) compared patients with AD, HD and PD on the California Verbal Learning Test and a selective reminding task. The groups were matched for severity of dementia using the Dementia Rating Scale. Recognition accuracy was found to be significantly greater in the HD and PD groups than in the AD group, providing further evidence for relatively preserved storage but impaired retrieval in the subcortical dementias. This same interpretation was made of the performance pattern that emerged in a recent comparison of semantic fluency in AD, PD and HD patients (Randolph, Braun, Goldberg & Chase, 1993). In that study, the HD and PD patients generated considerably more category items when provided with subcategory cues relative to an uncued condition. Thus, the provision of retrieval prompts improved the performance of patients with subcortical dementias. The AD patients, on the other hand, showed no such benefit from the cued condition.

Although recognition memory is generally much better than recall performance among HD patients (Brandt & Butters, 1994; Butters et al., 1985), there is some evidence to suggest that near-normal recognition memory may be material-specific. Moss, Albert, Butters and Payne (1986) administered a delayed recognition span task in which patients had to identify (i.e. recognize) the disk most recently added to an array of previously viewed disks. The materials used for the various stimulus conditions included blank disks (for a spatial condition) and disks marked by different colors, patterns, faces and words (for nonverbal and verbal conditions). Consistent with previous findings, HD patients demonstrated near-normal verbal recognition memory performance despite impaired free recall of the same words. Surprisingly, however, HD patients displayed impaired recognition performance in the spatial, color, pattern and facial conditions. It may be, therefore, that when recognition memory for nonverbal materials is assessed, or when challenging recognition memory tasks are employed, HD patients show recognition memory deficits not typically observed when traditional multiple-choice or yes/no verbal recognition memory tasks are used.

The possibility also exists that the relative sparing of recognition memory performance in the subcortical dementias is task-specific. Brandt, Corwin and Krafft (1992), using the Hopkins Verbal Learning Test, did not find that recognition accuracy was greater in HD than in AD. They did, however, find that AD patients had a more liberal ("yea-saying") response bias during yes/no recognition memory testing. This was especially true when the recognition foils were from the same semantic categories as the target items. This observation is consistent with the notion of a breakdown in the structure of the semantic network in AD. As noted earlier, there appears to be an erosion of the distinctions between category exemplars in AD (e.g. Martin, 1992). If one fails to appreciate the particular attributes that make an object distinct from other objects in its semantic category, both targets and related foils will produce a feeling of familiarity, leading to more "yes" than "no" responses on recognition memory testing. The fact that Delis et al. (1991) did not find a liberal response bias among their AD patients may be due to differences in the two studies in the number of distractors per target and in the statistical models used to evaluate response bias (Snodgrass & Corwin, 1988).

Butters and his colleagues have examined the performance profiles of amnesic patients and those with dementias of different etiologies on the Wechsler Memory Scale–Revised. Compared with patients with circumscribed amnesia, AD and HD patients had significantly lower Attention/Concentration Indices relative to their General Memory Indices. This was especially true for the HD patients. In addition, the amount of forgetting over a delay period (reflected in the difference between the General Memory Index and the Delayed Memory Index) was less in both demented groups than in the amnesics (Butters, Salmon, Cullum et al., 1988).

Recently, Tröster et al. (1993) reported that savings scores (i.e. percentage retained) between immediate and delayed recall of the Logical Memory and Visual Reproduction subtests were lower in AD patients than in equivalently demented HD patients. In fact, among mildly demented AD and HD patients, savings scores on these two tests correctly diagnosed 85% of the patients. Among moderately demented patients, however, this figure dropped to 74%. Similar results have been found among PD patients, who often show very little decline with delays at which AD patients decline precipitously (Mortimer, 1988). In one study, patients with PD forgot nothing between their immediate and delayed recalls of drawings (cited in Mortimer, 1988).

Several recent studies have explored the nature and extent of patients' errors on episodic memory tests. Kramer et al. (1988) administered the California Verbal Learning Test to probable AD patients, mildly demented HD patients, and moderately-to-severely demented HD patients. As expected on the basis of previous investigations of AD patients (e.g. Fuld et al., 1982), there was a high frequency of intrusion errors among the AD patients. Moreover, the AD patients made three times as many intrusion errors than did the other patients or the age-matched healthy subjects. The discrepancy in intrusion rate between AD patients and HD patients increased dramatically after a delay and on cued recall trials. In a subsequent study (Kramer, Levin, Brandt & Delis, 1989), AD, HD and PD patients were compared with each other on the California Verbal Learning Test. The results confirmed and extended the results of the previous study: AD patients had a higher rate of intrusions than did either of the subcortical groups, even after taking total recall into account.

More recently, Pillon, Deweer, Agid and Dubois (1993) failed to find group differences in overall memory performance between AD, HD and PD patients with the California Verbal Learning Test, which they attributed to a "floor effect". That is, the patients were all severely impaired on this instrument, and the fact that no performance differences emerged between the groups may be attributed to insufficient sensitivity of the test to detect differences at very low levels of performance. Nevertheless, intrusion errors during free recall and total number of intrusions across trials were much more common in the AD group than in the HD group; the PD patients had an intermediate level of intrusions that did not differ significantly from either of the other two groups.

It appears, then, that intrusion errors characterize the verbal memory performance of AD patients to a much greater extent than patients with subcortical dementia, such as HD or PD. This finding has recently been extended to the figural memory of AD and HD patients, using the Visual Reproduction subtest of the Wechsler Memory Scale (Jacobs, Salmon et al., 1990). The difference in the number of prior-item intrusion errors found in that study is particularly striking, because there are only four designs on this task (and only three on which prior-item intrusions can be made).

Implicit Memory

As noted earlier, AD patients perform well on tests of motor skill learning, repetition priming, and other implicit memory tasks that require more perceptual than conceptual analysis. Patients with subcortical dementia also display relatively intact implicit memory on many tasks, but the particular domains of preserved abilities and the degree to which aspects of implicit memory are spared differ among diseases.

Investigations of implicit memory in HD have revealed a pattern of preserved lexical, semantic and pictorial priming abilities (Bylsma, Rebok & Brandt, 1991; Shimamura, Salmon, Squire & Butters, 1987), but impaired motor, visuomotor and perceptual skill acquisition (Heindel, Butters & Salmon, 1988; Martone et al., 1984). When groups of HD and AD patients are compared directly, an interesting double dissociation emerges on two varieties of implicit memory: motor skill learning and lexical priming.

On a pursuit rotor task, in which subjects are instructed to maintain contact between a hand-held stylus and a rotating disk, AD patients improve with practice at the same rate as do healthy peers. However, HD patients are severely impaired on this task, even after adjusting the rotation speed to equate groups on initial performance (Heindel et al., 1989). Another implicit memory task that relies on motor programs and expectancies is weight-biasing. In this task, subjects are asked to rate the heaviness of a set of weights following exposure to either heavy or light weights. AD patients, like normal individuals, judge objects to be heavier after exposure to light weights, a phenomenon known as weight-biasing (Heindel, Salmon & Butters, 1991). The weight judgments of HD patients, in contrast, are not influenced by the heaviness of previously exposed weights (Heindel et al., 1991). Prism adaptation, a perceptual task requiring subjects to point to a target while wearing distorting prisms that laterally displace their vision, is also differentially affected among dementia populations, with preserved adaptation in AD and impaired adaptation in HD (Paulsen et al., 1993). Finally, there is evidence to suggest that implicit learning of an embedded sequence in the serial-response task is preserved in AD (Knopman & Nissen, 1987) and impaired in HD (Knopman & Nissen, 1991; Willingham & Koroshetz, 1993), although these patient groups have not been compared directly in a single study.

Studies of lexical and verbal priming produce the opposite pattern of results. On word-stem completion tasks, HD patients demonstrate normal priming, whereas AD patients are impaired (Shimamura, Salmon, Squire & Butters, 1987). Similar results are found on a semantic priming task involving paired associates (Salmon, Shimamura, Butters & Smith, 1988; Smith et al., 1988). In this paradigm, subjects judge whether pairs of words are related (e.g. *needle–thread*) and are later asked to say "the first word that comes to mind" in response to a stimulus word (e.g. *needle*). HD patients tend to respond with the previously paired word, whereas AD patients are just as likely to give another associate (e.g. *sewing* or *pin*).

Interpretations of this double dissociation (i.e. preserved motor and perceptual priming with impaired verbal priming in AD, and vice versa in HD) have been based on the known differences in the morbid anatomy of the two diseases. Specifically, the widespread neocortical pathology found in AD patients is thought to underlie their priming impairments, whereas neuronal loss in the basal ganglia (especially caudate nucleus) is thought to underlie the impaired motor learning in HD (Butters, Heindel & Salmon, 1990; Butters, Salmon, Heindel et al., 1988; Salmon & Heindel, 1992).

Comparisons of AD and PD patients have also revealed different patterns of impairment on implicit memory tasks. Bondi and Kaszniak (1991) studied AD and nondemented PD patients on three tasks: a fragmented-pictures test (i.e. identification of visually degraded pictures), word-stem completion priming, and pursuit-rotor tracking. A mirror-reading test was also administered to PD patients and normal control subjects. The AD patients were impaired on the word-stem completion taks, but showed normal learning of the pursuit-rotor tracking and improved at a normal rate on the skill-learning component of the fragmented-pictures test (i.e. they were better able to identify degraded pictures with practice). The PD patients evidenced a normal magnitude of word-stem completion priming, normal decreases over trials when reading mirror-transformed script, and a normal rate of improvement on the pursuit-rotor tracking task, but were selectively impaired on the skill-learning component of the fragmented-picture test. Thus, like HD patients, PD patients show preserved lexical priming and impaired priming on a complex visuoperceptual skill-learning task. Unlike HD patients, the nondemented PD patients in this study performed normally on mirror reading and pursuit-rotor tracking. These findings partially confirm the results of other studies, in which nondemented PD patients have shown normal priming on mirror reading, but a diminished magnitude of improvement across days on a pursuit-rotor task (Harrington, Haaland, Yeo & Marder, 1990).

Very few studies have compared directly the implicit memory of AD, HD and PD patients with comparable levels of dementia severity. Heindel et al. (1989), however, did just that. In their study, all three patient groups, as well as nondemented PD patients and two groups of normal control subjects (middle-aged and elderly), were compared on motor (pursuit-rotor learning) and lexical (word-stem completion) implicit memory tasks. The results confirmed previous findings of a double dissociation between AD and HD patients on the two tasks (preserved motor learning and impaired lexical priming in AD, and vice versa in HD). Interestingly, the demented PD patients were impaired, and the nondemented patients were intact, on both tasks. These results suggest that even among the subcortical dementias, there is some variability in the characteristics of implicit memory (i.e. more pervasive impairments in PD than in HD when equated for dementia severity). The pattern of findings is consistent with the notion that motor skill learning is dependent on an intact corticostriatal system (the system that is compromised in HD and PD but relatively preserved in AD), whereas lexical priming is dependent on the integrity of neocortical association areas (brain regions that are relatively unscathed in HD but severely compromised in AD). The fact that demented PD patients often show neuropathological changes typical of AD (Boller, Mizutani, Roessmann & Gambetti, 1980; Whitehouse, Hedreen, White & Price, 1983) is consistent with the findings of impaired lexical priming in this group of patients.

RETROGRADE AMNESIA AND REMOTE MEMORY

Impaired memory for events and information learned prior to the onset of one's illness is termed *retrograde amnesia*. Patients with alcoholic Korsakoff's syndrome characteristically display a temporally graded retrograde amnesia in which remote memories are better retained than those from the period immediately preceding their illness (Albert, Butters & Levin, 1979; Kopelman, 1989). Unlike amnesic Korsakoff patients, HD patients show a severe and generalized retrograde amnesia, producing a "flat" gradient of recollection as a function of decade (Albert, Butters & Brandt, 1981a,b).

Just as HD and AD patients are differentially impaired on numerous episodic and implicit memory tests, so too do they display qualitatively different patterns of remote memory. In one study (Beatty et al., 1988), mildly demented HD and AD patients were administered an updated version of the Boston Remote Memory Battery, which assesses memory for famous people and events from the 1940s to the 1980s. Although the AD patients had much lower scores overall, indicating a more pervasive retrograde amnesia than that observed in HD, their recall of events from the 1940s and 50s was significantly better than their recall from later decades. HD patients, in contrast, were equally impaired across decades, thereby confirming previous findings of a "flat" retrograde amnesia. The results may be interpreted as another manifestation of deficient retrieval in HD. Similar to their general impairment in retrieving newly stored material, HD patients appear to have difficulty retrieving stored knowledge about events from the remote and recent past. AD patients, whose memory deficits are characterized by greater storage and acquisition deficits than retrieval impairments, show a temporally graded amnesia not unlike that associated with Korsakoff's syndrome.

Kopelman (1989) compared AD and Korsakoff patients directly on tests of remote, autobiographical, and temporal–context memory. Both groups showed a temporal gradient across all measures, but the slope of the gradient was steeper among the Korsakoff patients than among those with AD. It has been argued that Korsakoff patients have a progressive anterograde deficit by virtue of their chronic alcoholism for the years immediately preceding their disease onset. The steep slope of their temporally graded memory impairment may therefore be attributed to an anterograde deficit superimposed on a "flat" retrograde amnesia.

Wilson, Kaszniak and Fox (1981) also found a remote memory impairment among AD patients. Interestingly, although they noted a trend for poorer recall of material from the 1960s and 70s than for earlier decades, they characterized the patients' performance as a "flat" retrograde amnesia. Because AD is a slowly progressive disease with an insidious onset, it is possible that the poor recall for the later decades represents an anterograde learning deficit corresponding to the very earliest stages of their disease. Their poor recall for the earlier periods would then be characterized as a "flat" retrograde memory impairment, quantitatively worse but qualitatively similar to that observed in HD. Alternatively, if the events of the 1960s and 1970s are construed as occurring prior to the onset of AD, then the patients' retrograde memories would be characterized as temporally graded, as observed in Korsakoff patients.

Given the suggestion that AD and HD patients have different patterns of retrograde memory impairment, Sagar et al. (1988) compared AD and PD patients' remote memory of both public and personal events, using both recall and recognition tests. Both groups demonstrated a temporal gradient in their recall of the content of public and personal remote memories, with poorer recall of more recent memories. Interestingly, when memory was assessed by recognition, or by recall for the date rather than the content of past events, the gradient was not apparent. Taken together, the findings from several studies suggest that AD patients may appear to have either a "flat" or a temporally graded pattern of retrograde memory, depending on the manner in which it is tested and the precision with which their disease onset may be ascertained. PD patients, like those with AD, may show a temporal gradient of retrograde amnesia under some conditions. In contrast, HD patients always appear to have a "flat" retrograde amnesia, whereas Korsakoff patients have a relative sparing of memory from the remote past.

SUMMARY

Recent research in the neuropsychology of dementia has revealed dissociable patterns of preserved and impaired memory abilities among different disease states. These findings clearly indicate that dementia is not a homogeneous disorder. Attempts to delineate specific impairments associated with specific diseases suggest that the disparate memory profiles observed are a function of the particular brain regions affected by each disease.

AD patients have great difficulty with encoding and acquisition, leading to extensive primary and secondary episodic memory impairments as measured by memory span and tests of long-term recall and recognition. Their memory performance is further marked by semantic memory dysfunction, excessive intrusion errors, and a rapid rate of forgetting. Despite these impairments, AD patients consistently demonstrate preserved implicit memory on priming paradigms employing relatively "automatic" processing, motor skill learning, and perceptual processing. Their distant remote memories also appear to be less affected than those from the more recent past. Overall, this pattern of impaired and relatively preserved abilities is attributed to the temporal–parietal and neocortical association areas compromised in AD.

The memory performance of HD patients, in contrast, is marked by greater retrieval than acquisition deficits. As in other subcortical dementia syndromes, HD patients display relatively intact primary memory and improve substantially when tested with recognition measures. They show better savings over time and make fewer intrusion errors than do AD patients. In the domain of implicit memory, HD patients show preserved lexical, semantic and pictorial priming, but are impaired on motor, visuomotor and perceptual skill acquisition. The remote memory of HD patients is generally characterized as a "flat" retrograde amnesia, with equivalently impaired memory across past decades. The pattern of impaired and preserved abilities is attributed to damage to the corticostriatal system in general and the caudate nuclei in particular.

ACKNOWLEDGEMENTS

This chapter is dedicated to our teacher and friend, Professor Nelson Butters. The work is supported, in part, by grants NS16375, AG05146 and AG00149 from the National Institutes of Health, and by the John Boogher Fellowship in Memory Disorders (J.B.R.).

REFERENCES

Albert, M.L., Feldman, R.G. & Willis, A.L. (1974). The subcortical dementia of progressive supranuclear palsy. *Journal of Neurology, Neurosurgery and Psychiatry*, **37**, 121–130.
Albert, M.S., Butters, N. & Brandt, J. (1981a). Patterns of remote memory in amnesic and demented patients. *Archives of Neurology*, **38**, 495–500.
Albert, M.S., Butters, N. & Brandt, J. (1981b). Development of remote memory loss in patients with Huntington's disease. *Journal of Clinical Neuropsychology*, **3**, 1–12.
Albert, M.S., Butters, N. & Levin, J. (1979). Temporal gradients in the retrograde amnesia of patients with alcoholic Korsakoff's disease. *Archives of Neurology*, **36**, 211–216.
American Psychiatric Association (1987). *Diagnostic and Statistical Manual of Mental Disorders*, 3rd edn. APA, Washington, DC.

Baddeley, A.D. (1986). *Working Memory*. Clarendon Press, Oxford.

Baddeley, A.D. (1992). Working memory, *Science*, **255**, 556–559.

Baddeley, A.D., Bressi, S., Della Sala, S., Logie R. & Spinnler, H. (1991). The decline of working memory in Alzheimer's disease: a longitudinal study. *Brain*, **114**, 2521–2542.

Baddeley, A., Della Sala, S. & Spinnler, H. (1991). The two-component hypothesis of memory deficit in Alzheimer's disease. *Journal of Clinical and Experimental Neuropsychology*, **13**, 372–380.

Baddeley, A.D. & Hitch, G.J. (1974). Working memory. In G. Bower (ed.), *The Psychology of Learning and Motivation: Advances in Research and Theory*, vol. 8. Academic Press, New York, pp. 47–90.

Baddeley, A., Logie, R., Bressi, S., Della Sala, S. & Spinnler, H. (1986). Dementia and working memory. *Quarterly Journal of Experimental Psychology*, **38A**, 603–618.

Bayles, K.A. & Tomoeda, C.K. (1983). Confrontation naming impairment in dementia. *Brain and Language*, **19**, 98–114.

Beatty, W.W., Goodkin, D.E., Monson, N., Beatty, P.A. & Herstgaard, D. (1988). Anterograde and retrograde amnesia in patients with chronic progressive multiple sclerosis. *Archives of Neurology*, **45**, 611–619.

Beatty, W.W., Salmon, D.P., Butters, N., Heindel, W.C. & Granholm, E. (1988). Retrograde amnesia in patients with Alzheimer's disease or Huntington's disease. *Neurobiology of Aging*, **9**, 181–186.

Becker, J.T. (1988). Working memory and secondary memory deficits in Alzheimer's disease. *Journal of Clinical and Experimental Neuropsychology*, **10**, 739–753.

Becker, J.T., Boller, F., Saxton, J. & McGonigle-Gibson, K.L. (1987). Normal rates of forgetting of verbal and non-verbal material in Alzheimer's disease. *Cortex*, **23**, 59–72.

Berg, L., McKeel, D.W., Miller, J.P., Baty, J. & Morris, J.C. (1993). Neuropathological indexes of Alzheimer's disease in demented and nondemented persons aged 80 and older. *Archives of Neurology*, **50**, 349–358.

Boller, F., Mizutani, T., Roessmann, U. & Gambetti, P. (1980). Parkinson disease, dementia, and Alzheimer disease: clinicopathological correlations. *Annals of Neurology*, **7**, 329–335.

Bondi, M.W. & Kaszniak, A.W. (1991). Implicit and explicit memory in Alzheimer's disease and Parkinson's disease. *Journal of Clinical and Experimental Neuropsychology*, **13**, 339–358.

Brandt, J. (1985). Access to knowledge in the dementia of Huntington's disease. *Developmental Neuropsychology*, **1**, 335–348.

Brandt, J. (1990). Cognitive impairments in Huntington's disease: insights into the neuropsychology of the striatum. In F. Boller & J. Grafman (eds), *The Handbook of Neuropsychology*. Elsevier Scientific Publishers, Amsterdam.

Brandt, J. (1991). The Hopkins Verbal Learning Test: development of a new memory test with six equivalent forms. *The Clinical Neuropsychologist*, **5**, 125–142.

Brandt, J. & Benedict, R.H.B. (1993). Dementia. In L. Squire (ed.), *Encyclopedia of Learning and Memory*. Macmillan Publishing, New York.

Brandt. J. & Butters, N. (1994). Neuropsychological characteristics of Huntington's disease. In I. Grant & K.M. Adams (eds), *Neuropsychological Assessment of Neuropsychiatric Disorders*, 2nd edn. Oxford University Press, New York.

Brandt, J. & Bylsma, F.W. (1993). The dementia of Huntington's disease. In R.W. Parks, R.F. Zec & R.S. Wilson (eds), *Neuropsychology of Alzheimer's Disease and Other Dementias*. Oxford University Press, New York, pp. 265–282.

Brandt, J., Corwin, J. & Krafft, L. (1992). Is verbal recognition memory really different in Huntington's and Alzheimer's disease? *Journal of Clinical and Experimental Neuropsychology*, **14**, 773–784.

Brandt, J., Folstein, S.E. & Folstein, M.F. (1988). Differential cognitive impairment in Alzheimer's disease and Huntington's disease. *Annals of Neurology*, **23**, 555–561.

Brandt, J., Spencer, M., McSorley, P. & Folstein, M. (1988). Semantic activation and implicit memory in Alzheimer's disease. *Alzheimer Disease and Associated Disorders*, **2**, 112–119.

Buschke, H. (1973). Selective reminding for analysis of memory and learning. *Journal of Verbal Learning and Verbal Behavior*, **12**, 543–550.

Butters, N., Granholm, E., Salmon, D.P., Grant, I. & Wolfe, J. (1987). Episodic and semantic memory: a comparison of amnesic and demented patients. *Journal of Clinical and Experimental Neuropsychology*, **9**, 479–497.

Butters, N., Heindel, W.C. & Salmon, D.P. (1990). Dissociation of implicit memory in dementia: neurological implications. *Bulletin of the Psychonomic Society*, **28**, 359–366.

Butters, N., Salmon, D.P., Cullum, C.M., Cairns, P., Tröster, A.I. & Jacobs, D. (1988). Differentiation of amnesic and demented patients with the Wechsler Memory Scale-Revised. *The Clinical Neuropsychologist*, **2**, 133–148.

Butters, N., Salmon, D.P. & Heindel, W.C. (1990). Processes underlying the memory impairments of demented patients. In E. Goldberg (ed.), *Contemporary Neuropsychology and the Legacy of Luria*. Erlbaum, Hillsdale, NJ, pp. 99–126.

Butters, N., Salmon, D.P., Heindel, W. & Granholm, E. (1988). Episodic, semantic, and procedural memory: some comparisons of Alzheimer and Huntington disease patients. In R.D. Terry (ed.), *Aging and the Brain*. Raven Press, New York, pp. 63–87.

Butters, N., Wolfe, J., Granholm, E. & Martone, M. (1986). An assessment of verbal recall, recognition and fluency abilities in patients with Huntington's disease. *Cortex*, **22**, 11–32.

Butters, N., Wolfe, J., Martone, M., Granholm, E. & Cermak, L.S. (1985). Memory disorders associated with Huntington's disease: verbal recall, verbal recognition, and procedural memory. *Neuropsychologia*, **23**, 729–743.

Bylsma, F.W., Rebok. G. & Brandt, J. (1992). Long-term retention of implicit learning in Huntington's disease. *Neuropsychologia*, **29**, 1213–1221.

Chan, A.S., Butters, N., Paulsen, J.S., Salmon, D.P., Swenson, M.R. & Maloney, L.T. (1993). An assessment of the semantic network in patients with Alzheimer's disease. *Journal of Cognitive Neuroscience*, **5**, 254–261.

Chan, A.S., Butters, N., Salmon, D.P. & McGuire, K.A. (1993). Dimensionality and clustering in the semantic network of patients with Alzheimer's disease. *Psychology and Aging*, **8**, 411–419.

Christensen, H., Hadzi-Pavlovic, D. & Jacomb, P. (1991). The psychometric differentiation of dementia from normal aging: a meta-analysis. *Psychological Assessment*, **3**, 147–155.

Cohen, N.J. & Squire, L.R. (1980). Preserved learning and retention of pattern-analyzing skill in amnesia: dissociation of knowing how and knowing that. *Science*, **210**, 207–210.

Corkin, S. (1982). Some relationships between global amnesias and the memory impairments in Alzheimer's disease. In S. Corkin, K.L. Davis, J.H. Growdon, E. Usdin & R.J. Wurtman (eds), *Aging Vol. 19. Alzheimer's Disease: A Report of Progress*. Raven Press, New York, pp. 149–164.

Craik, F.I.M. (1977). Age differences in human memory. In J.E. Birren & K.W. Schaie (eds), *Handbook of the Psychology of Aging*. Van Nostrand Reinhold, New York, pp. 384–420.

Craik, F.I.M. & Levy, B.A. (1976). The concept of primary memory. In W.K. Estes (ed.), *Handbook of Learning and Cognitive Processes. Vol. 4: Attention and Memory*. Erlbaum, Hillsdale, NJ, pp. 133–175.

Crook, T. & Larrabee, G.J. (1988). Age-associated memory impairment: diagnostic criteria and treatment strategies. *Psychopharmacology Bulletin*, **24**, 509–514.

Crook, T.H., Bartus, R.T., Ferris, S.H., Whitehouse, P., Cohen, G.D. & Gershon, S. (1986). Age-associated memory impairment: proposed diagnostic criteria and measures of clinical change (Report of a National Institute of Mental Health workgroup). *Developmental Neuropsychology*, **2**, 261–276.

Cummings, J.L. (ed.). (1990). *Subcortical Dementia*. Oxford University Press, New York.

Cummings, J.L. & Benson, D.F. (1984). Subcortical dementia: review of an emerging concept. *Archives of Neurology*, **41**, 874–879.

Cummings, J.L. & Benson, D.F. (1992). *Dementia: A Clinical Approach*, 2nd ed. Butterworth–Heinemann, Boston.

Delis, D.C., Kramer, J.H., Kaplan, E. & Ober, B.A. (1987). *The California Verbal Learning Test*. The Psychological Corporation, San Antonio.

Delis, D.C., Massman, P.J., Butters, N., Salmon, D.P., Cermak, L.S. & Kramer, J.H. (1991). Profiles of demented and amnesic patients on the California Verbal Learning Test: implications for the assessment of memory disorders. *Psychological Assessment: A Journal of Consulting and Clinical Psychology*, **3**, 19–26.

Deweer, B., Pillon, B., Michon, A. & Dubois, B. (1993). Mirror reading in Alzheimer's disease: normal skill learning and acquisition of item-specific information. *Journal of Clinical and Experimental Neuropsychology*, **15**, 789–804.

Duchek, J.M., Cheney, M., Ferraro, F. & Storandt, M. (1991). Paired associate learning in senile dementia of the Alzheimer type. *Archives of Neurology*, **48**, 1038–1040.

Evans, D.A., Funkenstein, H.H., Albert, M.S., Scherr, P.A., Cook, N.R., Chown, M.J., Hebert, L.E., Hennekens, C.H. & Taylor, J.O. (1989). Prevalence of Alzheimer's disease in a community population of older persons: higher than previously reported. *Journal of the American Medical Association*, **262**, 2551–2556.

Flowers, K.A., Pearce, I. & Pearce, J.M.S. (1984). Recognition memory in Parkinson's disease. *Journal of Neurology, Neurosurgery and Psychiatry*, **47**, 1174–1181.

Folstein, M.F., Folstein, S.E. & McHugh, P.R. (1975). 'Mini-Mental State': a practical method for grading the cognitive state of patients for the clinician. *Journal of Psychiatric Research*, **12**, 189–198.

Folstein, S.E., Brandt, J. & Folstein, M.F. (1990). Huntington's disease. In J.L. Cummings (ed.), *Subcortical Dementia*. Oxford University Press, New York, pp. 87–107.

Fuld, P.A., Katzman, R., Davies, P. & Terry, R.D. (1982). Intrusions as a sign of Alzheimer's dementia: chemical and pathological verification. *Annals of Neurology*, **11**, 155–159.

Fuld, P.A., Masur, D.M., Blau, A.D., Crystal, H. & Aronson, M.K. (1990). Object-memory evaluation for prospective detection of dementia in normal functioning elderly: predictive and normative data. *Journal of Clinical and Experimental Neuropsychology*, **12**, 520–528.

Grady, C.L., Haxby, J.V., Horwitz, B., Sundaram, M., Berg, G., Schapiro, M., Friedland, R.P. & Rapoport, S.I. (1988). Longitudinal study of the early neuropsychological and cerebral metabolic changes in dementia of the Alzheimer type. *Journal of Clinical and Experimental Neuropsychology*, **10**, 576–596.

Graf, P., Squire, L.R. & Mandler, G. (1984). The information that amnesic patients do not forget. *Journal of Experimental Psychology: Learning, Memory, and Cognition*, **10**, 164–178.

Grafman, J., Rao, S., Bernardin, L. & Leo, G.J. (1991). Automatic memory processes in patients with multiple sclerosis. *Archives of Neurology*, **48**, 1072–1075.

Granholm, E. & Butters, N. (1988). Associative encoding and retrieval in Alzheimer's and Huntington's disease. *Brain and Cognition*, **7**, 335–347.

Grober, E., Buschke, H., Kawas, C. & Fuld, P. (1985). Impaired ranking of semantic attributes in dementia. *Brain and Language*, **26**, 276–286.

Harrington, D.L., Haaland, K.Y., Yeo, R.A. & Marder, E. (1990). Procedural memory in Parkinson's disease: impaired motor but not visuoperceptual learning. *Journal of Clinical and Experimental Neuropsychology*, **12**, 323–339.

Harris, S.J. & Dowson, J.H. (1982). Recall of a 10-word list in the assessment of dementia in the elderly. *British Journal of Psychiatry*, **141**, 524–527.

Hart, R.P., Kwentus, J.A., Harkins, S.W. & Taylor, J.R. (1988). Rate of forgetting in mild Alzheimer's-type dementia. *Brain and Cognition*, **7**, 31–38.

Heindel, W.C., Butters, N. & Salmon, D.P. (1988). Impaired learning of motor skill in patients with Huntington's disease. *Behavioral Neuroscience*, **102**, 141–147.

Heindel, W.C., Salmon, D.P. & Butters, N. (1991). The biasing of weight judgments in Alzheimer's and Huntington's disease: a priming or programming phenomenon? *Journal of Clinical and Experimental Neuropsychology*, **13**, 189–203.

Heindel, W.C., Salmon, D.P., Shults, C.W., Walicke, P.A. & Butters, N. (1989). Neuropsychological evidence for multiple implicit memory systems: a comparison of Alzheimer's, Huntington's, and Parkinson's disease patients. *Journal of Neuroscience*, **9**, 582–587.

Hodges, J.R., Salmon, D.P. & Butters, N. (1991). The nature of the naming deficit in Alzheimer's and Huntington's disease. *Brain*, **114**, 1547–1558.

Huff, F.J., Corkin, S. & Growdon, J.H. (1986). Semantic impairment and anomia in Alzheimer's disease. *Brain and Language*, **28**, 235–249.

Hugdahl, K., Asbjørnsen, A. & Wester, K. (1993). Memory performance in Parkinson's disease. *Neuropsychiatry, Neuropsychology, and Behavioral Neurology*, **6**, 170–176.

Hughes, C.P., Berg, L., Danziger, W.L., Coben, L.A. & Martin, R.L. (1982). A new clinical scale for the staging of dementia. *British Journal of Psychiatry*, **140**, 566–572.

Jacobs, D., Salmon, D.P., Tröster, A.I. & Butters, N. (1990). Intrusion errors in the figural memory of patients with Alzheimer's and Huntington's disease. *Archives of Clinical Neuropsychology*, **5**, 49–57.

Jacobs, D., Tröster, A.I., Butters, N., Salmon, D.P. & Cermak, L.S. (1990). Intrusion errors on the visual reproduction test of the Wechsler Memory Scale and the Wechsler Memory Scale–Revised: an analysis of demented and amnesic patients. *The Clinical Neuropsychologist*, **4**, 177–191.

Keane, M.M., Gabrieli, J.D.E., Fennema, A.C., Growdon, J.H. & Corkin, S. (1991). Evidence for a dissociation between perceptual and conceptual priming in Alzheimer's disease. *Behavioral Neuroscience*, **105**, 326–342.

Knopman, D.S. & Nissen, M.J. (1987). Implicit learning in patients with probable Alzheimer's disease. *Neurology*, **37**, 784–788.

Knopman, D.S. & Nissen, M.J. (1991). Procedural learning is impaired in Huntington's disease: evidence from the serial reaction time task. *Neuropsychologia*, **29**, 245–254.

Knopman, D.S. & Ryberg, R. (1989). A verbal memory test with high predictive accuracy for dementia of the Alzheimer type. *Archives of Neurology*, **46**, 141–145.

Kopelman, M.D. (1985). Rates of forgetting in Alzheimer-type dementia and Korsakoff's syndrome. *Neuropsychologia*, **23**, 623–638.

Kopelman, M.D. (1989). Remote and autobiographical memory, temporal context memory and frontal atrophy in Korsakoff and Alzheimer patients. *Neuropsychologia*, **27**, 437–460.

Kral, V.A. (1962). Senescent forgetfulness: benign and malignant. *Journal of the Canadian Medical Association*, **86**, 257–260.

Kramer, J.H., Delis, D.C., Blusewicz, M.J., Brandt, J., Ober, B.A. & Strauss, M. (1988). Verbal memory errors in Huntington's and Alzheimer's dementias. *Developmental Neuropsychology*, **4**, 1–15.

Kramer, J.H., Levin, B., Brandt, J. & Delis, D.C. (1989). Differentiation of Alzheimer's, Huntington's and Parkinson's diseases on the basis of verbal learning characteristics. *Neuropsychology*, **3**, 111–120.

Lane, F. & Snowdon, J. (1989). Memory and dementia: a longitudinal survey of suburban elderly. In P. Lovibond & P. Wilson (eds), *Clinical and Abnormal Psychology*. Elsevier, New York, pp. 365–367.

Loftus, G.R. (1985). Observations: evaluating forgetting curves. *Journal of Experimental Psychology: Learning, Memory and Cognition*, **11**, 397–406.

Martin, A. (1992). Degraded knowledge representations in patients with Alzheimer's disease: implications for models of semantic and repetition priming. In L.R. Squire & N. Butters (eds), *Neuropsychology of Memory*, 2nd edn. Guilford, New York, pp. 220–232.

Martin, A., Brouwers, P., Cox, C. & Fedio, P. (1985). On the nature of the verbal memory deficit in Alzheimer's disease. *Brain and Language*, **25**, 323–341.

Martin, A., Brouwers, P., Lalonde, F., Cox, C., Teleska, P. & Fedio, P. (1986). Towards a behavioral typology of Alzheimer's patients. *Journal of Clinical and Experimental Neuropsychology*, **8**, 594–610.

Martin, A. & Fedio, P. (1983). Word production and comprehension in Alzheimer's disease: the breakdown of semantic knowledge. *Brain and Language*, **19**, 124–141.

Martone, M., Butters, N., Payne, M., Becker, J. & Sax, D.S. (1984). Dissociations between skill learning and verbal recognition in amnesia and dementia. *Archives of Neurology*, **41**, 965–970.

Massman, P.J., Delis, D.C., Butters, N., Dupont, R.M. & Gillin, J.C. (1992). The subcortical dysfunction hypothesis of memory deficits in depression: neuropsychological validation in a subgroup of patients. *Journal of Clinical and Experimental Neuropsychology*, **14**, 687–706.

Massman, P.J., Delis, D.C., Butters, N., Levin, B.E. & Salmon, D.P. (1990). Are all subcortical dementias alike? Verbal learning and memory in Parkinson's and Huntington's disease patients. *Journal of Clinical and Experimental Neuropsychology*, **12**, 729–744.

Masur, D.M., Fuld, P.A., Blau, A.D., Thal, L.J., Levin, H.S. & Aronson, M.K. (1989). Distinguishing normal and demented elderly with the Selective Reminding Test. *Journal of Clinical and Experimental Neuropsychology*, **11**, 615–630.

Mattis, S. (1988). *Dementia Rating Scale Manual*. Psychological Assessment Resources, Odessa, FL.

Mayeux, R., Stern, Y., Rosen, J. & Benson, D.F. (1983). Is "subcortical dementia" a recognizable clinical entity? *Annals of Neurology*, **14**, 278–283.

McDaniel, K.D. (1990). Thalamic degeneration. In J.L. Cummings (ed.), *Subcortical Dementia*. Oxford University Press, New York, pp. 132–144.

McGlone, J., Gupta, S., Humphrey, D., Oppenheimer, S., Mirsen, T. & Evans, D.R. (1990). Screening for early dementia using memory complaints from patients and relatives. *Archives of Neurology*, **47**, 1189–1193.

McKhann, G., Drachman, D., Folstein, M., Katzman, R., Price, D. & Stadlan, E.M. (1984). Clinical diagnosis of Alzheimer's disease: report of the NINCDS-ADRDA workgroup under the auspices of Department of Health and Human Services task force on Alzheimer's disease. *Neurology*, **34**, 939–944.

Miller, E. (1971). On the nature of the memory disorder in presenile dementia. *Neuropsychologia*, **9**, 75–78.

Mohs, R.C., Kim, Y., Johns, C.A., Dunn, D.D. & Davis, K.L. (1986). Assessing changes in Alzheimer's disease: memory and language. In L.W. Poon (ed.), *Handbook for Clinical Memory Assessment of Older Adults*. American Psychological Association, Washington, DC, pp. 149–155.

Monsch, A.U., Bondi, M.W., Butters, N., Salmon, D.P., Katzman, R. & Thal, L.J. (1992). Comparisons of verbal fluency tasks in the detection of dementia of the Alzheimer type. *Archives of Neurology*, **49**, 1253–1258.

Morris, J.C., Heyman, A., Mohs, R.C., Hughes, J.P., van Belle, G., Fillenbaum, G., Mellits, E.D. & Clark, C. (1989). The Consortium to Establish a Registry for Alzheimer's Disease (CERAD). Part 1. Clinical and neuropsychological assessment of Alzheimer's disease. *Neurology*, **39**, 1159–1165.

Morris, J.C., McKeel, D.W., Jr., Fulling, K., Torack, R.M. & Berg, L. (1988). Validation of clinical diagnostic criteria for Alzheimer's disease. *Annals of Neurology*, **24**, 17–22.

Morris, R.G. (1986). Short-term forgetting in senile dementia of the Alzheimer type. *Cognitive Neuropsychology*, **3**, 77–97.

Morris, R.G. & Baddeley, A.D. (1988). Primary and working memory functioning in Alzheimer-type dementia. *Journal of Clinical and Experimental Neuropsychology*, **10**, 279–296.

Morris, R.G. & Kopelman, M.D. (1986). The memory deficits in Alzheimer-type dementia: a review. *Quarterly Journal of Experimental Psychology*, **38A**, 575–602.

Mortimer, J.A. (1983). Alzheimer's disease and senile dementia: prevalence and incidence. In B. Reisberg (ed.), *Alzheimer's Disease*. The Free Press, New York, pp. 141–148.

Mortimer, J.A. (1988). The dementia of Parkinson's disease. *Clinics in Geriatric Medicine*, **4**, 785–797.

Moscovitch, M. (1982). A neuropsychological approach to perception and memory in normal and pathological aging. In F.I.M. Craik & S. Trehub (eds), *Aging and Cognitive Process*. Plenum Press, New York, pp. 55–78.

Moss, M.B., Albert, M.S., Butters, N. & Payne, M. (1986). Differential patterns of memory loss among patients with Alzheimer's disease, Huntington's disease, and alcoholic Korsakoff's syndrome. *Archives of Neurology*, **43**, 239–246.

Nebes, R.D. (1989). Semantic memory in Alzheimer's disease. *Psychological Bulletin*, **106**, 377–394.

Nebes, R.D., Boller, F. & Holland, A. (1986). Use of semantic context by patients with Alzheimer's disease. *Psychology and Aging*, **1**, 261–269.

Nebes, R.D., Brady, C.B. & Huff, F.J. (1989). Automatic and attentional mechanisms of semantic priming in Alzheimer's disease. *Journal of Clinical and Experimental Neuropsychology*, **11**, 219–231.

Nebes, R.D., Martin, D.C. & Horn, L.C. (1984). Sparing of semantic memory in Alzheimer's disease. *Journal of Abnormal Psychology*, **93**, 321–330.

Ober, B.A., Dronkers, N.F., Koss, E., Delis, D.C. & Friedland, R.P. (1986). Retrieval from semantic memory in Alzheimer-type dementia. *Journal of Clinical and Experimental Neuropsychology*, **8**, 75–92.

Ober, B.A., Shenaut, G.K., Jagust, W.J. & Stillman, R.C. (1991). Automatic semantic priming with various category relations in Alzheimer's disease and normal aging. *Psychology and Aging*, **6**, 647–660.

O'Connor, D.W., Pollitt, P.A., Roth, M., Brook, P.B. & Reiss, B.B. (1990). Memory complaints and impairment in normal, depressed, and demented elderly persons identified in a community survey. *Archives of General Psychiatry*, **47**, 224–227.

Paulsen, J.S., Butters, N., Salmon, D.P., Heindel, W.C. & Swenson, M.R. (1993). Prism adaptation in Alzheimer's and Huntington's disease. *Neuropsychology*, **7**, 73–81.

Peterson, L.R. & Peterson, M.J. (1959). Short-term retention of individual verbal items. *Journal of Experimental Psychology*, **58**, 193–198.

Pillon, B., Deweer, B., Agid, Y. & Dubois, B. (1993). Explicit memory in Alzheimer's, Huntington's and Parkinson's diseases. *Archives of Neurology*, **50**, 374–379.

Pillon, B., Dubois, B., Lhermitte, F. & Agid, Y. (1986). Heterogeneity of cognitive impairment in progressive supranuclear palsy, Parkinson's disease, and Alzheimer's disease. *Neurology*, **36**, 1179–1185.

Randolph, C., Braun, A.R., Goldberg, T.E. & Chase, T.N. (1993). Semantic fluency in Alzheimer's, Parkinson's and Huntington's disease: dissociation of storage and retrieval failures. *Neuropsychology*, **7**, 82–88.

Rao, S.M., Hammeke, T.A., McQuillen, M.P., Khatri, B.O. & Lloyd, D. (1984). Memory disturbance in chronic progressive multiple sclerosis. *Archives of Neurology*, **41**, 625–631.

Raskin, S.A., Sliwinski, M. & Borod, J.C. (1992). Clustering strategies on tasks of verbal fluency in Parkinson's disease. *Neuropsychologia*, **30**, 95–99.

Rebok, G. & Folstein, M.F. (1993). Dementia. *Journal of Neuropsychiatry and Clinical Neurosciences*, **5**, 265–276.

Rich, J.B. (1993). Pictorial and verbal implicit memory in aging and Alzheimer's disease. *Journal of Clinical and Experimental Neuropsychology*, **15**, 38.

Roediger, H.L. III (1990). Implicit memory: retention without remembering. *American Psychologist*, **45**, 1043–1056.

Sagar, H.J., Cohen, N.J., Sullivan, E.V., Corkin, S. & Growdon, J.H. (1988). Remote memory function in Alzheimer's disease and Parkinson's disease, *Brain*, **111**, 185–206.

Salmon, B.P. & Heindel, W.C. (1992). Impaired priming in Alzheimer's disease: neuropsychological implications. In L.R. Squire & N. Butters (eds), *Neuropsychology of Memory*, 2nd edn. Guilford, New York, pp. 179–187.

Salmon, D.P., Shimamura, A.P., Butters, N. & Smith, S. (1988). Lexical and semantic priming deficits in patients with Alzheimer's disease. *Journal of Clinical and Experimental Neuropsychology*, **10**, 477–494.

Schacter, D. (1987). Implicit memory: history and current status. *Journal of Experimental Psychology: Learning, Memory and Cognition*, **13**, 501–518.

Shimamura, A.P. (1986). Priming effects in amnesia: evidence for a dissociable memory function. *Quarterly Journal of Experimental Psychology*, **38A**, 619–644.

Shimamura, A.P., Salmon, D.P., Squire, L.R. & Butters, N. (1987). Memory dysfunction and word priming in dementia and amnesia. *Behavioral Neuroscience*, **101**, 347–351.

Slamecka, N.J. & McElree, B. (1983). Normal forgetting of verbal lists as a function of their degree of learning. *Journal of Experimental Psychology: Learning, Memory and Cognition*, **9**, 384–397.

Smith, S., Butters, N., White, R., Lyon, L. & Granholm, E. (1988). Priming semantic relations in patients with Huntington's disease. *Brain and Language*, **33**, 27–40.

Snodgrass, J.G. & Corwin, J. (1988). Pragmatics of measuring recognition memory: applications to dementia and amnesia. *Journal of Experimental Psychology: General*, **117**, 34–50.

Spinnler, H., Della Sala, S., Bandera, R. & Baddeley, A. (1988). Dementia, aging, and the structure of human memory, *Cognitive Neuropsychology*, **5**, 193–211.

Stuss, D.T. & Cummings, J.L. (1990). Subcortical vascular dementias. In J.L. Cummings (ed.), *Subcortical Dementia*. Oxford University Press, New York, pp. 145–163.

Terry, R. & Katzman, R. (1992). Alzheimer disease and cognitive loss. In R. Katzman & J.W. Rowe (eds), *Principles of Geriatric Neurology*. F.A. Davis Co, Philadelphia, pp. 207–265.

Tröster, A.I., Butters, N., Salmon, D.P., Cullum, C.M., Jacobs, D., Brandt, J. & White, R.F. (1993). The diagnostic utility of savings scores: differentiating Alzheimer's and Huntington's diseases with the Logical Memory and Visual Reproduction subtests. *Journal of Clinical and Experimental Neuropsychology*, **5**, 773–788.

Tulving, E. (1972). Episodic and semantic memory. In E. Tulving & W. Donaldson (eds), *Organization of Memory*. Academic Press, New York, pp. 382–403.

Tulving, E. & Colotla, V.A. (1970). Free recall of trilingual lists. *Cognitive Psychology*, **1**, 86–98.

Tulving, E., Schacter, D.L. & Stark, H.A. (1982). Priming effects in word-fragment completion are independent of recognition memory. *Journal of Experimental Psychology: Learning, Memory and Cognition*, **8**, 336–342.

Waugh, N.C. & Norman, D.A. (1965). Primary memory. *Psychological Review*, **72**, 89–104.

Wechsler, D. (1945). A standardized memory scale for clinical use. *Journal of Psychology*, **19**, 87–95.

Wechsler, D. (1987). *Wechsler Memory Scale – Revised* (manual). Psychological Corporation, New York.

Weingartner, H., Kaye, W., Smallberg, S., Cohen, R., Ebert, M.H., Gillin, J.C. & Gold, P. (1982). Determinants of memory failure in dementia. In S. Corkin, K.L. Davis, J.H. Growdon, E. Usdin & R.J. Wurtman (eds), *Aging: Vol. 19. Alzheimer's Disease: A Report of Progress*. Raven Press, New York, pp. 171–176.

Welsh, K.A., Butters, N., Hughes, J.P., Mohs, R. & Heyman, A. (1991). Detection of abnormal memory decline in mild cases of Alzheimer's disease using CERAD neuropsychological measures. *Archives of Neurology*, **48**, 278–281.

Welsh, K.A., Butters, N., Hughes, J.P., Mohs, R.C. & Heyman, A. (1992). Detection and staging of dementia in Alzheimer's disease. *Archives of Neurology*, **49**, 448–452.

Whelihan, W.M., Lesher, E.L., Kleban, M.H. & Granick, S. (1984). Mental status and memory assessment as predictors of dementia. *Journal of Gerontology*, **39**, 572–576.

Whitehouse, P.J. (1986). The concept of subcortical and cortical dementia: another look. *Annals of Neurology*, **19**, 1–6.

Whitehouse, P.J., Hedreen, J.C., White, C.L. & Price D.L. (1983). Basal forebrain neurons in the dementia of Parkinson disease. *Annals of Neurology*, **13**, 242–248.

Wilkie, F.L., Eisdorfer, C., Morgan, R., Loewenstein, D.A. & Szapocznik, J. (1990). Cognition in early human immunodeficiency virus infection. *Archives of Neurology*, **47**, 433–440.

Willingham, D.B. & Koroshetz, W.J. (1993). Evidence for dissociable motor skills in Huntington's disease patients. *Psychobiology*, **21**, 173–182.

Wilson, R.S., Bacon, L.D., Fox, J.H. & Kaszniak, A.W. (1983). Primary memory and secondary memory in dementia of the Alzheimer type. *Journal of Clinical Neuropsychology*, **5**, 337–344.

Wilson, R.S., Como, P.G., Garron, D.C., Klawans, H.L., Barr, A. & Klawans, D. (1987). Memory failure in Huntington's disease. *Journal of Clinical and Experimental Neurology*, **9**, 147–154.

Wilson, R.S., Kaszniak, A.W., Bacon, L.D., Fox, J.H. & Kelly, M.P. (1982). Facial recognition memory in dementia. *Cortex*, **18**, 329–336.

Wilson, R.S., Kaszniak, A.W. & Fox, J.H. (1981). Remote memory in senile dementia. *Cortex*, **17**, 41–48.

Wolfe, J., Granholm, E., Butters, N., Saunders, E. & Janowsky, D. (1987). Verbal memory deficits associated with major affective disorders: a comparison of unipolar and bipolar patients. *Journal of Affective Disorders*, **13**, 83–92.

Youngjohn, J.R. & Crook, T.H. (1993). Stability of everyday memory in age-associated memory impairment: a longitudinal study. *Neuropsychology*, **7**, 406–416.

Youngjohn, J.R., Larrabee, G.J. & Crook, T.H. (1992). Discriminating age-associated memory impairment from Alzheimer's disease. *Psychological Assessment*, **4**, 54–59.

Zec, R.F. & Vicari, S. (1990). Rey Auditory Verbal Learning Test: utility in dementia evaluations. *The Clinical Neuropsychologist*, **4**, 281.

Chapter 11

Schizophrenia

Peter McKenna
Fulbourn Hospital, Cambridge, UK
Linda Clare
University College, London, UK
and
Alan D. Baddeley
MRC Applied Psychology Unit, Cambridge, UK

INTRODUCTION

It may come as something of a surprise to find a chapter on schizophrenia in a book about memory disorders. Yet it is now accepted that neuropsychological deficits ranging from the subtle to the profound can be seen in many patients with the disorder. Recent research has indicated that memory impairment—sometimes pure and pronounced enough to constitute a "schizophrenia amnesia"—makes an important contribution to the pattern of impairment found. It may be that a detailed mapping of memory and other neuropsychological deficits in schizophrenia will shed some light on the nature of the underlying disease process. It is also possible that understanding this aspect of the psychology of schizophrenia will help make sense of the strikingly unusual symptoms of the disorder. Finally, the recognition that memory and other neuropsychological deficits are frequently present in schizophrenic patients may have implications for their management.

WHAT IS SCHIZOPHRENIA?

Schizophrenia is a disorder in which an individual—who may previously have been normal or who may have shown a lifelong pattern of poor social adjust-

Handbook of Memory Disorders. Edited by A.D. Baddeley, B.A. Wilson and F.N. Watts.
© 1995 John Wiley & Sons Ltd.

ment—develops one or more of a set of symptoms affecting thought, perception and behaviour. The range of these symptoms is wide, but they often cluster together in rather characteristic ways, this giving rise to the historical division of patients into those with paranoid, hebephrenic, catatonic or simple schizophrenia. In recent years the value of dividing schizophrenic symptoms into two broad "positive" and "negative" groups has also been recognised. Positive symptoms are those characterised by the *presence* of an abnormal phenomenon, and consist principally of delusions, hallucinations and formal thought disorder (incoherence of thinking so that speech becomes difficult to follow). Negative symptoms, those which are characterised by the *absence* or *diminution* of a normal function, comprise apathy, poverty of speech and a variety of abnormalities in the realm of emotional life which are subsumed under the term "affective flattening".

Schizophrenia is almost always a severe condition, and it is typically permanently disabling. Via a series of relapses and remissions of positive symptoms, the vast majority of patients evolve towards a state of enduring deterioration in which negative symptoms loom especially large. Even in mild cases, there is usually some degree of occupational decline and social isolation is common. In the worst affected cases, the patient becomes unable to look after himself or herself and is quite likely to require indefinite care and supervision.

The aetiology of schizophrenia remains, after decades of research, largely unknown. For much of this century, psychoanalytic and psychosocial theories held sway, and at one time the whole construct of the disorder as a medical illness was called into question. Currently, however, it is widely believed that schizophrenia represents some form of biological brain disease. Although definitive proof is lacking, several lines of evidence support such a contention. It is established beyond any reasonable doubt that there is a genetic predisposition to the disorder. Strong circumstantial evidence also points to a disturbance of brain neurochemistry, most likely affecting dopamine or some other neurotransmitter that interacts with it. In addition there are broad hints that structural and functional brain abnormalities can be detected in many patients with the disorder, even though these are generally rather subtle.

General Cognitive Impairment

Kraepelin (1913) and Bleuler (1911), the psychiatrists who originated the concept of schizophrenia, considered it to be a "functional" rather than an "organic" psychosis. This meant that, in contrast to disorders like dementia and delirium, higher cognitive functions were preserved. Both Kraepelin and Bleuler were certainly aware that patients with the most severe and chronic forms of schizophrenia could sometimes be unable to give correct answers to simple questions or seem unable to recall basic information. However, they assumed that this occurred because psychotic experiences and symptoms such as thought disorder were interfering with the use of faculties which remained fundamentally intact underneath.

After nearly a century of adherence to this dogma, evidence has begun to accumulate which points squarely to the fact that an intellectual decline takes place in some, possibly the majority of patients with schizophrenia. A number of early studies revealed that, as a group, patients with schizophrenia had a lower than expected IQ; these studies also suggested that this represented a decline from previously normal levels (see Payne, 1973). Subsequently it has been demonstrated that among chronically hospitalised "institutionalised" schizophrenic patients, obvious signs of overall intellectual impairment are commonplace (Owens & Johnstone, 1980). A proportion of such long-stay patients have been found to show exceptionally severe cognitive difficulties: as many as 25% exhibit age disorientation, underestimating their age by five years or more (Stevens, Crow, Bowman & Coles, 1978), a phenomenon which is typically part of a pattern of widespread neuropsychological deficits (Liddle & Crow, 1984).

There is good evidence that these deficits are not due to the drug treatment to which almost all schizophrenic patients have been exposed, often for long periods. Many of the relevant IQ studies considered by Payne (1973) were carried out before the era of drug treatment. In the studies of Crow and coworkers (Owens & Johnstone, 1980; Buhrich, Crow, Johnstone & Owens, 1988) both overall intellectual impairment and age disorientation were found to be unrelated to lifetime drug exposure. It should also be pointed out that there has never been any strong evidence that administration of antipsychotic drugs to normal individuals interferes greatly with memory or other cognitive functions (e.g. King, 1990).

Specific Neuropsychological Deficits

Although there is no doubt that schizophrenia is associated with a tendency to develop overall intellectual impairment, this is not obviously apparent in the large majority of patients with acute illnesses. Even among patients with the most severe and chronic illnesses, only a minority show anything approaching a full-blown dementia. In these circumstances, researchers have asked whether circumscribed neuropsychological deficits might be more characteristic of the disorder, by virtue of being demonstrable in most or even all patients and being present over and above any coexisting general poor intellectual performance.

Numerous aspects of neuropsychological function have been examined in schizophrenia. To summarise a substantial body of research (reviewed in more detail by Cutting, 1985), there is little evidence that basic perceptual processes are disturbed. The higher aspects of perceptual processing and several aspects of language function have been found to show impairment in some studies, but here the deficits tend to be on the whole minor. In addition, it has never been shown that any perceptual or linguistic impairment in schizophrenia is disproportionate to that expected on the basis of the general tendency to poor performance which characterises the disorder. The central aspects of motor control have not been subjected to nearly as much scrutiny; beyond the demonstration that schizophrenic patients are slow on reaction time tasks (Yates, 1973), little is known. Executive function in schizophrenia is discussed later in this chapter.

MEMORY IMPAIRMENT: A DISPROPORTIONATE DEFICIT?

The results of around 20 early studies of memory in schizophrenia produced a moderate consensus. Cutting (1985), reviewing the evidence then available, concluded that memory appeared to be intact in patients with acute schizophrenia, at least superficially, but that poor memory function, sometimes amounting to a marked amnesia, was common in patients with chronic, severe illness.

Credit for the first detailed exploration of the scope of memory impairment in schizophrenia belongs to Calev and his coworkers (Calev, 1984a,b; Calev, Venables & Monk, 1983; Calev, Berlin & Lerer, 1987; Calev, Korin, Kugelmass & Lerer, 1987). In a series of studies carried out mainly on chronic schizophrenic patients, these authors found evidence of substantial deficits in episodic memory tasks; these deficits affected both recall and recognition, although the former appeared to be of considerably greater magnitude. Evidence of retrograde amnesia was also found which extended back to remote events. These results were considered to be consistent with the presence of an amnesic syndrome in schizophrenia, although other interpretations—for example a deficit in the organisation of material to be remembered—were considered possible.

Since then a number of studies have suggested that memory is one of the major areas of neuropsychological deficit in schizophrenia (e.g. McKenna et al., 1990; Saykin et al., 1991; Goldberg et al., 1993b). In our own study (McKenna et al., 1990), we examined memory function in schizophrenia in as simple and straightforward a way as possible: a "user-friendly" battery was chosen (the Rivermead Behavioural Memory Test or RBMT; Wilson, Cockburn & Baddeley, 1985; Wilson, Cockburn, Baddeley & Hiorns, 1989), which is suitable for use in clinical populations and which does not make too many demands on attention and motivation. This was administered to a sample of 60 patients aged 18 to 68. These were selected to provide as far as possible a "snapshot" of schizophrenia as a whole: they were drawn in approximately equal numbers from acute wards and outpatient clinics; from a rehabilitation service for the more chronically ill; and from long-stay "back" wards whose residents are typically severely incapacitated.

Performance on the RBMT was expressed as a screening score, the number of tests passed out of a maximum of 12. As shown in Figure 11.1, the schizophrenic

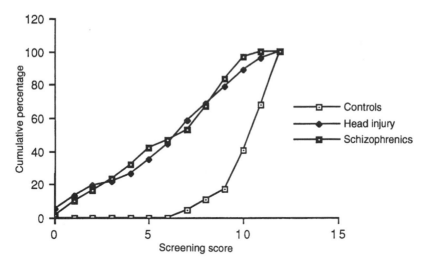

Figure 11.1 Cumulative RBMT screening scores for patients with schizophrenia, closed head injury and normal individuals. Reproduced from McKenna et al. (1990) by permission of Cambridge University Press

patients' performance was found to be obviously poorer than that of 118 normal individuals of comparable age range; nearly half the total sample had memory scores in the moderately or severely impaired range. Their performance was in fact no better than that of a sample of 176 patients with moderate or severe brain injury. Impairment was not restricted to chronic patients; substantial deficits were sometimes seen in acute or remitted patients as well. Mirroring the findings for overall cognitive impairment, memory impairment was found to be a function of severity and chronicity of illness; a correlation with overall intellectual impairment was also found.

Having demonstrated that memory impairment is prevalent in schizophrenia, it needs to be established whether or not this is disproportionate to the degree of overall intellectual impairment. In our study, a preliminary attempt to do this was made by comparing the patients' performance on the RBMT with their performance on two simple measures of overall intellectual function. The Mini-Mental State Examination (MMSE) (Folstein, Folstein & McHugh, 1975) is a widely used test of this type which covers orientation, memory, language, praxis and attention. Although unsophisticated in neuropsychological terms, it has the advantage that cutoffs for clinically significant levels of dementia have been established (Anthony et al., 1982). The Middlesex Elderly Assessment of Mental State (MEAMS) (Golding, 1989) is a similar test which begins with orientation and then goes on to cover language, memory, visuospatial function and executive function in a systematic way. As can be seen from Figure 11.2, while around half the sample of schizophrenic patients fell into the moderately or severely impaired range on the RBMT, only a much smaller proportion

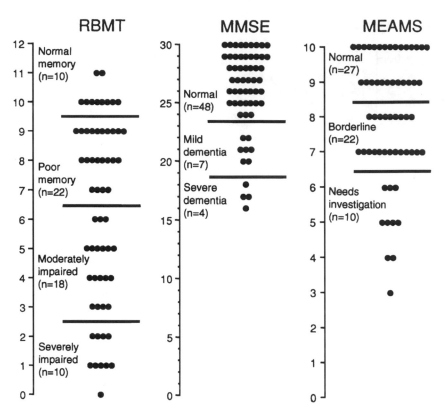

Figure 11.2 Distribution of scores for 60 schizophrenic patients on a memory test (RBMT) and two tests of general intellectual function (MMSE and MEAMS). Reproduced by permission from McKenna et al. (1990)

scored below the cutoffs for mild dementia and borderline function on the MMSE and MEAMS respectively. In this study the scores on the memory tests of the MEAMS were excluded from consideration.

This tentative finding has since been corroborated in a study by Saykin et al. (1991). These authors administered a wide-ranging battery of neuropsychological tests to a group of 36 schizophrenic patients and 36 normal controls. The raw scores for the patients were rescaled to standard equivalents by means of the technique of z-transformation, using the means and standard deviations of the control group. The z score profile for the patients is reproduced in Figure 11.3, in which the zero on the ordinate represents the mean for the control group. It can be seen that, while the schizophrenic patients performed significantly more poorly than the normals on all tests, in most cases the level was not drastically reduced—generally scoring fell between one and two standard deviations below the control group mean. Only the findings on the memory tests provided an exception, performance on these being depressed to a much greater degree.

It is difficult to ascribe poor memory performance in schizophrenia to factors

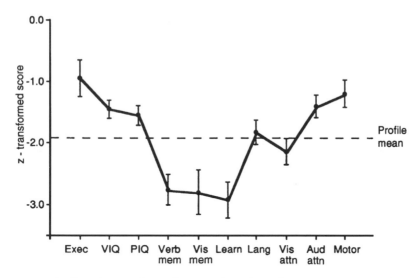

Figure 11.3 Profile of z-transformed scores for schizophrenic patients on a battery of neuropsychological tests. Exec = Wisconsin Card Sorting Test; VIQ = verbal IQ from WAIS; PIQ = performance IQ from WAIS; Verb Mem = logical recall from Wechsler Memory Scale; Vis Mem = design memory from Wechsler Memory Scale; Learn = verbal learning (two tasks); Lang = language (five tasks); Vis Attn = visuomotor processing and attention (three tasks); Aud Attn = auditory processing and attention (two tasks); Motor = motor coordination (two tasks). Reproduced by permission from Saykin et al. (1991)

like poor motivation, lack of cooperation or the distracting effects of psychotic symptoms. For cxample, the RBMT and the MEAMS are roughly similar in length of time taken for testing and in the degree of effort and concentration required, yet the schizophrenic patients in our study performed much more badly on the former than the latter. The patients in the study of Saykin and coworkers were drug-free at the time of testing, and this removes any doubt that memory impairment in schizophrenia is due to treatment factors.

THE PATTERN OF MEMORY IMPAIRMENT: THE CASE FOR A SCHIZOPHRENIC AMNESIA

It is clear from the studies described above that while memory is commonly impaired in schizophrenia, this impairment tends to occur in a setting of generalised poor neuropsychological test performance. In order to elucidate the pattern of memory impairment in the disorder—if there is a characteristic pattern—special strategies need to be adopted to minimise the "noise" such a background has the potential to introduce. In what follows, the approach taken will be first to try to obtain a rough outline of the different aspects of memory which are affected in schizophrenia, using the group studies that are available. These have generally employed acute or mixed samples of schizophrenic patients in which the overall level of memory impairment is typically not specified (and would not be expected to be great). Then, in order to get as clear a view as possible of the nature of memory deficit, these studies will be supplemented with the relatively little work that has employed the neuropsychological case study technique. Most of these latter studies derive from our own research in which we modified an approach previously employed for amnesic patients (see Baddeley, 1982) and selected schizophrenic patients who showed moderate or marked memory deficits in relative isolation. Fortunately, memory impairment in schizophrenia is common and disproportionate to the overall level of intellectual impairment, and so it is relatively easy to find suitable patients who also fulfil the requirements of being motivated, compliant and not too distracted by positive symptoms.

Short-Term Memory

Early studies of short-term memory in schizophrenia reached varying conclusions about its intactness (see Cutting, 1985). A number of more recent group studies, however, have argued that the forward digit span remains within normal limits (i.e. five or greater) (Kolb & Whishaw, 1983; McKenna et al., 1990; Goldberg et al., 1993b), at least in the vast majority of patients. A few studies, whilst in broad agreement with this finding, have suggested that a subtle degree of impairment can nevertheless be detected. For example, Gruzelier et al. (1988) found that a group of 36 schizophrenic patients had a mean forward digit span of 5.85, compared with 6.85 for a group of 29 educationally matched normal individuals. Corsi block span, a test of visuospatial immediate memory, was also slightly lower at 4.06 in the patients compared with 4.86 in the controls.

In a study using the neuropsychological case study design, we (Tamlyn et al., 1992) examined five patients who showed RBMT screening scores in the moderately or severely impaired range in conjunction with relatively preserved overall intellectual function, as judged by MMSE scores above the cutoff for mild dementia. These patients were all found to have forward digit spans in the range of 5–7, and their performance on the Corsi blocks was in all cases one or two items below their digit span, as in normal individuals. In addition, a serial position curve for these five patients was obtained by combining their average performance on 10 free-recall lists of 12 disyllabic words. This is shown in Figure 11.4 where their performance is compared with that of 42 normal individuals. A normal recency effect is apparent, combined with obvious impairment in the early and middle portions of the list. In fact, the resemblance to the pattern of performance of amnesic patients is striking.

Working Memory

The idea of an impairment in working memory is currently fashionable in schizophrenia research. To some extent this is a theoretical proposition, based

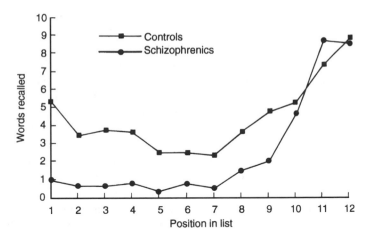

Figure 11.4 Serial position curve for word-list recall in five memory-impaired schizophrenic patients and normal individuals. Reproduced by permission from Tamlyn et al. (1992)

on a primate model of working memory (Goldman-Rakic & Friedman, 1991) which is somewhat different from the cognitive psychological conceptualisation of Baddeley (1986). However, a hint of working memory impairment was found in one study: Goldberg et al. (1993b) found that, whereas forward digit span was similar in schizophrenic patients and a control group consisting of their non-schizophrenic identical twins, there was a trend to poorer performance in reverse digit span. Reverse digit span is presumed to place a greater load on the central executive, and further evidence of impairment in this component of working memory has recently been obtained by Morice and Delahunty (in press). These authors administered a variety of span and other working memory tests to 18 schizophrenic patients and controls. They found no disturbance in the function of the articulatory loop, but clear evidence of a performance decrement in tasks placing demands on the central executive.

In our study (Tamlyn et al., 1992) the five generally memory-impaired schizophrenic patients studied individually showed phonological similarity and word-length effects consistent with undisturbed functioning of the articulatory loop component of working memory. There was thus no suggestion of impairment in at least one of the two slave systems of working memory. This study left open the question of impairment in the central executive component of working memory, a question that is returned to below.

Long-Term Memory

While it is accepted that schizophrenic patients show impairment on memory tests which tap long-term memory function, relatively few studies have investigated the various different subdivisions of this memory store. Goldberg et al. (1989) argued that the major impairment in schizophrenia was in recall, and

Calev (1984a,b) concluded that while recall and recognition were both impaired, recall was affected to a much greater degree. Calev et al. (1987a) also examined remote memory in schizophrenia, comparing the performance of 16 chronic schizophrenic patients and 16 normal controls on the Famous Events Questionnaire of Squire and Cohen (1979). They found that the patients showed significantly poorer performance, but no temporal gradient was observed.

In the five memory-impaired patients examined in detail by ourselves (Tamlyn et al., 1992), it was found that long-term memory impairments were widespread and often severe. Performance on a test of prose recall was well below the normal range in all cases. Recognition of words was obviously impaired in two of the five patients, and recognition of faces was impaired to a similar degree in three of them. In addition, scoring on tests of remote and autobiographical memory were depressed—on the latter test there was some suggestion of a temporal gradient with relative sparing of distant memories, although this was not clearly evident when each patient was considered individually.

Semantic Memory

The first study to examine semantic memory explicitly in schizophrenia was carried out by Koh and coworkers (see Koh, 1978). They used a sorting task in which words were required to be categorised according to common features; some of the words were related to each other (e.g. *lake, hill, valley, canyon,*) and some were unrelated to any of the others. When young, acute schizophrenic patients who were in remission were compared with nonschizophrenic psychiatric patients and normal controls, no major differences were found. However, the schizophrenics showed a tendency to utilise less categories and put more words in each category. Koh concluded that any impairment in semantic memory was minor and a reflection of the organising processes acting upon it rather than of the store *per se*.

More recent work has reached different conclusions. In our group study (Tamlyn et al., 1992), a preliminary examination of semantic memory was undertaken using the semantic processing test of Collins and Quillian (1969) (developed by Baddeley, Emslie and Nimmo-Smith (1992) as part of the Speed and Comprehension of Language Processing Battery). In this test, subjects have to indicate whether each of 50 sentences such as "Rats have teeth" and "Onions crush their prey" are true or false. Speed of verification is the usual measure and, as might be expected, errors are rarely made by normal individuals. The performance of 53 schizophrenic patients on this task was compared with that of 38 normal individuals of comparable age distribution (in this study the test was administered orally rather than in the usual written form). The speed of semantic processing for the two groups was highly significantly slower for the schizophrenic patients, and there was little overlap between the two groups: their mean verification time was 5.72 seconds per sentence (range 3.70–18.5) compared with 3.50 seconds per sentence (range 2.76–4.6) for the controls.

Slowness, which is characteristic of schizophrenic patients' performance on a range of tasks (e.g. Nelson et al., 1990), was not the only feature of their performance. They also made a considerably greater number of errors: 14 of the patients made three or more verification errors, with 5 of these making more than 10 errors. This was in marked contrast to the controls, none of whom made more than two errors.

The little further work in this area has tended to reinforce the view that there is a major deficit in semantic memory in schizophrenia. McKenna, Mortimer and Hodges (1994) administered a battery of semantic tests recently devised by Hodges, Salmon and Butters (1992) to patients with schizophrenia, and compared their performance with that of normal individuals and patients with Alzheimer's disease. The battery probes knowledge of well-known living and man-made items such as *fox* and *toaster* in a variety of ways—for example requiring subjects to name the items, sort them into categories and also to give definitions of them. Deficits were found on virtually all the subtests in schizophrenic patients, and their performance was found to be, on average, intermediate between that of normal individuals and patients with mild to moderate Alzheimer's disease.

Procedural Memory

Relatively few studies of procedural memory have been undertaken in schizophrenia. Early studies using a prototypical motor skill task, the pursuit rotor (reviewed by Eysenck & Frith, 1977) produced conflicting findings, although on balance they pointed to some impairment in the acquisition of the skill. More recently, however, Goldberg et al. (1993b) found no difference in the pursuit rotor performance of 15 schizophrenic patients and their non-schizophrenic identical twins; this was despite the patients showing significantly poorer episodic memory performance. These authors (Goldberg et. al., 1990), as well as Gras-Vicendon, Danion, Grange, Bilik, Willare-Schroeder, Sichel and Singer (unpublished), also found that groups of schizophrenic patients improved at the same rate as controls on a four-disc version of the Tower of Hanoi task, which the authors argued must involve procedural memory to some extent.

In our own study (Clare, McKenna, Mortimer & Baddeley, 1993), we examined the procedural memory performance of 12 schizophrenic patients who fulfilled the same requirements as those of Tamlyn et al. (1992) for demonstrating memory impairment in relative isolation. These were compared with 12 normal subjects individually matched for age, sex and estimated premorbid IQ (current IQ in the case of the normals). The patients and controls were examined in three diverse tasks of procedural memory—pursuit rotor tracking, jigsaw completion and reading mirror-transformed script. On pursuit rotor tracking and jigsaw completion, while overall performance was poorer than that of controls, the rate at which patients and controls acquired the skill was comparable, and the gains made were retained to a comparable extent across

two test sessions a week apart. In reading transformed script, not only was the
rate of acquisition and retention of the skill comparable in the patients and
controls, but the overall reading times did not differ significantly between the
two (however, there was a trend towards poorer performance in the patients).
The findings for pursuit rotor performance and reading transformed script are
shown in Figures 11.5, 11.6 and 11.7.

These findings invite the interpretation that procedural *learning* remains
intact in schizophrenia, whereas at the same time the mechanisms underlying
procedural *performance* are subject to the same tendency to poor cognitive
performance that characterises schizophrenic patients on many tasks.

Implicit Memory

Studies of implicit memory in schizophrenia are beginning to accumulate, but
the results so far have been conflicting. Using a modification of the California
Verbal Learning Test, Heinrichs and Bury (1991) claimed that both explicit and
implicit memory were impaired in schizophrenic patients. Randolph, Gold,
Goldberg and Weinberger (1991) also found impaired implicit memory in a task
involving word-stem completion. On the other hand, Myles-Worsley (1991)
found normal perceptual priming in a task requiring identification of repetitively
presented partially obscured words.

Perhaps the best designed of these group studies is that of Gras-Vincendon et

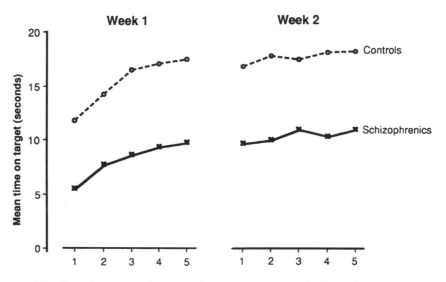

Figure 11.5 Pursuit rotor performance for memory-impaired schizophrenic patients and
matched controls. Reproduced by permission from Clare et al. (1993)

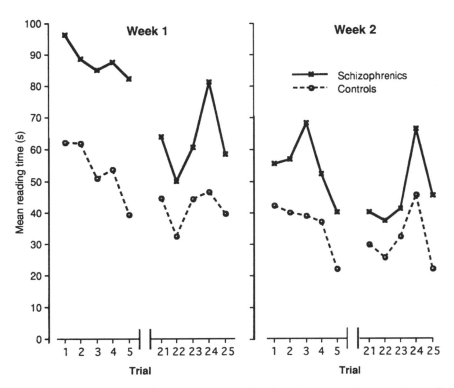

Figure 11.6 Performance of memory-impaired schizophrenic patients and matched controls on reading transformed script (nonrepeated items). Reproduced by permission from Clare et al. (1993)

al. (unpublished). They presented 24 schizophrenic patients and 24 matched normal controls with 30 words. The subjects first had to try to remember as many of the words as possible under a free-recall condition. This was followed by a repetition priming condition, in which the subjects were presented with three-letter stems of the 30 original words and 30 new words and asked to complete them with the first word that came to mind. It was found that the schizophrenic patients performed significantly more poorly than the controls in the free-recall task. In contrast there were no differences between the groups in the number of words completed with previously presented words.

This last finding appears to hold true when schizophrenic patients with substantial degrees of general memory impairment are considered. Clare et al. (1993) tested implicit memory in 10 of the 12 memory-impaired schizophrenic patients and controls described above, using a task involving priming in homophone spelling. All subjects were first asked 20 simple questions, the answers to 10 of which involved the less frequently occurring spelling of homophones of words (e.g. *buoy, wring*). Subjects were then asked to spell a list of 40 words; these contained the 10 primed homophones, 10 unprimed homophones, the

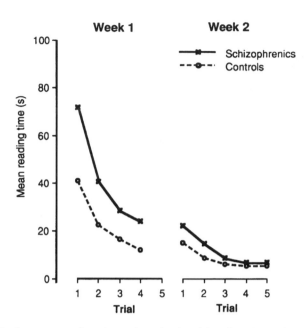

Figure 11.7 Performance of memory-impaired schizophrenic patients and matched controls on reading transformed script (repeated items). Reproduced by permission from Clare et al. (1993)

remaining 10 words which were the answers to the initial questions, and 10 other words with only one correct spelling. The subjects were tested again a week later, at which time they were asked to spell the same 40 words listed in a different order, without the priming questions being repeated. The results are summarised in Table 11.1. Both the patients and controls showed evidence of priming in week one, and this was less marked although still perhaps discernible a week later. Analysis of variance indicated there were no significant differences between the two groups.

To summarise, the pattern of memory impairment in schizophrenia seems to be one in which short-term memory and at least some aspects of working

Table 11.1 Priming in homophone spelling in schizophrenia: choice of less-frequent spelling as a function of priming during week 1

	Week 1			Week 2		
	Primed (%)	Unprimed (%)	Priming	Primed (%)	Unprimed (%)	Priming
Patients (n=10)	24.2	7.0	17.2	13.1	8.0	5.1
Controls (n=10)	32.5	18.5	14.0	16.0	15.3	0.7

Analysis of variance showed significant priming for the group as a whole ($F_{1,18}=7.05$; $p < 0.05$) and a significant week × priming interaction ($F_{1,18}=8.32$; $p = 0.01$). The priming effect operated in week one ($F_{1,36}=14.45$; $p < 0.001$), but became insignificant by week two ($F_{1,36}=0.41$; NS). There were no significant differences between patients and controls ($F_{1,18}=0.22$; NS) memory are preserved, this being coupled with a long-term memory impairment which encompasses episodic and semantic memory but which spares procedural and implicit memory. In many ways this pattern is similar in nature—but on average considerably milder in degree—to that seen in the classical amnesic syndrome. However, there is a glaring difference in that semantic memory seems to emerge as a major area of impairment in schizophrenia, whereas in the amnesic syndrome semantic memory has been considered to remain intact. It can certainly be pointed out that this view of the classical amnesic syndrome is an oversimplification: when acquisition of semantic knowledge immediately prior to or following onset of amnesia is studied, it is clear that deficits are present (e.g. see Squire, 1987). Nevertheless, the evidence so far suggests that in schizophrenia semantic information presumably acquired a long time prior to the onset of illness is affected.

EXECUTIVE DYSFUNCTION IN SCHIZOPHRENIA

In schizophrenia, a number of functional imaging studies over the last ten years have suggested the presence of "hypofrontality", although other studies have failed to confirm this (see Andreasen et al., 1992). This has stimulated interest in the possibility of a neuropsychological dysexecutive syndrome in schizophrenia, to the extent that most current theories of schizophrenic symptoms invoke some form of executive dysfunction (see below). As executive function plays a crucial part in the theory of working memory elaborated by Baddeley (1986), and is also currently considered to play an important role in long-term memory (Baddeley & Wilson, 1988; Baddeley, 1990), it is clear that the question of executive deficits in schizophrenia may be relevant to the finding of memory impairment in the disorder.

Poor performance on executive tasks is well documented in schizophrenia (e.g. Goldberg et al., 1987, 1988; Morice, 1990; Liddle & Morris, 1991). What is less clear is whether or not this poor performance reflects the presence of a specific neuropsychological deficit in schizophrenia, or whether it is merely a function of the overall intellectual decline that accompanies the disorder. In fact, none of the above studies made any real attempt to demonstrate that the executive deficits found were present over and above the level of general intellectual impairment of their patient groups. The current state of the evidence bearing on this point can perhaps best be summed up by contrasting, once again, group and single-case neuropsychological approaches.

Saykin et al. (1991) in the study described above, and Braff et al. (1991) in a similar study, administered a wide-ranging battery of neuropsychological tests to groups of 36 and 46 chronic schizophrenic patients respectively, and to normal controls. In both studies the principal test of executive function used was the Wisconsin Card Sorting test. It was found that, as expected, the patients performed significantly more poorly than the controls on all the tests. However, when the schizophrenic patients' scores on the tests were made comparable with each other (using the technique of z-transformation in the study of Saykin et al., and a different method involving demographically corrected t-scores in the study of Braff et al.) it was clear that the patients' performance on the Wisconsin Card Sorting test, whilst significantly poorer than the controls', was only modestly impaired—in fact it did not stand out in any way from their performance on most of the other tests (see Figure 11.3). In the study of Braff and coworkers, performance on another test sensitive to executive impairment—Part B of the Trail Making test—was considerably more impaired; however, this is a timed test.

Shallice, Burgess and Frith (1991) applied the neuropsychological case study approach to five chronically hospitalised schizophrenic patients. The patients were subjected to an extensive battery of tests: these included general measures, such as current and estimated premorbid IQ, and specific tests of visuospatial function, language, memory, and 12 tests generally accepted as being sensitive to executive dysfunction. They found that the patients showed a consistent pattern of severe impairment on the executive tests. In two of the patients this was against a background of preserved IQ, normal performance on tests of visual perception and language, and only scattered poor performance on memory tests. In a third patient, it was part of a pattern of widespread deficits coupled with a marked IQ decline. The remaining two patients showed executive deficits plus some degree of overall intellectual impairment. Shallice and coworkers argued that impaired executive function was thus the common denominator of schizophrenic neuropsychological impairment, being found in the setting of no, some or a great deal of overall impairment. Their findings in three patients who did not show any great overall intellectual deterioration are illustrated in Table 11.2, which highlights the contrast between the performance on executive tests and that on tests of visual perception and language.

IMPLICATIONS FOR UNDERSTANDING THE PATHOLOGICAL BASIS OF SCHIZOPHRENIA

The application of neuropsychological techniques to patients with schizophrenia indicates that there are two axes of impairment. One is a tendency to general intellectual impairment, which is manifested in many patients merely as a fall in IQ, but which becomes more noticeable as the severity and chonicity of illness increase. The other relates to specific neuropsychological deficits. Memory shows pronounced and frequently-observed effects, and executive function may or may not be affected to a comparable extent. It remains uncertain precisely what proportion of patients show specific rather than generalised deficits. It must be acknowledged, too, that in some patients with acute or mild illness there is no obvious impairment. It might be anticipated that this accumulation of knowledge would help to understand the nature of the brain pathology in schizophrenia, and that it would clarify the psychological disturbance which presumably underlies the development of the positive and negative symptoms of the disorder. However, rather than permitting pieces of the jigsaw to be fitted

Table 11.2 Performance of three chronic schizophrenic patients (H.E., H.S. and R.S.), without marked overall intellectual impairment, on executive and other neuropsychological tests (modified from Shallice et al., 1991)

	H.E. (age 44)	H.S. (age 66)	R.S. (age 55)
Visuospatial and language tests			
Visual tests			
Figure–ground discrimination	0	0	0
Dot-centering	0	0	0
Dot-counting	0	0	0
Cube analysis	0	0	0
Unusual views	0	0	3
Usual views	0	0	3
Naming from silhouettes	0	2	2
Copying a figure	0	2	0
Language tests			
Graded spelling	0	0	0
Graded naming	0	0	0
Naming from description	1	0	3
Token test	0	0	3
Tests sensitive to executive impairment			
Wisconsin Card Sorting test	3	0	3
Object-sorting	0	3	0
Cognitive Estimates test	3	0	3
Motor alternation	0	0	3
Money's Road Map test	0	3	3
Personal Orientation test	0	0	3
Self-ordered pointing	0	3	3
Stroop test: word-reading	0	3	3
Stroop test: colour-naming	2	3	0
Trail Making test (B)	3	2	0
FAS test (verbal fluency/1 min)	0	1	2

Scores 0–3 represent impairment indices derived from normative data on each of the tests. 0 = at or above 25th percentile; 1 = 10th to 25th percentile; 2 = 5th to 10th percentile; 3 = below 5th percentile. (Performance on memory tests was intermediate between that on perceptual and language tests and that on executive tests)

together, if anything the neuropsychological findings in schizophrenia make the picture more puzzling.

Many attempts have been made to relate overall intellectual impairment in schizophrenia to the presence of underlying brain dysfunction. In fact, while there has been an intense search for brain pathology in schizophrenia over the last 20 years, only one strong candidate has emerged: this is lateral ventricular enlargement which has finally been established as being present beyond reasonable doubt (Andreasen et al., 1990). Some studies have suggested that general intellectual impairment is associated with lateral ventricular enlargement in schizophrenia, but these are matched by an equal number which have not found this (see Lewis, 1990). The largest and most detailed examination of this issue found no evidence of association between the two (Owens et al., 1985).

If overall intellectual impairment is not closely linked to brain structure in schizophrenia, does the memory deficit found in the disorder point to a localised brain disorder? The schizophrenic pattern of memory impairment differs from that seen in dementia of Alzheimer type in which both short-term and long-term memory are affected at an early stage (Morris & Kopleman, 1986). In a number of ways it appears to resemble the memory impairment of classical amnesic syndrome (leaving aside the complicating factor of semantic memory impairment). Unfortunately, these findings do not make it possible to draw firm conclusions about underlying neuropathology. The amnesic syndrome itself is found in individuals who have sustained various types of brain damage, including Korsakoff's syndrome, bilateral temporal lobectomy, closed head injury (Baddeley et al., 1987) and frontal lobe lesions (Baddeley & Wilson, 1988). While it seems reasonable to speculate that schizophrenic memory impairment is likely to be a manifestation of discrete rather than generalised brain dysfunction, any more specific extrapolation from the neuropsychological to the neuroanatomical must be considered to be a hazardous undertaking.

Similarly, the neuropsychological approach to schizophrenia has so far provided little insight into the way in which symptoms are formed and maintained. It seems fairly clear that general intellectual impairment (Owens & Johnstone, 1980; Mortimer, Lund & McKenna, 1990), memory impairment (Tamlyn et al., 1992), and probably also executive impairment (Morrison-Stewart et al., 1992) are not closely linked with any particular classes of schizophrenic symptom. Clinical–neuropsychological correlations have been found in some studies, particularly with respect to ratings of negative symptoms and formal thought disorder. However, it is far from clear that some or all of these correlations are not artefactual, produced spuriously by common associations of both neuropsychological deficits and symptoms with factors like severity and chronicity of illness (see Mortimer et al., 1990).

Experimental attempts to unravel the neuropsychology of schizophrenia have proceeded alongside theoretical attempts to construct a cognitive neuropsychological model of schizophrenic symptoms (e.g. McKenna, 1987; Cutting, 1990; Gray, Rawlins, Hemsley & Smith, 1991; Frith, 1992). These latter approaches—which all make the central assumption that schizophrenic patients show specific neuropsychological deficits—have generally proved rather disappointing in their power to explain the range of schizophrenic symptoms. One account, however, may hold out some promise of achieving the psychological and neuropsychological integration necessary to arrive at explanations (or at least testable models) of schizophrenic symptoms. Frith (1992) has proposed an ingenious account of certain positive symptoms based on a particular kind of executive dysfunction—defective monitoring of willed intentions. He has also gone further and recognised that there may be potential to be exploited in relating schizophrenic symptoms to a fundamental disorder of knowledge. Drawing on Leslie's (1987) theory of first- and second-order representations of knowledge, he is able to elaborate neat explanations for a wide range of positive and negative schizophrenic symptoms. Of course, in a general sense, the concept of knowledge equates with that of semantic memory. It may thus be that the empirical finding of memory impairment in schizophrenia will ultimately have some impact on theories of schizophrenic symptoms.

IMPLICATIONS FOR CLINICAL PRACTICE

Memory impairment emerges from this discussion as an interesting peak in a landscape of neuropsychological dysfunction that characterises schizophrenia. As yet, however, there are still gulfs to be crossed in relating the schizophrenic memory deficit either to symptoms or to underlying biological brain disease. In the meantime, the findings do have some more immediate implications for clinical practice. The presence or possible presence of a memory impairment needs to be taken into account in working with people who are diagnosed as having schizophrenia, as it will affect the expectations one has of them, the nature of the help they are offered, and the way in which clinicians seek to educate them and their families or carers about their disorder.

Little is known about the natural history of memory and other neuropsychological deficits in schizophrenia, and it is uncertain whether they are static or progressive, or—of particular theoretical and practical importance—whether they can fluctuate, for example worsening and improving along with changes in positive symptoms. At present, however, the suspicion has to be that they are relatively fixed. Goldberg et al. (1993a) examined the effects of clozapine, a new antipsychotic drug which has been shown to be superior to conventional treatment, on symptoms and neuropsychological function in a group of 15 schizophrenic patients. Clozapine brought about highly significant improvements in both positive and negative symptoms. At the same time, however, no corresponding improvement was found in the patients' neuropsychological test performance.

Although it may thus be that the memory and other neuropsychological deficits that accompany schizophrenia are enduring, this does not necessarily mean that they are completely resistant to treatment. As in neurological disorders, they may be susceptible to rehabilitation and skills training. Cognitive remediation in schizophrenia is still in its infancy, and, as Green (1993) has noted in a recent review, the area suffers from a double liability: sparse data and limited theory. Nevertheless, encouraging results have been obtained with training on executive tests, and there are strong suggestions that improvements can be achieved in deficits in other domains of function, including memory.

REFERENCES

Andreasen, N.C., Swayze, V.W., Flaum, M., Yates, W.R., Arndt, S. & McChesney, C. (1990). Ventricular enlargement in schizophrenia evaluated with computed tomographic scanning. *Archives of General Psychiatry*, **47**, 1008–1015.

Andreasen, N.C., Rezai, D., Alliger, R., Swayze, V.W., Flaum, M., Kirchner, P., Cohen, G. & O'Leary, D.S. (1992). Hypofrontality in neuroleptic-naive patients and in patients with chronic schizophrenia. *Archives of General Psychiatry*, **49**, 943–958.

Anthony, J.C., LeReche, L., Niaz, U., Von Korff, M.R. & Folstein, M.F. (1982). Limits of the 'Mini-Mental State' as a screening test of dementia and delirium among hospital patients. *Psychological Medicine*, **12**, 397–408.

Baddeley, A.D. (1982). Amnesia: a minimal model and an interpretation. In L.S. Cermak (ed.), *Human Memory and Amnesia*. Erlbaum, Hillsdale, NJ.

Baddeley, A.D. (1986). *Working Memory*. Clarendon Press: Oxford.

Baddeley, A.D. (1990). *Human Memory: Theory and Practice*. Erlbaum: Hove.

Baddeley, A.D. & Wilson, B. (1988). Frontal amnesia and the dysexecutive syndrome. *Brain and Cognition*, **7**, 212–230.

Baddeley, A.D., Harris, J., Sunderland, A., Watt, K.P. & Wilson, B.A. (1987). Closed head injury and memory. In H.S. Levin, J. Grafman & H.M. Eisenberg (eds), *Neurobehavioral Recovery from Head Injury*. Oxford University Press, New York.

Baddeley, A.D., Emslie, H. & Nimmo-Smith, I. (1992). *The Speed and Capacity of Language Processing (SCOLP) Test*. Thames Valley Test Co., Bury St Edmunds, Suffolk.

Bleuler, E. (1911). *Dementia Praecox, or the Group of Schizophrenias* (translated 1950 by J. Zinkin). International Universities Press, New York.

Braff, D.L., Heaton, R., Kuck, J., Cullum, M., Moranville, J., Grant, I. & Zisook, S. (1991). The generalized pattern of neuropsychological deficits in outpatients with chronic schizophrenia with heterogeneous Wisconsin Card Sorting Test results. *Archives of General Psychiatry*, **48**, 891–898.

Buhrich, N., Crow, T.J., Johnstone, E.C. & Owens, D.G.C. (1988). Age disorientation in chronic schizophrenia is not associated with pre-morbid intellectual impairment or past physical treatments. *British Journal of Psychiatry*, **152**, 466–469.

Calev, A. (1984a). Recall and recognition in mildly disturbed shcizophrenics: the use of matched tasks. *Psychological Medicine*, **14**, 425–429.

Calev, A. (1984b). Recall and recognition in chronic nondemented schizophrenics: use of matched tasks. *Journal of Abnormal Psychology*, **93**, 172–177.

Calev, A. Berlin, H. & Lerer, B. (1987a). Remote and recent memory in long-hospitalised chronic schizophrenics. *Biological Psychiatry*, **22**, 79–85.

Calev, A. Korin, Y., Kugelmass, S. & Lerer, B. (1987b). Performance of chronic schizophrenics on matched word and design recall tasks. *Biological Psychiatry*, **22**, 699–709.

Calev, A., Venables, P.H. & Monk, A.F. (1983). Evidence for distinct memory pathologies in severely and mildly disturbed schizophrenics. *Schizophrenia Bulletin*, **9**, 247–264.

Clare, L., McKenna, P.J., Mortimer, A.M. & Baddeley, A.D. (1993). Long-term memory in schizophrenia: what is impaired and what is preserved? *Neuropsychologia*, **31**, 1225–1241.

Collins, A.M. & Quillian, M.R. (1969). Retrieval time from semantic memory. *Journal of Verbal Learning and Verbal Behavior*, **8**, 240–247.

Cutting, J. (1985). *The Psychology of Schizophrenia*. Churchill Livingstone, Edinburgh.

Cutting, J. (1990). *The Right Hemisphere and Psychiatric Disorders*. Oxford University Press, Oxford.

Eysenck, H.J. & Frith, C.D. (1977). *Reminiscence, Motivation and Personality*. Plenum Press, New York/London.

Folstein, M.F., Folstein, S.E. & McHugh, P.R. (1975). 'Mini-Mental State': a practical method for grading the cognitive state of patients for the clinician. *Journal of Psychiatric Research*, **12**, 189–198.

Frith, C.D. (1992). *The Cognitive Neuropsychology of Schizophrenia*. Erlbaum, Hove.

Goldberg, T.E., Greenberg, R.D., Griffin, S.J., Gold, J.M., Kleinman, J.E., Pickar, D., Schulz, S.C. & Weinberger, D.R. (1993a). The effect of clozapine on cognition and psychiatric symptoms in patients with schizophrenia. *British Journal of Psychiatry*, **162**, 43–48.

Goldberg, T.E., Kelsoe, J.R., Weinberger, D.R., Pliskin, N.H., Kirwin, P.D. & Berman, K.R. (1988). Performance of schizophrenic patients on putative neuropsychological tests of frontal lobe function. *International Journal of Neuroscience*, **42**, 51–58.

Goldberg, T.E., Ragland, J.D., Torrey, E.F., Gold, J.M., Bigelow, L.B. and Weinberger, D.F. (1990). Neuropsychological assessment of monozygotic twins discordant for schizophrenia. *Archives of General Psychiatry*, **47**, 1066–1072.

Goldberg, T.E., Torrey, E.F., Gold, J.M., Ragland, J.D., Bigelow, L.B. & Weinberger, D.R. (1993b). Learning and memory in monozygotic twins discordant for schizophrenia. *Psychological Medicine*, **23**, 71–85.

Goldberg, T.E., Weinberger, D.R., Berman, K.F., Pliskin, N.H. & Podd, M.H. (1987). Further evidence for dementia of prefrontal type in schizophrenia? A controlled study of teaching the Wisconsin Card Sorting Test. *Archives of General Psychiatry*, **44**, 1008–1014.

Goldberg, T.E., Weinberger, D.R., Pliskin, N.H., Berman, K.F. & Podd, M.H. (1989). Recall memory deficit in schizophrenia: a possible manifestation of prefrontal dysfunction. *Schizophrenia Research*, **2**, 251–257.

Golding, E. (1989). *The Middlesex Elderly Assessment of Mental State*. Thames Valley Test Co, Bury St Edmunds, Suffolk.

Goldman-Rakic, P.S. & Friedman, H.R. (1991). The circuitry of working memory revealed by anatomy and metabolic imaging. In H.S. Levin, H.M. Eisenberg & A.L. Benton (eds), *Frontal Lobe Function and Dysfunction*, Oxford University Press, Oxford.

Gras-Vincendon, A., Danion, J.-M., Grange, D., Bilik, M., Willard-Schroader, D., Sichel, J.-P. & Singer, L. Explicit memory, repetition priming, and cognitive skill learning in schizophrenia (submitted for publication).

Gray, J.A., Rawlins, J.N.P., Hemsley, D.R. & Smith, A.D. (1991). The neuropsychology of schizophrenia. *Behavioral and Brain Sciences*, **14**, 1–84.

Green, M.F. (1993). Cognitive remediation in schizophrenia: is it time yet? *American Journal of Psychiatry*, **150**, 178–187.

Gruzelier, J., Seymour, K., Wilson, L., Jolley, A. & Hirsch, S. (1988). Impairment on neuropsychological tests of temporohippocampal and frontohippocampal function in remitting schizophrenia and affective disorders. *Archives of General Psychiatry*, **45**, 623–629.

Heinrichs, R.W. & Bury, A.S. (1991). Impaired implicit memory in schizophrenia: a selective deficit? *Schizophrenia Research*, **4**, 385.

Hodges, J.R., Salmon, D.P. & Butters, N. (1992). Semantic memory impairment in Alzheimer's disease: failure of access or degraded knowledge? *Neuropsychologia*, **30**, 301–314.

King, D.J. (1990). The effect of neuroleptics on cognitive and psychomotor function. *British Journal of Psychiatry*, **157**, 799–811.

Koh, S.D. (1978). Remembering of verbal materials by schizophrenic young adults. In S. Schwartz (ed.), *Language and Cognition in Schizophrenia*, Wiley, New York.

Kolb, B. & Wishaw, I.Q. (1983). Performance of schizophrenic patients on tests sensitive to right or left frontal, temporal or parietal function in neurological patients. *Journal of Nervous and Mental Disease*, **171**, 435–443.

Kraepelin, E. (1913). *Dementia Praecox and Paraphrenia* (translated 1919 by R.M. Barclay). Livingstone, Edinburgh.

Leslie, A.M. (1987). Pretence and representation: the origins of 'theory of mind'. *Psychological Review*, **94**, 412–426.

Lewis, S.W. (1990). Computerised tomography in schizophrenia 15 years on. *British Journal of Psychiatry*, **157**, suppl. 9, 16–24

Liddle, P.F. & Crow, T.J. (1984). Age disorientation in chronic schizophrenia is associated with global intellectual impairment. *British Journal of Psychiatry*, **144**, 193–199.

Liddle, P.F. & Morris, D.L. (1991). Schizophrenic symptoms and frontal lobe performance. *British Journal of Psychiatry*, **158**, 340–345.

McKenna, P.J. (1987). Pathology, phenomenology and the dopamine hypothesis of schizophrenia. *British Journal of Psychiatry*, **151**, 288–301.

McKenna, P.J., Tamlyn, D., Lund, C.E., Mortimer, A.M., Hammond, S. & Baddeley, A.D. (1990). Amnesic syndrome in schizophrenia. *Psychological Medicine*, **20**, 967–972.

McKenna, P.J., Mortimer, A.M. & Hodges, J.R. (1994). Semantic memory and schizophrenia. In A. David & J. Cutting (eds), *The Neuropsychology of Schizophrenia*. Erlbaum, Hove.

Morice, R. (1990). Cognitive inflexibility and pre-frontal dysfunction in schizophrenia and mania. *British Journal of Psychiatry*, **157**, 50–54.

Morice, R. & Delahunty, A. (in press). Working memory impairment in schizophrenia. *Psychological Medicine*.

Morris, R.G. & Kopelman, M.D. (1986). The memory deficits in Alzheimer-type dementia: a review. *Quarterly Journal of Experimental Psychology*, **38A**, 575–602.

Morrison-Stewart, S.L., Williamson, P.C., Corning, W.C., Kutcher, S.P., Snow, W.G. & Merskey, H. (1992). Frontal and non-frontal neuropsychological test performance and clinical symptomatology. *Psychological Medicine*, **22**, 353–359.

Mortimer, A.M., Lund, C.E. & McKenna, P.J. (1990). The positive:negative dichotomy in schizophrenia. *British Journal of Psychiatry*, **156**, 41–49.

Myles-Worsley, M. (1991). Implicit versus explicit memory in schizophrenia. *Schizophrenia Research*, **4**, 389.

Nelson, H.E., Pantelis, C., Carruthers, J., Speller, J., Baxendale, S. & Barnes, T.R.E. (1990). Cognitive functioning and symptomatology in chronic schizophrenia. *Psychological Medicine*, **20**, 357–365.

Owens, D.G.C. & Johnstone, E.C. (1980). The disabilities of chronic schizophrenia—their nature and the factors contributing to their development. *British Journal of Psychiatry*, **136**, 384–393.

Owens, D.G.C, Johnstone, E.C., Crow, T.J., Frith, C.D., Jagoe, J.R. & Kreel, L. (1985). Lateral ventricular size in schizophrenia: relationship to the disease process and its clinical manifestations. *Psychological Medicine*, **15**, 27–41.

Payne, R.W. (1973). Cognitive abnormalities. In H.J. Eysenck (ed.), *Handbook of Abnormal Psychology*. Pitman, London.

Randolph, C., Gold, J.M., Goldberg, T.E. & Weinberger, D.R. (1991). Implicit memory function in schizophrenia. *Schizophrenia Research*, **4**, 391.

Saykin, A.J., Gur, R.C., Gur, R.E., Mozley, P.D., Mozley, L.H., Resnick, S.M., Kester, B. & Stafiniak, P. (1991). Neuropsychological function in schizophrenia: selective impairment in memory and learning. *Archives of General Psychiatry*, **48**, 618–624.

Shallice, T., Burgess, P.W. & Frith, C.D. (1991). Can the neuropsychological case-study approach be applied to schizophrenia? *Psychological Medicine*, **21**, 661–673.

Squire, L.R. (1987). *Memory and Brain*. Oxford University Press, Oxford.

Squire, L.R. & Cohen, N. (1979). Memory and amnesia: resistance to disruption develops. *Neuroscience*, **11**, 170–175.

Stevens, M., Crow, T.J., Bowman, M.J. & Coles, R.C. (1978). Age disorientation in schizophrenia: a constant prevalence of 25 per cent in a chronic mental hospital population? *British Journal of Psychiatry*, **133**, 130–136.

Tamlyn, D., McKenna, P.J., Mortimer, A.M., Lund, C.E., Hammond, S. & Baddeley, A.D. (1992). Memory impairment in schizophrenia: its extent, affiliations and neuropsychological character. *Psychological Medicine*, **22**, 101–115.

Wilson, B.A., Cockburn, J.M. & Baddeley, A.D. (1985). *The Rivermead Behavioural Memory Test*. Thames Valley Test Co., Bury St Edmunds, Suffolk.

Wilson, B.A., Cockburn, J.M., Baddeley, A.D. & Hiorns, R. (1989). The development and validation of a test battery for detecting and monitoring everyday memory problems. *Journal of Clinical and Experimental Neuropsychology*, **11**, 855–870.

Yates, A.J. (1973). Abnormalities of psychomotor functions. In Eysenck (ed.), *Handbook of Abnormal Psychology*. Pitman, London.

Chapter 12

Depression and Anxiety

Fraser N. Watts
MRC Applied Psychology Unit, Cambridge, UK

INTRODUCTION

The focus of this chapter will be on the impairment of memory performance in people who are depressed or anxious. There is reason to think that both depression and anxiety are associated with impairments in performance on a very broad range of cognitive tasks, and memory is among these. Though emotionally-based memory problems are generally less severe than neuropsychological ones, there are several reasons why they need to be considered in a handbook such as this.

Many of the patients who present with memory problems are likely to be depressed or anxious, whatever other difficulties they may have. The first diagnostic question that arises is whether the memory problems can be explained entirely in terms of the patient's emotional state, or whether organic factors are involved. However, whatever the answer to this question, emotional factors are still relevant. Even where an organic basis to the memory problem is detectable, the memory problems may be further exacerbated by the patient's depression and anxiety. The proper clinical management of the memory problem will often depend on taking this into account. Alternatively, if an organic basis of the memory problem is ruled out, it becomes even more important to look at the emotional aspects.

Questions about whether or not organic factors are involved might arise with an elderly person complaining of memory problems. Thus, the question might be whether he or she was showing the early signs of Alzheimer's disease, or was "just depressed". A variety of tests of memory have been developed to assist with this differential diagnosis, the assumption being that depression is associated with a lesser degree of memory impairment than organic memory disorders.

Handbook of Memory Disorders. Edited by A.D. Baddeley, B.A. Wilson and F.N. Watts.
© 1995 John Wiley & Sons Ltd.

While this assumption is probably correct, it would be a mistake to imagine that the performance of depressed patients on memory tests is normal and satisfactory. This chapter will describe and analyse the memory performance of such patients, though questions of distinguishing between organic and functional memory problems are dealt with more explicitly in Chapter 15.

When Alzheimer's disease is ruled out, the presenting memory problems will at least partly be those that are associated with "normal ageing" (see Chapter 8). However, given the frequency of depression in old age, it is quite likely that the elderly person will also be depressed, and the presenting memory problems will then be a compound of those associated with ageing and with depression. This is actually a "grey" area that is not well understood, as studies on memory in normal ageing have generally not taken care to ensure that the subjects studied are not also depressed. Indeed, it is possible that a great deal of what passes in the literature for the memory problems associated with old age is in fact a product of depression. Even if Alzheimer's disease is confirmed, it is highly probable that, at least in the early stages, the elderly person will be depressed about their failing mental powers and that this depression will exacerbate the memory problems.

Sometimes, patients who present with memory problems are well aware that they are depressed or anxious, and realise that this is the basis of their memory problems. Of course, patients may be wrong in putting their memory problems down to their emotional state, but in general there is a bias in patients towards organic explanations. Depressed patients frequently attribute their cognitive problems to a permanent loss of mental powers, and this causes them additional distress. However, it is also possible that patients "resist" an organic diagnosis even when this is obvious to everyone else, a stance that can be seen as a "defensive" move to ward off the distress associated with admitting organically based cognitive decline.

People most commonly come to the clinic with memory problems as their focal complaint when adequate memory functioning is important to their work. College students are among these, but those with intellectually demanding jobs may also present with worries about their memory performance. The fact that memory is important for everyday functioning can create a particular performance anxiety about memory. Slight memory problems can be perceived as much more serious than they really are, because of the anxiety associated with them. The perceived problems then become a source of further anxiety or depression, which can in turn exacerbate the actual memory problems.

There is theoretical as well as practical interest in looking at the memory problems associated with depression and anxiety. Memory problems arise in a great variety of contexts, and with very different aetiologies. Despite this, amnesias of different origins are often strikingly similar in their cognitive characteristics. Despite this, it would be wrong to assume that *all* memory problems are essentially similar in their characteristics. Those associated with depression and anxiety seem likely, on the face of things, to be somewhat different from those that have a neuropsychological basis. Hence, examining the nature of these memory problems may make a valuable contribution to developing a taxonomy of memory problems.

There is a broad range of memory phenomena associated with emotional states, which have been comprehensively reviewed in the recent *Handbook of Emotion and Memory Research and Theory* (Christianson, 1992). This chapter will have a relatively circumscribed focus. It will not be concerned with the autobiographical memory phenomena that arise in emotional states. For example, in post-traumatic stress disorder there are frequently disorders in the recall of traumatic events, most commonly of abnormal intrusiveness, though sometimes of repression (see Chapters 14 and 22). Also, there is a tendency for people with emotional disorders to selectively recall events that are consonant with their current mood state. This is a reasonably well replicated phenomenon in depression (for reviews see Teasdale & Barnard, 1993; Blaney, 1986; Dalgleish & Watts, 1990; Ucros, 1989). There is some evidence for a comparable phenomenon of mood-congruent memory in anxiety (Dalgleish & Watts, 1990; Eysenck, 1992) but evidence for this is much more patchy.

Though the issues raised by memory problems in states of anxiety and depression are similar, the literature on the two has proceeded rather separately, and has different strengths and weaknesses. Studies of memory problems in depression have more commonly focused on the simple question of whether such problems exist. Only in the last ten years, largely influenced by Ellis' processing resources theory (Ellis & Ashbrook, 1988), has the literature on impairments of memory in depression begun to have a theoretical focus; in contrast, the theory of Spence and Spence (1966) about how anxiety affected learning gave the anxiety literature a stronger theoretical focus at a much earlier stage. Because the effects of anxiety are much more selective than those of depression, and because anxiety often enhances memory performance rather than impairing it, the anxiety literature has not had to deal so much with the question of whether any impairment of anxiety on performance is due to low motivation, poor verbal productivity, or cautious response criteria.

This chapter focuses first on the memory problems associated with depression, because depressed patients are much more likely than anxious patients to present in the clinic complaining of memory problems. The literature on the effects of anxiety on memory will then be reviewed more briefly, largely to examine the similarities and differences.

ARE THERE MEMORY DISORDERS ASSOCIATED WITH DEPRESSION AND ANXIETY?

The first question about the relationship of depression and anxiety to memory that concerns the clinician is whether they really do produce an impairment in memory performance. It would be widely accepted that people who are depressed and anxious complain of poor memory, but is their memory really affected? It is a question that has been tackled more explicitly for depression than for anxiety.

Investigating this requires the use of designs that ensure that these emotional states are not being confounded with differences in intellectual ability. The majority of studies on anxiety have used correlational designs, whereas group designs have been used much more commonly in studies of depression. Both designs are, of course, perfectly acceptable, though correlational designs tend to be less sensitive. However, they raise different issues about how to control for other, extraneous variables which may be accounting for the results. To be specific, as Eysenck (1977, p. 232) points out, there is some evidence that scores on the Manifest Anxiety Scale (Taylor, 1953) are negatively correlated with intelligence. However, most studies have made no attempt to establish that the lower memory performance associated with anxiety is specifically due to the anxiety, rather than being due to undetected variation in intelligence. The group designs used in studies of memory problems in depression (see Watts, 1993) have more commonly matched groups on educational level or intelligence as a way of controlling for this.

A further complication is that there is evidence (e.g. Hodges & Durham, 1972) that the effects of anxiety on task performance are dependent on patients' level of general ability. Anxiety can enhance performance, but this is most likely to occur in high-ability subjects. In low-ability subjects, anxiety either has no effect, or a deleterious one. Because the majority of anxiety studies have been carried out on students, whereas more depression studies have been carried out on clinical patients, the intellectual levels of the subjects used in the two literatures are probably not comparable.

Those who are sceptical about whether depression is associated with memory problems have generally held one or both of the following positions:

1. Depressed people complain about their memory, but when it is objectively tested it is found to be intact.
2. People who are depressed may perform badly on memory tests, but this is not because their memory is impaired; it is just that their motivational problems or lack of confidence prevent them producing the memory material to which they have access.

There is a foundation of truth in these hypotheses. Depression seems to lead people to perceive their memory performance as being worse than it actually is. Also, it is probably very often the case that depressed patients underperform on memory tests through lack of motivation or confidence. However, a careful examination of the research evidence makes it difficult to sustain the position that there is *nothing more* than this to the apparent memory problems associated with depression.

The perceptions of depressed people certainly do not constitute an accurate guide to the extent to which they really have memory problems. Watts (1993, p. 115) summarises a considerable body of evidence showing that depressed people's complaints about their memory performance are more closely related to their mood state than to their objective performance on memory tests. For example, Williams, Little, Scates & Blockman (1987) found that depression was associated with memory complaints but not with significant impairments in objective memory performance.

There is some evidence (Chandler & Gerndt, 1989; Niederehe & Yoder, 1989) that there is a particular tendency in people who are both depressed *and* elderly for complaints about memory to outstrip objective memory problems. Watts (1993, p. 116) drew attention to the fact that, of studies that have failed to show that depression is associated with poor performance on memory tests, a disproportionate number appear to have been conducted on elderly subjects. It therefore seems that the clinician needs to be particularly wary, with elderly patients, of assuming that memory complaints are a good indication of actual memory performance.

Nevertheless, there is an abundance of evidence, from well-controlled studies, of an association between depression and poor memory performance. The controlled studies of clinical depression fall mainly into two groups. One compares depressed patients with matched normal controls. An early, influential study of this kind was that of Cronholm and Ottosson (1961) using matched surgical patients, a study that was substantially replicated by Sternberg and Jarvik (1976). Depression was found to be associated with poorer performance on memory for word pairs, for simple figures and for personal data about fictitious people, and this was found at both immediate and delayed testing.

A second kind of study compared the performance of depressed people when ill with their performance when recovered (e.g. Stromgren, 1977). Though the possibility of practice effects makes such studies inconclusive, the results from them corroborate the general picture of an association of depression with impaired performance on memory tests.

More recently, there have been studies showing that induced depressed mood produces an impairment of memory performance (e.g. Ellis, Thomas & Rodriguez, 1984). Studies of this kind have been reviewed by Ellis and Ashbrook (1988). The direction of causal effects in such studies is obviously much clearer, though there is always an element of uncertainty about the extent to which induced depressed mood corresponds to naturally occurring depression. Evidence from these various sources is sufficient to conclude that depression really is associated with poor memory performance.

Next, there is the question of whether this represents a memory *impairment* in depression, or whether poor memory performance can be explained in other ways. This latter idea has sufficient foundation in research evidence to give it plausibility. For example, there is evidence that errors of omission are particularly characteristic of depression (Henry, Weingartner & Murphy, 1973; Whitehead, 1973; Dannenbaum, Parkinson & Inman, 1988) and this is consistent with the view that depressed patients underperform for motivational reasons. However, Leight and Ellis (1981) found that induced depressed mood was associated with poor memory performance even when a forced-recall paradigm was used.

Also, Watts and Sharrock (1987) found that depressed and normal subjects differed as much in a cued recall test requiring minimal responses, as they did on free recall. There is also evidence (Watts, Morris & MacLeod, 1987) that depressed patients are impaired even on recognition memory.

A related hypothesis, that depressed patients underperform on memory tests because of a conservative response bias, has recently been put forward by Johnson and Magaro (1987, p. 32). Though there is no reason to dispute that there *is* a conservative response bias associated with depression, this does not fully explain the poor memory performance associated with depression. Studies of recognition memory provide the most appropriate methodology for investigating this. Unfortunately, the evidence is somewhat conflicting. Some studies have found depression to be associated with cautious response criteria, rather than discriminability (Miller & Lewis, 1977; Dunbar & Lishman, 1984). However, other studies have found that depression is associated with poor discriminability in recognition memory (Silberman et al., 1983; Watts, Morris & MacLeod, 1987). Which pattern of results is obtained may depend on procedural details. Specifically, Watts, Morris and MacLeod (1987) found that when subjects vocalised words after auditory presentation, depression was not associated with increased false alarms, though increased false alarms *were* found when vocalisation was not required. This is a matter which requires further investigation to disentangle. However, as Watts, Morris and MacLeod (1987) argued, there is at least some recognition memory data which is not explicable in terms of the response bias hypothesis.

There is one major body of research evidence which suggests that the memory problems of depressed patients are *selective*, in that they depend on the hedonic tone of the material concerned. The research literature on mood congruent memory in depression is very extensive, and several reviews are available (e.g. Teasdale & Barnard, 1993; Blaney, 1986; Bower, 1987; Dalgleish & Watts, 1990; Ellis & Ashbrook, 1989; Johnson & Magaro, 1987; Singer & Salovey, 1988; Ucross, 1989). Nondepressed subjects tend to show a memory bias in favour of positive material, whereas depressed subjects either fail to show this bias or show a bias towards negative material. Unfortunately, relatively few mood-congruency studies have also included neutral material. From those that have (e.g. Teasdale & Russell, 1983; Dunbar & Lishman, 1984) it is not clear that depressed patients' memory for positive material is any worse than their memory for neutral material. However, it is clear that negatively-toned material constitutes an exception to the general finding that depressed people perform poorly on memory tests.

This has important clinical and theoretical implications. Clearly, it makes it necessary to reject any simplistic hypothesis that depressed people are simply incapable of remembering as well as normal controls. It also has considerable potential value in memory assessment, though one that has not yet been fully exploited. Intact memory for negatively-toned material is, of course, one key way in which the memory problems of depressed patients differ from those of other amnesiacs. It would thus be particularly valuable to include such material in diagnostic tests seeking to elucidate whether a memory problem was organically based or due to depression. Though most memory tests designed to differentiate between organic and functional memory problems have used neutral material, it is arguable that negatively-toned material would do the job better.

ANALYSIS OF MEMORY DEFICITS IN DEPRESSION

In characterising the memory deficits in depression, or any other clinical condition, it is particularly interesting to understand the *limits* of the memory disorder; i.e. which tasks show an impairment and which do not. Such "differential deficit" hypotheses are the stuff of abnormal psychology, though the methodological problems in investigating them are formidable (Chapman & Chapman, 1973; Watts, 1989), and very few studies even attempt to deal with them. Not surprisingly, the literature is somewhat confused; it would make a simpler story if there were some tasks which *always* showed an effect of depression, and other tasks which *never* showed such an effect. Unfortunately, the situation is that some tasks are more likely to show an effect of depression than others. No doubt the memory problems of depressed patients vary from one case to another. However, the following review should enable the clinician to identify where the memory problems of a particular depressed patient are most likely to lie.

Short-Term Versus Long-Term Memory

The trend is for depressed subjects to show relatively intact performance on short-term memory tasks, but to be more consistently impaired on long-term memory tasks. The relevant studies do not necessarily presuppose an absolute distinction between two kinds of memory, short-term and long-term. However, they are consistent with the general proposition that the more long-term memory is required, the more likely there is to be a deficit.

Apparently the only study of sensory memory in depression is that of Colby and Gotlib (1988). They used a modified Sperling (1960) task in which a 3 × 4 array of characters was displayed. Under some conditions, subjects had to recall a specific row; in others, they had to recall the total display. The partial report data are normally assumed to be mainly a reflection of sensory store processes, while report of the whole display is assumed to reflect the capacity of short-term memory stores. Depressed subjects showed no impairment in partial recall, and thus would be regarded as having satisfactory sensory memory. However, they showed significant impairment in recall of the whole display, indicating limits in short-term store.

Also relevant to sensory memory are studies of the "memory comparison stage" (i.e. scanning and retrieval) in Sternberg's (1969) "additive factors" approach. Performance on memory comparison tasks can be subdivided further into indices of speed of scanning, and performance on nonscanning stages (encoding, binary decision, and response output). Most studies (Glass et al., 1981; Hilbert, Niederehe & Kahn, 1976; Koh & Wolpert, 1983) have found no association between depression and slow scanning performance. However, a more recent study by Brand and Jolles (1987) was able to demonstrate slower scanning in depressed subjects. They suggest that this may have been due to their employment of newly developed versions of the memory comparison task that were shorter and designed to be more acceptable in the clinic. There is more support for depression being associated with impaired performance on the nonscanning aspect of memory comparison tasks (e.g. Glass et al., 1981; Brand & Jolles, 1987). Glass and colleagues comment that depressed patients normally adopt a conservative response strategy in which they maintain accuracy at the expense of speed. Brand and Jolles found evidence that depression was associated with a less efficient search strategy involving greater reliance on controlled as opposed to automatic processing.

Another task which has been widely used in the assessment of short-term memory is *digit span*. The majority of studies have found no association between depression and digit span performance (Calev et al., 1989; Gass & Russell, 1986; Kopelman, 1986; Whitehead, 1973). Kopelman (1986) also examined "supra-span" (i.e. recall of a series two digits longer than digit span) and found no association with depression. Colby and Gotlib (1988) examined memory for series of digits, either with no delay, or with delays of 20 or 30 seconds. Under the normal condition of recall without delay, the performance of depressed and control subjects was virtually identical. However, a difference between groups appeared when a delay in recall was introduced. In so far as digit span can be taken as an indication of short-term memory, this is fairly clear evidence that short-term memory is generally intact, whereas difficulties arise with slightly longer-term recall. This claim is also supported by the work of Channon, Baker and Robertson (1993b) who tested depressed patients on a variety of working memory tests and found them to be impaired only when the central executive was involved, not on specific tests of articulatory loop functions. The only somewhat contradictory finding is apparently that of Dannenbaum, Parkinson and Inman (1988) who found that elderly depressed subjects showed an impairment on a *letter* span task.

The relevance of delay to depressive memory deficits is confirmed by Cohen et al. (1982) who found that depressed patients were impaired only in *delayed* recall of a set of trigrams. Also consistent with this general picture is the evidence of Henry, Weingartner and Murphy (1973) using a serial learning task, that the deficit of depressed patients appeared only from the second trial onwards. One plausible explanation of why long-term memory should be impaired, when short-term memory is apparently not, is that rehearsal processes do not operate normally in depression; i.e. depressed subjects either do not rehearse, or do not derive the usual benefit from it. It is consistent with this view that Berndt and Berndt (1980) found, on a Brown–Petersen task, that the differences between depressed and control subjects disappeared when rehearsal was prevented by requiring subjects to count backwards.

Thus it seems that it may make a critical difference to the detection of memory impairment in depression whether or not there is even a small (e.g. 30 seconds) delay, the introduction of a longer delay, such as 30 minutes, does not appear to introduce any additional problems. This has been found in several studies that have compared immediate with delayed recall of prose material (Coughlan & Hollows, 1984; Kopelman, 1986; Stromgren, 1977; Whitehead, 1973). The same is true of studies of delayed recall of a novel name and address (Kopelman, 1986), word lists in a Brown–Petersen task (Dannenbaum, Parkinson & Inman, 1988), and a battery of tests including word-pairs, figures and personal data (Sternberg & Jarvik, 1976). Though many of these studies have compared what is called "immediate" recall with delayed recall, in many cases the material has been sufficiently extended to exceed the limits of short-term memory in terms of quantity. Also, the duration of presentation has in many cases exceeded the temporal limits of short-term recall.

Of particular interest, because it included an alcoholic control group, is the study of Query and Megran (1984), using the Rey Auditory–Verbal Learning Test. Both depression and alcoholism affected initial recall. However, alcoholism, but not depression, was associated with a further impairment as a result of adding an interference task. It may be one of the relatively unusual features of the memory problems associated with depression that the long delays do not produce any greater deficit than very brief ones. The comparison of performance at different delays may therefore be of particular diagnostic value.

Comparison of Different Indices of Memory

Another approach to the analysis of memory deficits is to compare different indices of memory, to see which yield the greatest deficits. One comparison which has often been employed in the memory disorder literature is that between free recall and recognition. The literature on recognition memory, which has already been mentioned in connection with the question of a possible conservative response style in depression, is somewhat ambiguous. Deficits in recognition memory are demonstrable in depression, and these can be shown, on signal detection analysis to be attributable to d' rather than to β (Watts, Morris & MacLeod, 1987). However, it is clear that problems with recognition memory are less severe, and arise less often than those with free recall. Whitehead (1973) found that recovery from depression was associated with improvement in recall on a serial learning task, but not in recognition memory. Calev and Erwin (1985) and Watts and Sharrock (1987) have also both found depression to be associated with a deficit in free recall but not in recognition.

Unfortunately, the interpretation of this finding is not entirely clear. Some have argued that free recall requires a retrieval process whereas recognition memory does not. On that argument, it might be concluded that depressed subjects have a specific problem with retrieval. However, it also needs to be borne in mind that free recall is more generally demanding of processing resources than is recognition. That, rather than any specific retrieval deficit, may be the explanation of why problems are more likely to arise with free recall.

Another interesting comparison is of "explicit" with "implicit" measures of learning. As is apparent from other chapters in this handbook, the distinction has aroused considerable interest because many amnesic patients appear to have intact performance on implicit learning tasks, whereas performance on explicit learning tasks is impaired. The question arises of whether this is also true of the memory problems found in depression. Unfortunately, the relevant evidence is so far conflicting. Three studies (Danion et al., 1991; Hertel & Hardin, 1990; Peters, 1992) have found depression to be associated with deficits on explicit but not implicit tasks. However, a fourth study (Elliott & Greene, 1992) has found that depression was associated with a deficit on both explicit and implicit tasks. The discrepancy between the findings of Danion and colleagues and those of Elliott and Greene is particularly puzzling as the experiments are similar in many ways. Both studied clinical depressives, and both used word-stem completion as a measure of implicit memory. The discrepancy between the two studies also seems unlikely to be due to statistical power, as Danion and coworkers used larger groups of subjects than did Elliott and Greene. The study of Hertel and Hardin was rather different, in that it used students with high scores on the Beck Depression Inventory, and the implicit task required subjects to spell homophones.

At present, the balance of evidence suggests that if implicit tests of learning show an effect of depression at all, they do so less than explicit tests of recall. This seems to be one way in which the memory problems associated with depression are qualitatively similar to those associated with other amnesias.

Structure of Materials

When surveying inconsistencies in the literature between experiments that have and have not found an effect of depression on memory, it is a plausible interpretation that experiments that have failed to find an effect have often used highly structured material such as sentences or passages of prose (Ellis & Ashbrook, 1988). A substantial number of studies have investigated the hypothesis that depressed patients are poor at structuring materials, and show their most serious deficits with unstructured materials.

One specific hypothesis, which has been tested in several experiments, is that depressed subjects cluster material in terms of semantic categories less than control subjects do. Thus, for example, if a list is presented containing words drawn from several different semantic categories, and these are presented in "unclustered" order, it is possible to examine the extent to which these are recalled in clustered form. A series of studies have found that depressed subjects are less likely to show clustered recall (Calev & Erwin, 1985; Koh,

Kayton & Berry, 1973; Russell & Beekhuis, 1976; Weingartner et al., 1981). The only negative result here is apparently that of Silberman, Weingartner, Targum and Byrnes (1985). The relative lack of clustering at recall by depressed subjects is thus a reasonably well replicated finding.

A related line of research has investigated differential recall for word lists that vary in their level of structural organisation, though results here have been much more conflicting. A seminal experiment of Weingartner et al. (1981) found that depressed and control subjects differed little in their recall of words presented in clustered form, but that depressed subjects were at a disadvantage in recall of unclustered lists. Presumably, they were less able to impose structure for themselves when presented with unstructured material. However, several studies have now obtained the opposite result of depressed patients showing greater relative deficits for structured materials—i.e. Watts, Dalgleish, Bourke and Healy (1990) comparing clustered with unclustered lists, Peters (1992) comparing semantically related with unrelated words, and Levy and Maxwell (1968) comparing different levels of approximation to text.

There are also studies that have found greatest relative deficit for *medium* levels of structure. Watts et al. (1990) found this for medium approximation to text, compared with low or high approximation. They suggested that medium-structure lists may best repay efforts at structuring. Lists with no latent structure may show little dividend from efforts at structuring at presentation. On the other hand, lists presented in highly structured form do not require much ability to structure. Channon, Baker and Robertson (1993a) obtained results which were consistent with this view. The clearest difference between depressed and control subjects was for word lists in which words from different semantic categories were presented in random order. Differences were less marked both for lists in which words were clustered at presentation and for lists in which the words were semantically unrelated. Again, the intermediate level of structure seemed to show the most effect of depression.

The hypothesised deficit of depressed subjects in structuring material presented to them has also been explored in terms of how they handle prose material. Watts and Cooper (1989), using clinically depressed subjects, were able to demonstrate a deficit in recalling the prose passage "Circle Island", even though deficits with prose materials have been reported relatively rarely. Of particular interest was the fact that depressed subjects did not show the normal tendency for better recall of units of the story that were central to its gist. However, it was not the case that depressed subjects were relatively random in what units they recalled, as the effects of imageability of units on their recall was just as marked in depressed as in control subjects. The failure to show preferential recall of units central to the gist of the story suggests that depressed subjects were not processing the passage in a way that led them to discern its overall structure and to identify the place of individual units within it.

Similar conclusions can be drawn from the work of Ellis, Varner, Becker & Ottaway (1995), which varied whether or not a title was presented at the beginning of the story. Depressed subjects were at a particular disadvantage, compared with controls, when the title was omitted. They were also at a relative disadvantage when a different story had been presented immediately previously, suggesting a difficulty in switching from one structure to another. This study is also generally consistent with the view that depressed patients do not have the resources to structure materials adequately, especially under conditions where this is relatively demanding.

One of the interesting issues raised by the studies reviewed in this section is to what extent they present a clinic analogue of a memory problem that arises in real-life settings. For example, the failure of depressed patients to show the normal bias towards selective recall of important things may arise, not just with stories like "Circle Island", but in a wide range of everyday settings. If so, the practical handicap created by depressive memory problems may be much greater than sometimes appears from formal testing in the clinic.

Experimental Manipulation of Effortful Processing

A related approach to manipulating the processing effort involved in memory tasks has made use of the sentence-completion task, first used by Tyler, Hertel, McCallum and Ellis (1979) with normal subjects, though here again rather conflicting results have been obtained. Sentences are presented in which the last word has to be completed by the subject. In some cases, the last word fits easily and the sentence can be completed with low effort (e.g. "The frightened girl was awakened by the ... *dream*"). In other cases, there is no single word that obviously fits the gap, so more effort is needed to select an appropriate one. Normal subjects show better recall of words which have been used to complete "high effort" sentences. Ellis, Thomas and Rodriguez (1984) predicted, and found, that depressed subjects would show greatest relative impairment, compared with controls, for "high effort" sentences. They also obtained similar findings in an experiment in which "base" sentences (e.g. "The hungry child opened the door") were compared with "elaborated" sentences (e.g. "The hungry child opened the door of the refrigerator"). Normal subjects showed better recall for target adjectives from elaborated sentences than from base sentences, but depressed subjects did not show this. The assumption is that depressed subjects do not apply the processing resources to elaborated sentences that, in normal subjects, are responsible for the better recall.

These results of Ellis and colleagues were obtained with experimentally induced depression. Unfortunately, there have been difficulties in replicating the findings with other groups of subjects. It seems that they do *not* extend to students with high scores on the Beck Depression Inventory. Potts, Camp and Coyne (1989) attempted to replicate the differential effect of base and elaborated sentences with such depressed subjects, and failed to do so. Also, Hertel and Rude (1991a) carried out a series of studies attempting to replicate the sentence-completion effect, and failed to show that it was affected by depression. It can be concluded with reasonable confidence that the critical factor in this failure to replicate was the choice of subject population, because Hertel and Rude (1991a), in their second experiment, studied both a high BDI group and a group with experimentally induced depression. They were able to replicate the findings of Ellis, Thomas and Rodriguez, (1984) for the latter but not for the former. More serious, from a clinical point of view, is the work of Hertel and Rude (1991b) on the sentence-completion task using depressed patients. They also failed to find the kind of interaction between depression and sentence type that is demonstrable for experimentally induced depression. The present state of affairs is thus that this effect has been demonstrated only for experimentally induced depressed mood.

Nevertheless there are other experiments that are consistent with the general line of argument about depressed patients being most impaired in memory tasks requiring effortful processing. Weingartner et al. (1981) required subjects to produce a semantic associate to some words, and an acoustic one to others. Normal subjects showed better recall of semantically associated words, but this was not shown by depressed patients. Generating a semantic associate is probably in some sense more effortful, and it was here that depressed subjects showed their greatest deficit. Also, Roy-Byrne et al. (1986) reported two relevant experiments. In the first, depressed patients were presented with pairs of nouns and asked to make a comparative judgement about the items of each pair. Depressed patients were impaired in free recall of the word presented, which was regarded as an effortful task; in contrast, they were not impaired in recalling their judgements about the words, which was regarded as an automatic task. In similar vein, subjects were presented with a list of categorically similar words, in which some words were repeated. During presentation, they were asked to raise their right hand when they heard a word repeated. Depressed patients were again impaired on recall of the words, an effortful task. However, they were not impaired in their ability to recognise which words had been presented twice, which was regarded as a more "automatic" task. Similarly, Golinkoff and Sweeney (1989) showed that depressed subjects were impaired in paired-associate learning, but not in frequency judgements. Finally Calev, Nigal and Chazan (1989) have extended these ideas to a word-production task, finding that depressed subjects were more impaired with the effortful task of producing words belonging to a particular semantic category than with the more automatic task of producing words beginning with a common letter.

Manipulations Designed to Improve Performance

One of the main practical questions arising from this line of research is whether it leads to any strategies that can be used to help depressed patients improve their memory performance. Given that depressed patients, left to themselves, make only limited use of good encoding strategies, is it helpful to direct them explicitly to use better strategies?

Hertel and Hardin (1990) found that the inferior performance shown by depressed subjects on recognition memory disappeared when subjects were *supplied* with strategies. This occurred whether the strategies applied to a spelling task in which subjects were exposed to words, or to the recognition task itself. It was when subjects were left to generate their own strategies that those who were depressed showed a disadvantage in memory performance. This suggests that depressed subjects do not necessarily have a limit on their memory *capacity*; but that their *performance* is often undermined by a failure to adopt optimal strategies spontaneously.

Hertel and Rude (1991b) extended this perspective by examining the provision of strategies for the sentence-completion task already discussed. The interesting feature of this study was that under one condition subjects were required to repeat the word at the end of the sentence as a way of holding their attention to the task. Under this condition, depressed subjects showed no deficit whereas they did do so when this task requirement was not included. Again, this supports the view that depressed subjects can show normal memory performance under conditions which ensure that their processing resources are appropriately applied to the task in hand.

An alternative set of interventions focuses on memorial processes which operate normally in depressed subjects, such as imagery. Depressed subjects show the normal effect for imageable material to be better recalled (Watts & Cooper, 1989). Given this, it would be expected that imagery strategies would improve the memory performance of depressed subjects, and indeed this is the case (Watts, MacLeod & Morris, 1988b). Requiring subjects to form images of the material in a prose passage was presumably another way of ensuring that processing resources were effectively allocated.

There has so far been relatively little discussion of how these kinds of strategies can be used flexibly in the clinic to help depressed patients improve their memory performance. Students with study problems that arise from depression or anxiety are one relevant example. One well-developed method of helping students is the "PQ4R" method of Thomas and Robinson (1972), with its six stages of "preview, question, read, reflect, recite and review". This method is clearly of general benefit (Fraser, 1975), and it may be particularly valuable with students who are anxious or depressed. Watts (1985) has provided a more general discussion of the use of structuring encoding strategies to help with emotionally based study problems.

COMPARISON OF THE EFFECTS OF DEPRESSION AND ANXIETY

Though there are some similarities between the effects of depression and anxiety on memory performance, the contrasts are quite marked. These are apparent both when you examine which memory tasks are particularly sensitive to impairment, and also in terms of subjects' general orientation to the memory tasks. For example, as will be seen, there are reasons for thinking that depressed people apply relatively little cognitive effort, whereas anxious people show an unusually high level of cognitive effort.

A comparison of the effects of anxiety and depression is, of course, never a straightforward matter from a methodological point of view. The problem is that it is rare to achieve a complete dissociation between them. Even though anxiety frequently occurs without depression, many depressive states also involve anxiety. Given this, it is striking that the effects of depression and anxiety on memory should be as different as they apparently are. However, even where there are apparent similarities, it is possible that these are attributable to the anxiety that frequently co-occurs with depression. Another problem lies in the distinction between state and trait aspects of anxiety, as their relationship to memory performance is not always the same. In general, there is less evidence that trait anxiety impairs memory performance. The effects of state anxiety are probably more powerful. However, it is not always well documented that it is *anxiety* rather than general *arousal* that is affecting memory.

Digit Span

One striking empirical contrast between the effects of depression and anxiety is on short-term memory performance, of which the "digit span" task is the most commonly used index. As was seen in the previous section, though depression has marked effects on a wide variety of memory tasks, digit span is one task that shows little effect of depression. In contrast, digit span is the task that has most frequently been shown to be impaired by anxiety. This is a point at which a clear distinction needs to be made between trait anxiety and state anxiety (Mueller, 1976). *Trait* anxiety has often been found not to affect digit span. In contrast, there is reasonably reliable evidence that the state anxiety associated with situational stress has a deleterious effect on digit span performance (e.g. Dunn, 1968, see Eysenck, 1979). A weakness in many studies of the effects of anxiety on digit span is that subjects have been classified as high or low anxious on a post-hoc basis. In this connection, the studies of Idzikowski and Baddeley, which involved an experimental manipulation of public speaking anxiety (1983) and parachuting anxiety (1987), are important, as both showed an effect on digit span.

Unfortunately, digit span does not represent a pure index of short-term memory, and there are other tasks, better grounded in memory theory, for assessing the effect of anxiety on short-term memory performance. A step in this direction was taken in a recent study by Darke (1988) which showed an effect of anxiety, not only on the traditional digit span task, but also in a paradigm developed by Daneman and Carpenter (1980) in which subjects are required to recall the last words of a series of sentences. The best conclusion, on the available evidence, is that state anxiety has an adverse effect on short-term performance, whereas depression has little or no such effect.

The assumption that has generally been made about why anxiety interferes with digit span performance is that anxious thoughts occupy working memory and limit its capacity (e.g. Eysenck, 1977). This is an entirely plausible assumption. However, it would seem to apply equally to depressed subjects, who also have a lot of emotionally related intrusive thoughts. If it is indeed the case that digit span is affected less in depression than in anxiety, a more specific theory would be needed to explain this.

Though there has been relatively little investigation of *long-term memory* in anxiety, an interesting possibility is that state anxiety, at least, would show a pattern of results that has often been demonstrated for highly arousing materials, i.e. poor recall in the short term, but superior long-term recall (e.g. Bradley & Baddeley, 1990). This is a hypothesis that remains to be investigated as far as state anxiety is concerned. However, it is already clear that high *trait* anxious subjects do not show superior long-term recall (see Mueller, 1980, p. 66).

Paired-Associate Learning

A memory task that has been used extensively in research on the effects of anxiety is paired-associate learning, largely stimulated by the theory of Spence (1958). The idea was essentially that anxiety increased the probability of both correct and competing responses. Where the correct response is dominant, anxiety should lead to better performance. This can be achieved either by ensuring that there is an initial associative connection between the words of each pair, or by ensuring that there is little similarity within either the stimulus words or the response words. The evidence indicates that under these conditions, anxiety generally is associated with enhanced performance in paired-associate learning (see Eysenck, 1977, p. 221 ff.). In contrast, where more difficult paired-associate learning tasks are constructed in which, for example, the correct response is one that has an initial associative connection with a different stimulus word, anxiety tends to be associated with poorer performance. The study of Standish and Champion (1960) is an example of how anxiety can have opposite effects on differently constructed paired-associate learning tasks.

Though the pattern of effects of anxiety on paired-associate learning is generally consistent with Spence's theory, a variety of other interpretations are also possible. Saltz (1970) suggested that the data had been misread, and that the deleterious effects of anxiety on memory could equally well be explained in terms of greater sensitivity to failure in anxious subjects. One way of investigating this is to try to decouple the inherent difficulty of the task from success–failure experience, by giving false feedback. Weiner (1966) carried out this experiment, and their results appear to support the hypothesis that feedback is more important than inherent task difficulty; i.e. anxious subjects do worse on a task at which they are experiencing failure. This certainly shows that matters are more complicated than hypothesised by Spence. However, it would probably be an over-reaction to switch to an alternative simple view that experience of success and failure is all that matters.

The effect of varying the difficulty of paired-associate learning tasks has also been investigated in depression. Depressed subjects show greater impairment with more difficult paired associates. However, there is a clear divergence from the results with anxious subjects in that there is no indication that depressed subjects show *better* performance than controls in learning easy paired associates. For example, Kopelman (1986) found that, for difficult paired associates, the performance of depressed subjects was as bad as that of demented patients. For easy paired associates, depressed subjects showed a degree of impairment, but not as bad as that of demented patients. Comparable results were obtained by LaRue et al. (1986). There has been no attempt so far in the depression literature to establish exactly why depressed subjects show greater impairment on more difficult paired associates; for example whether it is due to the inherent difficulty of the task or to the experience of failure.

Effortful Processing

Another point of similarity between the effects of depression and anxiety on memory is that both seem to bias subjects towards processing strategies that are less effortful, less "structuring" or more superficial. The relevant evidence for the effects of anxiety has been well reviewed by Mueller (1980). This is an area in which there is reasonable convergence between the effects of anxiety and depression. Specifically, anxious subjects tend to show less clustering in recall, and in so far as they cluster at all are less likely to do it on the basis of semantic features (Mueller, 1976). However, replications of this kind of effect have not always been easy, and results seem to depend on procedural factors such as rate of presentation (Mueller, 1980, pp. 67–70). The literature on *arousal* differences (e.g. Schwartz, 1975) suggests that this is a point at which state anxiety has more effect than trait anxiety.

If anxious subjects do not spontaneously process semantic features, it might be predicted that they, like depressed subjects, would show differential responsiveness to semantic orienting instructions. As already noted, the one relevant study of depressed subjects showed that their performance benefited *less* than controls from semantic orientation (Weingartner et al., 1981). In contrast, the early studies of anxious subjects showed the opposite result—i.e. *more* benefit from semantic orientation (Mueller, 1978). Another study of depth of processing in face recognition found no interaction with anxiety (Mueller, Bailis & Goldstein, 1979). If depressed and anxious subjects do indeed show opposite results at this point, it would be of considerable interest. However, for that to be concluded with any confidence it would need to be shown in a single study in which exactly the same procedures were used for all groups. Unfortunately, even if it is assumed that depressed and anxious subjects have less natural orientation to semantic features than controls, it is not entirely clear what should be predicted from this about their responsiveness to semantic orienting instructions.

Processing Resources and Efficiency

At a more theoretical level, it is arguable that there are significant differences between the effects of depression and anxiety on memory, particularly in the role that cognitive "effort" plays in performance. It is helpful here to consider the processing efficiency theory of the cognitive effects of anxiety advanced by Eysenck (e.g. Eysenck & Calvo, 1992). This assumes that anxiety, through worry and other mechanisms, reduces the amount of processing capacity that is available for task performance. However, this does not necessarily lead to a fall-off in performance effectiveness, as additional cognitive effort may be made to compensate for depleted processing resources. Even if there is no fall-off in performance, it becomes less *efficient*, as a greater degree of effort has to be expended in order to maintain performance at normal levels. The two key propositions of the theory are: (1) that anxiety typically impairs processing *efficiency* more than performance *effectiveness*, and (2) that adverse effects of anxiety on task performance generally become stronger as task demands on working memory capacity increase.

The first proposition seems to represent an interesting point of divergence between the memorial effects of depression and anxiety, though the matter requires further investigation. The evidence cited by Eysenck and Calvo is not very extensive, and much of it is based on cognitive tasks other than memory. Also, there is as yet hardly any relevant evidence for depression.

Part of the evidence cited by Eysenck and Calvo supports the view that anxious subjects show greater *effort* during task performance. The evidence for this is partly based on self-report indices (e.g. Dornic, 1977) and partly on physiological indices (Weinberg, 1978). This seems a likely point of divergence between anxiety and depression. There is also evidence that effort-enhancing instructions are of most benefit to high-anxious subjects (e.g. Calvo, 1985; Eysenck, 1985). It is not clear that this necessarily follows from the theory; it might be argued that if the performance of anxious subjects is generally more effortful, they would show *less* additional benefit from effort-enhancing instructions. Though the assumption would be that the performance of depressed subjects is *less* effortful than controls, there is a similar ambiguity about the empirical predictions from this.

Eysenck and Calvo also make a set of predictions about dual-task performance. Attempting to combine two tasks has more adverse effects on both a central task (e.g. Calvo & Ramos, 1989) and a secondary task (e.g. Eysenck, 1982) in anxious subjects than in controls, and there is less spare capacity to respond to probes (e.g. Eysenck, 1989). Krames and MacDonald (1985) have reported an intriguing study of dual-task memory performance in depression. The primary task was recall of a word list; the secondary task was a digit load, of variable length. The depressed subjects showed no difference in recall of the digits, but were impaired on recall of the word lists. The most interesting aspect of the findings of Krames and MacDonald relates to the length of the digit load. Control subjects showed the normal effect of poorer recall of words under conditions of longer digit load. However, intriguingly, depressed subjects showed the opposite (i.e. *better* word recall with longer digit loads). Several studies have reported, in similar vein, that a concurrent task can increase the speed of psychomotor performance in depressives but not in controls (see Williams, Watts, MacLeod & Mathews, 1988, pp. 36–37). The interpretation that Krames and McDonald offered for this finding was that "when the demands of a task are increased, the depressed subject is forced to pay greater attention to the task at hand at the expense of whatever distracting schemata may be present" (p. 570). This counter-intuitive finding stands in need of replication. The only other similar study (Peters, 1992) obtained a different pattern of results. Clinically depressed subjects showed relatively little difference in performance with varying digit load, whereas the longer digit load significantly reduced the memory performance of control subjects. The pattern of results reported by Krames and McDonald is certainly not something that would be predicted for anxious subjects from Eysenck and Calvo's processing efficiency theory.

The processing-resources theory of depression which has been advanced by Ellis and Ashbrook (1988) begins by making a parallel assumption to that of Eysenck and Calvo; i.e. that fewer processing resources are available in depressed than in normal subjects. It is further assumed that, in depression, fewer processing resources are actually applied to the task in hand. Both of these assumptions seem likely to be correct. The work of Hertel and her colleagues, cited earlier, that constraining subjects' attention to the task in hand can normalise the performance of depressed subjects, is direct support for this additional proposition. In the nature of things, it is not easy to distinguish cmpirically between the hypotheses that processing resources are not *available*, and that they are not *allocated*. However, progress might be made by applying to depression the methodologies for studying processing efficiency (direct measures of effort and dual task methodologies) that Eysenck and Calvo cite in connection with anxiety.

The second proposition of Eysenck and Calvo, that the adverse effects of anxiety on task performance generally become stronger as task demands on working memory capacity increase, seems to apply equally to depression and anxiety. Ellis and Ashbrook (1988) cite a substantial body of evidence on depression that is consistent with this view, and Eysenck and Calvo (1992) cite comparable evidence for anxiety.

The Role of Emotional Thoughts

A further similarity in the processing-efficiency theory of anxiety (Eysenck & Calvo, 1992) and the processing-resources theory of depression (Ellis & Ashbrook, 1988) is that they assume a similar mechanism by which processing resources are depleted in the two cases. In both cases, it is assumed that processing resources are taken up by task-irrelevant emotionally-related thoughts.

A seminal paper in the anxiety literature was that of Wine (1971) who argued that effects of anxiety on performance were mediated by "ruminative, self-evaluative worry". Anxiety can be assumed to comprise both worry and more physiological aspects of anxiety. The available evidence suggests that it is worry which affects cognitive performance (e.g. Morris, Davies & Hutchings, 1981). The impact of worry on cognitive performance has continued to be a central assumption of cognitive theories of anxiety (e.g. Sarason, 1988; Eysenck, 1992).

In a parallel way, it can be assumed that the negative thoughts that are characteristic of depressed patients are equally important in affecting their level of task performance. For example, Ellis, Seibert and Herbert (1990) showed that induced depression was associated with thoughts rated as unfavourable, and Seibert and Ellis (1991) showed that students with induced moods of either sadness or happiness showed a higher level of task-irrelevant thoughts, and that there was a correlation between the frequency of such thoughts and performance on a memory task.

There is certainly plausibility in the assumption that it is the task-irrelevant, emotionally-related thoughts of depressed and anxious subjects which affect their memory performance. However, the correlational evidence in support of this is not wholly consistent. So far as anxiety is concerned, there have been a number of failures to show correlations between the frequency of intrusive thoughts and task performance, though there are indications that the subjective meaning attached to task-irrelevant thoughts may be more significant than their mere frequency (see Galassi, Frierson & Siegal, 1984). As far as depression is concerned, Watts, MacLeod and Morris (1988) reported evidence that intrusive thoughts ("mind-wandering") were correlated with performance on some tasks, while performance on others was correlated with patients' minds "going blank" rather than mind-wandering. For example, when memory for prose was examined under ordinary processing conditions, it showed a negative correlation with mind-wandering, but when subjects were required to form images while listening to those prose passages, performance correlated negatively with blanking.

At the present time, it would be reasonable to conclude that, though anxious and depressive thoughts contribute to the memory impairments of subjects concerned, they may not be capable of bearing the full burden of explanation. It seems likely, at least in depression, that there are problems concerned with the allocation of cognitive effort that are distinct from problems caused by negative thoughts.

CONCLUSIONS

The memory problems of depressed and anxious subjects have both now received considerable investigation, though it is curious and regrettable that there has been so little direct comparison of their effects. On the present evidence, it is reasonable to conclude that both groups of subjects have diminished processing resources available as a result of their emotional preoccupations. *Anxious* subjects tend to compensate for this by more effortful performance, and sometimes outperform normal controls. However, their performance is less "efficient" than that of controls. *Depressed* subjects, in contrast, show a failure to allocate processing resources to memory tasks, which compounds the problems created by the reduced resources they have available. The memory problems of depressed and anxious subjects are thus similar at some points, but interestingly different at others. Moreover, both of them seem likely to diverge from the memory problems of neuropsychological amnesics. However, there has been very little direct comparison of the memory problems of depressed and anxious subjects with those of other groups of amnesics.

REFERENCES

Berndt, D.J. & Berndt, S.M. (1980). Relationship of mild depression to psychological deficit in college students. *Journal of Clinical Psychology*, **36**, 868–874.

Blaney, P.H. (1986). Affect and memory: a review. *Psychological Bulletin*, **99**, 229–246.

Bower, G.H. (1987). Commentary on mood and memory. *Behaviour Research and Therapy*, **25**, 443–455.

Bradley, B.P. & Baddeley, A.D. (1990). Emotional factors in forgetting. *Psychological Medicine*, **20**, 351–355.

Brand, N. & Jolles J. (1987). Information processing in depression and anxiety. *Psychological Medicine*, **17**, 145–153.

Calev, A. & Erwin, P.G. (1985). Recall and recognition in depression: use of matched task. *British Journal of Clinical Psychology*, **24**, 127–128.

Calev, A., Ben-Tzvi, E., Shapira, B., Drexler, H., Carasso, R. & Lerer, B. (1989). Distinct memory impairments following ECT and imipramine. *Psychological Medicine*, **19**, 1110–1119.

Calev, A., Nigal, D. & Chazan, S. (1989). Retrieval from semantic memory using meaningful and meaningless constructs by depressed, stable bipolar and manic patients. *British Journal of Clinical Psychology*, **28**, 67–73.

Calvo, M.G. (1985). Effort, aversive representations and performance in test anxiety. *Personality and Individual Differences*, **6**, 563–571.

Calvo, M.G. & Ramos, P.M. (1989). Effects of test anxiety on motor learning: the processing efficiency hypothesis. *Anxiety Research*, **2**, 45–55

Chandler, J.D. & Gerndt, J. (1988). Memory complaints and memory deficits in young and old psychiatric inpatients. *Journal of Geriatric Psychiatry and Neurology*, **1**, 84–88.

Channon, S., Baker, J.E. & Robertson, M.M. (1993a). Effects of structure and clustering on recall and recognition memory in clinical depression. *Journal of Abnormal Psychology*, **102**, 323–326.

Channon, S., Baker, J.E. & Robertson, M.M. (1993b). Working memory in clinical depression: an experimental study. *Psychological Medicine*, **23**, 87–91.

Chapman, L.J. & Chapman, J.P. (1973). Problems in the measurement of cognitive deficit. *Psychological Bulletin*, **79**, 380–385.

Christianson, S.-A. (ed.) (1992). *The Handbook of Emotion and Memory Research and Theory*. Erlbaum, Hillsdale, NJ.

Colby, C.A. & Gotlib, I.H. (1988). Memory deficits in depression. *Cognitive Therapy and Research*, **12**, 611–627.

Coughlan, A.K. & Hollows, S.E. (1984). Use of memory tests in differentiating organic disorder from depression. *British Journal of Psychiatry*, **145**, 164–167.

Cronholm, B. & Ottosson, J.O. (1961). The experience of memory function after electroconvulsive therapy. *British Journal of Psychiatry*, **109**, 251–258.

Dalgleish, T. & Watts, F.N. (1990). Biases of attention and memory in disorders of anxiety and depression. *Clinical Psychology Review*, **10**, 589–604.

Daneman, M. & Carpenter, P. (1980). Individual differences in working memory and reading. *Journal of Verbal Learning and Verbal Behavior*, **29**, 450–456.

Danion, J.M., Willard-Schroeder, D., Zimmermann, M.A., Grange, D., Sclienger, J.L. & Singer, L. (1991). Explicit memory and repetition priming in depression: preliminary findings. *Archives of General Psychiatry*, **48**, 707–711.

Dannenbaum, S.E., Parkinson, S.R. & Inman, V.W. (1988). Short-term forgetting: comparisons between patients with dementia of the Alzheimer type, depressed, and the normal elderly. *Cognitive Neuropsychology*, **5**, 213–233.

Darke, S. (1988). Anxiety and working memory capacity. *Cognition and Emotion*, **2**, 145–154.

Dornic, S. (1977). *Mental load, effort and individual differences*. Reports from the Department of Psychology, University of Stockholm, no. 509.

Dunbar, G.C. & Lishman, W.A. (1984). Depression, recognition-memory and hedonic tone: a signal detection analysis. *British Journal of Psychiatry*, **144**, 376–382.

Dunn, J.A. (1968). Anxiety, stress and the performance of complex intellectual tasks: a new look at an old question. *Journal of Consulting and Clinical Psychology*, **32**, 669–673.

Elliott, C.L. & Greene, R.L. (1992). Clinical depression and implicit memory. *Journal of Abnormal Psychology*, **101**, 572–574.

Ellis, H.C. & Ashbrook, P.W. (1988). Resource allocation model of the effects of depressed mood states on memory. In K. Fiedler & J. Forgas (eds), *Affect, Cognition and Social Behavior*. Hogrefe, Toronto, pp. 25–43.

Ellis, H.C. & Ashbrook, P.W. (1988). The "state" of mood and memory research: a selective review. *Journal of Social Behaviour and Personality*, **4**, 1–21.

Ellis, H.C., Seibert, P.S. & Herbert, B.J. (1990). Mood state effects on thought listing. *Bulletin of the Psychonomic Society*, **28**, 147–150.

Ellis, H.C., Thomas. R.L. & Rodriguez, I.A. (1984). Emotional mood states and memory: elaborative encoding, semantics processing, and cognitive effort. *Journal of Experimental Psychology: Learning, Memory and Cognition*, **10**, 470–482.

Ellis, H.C., Varner, L.J., Becker, A.S. & Ottaway, S.A. (1995). Emotion and prior knowledge in memory and comprehension of ambiguous stories. *Cognition and Emotion*, **9**, in press.

Eysenck, M.W. (1977). *Human Memory: Theory, Research and Individual Differences*. Pergamon Press, Oxford.

Eysenck, M.W. (1979). Anxiety, learning and memory: a reconceptualization. *Journal of Research in Personality*, **13**, 363–385.

Eysenck, M.W. (1982). *Attention and Arousal: Cognition and Performance*. Springer-Verlag, Berlin.

Eysenck, M.W. (1985). Anxiety and cognitive-task performance. *Personality and Individual Differences*, **6**, 579–586.

Eysenck, M.W. (1989). Stress, anxiety and intelligent performance. In D. Vickers & P.L. Smith (eds), *Human Information Processing: Measures, Mechanisms and Models*. North Holland, Amsterdam.

Eysenck, M.W. (1992). *Anxiety: The Cognitive Perspective*. Erlbaum, Hove.

Eysenck, M.W. & Calvo, M.G. (1992). Anxiety and performance: the processing efficiency theory. *Cognition and Emotion* **6**, 409–434.

Fraser, L.T. (1975). Prose processing. In G.H. Bower (ed.), *Psychology of Learning and Motivation*, **9**, 1–48.

Galassi, J.P., Frierson, H.T. & Siegal, R.G. (1984). Cognitions, test anxiety, and test performance: a close look. *Journal of Consulting and Clinical Psychology*, **51**, 292–293.

Gass, C.S. & Russell, E.W. (1986). Differential impact of brain damage and depression on memory test performance. *Journal of Consulting and Clinical Psychology*, **54**, 261–263.

Glass, R.M., Uhlenhuth, E.H., Hastl, F.W., Matuzas, W. & Fischman, M.W. (1981). Cognitive dysfunction and imipramine in outpatient depressives. *Archives of General Psychiatry*, **38**, 1048–1051.

Golinkoff, M. & Sweeney, J.A. (1989). Cognitive impairments in depression. *Journal of Affective Disorders*, **17**, 105–112.

Henry, G.M., Weingartner, H. & Murphy, D.L. (1973). Influence of affective states and psychoactive drugs on verbal learning and memory. *American Journal of Psychiatry*, **130**, 966–971.

Hertel, P. & Hardin, T.S. (1990). Remembering with and without awareness in a depressed mood: evidence of deficits in initiative. *Journal of Experimental Psychology: General*, **119**, 45–59.

Hertel, P.T. & Rude, S.S. (1991a). Recalling in a state of natural or experimental depression. *Cognitive Therapy and Research*, **15**, 103–127.

Hertel, P.T. & Rude, S.S. (1991b). Depressive deficits in memory: focusing attention improves subsequent recall. *Journal of Experimental Psychology: General*, **120**, 301–309.

Hilbert, N.M., Niederehe, G. & Kahn, R.L. (1976). Accuracy and speed of memory in depressed and organic aged. *Educational Gerontology*, **1**, 131–146.

Hodges, W.F. & Durham, R.L. (1972). Anxiety, ability and digit span performance. *Journal of Personality and Social Psychology*, **24**, 401–406.

Idzikowski, C. & Baddeley, A.D. (1983). Waiting in the wings: apprehension, public speaking and performance. *Ergonomics*, **26**, 575–583.

Idzikowski, C. & Baddeley, A.D. (1987). Fear and performance in novice parachutists. *Ergonomics*, **30**, 1463–1474.

Johnson, M.H. & Magaro, P.A. (1987). Effects of mood and severity on memory processes in depression and mania. *Psychological Bulletin*, **101**, 28–40.

Koh, S.D., Kayton, L. & Berry, R. (1973). Mnemonic organization in young nonpsychotic schizophrenics. *Journal of Abnormal Psychology*, **81**, 299–310.

Koh, S.D. & Wolpert, E.A. (1983). Memory scanning and retrieval in affective disorders. *Psychiatry Research*, **8**, 289–297.

Kopelman, M.D. (1986). Clinical tests of memory. *British Journal of Psychiatry*, **148**, 517–525.

Krames, L. & McDonald, M.R. (1985). Distraction and depressive cognitions. *Cognitive Therapy and Research*, **9**, 561–573.

LaRue, A., D'Elia, L.F., Clark, E.O., Spar, J.E. & Jarvik, L.F. (1986). Clinical tests of memory in dementia, depression and healthy aging. *Psychology and Aging*, **1**, 69–77.

Leight, K.A. & Ellis, H.S. (1981). Emotional mood states, strategies and state-dependency in memory. *Journal of Verbal Learning and Verbal Behavior*, **20**, 251–266.

Levy, R. & Maxwell, A.E. (1968). The effect of verbal context on the recall of schizophrenics and other psychiatric patients. *British Journal of Psychiatry*, **114**, 311–316.

Miller, E. & Lewis, P. (1977). Recognition memory in elderly patients with depression and dementia. *Journal of Abnormal Psychology*, **86**, 84–86.

Morris, L.W., Davis, M.A. & Hutchings, C.H. (1981). Cognitive and emotional components of anxiety: literature review and a revised worry–emotionality scale. *Journal of Educational Psychology*, **73**, 541–555.

Mueller, J.H. (1976). Anxiety and cue utilization in human learning and memory. In M. Zuckerman and C.D. Spielberger (eds), *Emotions and Anxiety: New Concepts, Methods and Applications*. Erlbaum, Hillsdale, NJ.

Mueller, J.H. (1978).The effects of individual differences in test anxiety and type of orienting task on levels of organization in free recall. *Journal of Research in Personality*, **12**, 100–116.

Mueller, J.H. (1980). Test anxiety and the encoding and retrieval of information. In I.G. Sarason (ed.), *Test Anxiety: Theory, Research and Applications*. Erlbaum, Hillsdale, NJ.

Mueller, J.H., Bailis, K.L. & Goldstein, A.G. (1979). Depth of processing and anxiety in facial recognition. *British Journal of Psychology*, **70**, 511–515.

Niederehe, G. & Yoder, C. (1989). Metamemory perceptions in depressions of young and older adults. *Journal of Nervous and Mental Disease*, **177**, 4–14.

Peters, L. (1992). *Memory Deficits in Dysphoria and Clinical Depression*. Unpublished PhD thesis, University of New South Wales.

Potts, R., Camp, C. & Coyne, C. (1989). The relationship between naturally occurring dysphoric moods, elaborative encoding and recall performance. *Cognition & Emotion*, **3**, 197–205.

Query, W.T. & Megran, J. (1984). Influence of depression and alcoholism on learning, recall and recognition. *Journal of Clinical Psychology*, **40**, 1097–1100.

Roy-Bryne, P.J., Weingartner, H., Bierer, L.M., Thompson, K. & Post, R.M. (1986). Effortful and automatic cognitive processes in depression. *Archives of General Psychiatry*, **43**, 265–267.

Russell, P.N. & Beekhuis, M.E. (1976). Organization in memory: a comparison of psychotics and normals. *Journal of Abnormal Psychology*, **85**, 527–534.

Saltz, E. (1970). Manifest anxiety: have we misread the data? *Psychological Review*, **77**, 568–573.

Sarason, I.G. (1988). Anxiety, self-preoccupation and attention. *Anxiety Research*, **1**, 3–7.

Schwartz, S. (1975). Individual differences in cognition: some relationships between personality and memory. *Journal of Research and Personality*, **9**, 217–225.

Seibert, P.S. & Ellis, H.C. (1991). Irrelevant thoughts, emotional mood states and cognitive task performance. *Memory and Cognition*, **19**, 507–513.

Silberman, E.K., Weingartner, H., Laraia, M., Byrnes, S. & Post, R.M. (1983). Processing of emotional properties of stimuli by depressed and normal subjects. *Journal of Nervous and Mental Diseases*, **171**, 10–14.

Silberman, E.K., Weingartner, H., Targum, S.D. & Byrnes, S. (1985). Cognitive functioning in biological subtypes of depression. *Biological Psychiatry*, **20**, 654–661.

Singer, J.A. & Salovey, P. (1988). Mood and memory: evaluating the network theory of affect. *Clinical Psychology Review*, **8**, 211–251.

Spence, K.W. (1958). A theory of emotionally based drive (D) and its relation to performance in simple learning situations. *American Psychology*, **13**, 131–141.

Spence, J.T. & Spence, K.W. (1966). The motivational components of manifest anxiety: drive and drive stimuli. In C.D. Spielberger (ed.), *Anxiety and Behaviour*. Academic Press, London.

Sperling, G. (1960). The information available in brief visual presentations. *Psychological Monographs*, **74**, 1–29.

Standish, R.R. & Champion, R.A. (1960). Task difficulty and drive in verbal learning. *Journal of Experimental Psychology*, **58**, 361–365.

Sternberg, S. (1969). The discovery of processing stages: extensions of Donder's method. *Acta Psychologia*, **30**, 276–315.

Sternberg, D.E. & Jarvik, M.E. (1976). Memory functions in depression. *Archives of General Psychiatry*, **33**, 219–224.

Stromgren, L.S. (1977). The influence of depression on memory. *Acta Psychiatrica Scandinavica*, **5**, 109–128.

Taylor, J.A. (1953). A personality scale of manifest anxiety. *Journal of Abnormal Social Psychology*, **48**, 285–290.

Teasdale, J.D. & Barnard, P.J. (1993). *Affect, Cognition and Change*. Erlbaum, Hove.

Teasdale, J.T. & Russell, M.L. (1983). Differential effects of induced mood on the recall of positive, negative and neutral words. *British Journal of Clinical Psychology*, **22**, 163–171.

Thomas, E.L. & Robinson, H.A. (1972). *Improving Reading in Every Class*: *A Sourcebook for Teachers*. Allyn & Bacon, Boston.

Tyler, S.W., Hertel, P.T., McCallum, M.C. & Ellis, H.C. (1979). Cognitive effort and memory. *Journal of Experimental Psychology*: *Learning, Memory and Cognition*, **5**, 607–617.

Ucros, C.G. (1989). Mood state-dependent memory: a meta-analysis. *Cognition and Emotion*, **3**, 139–169.

Watts, F.N. (1985). Individual-centred cognitive counselling for study problems. *British Journal of Guidance and Counselling*, **13**, 238–247.

Watts, F.N. (1989). Experimental abnormal psychology. In G. Parry & F.N. Watts (eds), *Behavioural and Mental Health Research*: *A Handbook of Skills and Methods*. Erlbaum, Hove.

Watts, F.N. (1993). Problems of memory and concentrations. In C.G. Costello (ed.), *Symptoms of Depression*. John Wiley, New York.

Watts, F.N. & Cooper, Z. (1989). The effects of depression on structural aspects of the recall of prose. *Journal of Abnormal Psychology*, **98**, 150–153.

Watts, F.N., Dalgleish, T., Bourke, P. & Healy, D. (1990). Memory deficit in clinical depression: processing resources and the structure of materials. *Psychological Medicine*, **20**, 345–349.

Watts, F.N., MacLeod, A.K. & Morris, L. (1988a). A remedial strategy for memory and concentration problems in depressed patients. *Cognitive Therapy and Research*, **12**, 185–193.

Watts, F.N., MacLeod, A.K. & Morris, L. (1988b). Associations between phenomenal and objective aspects of concentration problems in depressed patients. *British Journal of Psychology*, **79**, 241–250.

Watts, F.N., Morris, L. & MacLeod, A.K. (1987). Recognition memory in depression. *Journal of Abnormal Psychology*, **96**, 273–275.

Watts, F.N. & Sharrock, R. (1987). Cued recall in depression. *British Journal of Clinical Psychology*, **26**, 149–150.

Weinberg, R.S. (1978). The effects of success and failure on the patterning of neuromuscular energy. *Journal of Motor Behaviour*, **10**, 53–61.

Weiner, B. (1966). The role of success and failure in the learning of easy and complex tasks. *Journal of Personality and Social Psychology*, **3**, 339–344.

Weingartner, H., Cohen, R.M., Murphy, D.L., Martello, J. & Gerdt, C. (1981). Cognitive processes in depression. *Archives of General Psychiatry*, **38**, 42–47.

Whitehead, A. (1973). Verbal learning and memory in elderly depressives. *British Journal of Psychiatry*, **123**, 203–208.

Williams, J.M., Little, M.M., Scates, S. & Blockman, N. (1987). Memory complaints and abilities among depressed older adults. *Journal of Consulting and Clinical Psychology*, **55**, 595–598.

Williams, J.M.G., Watts, F.N., MacLeod, C. & Mathews, A. (1988). *Cognitive Psychology and Emotional Disorders*. John Wiley, Chichester.

Wine, J. (1971). Test anxiety and direction of attention. *Psychological Bulletin*, **76**, 92–104.

Chapter 13

Memory Following Electroconvulsive Therapy

Connie Cahill
and
Chris Frith
MRC Cyclotron Unit, Hammersmith Hospital, London, UK

ECT AS A FORM OF TREATMENT IN PSYCHIATRY

In the 1920s, Von Meduna, a Hungarian psychiatrist, suggested that the induction of brain seizures would result in the alleviation of psychotic symptoms. This proposal was based on the observation that spontaneous brain seizures are often associated with a temporary remission of psychotic symptoms, and figures (later shown to be incorrect) suggesting an antagonism between schizophrenia and epilepsy. The proposal was taken up by Cerletti, an Italian neurologist, and his associate Bini in the 1930s who developed the first machine to induce seizures in human subjects. Thus, electroconvulsive therapy was first introduced as a therapeutic intervention for the psychotic disorders, schizophrenia and manic–depressive psychosis. However, widespread clinical application soon revealed that this treatment was more effective in the treatment of depressive illness, in which it brought about substantial reductions in chronicity and morbidity (Slater, 1951). Numerous clinical trials have since demonstrated that ECT has the potential for producing a rapid, if short-term, recovery from severe —particularly "endogenous type"—depressive illness (e.g. Clinical Psychiatry Committee, 1965; Johnstone et al., 1980). Most recently, analyses of the results of two major trials indicated that it was most effective in relieving symptoms in depressed patients with retardation and delusions (Buchan et al., 1992). In current practice its use is indicated in cases where there is immediate risk of

Handbook of Memory Disorders. Edited by A.D. Baddeley, B.A. Wilson and F.N. Watts.
© 1995 John Wiley & Sons Ltd.

suicide or the patient's physical health is endangered by their not eating or drinking (Gelder, Gath and Mayou, 1988).

The procedures used in the early decades of ECT administration were crude, hazardous and distressing for the patient. This contributed in large part to the public concern and debate over the ethics of the treatment, as well as providing a focus for the "anti-psychiatry movement", influential during the 1960s. Many clinicians therefore abandoned ECT in favour of the relatively safe and effective new drug therapies which became available for the treatment of depressive illness in the late 1950s. However, modern ECT procedures, which incorporate brief anaesthesia, muscle relaxants, and more control over shock intensity, are greatly improved and the treatment continues to be used. Indeed, in recent years there has been a revival of interest in this particular form of treatment in the USA.

The therapeutic effectiveness of ECT is believed to depend upon the induction of a grand mal cerebral seizure, sufficient in duration and generalisation to elicit persistent brain changes (Fink, 1990). This seizure is induced by an electric current delivered via electrodes, which may be placed on opposite sides of the head (referred to as "bilateral" ECT) or on the same side (typically the right, i.e. nondominant; known as "unilateral" ECT). Which of these two forms of treatment is the more effective has not been established conclusively. D'Elia and Raotma (1975) reviewed 29 studies appearing between 1962 and 1973 and concluded that the better controlled studies overwhelmingly supported equal efficacy between nondominant unilateral and bilateral treatments. However, reports of an inferior efficacy in unilateral treatment continue to emerge. On the whole, it appears that the likelihood of achieving a good outcome is greater with bilateral ECT, and there is also evidence to suggest that patients receiving bilateral treatment recover more rapidly (e.g. Gregory, Shawcross & Gill, 1985). In Great Britain clinical practice is overwhelmingly bilateral (see Pippard, 1992). Typically, a course of ECT consisting of 6–12 treatments, administered over a 3–5 week period, is required for the patient to reach a clinically significant level of recovery.

THE ASSESSMENT OF ECT-RELATED MEMORY DEFICITS

Research into the effects of ECT on memory functioning must take into account the fact that depressive illness is itself associated with impairment in memory function (Sternberg & Jarvik, 1976; Johnson & Magaro, 1987). It follows that the memory functioning of virtually all patients entering a study of the effects of ECT will manifest some degree of memory deficit as a consequence of their being depressed. Furthermore, because ECT is generally reserved for only the most severely depressed patients, it is highly likely that those study subjects receiving ECT will be significantly more depressed than a non-ECT depressed "control" group, and consequently, more memory-impaired from the outset. Assessment of *changes* in memory function must also consider that as treatment or time progresses changes may occur in memory functioning simply as a function of changes in patients' levels of depression. Thus, the investigator must find ways of separating out memory deficits due to depression from those caused by the treatment.

Various methodological procedures can be employed to achieve this end. Random allocation of subjects to ECT or non-ECT treatment groups can protect against pretreatment group differences in severity of depression and levels of memory dysfunction. Unfortunately, for ethical reasons, this is rarely permissible. Alternatively, administering baseline (i.e. pretreatment) assessments of both memory functioning and level of depression, and comparing these with post-ECT assessments, permits assessment of change in performance following the introduction of ECT. It also allows examination of whether changes in memory function are related to changes in the level of depression. Most of the studies of ECT are of this type. Incorporating a depressed control group of subjects who undergo the same testing procedures also provides a control for the possible effects of repeated testing and the passage of time. If any of these methodological constraints are to serve their purpose well, it is crucial that levels of depression are assessed in all study groups and at regular intervals, ideally in the same testing session as the memory assessments, and that this information is used in the analysis of results.

Finally, we should point out some of the hazards in determining long-term effects of ECT on memory functioning. Establishing such effects (i.e. effects that become evident weeks, months or years after treatment) is hampered by the lack of control the investigator has over events in the follow-up period. Typically, once a patient has completed the ECT treatment stage, management of their condition reverts to their clinician who will introduce whatever forms of treatment he or she thinks appropriate. This is likely to include prescription of antidepressant drugs. Since such drugs frequently have anticholinergic properties, they may well impair memory. When patients are reassessed at follow-up their level of psychological well-being may have altered considerably—for better or for worse—since they were last assessed. One cannot assume that patients have recovered by virtue of the ECT and remained well. Assessment of symptomatology and mood state at follow-up is therefore of critical importance.

Unfortunately, it is too often the case that levels of depression are not reported, making results of memory tests difficult to interpret. This methodological shortcoming is also a major source of difficulty for making comparisons between the results of one study and another. Other significant sources of difficulty include:

- Variation in the number of shocks administered
- Variations in the positioning of the electrodes
- Differences in the length of time between administration of ECT and memory testing

- Differences in the memory tests and measures used
- Differences in the levels of depression in the study groups

All these factors may well influence results in ways that remain largely unknown.

This chapter does not set out to review the literature on the effects of ECT on memory. Rather, we present results from those studies which incorporate as many as possible of the methodological procedures necessary for controlling potential confounding variables, and highlight the consistent trends in the data.

ANTEROGRADE MEMORY FUNCTIONING AFTER ECT

After ECT, patients will have difficulty learning new material. This impairment results from *anterograde* effects of the shock. Severe impairments in immediate or short-term memory are most likely to feature in the few hours after administration of ECT. Reports of impairments in immediate memory thereafter are variable, with the precise nature of the memory task proving critical. By contrast, substantial deficits are found consistently in the retention of information acquired for the first time shortly after shock.

Squire and Miller (1974) demonstrated this differential pattern of performance in immediate and delayed memory functioning (see Figure 13.1). They presented to patients receiving ECT, and a non-ECT depressed control group, a series of eight cards on which were printed drawings of common objects—photographs of human faces, nonsense line drawings and monosyllabic simple words. Recognition memory for these items was tested 30 minutes after presen-

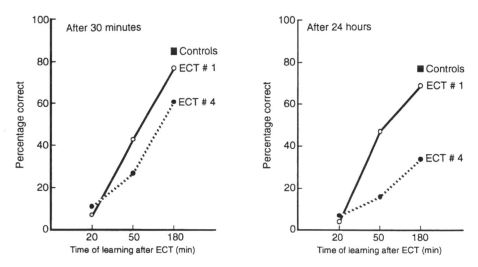

Figure 13.1 Performance of patients receiving bilateral ECT (*n*=9) on a recognition memory task. The control group (*n*=16) consisted of depressed patients not receiving ECT. Redrawn from data in Squire and Miller (1974)

tation. Different series of stimuli were presented at 20, 50 and 180 minutes after ECT. The results in the ECT group clearly indicated significantly reduced levels of recall relative to the controls in those series tested close to the administration of the shock, followed by consistent improvement across each succeeding testing interval; by the final (180-minute) post-shock test their performance was not significantly different from the depressed controls. Squire (1986) reported a replication of this finding in a study which tested recognition memory for a 10-word list tested after 15 minutes and four time points after ECT—45, 65 and 85 minutes, and 9 hours. Squire and Miller (1974) also cite a number of early studies of the effects of ECT on memory functioning which are consistent with these findings.

In contrast to these results indicating minimal effects on short-term recognition memory, Squire and Miller (1974) also reported that the same information which the patients recognised at acceptable levels on the day of ECT administration was not so readily available to them the following day, when their recognition performance was found to be significantly impaired relative to the same controls. These authors also reported that this deficit in the retention of material suffered a cumulative effect with the administration of more electroshocks, so that after the fourth treatment patients were less able to retain material after 24 hours than after their first treatment.

The general pattern of results reported in this "immediate" phase following ECT, consisting of relatively substantial impairment in long-term (24 hours) compared with short-term (30 minutes) memory functioning, is essentially one that carries forward and becomes more fully developed in studies examining medium-term effects (i.e. up to one week post-ECT).

Medium-Term Effects

As early as 1963, Cronholm and Ottosson reported that "ECT has an adverse influence mainly on the hypothetical memory variable 'retention', whereas another hypothetical variable 'learning' shows improvement parallel with the amelioration of depression". They studied the effects of a particularly short course of ECT (four electroshocks were administered) in a group of 35 patients one week after cessation of treatment. They found that, on average, their subjects' immediate reproduction of 30 word-pairs and 20 figures was, if anything, slightly (though not significantly) improved on pre-ECT performance; whereas their ability to reproduce this information after a 3-hour delay was significantly reduced and their "rate of forgetting" had increased significantly.

More recently, in one of the most methodologically sound studies to date, Horne, Pettinati, Sugerman and Varga (1985) examined changes in memory functioning following five electroshocks in a group of 48 depressed patients assigned randomly to either bilateral or nondominant unilateral ECT. Patients completed a battery of memory tests and the Hamilton Depression Rating Scale (Hamilton, 1960) within 24–48 hours of the fifth ECT in their course of treatment. Within the context of very significant clinical improvements in their depressive symptomatology (depression score pre-ECT = 23.3; post-ECT = 7), the bilateral group demonstrated large and statistically significant decrements in their performance on a number of memory tasks. Delayed recall of a short story (taken from Wechsler Memory Scale, 1945) 24 hours after its presentation was diminished by as much as 73.2% on pre-ECT performance; delayed recall of abstract designs (also from WMS) was less severely affected—down by 54%; and their immediate recall of the short story was also affected—down by 35%. However, no significant changes occurred on Digit Span (forward and backward), or the WMS paired-associates (i.e. eight pairs of words: four "easy", four "hard", with six learning trials).

Calev et al. (1991) obtained broadly similar results on testing a more severely depressed group of patients (mean depression score pre-ECT = 31.4). One day after their final electroshock (average number of shocks = 9), the patients were also very significantly improved in terms of depressive symptomatology (pre- to post-ECT comparison significant at the $p = 0.0001$ level). Yet they too demonstrated significant pre- to post-ECT decrements in the delayed retention of both verbal and visual stimuli—a deficit which these authors characterised as "more rapid forgetting". Again, deficits in immediate recall were apparent on a categorised word-list task, contrasting with no performance change pre- to post-ECT on digit span (tested forwards only). However, these investigators did find a significantly reduced level of performance post-ECT on their paired-associate learning task. This task used 10 pairs of unrelated nouns with four learning trials, which may well account for the discrepancy between their results and those of Horne et al. It seems likely that Calev et al.'s task was more difficult. The variation in the reports of deleterious effects of ECT on immediate or short-term memory functioning may be explained, at least partially, by the factor of difficulty.

It is clearly the case that different memory tests (and, by extension, different memory functions) may be more or less sensitive to the effects of ECT. We are not aware, for instance, of any study which reports a diminished performance pre- to post-ECT on digit span or Brown–Peterson type tasks. Rather it seems that those tasks which place a greater load on retrieval mechanisms are more vulnerable to the effects of this treatment. Hence, there is more evidence of impairment on recall as opposed to recognition tasks, and tasks involving delayed as opposed to immediate responding.

Despite using memory tasks very different from those traditionally reported, Frith et al. (1983) obtained results which could be explained in terms of the predominant deficit reported in the literature; i.e. a decrease in the amount of new information retained over a period of hours. This study is notable for its attempts at distinguishing (a) effects due to the administration of an electroshock, as opposed to all other aspects of ECT treatment, and (b) effects of ECT treatment as opposed to those associated with the patients' level of depression. These investigators randomly assigned 62 patients to either "real" (i.e. including electroshock) or "sham" (simulated electroshock) ECT and used outcome (in terms of depression score) as an independent variable in the analysis of their results. They found that immediate reproduction (i.e. after a 30-second interval during which subjects counted backwards in 7's) of a 20-word list was not significantly impaired relative to baseline (pre-ECT) performance in either the real or sham ECT groups. However, during the course of treatment the sham ECT group's performance improved to a significantly greater degree than that of the real ECT group on a learning-labels-for-faces task—possibly reflecting poor retention of material presented in previous trials in the real ECT group. Outcome did not influence these effects.

In reviewing these studies, it seems that another critical factor in determining whether or not effects on immediate memory function will be demonstrated is the latency between the administration of the electroshock and the time at which memory is tested. There is a strong suggestion that the impairments in immediate recall evident on the day following ECT may resolve within the following days. In what is a seriously limited study, since the results are based on data pooled from bilateral and unilateral ECT groups (which contained significantly different numbers of responders and nonresponders), Steif et al. (1986) nonetheless report data which may be illustrating this differential pattern. When memory functioning in their subjects was tested 24–36 hours after the seventh ECT session and compared with pretreatment levels of performance, both immediate and delayed memory functioning were significantly impaired on a combined measure based on word- and face-recognition tasks. However, and consistent with the results reported by Cronholm and Ottosson (1963), when retesting four days (on average) after the ECT course, immediate memory scores had returned to pre-ECT baseline levels, while delayed memory performance remained impaired (see Figure 13.2). On the basis of these results, Steif and colleagues suggested that "immediate memory performance is more sensitive than delayed memory performance to the interval from last treatment and that ECT has more persistent effects on the retention of information than on information acquisition". However, direct comparisons between subjects' performance within 24–36 hours after final ECT and that produced some days later, and measures to control for the effect of possible changes in level of depression, will be required in order to confirm the existence of such an effect.

Long-Term Effects

A "rule" which applies to all the results reported takes the form that the absence of a difference between pre- and post-ECT performance may not legitimately be interpreted as indicating "no effect of ECT". As Steif et al. (1986) point out, the improvement in memory functioning which should be associated with clinical recovery may have been offset by an impairment due to ECT, resulting in apparently unchanged performance. Whether or not this is the case can be answered either by comparing post-ECT results with a control group matched for depression at time of testing; or alternatively, by studies employing

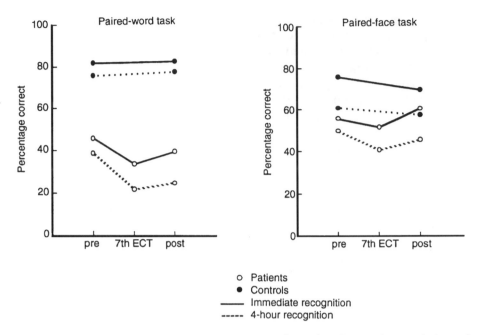

Figure 13.2 Performance of patients receiving ECT (*n*=17) and normal controls (*n*=20) on a paired-word and a paired-face recognition task administered on average 8 days prior to the start of ECT, 24–36 hours following the seventh ECT session, and 4 days following the end of treatment. ●=controls; ○=patients; ———=immediate recognition; - - -=4-hour recognition. Redrawn from data in Steif et al. (1986)

longer-term post-ECT assessments, which have the potential to assess whether the impairments apparent following ECT resolve in the follow-up period despite little or no change in clinical outcome.

In a large review of studies reporting long-term follow-up data for ECT-treated patients on memory tasks, Weeks, Freeman and Kendell (1980) concluded that, on average, return to baseline was achieved in approximately 72 days following cessation of treatment. Of the studies cited above, Frith et al. (1983) found that neither of the deficits present in the days following cessation of ECT treatment were still apparent at 6-month follow-up. On the learning-labels-for-faces task, both real and sham ECT groups reached a level of performance equal to the normal controls, while the real ECT group's performance on the word-list recognition task only managed to return to the baseline (i.e. pre-ECT, depressed) level. Frith and colleagues were able to report that depression scores for the ECT patients at 6-month follow-up were in the same range as when ECT treatment was terminated, and there was no effect of outcome on the follow-up data. Similarly, Calev et al.'s (1991) ECT patients were unchanged in terms of depressive symptom ratings at 6-month follow-up. Nevertheless, they surpassed their pre-ECT level of performance on those tasks on which they had demonstrated deficits post-ECT, when tested at this time (for example, see Figure

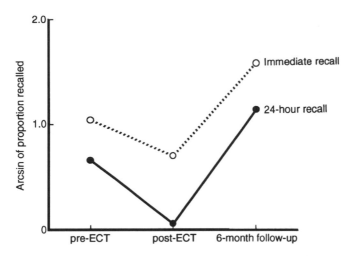

Figure 13.3 Performance of patients receiving bilateral ECT (*n*=10) on verbal paired-associates. Redrawn from data in Calev et al. (1991)

13.3). At 1-month follow-up they had reached their pre-ECT level of performance.

These findings of improved memory performance despite no significant changes in level of depression (post-ECT to follow-up) are important because they indicate that memory performance in these cases was independent of level of depression. It is therefore possible to interpret these results as demonstrating the resolution of real, ECT-induced deficits.

RETROGRADE MEMORY FUNCTIONING

Relatively few investigators have examined the *retrograde* effects of ECT; that is, the influence of this treatment on recall of material learned in the years before treatment. This may be due in part to a lack of standardised tests for the assessment of past memories. Studies are difficult to compare for this reason. Material covering different kinds of event and time periods have been used and, in some studies, no precise information is given about the content of the instrument used.

Retrograde memory functioning may be assessed for two classes of information: autobiographical memories and memory for public events. This section attempts to review these areas separately. A major source of variation in the retrograde effects of organic insults such as ECT derives from the timing of the three critical events: (a) when the to-be-remembered event occurred, (b) when the ECT was administered, and (c) when the memory was tested. These may be critical factors in determining the results obtained.

Autobiographical Memory Functioning

Janis (1950), and Janis and Astrachan (1951), assessed autobiographical memory function before ECT and 4, 10 and 14 weeks post-ECT. Both of these studies found that patients frequently failed to recall autobiographical details on retesting which had been spontaneously recalled pre-ECT. Furthermore, these authors noted that in some cases these items of information could not be elicited by cues provided by the examiner, suggesting that some autobiographical details had been lost from memory permanently. In 1981, Squire, Slater and Miller attempted to replicate these findings using a similar technique. However, the examples given of the kinds of topics covered in their "Personal Events" questionnaire do not refer to autobiographical material only; rather there is a mix of questions concerning autobiographical and public material (e.g. the names of school classmates, events or names associated with the Watergate scandal). Subjects were asked simply to recall their memories of such events which covered a period extending from the current (index) hospital admission to 20 years earlier. The same form of the test was used for testing one day before the ECT, one hour after the fifth ECT, one week after the termination of ECT (mean electroshocks administered = 9.1) and at 7-month follow-up. At no time was level of depression in either the ECT or non-ECT group assessed. Analysis of the number of facts recalled by subjects revealed that, before ECT commenced, the ECT group ($n = 10$) scores were not significantly different from those of depressed controls ($n = 7$). However, analysis of the scores for the ECT group pre- to post-treatment (a combination of one hour after the fifth ECT and one week after completion) showed that this group recalled significantly fewer details than they had done previously; by contrast, the depressed controls recalled significantly more on retesting after an approximately similar time lapse (one month). Examining the pattern of results across the various individual questions, Squire and colleagues found the responses for more recent events to be more significantly affected than remote memories. Furthermore, this effect was largely attributable to memory loss for one question—that referring to the day of the (index) hospital admission (which occurred 2–36 days prior to the start of ECT). Consistent with the reports of Janis and coworkers, Squire and colleagues found that reminders often failed to "jog" the patient's memory, and poor recall for this event was still evident at 7-month follow-up.

Further evidence of a limited temporal gradient effect on the recall of autobiographical information following ECT is provided by Calev et al. (1989). On testing 16 ECT patients with a similar questionnaire 18–24 hours after the seventh ECT, they found that, compared with patients receiving drug therapy (imipramine; $n = 10$), ECT patients forgot significantly more information concerning recent events (i.e. occurring in the last year) than more remote events (more than two years ago). However, the few details provided regarding questionnaire content suggest that the kinds of information solicited for these periods may have been different. If this were the case, the effect seen may be one relating to content of the questionnaire rather than an effect of time period.

Further complicating the picture is the fact that Calev et al. (1991) failed to replicate these findings in a larger group ($n = 27$) of ECT patients, though a slightly different time-period analysis was used on this occasion. They did, however, report significant decreases in the total amount of information recalled by patients after they had undergone ECT—an effect not demonstrated by their control subjects on retesting.

Memory for Public Events

Squire and coworkers have attempted to study this aspect of memory via a number of tasks including "Public Events" questionnaires (e.g. for news events during the 1950s, 60s and 70s, and recall of information concerning television programmes). Tests based on the latter material have the advantage that they can, to some degree, incorporate controls for timing and degree of public exposure to the information. Squire, Slater and Miller (1981) tested 18 ECT patients' recall of details about the plot, characters and actors' names, as well as details of episodes of series broadcast for one season only between 1967 and 1974. All subjects were tested in 1975/76, pre-ECT, one week post-ECT and at 7-month follow-up. No control patients were tested for comparison. The statistical analysis reported showed a significant and selective decrease in the number of facts recalled for the most recent programmes one hour after the fifth ECT, followed by constant improvement in scores, so that at 7 months the patients' performance was not significantly below their pre-ECT scores. In the same study, a broadly similar pattern was revealed in another group of 10 patients' recall performance (measured as percentage correct) on the public-events questionnaire. One hour after the fifth ECT, scores were below baseline (pre-ECT) for all time periods, though somewhat more so for the most recent period. The scores obtained for all time periods at succeeding test points were higher, with scores at 7 months almost equal to pre-ECT for the most recent period and scores for the more remote periods improved on baseline. Squire and colleagues interpreted these results as indicating a time-gradient effect, similar to that observed in other amnesic conditions.

Calev and coworkers studied the performance of both ECT-treated and depressed controls on similar questionnaires 18–24 hours post-ECT. Comparison of pre- and post-ECT (mean = 8.9 electroshocks) scores on a questionnaire covering the periods 1954–63, 1964–73, 1974–83 and the last year before ECT, revealed a highly significant post-ECT deficit, but no evidence of a time-gradient effect (Calev et al., 1991). Similar results were obtained when ECT subjects were tested 18–24 hours after seven ECT sessions, on a questionnaire covering the much more restricted time period 1973–85 (Calev et al., 1989). The scores of the depressed control subjects in this study, who were treated with a standard antidepressant drug (imipramine), were unchanged when retested.

There is thus good evidence that ECT impairs memory for past events in both the public and the private domains. It is possible that more recent memories are more severely affected, and that the effects of ECT dissipate with time since treatment. However, these observations need to be confirmed in studies that are better controlled.

SUBJECTIVE EXPERIENCE OF MEMORY IMPAIRMENT FOLLOWING ECT

Freeman and Kendell (1980) conducted an extensive survey of 166 patients who had ECT 6–18 months or 6 years previously, with a view to gathering information on (amongst other things) their past experience, and current feelings and attitudes towards the treatment. When questioned about their opinion regarding memory impairments following ECT, 30% agreed with the statement "My memory has never returned to normal" (63.1% disagreed with this statement); approximately the same percentages applied to the statement "ECT causes permanent changes to memory". However, exactly what the respondents may have understood this statement to mean is unclear. Did they mean their ability to remember new events was impaired? Or was it that they felt they could not remember events from the past—referring perhaps to the time surrounding their ECT treatment? Furthermore, the fact that only a minority of ECT patients complained of longstanding memory impairment suggests that a factor other than having experienced ECT may account for the differential reporting in the group.

Squire and Slater (1983) attempted to address these kinds of questions through a detailed examination of ECT patients' subjective experience of memory functioning in a prospective 3-year follow-up of patients prescribed bilateral ($n = 31$) or unilateral ($n = 28$) ECT. Patients' subjective experience of their memory function was assessed pre-ECT, and at one week, 7 months and 3 years post-ECT via a memory self-rating scale, a structured interview and a technique which required patients to indicate on a line representing a specified period of time any points or periods which they had difficulty remembering. A control group of depressed patients who underwent other forms of treatment was assessed during their hospital stay and 7 months later. The results on the self-rating scale indicated that, before ECT, all subjects reported memory impairments to a similar degree. Not surprisingly, one week post-ECT those receiving bilateral treatment only reported significantly more impairment relative to their baseline. At 7-month follow-up the depressed control group exhibited a significant improvement over their previous score, while by contrast, both ECT groups reported pre-ECT (i.e. suboptimal) level of functioning. Moreover, the overall memory self-rating score at 3-year follow-up (bilateral group only tested) remained at approximately this level, still significantly below that of the control group at 7 months.

Analysis of the data obtained from the time-line technique showed that at 7-month follow-up patients reported difficulty mainly in remembering events in the two years preceding ECT and in the 3 months after the start of treatment. Before ECT these patients had only reported problems for past events extending over the preceding 5 months.

These data substantiate the findings of Freeman and Kendell, and appear to indicate that patients who receive bilateral ECT will report experiencing memory impairment to a significantly greater extent than patients who have also experienced depression, but have not received ECT.

It is important to note, however, that the severity of depression in the study groups was not reported in this study. A number of studies have demonstrated that this may be a significant determinant of reported memory deficits. Cronholm and Ottosson (1963), for example, applied regression analyses to their data on ratings of depressive symptomatology and self-ratings of memory change. They found that the variable "experience of memory change" (i.e. subjective improvements in memory) was significantly related to "improvement in the depressive state". The same positive relationship between the reporting of memory difficulties and depressive state was reported by Frith et al. (1983), who found that subjective memory complaints were significantly worse for those who had a poor outcome (in terms of depressive symptoms) irrespective of whether they had received real or sham ECT. Indeed, there were indications that this factor may have been at work in the study of Squire and Slater cited above. Data from the structured interview indicated that there was a significant association between reports of memory problems and the report that ECT did not help at all, or helped for no longer than 3 months. These disclosures strongly suggest that these individuals continued to experience levels of depression at follow-up.

These studies suggest that complaints of long-term memory impairments may result from concurrent depression, rather than from long-term effects of ECT.

BILATERAL VERSUS UNILATERAL ECT

All of the results cited so far (with the exception of Steif et al., 1986) have referred to bilateral ECT. Unilateral nondominant ECT was introduced by Lancaster, Steinert and Frost (1958), who reported that memory impairment was less severe with this procedure at no cost to clinical outcome. Such a result can be explained on the grounds that:

- Verbal functions, including verbal memory, are largely subserved by the left hemisphere.
- The right hemisphere is implicated in abnormal, and particularly depressed, mood states.

Since the first reports of Lancaster and coworkers there have been a great many studies of the differential effects of the various forms of ECT. Unfortunately, the level of methodological rigour required by such studies in order to generate interpretable and reliable results is extremely high and rarely achieved. It is not surprising to find that contradictory findings can be cited. As noted earlier, even the basic issue of whether or not bilateral ECT is as effective as nondominant unilateral ECT is still a matter of research and debate.

However, in spite of these problems clear trends have emerged. Fromm-Auch (1982) reviewed the findings reported in the previous 16 years and identified the following results:

1. Impairment of both verbal and nonverbal functions with bilateral ECT.
2. Impairment of verbal functions with unilateral dominant ECT.
3. Impairment of nonverbal functions with less than five sessions of nondominant ECT, in contrast to improvement of these functions after five or more sessions of nondominant ECT.
4. No change or improvement of verbal memory functions with unilateral nondominant ECT.

Thus, bilateral ECT produces more impairment, and it seems that electrode placement interacts with the functional laterality of the brain, producing hemisphere-specific effects.

The results of Horne et al. (1985, cited above) suggest that the better outcome on memory tests in the unilateral ECT patients applies to tests of both short-term and long-term (i.e. delayed-recall) functioning. The performance of patients who received unilateral nondominant ECT did not decline from baseline on either short-term or long-term memory tests after five sessions of ECT.

EFFECTS OF OTHER ECT PARAMETERS

ECT administration may vary along a number of parameters, such as the kind of stimulus waveform used (sinewave or brief-pulse), or electrode placement (bitemporal, bifrontal, or temporoparietal, for example). An important research issue is whether variations in these parameters produce different degrees of relief from depression or memory impairment.

We are not aware of studies which have examined systematically the issue of electrode placement. For example, it is not known whether or not bifrontal ECT produces more impairment or a different pattern of impairment relative to bitemporal ECT. Though the studies cited in the section on anterograde deficits used different electrode placements, it is not possible to assess the effects of these different placements, simply because so many other factors were also varied. This is an issue which needs systematic investigation.

Similarly, very little research effort has been directed at the possible differential effects of different waveforms. Weiner, Roger, Davidson and Squire (1986) conducted an exemplary study in which depressed subjects were assigned randomly to either bilateral or unilateral ECT and to either sinewave or brief-pulse stimuli. Memory functioning and levels of depression were assessed before ECT, 2–3 days after the final ECT (mean = 9.5 sessions) and at 6-month follow-up. A control group of depressives not prescribed ECT was tested at similar time intervals. There were no significant differences between the groups in terms of age, years of education, socio-economic status, or baseline scores of depression. All groups were also equivalent in terms of degree of improvement measured on three separate scales over the course of treatment. Despite this high degree of similarity between the groups, significant group differences emerged when post-ECT scores were compared with baseline scores on measures of delayed (20-minute) recall. Consistent with the studies cited in the previous section, those receiving bilateral ECT demonstrated significantly greater decrements in performance than both the control and unilateral ECT subjects on a number of tasks including verbal paired-associates and retrograde memory tasks. The authors reported that sinewave ECT was similarly associated with greater deficits. Sinewave ECT subjects' deficits were significantly worse than those of both the control and brief-pulse ECT subjects on virtually all delayed memory tasks. By contrast, the performance of the brief-pulse ECT group was not significantly different from that of the control group on any of the delayed-memory tests. These findings have been supported by those of Squire and Zouzounis (1986) who also compared sinewave and brief-pulse ECT, albeit in a less methodologically sound study. They confirmed that sinewave ECT produced more impairment, but only in the short term.

SUMMARY AND CONCLUSIONS

The quality of memory functioning changes both during and following a course of ECT. Different patterns of deficit, or lack thereof, will emerge from studies examining memory at differing time-points. In the first hours following an electroshock, new learning may be severely compromised and the patient may have difficulty recalling recent events which preceded the onset of ECT treatment. This time period represents the low-point of functioning and from here on memory improves. In the days following an electroshock or termination of treatment, recognition memory should return to pre-ECT or near-normal levels of functioning, while tasks requiring free recall of new information may still be moderately impaired (depending to some extent on the load placed on retrieval processes). At this time, patients may continue to experience difficulty recalling public or personal events from the past (extending back over a few years), but most notably for events transpiring in the days before ECT was initiated.

At follow-up one month later, many patients will have attained a level of anterograde functioning close to their pre-ECT level or better. However, this level of functioning may represent a deleterious effect of ECT "masked" by improvements associated with recovery from depression.

At 6 months, post-ECT patients' level of anterograde memory functioning should have surpassed pretreatment levels (although we do not have the data available yet to establish whether this is likely to reach normal levels of functioning). Unfortunately, the results published to date indicate that, even at this stage of follow-up, patients may still not have recovered their memory for life-events which occurred close to the time of treatment.

It is clear from the results documented above that people who have undergone a course of ECT treatment can legitimately complain about its effects on memory functioning, particularly in the immediate and medium term. Complaints about long-term, permanent impairments of memory for new events are more difficult to interpret. Obviously the data presented above are based on group averages and it is conceivable that they may hide the occasional patient who does experience such a deficit. There is, however, reasonable evidence indicating that the subjective experience of sustained memory impairment is associated with a poor response to treatment, and thus ongoing depression, rather than to long-term effects of ECT.

REFERENCES

Buchan, H., Johnstone, E., McPherson, K., Palmer, R.L., Crow, T.J. & Brandon, S. (1992). Who benefits from electroconvulsive therapy? Combined results of the Leicester and Northwick Park Trials. *British Journal of Psychiatry*, **160**, 355–359.

Calev, A., Ben-Tzvi, E., Shapira, B., Drexler, H., Carasso, R. & Lerer, B. (1989). Distinct memory impairments following electroconvulsive therapy and imipramine. *Psychological Medicine*, **19**, 111–119.

Calev, A., Nigal, D., Shapira, B., Tubi, N., Chazan, S., Ben-Yehuda, Y., Kugelmass, S. & Lerer, B. (1991). Early and long-term effects of electroconvulsive therapy and depression on memory and other cognitive functions. *Journal of Nervous and Mental Disease*, **179**(9), 526–533.

Clinical Psychiatry Committee (1965). Clinical trials in the treatment of depressive illness: report to the Medical Research Council. *British Medical Journal*, **i**, 881–886.

Cronholm, B. & Ottosson, J.-O. (1963). The experience of memory after electroconvulsive therapy. *British Journal of Psychiatry*, **109**, 251–258.

D'Elia, G. & Raotma, H. (1975). Is unilateral ECT less effective than bilateral ECT? *British Journal of Psychiatry*, **126**, 83–89.

Fink, M. (1990). How does convulsive therapy work? *Neuropsychopharmacology*, **3**, 73–82.

Freeman, C.P.L. & Kendell, R.E. (1980). ECT. I: Patients' experiences and attitudes. *British Journal of Psychiatry*, **137**, 8–16.

Frith, C.D., Stevens, M., Johnstone, E.C., Deakin, J.F.W., Lawler, P. & Crow, T.J. (1983). Effects of ECT and depression on various aspects of memory. *British Journal of Psychiatry*, **142**, 610–617.

Fromm-Auch, D. (1982). Comparison of unilateral and bilateral ECT: evidence for selective memory impairment. *British Journal of Psychiatry*, **141**, 608–613.

Gelder, M., Gath, D. & Mayou, R. (1988). *Oxford Textbook of Psychiatry*. Oxford University Press, Oxford.

Gregory, S., Shawcross, C.R. & Gill, D. (1985). The Nottingham ECT study. A double-blind comparison of bilateral, unilateral and simulated ECT in depressive illness. *British Journal of Psychiatry*, **146**, 520–524.

Hamilton, M. (1960). Assessment of depression scale. *Journal of Neurology, Neurosurgery and Psychiatry*, **23**, 56–62.

Hamilton, M. (1967). Development of a rating scale for primary depressive illness. *British Journal of Social and Clinical Psychology*, **6**, 278–296.

Horne, R.L., Pettinati, H.M., Sugerman, A.A. & Varga, E. (1985). Comparing bilateral and unilateral electroconvulsive therapy in a randomised study with EEG monitoring. *Archives of General Psychiatry*, **42**, 1087–1092.

Janis, I.L. (1950). Psychologic effects of electric convulsive treatments. *Journal of Nervous and Mental Disease*, **111**, 359–382.

Janis, I.L. & Astrachan, M. (1951). The effects of electroconvulsive treatments on memory efficiency. *Journal of Abnormal and Social Psychology*, **46**, 501–511.

Johnson, M.H. & Magaro, P.A. (1987). Effects of mood and severity on memory processes in depression and mania. *Psychological Bulletin*, **101**, 28–40.

Johnstone, E.C., Deakin, J.F.W., Lawler, P., Frith, C.D., Stevens, M., McPherson, K. & Crow, T.J. (1980). The Northwick Park electroconvulsive therapy trial. *Lancet*, **ii**, 1317–1320.

Lancaster, N., Steinert, R. & Frost, I. (1958). Unilateral electroconvulsive therapy. *Journal of Mental Science*, **104**, 221–227.

Pippard, J. (1992). Audit of electroconvulsive treatment in two National Health Service regions. *British Journal of Psychiatry*, **160**, 621–637.

Slater, E. (1951). Evaluation of electroconvulsive therapy as compared with conservative methods in depressive states. *Journal of Mental Science*, **97**, 567–569.

Squire, L.R. (1986). Memory functions as affected by electroconvulsive therapy. *Annals of New York Academy of Sciences*, **462**, 307–314.

Squire, L.R. & Chace, P.M. (1975). Memory functions six to nine months after electroconvulsive therapy. *Archives of General Psychiatry*, **32**, 1557–1564.

Squire, L.R. & Miller, P.L. (1974). Diminution of anterograde amnesia following electroconvulsive therapy. *British Journal of Psychiatry*, **125**, 490–495.

Squire, L.R. & Slater, P.C. (1983). Electroconvulsive therapy and complaints of memory dysfunction: a prospective three-year follow-up. *British Journal of Psychiatry*, **14**, 791–801.

Squire, L.R., Slater, P.C. & Miller, P.L. (1981). Retrograde amnesia and bilateral electroconvulsive therapy. *Archives of General Psychiatry*, **38**, 89–95.

Squire, L.R. & Zouzounis, J.A. (1986). ECT and memory: brief pulse versus sine wave. *American Journal of Psychiatry*, **143**, 596–601.

Steif, B.L., Sackeim, H.A., Portnoy, S., Decina, P. & Malitz, S. (1986). Effects of depression and ECT on anterograde memory, *Biological Psychiatry*, **21**, 921–930.

Sternberg, D.E. & Jarvik, M.E. (1976). Memory functions in depression. *Archives of General Psychiatry*, **33**, 219–224.

Wechsler, D. (1945). A standardised memory scale for clinical use. *Journal of Psychology*, **19**, 87–95.

Weeks, D., Freeman, C.P.L. & Kendell, R.E. (1980). ECT. II: Enduring cognitive deficits? *British Journal of Psychiatry*, **137**, 26–37.

Weiner, R.D., Rogers, H.J., Davidson, J.R.T. & Squire, L.R. (1986). Effects of stimulus parameters on cognitive side effects. *Annals of New York Academy of Sciences*, **462**, 315–325.

Chapter 14

Functional Disorders of Autobiographical Memory

John F. Kihlstrom
Yale University, New Haven, USA
and
Daniel L. Schacter
Harvard University, Cambridge, USA

INTRODUCTION

The memory disorders most commonly encountered in the clinic are those associated with some form of damage to brain tissue. The amnesic syndromes linked to lesions of the medial portions of the temporal lobes, or the diencephalon, are classic examples of the type; so is the retrograde amnesia observed following a concussive blow to the head. In other cases, however, a clinically significant amnesia appears in the absence of any obvious defect in brain structure or function. These include episodes of amnesia or fugue following emotional trauma; amnesia is also observed in cases of multiple personality disorder. Functional amnesia may be defined as a memory loss that is attributable to an instigating event or process that does not result in insult, injury or disease affecting brain tissue, but that produces more forgetting than would normally occur in the absence of that instigating event or process (Schacter & Kihlstrom, 1989).

The functional amnesias may be further divided into pathological and non-pathological types. The pathological functional amnesias are those in which amnesia is either a diagnostic symptom of mental disorder, or occurs in the context of a diagnosable mental disorder. Psychogenic amnesia, psychogenic fugue, depersonalization and derealization, and multiple personality are of this

Handbook of Memory Disorders. Edited by A.D. Baddeley, B.A. Wilson and F.N. Watts.
© 1995 John Wiley & Sons Ltd.

type. Nonpathological functional amnesias are those which can be induced by psychological procedures in individuals who are free of any diagnosable mental disorder. The chief example of this category is posthypnotic amnesia, which may be induced in normal hypnotized subjects by means of a verbal suggestion (for reviews, see Kihlstrom, 1985; Kihlstrom & Barnhardt, 1993). This chapter is confined to those instances of functional amnesia most likely to be encountered in the clinic (for alternative surveys of this material, see Kihlstrom, Tataryn & Hoyt, 1993; Kopelman, 1987; Schacter & Kihlstrom, 1989; Spiegel, Frischholz & Spira, 1993).

FUNCTIONAL AMNESIA IN THE DISSOCIATIVE DISORDERS

Functional amnesia impairing autobiographical memory is a pathogonomic sign in a major class of mental illnesses known as the dissociative disorders. According to the fourth edition of the *Diagnostic and Statistical Manual for Mental Disorders* (DSM-IV; American Psychiatric Association, 1994; see also Cardena et al., 1993), the dissociative disorders consist of a group of related disorders that share symptoms reflecting a disturbance in the integrative functions of memory, consciousness, and/or identity. This category of mental illness began its existence, in the first edition of the *Diagnostic and Statistical Manual* (DSM; 1952) as *dissociative reaction*, a form of psychoneurotic disorder; in the second edition (DSM-II, 1968), dissociative disorder was classified as a subtype of *hysterical neurosis*, itself a type of neurosis; the third edition (DSM-III, 1980) and its revision (DSM-III-R, 1987) abandoned reference to both neurosis and hysteria, and listed the *dissociativ2ee disorders* as a major category of mental illness. DSM-III de-emphasized the importance of amnesia in the diagnosis of dissociative disorder, but DSM-III-R returned amnesia to its rightful place. DSM-IV renames some of the syndromes (for example, the psychogenic amnesia of DSM-III-R is now dissociative amnesia, multiple personality disorder is now dissociative identity disorder), and recognizes nonpathological phenomena of dissociation, such as trance and possession states, which are encountered in non-western cultures). As an aid to clinical practitioners, this chapter adopts the diagnostic labels of DSM-IV; Kihlstrom (1994) has provided a detailed summary of the history of this diagnostic category.

Historically, three distinct forms of dissociative disorder have been widely recognized: dissociative amnesia, dissociative fugue, and dissociative identity disorder. Amnesia for all or part of one's personal history is the hallmark of each of these syndromes. In dissociative amnesia, the core symptom is an inability to remember important personal information, typically a traumatic experience. In dissociative fugue, the core symptom is confusion about one's identity, loss of identity, or the assumption of a new identity. This amounts to forgetting who one is, not just what one has done. Interestingly, the change in identity is typically accompanied by a loss of memory for events and experiences associated with the former identity; and when the fugue state resolves, and the person reverts to his or her original identity, access to these memories is restored while autobiographical memories associated with the newly assumed identity are lost. Dissociative identity disorder resembles fugue, except that the shift between identities, and associated sets of autobiographical memories, is cyclical. It appears as if two or more separate identities exist within the same individual, alternating in control over experience, thought and action. Each of these identities (sometimes called *alter egos*, or simply *alters*) has its own fund of autobiographical memories, covering events and experiences that occurred while it was in control. Finally, the alter egos are separated by a symmetrical or asymmetrical amnesia, which may prevent one personality from knowing the actions, experiences, or even the existence of another.

Amnesia is also featured in several other forms of dissociative disorder, including those that are recent additions to the nomenclature. For example, in *ataque de nervios*, a culture-specific form of trance and possession disorder observed in Latin America, an individual under stress experiences somatic symptoms resembling panic followed by such behaviors as breaking objects or attacking other people; there is an amnesia for the episode after it has ceased (Lewis-Fernandez, 1994). Depersonalization disorder involves the sense that one's body or one's self is unreal; the person may also feel that his or her surroundings, or other people, are unreal—in which case we speak of derealization (Steinberg, 1991). The person retains his or her sense of identity in depersonalization and derealization, and presumably his or her fund of autobiographical memory as well (although this has not been systematically investigated); what is lost is the sense of familiarity—thus, as Reed (1974/1988; 1979) has noted, depersonalization and derealization are fundamentally anomalies of recognition.[1]

The importance of amnesia in the dissociative disorders is clearly indicated by the questions posed in structured clinical interviews, such as the Dissociative Disorders Interview Schedule (DDIS: Ross, 1989) and the Structured Clinical Interview for DSM-IV Dissociative Disorders (SCID-D: Steinberg, 1993; Steinberg, Rounsaville & Cicchetti, 1990) that have been developed to permit reliable diagnosis of these disorders.[2] The following extracts from the SCID-D indicate how dissociative disorders of memory and identity are assessed clinically. If the symptoms are not due to drugs, alcohol, or head trauma, positive answers contribute to the diagnosis of depersonalization, dissociative amnesia, dissociative fugue, or dissociative identity disorder. (For the full text of the structured interview and detailed instructions on scoring, see Steinberg (1993).)

Have you ever felt as if there were large gaps in your memory? Have there ever been hours or days that seemed to be missing, or that you couldn't account for? Has there ever been a time in which you had difficulty remembering your daily activities?

Have you ever found yourself in a place and been unable to remember how or why you went there? Have you ever traveled away from your home unexpectedly and been unable to remember your past?

Have you ever found yourself in a place away from your home and been unable to remember who you were? If so, did you experience any confusion or changes in your usual identity?

Have you ever been unable to remember your name, age, address, or other important personal information?

Have you ever felt as if there was a struggle going on inside of you? Have you ever felt as if there was a struggle going on inside you about who you really are? Have you ever felt confused as to who you are?

Have you ever felt as if, or found yourself acting as if, you were still a child? Have you ever acted as if you were a completely different person? Have you ever been told by others that you seem like a different person?

Have you ever referred to yourself (or been told by others that you referred to yourself) by different names? Have other people referred to you by different names?

Have you ever found things in your possession that seemed to belong to you, but you could not remember how you got them?

Have you ever felt as if you were possessed or controlled?

Has your mood ever changed rapidly, without any reason? Have you ever experienced (or been told of) rapid changes in your capabilities, or ability to function?

Have you ever felt as if you were living in the past, or reliving the past as though it were occurring in the present?

Do you ever talk to yourself or have ongoing dialogues with yourself? Are these dialogues similar to hearing voices or to thoughts? Does it feel as if they occur inside your head?

FUNCTIONAL AMNESIA AND THE STRUCTURE OF MEMORY

In view of these diagnostic questions, it is apparent that the memory impairment observed in the dissociative disorders covers a very broad spectrum. First and foremost, the dissociative disorders are marked by impairments in *episodic memory*. Episodic memory concerns people's knowledge of particular events that they themselves have experienced; it is inherently autobiographical (Tulving, 1983). A full-blown episodic memory describes an event that has occurred in the past, but it also makes reference to the spatiotemporal context—the time and place—in which that event took place; it also necessarily makes reference to the self as the agent or experiencer of the event in question. By contrast, *semantic memory* consists of generic knowledge about the world; with respect to oneself, it includes knowledge of one's own name, residence, occupation, family members, and other information that is not contingent on its association with a particular time and place; this self-referent semantic memory is tantamount to one's identity (Kihlstrom & Klein, 1994).

Considerations of the episodic–semantic distinction help to organize the subtypes of dissociative disorder. In pure cases of dissociative amnesia, there is a loss of episodic, but not of semantic, memory, about oneself. People forget what they did, or what happened to them, during a specified period of time; but they do not forget who they are. In most cases the amnesia is reversible, and access to the autobiographical memories covered by the amnesia is eventually restored. In dissociative fugue, there is a loss of self-referent semantic memory as well as of episodic memory: these patients forget who they are, as well as what they have done. If the patient assumes a new identity, a new set of autobiographical memories becomes associated with the new mental representation of self. When the fugue is resolved, and the new identity is lost, the associated autobiographical memories are lost as well. Something similar happens in dissociative identity disorder, except that there is a kind of alternation or exchange of identities and associated autobiographical memories. While the dissociative disorders involve profound impairments of autobiographical memory, and of self-referent semantic memory, other knowledge stored in memory appears to be relatively unimpaired. The individual's fund of world knowledge (non-self-referent semantic knowledge), and repertoire of cognitive and motoric skills (procedural knowledge) remain intact.

The Case of Mary Reynolds

Occasional case reports of dissociative identity disorder suggest that procedural knowledge also shifts with identity and episodic memory. For example, in the case of Mary Reynolds (James, 1890, pp. 359–363; see also Carlson, 1984; Kihlstrom, Tataryn & Hoyt, 1993), the first shift from her usual identity (which we will call Mary 1) to an alter ego (Mary 2) was accompanied by a virtually complete loss of declarative and procedural memory:

> Memory had fled. To all intents and purposes she was as a being for the first time ushered into the world. "All of the past that remained to her was the faculty of pronouncing a few words, and this seems to have been as purely instinctive as the wailings of an infant; for at first the words which she uttered were connected with no ideas in her mind." Until she was taught their significance they were unmeaning sounds.

However, for the most part this knowledge was quickly reacquired:

> The first lesson in her education was to teach her by what ties she was bound to those by whom she was surrounded, and the duties devolving upon her accordingly. This she was very slow to learn, and "indeed, never did learn...." The next lesson was to re-teach her the arts of reading and writing. She was apt enough, and made such rapid progress in both, that *in a few weeks* she had readily re-learned to read and write...(emphasis in the original).

Interestingly, there was apparently no further loss of semantic or procedural knowledge upon later shifts between personalities.

Although Mary 2 was thoroughly ignorant of the experiences, activities and knowledge of Mary 1, occasionally this information seemed to leak through the amnesic barrier. On one instance, for example, Mary 2 was prevented by her family from attending church services (about which she displayed no knowledge, in any event). That night she had a dream in which her dead sister led her towards a crowd, to which another figure read from a large book. The verses which Mary 2 quoted from memory the next morning were, of course, familiar passages from the Bible (of which Mary 2 claimed complete ignorance). The dead sister also appeared in other dreams reported in the second state, although Mary 2 never recognized her or acknowledged that she had once had a sister.

The marked savings in relearning displayed by Mary Reynolds, and the appearance of scenes known to her first identity in dreams reported by her second, are both reminiscent of the distinction between explicit and implicit memory familiar in studies of the organic amnesic syndromes (Schacter, 1987; Schacter, Chiu & Ochsner, 1993). Explicit memory refers to the individual's conscious recollection of a past event, as reflected in recall and recognition, while implicit memory refers to changes in the person's experience, thought or action that are attributable to an event, independent of conscious recollection. The explicit–implicit distinction, originally formulated in the context of episodic memory, can be extended to other domains as well (e.g. Kihlstrom, Mulvaney & Tobia, in press; Kihlstrom, Barnhardt & Tataryn 1992; Schacter et al., 1990). In the case of Mary Reynolds, savings suggest that much of her nonepisodic knowledge, semantic and procedural, was retained in storage and expressed implicitly, even though it was temporarily inaccessible to conscious retrieval.

One of the most interesting features of the functional amnesias concerns discrepancies between explicit and implicit expressions of autobiographical memory. To what extent do the memories lost to conscious recollection remain dynamically active? Unfortunately, despite all the attention currently being paid to the dissociative disorders, little systematic experimental work has been performed to investigate the disruptions of memory and identity that lie at their core. The review that follows is gleaned from those relatively few cases that have been studied quantitatively from the point of view of memory: we wish to underscore that this area is ripe for collaboration between researchers and clinicians. As knowledge accumulates, many of the generalizations made here may have to be altered.

DISSOCIATIVE AMNESIA AND FUGUE

In principle, dissociative amnesia and dissociative fugue should be easy to distinguish. The defining feature of dissociative amnesia is the loss of episodic memory; dissociative fugue also entails amnesia, but involves a change in identity (and sometimes physical relocation) as well.

In fact, however, the boundaries between amnesia and fugue are blurred. For example, Nemiah (1979) distinguished three forms of psychogenic amnesia: *systematized*, covering only specific events and related material; *localized*, covering a period of hours or weeks; and *generalized*, covering the person's entire life; in this last instance, amnesia obviously verges on fugue. For good measure, Fisher (1945; Fisher & Joseph, 1949) distinguished three types of fugues: amnesia with change in identity and relocation; amnesia with loss but no change in identity; and a reversion to an earlier period of one's life, with an amnesia covering one's life history subsequent to that period; this last type verges on amnesia, completing the circle.

Except for cases of very limited (and probably very transitory) amnesia, it appears that most psychogenic losses of autobiographical memory are associated with some alteration of identity. Of course, this is an empirical question, and deserving of systematic research in the future. For the present, amnesia and fugue are usually treated together, sometimes under the label of *functional retrograde amnesia* (Schacter & Kihlstrom, 1989; for other reviews, see also Keller & Shaywitz, 1986; Loewenstein, 1991).

Clinical Description

Dissociative amnesia, regardless of whether it is accompanied by fugue, is typically retrograde in nature, usually covering the precipitating incident and events that occurred previously. In the classic instance, the amnesia covers some traumatic event, such as physical or sexual assault, combat, or natural disaster. In other cases it covers an extended period of time leading up to the trauma. It has been claimed that dissociative amnesia frequently occurs in association with post-traumatic stress disorder (PTSD; see Herman, 1992); sometimes it is observed in the perpetrators as well as the victims of crimes (Schacter, 1986). There may be some element of anterograde amnesia as well, covering the period beginning with the trauma and ending about the time that the patient comes to clinical attention—perhaps it is at this point that the patient discovers he or she is amnesic, and seeks help. Continuous functional anterograde amnesias, resembling the organic amnesic syndromes, are rare—although Janet (1893) reported a case in which memory of the traumatic event was preserved intact, while the patient was unable to remember events that occurred subsequently.

Recovery from dissociative amnesia and fugue has not been well studied, but appears to proceed in stages. Typically patients are discovered when they spontaneously become aware of their memory deficit, or when they fail to respond appropriately to questions (e.g posed by police or medical personnel) about their identity, background and recent activities. Most dissociative amnesias and fugues resolve spontaneously, or when the patient is identified independently and brought into contact with family and friends. In some cases the patient recovers his or her memory and identity suddenly; in other cases, memory returns more gradually, often with other people helping to fill in the gaps. Sometimes there is an intermediate stage where the person first comes to appreciate his or her loss of memory and identity, and then regains it. When the amnesia resolves, and the patient has recovered those memories that were previously lost, he or she is frequently left with an amnesia covering the episode itself.

The Case of Sharon

A representative case of amnesia and fugue is that of Sharon, a 34-year-old woman who was found lying unconscious, naked, and near starvation in a park, her skin covered with sores and rat bites (Eisen, 1989). She could not identify herself, nor could she give an account of how she came to be in the park. After seven months of hospitalization, media exposure led to her identification by, and reunion with, her family, whom she accepted as her own but did not actually recognize. During subsequent hypnotherapy, Sharon recovered her identity and pre-fugue memory, as well as memories of the fugue state itself. After a difficult life with her family of origin, Sharon had graduated from high school and taken an office job. She was seduced by her supervisor, who was married, and eloped with him to live in another state. After eight years, all contact with her family ceased. Five years after that, a period in which she was held virtually a prisoner in her house, she apparently escaped—later to be found in the park.

Over the years, a number of case series of amnesia and/or fugue have been reported. Dissociative amnesia and fugue are rare, with a reported incidence ranging from less than 1% (Abeles & Schilder, 1935) to less than 2% (Kirshner, 1973) among psychiatric patients. Sometimes the episode is instigated by a clearly traumatic event, or an extremely stressful environment. For example, Sargent and Slater (1941) found amnesia in over 14% of a consecutive series of combat soldiers hospitalized during the Second World War. Fully 35% of those exposed to the most extreme combat stress had amnesia for their experiences, compared with 6% amnesic among those whose experiences had been "trifling". About 25% of the cases had suffered head injury, but this was deemed insufficient to account for the memory disorder. Trauma, abuse, deprivation, and neglect often figure prominently in the childhood histories of these patients, although it should be noted that this information is usually based on retrospective self-reports, and is therefore not necessarily valid.

Experimental Studies of Memory in Amnesia and Fugue

Although there are many vivid clinical descriptions of dissociative amnesia and fugue, few cases have been subject to formal analysis using experimental techniques developed in the laboratory. One of the reasons is the difficulty of catching such cases before they have been resolved, and the amnesia has reversed. Still, a few attempts have been made, and these provide models of the sorts of investigations that should be attempted as the opportunity arises.

The Case of P.N.

This 21-year-old-male was hospitalized complaining of back pain (Schacter, Wang, Tulving & Freedman, 1982), at which time he realized that he could not identify himself or remember anything of his past. However, he knew where he was and the names of prominent persons in contemporary sports and politics; he also had an island of memory for a period when he had worked as a courier. The patient was identified through media coverage, although he did not immediately recognize his family members. Neurological examination was unremarkable, except that a myelogram revealed a herniated disk, which was successfully treated by laminectomy. The fugue episode, which had apparently begun four days earlier following the funeral of P.N.'s grandfather, resolved the next evening.

During the amnesic period, and again three weeks after recovery, P.N. completed two formal tests of memory function, and his performance was compared with that of a control subject matched for age, gender, education and IQ. In the first test, he was asked to recognize the faces of individuals who became famous during the decades from 1920 to 1979. His performance on this task was approximately equal to that of the control patient; most important, there was no change between testing sessions. In the second, P.N. was presented with a common English word, and asked to recall a personal experience related to that cue. When recall was unconstrained with respect to temporal epoch, only a small minority of P.N.'s memories came from the period of time prior to the onset of the fugue; by contrast, the vast bulk of the control subject's memories came from a comparable period. When forced to recall events from the period covered by the fugue, P.N. could do so, although most of these events came from his island of memory; his response latencies were much longer than the control subject's. After the fugue resolved, P.N.'s performance in both conditions was comparable to the control's, and there was no bias towards events located in his previous island of memory.

The Case of Patient K

Most dissociative amnesias are content-specific and time-general, affecting a broad swath of autobiographical memory and (at least sometimes) personal identity. Thus, the memory deficit typically covers material that is directly self-relevant. However, two very interesting cases have been reported in which the content of the amnesia is quite general, but the period of time covered by it is very specific (Treadway, Cohen, McCloskey & Gordon, 1992). Patient K, a 53-year-old-male, was electrocuted in a household accident in 1984; when he regained consciousness, he thought the year was 1945, and that he was 14 years old and resided in his hometown. He did not recognize his wife and children, and he had no awareness that his father had died. His last memory was of being hit on the head with a baseball bat in August 1945. Eight years later, in 1992, the amnesia still had not remitted, and patient K still perceived himself as a 14-year-old boy (and was quite surprised when he saw himself in the mirror every morning!). In addition to his autobiographical memory, patient K also lost a number of adult skills, such as shaving, driving and operating various electronic devices. When tested with techniques similar to those employed with P.N., patient K showed excellent memory for famous people and public events up to 1945, but none for persons and events who became famous afterwards.

The Case of Patient F

Patient F, a woman also studied by Treadway et al. (1992), showed similar features. In 1976, at age 39, she suffered a large coronary aneurism; upon regaining consciousness, she thought the year was 1960 and she was 23 years old. She remembered that she was married and had three children, but she identified them as two to five years old when in fact they were aged 16 to 19; she had no knowledge of her fourth child, and she described as new the house in which she had lived for 16 years. Like patient K, patient F had excellent memory for famous persons and events up to 1960, but not afterwards. She did not know how to operate a dishwasher acquired sometime after 1960. There was little or no remission of this amnesia over the next 16 years. Interestingly, in both cases the amnesia effectively blotted out a stressful period in the patients' lives, and returned them to happier times. Patient K's personal and family life took a dramatic turn for the worse in September 1945, and again in 1984; patient F was under considerable stress in 1961, and went through a major family crisis in 1976.

These cases illustrate how the systematic application of techniques derived from the experimental laboratory can shed light both on the nature of the individual case and on general principles of memory organization and function.[3] For example, Treadwell et al. (1992) argue from patients F and K that autobiographical memory is organized around landmark events that define major epochs in a person's life. Loss of access to the landmark events entails loss of everything in between—much as in a verbal-learning experiment, where forgetting tends to occur within conceptual categories. P.N. illustrates another form of landmark: during the time of his fugue, he retained an island of memory defined by his employment as a courier. The importance of such landmarks in organizing autobiographical memory deserves further investigation, in both patients and normals.

Explicit and Implicit Memory During Fugue

By definition, amnesia and fugue entail impairments of explicit memory: these patients cannot consciously recollect who they are or what they have been doing.

The question arises, then, whether they have any implicit memory for such information. In other words, are there aspects of their experience, thought and action that are affected by events, and other information, which they cannot consciously remember? Of course, dissociations between explicit and implicit memory are commonly observed in cases of organic amnesia. Unfortunately, except for a few studies of dissociative identity disorder (discussed below), there is no experimental evidence on this question. However, several individual case reports of amnesia and fugue do suggest that the answer is affirmative: this is clearly a matter deserving more experimental attention.

An early illustration of an explicit–implicit dissociation is Janet's (1904) case of Madame D. She was treated for an amnesia (without fugue or loss of identity) whose onset followed a stranger's report, later proved false, that her husband had died (for a secondary account, see Prince, 1906, pp. 257 ff. and Appendix E). She had intact autobiographical memory up until Bastille Day of that year (perhaps another landmark forming a boundary between memory and amnesia), but no memory for the six weeks between the holiday and the hoax. Nevertheless, she had dreams about the episode at night—day residues that are clear evidence that memory for the episode was retained and dynamically active. Similar hints are found in James's (1890) famous case of Ansel Bourne, an itinerant preacher who during a fugue was known as A.J. Brown, a storekeeper (for an alternative account, see Kenney, 1986). First, note the similarity in first and last initials: A. Bourne and A. Brown. Moreover, A.J. Brown was a devoted churchgoer, a habit perhaps carried over from his life as Ansel Bourne; and once during services gave testimony about a religious conversion he had experienced as Bourne, while attributing it to his life as Brown.

More recent case studies also provide tantalizing evidence of explicit–implicit dissociations affecting identity and autobiographical memory. Thus, patient P.N. referred to himself as "Lumberjack", a nickname bestowed on him during the period covered by his amnesia, without any apparent awareness of the origins of the moniker (Schacter, Wang, Tulving & Friedman, 1982). Another man, who fell amnesic after murdering his wife, showed a specific deficit in recognizing women's names and faces (Gudjonsson & MacKeith, 1983). Patient Jane Doe, unable to identify herself or give any helpful information, was asked on several occasions to dial a telephone randomly: she dialed the same number consistently, which proved to be her mother's (Lyon, 1985). Patient M.R., a victim of homosexual rape, gave a large number of sexual responses to the Rorschach inkblots; he also became distressed, and attempted suicide, after viewing card 18BM of the Thematic Apperception Test, which can be interpreted as depicting one person attacking another from behind (Kaszniak, Nussbaum, Berren & Santiago, 1988). Patient C.M., a rape victim studied by Christianson and Nilsson (1989), became upset when returned to the scene of her assault (without recognizing its significance); she also reported the intrusion of the words "bricks" and "bricks and the path" into her stream of consciousness—again, without any awareness that she had actually been assaulted on a path constructed from crumbled bricks; her amnesia remitted when she went jogging on a road whose texture resembled that of the road on which she had been jogging when attacked. In each case, the patient's behavior is clearly attributable to some feature of an event covered by his or her amnesia.

Implicit memory can also be expressed through psychophysiological responses. In a study of organic amnesics, Bentin, Moscovich and Heth (1992) found differential P300 components in the event-related potentials elicited by items from a studied wordlist, compared with controls, even though none of the list items was recalled. However, an early case study of dissociative amnesia revealed no such differences (Wiggins, Lombard, Brennan & Heckel, 1964). The patient was amnesic for a period beginning on New Year's Day (another landmark?), shortly before he resigned from his job and embarked on a financial venture of dubious legality. When questioned about his activities during the period covered by the amnesia (which had been uncovered independently), he showed no differential electrodermal responses to critical and neutral questions. On the other hand, Gudjonsson (1979) employed electrodermal responses to determine the month in which the amnesic patient P had been born, her age, primary school, and the road on which she had lived as a child; from this information the patient was tentatively identified. Although she rejected the identity as unfamiliar, she also gave differential electrodermal responses to that name, compared with other names selected from the records of her probable primary school. In a later account of this same patient, renamed Miss Blank, Gudjonsson and Hayward (1982) found elevated levels of voice stress when her Rorschach responses had death themes, even though she had no awareness that her fugue had followed a suicide attempt.

DISSOCIATIVE IDENTITY DISORDER

Dissociative identity disorder, more popularly known as *multiple personality disorder* (MPD), is one of the most dramatic of all psychopathological syndromes. Not only does the patient exhibit, in alternation, two or more radically different identities, with correspondingly different personalities and autobiographical memories; but these alter egos are also separated by an amnesic barrier such that one or more of the alter egos appears to be unaware of the experiences, thoughts and actions of the others. Once considered to be very rare (Sutcliffe & Jones, 1962; Taylor & Martin, 1944), this syndrome is now diagnosed with considerable frequency, raising concerns that many cases are the product of iatrogenesis and cultural suggestion (for other reviews, see Bliss, 1986; Kihlstrom, Tataryn & Hoyt, 1993; Kluft, 1991; Putnam, 1989; Ross, 1990; Schacter & Kihlstrom, 1989).

Clinical Description

Dissociative identity disorder resembles fugue in that the fate of autobiographical memory is closely related to the individual's identity, but there is an alternation among identities, with corresponding changes in the accessibility of autobiographical memory. In a series of 100 cases (Putnam et al., 1986), the mean number of alter egos was 13—a figure that may be inflated by the application of DSM-III criteria for multiple personality disorder, which do not require evidence of interpersonality amnesia; evidence of interpersonality amnesia was obtained in 98 of the cases, but that does not mean that within every case, some form of amnesia separated every alter ego from at least one other alter ego. The situation is complicated, however, by the fact that the amnesia is often asymmetrical. For example, in the classic case of Miss Beauchamp (Prince, 1906; see also Rosenzweig, 1987, 1988), in which there were four identities, the alter ego known as BI (the original Miss Beauchamp, also called "the Saint" by Prince) was largely ignorant of BII (BI when hypnotized), BIII (Sally, "the Idiot"), or BIV ("the Realist"); BII knew about BI and BIV, but not BIII; and BIII knew about BIV but not BI or BII. BIV knew nothing about BI, BII or BIII.

Moreover, the amnesia may be incomplete. In examining Miss Beauchamp, Prince found that fragments, or abstract representations of certain memories seemed to leak through the amnesic barrier, allowing one alter ego to refer to events and experiences known to another. Prince (1906, pp. 253ff) described three classes of such intrusions, permitting BIII to access knowledge associated with BI, even though BIII was ordinarily unaware of BI's existence or autobiographical record:

- Spontaneous memory flashes, in which one alter ego remembered something that belonged to the autobiography of another (similar to A.J. Brown's reference to an event in the life of Ansel Bourne as if it were his, Brown's, own)
- Phenomena of abstraction, in which one personality employed a kind of self-induced hypnosis to access the memories of another
- Visions, apparently similar to flashbulb memories (Brown & Kulik, 1977; Winograd & Neisser, 1992), representing isolated scenes.

Similar phenomena breached the amnesia of BIV for the life of BI.

Experimental Studies of Memory in Dissociative Identity Disorder

As with dissociative amnesia and fugue, it is remarkable how seldom the amnesia in dissociative identity disorder has been studied with techniques derived from the laboratory study of memory. In the cases of dissociative identity disorder the absence of formal experimentation is particularly unfortunate, because the amnesic barrier between identities raises so many interesting questions about the organization of autobiographical memory. Can the clinical impression of symmetrical or asymmetrical amnesia be verified with laboratory techniques? To what extent is autobiographical memory and other knowledge shared implicitly between personalities? To what extent are autobiographical memories linked to specific mental representations of the self as the agent or experiencer of the events in question? Only a few cases have received experimental analysis with these sorts of questions in mind.[4]

The Case of I.C.

One approach to these questions involves sampling autobiographical memory in each alter ego. The sole published example of this type is the experimental case study of patient I.C. reported by Schacter, Kihlstrom, Canter Kihlstrom and Birren (1989). This patient, who in ordinary life was an extremely high-functioning woman 24 years of age, married with one child, presented with four alter egos in addition to I.C., her normal personality: Heather, Joan, Gloria and Alpha. All four alter egos were aware of each other and of I.C.; I.C. had no awareness of any of the others. The experiment involved the recall of autobiographical memories cued by common words, in a manner similar to patient P.N., the case of functional retrograde amnesia studied by Schacter et al. (1982); she also completed a survey of early childhood recollections. In both instances, her performance was compared with that of control groups totaling 30 age-matched, normal women.

In an unconstrained version of the autobiographical cueing task, I.C. was presented with the cues and asked to recall related episodes from any time in her life. Like the controls, she showed a recency bias, preferring to recall events from the immediately past year; however, this bias was much stronger in I.C.: 67% of her memories were dated within the past year, compared with only 44% for the controls; and 96% of her memories were dated within the past 10 years, compared with only 64% for the controls.

I.C. recalled only a single memory more than 10 years old (i.e. dating from age 14 years or earlier). This memory came from when she was 12 years old. By contrast, the controls recalled more than 36% of their memories from a comparable period in their lives. In a second phase, the cues were repeated, with the constraint that the memories retrieved had to be of events occurring before age 12: in this case, she was able to produce memories to only 21% of the cues, compared with 86% for the controls; all of these memories were of events occurring between ages 10 and 12. In a third phase, employing a new set of cues, memory was constrained to the years prior to age 10: I.C. failed to produce even a single memory, whereas the controls produced memories to almost 90% of the cues. Her earliest recollection was dated at age 12, compared with age 4 for the controls (see also Kihlstrom & Harckiewicz, 1982).

When compared with age-matched controls, then, I.C. showed a striking recency bias, accompanied by a profound deficit in memory for her childhood experiences. The recency bias seems explicable in terms of the anchoring effect of a landmark event: her first hospitalization for MPD had occurred only a year earlier. The deficit in childhood memory is more puzzling. In line with recent speculations about the origins of dissociative disorder in childhood histories of physical and sexual abuse (for which, again, the primary evidence is retrospective self-report, and thus of uncertain validity), it is possible that this entire period of I.C.'s life had been repressed. On the other hand, while there was some evidence of sexual abuse in I.C.'s life, there were reasons to think it had begun in adolescence, not childhood. This raises the possibility that, contrary to appearance, I.C. was not the patient's original personality at all, but rather an alter ego that began to emerge in late childhood or early adolescence. Thus, there were no autobiographical memories associated with this particular mental representation of self. Evidence bearing on this speculation might have been provided by repeating the experimental procedures with other alter egos, but this was not possible at the time, and the patient has since been lost to follow-up.

The Case of Jonah

The pioneering experimental case study of amnesia in multiple personality was reported by Ludwig et al. (1972). In this case, a 27-year-old man presented with four personalities: Jonah, Sammy, King Young, and Usoffa Abdullah. Jonah was amnesic for the other three, each of whom had full knowledge of his experiences and limited awareness of each other. During Jonah's hospitalization, Ludwig et al. performed a series of laboratory tests to document and explore this pattern of amnesia. For example, Jonah could not recall paired associates taught to other personalities, although they could each remember items taught to Jonah; moreover, neither Sammy, King Young nor Usoffa were able to recall items taught to either of the other two alter egos. A similar pattern of performance was observed when measuring electrodermal responses to emotion-laden words selected as distinctly meaningful to each personality. Thus, Sammy, King Young and Usoffa responded differentially to their own words, and to Jonah's, but not to each other's; Jonah responded only to his own words.

In both of these procedures, the responses are consistent with the pattern of symmetrical awareness and memory evident on clinical examination. However, other tasks seemed to indicate that the amnesic barrier was to some extent permeable. Thus, when one personality was asked to learn (as opposed to merely recall) the paired-associates learned by another, the second personality showed considerable savings compared with the first one. Similar interpersonality savings were shown on the block-design subtest of the Wechsler Adult Intelligence Scale (Jonah, tested first, received the lowest score on this test; King Young, tested last, received the highest score), and on the logical memory subtest of the Wechsler Memory Scale (the first personality tested with a particular story remembered the fewest items, while the last personality tested remembered the most). Conditioned emotional responses (with shock US signalled by a different CS in each personality) established in one personality transferred to the others, with one major exception: Usoffa, the personality which showed the greatest difficulty in conditioning, showed the least transfer to and from the other personalities.

Ludwig et al. (1972) interpreted their results in terms of the emotional valence of the stimulus material: affectively neutral material generalized among all the personalities, while affectively charged material transferred from Jonah to the others, but not the reverse. However, as the investigators themselves noted, this interpretation was somewhat strained, as it is hard to see the emotional significance of some tasks, such as paired-associate learning, logical memory and block design, where evidence of transfer was obtained. In retrospect, the pattern of results seems to indicate a set of dissociations between explicit and implicit memory: Jonah lacks conscious recollection of the experiences of the other personalities, although the other personalities have conscious recollection of Jonah's experiences—an asymmetrical amnesia; but when the memory task does not require conscious recollection, the amnesic barrier is breached, and one personality can show changes in behavior that are attributable to events experienced by another.

A Series of Cases

The distinction between explicit and implicit memory is also helpful in understanding the results of a study of nine patients reported by Silberman et al. (1985). The patients were selected in such a manner that each had at least two alter egos that were mutually amnesic; 10 normal subjects served as controls. Each individual was presented with four matched wordlists, two to each alter ego. The hypothesis was that within each alter ego the lists would show mutual interference, reducing recall; across alter egos, the amnesic barrier would reduce interlist interference. However, this was not the outcome: although each alter ego denied awareness of its counterpart's learning experiences, retroactive and proactive interference was not reduced between, as compared to within, alter egos (in fact it was increased, but that may have been an artifact of an anomaly in the procedure).

Interestingly, recognition was excellent in terms of the subjects' ability to distinguish between items that had been presented to any personality versus those that were entirely new; however, the alter egos were unable to discriminate between items that had been presented to themselves and those that had been presented to their counterparts; that is, each alter ego showed a form of source amnesia (Evans, 1979; Evans & Thorn, 1966; Schacter, Harbluk & McLachlan, 1984; Shimamura & Squire, 1987), in which they were able to remember items but unable to indicate the circumstances under which they had been encountered. Silberman et al. (1985) concluded that the dissociation between alter egos was incomplete, permitting memory to transfer from one to the other. However, since both interference effects and source amnesia are implicit expressions of memory, another interpretation is that the dissociation between alter egos affects explicit memory but not implicit memory.

The Case of Margaret

The explicit–implicit distinction is also relevant to a case reported by Dick-Barnes, Nelson & Aine (1987), in which there were three identities separated by an asymmetrical amnesia: Margaret was unaware of either Rachel or Dee, though Rachel and Dee were both aware of each other and Margaret. Both a verbal learning task and a pursuit-rotor learning task showed evidence of interpersonality transfer. Pursuit-rotor learning, as an instance of skill acquisition, involves an implicit expression of memory: one does not require conscious recollection of the learning experience in order to display a cognitive or motor skill. In this study, the same pursuit-rotor task was learned by all subjects, and the savings in learning shown across alter egos were similar to the savings shown by Jonah on block-design.

Interpretation of the verbal-learning task in terms of explicit versus implicit memory must remain tentative. At the time of study, each alter ego was presented with a separate list of paired associates, until a criterion of learning had been reached; at the time of test, each alter ego was presented with the stimulus terms, and asked to provide the response. Ordinarily, such a test would count as explicit memory. However, it is now generally understood that every memory task has both explicit and implicit components to it. In particular, performance on paired-associate learning can be influenced by priming of the association between cue and target, independent of conscious recollection. In this case, the interpersonality transfer of learning may have been mediated by such priming effects. If so, the outcome would count as evidence of implicit, rather than explicit, memory.

The Case of Alice

Although the results of the foregoing studies are interpretable in terms of the distinction between explicit and implicit memory, none of them were designed with this distinction in mind. To date, the lone published study which has this feature was reported by Nissen et al. (1988). In this case, a woman presented with 22 alter egos, of which eight were subjected to formal testing. Although the pattern of interpersonality amnesia was somewhat complicated, most of the eight alter egos had no awareness of, or memory for, the others. This clinical observation was confirmed by two studies of explicit memory: the paired-associate learning test of the Wechsler Memory Scale and a test of Yes–No recognition for a list of words. In both cases, one alter ego failed to remember items that had been presented to another personality.

As expected, several tests of implicit memory gave evidence of interpersonality transfer: forced-choice recognition (which can be mediated by priming effects), repetition priming in perceptual identification and in word-fragment completion, sequence learning in serial reaction time, and proactive interference in paired-associate learning. Thus, when presented with a word quickly followed by a masking stimulus, one personality was more likely to identify the item if it had previously been presented to another personality. As another example, one personality found it easier to complete difficult word fragments (such as $a \_ \_ a \_ \_ in$) when the target word had previously been studied by another personality. On the other hand, several other tests of implicit memory gave contrary findings: successive story recall, repetition priming in stem completion, interpretation of ambiguous texts and sentences. For example, there were no priming effects when subjects were asked to complete three-letter stems with legal English words.

To some extent, the dissociation between explicit and implicit memory observed in this patient is consistent with inferences derived from the other cases; but the dissociation among measures of implicit memory is puzzling. Of course, there are differences in the cognitive requirements of the various tasks, even between such formally similar tasks as word-fragment completion (in which there is only one possible correct response) and word-stem completion (in which there are many possible correct responses). Such differences have been observed to affect the performance of normal subjects on implicit memory tasks (Roediger, 1990), and they probably affect the performance of dissociative disorder patients as well. For now, however, investigators interested in implicit memory between alter egos are advised to employ multiple measures of both explicit and implicit memory in their studies. They should also employ multiple patients, after the manner of Silberman et al. (1985), in order to assess the generalizability of experimental results.

The Case of Ms A

Although the report by Nissen et al. (1988) provides the clearest test to date of the hypothesis that implicit memory is spared in multiple personality disorder, all of the cases reviewed involve laboratory tests of memory, and thus lie at some distance from the problem of everyday autobiographical memory in these patients. This regrettable situation is perhaps necessary, insofar as proper experimental studies of memory require rigorous control over the conditions of encoding and retrieval. Even so, the possibility of conducting laboratory studies of explicit or implicit memory for events in the real world outside the laboratory is raised by a study conducted by Loewenstein and his colleagues, involving the technique of experiential sampling in a woman who initially presented with five, and later 21, alter egos (Loewenstein et al., 1987). In this study, the investigators outfitted the patient with an electronic pager which prompted her to fill out a diary recording such information as the time and place, which personality was in control at the moment, whether a switch in personality had occurred since the last signal, other individuals present, activities, and ratings of current mood and physical symptoms. These instructions were given to all 21 alter egos, although in the final analysis four of the personalities accounted for the bulk of responses to the pager. The resulting log provides a unique "online" record of the alternating personalities in dissociative identity disorder, and their activities and experiences. Unfortunately, none of this information was used in a study of interpersonality memory and amnesia—except that reports of lost time or amnesia were used to infer personality switches between signals. However, the potential value of such a study is obvious, and investigators with an interest in this syndrome are encouraged to consider the experiential sampling technique when designing future memory experiments.

NONDISSOCIATIVE FUNCTIONAL AMNESIA

The functional amnesias are almost wholly identified with the dissociative disorders, a diagnostic category which itself is identified with a hypothetical process called dissociation.[5] The first theoretical explanation of dissociation was presented by Janet (1889, 1907) in his descriptive and theoretical accounts of hysteria (for a secondary account see Ellenberger, 1970; for updated versions of dissociation theory, see Hilgard, 1977/1986; Kihlstrom, 1992). Janet analyzed mental life into a large number of content-specific elementary structures, called psychological automatisms, which combine perception and action. Ordinarily, Janet believed, the individual's repertoire of psychological automatisms is bound together into a single unified stream of consciousness. But in periods of stress a particular automatism, or set of related automatisms, could be split off from the rest, continuing to function but isolated from conscious awareness and voluntary control. Thus, dissociated psychological automatisms continued to influence experience, thought and action, but did so subconsciously, as hysterical accidents.

Janet held that the essential characteristic, or stigma, of hysteria was a narrowing of the field of consciousness, construed as analogous to the distinction between central and peripheral visual fields. In dissociative amnesia and fugue, and in the amnesia of dissociative identity disorder, the memories in question have been barred from conscious access; nevertheless, the critical memories have been well encoded and remain available in storage. Accordingly, these amnesias may be reversible, and even if they are not memory for the events covered by amnesia may be expressed implicitly in the person's ongoing experience, thought, and action outside of awareness. As such, the classical functional disorders, whose underlying mechanism is described as dissociative, may be construed as disorders of memory retrieval.

It is important to note that the functional disorders of memory are not necessarily dissociative in nature, and they do not necessarily reflect a disruption of memory retrieval. For example, some functional amnesias may reflect a mechanism of repression rather than dissociation (Rapaport, 1942; for coverage of the recent literature, see Singer, 1990). Both repression and dissociation reflect a lack of conscious accessibility to certain memories; in principle, both are reversible, and thus would seem to reflect disruptions in retrieval. In the case or repression, however, the memories in question are affect-laden, and are excluded from consciousness for purposes of defense against anxiety; dissociation, by contrast, can affect any sort of memory, positive and neutral as well as negative, and is not defensive in nature. While repression is the cornerstone of

Freud's psychoanalytic theory, it is not associated with particular psychiatric syndromes as dissociation is: there is no group of "repressive disorders" listed in DSM-IV. But repression has been implicated in the memory disorders of individuals suffering from post-traumatic stress disorder (Herman, 1992), and certainly deserves further investigation as a memory mechanism.

Of course, traumatic stresses can induce amnesia by means other than repression—although the evidence from both field and laboratory studies indicates that memory for peripheral, rather than central, details of the episode will be lost (Christianson, 1992a; Christianson & Nilsson, 1989, 1992; for a review of the effects of emotion on memory, see Christianson, 1992b). Rarely does the amnesia cover the entire event. To the extent that the forgetting qualifies as amnesia, however, it is clearly functional in nature: the forgetting occurs in the absence of any insult, injury or disease affecting brain tissue. The commonest interpretation of these memory deficits is in terms of the Yerkes–Dodson Law or its updated version, the Easterbrook cue-utilization hypothesis (Anderson, 1990; Neiss, 1988, 1990; Christianson, 1992a). Yerkes and Dodson (1908) proposed that increases in arousal from low to moderate to high levels initially increase, and then decrease, performance. Easterbrook (1959) hypothesized that increasing arousal progressively decreased the amount of attention devoted to events, thus impairing the processing of first peripheral, and then central, information. In either case, very high levels of arousal would have the effect of decreasing the resources devoted to information-processing at the time of encoding, resulting in a permanent deficit in memory (one ambiguity in these proposals is that they would seem to predict amnesia for highly arousing *positive* as well as negative events).

Interestingly, it appears that while high arousal has deleterious effects on memory shortly after the target event, memory for that event may be improved over long retention intervals (Revelle & Loftus, 1992). This phenomenon, sometimes known as *reminiscence*, would appear to contradict the idea that arousal-induced amnesias are permanent, and deserves further study.

Emotional states other than fear can produce functional amnesias. For example, Ellis and Ashbrook (1988; see also Ellis, 1990) have argued that depressed mood prevents the deployment of adequate attentional resources at the time of encoding, resulting in a profound deficit in memory. Such an effect would be permanent instead of reversible, although it would not necessarily affect performance on implicit memory tasks that are insensitive to variations in encoding. (For a review of the effects of emotion on implicit memory, see Tobias, Kihlstrom & Schacter (1992).) Of course, insofar as depression reflects low levels of emotional arousal, this outcome might be predicted on the basis of the Yerkes–Dodson Law. Another form of emotionally induced functional amnesia is mood-dependent memory (Bower, 1981; Eich & Metcalfe, 1989). It has now been established that memories encoded in one emotional state (e.g. sadness) are more accessible if retrieval takes place in that same state, as opposed to its hedonic opposite (e.g. happiness) or a neutral state. The relative weakness and unreliability of these effects in the laboratory may be due to the difficulty in inducing profound emotional states in such a setting. But in cases of major psychopathology encountered in the clinic, especially bipolar affective disorder (so-called manic–depressive illness), the amnesia induced by changes in emotional states may be profound. Again, the amnesias resulting from mania or depression count as functional in nature, because the instigating events do not result in any insult, injury or disease affecting brain tissue.

WHAT'S FUNCTIONAL ABOUT FUNCTIONAL AMNESIA?

Of course, both arousal and emotion are the products of underlying psychobiological processes that may affect memory more or less directly (LeDoux, 1992; McGaugh, 1992; Nilsson & Archer, 1992). Similarly, it should be noted that many episodes of functional amnesia, fugue and depersonalization begin with a physical injury involving the head. In addition, there is some evidence (admittedly controversial, and some as yet unpublished; for an overview, see Putnam, 1989, 1991) that patients with dissociative identity disorder show alterations in brain organization and neurochemistry that correspond to their changes in identity. If so, should these memory disorders still be labelled functional as opposed to organic (Spitzer et al., 1992)? Answering this question depends on what is meant by the very label *functional*, and in this respect there are at least three possibilities.

First, there is the formal neurological distinction between the structural or anatomical and the functional or physiological (Reynolds, 1990). This view distinguishes between those disorders that are due to lesions in brain tissue (presumably observable on autopsy, or by means of contemporary brain-imaging techniques) and those that result from anomalies of neurochemistry in a structurally intact brain. Obviously, in both cases the disease is organic in nature. The second, more colloquial, use refers to the distinction between those diseases whose organic basis is known and those whose organic basis, while presumed, has not yet been established. In this sense, the history of medicine is a chronicle of shifts from the functional to the organic, and psychopathology is no exception. In the same way that general paresis, or paralytic dementia, is now known to be caused by the syphilitic spirochete, schizophrenia—once labelled as a "functional" psychosis—is rapidly being traced to anomalies of neurotransmitter function.

The category *neurosis* (now banished, along with psychosis, from DSM) illustrates a third construal of the functional disorders: not only is no organic cause (e.g. brain insult, injury or disease) known; rather, the primary cause is presumed to be psychosocial rather than biological in nature. The functional amnesias, whether attributed to dissociation, repression or something else, lie squarely in the domain of the neuroses; and for more than 100 years their causes have been presumed to be mental rather than physical in nature: Breuer and Freud (1893–95, p. 7) wrote that "Hysterics suffer mainly from reminiscences". In part, this version of the organic—functional distinction in psychopathology is an expression of Cartesian dualism, with its categorical distinction between mind and body. And, of course, it was abetted by the rise of Freudian psychoanalysis to dominance in psychopathology, which increased the alienation of psychiatry and clinical psychology from neurology. But in part, it also reflects the three levels at which any behavioral phenomenon can be analyzed: biological, psychological and social. By attributing hysterical symptoms to reminiscences, Breuer and Freud expressed a clear preference for a psychological explanation in terms of memory, conflict and anxiety.

In the final analysis, however, all construals involving the term *functional*—structure versus function, proven organic versus hypothetically organic, and somatogenic versus psychogenic—are fundamentally false. Neuroanatomical changes have neurophysiological consequences; neurological patients have problems in living that must be dealt with psychologically and socially; and the effects of the external environment are mediated by mental structures and processes that themselves have their physical basis in the structures and processes studied by neuroscience. We assume that the functional amnesias are associated with (correlated with) changes in brain state, and we can look forward to the day when we know as much about the psychobiology of fugue states and multiple personality as we do about the amnesic syndrome.

In the case of the functional amnesias, however, the most immediate causes do not lie in the nervous system, and the most direct and parsimonious explanations are not at the biological level. Perhaps the term *functional* is too vague, or has outlived its usefulness; but it still has value, in directing the attention of clinicians and researchers to the individual's social environment, and the cognitive structures and processes that mediate the individual's response to environmental events.

ACKNOWLEDGEMENTS

Preparation of this chapter, and the point of view represented therein, was supported in part by grants MH-35856 from the National Institute of Mental Health and AG-08441 from the National Institute on Aging. We thank John Allen, Melissa Birren, Lawrence Couture, Elizabeth Glisky, Martha Glisky, Heather Law, Shelagh Mulvaney and Victor Shames for comments and discussion.

NOTES

1. Depersonalization and derealization are psychopathological syndromes in their own right, but they are also nonspecific symptoms that are essentially independent of psychiatric diagnosis (Steinberg, 1991). Experiences of depersonalization and derealization are reported with some frequency in the normal population, and have been studied in survivors of disasters, violence, and other traumatic experiences: near-death

(Noyes & Kletti, 1977), building collapses (Wilkinson, 1983), tornadoes (Madakisira & O'Brien, 1987), airplane crashes (Sloan, 1988) and earthquakes (Cardena & Spiegel, 1993) are a few examples of a potentially rich area of research. This literature is not reviewed in this chapter, as it rarely deals with issues of memory *per se*.

2. There are also a number of instruments available for screening purposes, prior to a formal diagnostic interview (for a review, see Kihlstrom, Glisky & Angiulo, 1993; Steinberg, 1994). Of these, the Mini-SCID-D, an abbreviated version of the SCID-D, most closely conforms to the standard (DSM) diagnostic criteria for dissociative disorder; certainly it contains the most detailed assessment of memory functions.

3. Cases of dissociative amnesia are difficult to study—they occur unexpectedly, and they tend to resolve rapidly. However, researchers can be prepared to conduct case studies, or even more extensive investigations, as the occasion arises. For example, Cardena and Spiegel (1993) seized the opportunity to study dissociative symptoms in reaction to the 1989 Loma Prieta earthquake in California. One week after the earthquake, a sample of Bay Area residents who had experienced the earthquake showed high levels of depersonalization and derealization, which had abated on follow-up four months later. Interestingly, there was no evidence of partial or complete amnesia for the event; to the contrary, many respondents complained of detailed, intrusive memories of the event (perhaps similar to flashbulb memories?), as well as of everyday memory problems. It may be that levels of trauma experienced by these subjects were not sufficient to induce amnesia; or amnesia may have been prevented, or overcome, by accounts in the media and memories shared by friends and colleagues.

4. There have been experimental case studies of dissociative identity disorder which have focused on variables other than memory, such as responses to personality tests and psychophysiological assessments. For surveys, see Kihlstrom, Tataryn & Hoyt (1993) and Schacter & Kihlstrom (1989).

5. Other diagnostic categories sharing this property are the conversion disorders and the somatization disorders—which, along with the dissociative disorders, comprise what has been known as hysteria since the 19th century. For a history of the diagnosis of hysteria, and an argument for moving the conversion disorders from the somatoform to the dissociative category, see Kihlstrom (1992, 1994).

REFERENCES

Abeles, M. & Schilder, P. (1935). Psychogenic loss of personal identity. *Archives of Neurology & Psychiatry*, **34**, 587–604.

American Psychiatric Association (1994). *Diagnostic and Statistical Manual of Mental Disorders*, 4th edn. American Psychiatric Press, Washington, DC.

Anderson, K.J. (1990). Arousal and the inverted-U hypothesis: a critique of Neiss's "Reconceptualizing arousal". *Psychological Bulletin*, **107**, 96–100.

Bentin, S., Moscovitch, M. & Heth, I. (1992). Memory with and without awareness: performance and electrophysiological evidence of savings. *Journal of Experimental Psychology: Learning, Memory and Cognition*, **18**, 1270–1283.

Bliss, E.L. (1986). *Multiple Personality, Allied Disorders, and Hypnosis*. Oxford University Press, New York.

Bower, G.H. (1981). Mood and memory. *American Psychologist*, **36**, 129–138.

Braun, B.G. & Frischholz, E.J. (1992). Remembering and forgetting in patients suffering from multiple personality disorder. In S.-A. Christianson (ed.), *Handbook of Emotion and Memory: Research and Theory*. Erlbaum, Hillsdale, NJ, pp. 411–428.

Brown, R. & Kulik, J. (1977). Flashbulb memories. *Cognition*, **5**, 73–99.

Cardena, E., Lewis-Fernandez, R., Bear, D., Pakianathan, I. & Spiegel, D. (in press).

Dissociative disorders. In *DSM-IV Sourcebook*. American Psychiatric Press, Washington, DC.

Cardena, E. & Spiegel D. (1993). Dissociative reactions to the San Francisco Bay Area earthquake of 1989. *American Journal of Psychiatry*, **150**, 474–478.

Carlson, E.T. (1984). The history of multiple personality in the United States: Mary Reynolds and her subsequent reputation. *Bulletin of the History of Medicine*, **58**, 72–82.

Christianson, S.-A. (1992a). Emotional stress and eyewitness memory: critical review. *Psychological Bulletin*, **112**, 284–309.

Christianson, S.-A. (1992b). *Handbook of Emotion and Memory*. Erlbaum, Hillsdale, N.J.

Christianson, S.-A. & Nilsson L.-G. (1984). Functional amnesia as induced by psychological trauma. *Memory and Cognition*, **12**, 142–155.

Christianson, S.A. & Nilsson, L.G. (1989). Hysterical amnesia: a case of aversively motivated isolation of memory. In T. Archer & L.G. Nilsson (eds), *Aversion, Avoidance and Anxiety*. Erlbaum, Hillsdale, NJ, pp. 289–310.

Dick-Barnes, M., Nelson, R. & Aine, C.J. (1987). Behavioral measures of multiple personality: the case of Margaret. *Journal of Behavior Therapy and Experimental Psychiatry*, **18**, 229–239.

Easterbrook, J.A. (1959). The effect of emotion on cue utilization and the organization of behavior. *Psychological Review*, **66**, 183–201.

Eich, J.E. & Metcalfe, J. (1989). Mood independent memory for internal versus external events. *Journal of Experimental Psychology: Learning, Memory and Cognition*, **15**, 443–455.

Eisen, M.R. (1989). Return of the repressed: hypnoanalysis of a case of total amnesia. *International Journal of Clinical and Experimental Hypnosis*, **37**, 107–119.

Ellenberger, H.F. (1970). *The Discovery of the Unconscious: The History and Evolution of Dynamic Psychiatry*. Basic Books, New York.

Ellis, H.C. (1990). Depressive deficits in memory: processing initiative and resource allocation. *Journal of Experimental Psychology: General*, **119**, 60–62.

Ellis, H.C. & Ashbrook, P.W. (1988). Resource allocation model of the effects of depressed mood states on memory. In K. Fiedler & J. Forgas (eds), *Affect, Cognition and Social Behavior*. Hogrefe, Toronto, pp. 25–43.

Evans, F.J. (1979). Contextual forgetting: posthypnotic source amnesia. *Journal of Abnormal Psychology*, **88**, 556–563.

Evans, F.J. & Thorn, W.A.F. (1966). Two types of posthypnotic amnesia: recall amnesia and source amnesia. *International Journal of Clinical and Experimental Hypnosis*, **14**, 162–179.

Fisher, C. (1945). Amnesic states in war neuroses: the psychogenesis of fugues. *Psychoanalytic Quarterly*, **14**, 437–468.

Fisher, C. & Joseph, E. (1949). Fugue with loss of personal identity. *Psychoanalytic Quarterly*, **18**, 480–493.

Gudjonsson, G.H. (1979). The use of electrodermal responses in a case of amnesia (a case report). *Medicine, Science and the Law*, **19**, 138–140.

Gudjonsson, G.H. & Haward, L.R.C. (1982). Case report—Hysterical amnesia as an alternative to suicide. *Medicine, Science and the Law*, **22**, 68–72.

Gudjonsson, G.H. & MacKeith, J.A.C. (1983). A specific recognition deficit in a case of homicide. *Medicine, Science and the Law*, **23**, 37–40.

Herman, J.L. (1992). *Trauma and Recovery: The Aftermath of Violence—from Domestic Abuse to Political Terror*. Basic Books, New York.

Hilgard, E.R. (1977). *Divided Consciousness: Multiple Controls in Human Thought and Action*. Wiley-Interscience, New York.

James, W. (1890). *Principles of Psychology*. Holt, New York.

Janet, P. (1893). Continuous amnesia (in French). *Revue Generale des Sciences*, **4**, 167–179.

Janet, P. (1904). Amnesia and the dissociation of memories by emotion (in French). *Journal de Psychologie Normal et Pathologique*, **1**, 417–453.

Janet, P. (1907). *The Major Symptoms of Hysteria*. Macmillan, New York.

Kaszniak, A.W., Nussbaum, P.D., Berren, M.R. & Santiago, J. (1988). Amnesia as a consequence of male rape: a case report. *Journal of Abnormal Psychology*, **97**, 100–104.

Keller, R. & Shaywitz, B.A. (1986). Amnesia or fugue state: a diagnostic dilemma. *Journal of Developmental and Behavioral Pediatrics*, **7**, 131–132.

Kenney, M.G. (1986). *The Passion of Ansel Bourne: Multiple Personality in American Culture*. Smithsonian Institution Press, Washington, DC.

Kihlstrom, J.F. (1985). Posthypnotic amnesia and the dissociation of memory. In G.H. Bower (ed.), *The Psychology of Learning and Motivation*, vol. 19. Academic Press, New York, pp. 131–178.

Kihlstrom, J.F. (1990). The psychological unconscious. In L. Pervin (ed.), *Handbook of Personality: Theory and Research*. New York, pp. 445–464.

Kihlstrom, J.F. (1992). Dissociative and conversion disorders. In D.J. Stein & J. Young (eds), *Cognitive Science and Clinical Disorders*. Academic Press, San Diego, pp. 247–270.

Kihlstrom, J.F. (1994). One hundred years of hysteria. In S.J. Lynn & J.W. Rhue (eds), *Dissociation: Theoretical, Clinical and Research Perspectives*. Guilford, New York, pp. 365–394.

Kihlstrom, J.F. & Barnhardt, T.M. (1993). The self-regulation of memory, for better and for worse, with and without hypnosis. In D.M. Wegner & J.W. Pennebaker (eds), *Handbook of Mental Control*. Prentice-Hall, Englewood Cliffs, NJ, pp. 88–125.

Kihlstrom, J.F., Barnhardt, T.M. & Tataryn, D.J. (1992). Implicit perception. In R.F. Bornstein & T.S. Pittman (eds), *Perception Without Awareness*. Guilford, New York, pp. 17–54.

Kihlstrom, J.F. & Harackiewicz, J.M. (1982). The earliest recollection: a new survey. *Journal of Personality*, **50**, 134–148.

Kihlstrom, J.F. & Klein, S.B. (1994). The self as a knowledge structure. In R.S. Wyer & T.K. Srull (eds), *Handbook of Social Cognition*, vol. 1, 2nd edn. Erlbaum, Hillsdale, NJ, pp. 153–208.

Kihlstrom, J.F., Mulvaney, S. & Tobias, B.A. (in press). The emotional unconscious. In E. Eich (ed.), *Counterpoints: Cognition, Memory and Language*. Simon & Schuster International, London.

Kihlstrom, J.F., Tataryn, D.J. & Hoyt, I.P. (1993). Dissociative disorder. In P.J. Sutker & H.E. Adams (eds), *Comprehensive Handbook of Psychopathology*, 2nd edn. Plenum, New York, pp. 203–234.

Kirschner, L.A. (1973). Dissociative reactions: an historical review and clinical study. *Acta Psychiatrica Scandinavica*, **49**, 698–711.

Kluft, R.P. (1991). Multiple personality disorder. *American Psychiatric Press Review of Psychiatry*, **10**, 161–188.

Kopelman, M.D. (1987). Amnesia: organic and psychogenic. *British Journal of Psychiatry*, **150**, 428–442.

LeDoux, J.E. (1992). Emotion as memory: anatomical systems underlying indelible memory tracts. In S.-A. Christianson (ed.), *Handbook of Emotion and Memory: Research and Theory*. Erlbaum, Hillsdale, NJ, pp. 269–288.

Lewis-Fernandez, R. (1994). The role of culture in the configuration of dissociative states: a comparison of Puerto Rican ataque de nervios and Indian "possession syndrome". In D. Spiegel (ed.), *Dissociation: Culture, Mind and Body*. American Psychiatric Press, Washington, DC, pp. 123–167.

Loewenstein, R.J. (1991). Psychogenic amnesia and psychogenic fugue: a comprehensive review. *American Psychiatric Press Review of Psychiatry*, **10**, 189–222.

Loewenstein, R.J., Hamilton, J., Alagna, S., Reid, N. & deVries, M. (1987). Experiential sampling in the study of multiple personality disorder. *American Journal of Psychiatry*, **144**, 19–24.

Loftus, E.F. & Burns, T.E. (1982). Mental shock can produce retrograde amnesia. *Memory and Cognition*, **10**, 318–323.

Ludwig, A.M., Brandsma, J.M., Wilbur, C.B., Bendfeldt, F. & Jameson, D.H. (1972). The objective study of multiple personality: or, are four heads better than one? *Archives of General Psychiatry*, **26**, 298–310.

Lyon, L.S. (1985). Facilitating telephone number recall in a case of psychogenic amnesia. *Journal of Behavior Therapy & Experimental Psychiatry*, **16**, 147–149.

Madakasira, S. & O'Brien, K. (1987). Acute posttraumatic stress disorder in victims of a natural disaster. *Journal of Nervous and Mental Disease*, **175**, 286–290.

McGaugh, J.L. (1992). Affect, neuromodulatory systems, and memory storage. In S.-A. Christianson (ed.), *Handbook of Emotion and Memory: Research and Theory*. Erlbaum, Hillsdale, NJ, pp. 245–268.

Neiss, R. (1988). Reconceptualizing arousal: psychological states in motor performance. *Psychological Bulletin*, **103**, 345–366.

Neiss, R. (1990). Ending arousal's reign of error: a reply to Anderson. *Psychological Bulletin*, **107**, 101–105.

Nemiah, J.C. (1979). Dissociative amnesia: a clinical and theoretical reconsideration. In J.F. Kihlstrom & F.J. Evans (eds), *Functional Disorders of Memory*. Erlbaum, Hillsdale, NJ, pp. 303–324.

Nilsson, L.-G. & Archer, T. (1992). Biological aspects of memory and emotion: affect and cognition. In S.-A. Christianson (ed.), *Handbook of Emotion and Memory: Research and Theory*. Erlbaum, Hillsdale, NJ, pp. 289–306.

Nissen, M.J., Ross, J.L., Willingham, D.B., Mackenzie, T.B. & Schacter, D.L. (1988). Memory and awareness in a patient with multiple personality disorder. *Brain and Cognition*, **8**, 117–134.

Noyes, R. & Kletti, R. (1977). Depersonalization in response to life-threatening danger. *Comprehensive Psychiatry*, **18**, 375–384.

Prince, M. (1906). *The Dissociation of a Personality: A Biographical Study in Abnormal Psychology*. Longmans Green, New York.

Putnam, F.W. (1989). *Diagnosis and Treatment of Multiple Personality Disorder*. Guilford, New York.

Putnam, F.W. (1991). Dissociative phenomena. *American Psychiatric Press Review of Psychiatry*, **10**, 145–160.

Putnam, F.W., Guroff, J.J., Silberman, E.K., Barban, L. & Post, R.M. (1986). The clinical phenomenology of multiple personality disorder: review of 100 recent cases. *Journal of Clinical Psychiatry*, **47**, 285–293.

Rapaport, D. (1942). *Emotions and Memory*. International Universities Press, New York.

Reed, G. (1979). Anomalies of recall and recognition. In J.F. Kihlstrom & F.J. Evans (eds), *Functional Disorders of Memory*. Erlbaum, Hillsdale, NJ, pp. 1–28.

Reed, G. (1988). *Psychology of Anomalous Experience*, rev. edn. Prometheus, Buffalo, NY. Original edition published 1974.

Revelle, W. & Loftus, D.A. (1992). The implications of arousal effects for the study of affect and memory. In S.-A. Christianson (ed.), *Handbook of Emotion and Memory: Research and Theory*. Erlbaum, Hillsdale, NJ, pp. 113–150.

Reynolds, E.H. (1990). Structure and function in neurology and psychiatry. *British Journal of Psychiatry*, **157**, 481–490.

Roediger, E.H. (1990). Implicit memory: retention without remembering. *American Psychologist*, **45**, 1043–1056.

Rosenzweig, S. (1987). Sally Beauchamp's career: a psychoarcheological key to Morton Prince's classic case of multiple personality. *Genetic, Social and General Psychology Monographs*, **113**, 5–60.

Rosenzweig, S. (1988). The identity and ideodynamics of the multiple personality "Sally Beauchamp": a confirmatory supplement. *American Psychologist*, **43**, 45–48.

Ross, C.A. (1990). *Multiple Personality Disorder: Diagnosis, Clinical Features, and Treatment*. Wiley, New York.

Sargent, W. & Slater, E. (1941). Amnesic syndromes in war. *Proceedings of the Royal Society of Medicine*, **34**, 757–764.

Schacter, D.L. (1986). Amnesia and crime: how much do we really know? *American Psychologist*, **41**, 286–295.

Schacter, D.L. (1987). Implicit memory: history and current status. *Journal of Experimental Psychology: Learning, Memory and Cognition*, **13**, 501–518.

Schacter, D.L., Chiu, C.-Y.P. & Ochsner, K.N. (1993). Implicit memory: a selective review. *Annual Review of Neuroscience*, **16**, 159–182.

Schacter, D.L., Harbluk, J.L. & McLachlan, D.R. (1984). Retrieval without recollection: an experimental analysis of source amnesia. *Journal of Verbal Learning and Verbal Behavior*, **23**, 593–611.

Schacter, D.L. & Kihlstrom, J.F. (1989). Functional amnesia. In F. Boller & J. Grafman (eds), *Handbook of Neuropsychology*, vol. 3. Elsevier Science, New York, pp. 209–231.

Schacter, D.L., Kihlstrom, J.F., Canter Kihlstrom, L. & Birren, M. (1989). Autobiographical memory in a case of multiple personality disorder. *Journal of Abnormal Psychology*, 1989, 508–514.

Schacter, D.L., Rapscak, S.Z., Rubens, A.B., Tharan, M. & Laguna, J. (1990). Priming effects in a letter-by-letter reader depend upon access to the word form system. *Neuropsychologia*, **10**, 1079–1094.

Schacter, D.L., Wang, P.L., Tulving, E. & Friedman, M. (1982). Functional retrograde amnesia: a quantitative case study. *Neuropsychologia*, **20**, 523–532.

Shimamura, A.P. & Squire, L.R. (1987). A neuropsychological study of fact memory and source amnesia. *Journal of Experimental Psychology: Learning, Memory and Cognition*, **13**, 464–473.

Silberman, E.K., Putnam, F.W., Weingartner, H., Braun, B.G. & Post, R.M. (1985). Dissociative states in multiple personality disorder: a quantitative study. *Psychiatry Research*, **15**, 253–260.

Singer, J.L. (1990). *Repression and Dissociation: Implications for Personality Theory, Psychopathology, and Health*. University of Chicago Press, Chicago.

Sloan, P. (1988). Post-traumatic stress in survivors of an airplane crash landing: a clinical and exploratory research intervention. *Journal of Traumatic Stress*, **1**, 35–47.

Spiegel, D., Frischholz, E.J. & Spira, J. (1993). Functional disorders of memory. *American Psychiatric Press Review of Psychiatry*, **12**, 747–782.

Spitzer, R.L., First, M.B., Williams, J.B.W., Kendler, K., Pincus, H.A. & Tucker, G. (1992). Now is the time to retire the term "organic mental disorders". *American Journal of Psychiatry*, **149**, 240–244.

Steinberg, M. (1991). The spectrum of depersonalization: assessment and treatment. *American Psychiatric Press Review of Psychiatry*, **10**, 223–247.

Steinberg, M. (1993). *Interviewer's Guide to the Structured Clinical Interview for DSM-IV Dissociative Disorders*. American Psychiatric Press, Washington, DC.

Steinberg, M. (1994). Systematizing dissociation: symptomatology and diagnostic assessment. In D. Speigel (ed.), *Dissociation: Culture, Mind and Body*. American Psychiatric Press, Washington, DC, pp. 59–88.

Steinberg, M., Rounsaville, B. & Cicchetti, D.V. (1990). The structured clinical interview for DSM-IIIR dissociative disorders: preliminary report on a new diagnostic instrument. *American Journal of Psychiatry*, **147**, 76–82.

Sutcliffe, J.P. & Jones, J. (1962). Personal identity, multiple personality, and hypnosis. *International Journal of Clinical and Experimental Hypnosis*, **10**, 231–269.

Taylor, W.S. & Martin, M.F. (1944). Multiple personality. *Journal of Abnormal and Social Psychology*, **39**, 281–300.

Thigpen, C.H. & Cleckley, H.M. (1957). *The Three Faces of Eve*. Popular Library, New York.

Treadway, M., Cohen, N.J. & McCloskey, M. (1992). Landmark life events and the organization of memory: evidence from functional retrograde amnesia. In S.-A. Christianson (ed.), *Handbook of Emotion and Memory: Research and Theory*. Erlbaum, Hillsdale, NJ, pp. 389–410.

Tulving, E. (1983). *Elements of Episodic Memory*. Oxford University Press, Oxford.

Wiggins, S.L., Lombard, E.A., Brennan, M.J. & Heckel, R.V. (1964). Awareness of events in case of amnesia. *Archives of General Psychiatry*, **11**, 67–70.

Wilkinson, C.B. (1983). Aftermath of a disaster: the collapse of the Hyatt Regency Hotel skywalks. *American Journal of Psychiatry*, **140**, 1134–1139.

Wilson, G., Rupp, C. & Wilson, W.W. (1950). Amnesia. *American Journal of Psychiatry*, **106**, 481–485.

Yerkes, R.M. & Dodson, J.D. (1908). The relation of strength of stimulus to rapidity of habit-formation. *Journal of Comparative Neurology and Psychology*, **18**, 459–482.

Section III

Assessment of Memory Problems

Chapter 15

The Assessment of Memory Disorders

Andrew R. Mayes
Royal Hallamshire Hospital, Sheffield, UK

INTRODUCTION

Memory assessment procedures are used for both clinical and research purposes. Clinical assessment itself has several aims, not all of which may apply to any given patient. First, it may involve determining how memory deficits change over time so as to identify whether spontaneous recovery is occurring, whether there is progressive deterioration, or whether there has been improvement in response to cognitive intervention or drug therapy.

Second, the aim may be to assess patients for impairment or for diagnostic purposes. For example, it is often important to know whether memory impairments have an organic cause, are psychogenic in origin, or are a mixture of the two, and whether they are caused at least partially by poor motivation, poor concentration, reduced intelligence, impaired ability to plan encoding and/or retrieval operations, by a "pure" memory deficit, or some combination of these. Diagnostic goals, therefore, require more detailed testing than that required to determine whether memory has changed because successful diagnosis necessitates a fuller description of the pattern of memory and cognitive performance of the patient.

Third, the aim may be to provide a detailed case description of the patient. For example, head-injured patients may be referred to the clinician in order to find out whether their impairments are too severe to allow a return to work and to assess the effects of the memory and cognitive impairments on daily living. Such assessments are essential for medicolegal cases, where it is vital to specify not only the cognitive and memory deficits and to show that they have been

Handbook of Memory Disorders. Edited by A.D. Baddeley, B.A. Wilson and F.N. Watts.
© 1995 John Wiley & Sons Ltd.

caused by brain injury, but also to determine the patient's chances of some degree of recovery from the impairments and their effects on the patient's lifestyle. Assessment of such effects depends on measuring the severity of the deficits, but may be best served by getting patients' relatives to rate the severity of the patients' disorders and the likely effects of these on daily living.

The fourth aim of clinical assessment is to determine whether patients are likely to respond to rehabilitation and, if so, what kind is likely to be most effective. Assessment of the effects of rehabilitation obviously involves the first aim of clinical assessments, which is the assessment of change in memory over time.

Memory assessment procedures are also used for research purposes. Research into memory disorders aims to ascertain the kinds of independent memory disorders that exist, relate these to the brain lesions that cause them when the disorders are organic in origin, and try to identify the functional deficits that underlie the disorders. This last aim involves not only using a variety of learning and memory tests, but also using non-mnemonic tests that tap motivation, attention and cognitive processing abilities. Memory involves a complex set of encoding processes which construct a represention of the information that is subsequently stored and retrieved. There is evidence that these processes can be *explicit*, in which case the subject is aware of what is being represented, or *implicit*, in which case the subject has no awareness of what is being represented (see Mayes, 1988). The storage processes that are automatically triggered in the normal brain by encoded information and which may continue for some time after encoding has occurred are still not well understood, although there have been some dramatic advances in the last decade (see Squire, Weinberger, Lynch & McGaugh, 1991). Finally, retrieval, to some extent like encoding, seems to involve both relatively automatic and also more effortful processes. In order to determine precisely which of these processes have to be disturbed in order to produce a given memory deficit requires a careful analysis of which cognitive, memory, attentional and motivational processes are disturbed and which are intact.

CRITERIA THAT STANDARD TESTS SHOULD FULFIL

Both research and clinical goals may depend on the use of publicly available, standard tests and tests that have been specially constructed to answer specific questions. Whereas the interpretation of patients' scores on standard tests is based on norms, interpretation of scores on specially constructed tests depends on comparing patients' scores with those of matched control subjects. In general, research uses a much higher proportion of specially constructed tests than does clinical work. Nevertheless, even research is critically dependent on widely used, standard tests because researchers in different laboratories need to know that they are talking about the same thing. If standard memory tests are to be useful, they should ideally be reliable, valid, sensitive, cover a broad range of performance levels, be standardized with comprehensive norms, and tap all of those kinds of memory that can be independently affected by differently located brain lesions. Tests are also likely to be more effective if they are interesting for patients to do. In many clinical situations, it is also important that tests should be reasonably quick.

It is clear that some of these criteria are in tension with others. For example, brevity is in tension with sensitivity and range because sensitivity and range are, in part, functions of the number of items in a test, and tests with many items take longer to administer. No test can, therefore, satisfy all criteria so it is important to select standard tests according to one's aims. For research it is appropriate to use time-consuming tests that are more sensitive and tap a wide range of processes, whereas for some clinical purposes it is best to use tests that are quicker, less sensitive, and which tap a narrower range of processes.

Surprisingly little attention has been paid to the reliability of memory tests, and yet when addressing certain theoretical issues it is desirable to use highly reliable tests. Thus, patients' performances on a test across different occasions would not be expected to be particularly consistent if the test has a low test–retest reliability. Inconsistent performance across occasions might therefore not be indicative of pathologically variable memory in a patient unless normal subjects have been shown to perform in a significantly more consistent manner. It is also possible that tests of item-specific implicit memory (priming) are typically less reliable than those of recognition and recall (explicit memory). If this is true, patients' performance on different tests of priming should show lower intercorrelations than different tests of explicit memory, not because of differences in the underlying memory processes, but simply because of the use of unreliable tests. Tulving and Schacter (1990) have demonstrated the hyper-specificity of word-fragment completion priming appropriately by showing that the correlation between two completion performances using different letter cues is zero whereas it rises to 0.9 when the same cues are used (indicating that the task has high test–retest reliability). In contrast, they argue that with similar explicit memory tasks using different cues good performance on one test predicts good performance on the other.

It is unclear what would count as validation of a memory test except that subjects who perform badly on it should either describe themselves, or more convincingly be described by others who know them well, as having poor memory. Two points should be made about this. The first is that the assessment of a close relative should provide better validation because some patients are known to be impaired at recognizing that they have poor memory (see Kapur, 1988). The second point is that the relative's assessment should be of the kind of memory that is tapped by the test. This leaves open the possibility that patients might perform normally on a set of memory tests and close relatives neverthe-less still claim that the patients show a memory problem in everyday life. Most researchers into memory disorders can provide anecdotal accounts to this effect. One interpretation is that everyday memory may involve some processes that are not tapped by currently available tests. For example, some patients with temporal lobe epilepsy or lesions of the anterior temporal lobes may perform relatively normally on tests of recall and recognition given shortly after a learning episode, but show deficits when tested at much longer delays (Martin et al., 1991). Partly for reasons of convenience, tests of this kind are rarely given and there is certainly no standardized test of this kind.

New memory tests are often cross-validated against others that are already established. As with validating by using relatives' assessments, this is acceptable provided the same kinds of memory are being tapped. Implicit in all of the above is the notion that tests should have ecological validity, especially if they are being used for clinical purposes. Ecological validity is best assessed either by getting relatives' reports of how bad memory is in everyday life, or by observing the frequency of everyday life memory failures directly—as was done with the Rivermead Behavioural Memory Test (Wilson et al., 1985).

A memory test may also fail to reveal an expected deficit if it is insensitive. Sensitivity is the ability of a test to tap differences and changes in the strength of an underlying process, and the test-related factors that determine it are not well understood. Nevertheless, it is likely to be greatly reduced when performance is close to floor or ceiling levels, and when a test has poor test–retest reliability. Apart from these factors, it must be influenced by how pure a measure the test provides of the underlying memory process. In other words, it depends on how valid a measure the test provides of the relevant process. Performance on some tests may be more strongly determined by irrelevant factors than the process that should be being measured. The issue may be of theoretical importance. For example, amnesic people sometimes show significantly impaired explicit memory and an insignificant trend towards worse performance on a test of priming. If explicit memory tests are very sensitive and priming tests very insensitive, this pattern of results could mean that the patients are impaired at priming as well as explicit memory. This would conflict with many people's view that amnesic people show preservation of priming. One way of addressing this issue would be to determine whether manipulations other than brain damage have equivalent effects on performance with the two kinds of test.

Given that one of the aims of memory testing is to determine how impaired or supernormal performance is, it is clear that this aim cannot be fully achieved if good performers score at ceiling levels and many patients score at floor levels. Memory tests need to be sensitive over a wide range of strengths of the underlying process. In general, there are more likely to be problems (a) with ceiling effects with tests of recognition as these may be rather easy for normal subjects, and (b) with floor effects with tests of recall as patients often fail totally, especially when delays are introduced. Sometimes, a test may be associated with both floor and ceiling effects. For example, the Warrington Word Recognition Test (WRT) (Warrington, 1984) is too easy for young, intelligent normal subjects many of whom score 49 or 50 out of 50, whereas there are quite a few amnesic people who score around chance levels. Just as the young normal subjects who achieve ceiling level scores probably differ in their memory abilities, the patients also probably differ in the severity of their verbal antero-grade amnesia. This is a hard problem to solve if only one memory test is used, so it may be necessary to develop tests with several levels of difficulty.

Memory varies as a function of a number of factors that vary in the normal population. Most obviously it varies as a function of age and intelligence. If a memory test is going to be useful in assessing a patient without the use of control group, norms need to be available for a range of age and intelligence levels so that it is possible to identify how many standard deviations below the mean level of a normal group, matched on age and intelligence, the patient falls. With tests of retrograde amnesia, performance is also likely to be strongly influenced by an individual's cultural background, and this may be true to a lesser extent for certain tests of anterograde amnesia—such as the Logical Memory subtest of Wechsler Memory Scale (WMS) (1945). Identification of memory impairment depends on reference to norms. For example, patients are often accepted as having organic amnesia if they fall more than a certain number of standard deviations below the mean performance of a matched normal population. Although the exact number of standard deviations varies and is in any case arbitrary, patients are typically regarded as having amnesia when their memory scores fall at least one and a half to two standard deviations below the mean score of normal subjects matched to them on intelligence and age.

One interesting corollary of this criterion of amnesia is that a person can fall more than two standard deviations below the mean memory test score of a matched sample from the normal population and show no evidence of brain damage. For example, in an unpublished study, Mayes, Hindmarch and Chap man gave Warrington's (1984) Recognition Memory Test (RMT) for faces to 100 Liverpool University students aged between 18 and 35. None of the students had a history of head injury, epilepsy or birth injury. Their mean score on the face-recognition test was 43.0 with a standard deviation of 4.6. The worst score on the face-recognition test was 29, four more subjects scored 33 or less, and one scored 34. These five subjects scored over two standard deviations below the mean of a group of similar people. Their bad performance was not a one-off occurrence, perhaps caused by poor attention on the first test occasion, because on a second series of tests, given over a month later, they performed very badly again on a series of similar face-recognition tests. Magnetic resonance imaging (MRI) confirmed that the brains of the poor face-recognizers showed no signs of having been damaged.

If subjects without brain damage can perform two or more standard devia-tions above or below the mean of an equivalent normal group, there is one important implication for procedures that assess the memory deficits caused by brain damage. Such assessments are typically made after brain damage has occurred. It was argued above that a memory assessment may fail to reveal a real deficit either if the wrong kinds of memory are tapped or if the tests used are insensitive. A third reason is that before brain damage occurred the patient's level of memory performance was well above the mean level shown by a matched control group and has now fallen to the mean level or insignificantly below it. This may be uncommon and, therefore, not usually clinically crucial; but some kind of appraisal from relatives of how good memory was pre-morbidly, although perhaps not very reliable, may indicate whether or not this problem needs to be considered seriously.

If memory were a function of a unitary brain system, then performance on all valid, reliable and sensitive tests should intercorrelate strongly. However, there is now compelling evidence that different kinds of memory disorder can occur independently of each other, presumably because they are caused by damage to different brain systems. On current evidence, something like seven or eight groups of memory disorders can be identified. These include:

- Disorders of immediate memory
- Disorders of previously well-established, primarily semantic memory.
- Disorders which probably reflect disturbed ability to plan encoding and retrieval operations, and that are caused by damage to the prefrontal associa-tion neocortex
- The amnesic disorders
- Disorders of skill learning and memory
- Disorders of classical conditioning (and perhaps of instrumental conditioning)
- Disorders of nonassociative kinds of memory, such as habituation
- Disorders of item-specific implicit memory or priming.

This listing is provisional because it supposes that the kinds of disorder within each group have more in common with each other than they do with disorders in other groups. The supposition would be supported if the disorders are caused by lesions in adjacent brain regions that share a similar neural architecture and involve functionally similar kinds of memory. It is assumed by most researchers that memories are stored in the same brain regions which process that informa-tion, so detailed assessments of memory need to take seriously the possibility that, in addition to poor memory for certain kinds of information, patients may be impaired at encoding and/or retrieving the same kind of information or some facets of it. Most important of all, standard memory tests need to tap the different kinds of memory that the lesion literature suggests exist. The kinds of memory disorder involved are considered more fully in Chapters 1 and 2.

Memory can then break down in several independent (or largely independent) ways following different kinds of brain damage. Assessment batteries should be able to identify which aspects of memory are affected in any given patient, and how severely they are affected. Ideally, they should identify whether the deficit results from an encoding, storage or retrieval deficit. If there is an encoding and/or retrieval impairment, the nature of this deficit needs to be more fully specified. It also needs to be determined whether the problem is caused by a brain lesion, whether it is hysterical (and therefore presumably unconsciously motivated), or whether it represents frank malingering. To show that the problem is organic it is not sufficient to show that there has been brain damage.

Finally, there need to be tests that can predict the severity of everyday memory problems that affect independence and employment.

STANDARD TESTS OF ANTEROGRADE MEMORY

A large number of standard tests of memory have been developed and most of them are tests of amnesia. This section will review some of the more widely used or more recently introduced of these tests. Several similar reviews have been made by Mayes (1986), Kapur (1988), Mayes and Warburg (1992), and Parkin and Leng (1993), while the use of such tests is well-illustrated in the chapter on the amnesic syndrome by O'Connor, Verfaellie and Cermak (Chapter 3).

Some consideration will be given to how well the tests fulfil the criteria that have been outlined, but it should be remembered that which test is most appropriate depends on what one's aims are. For research purposes, it is important to determine how selective an amnesia is, and Squire and Shimamura (1986) have suggested that this might be determined by the administration of the WAIS (use of the WAIS–R would now be advisable), a Dementia Rating Scale, the Boston Naming test, tests sensitive to frontal lobe function, as well as standard tests sensitive to the memory deficits found in amnesia. Parkin and Leng (1993) discuss which tests, sensitive to frontal lobe damage, are most suitable. Although the WAIS–R includes the digit span subtest, which taps a kind of short-term memory, it might also be desirable to measure previously well-established semantic memory and item-specific implicit memory (priming). Similar information may be desirable for detailed case studies, but probably not for other clinical purposes.

The Wechsler Memory Scale–Revised (WMS–R)

The WMS (Wechsler, 1945) was the first of the memory test batteries and achieved great popularity that was based not so much on its heavily criticized intrinsic properties (Lezak, 1983; Erickson & Scott, 1977) as on its convenience of use, its wide availability, the extensive literature that provides its normative base, and the fact that it has some neuropsychological validity (e.g. Skilbeck & Woods, 1980). The test comprises seven subtests, takes about 25 minutes to give, and exists in two alternative forms, although Form II is poorly standardized and its equivalence to Form I is in doubt.

The WMS has been criticized on several grounds:

1. All of its subtests are verbal with the exception of Visual Reproduction, which has been shown to contain drawings that are highly verbalizable. Patients with Memory Quotients as high as 140 have been described although they almost certainly had a disturbance of nonverbal memory (see Kapur, 1988).

2. It contains two subtests, Digit Span and Mental Control, performance on which is unaffected in pure amnesia.
3. It contains no tests of recognition, so it is incapable of determining whether a patient has an amnesia or a deficit of the kind that might be caused by frontal lobe lesions.
4. The battery contains no delayed memory testing, although there is certainly evidence that some forms of amnesia at least are most sensitive to such testing (e.g. see Pigott & Milner, 1993). Immediate testing also means that performance is partly determined by short-term memory which should be preserved in amnesics.

The insensitivity of the WMS to amnesia is perhaps illustrated by a study of McAndrews, Glisky and Schacter (1987) who found that two subgroups of amnesics differed in how well they performed on a priming task for previously novel material after a week's delay. The two groups' scores on the WMS did not differ, but the group that performed worse on the priming task also performed worse on specially devised tests of recall and recognition.

Partly in response to criticisms of the WMS, the battery was revised and has now been superseded by the WMS–R, although patients' results are still sometimes reported in terms of their WMS scores. The WMS–R takes about 50 minutes to administer, unless delayed recall testing is omitted in which case it takes about 30 minutes. The battery includes an extended orientation/information section from the WMS, and the following additional subtests have been retained from the earlier battery although some items have been changed or increased: Digit Span (a test of short-term memory); Logical Memory (which taps immediate recall of two short prose passages); Paired-Associate Learning (which involves three trials with a list of ten word pairs, half strongly and half weakly associated, with testing requiring the patient to recall the second word when given the first); and Visual Reproduction (which taps immediate reproduction of geometric designs). Delayed-recall versions of the last three subtests have been added, as have tests of spatial memory span and visual paired-associate learning and a test of recognition for geometric visual patterns. Scoring and interpretation have been revised and more extensive norms have been prepared for both normal and clinical populations, using stratified sampling techniques, for age, sex, race and geographical region for the American population. Scores from the tests are used to calculate a general memory index, a verbal memory index, a visual memory index, a delayed memory index, and an attention/concentration index, each with a mean of 100 and a standard deviation of 15. Patients' scores on subtests, and across subtests, can be compared with the population norms for their age group. The manual provides considerable information on reliability, validity, and the performance of selected clinical groups on the different indices.

The WMS–R represents an improvement on the WMS, but not as extensive an improvement as might have been hoped. The improvements include the provision of more normative data and the ability to test both delayed and non-verbal memory. There is also a large amount of information on the WMS–R being published as illustrated by the special issue of *The Clinical Neuropsychologist* (1988, vol. 2, part 2), which includes some of the early validation studies. Set against this are several problems or deficiencies. The test costs more and the full battery takes a long time to administer, which is a disadvantage for some clinical uses. The short form omits one of the battery's improvements: delayed-memory testing. There is now no equivalent alternative form so the test should not be used for monitoring memory change. There is still inadequate testing of recognition. Indeed, there are no tests of verbal recognition, which constitutes a serious omission. Several factor analytic studies of the battery have been performed and these do not always support the validity of the indices. For example, Roth, Conboy, Reeder and Boll (1990) identified three distinct, but strongly correlated factors: attention/concentration, immediate memory, and delayed memory. Their study suggests that the WMS–R fails to identify distinct factors reflecting visual and verbal memory, so the visual tests may need to be modified.

The Rivermead Behavioural Memory Test (RBMT)

This battery (see Wilson, Cockburn & Baddeley, 1985) comprises 12 subtests: recalling a name; spontaneously remembering where something has been hidden; asking a specific question in response to a cue (a test of prospective memory not included in other batteries); recognition of 10 recently shown pictures; immediate and delayed recall of a story; recognition of five unfamiliar faces; immediate and delayed recall of a route; remembering a message; questions about orientation in time, place and person. The tests are performed in a fixed order with intervening subtests filling the gap between presentation and test for some subtests. The varied nature of the tasks reduces interference and the whole test takes about 25 minutes to complete. There are four alternative equivalent versions of the test. The test has high face validity and is enjoyable for most people to do.

Two methods of scoring the battery have been developed. First, the simpler method involves deriving a screening score by allocating one point for successful performance on each subtest and no points for inadequate performance. The average normal person will obtain a perfect or nearly perfect score, and the cutoff for abnormality is set at three or more failures. Second, the more sensitive profile score is based on weighting the raw scores for the tests so as to provide a wider range of scores and less of a ceiling effect than the screening score, although more work needs to be done to determine its significance.

Development of the RBMT was directed towards tapping the everyday memory demands likely to be encountered by brain-damaged people. The test was originally standardized on a large group of patients and normal subjects. This revealed good inter-rater reliability and reliability between the parallel forms of the test, which make the RBMT the standard test of choice for measuring memory change. The battery has been validated by comparing RBMT performance not only with performance on other tests, but also with ratings of amount of forgetting as assessed by therapists, using a checklist of behaviours during sessions. Correlations of the RBMT with other tests are variable, but the correlations of RBMT scores with number of observed memory lapses made by individual patients are better than those of other standard tests and support the claim that this test is ecologically valid in that it measures everyday memory performance well. It has also been shown that the test is a particularly good indicator of the recovery status of amnesic and head-injured patients (Wilson, 1991; Schwartz and McMillan, 1989). Finally, the test has recently been adapted for use with children (Aldrich & Wilson, 1991; Wilson, Chalian, Besag & Bryant, 1993), which sets it apart from other standard tests.

The Adult Memory and Information Processing Battery (AMIPB)

The battery (see Coughlan & Hollows, 1985) comprises six subtests:

1. Immediate and delayed story recall with detailed guidelines not dissimilar to the WMS–R logical memory test.
2. Copying a complex figure followed by its immediate reproduction, and then reproduction after 30 minutes.
3. Word-list learning, in which a list of 15 words is presented for immediate recall on up to a maximum of five trials, followed by a single trial with a second list, and then a final recall attempt with the first list.
4. Design learning, in which subjects have to learn a design and reproduce it by connecting dots in a four by four array.
5. Information processing part A, in which subjects have to cancel the highest number in a list consisting of five two-digit numbers, followed by a motor speed task in which subjects merely have to cancel numbers as fast as they can.
6. Information processing part B, in which subjects are required to perform a more complex number cancellation than in (5), which is again followed by a motor speed task.

This battery, which typically takes about 45 minutes to give, is less well known than the ones described earlier. This does not relate to its intrinsic quality, but to the fact that it is published by its first author, is not advertised by him, and can only be obtained from him at St James's Hospital, Leeds. Detailed scoring instructions and norms are provided in the manual and the test exists in two parallel forms. The norms are provided for individual subtests, together with suggested cutoff points for the different age ranges, so it is possible to give subjects only part of the battery. Standardization was carried out on about 180 subjects for each parallel form of the test, and data are provided on age, sex, social class, and academic status of the sample. Correlations with other memory tests, test–retest correlations and inter-test correlations are generally satisfactory. Useful data on a group of depressed patients have also been gathered. A group of neurological patients was also found to show a significantly higher incidence of poor scores on most measures, but these data are somewhat limited in value because this group was of mixed aetiology.

The battery is useful because it taps both verbal and nonverbal memory, and delayed memory performance with both verbal and nonverbal materials. The learning tests are useful because they tap performance over several trials and also enable an assessment of sensitivity to interference to be made. The battery does not, however, tap recognition so it should be given with other tests that do this. Also, according to Kapur (1988), the 30-minute delayed recall of the complex figure runs the risk of producing floor-level performances in many neurological patients. Indeed, as he points out, at least one control subject scored zero at this delay.

The Luria–Nebraska Memory Scale (LNMS)

The LNMS (see Golden, Hammeke & Purisch, 1980) forms part of the larger Luria–Nebraska neuropsychological examination, and follows its general principles in so far as each test involves the brief administration of one or two items. This enables a relatively wide range of memory functions to be sampled quickly, in contrast with the usual strategy of using much more extensive observations of a more limited range of tasks.

Despite the inevitable limitations on the battery's sensitivity and reliability, the LNMS provides an initial screening that takes about 15 minutes to give, which may serve to highlight the memory processes that should be examined in greater detail. Its usefulness is increased because it contains tasks not available in other standard batteries, such as asking subjects to predict how many words in a list they are likely to remember (a task of metamemory, impairment on which may indicate dysfunction in the frontal lobes or related systems), word–picture association, and memory for hand position. The main drawback of the battery is that the norms, provided in the manual, are insufficient for the confident interpretation of failure on its tests. Also, there is only one form of the battery.

The Recognition Memory Test (RMT)

The RMT (see Warrington, 1984) comprises a recognition test for words and an equivalent test for faces. The two subtests are administered in a similar manner. Subjects are shown 50 words or 50 faces (unknown men) one at a time for three seconds each and asked to judge whether each item is pleasant or unpleasant by responding "yes" or "no" respectively. Immediately after the 50 items have been presented, the subject is given a two-alternative forced-choice recognition test in which the distractors are broadly similar to the target items and drawn from the same general source as the previously presented items.

The test takes about 15 minutes to give and was devised to detect minor degrees of memory deficit across a wide range of the normal population. It should be able to identify both verbal and nonverbal material-specific amnesias. Performance on recognition tests is also believed to be less vulnerable to the effects of anxiety and depression (Coughlan & Hollows, 1984). The battery was standardized on patients with right- and left-hemisphere lesions as well as normal control subjects, and both age- and sex-related norms are provided.

The RMT fills an important gap left by the previous batteries; that is, the adequate testing of recognition. As there is some evidence that performance on recognition and free-recall tests can be affected independently by brain lesions, it is of interest that, in a factor analytic study of 156 people who were given the WMS and the RMT, recognition was identified as a separate factor from recall (Compton, Sherer & Adams, 1992). The test is increasingly used because workers appreciate that it is important to tap both.

The battery nevertheless has some drawbacks. First, as Kapur (1988) has pointed out, the "faces" in the face recognition test are amenable to some degree of verbal encoding because of the inclusion of distinctive pieces of clothing in the pictures. This possibility is supported by the finding that face recognition is affected by left-hemisphere lesions as well as right, whereas word recognition is only affected by left-hemisphere lesions.

Second, young control subjects perform close to ceiling levels particularly on the word-recognition test, so that memory deficits in young, mildly impaired patients may not be detected. It has been suggested by Parkin and Leng (1993) that using the test upside down successfully reduces ceiling effects and so obviates this problem, except that one would have to run control subjects as this form of the test obviously is not standardized. The test also suffers from floor effects because severely impaired patients score at chance on both subtests and yet it is probable that the severity of their memory impairments varies considerably.

Third, it is the present author's experience that normal subjects perform worse on the face-recognition test than they do on the word-recognition test, and that variability of scoring is greater on the face-recognition test. In an unpublished study by Mayes, Hindmarch and Chapman, the mean and standard deviation of scores on the face-recognition test of 100 students were 43.0 and 4.6 respectively, whereas their mean and standard deviation on the word-recognition test were 47.8 and 2.5 respectively. This suggests that one should be cautious before accepting that low scores on the face-recognition test reflect an abnormality, and that it may sometimes be necessary to run a control group.

Fourth, there is no parallel version of this test available, so it is inappropriate for monitoring memory change.

Finally, Kapur (1987) has argued that no reliability estimates have been worked out for the test. It should also be pointed out that, with two-alternative forced-choice recognition, scoring is likely to be influenced by guessing to an increasing degree as memory gets worse.

A New Recall and Recognition Battery for Verbal and Nonverbal Material

Until recently there were no "recognition" alternatives to the RMT, although Parkin and Leng (1993) do refer to the Continuous Recognition test (see Hannay & Levin, 1988) in which subjects are shown a series of items and have to differentiate between repeated and nonrepeated items. The main value of such tests is that they easily vary difficulty level by changing the spacing between repetitions, and, because they use a yes/no recognition procedure, they provide measures of both sensitivity and bias in recognition memory.

Fortunately, a battery has been issued that may fill several gaps left by available standard memory tests (Baddeley et al., 1994). The battery should provide a means of tapping immediate and delayed recall and immediate recognition for both verbal and nonverbal materials. It comprises four main subtests.

First, there is the People test, which involves presenting photographs, occupations and names of four people (for example, a picture of Jim Green, a doctor). The subject is required to repeat the names, and is subsequently cued for recall by being given the person's profession (for example, what was the doctor's name?). Subjects are given three learning and test trials unless they reach criterion first. They are then given a delayed-recall test after a delay of 10 minutes.

Second, there is the Shapes test, which involves the presentation of four different versions of crosses that subjects are required to copy and then immediately reproduce from memory. There are three learning trials unless subjects achieve a perfect score on an earlier trial. Subjects then make a further recall attempt after a 10 minute delay. Third, there is the Names test, which taps recognition for people's names. Subjects are shown 12 names and are then given a four-choice forced-choice recognition test. There are two parts to the test. The easy section contains test items like *Sarah Boggis* (target), *Sarah Harris, Sarah Taylor* and *Sarah Wright*, whereas the harder section contains test items like *Matthew Brownhill, Matthew Brownlow, Matthew Brownell*, and *Matthew Brownlee* (target).

Fourth, there is the Doors test, which is the nonverbal equivalent of the Names test. The selection of material—coloured photographs of doors—even in the easy version makes the use of verbal strategies impracticable.

The battery has been standardized on a stratified sample of 237 normal subjects and has been found to be acceptable to patients. A number of measures can be derived from the tests, including an overall measure of episodic learning and memory, and separate measures of recall, recognition, visual and verbal memory, learning and forgetting. It is also possible to determine whether any deficit is likely to be caused by poor memory, severely impaired perception or response production. The normative data show that both recognition and recall decline with age, but that the rate of decline seems to be somewhat faster for recall.

Although the test is too recent to be fully appraised, it has several very promising features. First, it is patient-friendly and has high face validity. For example, the use of names with the verbal tests makes it unlikely that performance will be assisted by visual imagery, which could introduce a nonverbal component. Similarly, the use of crosses with the Shapes test makes it unlikely that verbal coding will assist performance, and recognition of the doors would probably not be helped by verbal coding strategies. Second, the separate checks on patients' perceptual and response capacity are very useful in screening for selective memory impairments. Third, the tests are likely to be sensitive over a wide range. This may be particularly so with the recognition tests that have both easy and difficult versions and use forced four-choice recognition. Finally, the battery is more comprehensive than previous ones. It should enable one to identify material-specific forms of amnesia and distinguish these from memory disorders caused by dysfunction of the frontal lobe system. It should also enable one to determine whether memory deficits are more severe when tested after a delay. The only things that one might wish for are delayed-recognition tests to match the recall ones, and parallel, equivalent forms of the battery.

The Williams Memory Battery

This battery (see Williams, 1968) has three parallel forms with each form comprising tests of digit span, peg-board position learning, word-definition learning, delayed (7–10 minutes) recall of pictures (followed by cued recall and recognition testing dependent on the subject's level of performance), and a brief assessment of knowledge of past personal events such as the features of the patient's first school.

Williams collected standardization data from 50 normal subjects. She found that the three forms were equivalent although, with repeat testing, performance on digit span tended to improve whereas that on delayed picture recall became worse. It was also shown that delayed picture recall was one of the best measures for discriminating between psychiatric and organic patients although, unfortunately, no specific diagnostic information was provided on the organic patients.

The battery is user-friendly and has been popular with clinicians, who now use mainly the delayed picture-recall test perhaps because patients like it and because it taps performance over a wide range. The qualitative impression of the relative efficiency of free recall, cued recall and recognition is perceived as useful for purposes of diagnosis and rehabilitation assessment.

The battery does, however, have limitations, which have been pointed out by Kapur (1988). First, the standardization data are inadequate, particularly with respect to the age ranges of both normal and patient samples. Second, the main surviving test, the delayed picture-recall test, has several weaknesses. There is insufficient guidance about the exposure for the set of pictures, absence of control data on the extent to which subjects can succeed on cued recall by guessing alone, and some confounding of cued recall and recognition because subjects may succeed at recognition on the basis of information from the cues alone.

Further Individual Tests

There are several individual tests that are widely used, some of which have been incorporated in slightly modified forms into the foregoing batteries. A few of these will be outlined briefly.

The Auditory Verbal Learning Test (AVLT)

The AVLT (see Rey, 1964) involves five presentations of a 15-word list with an immediate-recall test after each presentation. One trial of a second word list is then given, followed by an immediate-recall test. Another recall test for the first list is then given, and then, after a 30-minute delay, a delayed-recall test of the first list is given, followed by a recognition test. Although earlier norms (see Lezak, 1983) are best regarded as aids to diagnosis rather than a representative sampling of clinical and normal populations, Query and Megran (1983) have published more detailed normative data on the test from subjects with an age range from 19 to 81 years. As Kapur (1988) reports, the test has also been shown to discriminate between patients classified as impaired or unimpaired on the WMS. The test does make possible a number of useful memory measures. Normal young subjects do, however, score close to ceiling on the recognition test, so this part of the AVLT may be insensitive to mild impairments in young subjects.

A version of the AVLT has been incorporated by Coughlan and Hollows into the AMIPB and, in recent years, a variant of the test has been developed which possesses some advantages over the original. This is the *California Verbal Learning Test*, (CVLT, Delis, Kramer, Kaplan & Ober, 1987), which has a very similar structure to the AVLT. The first list comprises 16 words in four categories with four words in each category (tools, clothes, spices, fruits). The second has words drawn from two categories that are the same as in the first list (spices, fruits) and two categories that are different. In addition to the measures provided by the AVLT, the CVLT thus also makes possible measures of organizing strategy and different kinds of interference. The recognition test is also used to give measures of both sensitivity and bias. Unlike the AVLT, it is possible to score the CVLT either by hand or by using a scoring disk.

The Benton Revised Visual Retention Test (BVRT)

The BVRT (see Benton, 1974) comprises a series of 10 figures consisting of line drawings of geometric shapes, either one or three on a card. Some parts of the figures are easily verbalizable (such as triangles) whereas other parts are more complex, although some degree of verbalization may still be possible with these (for example, " a vee shape with straight sides at the top"). There are three alternative procedures for administering the test: 10-second exposure of each figure followed by immediate recall; 5-second exposure of each figure followed by immediate recall; and 10-second exposure, then 15 seconds unfilled delay followed by recall. There are three alternative forms of the test and the norms cover variations in age and educational level.

As a test of nonverbal recall the BVRT has two drawbacks. Apart from the possibility of verbalization already referred to above, the test also lacks control for differences in copying ability.

The Rey–Osterrieth Complex Figure Test (CFT)

Variants of this test (see Rey, 1941; Osterrieth, 1944) have been incorporated in batteries such as the AMIPB, and various methods of administration and scoring have been described by Lezak (1983). Typically, Rey's complex line drawing is presented and subjects are asked to copy it. The drawing is then removed and the subject immediately attempts to reproduce it. After a delay, usually between 10 and 30 minutes, subjects are asked to reproduce the figure again.

A variant of the CFT has been developed that attempts to get poor subjects up to a criterion level by having them trace the figure subcomponent by subcomponent. This variant also contains the following additional components: (a) a five-alternative forced-choice recognition test to tap delayed memory for the figure; (b) a test that assesses delayed memory for the spatial arrangement in which subjects have to place subcomponents of the figure in their correct locations; and (c) a delayed spatial recognition task in which subjects have to identify which part of the figure is in the wrong place (Diamond, personal communication).

Normative data on the CFT are sparse with respect to both subject numbers and range of age groups tested. Bennet-Levy (1984) provided normative data that took account of intelligence, but his sample had a mean age of 29 years so it did not sample the age range widely. As well as the two Rey-type figures in the AMIPB, Taylor (1979) has prepared an alternative figure although, as Parkin and Leng (1993) indicate, after a delay it is more difficult to recall the Rey figure than Taylor's alternative.

ASSESSMENT OF RETROGRADE AMNESIA

Fewer tests for retrograde amnesia have been developed than for anterograde amnesia. One reason for this may be that such tests tend to be more culture-

and country-specific than equivalent tests of anterograde amnesia. Nevertheless, memory for events and facts experienced premorbidly may be affected in several different ways following brain damage because such disturbances probably occur in frontal lobe dysfunction as well as in semantic memory disorders and amnesia. Tests of semantic memory are discussed by Patterson and Hodges in Chapter 7 so will not be further discussed here, except to suggest that it is desirable for such tests not only to be hard enough to avoid ceiling effects in normal subjects, but also match across different semantic categories on features such as frequency, familiarity, complexity, intracategory similarity, age of acquisition and so on. Only by using such matching can one be sure that category-specific effects are not artefactual.

As with semantic memory deficits, there is some evidence that amnesic-type disorders may affect autobiographical and public-event information differentially (see Chapter 18). It is therefore important to develop tests that are sensitive to autobiographical memories that were acquired premorbidly, as has been done by Kopelman, Wilson and Baddeley (1989a). Their *Autobiographical Memory Interview* (AMI) comprises two subtests. First, a "Personal Semantic Memory Schedule" taps memory for personal facts in four sections: background information, childhood, young adulthood, and the recent past. Each section is scored out of 21 and subjects have to give their knowledge of personal facts involving things like schools attended, friends, addresses, place and date of marriage, and facts about a journey made in the last year. The patient's responses are checked against information provided by someone like a near relative who knows the patient well. Second, an "Autobiographical Incidents Schedule" taps episodic memories by using the autobiographical cueing technique. In this technique, subjects are asked to recall past episodes in their lives that are associated respectively with childhood, young adulthood and the recent past. Other tests of autobiographical memory are discussed by Parkin and Leng (1993).

Patients' performance on such autobiographical memory tests should be compared with their performance on tests of public-event information. Such tests are illustrated by the *Price Estimation Test* of Wilson and Cockburn (1988), which requires subjects to estimate the current price of common items such as a loaf of bread. Amnesic subjects underestimate prices, with more affected patients producing more extreme underestimates. Kopelman, Wilson and Baddeley (1989b) have used two other tests that tap public-event-related information. The first is a *Famous Personalities Test* initially reported by Stevens (1979). This comprises 160 names, 20 of which are very famous and not included in the score, 60 of which are fictitious, and the remaining 80 of which were well known at some time from the 1930s onwards (although names need to be introduced for the 1980s and 90s). The second test is a *News Events Test* consisting of 50 pictures of memorable news events (ten for each decade between 1935 and 1984), which the subject is asked to describe. Kapur, Young, Bateman and Kennedy (1989) have developed a *Dead-or-Alive Test* in which subjects are given the names of famous people and asked to indicate whether each one is dead or alive, and if dead, to indicate how and when they died. This test is easy to update and currently includes people famous from the 1960s up to the 90s. As Parkin and Leng (1993) report, the test is an effective means of demonstrating a temporal gradient of retrograde amnesia in amnesic people, and provides several measures, one of which—memory for temporal order—may dissociate from other measures of premorbid memory.

Several further points should be made about tests of retrograde amnesia. First, they should tap not only recognition, but also free—and perhaps cued—recall, because it is possible that some patients will be relatively selectively impaired on free-recall tests (or even on recognition tests). Two such tests have recently been developed: one taps memory associated with the names of famous people, and the other taps memory associated with the names of famous events such as the Ronan Point and Piper Alpha disasters (Mayes et al., 1994). These tests tap memory for the names of the famous people and events using a forced four-choice recognition test in which each famous item must be distinguished from three plausible but unfamous items. Subjects try to recall details about the famous names and events, including information about their time of chief fame (for the famous names) or the year of their occurrence (for the events). Ideally, tests should be developed that tap free recall or recognition for identical information. For example, one could either recall what Francis Chichester was famous for or respond to a forced-choice recognition test comprising several areas in which he may have been famous.

Second, although anterograde memory assessment comprises both verbal and nonverbal tests, this is not true of retrograde memory assessments, which are all basically verbal. Complex pictorial representations of events are used, but it can, of course be argued that these are highly verbalizable. It would be relatively easy to construct a forced-choice recognition test in which each test item consisted of a face famous from the premorbid period and several similar, but unknown faces. But it would be far harder to construct a nonverbal free-recall test unless subjects can be induced either to draw or to describe the faces of famous people like John Kennedy or Madonna (and such abilities may depend at least partially on verbal encodings of facial features of the famous).

Third, standardization of a test will not only be geographically specific, but it will also be temporally specific. For example, 30 years from now few people will remember who Francis Chichester was, and the price of bread will probably be several times what it was in the early 1990s so that amnesic people will estimate its price at more than its current level. This means that tests like these would have to be restandardized at least every ten years. Standardization and restandardization should take into account (a) regional and cultural variations, (b) variations in education and intelligence, and (c) variations in age—all of which are likely to influence performance at least on public-information tests. Intelligence is an interesting factor because it seems probable that, if it has declined, then premorbid intelligence is likely to be the main influence on retrograde amnesia, whereas postmorbid intelligence is likely to be a stronger influence on anterograde amnesia.

Fourth, there has been considerable discussion of whether the underlying causes of anterograde and retrograde amnesia are the same (see Mayes, 1988).

Some of this discussion has related to whether degree of impairment on the two kinds of test is correlated in amnesics. But such comparisons have typically compared tasks that differ not only with respect to whether they tap premorbid or postmorbid memories, but also with respect to the kind of information for which memory is being tapped. It is important, therefore, to compare tests of pre- and postmorbid memory that tap memory for the same kind of information. For example, if event memory is being tested, then events encountered in both the pre- and postmorbid periods could be included so that the memories would only differ with respect to whether they were acquired pre- or postmorbidly. The absence of a correlation between pre- and postmorbid memories on a test like this would provide strong evidence that retrograde and anterograde amnesia dissociate in amnesic patients.

HYSTERICAL AMNESIA, MALINGERING AND ITEM-SPECIFIC IMPLICIT MEMORY

Memory disorders can result directly from brain damage and reflect the best performance of which the patient is capable.

Alternatively, they may arise because patients are motivated not to remember without being aware that they are so motivated. This condition is known variously as "hysterical amnesia" or "functional amnesia", and includes fugue states and cases of multiple personality (see Chapter 14). It may occur even when there is clear evidence of brain damage to those regions associated with amnesia. It is typically associated with retrograde rather than with anterograde amnesia (although it is clearly associated with the latter in multiple personality disorder), and is most likely to arise in individuals who either have a personality disorder or who have experienced emotionally traumatic events. Nevertheless, there may be some cases of hysterical amnesia where it is difficult to identify a motivational basis for the forgetting that is apparent in the emotional history of the patient.

Forgetting may, of course, be simulated by patients who are fully aware of what they are doing. One motive for doing this would be financial gain in medicolegal cases. Malingering is as likely to corrupt tests of anterograde amnesia as it is to corrupt tests of retrograde amnesia.

It is important to discriminate between the foregoing causes of apparently impaired remembering not only for clinical purposes, but also for theoretical reasons. For example, it is important to establish that cases with selective retrograde amnesia are not hysterical or malingering.

Hysterical amnesia differs from malingering in that the people concerned are supposedly unaware of what they are doing. This is not easy to determine. It is also uncertain whether the two conditions are associated with different patterns of memory performance when they are compared within the premorbid or postmorbid domains. Until it is shown that hysterical amnesia and malingering are associated with different performance patterns in the same memory domains, it seems sensible to use studies of memory performance differences between simulators and amnesic people to develop appropriate tests of "non-organic memory disorders". ("Simulated memory disorders" may be a better term, especially if certain brain dysfunctions actually lead to either aware or unaware simulation.)

In the domains of both post- and premorbid memory, three approaches might be tried. The first would involve attempts to eliminate the deficit by using amytal testing or hypnosis. The second would attempt to show that cases with "non-organic memory disorders" show more evidence of memory when tested indirectly than do organic amnesics with deficits that seem superficially to be no more severe. This would involve investigation of item-specific implicit memory for premorbidly experienced information. Unfortunately, it is not known to what extent people with organic amnesia will show normal implicit memory for premorbidly acquired information. Evidence of implicit memory for items for which subjects fail to show explicit memory is not necessarily a sign that the poor explicit memory performance is consciously or unconsciously engineered.

The third approach would attempt to show that the performance pattern of nonorganic cases is different from those found in organic cases. What has been noted here is that simulators tend to exaggerate the badness of their performance in certain areas over the levels of impairment that are found in people with organic amnesia. For example, Schacter (1986) showed that simulators make significantly less accurate feeling-of-knowing judgements than do genuine forgetters (although it should be noted that Janowsky, Shimamura and Squire (1989) have reported that patients with frontal lobe lesions *do* show a similar problem); and, more recently, Baker et al. (1993) showed that, whereas genuinely amnesic people showed impaired cued recall only after a short *filled* delay, simulators showed an impairment following an *unfilled* delay as well. They also tended to perform worse overall than those with a genuine amnesia.

These and other similar results suggest that simulators can be fooled, but the likelihood of this must be a function of the sophistication of their knowledge. A clever person, out for financial gain in a medicolegal case, might be very hard to detect if he or she has read the appropriate texts. The scenario bears an interesting resemblance to the evolutionary competition of predator–prey pairs.

PROBLEMS AND FUTURE DIRECTIONS FOR TEST DEVELOPMENT

Appropriate assessment of a memory disorder depends on having the correct theory of what characterizes processing deficits that cause the disorder, but the discovery of the correct theory depends on use of relatively good assessment procedures. The way out of the dilemma is to be aware of it, and to use assessment procedures that would be reasonably appropriate if any one of a number of the most plausible theories were correct. This suggests that one would be wise to use standard tests that are likely to tap as many memory processes as are feasible given one's constraints. For example, inclusion of delayed-memory tests would be advisable as these may be more sensitive to amnesia, particularly if it is mild as in patients with hippocampal sclerosis (e.g. Hermann et al., 1992). Recent work by De Renzi and Lucchelli (1993) suggests that some patients with temporal lobe damage may not show deficits even at delays of an hour or more, but display clear anterograde memory deficits at delays of several weeks. It would be very useful to have a standardized test that would assess memory at these delays in a quick, efficient fashion.

One also needs to consider carefully the underlying processes that may mediate performance on assessment tests. Performance on any memory test is likely to depend on more than one memory process. For example, although performance on free-recall and recognition tests has been shown to dissociate, both kinds of test are probably mediated by several memory processes, the weightings of which will vary as a function of the particular form of the test used. For example, in unpublished work, Isaac and Mayes have found that amnesic people show pathologically fast forgetting of stories and semantically organized word lists, but lose free recall of lists of unrelated words at a normal rate (see also Haist, Shimamura & Squire, 1992). Clearly, recall tests of organized and unrelated word lists must be mediated to some extent by nonoverlapping processes that can be dissociably affected by brain lesions.

There are currently no tests than can be confidently used to predict whether a patient will respond to memory rehabilitation, and, if so, what kinds of rehabilitation will be most effective. Much more research is needed on the kinds of memory strategies used by normal and brain-damaged people, which strategies lead to the best memory performance, and what factors determine the ability of patients to adopt the best strategies, before useful standard tests can be developed. For example, it would be useful to have techniques to identify the extent to which patients, spontaneously or under instruction, attend to the spatiotemporal context of material they must remember, use visual imagery strategies, and generate cues to aid recall.

One factor that is believed to determine the degree to which patients are able to adopt more efficient mnemonic strategies is the accuracy of their insight into the workings of their memory both at a specific and at a general level. Janowsky et al.'s (1989) task that measures the accuracy of feeling of knowing judgements could be used to measure metamemory of a specific kind, although this task unfortunately does not exist in standardized form. There are also several questionnaires about everyday memory and metamemory (Herrmann, 1984) that tap metamemory of the general kind, but these have been insufficiently validated for clinical use. There is evidence that the accuracy of metamemory is compromised by frontal lobe dysfunction (see Mayes, 1988), so standardized tests of metamemory should convey important diagnostic information as well as give a useful guide as to the likely effectiveness of rehabilitation.

Confabulation also results from frontal lobe dysfunction (Kapur, 1988), but there is currently no standardized way of assessing this symptom. It might be assessed by looking at errors of commission with tasks like the delayed recall of short prose passages, but it would probably be more useful to quantify the frequency of commission errors in naturalistic settings. This remains to be done.

Probably all of the standard tests discussed here would benefit from having improved normative data. More needs to be known about the performance of both normal and brain-damaged populations on existing tests. For example, more needs to be known about the strength of the association between different tests and different measures of intelligence. It is also most important to clarify which tests measure processes that dissociate from each other in brain-damaged patients.

Collection of these kinds of normative data would be facilitated if tests were presented in an automated fashion on computer. It is now possible to present nonverbal tests as easily as verbal ones on light and easily transportable computers. The advantages are that tests can be precisely standardized, the reaction time of responses accurately timed, and detailed analysis of results can be performed with great ease. Use of computerized testing will enable busy clinical psychologists to collect useful patient data, which it may be possible to pool centrally as the data collected at different locations will be comparable. Also, it will be far easier to modify and extend existing standard test protocols and to update norms. The development of computerized memory batteries should, therefore, be a powerful means of advancing both research and clinical work. The result will not necessarily be a reduction in the number of batteries used, but the ones that will be should have better norms and tap a wider range of dissociable memory processes.

SUMMARY

Brain damage causes several independent kinds of memory disorders. The number of these disorders and their characteristics are still only known in outline. Appropriate assessment procedures are vital not only for increasing theoretical understanding of these disorders, but also for clinical purposes. Assessment procedures need to work hand in hand with developing theoretical understanding of the disturbed processes that underlie the disorders, because the aim is to assess how severe are the disorders of these processes.

The best procedures will be those that remain appropriate if any one of several plausible theoretical accounts turns out to be correct. But it is also likely that assessment procedures will change as knowledge advances. Whatever procedures are used, it is important that the tests employed be reliable, valid and sensitive, allow performance to vary over a wide range without producing floor or ceiling effects, and be standardized with respect to suitable normal groups. It is also highly desirable that several equivalent forms of standardized tests be developed. This will be of use not only in clinical contexts, where the aim may be either to plot deterioration or to monitor the effects of treatment, but also in determining whether memory-disordered patients show more variable performance over time than do normal people. Development of knowledge and clinical advances will be faster if the best tests are universally adopted so that findings in different centres can be directly compared. Unfortunately, personal experience suggests that this goal may be difficult or impossible to achieve in the near future. A sceptic might reply that it is better this way because, in our present state of relative ignorance, there is a risk that very inadequate tests may become entrenched and retard the development of knowledge rather than accelerate it.

Psychological assessment of memory disorders in patients should be accompanied wherever possible with assessment of brain damage and dysfunction. Structural damage can be assessed most sensitively by MRI, which now permits the volumetric measurement of structures such as the hippocampus and amygdala as well as the determination of whether or not apparently intact brain regions show tissue abnormalities. Functional abnormalities that may sometimes appear even in structurally normal regions may be detected by positron emission tomography (PET), single photon emission tomography, and functional MRI.

REFERENCES

Aldrich, F.K. & Wilson, B.A. (1991). Rivermead Behavioural Memory Tests for Children (RBMT–C): a preliminary evaluation. *British Journal of Clinical Psychology*, **30**, 161–168.

Baddeley, A., Emslie, H. & Nimmo-Smith, I. (1994). *The Doors and People Test*. Thames Valley Test Co., Bury St Edmunds, Suffolk.

Baker, G.A., Hanley, J.R., Jackson, H.F., Kimmance, S. & Slade, P. (1993). Detecting the faking of amnesia: performance differences between simulators and patients with memory impairment. *Journal of Clinical and Experimental Neuropsychology*, **15**, 668–684.

Bennet-Levy, J. (1984). Determinants of performance on the Rey-Osterrieth complex figure test: an analysis, and a new technique for single case assessment. *British Journal of Clinical Psychology*, **23**, 109–119.

Benton, A.L. (1974). *Revised Visual Retention Test*. The Psychological Corporation, New York.

Compton, J.M., Sherer, M. & Adams, R.L. (1992). Factor analysis of the Wechsler Memory Scale and the Warrington Recognition Memory Test. *Archives of Clinical Neuropsychology*, **7**, 165–173.

Coughlan, A.K. & Hollows, S.E. (1985). *The Adult Memory and Information Processing Battery*. A.K. Coughlan, St James's Hospital, Leeds.

Delis, D.C., Kramer, J.H., Kaplan, E. & Ober, B.A. (1987). *CVLT: California Verbal Learning Test*. The Psychological Corporation, San Antonio.

De Renzi, E. & Lucchelli, P. (1993). Dense retrograde amnesia, intact learning capability and abnormal forgetting rate: a consolidation effect? *Cortex*, **29**, 449–466.

Erickson, R.C. & Scott, M.L. (1977). Clinical memory testing: a review. *Psychological Bulletin*, **84**, 1130–1149.

Golden, L.J., Hammeke, T.A. & Purisch, A.D. (1980). *The Luria–Nebraska Neuropsychological Examination*. Western Psychological Services, Los Angeles.

Haist, F., Shimamura, A.P. & Squire, L.R. (1992). On the relationship between recall and recognition memory. *Journal of Experimental Psychology: Learning, Memory and Cognition*, **18**, 691–702.

Hannay, H.J. & Levin, H.S. (1988). Visual continuous recognition memory in normal and closed-head-injured adolescents. *Journal of Clinical and Experimental Neuropsychology*, **11**, 444–460.

Hermann, B.P., Wyler, A.R., Somes, G., Berry, A.D. & Donhan, F.C. (1992). Pathological status of the mesial temporal lobe predicts memory outcome from left anterior temporal lobectomy. *Neurosurgery*, **31**, 652–657.

Herrmann, D.J. (1984). Questionnaires about memory. In J.E. Harris & P.E. Morris (eds), *Everyday Memory, Actions and Absentmindedness*. Academic Press, London.

Janowsky, J.S., Shimamura, A.P. & Squire, L.R. (1989). Memory and metamemory: comparisons between patients with frontal lobe lesions and amnesic patients. *Psychobiology*, **17**, 3–11.

Kapur, N. (1987). Some comments on the technical acceptability of Warrington's Recognition Memory Test. *British Journal of Clinical Psychology*, **26**, 144–146.

Kapur, N. (1988). *Memory Disorders in Clinical Practice*. Butterworths, London.

Kapur, N., Young, A., Bateman, D. & Kennedy, P. (1989). A long-term clinical and neuropsychological follow-up of focal retrograde amnesia. *Cortex*, **25**, 671–680.

Kopelman, M.D., Wilson, B.A. & Baddeley, A.D. (1989a). *Autobiographical Memory Interview*. Thames Valley Test Co., Bury St Edmunds.

Kopelman, M.D., Wilson, B.A. & Baddeley, A. (1989b). The autobiographical memory interview: a new assessment of autobiographical and personal semantic memory in amnesic patients. *Journal of Clinical and Experimental Neuropsychology*, **11**, 724–744.

Lezak, M.D. (1983). *Neuropsychological Assessment*. Oxford University Press, New York.

MacAndrews, M.P., Glisky, E.L. & Schacter, D.L. (1987). When priming persists: long-lasting implicit memory for a single episode in amnesic patients. *Neuropsychologia*, **25**, 497–506.

McCarthy, R.A. & Warrington, E.K. (1990). *Cognitive Neuropsychology*. Academic Press, London.

Martin, R.C. et al. (1991). Impaired long-term retention despite normal verbal learning in patients with temporal lobe dysfunction. *Neuropsychology*, **5**, 3–12.

Mayes, A.R. (1986). Learning and memory disorders and their assessment. *Neuropsychologia*, **24**, 25–39.

Mayes, A.R. (1988). *Human Organic Memory Disorders*. Cambridge University Press, Cambridge.

Mayes, A.R., Downes, J.J., McDonald, C., Poole, V., Rooke, S., Sagar, H.J. & Meudell, P.R. (1994). Two tests for assessing remote public knowledge: a tool for assessing retrograde amnesia. *Memory*, **2**, 183–210.

Mayes, A. & Warburg, R. (1992). Memory assessment in clinical practice and research. In J.R. Crawford, D.M. Parker & W.W. McKinley (eds), *A Handbook of Neuropsychological Assessment*. Erlbaum, Hove.

Osterrieth, P.A. (1944). Le test de copie d'une figure complexe. *Archives de Psychologie*, **30**, 206–356.

Parkin, A.J. & Leng, N.R.C. (1993). *Neuropsychology of the Amnesic Syndrome*. Erlbaum, Hove.

Pigott, S. & Milner, B. (1993). Memory for different aspects of complex visual scenes after unilateral temporal- or frontal-lobe resection. *Neuropsychologia*, **31**, 1–15.

Query, W.T. & Megran, J. (1983). Age-related norms for the AVLT in a male patient population. *Journal of Clinical Psychology*, **39**, 136–138.

Rey, A. (1941). L'examen psychologique dans les cas d'encephalopathie traumatique. *Archives de Psychologie*, **28**(112), 286–340.

Rey, A. (1964). *L'examen Clinique en Psychologie*. Presses Universitaires de France, Paris.

Roth, D.L., Conboy, T.J., Reeder, K.P. & Boll, T.J. (1990). Confirmatory factor analysis of the Wechsler Memory Scale–Revised in a sample of head-injury patients. *Journal of Clinical and Experimental Neuropsychology*, **12**, 834–842.

Schacter, D.L. (1986). Amnesia and crime: what do we really know? *American Psychologist*, **41**, 286–295.

Schwartz A.F. & McMillan, T.M. (1989). Assessment of everyday memory after severe head injury. *Cortex*, **25**, 665–671.

Skilbeck, C.E. & Woods, R.T. (1980). The factorial structure of the Wechsler Memory Scale: samples of neurological and psychogeriatric patients. *Journal of Clinical Neuropsychology*, **2**, 293–300.

Squire, L.R. & Shimamura, A.P. (1986). Characterizing amnesic patients in neurobehavioral study. *Behavioral Neuroscience*, **100**, 866–877.

Squire, L.R., Weinberger, N.M., Lynch, G. & McGaugh, J.L. (1991). *Memory: Organization and Locus of Change*. Oxford University Press, New York.

Stevens, M. (1979). Famous personality test: a test for measuring remote memory. *Bulletin of the British Psychological Society*, **32**, 211.

Taylor, L.B. (1979). Psychological assessment of neurosurgical patients. In T. Rasmussen & R. Marino (eds), *Functional Neurosurgery*. Raven Press, New York.

Tulving, E. & Schacter, D.L. (1990). Priming and human memory systems. *Science*, **247**, 301–306.

Waldeman, B.W., Dickson, A.L. & Kazelskis, R. (1991). The relationship between intellectual function and performance on the Wechsler Memory Scale. *Journal of Genetic Psychology*, **152**, 57–69.

Warrington, E.K. (1984). *Recognition Memory Test*. NFER–Nelson, Windsor.

Warrington, E.K. & McCarthy, R.A. (1983). Category-specific access dysphasia. *Brain*, **106**, 859–878.

Wechsler, D. (1945). A standardized memory scale for clinical use. *Journal of Psychology*, **19**, 87–95.

Wechsler, D. (1955). *Adult Intelligence Scale*. Psychological Corporation, New York.

Wechsler, D. (1987). *Wechsler Memory Scale–Revised*. Psychological Corporation, San Antonio.

Williams, M. (1968). The measurement of memory in clinical practice. *British Journal of Social and Clinical Psychology*, **7**, 19–34.

Wilson, B.A. (1991). Long-term prognosis of patients with severe memory disorders. *Neuropsychological Rehabilitation*, **1**, 117–134.

Wilson, B.A., Chalian, R.I., Besag, F.M.C. & Bryant, T. (1993). Adapting the Rivermead Behavioural Memory Test for use with children aged five to ten years. *Journal of Clinical and Experimental Neuropsychology*, **15**, 474–486.

Wilson, B.A. & Cockburn, J. (1988). The prices test: a simple test of retrograde amnesia. In M.M. Gruneberg, P.E. Morris & Sykes, R.N. (eds), *Practical Aspects of Memory: Current Research and Issues*, vol. 2. John Wiley, Chichester.

Wilson, B., Cockburn, J. & Baddeley, A. (1985). *The Rivermead Behavioural Memory Test*. Thames Valley Test Co., Bury St Edmunds.

Chapter 16

Behavioural and Self-Report Methods

Robert G. Knight
and
Hamish P.D. Godfrey
University of Otago, Dunedin, New Zealand

INTRODUCTION

Assessment of the memory-impaired patient in clinical practice has a number of objectives. The clinician may wish to determine how a client's current memory performance compares with that of a person of similar age and background. A further aim might be to establish whether other cognitive deficits, such as intellectual decline or perceptual defects, are significant in the patient's presenting problems. Traditional standardised neuropsychological tests are an effective means of answering such diagnostic questions. For clinicians working to rehabilitate patients with memory failure, however, these formal methods of assessment have limitations. In particular, they do not directly document the problems that patients are having in their everyday lives. Such tests do not reveal what patients actually can or cannot do, and how much awareness they have of their deficits. Nor is it possible to construct a view of how these deficits affect significant others in the patient's social environment. In short, although traditional tests of memory supply important diagnostic data, they do not provide information about the practical aspects of patients' impairments. To achieve a comprehensive understanding of the patient's problems and to formulate meaningful targets for therapy, traditional tests of neuropsychological functioning must be augmented by behavioural interviewing, symptom checklists for clients and caregivers, and behavioural measures of everyday memory.

This chapter reviews some of these measures. At the outset it must be

Handbook of Memory Disorders. Edited by A.D. Baddeley, B.A. Wilson and F.N. Watts.
© 1995 John Wiley & Sons Ltd.

acknowledged that terms like "the behavioural assessment of memory" are not readily defined. Our goal in this chapter is to introduce measures that have been constructed to evaluate memory in everyday life with a high degree of ecological validity. Our concern is to draw the attention of workers in rehabilitation settings to the usefulness of practical memory tasks in the process of implementing interventions for the memory-impaired.

BEHAVIOURAL ASSESSMENT OF MEMORY DEFICITS

Involvement in the management of patients with memory problems soon reveals the need for measures that provide data on their performance of everyday memory tasks. For example, some years ago, in our work with alcoholic Korsakoff patients living in a long-stay psychiatric ward, the limitations of conventional psychometric tests of memory skills quickly became apparent. A major limitation was that tests such as the Wechsler Memory Scale–Revised (WMS–R) do not provide the kind of behavioural information relevant to real-world performance necessary for setting rehabilitation goals. The WMS–R manual has many excellent features, but it is devoid of any ecologically valid criterion-referenced data. Such traditional tests have been constructed and standardised to provide normative data about individual clients and to assist in the identification of modality or material-specific deficits. Thus these tests can be used to determine how many standard deviations below average an individual has scored. A standard score of -1.5 on the General Memory Index of the WMS–R defines precisely how severe the problem is relative to normal performance, but this information cannot be translated into some indication of what the patient can actually learn or retain in everyday life. Neuropsychological data of the kind provided by the WMS–R are of value, but the process of supporting and rehabilitating dysmnesic patients necessitates obtaining more practical information. For example, care staff typically find information about the ability of patients to remember their way about the hospital or to follow a simple set of instructions more helpful than the results of laboratory-based tests of cognition. They can use this information to set limits or goals for their patients.

Another advantage of behaviourally based memory tests is their high face validity for clients, caregivers and therapists. This makes it more likely that the person tested will be motivated to perform well and receive appropriate encouragement from others to perform at their best during a testing session. The need to memorise lists of paired associates, nonsense syllables, or geometric designs is not something that people encounter often in their adult lives. Thus they are apt to dismiss tests based on traditional laboratory procedures as irrelevant and childish.

In the rehabilitation of individual patients, clinicians will often need to construct practical memory tasks that are relevant to a client's specific needs and to the setting in which therapy is taking place. The experience that applied psychologists have had with the behavioural assessment of a variety of problem behaviours and deficits strongly reinforces the importance of defining and measuring specific behavioural targets for individual clients. This requires that clinicians be able to determine through the medium of behavioural interviewing and observation precisely what problems the client is encountering. For a particular patient this may mean developing a strategy to overcome problems in their workplace. For example, an alcoholic client may present as relatively unimpaired on the WMS–R, but have considerable difficulty operating as a spray painter because of his/her inability to remember technical aspects of how to mix paints and solvents. A dementing patient may have difficulty learning the way about a care facility to which he/she has just been admitted. In both these instances the assessment will involve structuring a behavioural test that incorporates the distinctive features of the client's deficits. Such a test can be used to define specific behavioural goals for the client and to monitor change in performance over time.

Constructing a behavioural method for assessing memory can be a test of a clinician's initiative and ingenuity, and is dependent on the ability to make an accurate clinical appraisal of the patient's needs. Developing a customised procedure sensitive to the deficits of an individual client can be time-consuming, but the advantages for practical case management can be considerable. One disadvantage is that the expense and time involved in developing some sort of normative database for a one-off measure can be considerable. In the clinical context, however, this often does not matter; rehabilitation goals can be set without reference to normative standards. Where some comparative data are necessary, a matched comparison subject or a small group of controls can be tested. For example, it is sometimes possible to enlist the aid of workmates of a client to establish a desirable level of skill performance at work.

As an example of such a specific behavioural test, in the course of a study on the use of cognitive retraining with Korsakoff patients we constructed a simple test of memory for instructions. Patients were requested to deliver an envelope to a secretary's office and collect a pencil and eraser from another office (Godfrey & Knight, 1985; Knight & Godfrey, 1985). This test could be administered in a standardised manner and the performance of our amnesic patients then compared with that of nonamnesic alcoholics living in the same ward. The difficulty level could therefore be set appropriately for our group of Korsakoff patients. Although the procedure could not be exactly replicated in another clinical setting, the general method is capable of modification for use almost anywhere. It proved a simple test to administer, and allowed us to feed back to nursing staff some straightforward information about the practical limits in a patient's instrumental memory skills.

Standardised Behavioural Memory Tests

Ad hoc methods of behavioural assessment have recently been supplemented by the publication of standardised behavioural memory tests, which have demonstrated psychometric credentials and normative results to aid the interpretation of findings for individual clients. We now consider two such test batteries.

The Rivermead Behavioural Memory Test (RBMT)

This measure comprises 12 items, each of which is a practical test of memory selected by Barbara Wilson and her colleagues at the Rivermead Rehabilitation Centre, Oxford (Wilson, 1987; Wilson, Baddeley & Cockburn, 1988; Wilson, Cockburn & Baddeley, 1985; Wilson, Cockburn, Baddeley & Hiorns, 1989) on the basis of their experience with the assessment and remediation of brain-injured patients. Each of the items is administered in a standardised manner and four parallel versions of the test have been prepared. The 12 items are described briefly below:

1. *Remembering a name*. Subjects are shown the picture of a person and told the person's name. They are then tested for recall of both the first name and surname after a delay.
2. *Remembering a hidden belonging*. Subjects are asked for something of minimal value, such as a comb, which is placed somewhere in the examiner's room. They are then instructed to ask for the hidden object and remember where it was located, when the examiner says "We have now finished this test".
3. *Remembering an appointment*. In this test, the examiner sets a timer for 20 minutes, and tells the subject to ask about their next appointment when it sounds.
4. *Picture recognition*. This measure is a 2-choice delayed-recognition test of 10 line drawings of common objects.
5. *Immediate recall of a newspaper article*. A short prose passage is read to the subject and recall tested immediately.
6. *Delayed recall of the newspaper article*. The information presented in the course of the previous item is tested again after a 20-minute delay.
7. *Face recognition*. Subjects are tested on their ability to complete a 2-choice recognition test of five photographs of faces.
8. *Remembering a new route* (*immediate*). A short path between a number of specific locations in the testing room is demonstrated by the examiner. Subjects are instructed to retrace the examiner's route.
9. *Remembering a new route* (*delayed*). Ability to recall the route traced out by the examiner in the previous item is tested after a 20-minute delay.
10. *Delivering a message*. When demonstrating the route in item 8, the examiner deposits an envelope labelled "message" at a particular location. On both the immediate and delayed tests of route recall, the subject is required to take the envelope and leave it in a specified place further along the route.
11. *Orientation*. Nine questions testing the subject's orientation for time and place administered.
12. *Date*. The ability of subjects to give the correct date is scored separately from the other orientation items.

For each of the 12 items a cutoff score that best discriminated between brain-injured and control subjects was formulated, and this can be used to assign a pass/fail score to each item. The sum of the items passed is designated the *screening score* (ranging from 0 to 12). In addition, the raw scores are allocated either 2 points (normal), 1 point (borderline), or 0 points (abnormal) and these points can be summed to provide a standardised *profile score* (ranging from 0 to 24). Wilson et al. (1989) reported 100% inter-rater agreement in an evaluation of 10 different raters for both the screening and profile scores. Estimates of reliability based on correlations between the alternative forms of the test are generally satisfactory. For the pooled data from 118 patients tested twice, the correlation between screening scores was 0.78 and between profile scores 0.85. The lower screening score correlation was the product of relatively low correlation (0.67) between version A and D of the test battery; other screening score correlations exceeded 0.80.

Evidence for the validity of the RBMT comes from a variety of sources. One indication of the validity of this measure is the success with which it discriminates between brain-injured and normal subjects. Wilson et al. (1989) found that 176 brain-injured patients tested at the Rivermead Rehabilitation Centre scored significantly lower on each of the items than 118 healthy controls. To illustrate the sensitivity of individual items, an effect size (ES) score has been computed for each score (using the results in Table 3 of Wilson et al., 1989) by subtracting the patient scores from the control mean scores, and dividing by the control standard deviation. The resulting ES values (Table 16.1) provide a standardised index of the difference between the group means. Thus the ES computed for the screening score total of 2.98, indicates that the separation between the patient

Table 16.1 Effect sizes for the item and total scores on the RBMT

RBMT	Effect size
Item profile scores	
Name	1.09
Hidden belonging	1.32
Remembering appointment	1.20
Picture recognition	5.11
Newspaper article (immediate)	0.70
Newspaper article (delayed)	1.23
Route recall (immediate)	1.53
Route recall (delayed)	1.29
Message	1.36
Face recognition	1.77
Orientation	1.63
Date	1.11
Total scores	
Screening score	2.98
Profile	3.56

and control means is nearly three control-group standard deviations in magnitude. Using this index it can be seen that all the items with the exception of the immediate recall test of the newspaper prose passage have effect sizes in excess of one standard deviation. The most successful item is the picture recognition test where almost all the control subjects obtained 2-point scores (M = 1.99, SD = 0.09), whereas the patients' average was 1.53 (SD = 0.76). Overall, the level of discrimination between brain-injured subjects and healthy controls is good. The authors caution, however, that the RBMT was designed to be a test on which most healthy normal subjects would perform easily and thus score at a ceiling level. Goldstein and Polkey (1992) found that the RBMT failed to discriminate between patients who had undergone either a radical or more circumscribed temporal lobectomy. Scores on the logical memory subtest of the WMS, however, did distinguish between the two groups. Accordingly, the RBMT may not be sensitive to mild deficits in younger clients or to subtle differences between groups of neurologically impaired patients.

Concurrent validity has been assessed in a number of studies reporting correlations between the RBMT and other neuropsychological tests of memory. Wilson et al. (1989) reported some encouraging correlations between the RBMT total scores and other measures of secondary memory, including Warrington's (1984) Recognition Memory Test for words (0.60, 0.63) and faces (0.41, 0.43), and a paired associate learning test (0.60, 0.62). They found that correlations with tests of primary memory were, as might be expected, somewhat lower, ranging from 0.24 to 0.30. Similarly, Goldstein and Polkey (1992) reported correlations of 0.44 and 0.49 between the RBMT and scores on the WMS logical memory subtest, and 0.38 between the Rey Complex Figure test and the RBMT, for their sample of temporal lobectomy cases. These results suggest that there is strong association between performance analogue tests of everyday memory performance and traditional laboratory-based tests of secondary memory.

Correlations between RBMT scores, and patients' and relatives' ratings of memory loss, have been reported in several studies, providing additional information about the validity of the test. Results from four studies are summarised in Table 16.2. In all studies there was a significant association between RBMT scores and relatives' ratings of the patients' memory impairments. Significant correlations between self-ratings and RBMT scores were also found for Lincoln and Tinson's (1989) stroke patients, and Schwartz and McMillan's (1989) severely head-injured patients. The lack of significant correlations in Goldstein and Polkey's study may be the result of the relatively milder degree of impairment in their sample as evidenced by the patients' higher RBMT scores and lower ratings of deficit on the Everyday Memory Questionnaire than those reported in the other studies.

In summary, there is encouraging evidence for the usefulness of the RBMT in clinical practice. Shortened versions of the RBMT that can be used with patients who have perceptual deficits (Cockburn, Wilson, Baddeley & Hiorns, 1990a) or dysphasia (Cockburn, Wilson, Baddeley & Hiorns, 1990b) have been constructed, and norms for these groups of patients established. A children's

Table 16.2 Correlations between the RBMT and subjective ratings of memory impairments

	Patients' RBMT screening score		Correlations	
	Mean	SD	Screening	Profile
Wilson et al. (1989)	6.4	3.4		
Relative: MC			−0.57	−0.57
Self: MC			−0.43	−0.44
Lincoln & Tinson (1989)	5.3	2.7		
Self: EMQ			−0.46	
Goldstein & Polkey (1992)	7.13*			
Relative: EMQ			−0.38	−0.41
Self: EMQ			NS	NS
Schwartz & McMillan (1989)	6.62	3.1		
Relative: SMQ			0.39	
Self: SMQ			0.54	
Relative: EMQ			0.53	
Self: EMQ			0.49	

* Weighted average of 46 patients.
RBMT=Rivermead Behavioural Memory Test; MC=Memory Checklist; SMQ=Subjective Memory Questionnaire; EMQ=Everyday Memory Questionnaire.

version of the test has also been developed and is undergoing preliminary evaluation (Aldrich & Wilson, 1991). The usefulness of the test in evaluating the long-term effectiveness of rehabilitation has been demonstrated in a follow-up study of 25 head-injured clients. The strength of the test is its ability to screen for problems in the performance of everyday memory skills and to suggest appropriate goals for remediation. In addition, it provides a means of documenting the severity of memory impairment which patients, caregiver and other professionals can readily understand. It is apparent that such a measure is less sensitive to mild deficits than are traditional neuropsychological tests of memory. In this regard it is notable that the most successful item identified by the ES analysis in Table 16.1 is Picture Recognition, a task closely derived from traditional laboratory-based tests. The discriminatory power of this test is largely a function of the authors' decision to use relatively simple items and short delay periods. The sensitivity of the RBMT is also partly the product of the narrow range of item scores used in the profile and screening totals. For this reason the RBMT is likely to be more useful in rehabilitation settings than in the experimental investigation of organic amnesia.

Memory Assessment Clinic (MAC) Battery

Crook, Larrabee and colleagues have reported the construction of a battery of eight subtests designed to assess everyday memory using computer technology (Crook & Larrabee, 1988; Larrabee & Crook, 1989; Crook, Youngjohn, Larrabee & Salama, 1992). An impressive range of normative and psychometric data is now available for this battery. The MAC tests are all administered "in a standardized manner on a 19-in color monitor with a touchscreen, interfaced with a computer equipped with a 20 megabyte hard-disk drive, a laser-disk player, and customized computer graphics hardware" (Crook et al., 1992, p. 125). No responses are made on the keyboard; subjects indicate their responses verbally, on the touchscreen, or using a telephone (see below). The equipment necessary for the operation of such a computer-assisted testing process is expensive, but the MAC battery provides an example of the ingenious use of modern technology to simulate everyday memory tasks. A brief description of the MAC tests follows:

1. *Name–face association.* Subjects are shown live recordings on the computer screen of 14 individuals introducing themselves using common first names. The recorded individuals are then shown in a different order, giving the name of the city in which they live, and the subject is asked to recall their names. Three learning trials are administered and recall of the name–face pairs tested on each occasion. Recall is then retested after a 40-minute delay. Incidental learning may also be tested.

2. *Face matching.* This test uses a classic non-matching-to-sample procedure whereby subjects are required to indicate on the touchscreen monitor which face has been added to a previously displayed array of facial photographs. One photograph is shown on the first trial, and a new photograph is added on each of 25 successive trials.

3. *Face recognition.* Subjects are shown 156 photographs of faces, 50 of which are shown twice. Their task is to detect the repetitions.

4. *Telephone numbers.* Subjects are shown on the computer screen a series of 3, 7 or 10 digits and asked to read each one aloud. They then dial the numbers from memory on the telephone apparatus connected to the computer. West and Crook (1990) developed an interference condition in which subjects heard an engaged signal after they had dialled and were instructed to redial. This procedure was found to be especially sensitive to the effects of aging.

5. *Grocery list.* This test uses a 5-trial version of Buschke's (1973) selective reminding procedure with a list of 15 grocery items. A 40-minute delay recall trial is also administered.

6. *Name associates.* On each of five trials, subjects are presented with a series of six pairs of first and last names in a format similar to the WMS paired associates procedure. After each learning trial, recall is tested by presenting the last name and asking the subjects to provide the first.

7. *News.* A 6-minute television news broadcast is shown to subjects, who are then tested with 25 multichoice questions (Crook, Youngjohn & Larrabee, 1990).

8. *Divided attention.* In this behavioural test, participants listen to weather and traffic reports while performing a simulated driving task. The driving task involves responding to traffic signals, allowing calculation of reaction times

(Crook et al., 1992). After each simulated radio broadcast, immediate recall is tested in much the same way as for the WMS logical memory test.

9. *Misplaced objects*. This test is a more extensive computer version of the RBMT hidden belongings test. The subjects are shown a 12-room schema of a house on the computer screen together with 20 common items. They are asked to put each of the items into a room (no more than two items per room) and are later asked to recall the location of each item.

Like the RBMT, the MAC battery is a mixture of tasks with high face and ecological validity, some novel, others based on traditional laboratory tasks. The telephone dialling test, for example, is an interesting adaptation of the traditional digit span test. The computer guarantees a standardised administration procedure and allows a number of different scores to be calculated accurately and rapidly. Administration of the full battery takes about 1.5 hours (West Crook & Barron, 1992). Alternative forms of the various tests are available (Crook, Johnson & Larrabee, 1990) and translated versions of the battery are available in several languages (Crook et al., 1992).

Youngjohn, Larrabee and Crook (1992) reported test–retest reliabilities for 115 healthy volunteers of above-average intelligence and education tested on two occasions 21 days apart. On traditional neuropsychological tests the reliability estimates were moderate: 0.55 for the Logical Memory test, 0.72 for Paired Associate Learning, and 0.53 and 0.57 for the Benton Visual Retention test. Results from the MAC battery were of similar magnitude. Reliabilities for object location, divided attention, name–face associations, name associates, and grocery list ranged from about 0.70 to 0.85. Indices from the face-matching, telephone-dialling and face-recognition tasks had reliability estimates in the range 0.30 to 0.60. On the majority of the traditional and computerised test score indices, there were significant practice effects over the 3-week period, indicating the necessity for alternative forms for use when repeated testing is indicated. With the exception of the face-recognition tests, the MAC battery measures had retest reliability coefficients in the same range as comparable traditional neuropsychological tests. The relatively moderate correlations may have been the result of using a relatively homogeneous normal sample of subjects with a consequently restricted score range and the use of a retest procedure where practice effects are a considerable factor.

Evidence has accumulated for the validity and usefulness of the MAC battery in the assessment of age-related decline in memory functions, which in turn substantiates the clinical sensitivity of the various tests (e.g. Crook et al., 1992; Crook & West, 1990; Larrabee & Crook, 1989; West et al., 1992). Crook et al. (1992) report a normative base for the battery that comprises over 2500 normal volunteers tested in the United States. Factor analysis of the battery (Crook & Larrabee, 1988; Larrabee & Crook, 1989) has revealed that the battery assesses dimensions labelled verbal memory, visual memory, psychomotor speed, attention, and vigilance. To date the MAC battery has primarily been used to investigate normal memory functioning, although its potential as a diagnostic instrument in the detection of dementia has been explored (Youngjohn, Larrabee & Crook, 1992). The battery requires technical resources that may limit its routine deployment in many clinical assessment services. Nonetheless it is an interesting illustration of the way in which computer-assisted assessment procedures can be used to test everyday memory functions in an ecologically valid manner.

Conclusions

As clinical neuropsychologists have broadened their involvement in working with neurological cases to include long-term case management and rehabilitation, the need for measures that are directly relevant to everyday behaviour has become more urgent. The standardised measures that have emerged recently represent a useful blend of traditional memory tasks with behaviourally-referenced tests of everyday memory. Such measures have a greater ecological validity and are thus frequently more valuable in rehabilitation work than tests evolved from laboratory-based procedures (Wilson, 1991).

In the process of designing assessment procedures for individuals or groups of patients with special needs, we would encourage clinicians to develop specific measures that are relevant to their clinical setting and practice. Although the memory tests that make up measures like the RBMT or MAC battery are suitable for use with many clients, it is often necessary to develop tests that more precisely measure the distinctive employment-related or routine memory problems of an individual client. If a person needs to remember a sequence of operations in the assembly of an electronic device, then this can form the basis of a memory test. If the concern is that a mildly demented patient learn their way about a new residential home, then a simple and situation-specific orientation test can be devised to monitor their progress. If a head-injured person needs to learn to use external aids, such as a diary to help them remember their daily routine, then their ability to record and keep appointments should be assessed directly. Measures of baseline deficits, progress in therapy, and clinical outcome must be relevant to treatment goals.

In developing specific behavioural tests, there are some basic rules to follow. The patient's deficits on the basis of self and collateral reports should be specified, with clear behavioural referents. Measures would be chosen that are likely to be sensitive to therapeutic objectives. Wherever possible, multiple sources of information relevant to each problem should be collected. Thus behavioural tests should be employed with self-report scales, or validated against relatives' reports. Measurement procedures should be administered in a standardised manner so that sources of extraneous variance can be limited wherever possible. It is important to bear in mind that the measures should be as simple and easy to use as possible. Elaborate procedures that are time-consuming and expensive, or require extensive training, are likely to be abandoned as impractical very readily. There is little room in the realities of clinical practice for lengthy assessment procedures with little immediate clinical benefit.

SELF- AND COLLATERAL-REPORT METHODS

An important initial stage in clinical assessment is to obtain a clear description of the difficulties experienced by a patient with memory impairments. There are two immediate sources of information that the clinician can access: significant others (relatives, nurses, etc.) who know the client well, and the patient him- or herself. The clinician's task is to determine how the problem is experienced both by patients and by those who live or work with them. The use of collateral and self-report questionnaires allows clinicians to supplement their interview with a systematic review of the possible consequences of the memory failure. One important opportunity that is created when comparable information is obtained from both patients and collaterals is the ability to detect discrepancies in the accounts of the disorder obtained from different sources. In particular, this relates to the extent to which patients appreciate the changes that have occurred in their ability to remember or learn new information. Brain damage frequently results in a loss of insight. Demented patients, for example, may overestimate their abilities, and this may become obvious when their self-report is contrasted with their test performance or observed behaviour. There has recently been considerable interest in assessing patients' awareness of their memory skill, or their *metamemory*. Evaluating the congruence between a patient's self-report, collateral reports and objective tests of memory skills allows the clinician to make an estimate of a patient's insight into his or her cognitive disabilities.

Collateral Report Scales

Reports on a patient's observed level of everyday memory functioning provide a useful means of evaluating the *clinical significance* of an objectively documented memory impairment. Such information is usually obtained from either a friend, relative or health professional (i.e. a person in regular contact with the patient), who is asked to complete a standardised memory questionnaire or rating scale. The validity of collateral reports has generally been found to be high. For example, collateral reports discriminate memory-impaired patients from normal control patients, and correlate with patients' performance on objective memory tests (e.g. Goldstein & Polkey, 1992; Schwartz & McMillan, 1989; Wilson et al., 1989). Several memory checklists for use by health professionals or relatives have been published. We now describe two such scales.

Memory Checklist

This clinician checklist (Wilson, Cockburn, Baddeley & Hiorns 1989; see also

Sunderland, Watts & Baddeley, 1986) was developed in conjunction with the RBMT. It comprises 19 items grouped into three domains. The first group of items concerns forgetting ("Did he/she forget *things* he/she *was told* yesterday or a few days ago and have to be reminded of them?"). The second group focuses on conversation ("Did he/she get *details* of what someone had said *confused*?"), and the third on actions ("Did you observe the patient *getting lost* on a journey or in a building where he/she has been before?"). In a validation study in which 80 patients were rated by therapists after each of four daily rehabilitation sessions for a 2-week period, Wilson et al. (1989) found correlations between the RBMT and the number of observed memory lapses of -0.71 for the Screening score and -0.75 for the Profile score. Checklist errors also correlated substantially with scores on the Warrington Recognition Memory test. The results of this study suggested that the Memory Checklist is a valid means of collecting data on patients' memory performance in their every day lives.

Inpatient Memory Impairment Scale (IMIS)

This brief observation rating scale was originally designed for use by nursing staff in assessing hospitalised memory-impaired patients (Knight & Godfrey, 1984). The scale includes 10 items describing memory-related behaviours such as remembering names, recall of recent personal history and remembering directions. Behaviours are rated for frequency of occurrence using a 6-point scale ($0 = always$ to $5 = not at all$). A generalisability analysis, using data from 20 dysmnesic alcoholic patients, found this scale to have high internal consistency (rho-squared $= 0.96$), and high inter-rater reliability if two or more raters are used (rho-squared $= 0.86$). The concurrent validity of the scale was supported by high and statistically significant correlations between nurse ratings of patients on the IMIS and patients' test performance on the Wechsler Memory Scale ($r = 0.68$), a battery of practical memory tasks ($r = 0.77$) and a battery of experimental memory tasks ($r = 0.77$; Knight & Godfrey, 1984). The scale has been found to discriminate amnesic patients from chronic alcoholic patients and psychiatric patients (Godfrey & Knight, 1988). A revised version of the scale, the Memory Impairment Scale (MIS), has been developed for assessing community-based patients. Relatives ratings of head-injured patients on the MIS have been found to discriminate this patient group from matched normal control subjects, supporting the discriminant validity of the scale (Marsh, Knight & Godfrey, 1990).

Self-Report Scales

Research before the early 1980s tended to focus on the development of self-report measures for assessing memory in neurologically intact individuals (e.g. Herrman, 1982). More recently, a large number of memory self-report questionnaires and rating scales have been developed for clinical use with neurologically impaired patients (e.g. McGlone & Wands, 1991; Sunderland, Watts & Baddeley, 1986; Zelinski & Gilewski, 1991). One of the best developed of these scales is described below.

Memory Assessment Clinics Self-Rating Scale (MAC–S)

This measure (Crook & Larrabee, 1992) includes two subscales: an "Ability" subscale including 21 items designed to assess memory ability, and a "Frequency of Occurrence" subscale including 24 items designed to assess frequency of memory problems. The Ability subscale includes items such as "Where you have put objects (such as keys) in the home or office", "Verbal directions to a geographical location given minutes earlier" and "Details of family events that occurred during the past year". The Frequency of Occurrence subscale includes items such as "Forget the name of a familiar object", "Miss the point someone else is making during a conversation" and "Dial a number and forget whom you were calling before the phone is answered". Four global items are included in the scale:

- The first item asks the respondent to compare her/his memory with "the average individual".
- The second asks the respondent to compare her/his memory with "the best it has ever been".
- The third asks the respondent to compare her/his current memory speed with "the best your memory has ever been".
- The fourth asks the respondent to rate her/his concern or distress about memory "at this time".

All items are rated on 5-point Likert scales.

Items included in the revised version of the scale were selected on psychometric criteria from a pool of 102 items. Factor analysis of these items with a sample of 343 normal subjects produced five Ability factors and five Frequency of Occurrence factors (Winterling, Crook, Salama & Gobert, 1986). The Ability factors were labelled Everyday Task-Oriented Memory, Remote Memory, Reading Recall, Numerical Recall, and Word Recall. The Frequency of Occurrence factors were labelled Concentration, Everyday Task-Oriented Memory, Word Recall, Spatial Memory, and Facial Recognition. The pool of 102 items was reduced to the 49 comprising the revised scale by eliminating items which failed to load significantly on any factor and items which were redundant (Crook & Larrabee, 1990). The revised scale has a factor structure very similar to that found for the original 102-item pool. Factor scores were minimally affected by age or sex of respondent, their self-reported level of depression, or educational level. Crook and Larrabee (1992) evaluated the 3-week test–retest reliability of the scale which was found to be high for Ability subscale (0.82–0.90) and Ability Total scores (0.88–0.94), and for Frequency of Occurrence subscale (0.82–0.89) and Total scores (0.89–0.92). Retest reliability for the global ratings items was moderately high but varied significantly across items (mean of 0.57, range of 0.22 to 0.85). Preliminary evidence for the concurrent validity of the MAC–S is provided by Larrabee, West and Crook (1991), who found canonical correlations between self-rated memory and objective memory test performance accounting for approximately 30% of common variance in scores from a sample 125 normal adults. Normative data for this measure are provided in Crook and Larrabee (1992).

The clinical utility of this measure for assessing Alzheimer's patients has been demonstrated by Feher et al. (1991). In this study, self-report evaluations of patients' memory functioning were obtained from both patients (MAC–S) and a family member (MAC–F). Family ratings on the MAC–F were found to correlate significantly with patients' scores on the Logical Memory and Paired Associate Learning subscales of the Wechsler Memory Scale, and patients scores on the Benton Visual Retention Test. Patients' scores on the MAC–S failed to correlate significantly with either their objective test performance or family ratings on the MAC–F suggesting that the Alzheimer's patients lacked insight about their memory functioning. Interestingly, the discrepancy between patients' and family members' reports of patients' level of memory functioning was significantly associated with the severity of the patients' dementia and their objective test performance. These findings support the validity of the discrepancy score as a means of assessing patients' level of insight about their memory functioning.

The Utility of Self-Report Scales

In contrast to collateral reports, memory-impaired patients themselves are often unable to provide an accurate report of their level of everyday memory functioning. When patient self-report has been compared with patient performance on objective memory tests, the degree of association between these measures has been low and inconsistent (e.g. Sunderland, Harris & Baddeley, 1983). Furthermore, patients often report their level of memory functioning to be comparable to that of normal controls even when objective testing indicates that they have impaired memory ability (e.g. Feher et al., 1991).

Although patient self-report may not be useful for assessing their actual memory ability, it may provide important clinical information about a patient's degree of *insight* about their memory functioning (metamemory). Recent studies have supported the validity of patient self-report as a measure of insight (e.g. Feher et al., 1991; Godfrey, Partridge, Knight & Bishara, 1993), and have documented consistent differences in level of insight in memory disorders of differing aetiology. For example, Squire and Zouzounis (1988) found that amnesic Korsakoff patients underestimated the severity of their memory problems, suggesting that they lacked insight, whereas amnesics of a different aetiology accurately reported their level of memory problems. These findings suggest that comparing a patient's self-report of memory problems with collateral reports and the patient's objective test performance provides a valid measure of a patient's degree of insight about their memory impairment.

Patient insight about their memory problems may change over time. For example, Godfrey et al. (1993) found that head-injured patients assessed at 6 months following injury lacked insight about their neuropsychological symptoms and termed this "Post-Traumatic Insight Disorder". However, at longer follow-ups one and 2–3 years after injury, patients were aware of their neuropsychological symptoms. These findings indicate that some dysmnesic patients have a transient insight disorder which may persist for several months. The clinical implication of these findings is that patient and collateral reports of patients' memory functioning should always be documented along with objective test performance. A discrepancy between patient report with collateral report and objective test results suggests that the patient lacks insight about their memory disorder. Repeated testing over a period of several months is necessary to determine both the changes in the patient's memory ability and changes in his or her level of insight disorder.

Depression is common among neurologically impaired patients. This has prompted concern that the general negative outlook associated with depression may bias patient self-reports of their level of everyday memory functioning. Alternatively, however, patient reports of depressive and memory-related symptomatology may be meaningfully associated without necessarily calling into concern the validity of these reports. For example, many head-injured patients become reactively depressed as they become aware of their neuropsychological symptoms, and so reports of symptomatology and depression are highly associated (Godfrey et al., 1993). In clinical practice a careful qualitative analysis of patients' reports of memory symptoms may clarify the extent to which these reports reflect depression or genuine amnesic symptomatology. Depressogenic complaints may be discriminated from genuine symptoms in that the former tend to be reported as a uniform level of impairment across symptoms, including those that a clinician would expect to be unimpaired such as attention, concentration, immediate and remote memory (Squire & Zouzounis, 1988). These findings highlight the need for clinicians to undertake a careful qualitative examination of depressed patients' reports of symptoms of memory impairment to determine to what extent such reports are biased by the depressive disorder.

SUMMARY

The formulation of a memory problem in terms useful for clinical intervention requires information from a variety of sources. Traditional neuropsychological testing helps establish the presence and severity of memory impairment and any other cognitive dysfunctions the patient may have. It is important, however, that such testing is supported by an accurate functional analysis of the patient's deficits. In this chapter we have been concerned with ways of supplementing the results from traditional tests. Behavioural assessment, in which the clinician uses behavioural tests to evaluate the impaired patient's everyday memory skills, is an important part of designing a rehabilitation programme. The task for the clinician is to construct bahavioural tests that are relevant to a particular patient's deficits and personal circumstances. In doing this it may be possible to make use of or adapt published tests such as the RBMT or MAC battery. Sometimes it will be necessary to devise a behaviour test that is specific to an individual's problem. Constructing a valid personalised measure relies on the clinician's ability to identify a relevant situation, and develop stimuli of a suitable difficulty level. Behavioural tests can be used to document more precisely a patient's everyday functioning, to set treatment goals, and to monitor rehabilitation progress.

Memory checklists provide important information about the clinical impact of a memory problem on patients themselves and on those who are in contact with them. They allow the clinician to assess systematically the domain of possible consequences that a memory disorder may bring. In addition, comparison of self-report with information from significant others provides the clinician with information about the patient's perception or awareness of the extent of their problems. In some cases, notably in patients in the early stages of recovery from head trauma or patients developing Alzheimer's dementia, insight is a matter of major clinical significance. In this situation, it is important to contrast the patient's view of the disability with results from relatives' ratings and scores on neuropsychological tests. Memory rating scales and checklists can therefore play a significant role in the comprehensive assessment of the memory-impaired patient.

REFERENCES

Aldrich, F.K. & Wilson, B.A. (1991). Rivermead Behavioural Memory Test for Children (RBMT-C): a preliminary evaluation. *British Journal of Clinical Psychology*, **30**, 161–168.
Buschke, H. (1973). Selective reminding for analysis of memory and learning. *Journal of Verbal Learning and Verbal Behavior*, **12**, 543–550.
Cockburn, J., Wilson, B.A., Baddeley, A.D. & Hiorns, R. (1990a). Assessing everyday memory in patients with perceptual deficits. *Clinical Rehabilitation*, **4**, 129–135.
Cockburn, J., Wilson, B.A., Baddeley, A.D. & Hiorns, R. (1990b). Assessing everyday memory in patients with dysphasia. *British Journal of Clinical Psychology*, **29**, 353–360.
Crook, T.H., Johnson, B.A. & Larrabee, G.J. (1990). Evaluation of drugs in Alzheimer's disease and age associated memory impairment. In O. Benkert, W. Maier & K. Rickels (eds), *Methodology of the Evaluation of Psychotropic Drugs*. Springer-Verlag, Heidelberg, pp. 37–55.
Crook, T.H. & Larrabee, G.J. (1988). Interrelationships among everyday memory tests: stability of factor structure with age. *Neuropsychology*, **2**, 1–12.
Crook, T.H. & Larrabee, G.J. (1990). A self-rating scale for evaluating memory in everyday life. *Psychology and Aging*, **5**, 48–57.
Crook, T.H. & Larrabee, G.J. (1992). Normative data on a self-rating scale for evaluating memory in everyday life. *Archives of Neuropsychology*, **7**, 41–51.

Crook, T.H., Youngjohn, J.R. & Larrabee, G.J. (1990). The TV News Test: a new measure of everyday memory for prose. *Neuropsychology*, **4**, 135–145.

Crook, T.H. Youngjohn, J.R., Larrabee, G.J. & Salama, R. (1992). Aging and everyday memory: a cross-cultural study. *Neuropsychology*, **6**, 123–136.

Feher, E.P., Mahurin, R.K., Inbody, S.B., Crook, T.H. & Francis, J.P. (1991). Anosognosia in Alzheimer's disease. *Neuropsychiatry, Neuropsychology and Behavioural Neurology*, **4**, 136–146.

Godfrey, H.P.D. & Knight, R.G. (1985). Cognitive rehabilitation of memory function in dysmnesic alcoholics. *Journal of Consulting and Clinical Psychology*, **53**, 555–557.

Godfrey, H.P.D. & Knight, R.G. (1988). Inpatient memory impairment scale: a cross-validation and extension study. *Journal of Clinical Psychology*, **44**, 783–786.

Godfrey, H.P.D., Partridge, F.M., Knight, R.G. & Bishara, S.N. (1993). Course of insight disorder and emotional dysfunction following closed head injury: a cross-sectional follow-up study. *Journal of Clinical and Experimental Neuropsychology*, **15**, 503–515.

Goldstein, L.H. & Polkey, C.E. (1992). Behavioural memory after temporal lobectomy or amygdalo-hippocampectomy. *British Journal of Clinical Psychology*, **31**, 75–81.

Herrman, D.J. (1982). Know thy memory: the use of questionnaires to assess and study memory. *Psychological Bulletin*, **92**, 434–452.

Knight, R.G. & Godfrey, H.P.D. (1984). Reliability and validity of a scale for rating memory impairment in hospitalised amnesics. *Journal of Consulting and Clinical Psychology*, **5**, 769–773.

Knight, R.G. & Godfrey, H.P.S. (1986). The assessment of memory impairment: the relationship between different methods of evaluating dysmnesic deficits. *British Journal of Clinical Psychology*, **24**, 125–131.

Larrabee, G.J. & Crook, T.H. (1989). Dimensions of everyday memory in age-associated memory impairment. *Psychological Assessment: A Journal of Consulting and Clinical Psychology*, **1**, 92–97.

Larrabee, G.J., West, R.L. & Crook, T.H. (1991). The association of memory complaint with computer-simulated everyday memory performance. *Journal of Clinical and Experimental Neuropsychology*, **13**, 484–496.

Lincoln, N.B. & Tinson, D.J. (1989). The relation between subjective and objective memory impairment after stroke. *British Journal of Clinical Psychology*, **28**, 61–65.

McGlone, J. & Wands, K. (1991). Self-report of memory in patients with temporal lobe epilepsy and temporal lobectomy. *Cortex*, **2**, 19–28.

Marsh, N.V., Knight, R.G. & Godfrey, H.P.D. (1990). Long-term psychosocial adjustment following very severe closed head injury. *Neuropsychology*, **4**, 13–28.

Schwartz, A.F. & McMillan, T.M. (1989). Assessment of everyday memory after severe head injury. *Cortex*, **25**, 665–671.

Squire, L.R. & Zouzounis, J.A. (1988). Self-rating of memory dysfunction: different findings in depression and amnesia. *Journal of Clinical and Experimental Neuropsychology*, **10**, 727–738.

Sunderland, A., Harris, J.E. & Baddeley, A.D. (1983). Do laboratory tests predict everyday memory? A neuropsychological study. *Journal of Verbal Learning and Verbal Behavior*, **22**, 341–357.

Sunderland, A., Watts, K. & Baddeley, A.D. (1986). Subjective memory assessment and test performance in elderly adults. *Journal of Gerontology*, **41**, 376–384.

Warrington, E.K. (1984). *The Recognition Memory Test*. NFER–Nelson, Windsor.

West, R.L., Crook, T.H. & Barron, K.L. (1992). Everyday memory performance across the lifespan: effects of age and noncognitive individual differences. *Psychology and Aging*, **7**, 72–82.

West, R.L. & Crook, T.H. (1990). Age differences in everyday memory: laboratory analogues of telephone number recall. *Psychology and Aging*, **5**, 520–529.

Wilson, B.A. (1987). *Rehabilitation of Memory*. Guilford Press, New York.

Wilson, B.A. (1991). Neuropsychological rehabilitation. *Neuropsychology*, **5**, 281–291.

Wilson, B.A., Baddeley, A.D. & Cockburn, J. (1988). The trials, tribulations and triumphs in the development of a test of everyday memory. In M.M. Gruneberg, P.E. Morris & R.N. Sykes (eds), *Practical aspects of memory: Current Research and Issues. Vol. 1: Memory in Everyday Life*. John Wiley, Chichester, pp. 249–254.

Wilson, B.A., Cockburn, J. & Baddeley, A.D. (1985). *The Rivermead Behavioural Memory Test*. Thames Valley Test Company, Titchfield.

Wilson, B.A., Cockburn, J., Baddeley, A.D. & Hiorns, R. (1989). The development and validation of a test battery for detecting and monitoring everyday memory problems. *Journal of Clinical and Experimental Neuropsychology*, **11**, 855–870.

Winterling, D., Crook, T., Salama, M. & Gobert, J. (1986). A self-rating scale for assessing memory loss. In A. Bes, J. Cahn, S. Hoyer, J.P. Marc-Vergnes & H.M. Wisniewski (eds), *Senile Dementias: Early Detection*. John Libbey Eurotext, London/Paris, pp. 482–487.

Youngjohn, J.R., Larrabee, G.J. & Crook, T.H. 91992). Test–retest reliability of computerized, everyday memory measures and traditional memory tests. *Clinical Neuropsychologist*, **6**, 276–286.

Zelinski, E.M. & Gilewski, M.J. (1990). Memory Functioning Questionnaire: concurrent validity with memory performance and self-reported memory failures. *Psychology and Aging*, **5**, 388–399.

Chapter 17

Separating Memory from other Cognitive Problems

Diane B. Howieson
and
Muriel D. Lezak
Oregon Health Sciences University, Portland, USA

INTRODUCTION

The clinician is often asked to evaluate patients' memory or learning problems, even when memory is not the actual problem. A man's neighbor once referred him for a neuropsychological evaluation on the basis of a recently developed "memory" impairment. When the neighbor and his friend arrived for the evaluation, the neighbor explained that the friend apparently forgot to go to bed at night. It seems the friend had become unusually active and agitated with little apparent sleep for several weeks and the neighbor became concerned. Although this example may be unusual, it is not uncommon for patients and the people close to them to attribute a variety of cognitive and behavioral problems to memory problems. More often, a spouse brings her husband for evaluation complaining that he does not remember to do anything she has asked. When it turns out that the memory problem is confined to this one category of information, the clinician begins to suspect that the problem lies elsewhere.

Memory complaints provide fascinating and sometimes amusing insights into the complexities and vagaries of human relationships as well as the human mind, but they can present neuropsychologists with serious diagnostic challenges. This chapter focuses on the variety of cognitive problems that (secondarily) produce what patients or those dealing with them experience as poor memory. As more is learned about how the brain functions, it becomes increasingly difficult to distinguish between theoretical concepts of memory and other cognitive func-

Handbook of Memory Disorders. Edited by A.D. Baddeley, B.A. Wilson and F.N. Watts.
© 1995 John Wiley & Sons Ltd.

tions (Lezak, 1995). At the practical level, however, the clinician is able to make distinctions that have important implications for counseling and remediation.

The major sources of the *experience* of memory impairment when new learning and retention actually are spared are *information registration deficits* and *executive function disorders*. These neuropsychological abnormalities can occur discretely or in combination to affect the efficiency of the learning/memory system. Obviously, the more the problem is compounded, the more impaired will be the patient's memory performance.

INFORMATION REGISTRATION

Memory functions are dependent on attention and information processing for proper registration of information to be learned. *Attention* refers to the patient's ability to attend to and grasp all of a specific stimulus. *Information processing* refers to the ability to extract the meaning of the stimulus based on past experiences. Some types of information processing are relatively automatic while others require effort and strategies. Reductions in attention and information processing produce marked limitations on memory.

Attention

Many diffusely brain-injured patients have impaired attention (Morrow, Robin, Hodgson & Kamis, 1992; Rao, Leo, Bernardin & Unverzagt, 1991; Stuss et al., 1989; Van Gorp, Miller, Satz & Visscher, 1989). Many patients with limited attention attend adequately to tasks so that their impairment is obvious only on examination. The patient may be limited in attentional capacity, in the ability to direct attention, in the ability to divide attention to more than one stimulus, or in the ability to sustain attention. As attentional tasks increase in complexity they are often referred to as "tests of concentration" and "mental tracking". Although many of them involve more complex mental operations as well, attention is a prominent contributing process.

Attentional Capacity

Simple attention span is most frequently examined with a digit repetition task which tests how many numbers a person can attend to at once and repeat in sequence. The Digit Span tests from the Wechsler Intelligence Scales (WIS) (Wechsler, 1955, 1981) and the Wechsler Memory Scales (WMS) (Wechsler, 1945, 1987) assess repetition of digits both forward and backward. The latter task involves a mental tracking component which distinguishes it from the simple span measure. A more subtle disorder may be detected by increasing the demands of the task, such as using a sentence repetition task which increases the informational load (Benton & Hamsher, 1976, 1989; Spreen & Strauss,

1991). A visual measure of attention span may be obtained by the Corsi Cube test (Milner, 1971) or the WMS Visual Memory Span test (Wechsler, 1987) in which the patient reproduces spatially arranged patterns of increasing length as demonstrated by the examiner.

These tests of attention require intact short-term memory. Most brain-injured patients have intact short-term memory when recall follows reception immediately with neither delay nor interference. When their attention is directed away from tasks by an interpolated activity, retention, even for relatively brief intervals, becomes tenuous. Therefore, poor performance on a simple digit span task is more likely to represent an attention impairment rather than a true memory impairment. Patients with actual short-term memory impairment do exist (Warrington & Shallice, 1984; Vallar & Shallice, 1990; Vallar & Papagno, this volume), so this possibility should be evaluated.

Attentional capacity is resistant to the effects of many brain disorders. It may be restricted in the first months following head trauma but it is likely to return to normal during later states (Lezak, 1979; Ponsford & Kinsella, 1992; Scherer, Klett & Winnes, 1957). Most mildly demented Alzheimer's patients have normal capacity for reciting a string of digits (Storandt, Borwinick & Danziger, 1986), although not all (Freed, Corkin, Growdon & Nissen, 1989). However, when the information becomes more complex, as in sentence span tests, or more information is presented than can normally be grasped at once, as in supraspan tests (Benton, Hamsher, Varney & Spreen, 1983; Milner, 1970; see also Lezak, 1995), the reduced attentional capacity of many brain-injured persons becomes evident.

Directed Attention

In most settings an individual attending to a task must direct attention to the relevant material and ignore extraneous information, such as when required to read a book while riding a crowded bus. Normally, the clinician examines the patient in an environment relatively free from distraction in order to minimize this factor. Although ideal in one respect and expected when administering standardized tests, this arrangement differs, often radically, from the clatter and clutter of most patients' everyday situations and may mask the problem to be assessed. Therefore, the clinician may wish to interact with the patient in an environment with extraneous noise or activity and observe the patient's ability to be free from distraction. Some tests are designed with distraction included for this reason.

The Stroop test (Dodrill, 1978; Stroop, 1935) is a difficult task involving directed attention in addition to other processes. As a baseline measure of speed of responding, the patient is asked to read a page of color names. For the critical condition the patient is instructed to name the color in which color words are presented, such as saying "green" when the word "red" is printed in green ink. For literate adults, reading the words is prepotent over naming the ink color: therefore, attention must be directed to the color in which the words are printed while inhibiting the prepotent response.

Sustained Attention

Another aspect of attention that may be disrupted by brain injury, which frequently involves the frontal lobes (Stuss & Benson, 1987), is the ability to sustain attention. Many neuropsychological tests require this ability. The WMS Mental Control tests and Subtracting Serial Sevens (Strub & Black, 1985) provide measures of sustained attention as well as other mental operations.

Clinical evaluations of sustained attention often involve vigilance tasks in which stimuli—both targets and foils—are introduced over an extended period of time and the patient must indicate each target occurrence. Visual versions are usually in the form of cancellation tests consisting of rows of letters or numbers with instructions to the patient to cross out target items. Auditory forms are available in which subjects tap or press a computer key when they hear the designated target letter or word. Complex variations may be devised by asking the patient to indicate when two or more conditions have been fulfilled, such as when two numbers occur in succession on a tape presentation. The Letter Cancellation test (Diller et al., 1974) and Vigilance test (Strub & Black, 1985) are examples of this kind.

Divided Attention

Another aspect of attention that is sensitive to brain injury (Nestor, Parasuraman & Haxby, 1991; Stuss et al., 1989) or normal aging (Baddeley, 1986; Greenwood & Parasuraman, 1991) is divided attention or the ability to attend to more than one stimulus simultaneously. Practically, problems in this area show up as an inability to follow a recipe while the children are talking, or difficulty following a conversation when surrounded by a chattering crowd. However, deficiencies in dividing attention may also be at the heart of the "misplaced keys (wallet, glasses, etc.)" complaint: upon entering their homes these are patients who become immediately distracted (by the dog, the mail on the doormat, the children) and lay down their keys without registering where they put them. Almost inevitably they will attribute this latter problem to "poor memory".

Oral arithmetic stories provide one means of examining for this problem as subjects must perform a second or third set of operations while keeping practical solutions in mind. Take the problem "Mary has thirteen stamps and Jane has five. How many would Mary have to give to Jane for them to have the same number?" To solve this, several sequential calculations must be performed while retaining the question.

Difficulties in doing more than one thing at a time may also show up on list-producing tasks, whether they involve learning a series of items or generating items *de novo*. On these tasks patients who may be having no difficulty fulfilling the task requirements, whether they be to learn words or generate line patterns (e.g. the Ruff Figural Fluency Test: Ruff, Light & Evans, 1987), will repeat an abnormally large number of responses just given within the last minute or even last 10–15 seconds. In these repetitions, the patients demonstrate difficulty keeping track of their responses while performing an ongoing task. These repetitions are distinguishable from true perseverations as perseverating patients typically produce very few different responses, and once they begin perseverating, some if not all of the elements of succeeding responses will be perseverations.

The Trail Making test is a frequently used measure of divided attention or mental tracking (Lezak, 1995). In Part A the patient is asked to draw a line connecting in sequence a random display of numbered circles. The level of difficulty is increased in the second part (B) by having the patient again sequence a random display of circles with numbers and letters, going from 1 to A to 2 to B to 3 and so forth. The performance is measured for speed and the patient must be able to keep both sequences in mind to perform the task efficiently and quickly. The test also requires visual scanning, flexibility in shifting from set to set, and fine motor coordination and speed.

Contributions to Memory

It is often difficult to distinguish between a primary memory disorder and a more general impairment in attention or concentration secondarily disrupting memory. Several theorists (Luria, 1971; Stuss & Benson, 1987) have described the frontal lobe memory disorder as more a deficit in attention and other control functions than memory *per se*. Some cases sort themselves out, such as when a patient performs well on one class of tests and not on another. Some amnesic patients appear to have normal attention (Butters et al., 1992), and several studies have shown that the memory deficit in mild Alzheimer's disease occurs in patients without impaired sustained attention (Lines et al., 1991) or directed attention (Nebes & Brady, 1989). Often patients perform poorly on both attentional and memory tasks, thus making the distinction more difficult. Reductions in attentional capacity as well as memory may be seen in patients with diffuse brain dysfunction, such as from severe closed head injury, schizophrenia, metabolic encephalopathy, or severe dementia of the Alzheimer's type.

Some memory tasks place heavy demands on attention. Because of their length, some memory tasks require intact sustained attention. For example, in continuous-memory recognition tests (Hannay, Levin & Grossman, 1979; Trahan and Larrabee, 1988) patients see a long sequence of items out of which they must identify those already seen. Any loss of attention during the early (acquisition) phase of the task could affect performance on the remainder of the task. The performance demands of some visuographic memory tasks are substantial and may divide attention. Drawing geometric designs from memory would be expected to produce interference for those patients who labor with the drawing component of the task.

The clinician may choose to minimize the influence of attentional factors by test selection. Some tests are constructed to ensure that the patient overtly attends to material to be learned. The CERAD Word List Task (Morris et al.,

1989) requires that the patient read aloud each of the to-be-recalled words, which ensures registration of the words. One could argue that the act of reading divides the patient's attention between the performance and memory requirements of the test. However, reading is relatively automatic and the interference would be expected to be small. The examiner may wish to select a memory test with a simple response mode. For example, rather than having patients draw geometric designs, visuospatial memory can be examined having patients place items in their learned position on a spatial grid. The original 7/24 (Barbizet & Cany, 1968) and modified 7/24 Spatial Recall (Rao et al., 1984) tests as well as the Visual Spatial Learning test (Malec, Ivnik & Hinkeldey, 1991) examine memory for the location of stimulus items on a grid.

Information Processing

Many traumatically brain-injured patients, especially those whose damage is diffusely distributed, have reduced ability to process information as rapidly as it is presented to them. They may fail to recall elements of a conversation or the evening's news because they have not been able to assimilate the information as it was presented. Others with more focal and lateralized lesions may no longer be able to process verbal or nonverbalizable information adequately. If not properly examined, these deficits can be misinterpreted as due to memory failures.

It is generally accepted that memory deficits that are specific to either verbal or nonverbal material cut across sensory modalities. Most memory tests used clinically confound the type of material to be learned (verbal and nonverbal) with modality of presentation (aural or visual). That is, most verbal memory tests consist of having the patient recall material that has been read by the examiner, and most nonverbal tasks require the patient to draw from memory or recognize material presented visually. It is possible to disassociate these two factors, such as asking the patient to recall the names of a set of visually presented objects or pictures or to recall a series of familiar sounds, such as a bell, bird song, and paper rustling.

Speed

Information processing speed can be assessed using a variety of timed tasks. One of the more demanding tests is the Paced Auditory Serial Addition Task (PASAT) (Gronwall, 1977; Gronwall & Sampson, 1974), which has been used extensively to detect subtle disorders in a variety of patient populations with mild brain dysfunction. Although originally developed for patients with mild traumatic brain injury, the PASAT has also been used in other conditions in which brain damage tends to be diffuse, such as AIDS, toxic encephalopathy, and multiple sclerosis. The task requires that the patient report aloud the sum of consecutive pairs of numbers presented at a fixed rate by a tape-recorder. For example, if the numbers "2–7–4–1" are heard in that sequence, the subject should say "9" after hearing the "7", then "11" after hearing the "4", and so on. The task difficulty results from the necessity to inhibit the easier response of adding the last number presented on the tape with the last summation generated by the patient. The level of difficulty can be heightened by speeding up the rate of presentation of numbers. Like most complex tasks, it requires a number of cognitive operations in addition to information processing: sustained as well as divided attention, calculations, and inhibition of a prepotent response.

Verbal Deficits

Patients may have deficits that are specific to the nature of the information to be learned. Many patients with left hemisphere lesions have language impairments and patients with right hemisphere lesions often have visuospatial impairment. Even patients with intact fluent speech who appear to follow a casual conversation may have subtle language processing deficits. The Token Test (Boller & Vignolo, 1966; De Renzi & Vignolo, 1962) is sensitive to disrupted language processing that is not readily recognizable (Lezak, 1995). The test consists of series of oral commands using "tokens" of varying shapes, sizes and colors. The patient follows commands of increasing length and syntactic complexity. Unlike most information conveyed in social conversations, the commands given during this test lack contextual cueing or redundancy of information, thus bringing to light even fairly subtle comprehension problems.

Nonverbal Deficits

Likewise, patients may have deficits that are specific to processing of visuospatial information. The WIS tests include constructional tasks involving reconstructing designs with blocks and assembling puzzle pieces (Wechsler, 1944, 1955, 1981). The Complex Figure test requires more complex visuospatial processing when drawing from memory this difficult geometric design (Rey, 1964) or one of the alternative forms (Loring, Lee & Meador, 1988; Meador, Taylor & Loring, 1988, 1989, 1990; Taylor, 1979). Lesions of the posterior cerebral cortex frequently tend to be associated with difficulty with constructions, with right hemisphere lesions producing greater deficits than left hemisphere lesions. The geometric designs used in many memory tests, such as the Benton Visual Retention test (Benton, 1974; Sivan, 1991) and the Memory for Designs test (Graham & Kendall, 1960), lend themselves to verbal labels and thus are not useful measures of nonverbal functions.

Contributions to Memory

The role of slow information processing on memory performance can be examined by comparing performances on tests in which speed is essential and in which speed is relatively irrelevant. Many patients react as though overwhelmed when presented with story recall tasks, such as in the WMS. They experience it as too much information too fast. To test the limits on such a task, the examiner should slow down the pace, particularly pausing between sentences. Ideally, story recall tests would allow ample information processing by presenting the story more than once, such as with Babcock Story Recall format (Babcock, 1930; Rapaport, Gill & Schafer, 1968). Patients may show better performance on a word-list learning task in which the pace of presentation is naturally slower.

Material-specific processing deficits affect performance on memory tests in which language or visuospatial information is to be learned. Aphasic patients often perform poorly on verbal memory tests, which require both language and memory capacities. Language impairment can affect the patient's comprehension of the material or ability to produce the correct verbal response.

Aphasic stroke patients with extensive damage to the left temporal lobe—involving language areas on the convexity and memory structures more anterior and mesial—may sustain both memory and language impairments. Both of these areas play important but different roles in the verbal memory impairment. Aphasic patients tend to perform more poorly than nonaphasic patients on word-list learning, paired word associates learning, and prose recall tasks. However, some aphasic patients perform better on the prose tasks because they benefit from contextual information. Others process the grammatical and syntactical information too slowly and perform better on word-list tasks.

For some patients it may be impossible to assess the relative contribution of language impairment on verbal memory performance. One attempt consists of assessing memory with tasks with minimal verbal characteristics, such as memory for complex geometric designs or for faces (Warrington, 1984). Aphasic patients are at a disadvantage even on these tasks because of their disrupted ability to encode material using both verbal mediation and visual imagery. The difference in performance of a language-impaired patient on a verbal memory task compared with a nonverbal memory task will provide an indication of the material-specificity of the impairment.

Patients with visuospatial disorders who have difficulty drawing a geometric design will be disadvantaged in recalling the design because here memory becomes confounded with processing demands. Some examiners have advocated calculating the memory score in relation to the copy score (Brooks, 1972; Snow, 1979), thereby factoring out as much as possible the constructional component from the memory performance. However, if a patient is unable to copy the design within at least the *low average* range, a subsequent recall score is of dubious value. Some frequently used memory tests require the copying of relatively simple geometric designs, thereby minimizing the processing and constructional requirements. The Benton Visual Retention test and, to a lesser extent, the WMS Visual Reproduction test fall in this category. However, even the Visual Reproduction designs are too difficult for healthy very elderly persons (Howieson, Kaye & Howieson, 1991).

EXECUTIVE FUNCTIONS

The distinction between memory and other cognitive functions is perhaps most difficult when describing the motivating, control and regulatory behaviors that are necessary for all goal-directed activities including memory. In neuropsychological terms, executive functions refer to those abilities necessary to formulate goals and carry them out effectively (Lezak, 1982; Stuss & Benson, 1987). These are difficult tasks for many patients with extensive frontal lobe or diffuse brain injuries (Luria, 1980). Executive deficits can also be found in patients with limbic system disorders, organic solvents damage, Parkinson's disease, and right hemisphere damage (Lezak, 1982). The major categories of executive behaviors are (1) volition, (2) planning, (3) executing activities, and (4) self-monitoring (Lezak, 1995). A deficiency in any of these task-oriented behaviors can interfere with the ability to succeed in all but the simplest of cognitive tasks. Some executive functions have particular bearing on memory performance.

Volition

An individual must be aware of self and surroundings to be able to have the capacity to formulate a goal and exercise self-will. The ability to create motives involves the interaction of an appreciation of personal or social needs based on past experiences and self-identity with the capacity to be motivated (Lezak, 1982). Some brain-injured patients have greatly diminished capacity for self-generating activity. They may have a reasonable plan of action but fail to initiate the plan. These patients typically look their best in a formal evaluation where they can respond to the structure and motivation provided by the examiner. By their very nature, most examiner-administered tests require little self-generation by the patient (Lezak, 1982). Left on their own these patients lack the capacity to carry on, and appear apathetic.

Planning

Tasks that best assess executive functions are sufficiently complex to require planning or strategies to maximize performance. Examples include mazes, constructional tasks, and complex problem-solving tests such as the Twenty Questions parlor game, which was modified for neuropsychological use by Laine and Butters (1982). Patients who have difficulties on these tests may also fail to use strategies to facilitate their recall during memory testing.

Executing

Carrying out activities requires the capacities to initiate behavior and modify that behavior through switching, maintaining, or stopping behavior in an integrated manner according to an analysis of appropriate actions (Lezak, 1982).

The Category Test (Halstead, 1947) and the Wisconsin Card Sorting Test (Berg, 1948; Grant & Berg, 1948; Heaton et al., 1993) are both designed to measure flexibility of thinking and appropriate switching of behavior. They present patterns of stimuli and require the patients to select a response based on a principle or concept learned through feedback about the correctness of previous responses. The patients must realize when a shift in principles occurs and act accordingly. These tasks also assess capacity for concept formation. Deficits in modulation of behavior may result in inconsistent responses, perseverations, and impersistence.

Some brain-injured patients lack the ability to persist with lengthy or complex tasks. There are few open-ended tests that measure persistence. The Tinker Toy Test (Bayless, Varney & Roberts, 1989; Lezak, 1982, 1994b) was designed to measure planning and persistence. Patients are instructed simply to make what they want with these basic construction materials and thus must decide what to build and how to design it. Severely impaired patients begin the task without a plan and their final product may be the result of serendipity.

Impersistence can also be seen on word or design generation tests (usually called *fluency tests*) when patients stop generating items prematurely. These patients will often perform adequately if frequently prompted by the examiner.

Self-monitoring

Another executive function necessary for successful performance on cognitive tasks is the capacity to monitor and self-correct spontaneously and reliably. The person who is able to regulate the relevance and accuracy of most responses on tests will have an advantage over those who make careless errors or contaminate their performance with perseverative or extraneous responses. Some brain-injured patients, particularly those with frontal lobe damage, are impulsive and trade accuracy of performance for speed.

Impulsivity can be seen on Part B of the Trail Making test when a patient fails to shift set and gives the easier response. Maze-tracing tests may also elicit impulsivity as the patient changes into turns that lead to blind alleys. Observations of test-taking behavior differentiate those patients who regularly check their work—such as a reconstructed design on the WAIS Block Design test or copy of the Complex Figure—from those who do not. Requiring patients to complete a page of arithmetic calculations at their leisure (e.g. see Lezak, 1995) frequently brings out carelessness tendencies in patients who demonstrate adequate arithmetic skills but make—*and leave*—small computational errors on the page.

Contributions to Memory

When are deficits in volition, planning, persistence or self-monitoring on memory tests a primary feature of the memory disorder and when are they associated impairments? The executive deficit might be primary, but it can also occur in conjunction with a true memory disorder. The difficulty in making this distinction is illustrated by Baddeley and Wilson (1988) in their analysis of a man with a frontal syndrome due to a closed head injury sustained in a traffic accident. They concluded that this patient's memory disorder resembled a classic memory disorder but that it occurred in combination with a frontal syndrome. Trauma patients might be expected to have frontal syndromes because many sustain damage to the frontal lobes as well as to memory areas of the anterior/medial temporal lobes. It has been proposed that memory disorders of frontal-lobe patients are related to problems in attention and retrieval rather than to deficits in storage or consolidation, as seen in memory-impaired patients with medial temporal lobe and diencephalic areas affected (Shimamura, Janowsky & Squire, 1991).

Perhaps the best example of the interaction of executive and memory deficits occurs with the Korsakoff syndrome. Korsakoff patients have a severe memory impairment that interferes dramatically with daily activities, but it is the pervasive executive disorders that render them socially dependent and unable to carry out ordinary constructive activities (Lezak, 1994). Memory impairment is related presumably to lesions of primary memory areas, the dorsal–medial nucleus of the thalamus and mammillary bodies, but Korsakoff patients have frontal atrophy as well (Shimamura, Janowsky & Squire, 1991). Moscovitch (1982) showed that the Korsakoff patient's poor performance on one memory task—release from proactive interference—is related more to impairment of frontal functions than to the amnesic disorder.

Failure to use stratagies, to manipulate and organize information, will also limit recall on memory tests. These strategies may include chunking information (such as digits to recall), making meaningful associations between unrelated items to be recalled (such as difficult paired associates), or using semantic attributes to facilitate recall of related bits of information (such as words from a list). Several memory tests developed for clinical applications provide useful information about the use of strategies. The California Verbal Learning Test (Delis, Kramer, Kaplan & Ober, 1983, 1986, 1987) assesses the patient's use of semantic categorizing in the course of memory testing. The items to be learned are a "shopping list" consisting of 16 words, four from each of four object categories: fruits, spices, tools and clothing. The items are presented in random order with both uncued and category-cued recall trials. The uncued performances can be evaluated for semantic clustering, an effective recall strategy. Thus, patients who cluster according to categories tend to perform better than those who do not. Absence of semantic strategy may reflect impaired executive functioning as typified by frontally damaged patients, or it may be the product of a breakdown in semantic knowledge, such as with Alzheimer's disease.

A less structured word list can also provide important information about the use of memory strategies. The commonly used Auditory Verbal Learning Test (Lezak, 1995; Rey, 1964) consists of 15 unrelated words which the patient hears in the same order for each of five trials, with no restriction on order of recall. On first hearing the list, intact subjects show both recency and primacy effects, recalling most often the first few words and the last few words, with perhaps a few in the middle. As trials are repeated, most intact subjects begin to organize the words according to associations and their recall demonstrates these clusters. They also begin to recall first the words they haven't given before so they make sure not to forget them. These self-employed strategies assist the patient. We advocate inquiring of the patient who performs poorly on such a task whether they used any particular method for learning the words.

Deficits in self-monitoring can play havoc with memory. Both psychiatric patients and those with a frontal-lobe injury may have difficulty distinguishing accurate memories from internal associations. Some patients elaborate a completely faulty ending to a story they have been asked to remember, or interject associative material here and there. In some instances, if the examiner questions their response, these patients are able to specify the elaborated portion, thereby displaying some capacity to distinguish between external stimuli and their mental contents. Most people have a relatively accurate sense of confidence about the accuracy of memories, often referred to as the "feeling-of-knowing", and inhibit these associations.

Impersistence can also result in poor memory performance. These patients may readily recall a few elements of a story to be learned and then stop—sometimes stating, sometimes implying, "that's enough"—without attempting to expand the recall.

CONCLUSIONS

Most cognitive tasks involve a composite of mental operations. It is often difficult to specify where one ends and another takes over. Several models have been proposed to relate the cognitive functions discussed in this chapter. The information-processing model proposed by Schneider and Shiffrin (1977) relates attention and information processing by suggesting that divided attention is dependent on adequate speed of information processing. In fact, models of information processing include a stage in which stimuli are compared with memory stores for familiarity. Information processing is also a key element of some theories of memory (Cermak, 1972; Craik & Lockhart, 1972). Shallice (1982) has proposed a model of executive control over attentional resources which regulates the use of attentional resources in a goal-directed fashion, while Baddeley (1986) has proposed a model of working memory that includes inherent attentional and executive functions.

Memory tasks certainly have multiple demands and it is not always easy to dissociate memory from other cognitive functions. Clearly, some patients' cognitive impairments are restricted to memory alone. However, the majority of brain-injured patients with memory impairment have other cognitive deficits as well. If, for example, the patient has difficulty with attention or self-monitoring across a range of tasks, then poor performance on memory test may be at least partly attributable to these other cognitive problems. Some distinctions are difficult, such as between attention span and short-term memory. The clinician is challenged with making the correct distinctions so that necessary counseling and possibly remediation can be accurately directed.

REFERENCES

Babcock, H. (1930). An experiment in the measurement of mental deterioration. *Archives of Psychology*, **117**, 105.

Baddeley, A.D. (1986). *Working Memory*. Oxford University Press, Oxford.

Baddeley, A. & Wilson, B. (1988). Frontal amnesia and the dysexecutive syndrome. *Brain and Cognition*, **7**, 212–230.

Barbizet, J. & Cany, E. (1968). Clinical and psychometrical study of a patient with memory disturbances. *International Journal of Neurology*, **7**, 44–54.

Bayless, J.D., Varney, N.R. & Roberts, R.J. (1989). Tinker Toy Test performance and vocational outcome in patients with closed head injuries. *Journal of Clinical and Experimental Neuropsychology*, **11**, 913–917.

Benton, A.L. (1974). *The Revised Visual Retention Test*. Psychological Corporation, New York.

Benton, A.L. & Hamsher, K. deS. (1989). *Multilingual Aphasia Examination*. AJA Associates, Iowa City, Iowa.

Benton, A.L., Hamsher K. deS., Varney N.R. & Spreen, O. (1983). *Contributions to Neuropsychological Assessment*. Oxford University Press, New York.

Berg, E.A. (1948). A simple objective test for measuring flexibility in thinking. *Journal of General Psychology*, **39**, 15–22.

Boller, F. & Vignolo, L.A. (1966). Latent sensory aphasia in hemisphere-damaged patients: an experimental study with the Token Test. *Brain*, **89**, 815–831.

Brooks, D.N. (1972). Memory and head injury. *Journal of Nervous and Mental Disease*, **155**, 350–355.

Cermak, L.S. (1972). *Human Memory: Research and Theory*. Ronald Press, New York.

Craik, F.I.M. & Lockhart, R.S. (1972). Levels of processing: framework for memory research. *Journal of Verbal Learning and Verbal Behavior*, **11**, 671–684.

Delis, D.C., Kramer, J.H., Kaplan, E. & Ober, B.A. (1986). *California Verbal Learning Test*. Psychological Corp., San Antonio, TX.

Delis, D.C., Kramer, J.H., Kaplan, E., and Ober, B.A. (1983/1987). *California Verbal Learning Test, Form II (Research Edition)*. Psychological Corp., San Antonio, TX.

De Renzi, E. & Vignolo, L.A. (1962). The Token Test: a sensitive test to detect disturbances in aphasics. *Brain*, **85**, 665–678.

Diller, L., Ben-Yishay, Y., Gerstman, L.J., Goodkin, R., Gordon, W. & Weinberg, J. (1974). *Studies in Cognition and Rehabilitation in Hemiplegia* (Rehabilitation Monograph No. 50). New York University Medical Center Institute of Rehabilitation Medicine, New York.

Dodrill, C.B. (1978). A neuropsychological battery for epilepsy. *Epilepsia*, **19**, 611–623.

Freed, D.M., Corkin, S., Growdon, J.H. & Nissen, M.J. (1989). Selective attention in Alzheimer's disease: characterizing cognitive subgroups of patients. *Neuropsychologia*, **27**, 325–339.

Freides, D. & Avery, M.E. (1972). Narrative and visual spatial recall: assessment incorporating learning and delayed retention. *The Clinical Neuropsychologist*, **5**, 338–344.

Graham, F.K. & Kendall, B.S. (1960). Memory-for-Designs Test, Revised general manual. *Perceptual Motor Skills*, **11**, 147–188 (Monograph Supplement no. 2-VII).

Grant, D.A. & Berg, E.A. (1948). A behavioral analysis of degree of reinforcement and ease of shifting to new responses on a Weigl-type card-sorting problem. *Journal of Experimental Psychology*, **38**, 404–411.

Greenwood, P. & Parasuraman, R. (1991). Effects of aging on the speed of attentional cost of cognitive operations. *Developmental Neuropsychology*, **7**, 421–434.

Gronwall, D.M.A. (1977). Paced Auditory Serial-Addition Task: a measure of recovery from concussion. *Perceptual and Motor Skills*, **44**, 367–373.

Gronwall, D.M.A. & Sampson, H. (1974). *The Psychological Effects of Concussion*. University Press/Oxford University Press, Auckland.

Halstead, W.C. (1947). *Brain and Intelligence*. University of Chicago Press, Chicago.

Hannay, H.J., Levin, H.S. & Grossman, R.G. (1979). Impaired recognition memory after head injury. *Cortex*, **15**, 269–283.

Heaton, R.K., Chelune, G.J., Talley, J.L., Kay, G.C. & Curtiss, G. (1993). *Wisconsin Card Sorting Test Manual: Revised and Expanded*. Psychological Assessment Resources Inc., Odessa, FL.

Heaton, R.K., Grant, I. & Matthews, C.G. (1991). *Comprehensive Norms for an Expanded Halstead–Reitan Battery: Demographic Corrections, Research Findings, and Clinical Applications*. Psychological Assessment Resources Inc., Odessa, FL.

Howieson, D.B., Kaye, J. & Howieson, J. (1991). Cognitive status in healthy aging. *Journal of Clinical and Experimental Neuropsychology*, **13**, 28.

Laine, M. & Butters, N. (1982). A preliminary study of problem solving strategies of detoxified long-term alcoholics. *Drug and Alcohol Dependence*, **10**, 235–242.

Lezak, M.D. (1979). Recovery of memory and learning function following traumatic brain injury. *Cortex*, **15**, 63–70.

Lezak, M.D. (1982). The problem of assessing executive functions. *International Journal of Psychology*, **17**, 281–297.

Lezak, M.D. (1994). Domains of behavior from a neuropsychological perspective: the whole story. In W. Spaulding (ed.), *41st Nebraska Symposium on Motivation*. University of Nebraska, Lincoln, Nebraska.

Lezak, M.D. (1995). *Neuropsychological Assessment*, 3rd edn. Oxford University Press, New York.

Lines, C.R., Dawson, C., Preston, G.C., Reich, S., Foster, C. & Traub, M. (1991). Memory and attention in patients with senile dementia of the Alzheimer's type and in normal elderly subjects. *Journal of Clinical and Experimental Neuropsychology*, **13**, 691–702.

Loring, D.W., Lee, G.P. & Meador, K.J. (1988). Revising the Rey–Osterrieth: rating right hemisphere recall. *Archives of Clinical Neuropsychology*, **3**, 239–247.

Luria, A.R. (1971). Memory disturbance in local brain lesions. *Neuropsychologia*, **9**, 367–376.

Luria, A.R. (1980). *Higher Cortical Functions in Man*, 2nd edn. Basic Books, New York.

Malec, J.F., Ivnik, R.J. & Hinkeldey, N.S. (1991). Visual Spatial Learning Test. *Psychological Assessment*, **3**, 82–88.

Meador, K.J., Taylor, H.S. & Loring, D.W. (1990). Medical College of Georgia (MCG) Complex Figures. Unpublished test material, Department of Neurology, Medical College of Georgia, Augusta, Georgia.

Milner, B. (1970). Memory and the medial regions of the brain. In K.H. Pribram & D.E. Broadbent (eds), *Biology of Memory*. Academic Press, New York, pp. 29–50.

Milner, B. (1971). Interhemispheric differences in the localization of psychological processes in man. *British Medical Bulletin*, **27**, 272–277.

Morris, J.C., Heyman, A., Mohs, R.C., Hughes, J.P., van Belle, G., Fillenbaum, G., Mellits, E.D. & Clark, C. (1989). The consortium to establish a registry for Alzheimer's disease (CERAD). Part I: Clinical and neuropsychological assessment of Alzheimer's disease. *Neurology*, **39**, 1159–1165.

Morrow, L.A., Robin, N., Hodgson, M.J. & Kamis, H. (1992). Assessment of attention and memory efficiency in persons with solvent neurotoxicity. *Neuropsychologia*, **30**, 911–922.

Moscovitch, M. (1982). Multiple dissociations of function in amnesia. In L.S. Cermak (ed.), *Human Memory and Amnesia*. Erlbaum, Hillsdale, NJ, p. 337–370.

Nebes, R.D. & Brady, C.B. (1989). Focused and divided attention in Alzheimer's disease. *Cortex*, **25**, 300–315.

Nestor, P.G., Parasuraman, R. & Haxby, J.V. (1991). Speed of information processing and attention in early Alzheimer's dementia. *Developmental Neuropsychology*, **7**, 242–256.

Ponsford, J. & Kinsella, G. (1992). Attentional deficits following closed-head injury. *Journal of Clinical and Experimental Neuropsychology*, **14**, 822–838.

Rapaport, D., Gill, M.M. & Schafer, R. (1968). *Diagnostic Psychological Testing*. Rev. edn, R.R. Holt (ed.), International Universities Press, New York.

Rao, S.M., Hammeke, T.A., McQuillen, M.P., Khatri, B.O. & Lloyd, D. (1984). Memory disturbance in chronic progressive multiple sclerosis. *Archives of Neurology*, **41**, 625–631.

Rao, S.M., Leo, G.L., Bernardin, L. & Unverzagt, F. (1991). Cognitive dysfunction in multiple sclerosis. I: Frequency, patterns and prediction, *Neurology*, **41**, 685–691.

Rey, A. (1964). *L'Examen Clinique en Psychologie*. Presses Universitaires de France, Paris.

Ruff, R.M., Light, R.H. & Evans, R.W. (1987). The Ruff Figural Fluency Test: a normative study with adults. *Developmental Neuropsychology*, **3**, 37–52.

Scherer, I.W., Klett, C.J. & Winnes, J.F. (1957). Psychological changes over a three-year period following bilateral prefrontal lobotomy. *Journal of Consulting Psychology*, **19**, 291–298.

Schneider, W. & Shiffrin, R.M. (1977). Controlled and automatic human information processing. I: Detection, search and attention. *Psychological Review*, **84**, 1–66.

Shallice, T. (1982). Specific impairments of planning. In D.E. Broadbent & L. Weiskrantz (ed.), *The Neuropsychology of Cognitive Function*. The Royal Society, London, pp. 199–209.

Shimamura, A.P., Janowsky, J.S. & Squire, L.R. (1991). What is the role of frontal lobe damage in memory disorders. In H.M. Levin, H.M. Eisenberg & A.L. Benton (eds), *Frontal Lobe Function and Dysfunction*. Oxford University Press, New York.

Sivan, A.B. (1991). *Benton Visual Retention Test*, 5th edn. The Psychological Corporation, San Antonio, TX.

Snow, W.G. (1979). The Rey–Osterrieth Complex Figure Test as a measure of visual recall. Paper presented at the meeting of the International Neuropsychological Society, New York.

Spreen, O. & Strauss, E. (1991). *A Compendium of Neuropsychological Tests*. Oxford University Press, New York.

Storandt, M., Botwinick, J. & Danziger, W.L. (1986). Longitudinal changes: patients with mild SDAT and matched healthy controls. In L.W. Poon (ed.), *Handbook for Clinical Memory Assessment of Older Adults*. American Psychological Association, Washington, DC.

Stroop, J.R. (1935). Studies of interference in serial verbal reactions. *Journal of Experimental Psychology*, **18**, 643–662.

Strub, R.L. & Black, F.W. (1985). *Mental Status Examination in Neurology*, 2nd edn. F.A. Davis, Philadelphia.

Stuss, D.T. & Benson, D.F. (1987). The frontal lobes and control of cognition and memory. In E. Perecman (ed.). *The Frontal Lobes Revisited*. IRBN Press, New York, pp. 141–158.

Stuss, D.T., Stethem, L.L., Hugenholtz, H., Picton, T., Pivik, T. & Richard, M.T. (1989).

Reaction time after head injury: fatigue, divided and focused attention, and consistency of performance. *Journal of Neurology, Neurosurgery and Psychiatry*, **52**, 742–748.

Taylor, L.B. (1979). Psychological assessment of neurosurgical patients. In T. Rasmussen & R. Marino (eds), *Functional Neurosurgery*. Raven Press, New York.

Trahan, D.E. & Larrabee, G.J. (1988). *Continuous Visual Memory Test*. Psychological Assessment Resources Inc., Odessa, FL.

Vallar, G. & Shallice T. (1990). *Neuropsychological Impairments of Short-Term Memory*. Cambridge University Press, Cambridge.

Van Gorp, W.G., Miller, E.N., Satz, P. & Visscher, B. (1989). Neuropsychological performance in HIV-1 immunocompromised patients. *Journal of Clinical and Experimental Neuropsychology*, **11**, 763–773.

Warrington, E.K. (1984). *Recognition Memory Test*. National Foundation for Educational Research–Nelson, Windsor.

Warrington, E.K. & Shallice, T. (1984). Category specific semantic impairments. *Brain*, **107**, 829–854.

Wechsler, D. (1944). *The Measurement of Adult Intelligence*, 3rd edn. Williams & Wilkins, Baltimore.

Wechsler, D. (1945). A standardized memory scale for clinical use. *Journal of Psychology*, **19**, 87–95.

Wechsler, D. (1955). *WAIS Manual*. Psychological Corp., New York.

Wechsler, D. (1981). *WAIS-R Manual*. Psychological Corp., New York.

Wechsler, D. (1987). *Wechsler Memory Scale–Revised Manual*. Psychological Corp., San Antonio, TX.

Chapter 18

The Assessment of Psychogenic Amnesia

Michael D. Kopelman
Guy's and St Thomas's Medical School, London, UK

INTRODUCTION

Psychologically based amnesia encompasses instances of persistent memory impairment, such as occurs in depression or (in extreme form) in a depressive pseudo-dementia. Alternatively, it can entail transient or discrete episodes of memory loss. The former is considered in Chapter 12, and the latter is the subject of the present account. Such transient amnesias can be situation-specific, as occurs in amnesia for offences, occasionally in post-traumatic stress disorder, and in amnesia for childhood sexual abuse. In other cases, the transient amnesia can involve a more global memory deficit, often accompanied by a loss of the sense of personal identity, such as occurs in a psychogenic "fugue" state. Whilst these latter instances are the stuff of film and fiction (usually in grossly distorted form), it is important to recognise that situation-specific amnesia is much more commonplace, coming to the attention of clinical and forensic psychologists, psychiatrists and neurologists. The only general rule is that assessment is seldom straightforward.

Various forms of terminology are commonly used in discussing this issue. The present writer favours the term "psychogenic amnesia", because it does not make any assumptions about the degree to which memory loss results from unconscious processes ("hysterical amnesia"), rather than motivated/deliberate/conscious processes ("simulated" or "factitious" amnesia). The term "functional amnesia" is somewhat misleading in that there are, of course, deficits in function (or "process") in organic amnesia, and the salient feature of psychogenic amnesia is that, in some sense, it is always "dysfunctional".

Handbook of Memory Disorders. Edited by A.D. Baddeley, B.A. Wilson and F.N. Watts.
© 1995 John Wiley & Sons Ltd.

This chapter discusses situation-specific and global psychogenic amnesia in turn, by considering amnesia for offences and psychogenic fugue states as examples of each. This is followed by three brief case-histories which illustrate putative indicators of psychogenic and organic amnesia, as well as the potential hazards of these indicators.

SITUATION-SPECIFIC MEMORY LOSS: AMNESIA FOR OFFENCES

Defendants commonly claim amnesia for their alleged crimes, in which case psychologists and psychiatrists are often asked to assess the relevance of this amnesia. Consequently, it is regrettable that there is a relative dearth of studies investigating this intriguing form of forgetting, contrasting with investigations of eye-witness testimony, for which there is a burgeoning literature (e.g. Loftus, 1979; Wells and Loftus, 1984; Gruneberg, Morris & Sykes, 1988).

Prevalence and Characteristic Features of Amnesia for Offences

Amnesia has been reported most commonly in cases of homicide. Table 18.1 summarises the rates of amnesia obtained in several studies, which arose in different settings: between 25% and 45% of these offenders claimed amnesia for the killing. Somewhat higher figures were obtained if vaguer descriptions of memory loss were accepted: 60–70% in two of the studies (Bradford & Smith, 1979; Tanay, 1969).

Claims of amnesia also arise following other types of crime. Table 18.2 summarises the results of three studies in very different settings. Violent crime appears to be particularly associated with amnesia, although the definitive prevalence study, examining rates of amnesia following a range of differing offences (which have not necessarily come to court), has never been conducted. In Table 18.2 the association of amnesia with violent crime was evident in all

Table 18.1 Amnesia for the offence among those convicted of homicide

Study	Number	Amnesic(%)
Leitch, 1948	51	31
Guttmacher, 1955	36	33
O'Connell, 1960	50	40
Bradford & Smith, 1979	30	47
Taylor & Kopelman, 1984	34	26
Parwatikar et al., 1985*	105	23

*Pretrial evaluations only; rate for convicted homicides not given

Table 18.2 Relationship between type of offence and amnesia for offending (percentage of amnesic patients)

Crime	Hopwood & Snell (1933) Maximum security hospital, UK	Lynch & Bradford (1980) Forensic psychiatry service, Canada	Taylor & Kopelman (1984) Remand prison, UK
Homicide/attempted homicide	90	23	47
Other violence	8	63	53
Nonviolent crime	2	14	0
Total	100	100	100

three studies, although it has to be emphasised that these are biased samples, containing very high proportions of violent offenders.

A longitudinal study of this type of amnesia has not been completed to date and, in its absence, there are very conflicting views on its persistence (Leitch, 1948; O'Connell, 1960; Bradford & Smith, 1979). However, such amnesia does generally encompass a relatively brief time-span—always less than a day, and usually less than half an hour, according to Bradford and Smith (1979)—although occasional instances have been reported of amnesia for offences committed over an extended period, such as fraud (Kopelman et al., 1994b).

Principal Factors Associated with Amnesia for Crime

Violent Crime

Amnesia has been reported in cases of homicide, rape, assault, arson, armed robbery, and criminal damage (Hopwood & Snell, 1933; Lynch & Bradford, 1980; Taylor & Kopelman, 1984; Kopelman, 1987a). The association with violent crime may be secondary to the extreme emotional arousal and/or alcohol abuse commonly involved in such offences. It is intriguing that studies of the victims and eyewitnesses of offences have also revealed that impaired recall is related to the violence of the crime (e.g. Kuehn, 1974; Clifford & Scott, 1978; Yuille & Cutshall, 1986).

Extreme Emotional Arousal

High arousal appears to be particularly important in homicide cases where the offence was unpremeditated (Hopwood & Snell, 1933; O'Connell, 1960; Bradford & Smith, 1979; Taylor & Kopelman, 1984). In these cases the victim is usually closely related to the offender—in one series the victim was a lover, wife, close friend or family member in 88% of the cases (Taylor & Kopelman, 1984). There is often an accompanying diagnosis of depression, and sometimes a diagnosis of schizophrenia.

A 40-year-old Egyptian was married to an English woman with two young children. When he discovered that his wife was having an affair with a musician, he became depressed, and he was treated with an antidepressant as an outpatient at his local hospital. During the afternoon of the offence, he had a furious row with his wife, during which he threatened to kill the musician. Later, he could recall going to kiss his daughter good night, but he could not remember anything after that until the police arrived. However, he had in the meantime telephoned the police, and he was subsequently charged with the murder of his wife by stabbing.

Alcohol Abuse and Intoxication

There is commonly a history of chronic alcohol abuse and/or acute intoxication at the time of the offence in amnesic subjects (Table 18.3). Three studies have also implicated abuse of other drugs, although the types of drugs involved were not specified (Bradford & Smith, 1979; Lynch & Bradford, 1980; Parwatikar, Holcomb & Meninger, 1985). Alcohol could produce amnesia either from a so-called "blackout" or as a state-dependent phenomenon (Goodwin, Crane & Guze, 1969).

A 20-year-old man had consumed eight or more pints of beer plus three whiskies in the course of an evening. The last thing he could recall was being in a nightclub with friends, who had been threatened by a rival gang, and who were then pacified by attendants. Continuous memory returned early the following morning, whilst he was being interviewed in the police station, although there were "islets" of preserved memory in-between: peering down from a roof above a shop, being kicked by a policeman whilst up on the roof, being made to descend a ladder with handcuffs on. He had no idea how he had climbed up the roof or why. The accused was charged with assaulting a police officer whilst under the influence of alcohol. Eight months after the offence, there had been some infilling of memory between the "islets", and shrinkage of the amnesic gap from about six hours to approximately two hours.

Table 18.3 Relationship between alcohol and amnesia for crime

Study	Amnesic cases(%)	Nonamnesic cases(%)
Chronic abuse		
Hopwood & Snell, 1933	38	No comparison group
Lynch & Bradford, 1980	72	No comparison group
Taylor & Kopelman, 1984	42	10
Parwatikar et al., 1985	71	58
Intoxicated at time of offence		
O'Connell, 1960	30	13
Bradford & Smith, 1979	30	10
Taylor & Kopelman, 1984	42	20
Parwatikar et al., 1985*	87	42

* The figure given is for alcohol and/or drug abuse in this study.

Depressed Mood

Various authors have reported that depressed mood occurs with some frequency in patients claiming amnesia (Hopwood & Snell, 1933; Taylor & Kopelman, 1984; Parwatikar, Holcomb & Meninger, 1985). This is illustrated by the first case-history given above, and it is a similar finding to that obtained in studies of fugue states (see below). An association between depression and shoplifting has also been described (Gibbens, Palmer & Prince, 1971), the latter subjects sometimes claiming amnesia for their offences.

Acute Psychosis / Delusional Memory

Some studies report that a small group of subjects are found who have committed offences during floridly psychotic episodes (e.g. Taylor & Kopelman, 1984). These offences often consist of criminal damage or minor acts of aggression, but the account given of them by their perpetrator, although stated with apparent conviction, is at complete variance with what others had observed.

> A young man, who had a history of recurrent hospital admissions for schizophrenia, reported that he had gone into a fish-and-chip shop, that he had looked into the eyes of a Chinese serving woman, and that he had asked for cod roe. He said the lights had then become bright, and that he had fainted, and he could not remember anything else. In fact, there had been no loss of consciousness or altercation—he had suddenly picked up a bar and started smashing the ovens.

In very occasional cases, such anomalous or even delusional memories may result in charges being brought inappropriately:

> A sailor claimed that he had killed an acquaintance at sea, following an angry dispute; and he gave a detailed and consistent account of the killing. He was charged with murder, but it emerged that he had been floridly psychotic at the time of his confession, and that he was referring to a voyage three years earlier, when nobody had been lost at sea. Eventually he was acquitted, and his "confession" was attributed to a delusional memory; but by that stage he had already served a lengthy period in prison on remand.

Organic Brain Disorder and Amnesia for Offences

Although relatively rare, organic brain disease has important legal implications when it is a concomitant of amnesia for crime. Hopwood and Snell (1933) reported that 20% of their cases had a history of head injury, 12% previous amnesia, and 9% epilepsy. In contrast, other studies have failed to find an increased frequency of organic disorder or EEG abnormalities in amnesic offenders, relative to nonamnesic offenders (Bradford & Smith, 1979; Taylor & Kopelman, 1984). However, the amnesic samples in these series were relatively small, and the base rates for organic disorder would have been low. Taken together, they indicate that, although alcohol and/or drug intoxication are relatively common occurrences in crime, frank neurological disease is rare.

Nevertheless, it is very important to exclude any brain disease because, although amnesia *per se* does not affect a subject's fitness to plead or the question of responsibility in English law and many other jurisdictions, these issues often become pertinent in cases in which an organic factor is implicated, such as epilepsy, hypoglycaemia, head injury or sleepwalking (Fenwick, 1990, 1993).

Epilepsy

Epileptic automatisms or postictal confusional states occasionally result in crime. When this occurs, EEGs subsequently reveal that the seizure activity always involves the hippocampal and parahippocampal structures bilaterally as well as the mesial diencephalon (Fenton, 1972). As these structures are crucial for memory formation, amnesia for the period of automatic behaviour is always present and is usually complete (Knox, 1968). There is no automatism without amnesia. Consequently, assessment requires obtaining a convincing history of both epilepsy and amnesia.

> In the case of *R vs Sullivan* (reported by Fenwick, 1990), Sullivan was a known epileptic who, during a complex partial seizure, attacked and seriously injured an elderly neighbour. He had no memory whatsoever for the offence and, in a decision which caused some controversy at the time, the judge ruled that, if automatism were upheld, this would be a case of "insane automatism" as there was an underlying disease of the brain. As a successful plea of "insane automatism" would have meant that the Court be compelled to send Sullivan to hospital—possibly a secure hospital—his defence lawyers advised him to plead guilty, despite the fact that he could not remember the offence and had had no control over it. An appeal went to the House of Lords, but was rejected.

Hypoglycaemia

Patients with insulin-treated diabetes, alcohol intoxication, the "dumping" syndrome, insulinoma, or subjects abusing insulin, may suffer hypoglycaemia. Insulin abuse has been implicated in a number of serious offences, including violent crimes against children (Scarlett et al., 1977; Lancet, 1978). Where hypoglycaemia results from the administration of an external agent such as insulin, the case for a "sane" automatism can be argued; if upheld, this results in acquittal (in England and Wales and many other countries).

Head Injury

Where head injury is associated with amnesia for an offence, there is usually a relatively brief period of retrograde amnesia, which may shrink through time, a longer period of post-traumatic amnesia (PTA), and there may be islets of preserved memory within the amnesic gap. Occasionally, there is a particularly vivid memory for images or sounds occurring immediately before the injury, on regaining consciousness, or during a lucid interval before the onset of PTA (Russell & Nathan, 1946; Lishman, 1987). The length of PTA is assumed to reflect the extent of diffuse brain pathology, resulting from rotational forces, and it is predictive of eventual cognitive, social and psychiatric outcome (Lishman, 1968; Schacter & Crovitz, 1977; Brooks, 1984).

A 25-year-old man was charged with causing death by reckless driving, following an evening of moderate drinking at a public house. The last thing he recalled was opening a rear door for a girlfriend, and continuous memory returned 30 hours later, following his discharge from hospital. The car had struck a tree, subjecting the car to severe rotational forces. The subject had vivid "islets" of memory of lying in the street beside a passenger door, of being driven away in an ambulance with an unconscious woman beside him, of being examined by a doctor, and of being visited in the hospital by his girlfriend. He had no memory of driving the car or how the accident took place. The prosecution wanted to dispute the authenticity of the defendant's amnesia, but in this case it was easy to argue that the pattern of RA and PTA were consistent with the nature of the head injury, which had involved a few minutes' loss of consciousness, especially as the statements of witnesses and the medical records confirmed that the defendant had complained of confusion and memory loss almost immediately after regaining consciousness.

A 24-year-old man was struck violently on the head with an implement during a scuffle at a fair on a bank holiday. He bled profusely, and, subsequently, he could remember nothing of the next one hour and a quarter, except for a brief "islet" of memory of his head being bandaged. He was found by a police officer, who reported that he appeared confused and amnesic for what had occurred. His subsequent EEG showed bitemporal slow waves, consistent with a severe blow to the head. During the amnesic period, the subject had obtained a firearm and had threatened a family previously unknown to him. Because the blow to the head, the consistent claim of amnesia, the police officer's description, and the EEG were all compatible, the case for a "sane automatism" was argued. Unfortunately, the prosecution's case collapsed, and a jury was not given the opportunity to decide upon this.

Sleepwalking

Somnambulism occurs most commonly in childhood and adolescence, and occasionally occurs in adult life, especially when precipitated by fatigue, mental stress, sleep deprivation, drugs or alcohol, or a change in the sleeping environment (Kales, Soldatos et al., 1980; Howard & d'Orbán, 1987; Fenwick, 1990). It most commonly occurs within two hours of falling asleep, and this also applies if the subject is awoken in the middle of the night and then falls asleep again. Episodes usually last only a few minutes.

There are a substantial number of case reports in the medical and legal literature of violent attacks during sleepwalking, often involving strangulation, attempted strangulation, or the use of available implements as weapons, with a sleeping partner as the victim (Howard & d'Orbán, 1987; Fenwick, 1990). Most commonly in these case reports, there has not been any previous hostility between the offender and the victim, and the behaviour is entirely out of character. Characteristically, episodes of violence accompanying sleepwalking terminate in the subject appearing confused on awakening, recalling relatively little detail of any accompanying dream, but being aware of a sense of acute dread or terror in such a dream (so-called "night terrors"; Kales, Kales et al., 1980). This arises because sleepwalking and night terrors characteristically occur in stage four of slow-wave sleep, shortly before a transition to rapid-eye-movement (REM) sleep. Later in the night, dreams and possibly nightmares occur in association with REM sleep: the subject is paralysed and does not sleepwalk during these, and, on awakening, there is little or no confusion and the subject can recall his or her dreams very well.

Until recently, offences committed during sleepwalking constituted a form of "sane automatism" implying acquittal; but more recently, although the literature suggests that violent attacks during sleepwalking are unlikely to recur, they have been regarded as a form of "insane automatism", as no external agent is involved.

> A 25-year-old policeman shared a home with his uncle, who was resistant to all attempts at modernisation that the young policeman wanted to institute. Relations between them were difficult. The policeman had a past history of sleepwalking and, on the night of the alleged offence, he reported that, approximately ninety minutes after going to bed, he woke up to find himself in the kitchen with a cord tightly bound around his uncle's neck. Many of the details in the accused's account were consistent with sleepwalking and a night terror, but there were anomalies which both expert witnesses felt should be put to a jury. Curiously, on arrival in Court, the policeman had changed his story: he now said that the uncle had been attempting suicide, and it had been fortunate that he had been sleepwalking at the time, and that he had woken up in time to save his uncle. Despite this somewhat surprising account, the policeman was acquitted, not on the grounds of an "automatism", but because there was "reasonable doubt" as to who had put the cord around the uncle's neck.

Other Organic Brain Disorders

Other disorders which produce a discrete or transient episode of memory loss, such as toxic or post-ECT confusional states, transient ischaemic episodes, or the transient global amnesia (TGA) syndrome, are very unlikely to be associated with crime. Similarly, organic disorders which produce chronic or persistent amnesia are very seldom associated with crime, although occasional instances do occur (e.g. Brooks, Murphy, Janota & Lishman, 1987).

Authentic Amnesia or Deliberate Malingering?

Many observers consider that the amnesia claimed by offenders is a deliberate strategy to try to avoid the legal consequences of their offence. In view of this,

Hopwood and Snell (1933) conducted a retrospective review of follow-up information in the case notes of 100 Broadmoor prisoner/patients who, at the time of their trials, had claimed amnesia for their offences; they concluded that 78% of the amnesias had been "genuine", 14% had been "feigned", and 8% were "doubtful". On the other hand, following a review of the literature, Schacter (1986a) argued that "many claims of amnesia after crimes are simulated". Longitudinal studies would help indicate the consistency of offenders' claims through time, and there are methods whereby the more flagrant simulators might be detected (Schacter, 1986b; Brandt, 1992), but there is a dearth of evidence on this issue. However, there are a number of reasons for supposing that many cases of amnesia are authentic, although the issue may be less clearcut than it sometimes appears.

First, there may not be any distinct demarcation between "conscious" malingering and motivated or "unconscious" forgetting ("hysteria"). O'Connell (1960) favoured the view that the difference between them was a matter of degree rather than kind, and he provided examples of what he called the "passive disregard" by offenders towards their crimes. This was evident in the remarks of both amnesic and nonamnesic subjects. One nonamnesic offender, for example, described letting the memory "drift into the background...like putting something into... a safe and locking it away". By comparison, amnesic subjects described having "buried everything about (the) case" and feeling that recollection would be "so {horrifying} that I just can't remember anything" or that "there is something in my mind... it seems to be forming a picture and then... my head hurts... {and} it gets all jumbled up again".

Secondly, many amnesic cases have been described in the literature, who either have reported their own crime or failed to take measures to avoid their capture (Hopwood & Snell, 1933; Leitch, 1948; Gudjonsson & MacKeith, 1983; Taylor & Kopelman, 1984; Gudjonsson & Taylor, 1985). This makes an account of amnesia as simulation to avoid punishment seem less plausible. This was true of the first case-history given above; and Gudjonsson and MacKeith (1983) reported a similar incident:

> A 67-year-old man had apparently battered his wife to death without any apparent motive, before telephoning the police and giving himself up. On their arrival, he reported that he had no memory of the actual attack, but that he recalled standing over the body realising that he had been responsible for his wife's death. His memory had not cleared by the time of the Court hearing.

Thirdly, it should be noted that the factors which have been associated with amnesia in offenders overlap with those which have been implicated in cases of impaired recall by the victims or eyewitnesses of crime—notably violent crime, extreme emotional arousal and alcohol intoxication (see, e.g., Kuehn, 1974; Clifford & Scott, 1978; Yuille & Cutshall, 1986; Deffenbacher, 1988; Yuille, 1987).

Fourthly, it should be reiterated that, in English law (and in many other, but not all, jurisdictions), amnesia per se does not constitute either a barrier to trial or any defence. For amnesia to contribute to the question of responsibility, other issues have to be raised, such as epilepsy or other forms of organic brain disease. Most lawyers are aware of this, but, nevertheless, their clients continue to plead amnesia even in instances where recall of what actually happened would be helpful to their cause.

Assessment of Amnesia and its Causes

During an assessment interview, it is valuable to establish the duration of the amnesic gap, whether there are any islets of preserved memory within it, and whether there has been any loss of memory for time-periods preceding or following the episode. It can be extremely useful to establish from the available records at what point the accused first complained of amnesia, and how consistent his or her description of the amnesia has been. It is important to obtain any available evidence about the subject's behaviour at the time of and after the offence, and to obtain details about the background circumstances of the offence; e.g. the nature of the relationship with a victim, any immediately precipitating factors such as alcohol or drug intoxication, and whether there was any evidence of premeditation or an attempt to cover up the offence. Any past or concurrent history of head injury, epilepsy, hypoglycaemia, or sleep-walking is extremely important to establish, because of the implications for "automatism", and a detailed alcohol and drug history needs to be established. A medical assessment may reveal physical stigmata of alcohol and drug abuse and, if there is any suspicion of current memory impairment, a detailed cognitive assessment is obviously required. Interviewing relatives and other informants, inspection of the relevant legal documents and medical records, and the results of social and probation enquiries, can be every bit as important as the findings on any clinical or neuropsychological assessment. Blood test and urine analysis may reveal unadmitted or understated alcohol or drug abuse. An EEG should be arranged if there is any suspicion of epilepsy, and a CT or MRI scan if there is any suggestion of a structural lesion or a degenerative disorder. In the latter case, a cognitive assessment will also be required.

In the past, various psychophysiological measures, personality assessments, hypnosis, and Amytal abreactions have been proposed to differentiate either organic from psychogenic amnesia or authentic ("unconscious"/"hysterical") from simulated ("conscious") amnesia (Bradford & Smith, 1979; Lynch & Bradford, 1980; Parwatiker, Holcomb & Meninger, 1985; Powell, Gudjonsson & Mullen, 1983). More recently, various experimental procedures have been advocated, many of which are based on the principle that "simulators" or "fakers" will fail at relatively easy test items on specific memory tasks, where patients with either an organic or an hysterical amnesia would succeed. For example, Brandt, Rubinsky and Lassen (1985) suggested that simulators score below chance at recognition memory tests; and Wiggins and Brandt (1988) argued that they show relatively poor recognition memory compared with recall performance. Wiggins and Brandt (1988) also suggested that simulators showed normal primacy and recency effects, whereas the latter may be absent in patients with organic amnesia. Schacter (1986b) predicted that simulators may fail to show normal priming effects on memory tasks, a prediction which was confirmed by Horton, Smith, Barghout and Connolly (1992) in a recent laboratory study. Furthermore, Schacter (1986c) produced experimental evidence, indicating that simulators show abnormally low "feelings-of-knowing", in that they say that neither cueing, recognition testing, nor additional time would help their performance, unlike subjects who genuinely cannot remember test material. With regard to tests of retrograde memory, Wiggins and Brandt (1988) argued that simulators show abnormally poor performance on tests of autobiographical memory, and produce more implausible responses, whilst manifesting relatively mild impairment on tests of public event memory or anterograde memory.

Summary of Issues in Amnesia for Offending

Amnesia is most commonly seen in homicide cases in which it is claimed by 25–45% of offenders, but it may also follow other types of violent crime and, occasionally, nonviolent crime. It is particularly associated with states of extreme emotional arousal, alcohol intoxication and depressed mood, and it is occasionally associated with episodes of florid psychosis. Overt brain disease is seldom the cause of amnesia for crime, but it remains essential to identify disorders such as epilepsy, head injury or hypoglycaemia, because of their potentially crucial medicolegal importance. In the absence of brain disease, the presence of amnesia does not carry any legal implications in English law or many other jurisdictions. Many amnesic subjects have either reported their offence themselves or have made no attempt to conceal it, which argues against the view that these amnesias are deliberately simulated to avoid punishment. Detailed, longitudinal studies are required to elucidate further the precipitants, characteristics and outcome of this intriguing form of amnesia.

GLOBAL AMNESIA: PSYCHOGENIC FUGUE

A "fugue state" refers, in essence, to a syndrome consisting of a sudden loss of all autobiographical memories and the sense of self or personal identity, usually associated with a period of wandering, for which there is a subsequent amnesic gap upon recovery (Kopelman 1987b). Fugue states usually last a few hours or days only, and they appear to have occurred more commonly earlier in the century, particularly in wartime (Hunter, 1964).

A review of the earlier literature on psychogenic fugue states (Kopelman, 1987b) suggested that three main factors predisposed to such episodes (Table 18.4). First, fugue states are always preceded by a severe, precipitating stress

Table 18.4 Psychogenic amnesia: factors predisposing to fugue states

---

Predisposing stress (e.g. marital discord, financial problems, offending,
    war stress)
Depressed mood
Suicide attempts
Past history of head injury
Past history of alcohol abuse
Epilepsy
Other neurosis
Other organic disorder
Tendency to lie

---

such as marital or emotional discord (Kanzer, 1939), bereavement (Schacter, Wang, Tulving & Freeman, 1982), financial problems (Kanzer, 1939), a charge of offending (Wilson, Rupp & Wilson, 1950), or stress during wartime (Sargant & Slater, 1941; Parfit & Gall, 1944). Secondly, depressed mood is an extremely common antecedent for a psychogenic fugue state. Berrington, Liddell and Foulds (1956) wrote: "In nearly all fugues, there appears to be one common factor, namely a depressive mood. Whether the individual in the fugue is psychotic, neurotic, or even psychopathic, a depression seems to start off the fugue." For example, Schacter et al.'s (1982) patient was in a depressed mood, because he had just attended the funeral of his grandfather of whom he had been particularly fond. In fact, many patients in a "fugue" have been contemplating suicide just before the episode or do so following recovery from it (Abeles & Schilder, 1935; Stengel, 1941). For example, Abeles and Schilder (1935) described a woman who deserted her husband for another man: after a week she determined to return to her family but, as she descended into the railway underground station, she was contemplating suicide. The authors tersely reported that "instead amnesia developed". The third factor which commonly precedes a fugue state is a history of a transient, organic amnesia: Stengel (1941) reported that 10% of his sample had a history of epilepsy, and Berrington et al. (1956) reported that 16 of their 37 cases had previously experienced a severe head injury, and a further three cases had suffered a head injury of unknown severity. In brief, it appears that patients who have experienced a previous, transient organic amnesia, and who have become depressed and/or suicidal, are particularly likely to go into a "fugue" in the face of a severe, precipitating stress.

A confounding factor, however, is that several authors have noted that some of their patients appeared to be somewhat unreliable personalities with a possible legal motive for wanting to claim amnesia (Stengel, 1941; Wilson et al., 1950; Berrington et al., 1956). Kopelman (1987b) gave the example of a man who reported about ten or twelve fugue episodes, several of which were well-documented in medical records, and who also had a past history of depression and suicide attempts as well as transient amnesia following epileptic seizures and ECT. Unfortunately, this gentleman claimed amnesia for a period of a few hours, during which he was involved in a motor accident whilst driving when disqualified, without any insurance, whilst under the influence of alcohol, making assessment (for a medicolegal report) particularly difficult.

Clinical and Neuropsychological Factors

The clinical and neuropsychological phenomena of psychogenic amnesia often bear interesting resemblances to organic amnesia. For example, there may be islets or fragments of preserved memory within the amnesic gap. A woman, who was due to meet her husband to discuss divorce, recalled that she was "supposed to meet someone" (Kanzer, 1939). A young man, who slipped into a fugue following his grandfather's funeral, recalled a cluster of details from the year which he described (after recovery) as having been the happiest of his life (Schacter, Wang, Tulving & Freeman, 1982). The subject may adopt a detached attitude to these memory fragments, describing them as "strange and unfamiliar" (Coriat, 1907). In many cases, semantic knowledge remains intact (e.g. foreign languages, and the names of streets, towns, and famous people; see Kanzer, 1939; Schacter et al., 1982), whereas in others it is also implicated (Coriat, 1907; Abeles & Schilder, 1935; Kanzer, 1939). Similarly, performance at verbal-learning tests has been reported as unaffected (Abeles & Schilder, 1935; Kopelman, Christensen, Puffett & Stanhope, 1994a), mildly impaired (Schacter et al., 1982), or more severely impaired (Gudjonsson & Taylor, 1985). Memory for skills is often preserved (e.g. Coriat, 1907), but in the Padola hearing in 1959 (Bradford & Smith, 1979), retention of a rudimentary knowledge of aerodynamics and of other skills (e.g. solving jigsaw puzzles) was taken as evidence against an organic amnesia—a frankly erroneous interpretation in the light of contemporary findings demonstrating preserved procedural memory in organic amnesia. Sometimes, memory retrieval may be facilitated by chance cues in the environment (e.g. Abeles & Schilder, 1935; Schacter et al., 1982), but deliberate cueing is often unsuccessful (Coriat, 1907; Kanzer, 1939) and the results of Amytal abreaction are often disappointing (Lennox, 1943; Adatto, 1949; Kopelman et al., 1994a,b).

> Recently, a middle-aged man arrived in the Accident and Emergency Department of a central London hospital, complaining that he did not know who or where he was. He had only a vague memory of walking through South London during the preceding night, and he complained of sore feet. It was a Monday evening, and it emerged that, having attended a birthday party on the Saturday evening, where he claimed to have consumed only a small amount of alcohol, he left home early on Sunday morning to go to a building job. At some point, he thought that he had fallen over and banged his head. It appeared that he had been wandering throughout the next 36 hours. His relatives, who had been telephoning all the casualty departments in Central London, soon arrived, but he claimed that he was unable to recognise them. In addition, many aspects of semantic as well as autobiographical memory were lost: for example, he was unable to explain what a telephone was for. He was admitted initially to a medical ward, and later trans-

ferred to a psychiatric ward. We were strongly suspicious that his amnesia was either simulated or the result of an alcoholic blackout, although his family confirmed that he had not consumed much alcohol at the party. However, chance cues appeared to trigger the return of his memories. First, he saw a book on the medical ward by a man called Holmes, and this reminded him that he had recently discovered that a close friend of that name had terminal cancer. On transfer to the psychiatric ward, he was reminded that he had been briefly admitted to another psychiatric unit some years earlier: and, after this, his memories rapidly returned.

Clinical Assessment

In differentiating a global psychogenic amnesia from an organic amnesia, clinical factors may be important indicators, such as the rate and the circumstances of the onset of memory loss, whether there is loss of the sense of personal identity (rare in organic amnesia except in advanced dementia), and whether new learning is affected (often spared in psychogenic amnesia, although not necessarily). In TGA and organic confusional states, repetitive questioning (e.g. "Where am I?" or "What am I doing here?") is a characteristic feature, whereas personal identity is seldom lost; in psychogenic fugue, personal identity is lost but repetitive questioning is rare (Hodges & Ward, 1989; Kopelman, Panayiotopoulos and Lewis, 1994). If TGA attacks are frequent and brief (an hour or less), they are likely to have an epileptic basis (Hodges & Warlow, 1990), which Kapur (1990) has termed "transient epileptic amnesia" (TEA). On the other hand, TGA episodes are preceded by a precipitating stress in 14–33% of cases (Hodges & Ward, 1989; Miller et al., 1987), and it is misleading to assume that such stressors mean that an amnesia must be psychogenic.

Neuropsychological testing can be helpful. The same types of test are available for attempting to differentiate unconscious or "hysterical" amnesia from deliberate simulation as was the case in the assessment of offenders. Generally, these procedures seek to establish a disproportionate impairment on tests of recognition memory (relative to recall memory), failure on the easiest items of IQ tests, impaired "feelings-of-knowing", or failure to demonstrate normal psychological phenomena such as intact priming or procedural memory (Brandt, Rubinsky & Lassen, 1985; Brandt, 1992; Gudjonsson & Schakleton, 1986; Schacter, 1986b). An aberrant pattern of retrograde memory loss, particularly involving autobiographical memory, can be especially helpful in differentiating psychogenic from organic memory loss. For example, Kopelman (1994) cited a male patient who reported a virtually complete loss of autobiographical memories for a 12-year period preceding and including allegations of a sexual offence to a child: following a year's therapy in a forensic psychiatric unit, which included regular contextual cueing, this man's memories started to return. Patient A.T., described below, showed a disproportionate deficit in remote, autobiographical memories associated with an anomalous "temporal gradient" (a pronounced "recency effect").

Summary of Issues in Psychogenic Fugue

Fugue states tend to arise in subjects who have had a previous transient, organic amnesia, and who are depressed and possibly suicidal, and who are faced with a severe precipitating stress. Unlike transient organic amnesia, there is usually a loss of the sense of personal identity; but repetitive questioning during or immediately after the episode seldom occurs. There can be very variable effects upon new learning, semantic memory, or aspects of implicit memory. The question of deliberate simulation often arises, and the same types of neuropsychological assessment are available as have been used in amnesia for crime. However, because of the rarity of the disorder, only two studies have employed such procedures in this context (Schacter et al., 1982; Kopelman et al., 1994a).

THE NATURE OF PSYCHOGENIC AMNESIA

Leaving aside deliberate simulation, various mechanisms have been proposed to account for psychogenic amnesia. These include repression, dissociative states, a failure of initial encoding, an encoding–retrieval interaction, and state- or context-dependent retrieval deficits. These various theories can be grouped into those which place emphasis on the failure of memory at the time of initial encoding, which may be particularly true of amnesic offenders where severe alcoholic or drug intoxication is implicated, and those which place emphasis on a failure of memory retrieval. The latter is possibly more true of those unpremeditated homicide cases, which take place in a state of extreme emotional arousal, although in these cases the possibility of an interaction between encoding and retrieval factors cannot be excluded. In the present author's experience, a complete absence of any recollection is extremely rare, where organic brain disease, intoxication, or obvious simulation have been excluded. On detailed assessment, subjects often show some degree of "knowledge" or "recognition" of certain memories without explicit recollection, in a manner analogous to that seen in studies of amnesic patients or healthy subjects who have failed to remember something (Gardiner & Parkin, 1990). For example, as discussed above, O'Connell (1960) pointed to the qualitative similarities between what he called the "passive disregard" of those who deliberately put an unpleasant or traumatic memory to the back of their mind, and those subjects who, although claiming amnesia, describe the memory as being on the verge of "forming a picture". The Egyptian homicide case, cited above, and Gudjonsson and MacKeith's (1983) patient both "knew" that they must have committed their respective offences (although, in part, this was from the evidence before their eyes). Patient A.T. described below "recognised" a hotel on being taken back there, after it had been discovered that she had stayed there shortly after the onset of her amnesia; but she could recollect nothing about her time there, even after recovery of most of her earlier memories.

In short, there is a continuum in levels of awareness in memory (Figure 18.1), and patients with psychogenic amnesia do not necessarily fall at the extremes of either fully deliberate simulation or completely "unconscious" amnesia. The intriguing overlap between the factors (extreme emotional arousal, violence, alcohol) which produce impaired recall by the eyewitnesses and victims of offences as well as the perpetrators of the crime, and the pervasiveness of depressed mood in both fugue states and amnesia for crime, should, perhaps, direct further investigation of this topic.

Case Histories

Three recent case histories will illustrate some of the difficulties in assessment.

Patient S.D. (Kopelman, Panayiotopoulos & Lewis, 1994c) came complaining that "I'm having fugues, Doc", having had a diagnosis of psychogenic amnesia made elsewhere. However, he gave a typical history of episodes of transient global amnesia (TGA), in which he asked repetitive questions, appeared perplexed and confused, and was fully aware of who he was. There were eight or nine of these episodes during the course of a year, and they had all lasted

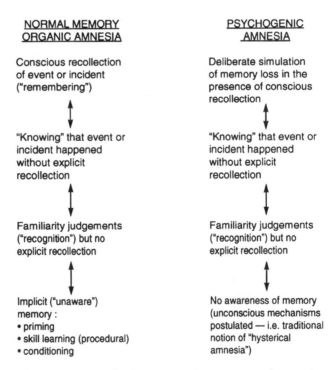

Figure 18.1   Levels of awareness in memory and amnesia

between half an hour and an hour. The brevity and frequency of the attacks suggested an epileptic basis (Hodges & Warlow, 1990), although there was no previous history of epilepsy, and two standard EEGs had been normal. A sleep EEG showed frequent mid-temporal sharp and slow-wave complexes, arising independently in the right and left hemispheres, and treatment with an anticonvulsant eliminated the attacks. There had been a stressful life event—S.D. had lost his job as a company director a year earlier—but this is commonly evident in patients with TGA (Hodges & Ward, 1989; Miller et al., 1987). Neuropsychological testing showed that this patient had a residual, interictal anterograde memory impairment, but relatively intact retrograde memory, contrasting with the neuropsychological findings in an earlier patient (Kapur et al., 1989) who had "transient epileptic amnesia" (TEA).

Patient A.T. (Kopelman et al., 1994a) "came round" on the London Undergound unaware of who or where she was. She carried a bag, containing some clothes and an envelope addressed to a name (which subsequently turned out not to be hers). She was taken to the nearest hospital, before being transferred to the present author's unit. Detailed assessments were conducted during the course of the following year, first as an inpatient, and later as an outpatient. She had a North American accent, but it took us 15 months to find out who she was with the help of Scotland Yard's Missing Persons Bureau. The duration of the amnesia suggested fabrication, but A.T. performed normally on virtually all tests of anterograde memory, including recognition and priming tasks. However, she showed an extremely severe impairment of retrograde memory on both autobiographical and public-information tasks, but with a prominent "recency effect" which was quite different from the temporal gradient normally seen in patients with organic amnesia. After she had been identified, she failed to show normal word-completion "priming" for the names of people and places she had known before the onset of her amnesia, although word-completion priming for post-onset names was normal. Moreover, on a recognition version of this test, her "feelings-of-knowing" for pre-onset names and places were no greater than for "baseline" items (unknown to her), which was interpreted as an aberrant finding. After discovering the circumstances of her disappearance from the United States, and following further information from her family, it seemed to us likely that she had indeed experienced an authentic fugue state lasting approximately a week, but that, thereafter, she was at least partially simulating, despite her excellent performance on most of the laboratory-designed tests for "faking".

Patient K.G. (Kopelman et al., 1994b) was a 55-year-old man, who had been charged with embezzlements from his workplace that had taken place during the course of approximately one year. He claimed amnesia for the offences. In addition, he described two "fugue" episodes, when he went wandering for several hours, and had no memory of what he had done during that time. The first of these occurred the day after he was charged with the offence, and the second happened the day after the police had searched his home. K.G. also complained of a progressive memory impairment, which was, initially, of relatively mild severity, and which was also complicated by his concomitant complaint of depression. Neuropsychological testing did not provide any evidence of fabrication, but it did indicate an impairment in anterograde memory, which slowly became worse through time. K.G. served a short prison sentence, during which he developed transient neurological signs, after which an MRI scan revealed multiple, small cortical and subcortical infarcts, including a larger one in the left hippocampus and parahippocampal gyrus. In brief, the circumstances of his disappearances seemed to indicate authentic "fugue" episodes, and the clinical and neuropsychological evidence confirmed a mild-to-moderate organic memory impairment of vascular aetiology. In the circumstances, K.G.'s continuing amnesia for his alleged embezzlement (he now claims that a colleague took advantage of his incapacity) is extremely difficult to evaluate.

CONCLUSIONS

In considering this topic, there have been two main issues: (a) differentiating organic from psychogenic amnesia; and (b) within psychogenic amnesia, differentiating motivated or "unconscious" forgetting ("hysterical amnesia") from deliberate simulation. In discussing amnesia for offences (as an example of situation-specific amnesia) and psychogenic fugue states (as an example of global amnesia), it has been argued that underlying or concomitant organic factors are relatively rare, aside from alcohol and drug intoxication, but it is extremely important to establish them when present, because they have implications for "automatism" as well as for the patient's wellbeing (e.g. patients S.D. and K.G.). Differentiating "hysterical" from simulated amnesia is much more problematic, especially as many patients with psychogenic amnesia show some degree of "knowing" or "recognition" in the absence of conscious recollection (Coriat, 1907; Kanzer, 1939; O'Connell, 1960). Moreover, evidence of simulation may not exclude the possibility that an initially "hysterical" amnesia was later put to use, when the subject realised the benefit of his or her "script" (case A.T.).

The circumstances and clinical features of the amnesia, the evidence of informants, legal documents, and medical records, are at least as important to the overall assessment as the pattern of performance on neuropsychological tests (case S.D.). However, many tests have been advocated for differentiating between organic memory loss, "hysterical" amnesia, and deliberate simulation, which usually rely upon simulators failing relatively easy items (e.g. in recognition memory or on IQ tests) or failing to demonstrate phenomena which are preserved in organic amnesia (priming, procedural memory). However, these tasks do not always succeed in detecting simulation (case A.T.). A disproportionately severe loss of autobiographical memory with an aberrant temporal gradient may be suggestive of psychogenic amnesia rather than organic memory loss (case A.T.; but see Kapur et al., 1992; Markowitsch et al., 1994); and the absence of "feelings-of-knowing" (Schacter, 1986b) suggests deliberate simulation. In general, it is probably accurate to state that where the neuropsychological deficit is very discrepant from what would be expected in organic amnesia, the disorder is more likely to result from simulation or fabrication than from an "authentic", "hysterical" or "unconscious" process.

ACKNOWLEDGEMENT

The author is grateful to Miss C. Hook for patiently typing the manuscript. His work is supported by the West Lambeth Community Care Trust.

REFERENCES

Abeles, M. & Schilder, P. (1935). Psychogenic loss of personal identity. *Archives of Neurology and Psychiatry*, **34**, 587–604.

Adatto, C.P. (1949). Observations on criminal patients during narcoanalysis. *Archives of Neurology and Psychiatry*, **62**, 82–92.

Berrington, W.P., Liddell, D.W. & Foulds, G.A. (1956). A reevaluation of the fugue. *Journal of Mental Science*, **102**, 281–286.

Bradford, J. & Smith, S.M. (1979). Amnesia and homicide: the Podola case and a study of thirty cases. *Bulletin of the American Academy of Psychiatry and the Law*, **7**, 219–231.

Brandt, J. (1992). Detecting amnesia's imposters. In L.R. Squire & N. Butters (eds), *Neuropsychology of Memory*, 2nd edn. Guilford Press, New York.

Brandt, J., Rubinsky, E. & Lassen, G. (1985). Uncovering a malingered amnesia. *Annals of New York Academy of Sciences*, **444**, 502–503.

Brooks, D.S., Murphy, D., Janota, I. & Lishman, W.A. (1987). Early onset of Huntington's chorea—diagnostic clues. *British Journal of Psychiatry*, **151**, 850–852.

Brooks, N. (1984). Cognitive deficits after head injury. In N. Brooks (ed.), *Closed Head Injury: Psychological, Social and Family Consequences*. Oxford University Press, Oxford.

Clifford, B.R. & Scott, J. (1978). Individual and situational factors in eyewitness testimony. *Journal of Applied Psychology*, **63**, 852–859.

Coriat, I.H. (1907). The Lowell case of amnesia. *Journal of Abnormal Psychology*, **2**, 93–111.

Deffenbacher, K. (1988). Eyewitness research: the next ten years. In M. Gruneberg, P. Morris & R. Sykes (eds), *Practical Aspects of Memory*, vol. 1. Wiley, Chichester.

Fenton, G.W. (1972). Epilepsy and automatism. *British Journal of Hospital Medicine*, **7**, 57–64.

Fenwick, P. (1990). Automatism, medicine and the law. *Psychological Medicine Monographs*, Suppl 17. Cambridge University Press, Cambridge.

Fenwick, P. (1993). Brain, mind and behaviour: some medico-legal aspects. *British Journal of Psychiatry*, **163**, 565–573.

Gardiner, J.M. & Parkin, A.J. (1990). Attention and recollective experience. *Memory and Cognition*, **18**, 579–583.

Gibbens, T.C.N., Palmer, C. & Prince, J. (1971). Mental health aspects of shoplifting. *British Medical Journal*, **iii**, 612–615.

Goodwin, D.W., Crane, J.B. & Guze, S.E. (1969). Phenomenological aspects of the alcoholic "blackout". *British Journal of Psychiatry*, **115**, 1033–1038.

Gruneberg, M., Morris, P. & Sykes, R. (1988). *Practical Aspects of Memory*. John Wiley, Chichester.

Gudjonsson, G.H. & MacKeith, J. (1983). A specific recognition deficit in case of homicide. *Medicine, Science and the Law*, **23**, 37–40.

Gudjonsson, G.H. & Shakleton, H. (1986). The pattern of scores on Raven's Matrices during "faking bad" and "non-faking" performance. *British Journal of Clinical Psychology*, **25**, 35–41.

Gudjonsson, G.H. & Taylor, P.J. (1985). Cognitive deficit in a case of retrograde amnesia. *British Journal of Psychiatry*, **147**, 715–718.

Guttmacher, M.S. (1955). *Psychiatry and the Law*. Grune & Stratton, New York.

Hodges, J.R. & Ward C.D. (1989). Observations during transient global amnesia: a behavioural and neuropsychological study of five cases. *Brain*, **112**, 595–620.

Hodges, J. & Warlow, C.P. (1990). The aetiology of transient global amnesia. *Brain*, **113**, 639–657.

Hopwood, J.S. & Snell, H.K. (1933). Amnesia in relation to crime. *Journal of Mental Science*, **79**, 27–41.

Horton, K.D., Smith S.A., Barghout, N.K. & Connolly, D.A. (1992). The use of indirect memory tests to assess malingered amnesia: a study of metamemory. *Journal of Experimental Psychology: General*, **121**, 326–351.

Howard, C. & d'Orbán, P.T. (1987). Violence in sleep: medico-legal issues and two case reports. *Psychological Medicine*, **17**, 915–925.

Hunter, I.M.L. (1964). *Memory*. Penguin, Harmondsworth.

Kales, A., Soldatos, C.R., Caldwell, A.B., Dales, J.D., Humphrey, F.J., Charney, D.S. & Schweitzer, P.K. (1980). Somnambulism. *Archives of General Psychiatry*, **37**, 1406–1410.

Kales, J.D., Kales, A., Soldatos, C.R., Caldwell, A.B., Charney, D.S. & Martin, E.D. (1980). Night terrors. *Archives of General Psychiatry*, **37**, 1413–1417.

Kanzer, M. (1939). Amnesia: a statistical study. *American Journal of Psychiatry*, **96**, 711–716.

Kapur, N. (1990). Transient epileptic amnesia: a clinically distinct form of neurological memory disorder. In H.J. Markowitsch (ed.), *Transient Global Amnesia and Related Disorders*. Hogrefe and Huber, Lewiston, NY.

Kapur, N., Ellison, D., Smith, M., McLellan, L. & Burrows, E.H. (1992). Focal retrograde amnesia following bilateral temporal lobe pathology: a neuropsychological and magnetic resonance study. *Brain*, **116**, 73–86.

Kapur, N., Young, A., Bateman, D. & Kennedy, P. (1989). Focal retrograde amnesia; a long-term clinical and neuropsychological follow-up. *Cortex*, **25**, 387–402.

Knox, S.J. (1968). Epileptic automatism and violence. *Medicine, Science and the Law*, **8**, 96–104.

Kopelman M.D. (1987a). Crime and amnesia: a review. *Behavioural Sciences and the Law*, **5**, 323–342.

Kopelman, M.D. (1987b). Amnesia: organic and psychogenic. *British Journal of Psychiatry*, **150**, 428–442.

Kopelman, M.D. (1994). The Autobiographical Memory Interview (AMI) in organic and psychogenic amnesia. *Memory*, **2**, 211–235.

Kopelman, M.D., Christensen, H., Puffett, A. & Stanhope, N. (1994a). The Great Escape: a neuropsychological study of psychogenic amnesia. *Neuropsychologia*, **32**, 675–691.

Kopelman, M.D., Green, R.E.A., Guinan, E.M., Lewis, P.D.R. & Stanhope, N. (1994b). The case of the amnesic intelligence officer. *Psychological Medicine* (in press).

Kopelman, M.D., Panayiotopoulos, C.P. & Lewis, P. (1994c). Transient epileptic amnesia differentiated from psychogenic "fugue": neuropsychological, EEG and PET findings. *Journal of Neurology, Neurosurgery and Psychiatry*, **57**, 1002–1004.

Kuehn, L.L. (1974). Looking down a gun barrel: person perception and violent crime. *Perceptual and Motor Skills*, **39**, 1159–1164.

Lancet (1978). Editorial: Factitious hypoglycaemia. *Lancet*, **i**, 1293.

Leitch, A. (1948). Notes on amnesia in crime for the general practitioner. *Medical Press*, **219**, 459–463.

Lennox, W.G. (1943). Amnesia, real and feigned. *American Journal of Psychiatry*, **99**, 732–743.

Lishman, W.A. (1968). Brain damage in relation to psychiatric disability after head injury. *British Journal of Psychiatry*, **114**, 373–410.

Lishman, W.A. (1987). *Organic Psychiatry*, 2nd edn. Blackwell, Oxford.

Loftus, E.F. (1979). *Eyewitness Testimony*. Harvard University Press, Cambridge, MA.

Lynch, B.E. & Bradford, J.M.W. (1980). Amnesia—its detection by psychophysiological measures. *Bulletin of the American Academy of Psychiatry and the Law*, **8**, 288–297.

Markowitsch, H.J., Calabrese, P., Haupts, M., Durwen, H.F., Liess, J. & Gehlen, W. (1994). Searching for the anatomical basis of retrograde amnesia. *Journal of Clinical and Experimental Neuropsychology* (in press).

Miller, J.W., Petersen, R.C., Metter, E.J., Millikan, C.H. & Yanagihara, T. (1987). Transient global amnesia: clinical characteristics and prognosis. *Neurology*, **37**, 733–737.

O'Connell, B.A. (1960). Amnesia and homicide. *British Journal of Delinquency*, **10**, 262–276.

Parfitt, D.N. & Gall, C.M.C. (1944). Psychogenic amnesia: the refusal to remember. *Journal of Mental Science*, **90**, 511–527.

Parwatikar, S.D., Holcomb, W.R. & Meninger, K.A. (1985). The detection of malingered amnesia in accused murderers. *Bulletin of the American Academy of Psychiatry and the Law*, **13**, 97–103.

Powell, G.E., Gudjonsson, G.H. & Mullen, P. (1983). Application of the guilty-knowledge technique in a case of pseudologia fantastica. *Personality and Individual Differences*, **4**, 141–146.

Russell, W.R. & Nathan, P.W. (1946). Traumatic amnesia. *Brain*, **69**, 280–300.

Sargant, W. & Slater, E. (1941). Amnesic syndromes in war. *Proceedings of the Royal Society of Medicine*, **34**, 757–764.

Scarlett, J.A., Mako, M.E., Rubenstein, A.H., Blix, P.M., Goldman, J., Horowitz, D.L., Tager, H., Jaspan, J.B., Stjemholm, M.R. & Olefsky, J.M. (1977). Factitious hypoglycaemia. *New England Journal of Medicine*, **297**, 1029–1032.

Schacter, D.L. (1986a). Amnesia and crime: how much do we really know? *American Psychologist*, **41**, 286–295.

Schacter, D.L. (1986b). On the relation between genuine and simulated amnesia. *Behavioral Sciences and the Law*, **4**, 47–64.

Schacter, D.L. (1986c). Feelings-of-knowing ratings distinguish between genuine and simulated forgetting. *Journal of Experimental Psychology: Learning, Memory and Cognition*, **12**, 30–41.

Schacter, D.L. & Crovitz, H.F. (1977). Memory function after closed head injury: a review of the quantitative research. *Cortex*, **13**, 150–176.

Schacter, D.L., Wang, P.L., Tulving, E. & Freeman, M. (1982). Functional retrograde amnesia: a quantitative case study. *Neuropsychologia*, **20**, 523–532.

Stengel, E. (1941). On the aetiology of the fugue states. *Journal of Mental Science*, **87**, 572–599.

Tanay, E. (1969). Psychiatric study of homicide. *American Journal of Psychiatry*, **125**, 252–258.

Taylor, P.J. & Kopelman, M. (1984). Amnesia for criminal offences. *Psychological Medicine*, **14**, 581–588.

Wells, G.L. & Loftus, E.F. (1984). *Eyewitness Testimony: Psychological Perspectives*. Cambridge University Press, Cambridge.

Wiggins, E.C. & Brandt, J. (1988). The detection of stimulated amnesia. *Law and Human Behaviour*, **12**, 57–78.

Wilson, G., Rupp. C. & Wilson, W.W. (1950). Amnesia. *American Journal of Psychiatry*, **106**, 481–485.

Yuille, J.C. (1987). The effects of alcohol and marijuana on eyewitness recall. Paper presented at the Conference on Practical Aspects of Memory, Swansea, UK (unpublished).

Yuille, J.C. & Cutshall, J.L. (1986). A case study of eye-witness memory of a crime. *Journal of Applied Psychology*, **71**, 291–301.

Section IV

Management of Memory Problems

Chapter 19

Management and Remediation of Memory Problems in Brain-Injured Adults

Barbara A. Wilson
MRC Applied Psychology Unit, Cambridge, UK

INTRODUCTION

BW: "Do you have a girlfriend?"
JB: "No, because I wouldn't recognise her if I saw her again"

The reply of the young man quoted above, who obviously has some insight into the nature of his memory difficulties, illustrates the isolation and loneliness experienced by many people whose memory has been impaired as a result of brain injury.

It needs emphasising that there are large numbers of people like J.B. in our society. Some 36% of people with severe head injury will have significant and permanent memory impairments. In the United Kingdom these figures reflect about 2500 new cases each year, and over four times that number in the USA.

Some 10% of people over the age of 65 years have dementia, with memory impairment an almost inevitable consequence. About 34% of people with multiple sclerosis have moderate or severe memory problems, as do 70% of people with AIDS and 10% of people with temporal lobe epilepsy. In addition, memory impairment is commonly seen after Korsakoff's syndrome and encephalitis, and is not uncommon after stroke, cerebral tumour, myocardial infarction, meningitis and carbon monoxide poisoning.

Despite these large numbers, and the severity of impairment experienced by people with brain damage, few will receive help in managing problems they will

Handbook of Memory Disorders. Edited by A.D. Baddeley, B.A. Wilson and F.N. Watts.
© 1995 John Wiley & Sons Ltd.

confront each day of their lives, few will be given guidance as to how to reduce the effect of their handicap on their everyday functioning.

Among neurologists, and many neuropsychologists working with these patients, the prevailing attitude seems to suggest that little or nothing can be done to alleviate the problems of brain-injured people. In contrast, relatives live in the hope, and sometimes indeed the expectation, that memory functioning can be restored if the right drug or relevant set of exercises can be administered.

Neither of these views is correct. Although it is a fact that there is no known way that lost memory functioning can be restored in patients with organic amnesia once the period of natural recovery is over, it is nevertheless true that patients and their families can be helped to cope with everyday difficulties they are likely to experience. The lives of brain-injured people can be made much more tolerable by teaching them, for example, to bypass certain problems or compensate for them, or use their residual skills more efficiently.

CONCERNS OF PATIENTS AND RELATIVES

In Chapter 17 of this volume, Howieson and Lezak provide an example of a patient seen for an evaluation of a recently developed "memory" impairment, the main symptom of which was "forgetting" to go to bed at night. The man's higher than usual level of nocturnal activity and agitation had concerned his neighbour who wrongly attributed the unusual behaviour to a poor memory. This erroneous explanation is not uncommon: relatives of language-impaired people may regard the impairment as "forgetting the meaning of words"; unilateral neglect may be described as "forgetting to look to the left"; and agnosia may be thought of as "forgetting what objects are used for". Howieson and Lezak describe how clinicians may differentiate between memory and other disorders.

Memory-impaired people typically show a normal (or nearly normal) short-term memory as measured by digit span or the recency effect in free recall, they have problems in learning and remembering new information, and experience a period of retrograde amnesia (Baddeley, 1990). Many will have additional cognitive problems such as poor attention or slow information processing, although some of them will present with a pure amnesic syndrome in which all cognitive abilities are intact except for delayed memory.

Organic memory impairment is usually diagnosed on the basis of performance on neuropsychological tests and will show up, for example, in poor scoring on tests of recall and recognition despite reasonable digit span. Patients and their relatives do not, however, complain about inability to perform these tests. They are much more likely to focus on difficulties that occur in daily living, the things that cause concern for not only memory-impaired people but also those with whom they come in contact. The mother of a young man with a pure amnesic syndrome described her son's problems in the following way:

He never remembers where the car is parked and gets embarrassed if he has to look in his book ... . He gets confused about arrangements with his friends. He double-books. For example, he records one appointment at home and then meets someone in the street and arranges another meeting with that person. He loses everything, pencils, his wallet, everything! It would be worse except I move things to obvious places. He never remembers what he has spent his money on and he forgets to carry out any plans he has made himself, like sorting out his videotapes.

In a series of answers to questionnaires prepared by Sunderland, Harris and Baddeley (1984) for head-injured people with memory impairment and their relatives, the most common problems reported by head-injured people themselves were:

- Inability to cope with a change in routine
- Having to check whether they had done something they meant to do
- Forgetting what they had been told
- Forgetting what they had just said
- Inability to follow the thread of a newspaper story
- Forgetting to tell someone something important
- Getting lost on a journey or walk they had been on only once or twice before
- Repeating something they had just said.

Problems most often reported by the relatives, when describing the head-injured people, were:

- Forgetting where they had put something
- Failing to recognise places they had been to before
- Rambling on about unimportant or irrelevant things
- Being unable to pick up a new skill
- Not finding a word on the tip-of-the-tongue
- Forgetting what happened yesterday
- Getting details mixed up
- Repeating a story or joke.

When a mother said of her son, "If he tells me that story about the greenhouse once more, I'll kill him!" she was reflecting what is perhaps the most distressing or most annoying characteristic of people with memory problems. Even those of us who see severely amnesic people for only a few hours each week can feel an increasing annoyance when the same story or phrase is repeated every two or three minutes. One patient, for example, says every few minutes that he has just woken up or just regained consciousness. He repeatedly interrupts conversations to inform the addressee of, what is to him, this important fact, thus making testing or therapy extremely difficult.

In addition to the frustration caused by repetition, relatives may fail to understand that some of the difficulties observed are a direct result of memory impairment. The wife of a man with a dense amnesia said, "I know he has problems remembering, but when I asked him to do the weeding in the garden he cut down the roses! That's not *memory*, is it?". Another characteristic that is difficult for relatives to understand is that the memory-impaired person can remember incidents or episodes from long ago yet cannot remember more recent events.

While some memory-impaired people may also be concerned about these difficulties, many of them will in fact have poor insight into the nature of their problems, thus causing them to underestimate the extent of their impairment (Sunderland, Harris & Baddeley, 1984; Wilson, Cockburn & Baddeley, 1989). The subjects in the Sunderland et al. study were living at home and their relatives' ratings of memory impairment correlated better with objective tests of memory than did those of the head-injured patients. Wilson and colleagues were looking at subjects attending a rehabilitation centre and they found little difference between the ratings of relatives and patients. However, ratings from therapists working at the centre showed a significant correlation with scores on an objective memory test whereas those from patients and relatives did not.

One area of concern to memory-impaired people is their fear of "going crazy". They may describe this as, "I'm losing my marbles" or "I don't want people to think I'm a nutter". Their interpretation of the fact that they are seeing a psychologist may be unduly fearful and reinforce their anxiety, so it is necessary to provide explanation and reassurance to allay such feelings. Explanations of this kind should always be accompanied by a written summary.

RECOVERY OF MEMORY FUNCTION AFTER BRAIN INJURY

Not surprisingly, memory-impaired people and their relatives exhibit much concern over the extent of improvements and the possibility of recovery, especially in the early stages after brain injury. When asked questions along these lines it is likely that most health service professionals hedge their bets, saying something that suggests that some improvement will take place but indicating that the extent of recovery remains unknown. Indeed, comparatively little is known about the long-term prognosis of memory disorders. On the one hand we have studies that show families reporting a high incidence of memory impairment continuing several years after the insult (e.g. Brooks, 1984; Oddy, 1984; Brooks, Campsie, Symington et al., 1987), while on the other hand we have studies showing significant recovery of memory functioning taking place during the first year after brain injury (Lezak, 1979). We know that one densely amnesic patient, H.M., did not show recovery or indeed improvement over a 30-year period (Scoville & Milner, 1957; Freed, Corkin & Cohen, 1987), and that another patient with a short-term memory impairment, T.B., showed a dramatic recovery at least two years after insult (Wilson & Baddeley, 1993). Victor, Adams and Collins (1989) found that 74% of a sample of 104 Korsakoff patients showed some degree of recovery over a 3 year period following admission, and 21% of their sample seemed to show a more or less complete recovery.

What can we say to those who ask us about improvement or recovery? The answer depends in part on the cause of the memory impairment. We would not expect changes for the better among people suffering from Alzheimer's or Huntington's disease, although it might be possible to slow down the rate of deterioration (Arkin, 1991, 1992). However, caution must be shown in our response to a direct question from a sufferer or carer because a lack of improvement does not necessarily mean that a patient with either of these diseases cannot learn some new skills or new information.

For patients in post-traumatic amnesia following head injury, we can expect considerable improvement and in some cases complete recovery. In a recent follow-up study of 54 brain-injured patients who were referred for memory therapy between the years 1979 and 1985 (29 with traumatic head injury, 10 with cerebral vascular accidents, 4 with encephalitis, 3 with Korsakoff's syndrome and 8 with other diagnoses), changes in memory functioning, dependence on aids and strategies, vocational outcome, and current social situations of the subjects were investigated (Wilson, 1991). Of the original group, seven had died (including two suicides), three could not be contacted, and one refused to participate in the study (although she supplied some information by letter). Thus 43 subjects were seen and reassessed.

Using the Rivermead Behavioural Memory Test (RBMT) (Wilson, Cockburn & Baddeley, 1985) as the measure of memory improvement, 13 subjects (30.2%) showed a fairly substantial improvement (3 or more screening points), 26 subjects (60%) showed little evidence of significant change since finishing formal rehabilitation, and 4 (9.3%) had declined. One of the last group had sustained a second head injury and another was in fact elderly, but there seemed to be no explanation for the deterioration in the memory of the other two who were both fairly young head-injured people.

Although only a third improved since the end of rehabilitation, many subjects had improved *during* rehabilitation. It was encouraging to find that most subjects were using more aids, strategies and techniques to compensate for their difficulties compared with the numbers they were using before and immediately at the end of rehabilitation. Furthermore, those subjects who were using six or more strategies were significantly more likely to be living independently (i.e in paid employment, living alone, or in full-time education) than those using less than six strategies ($\chi^2 = 10.87$, $p < 0.001$).

Most subjects including those who had improved, were left with residual memory deficits so the term "recovery" should be avoided. Nevertheless, the long-term prognosis was less bleak than anticipated several years earlier. Only 9 of the 43 were in long-term care while 15 were in paid employment. Most were coping better than when last seen. However, the figures should not hide the fact that many individuals in the group were lonely, unhappy, and still very handicapped by their brain injury and memory impairment.

HELPING MEMORY-IMPAIRED PEOPLE AND THEIR FAMILIES

While sensitivity to the fears and anxieties of families of brain-injured people is required on the part of professional health workers at all times, it is particularly necessary when the family of a head-injured person comes to memory therapy for the first time. In these very early stages, when families will be wondering about short-term and long-term developments, it is essential to keep all doors open and not close them—as once happened in the case of a mother visiting a psychiatrist after her son had attempted suicide by carbon monoxide poisoning. The psychiatrist, when referring to the son, told the mother, "What you see is what you get. He won't change from how he is now." In fact that young man went on to make good progress and regained some memory functioning over a period of a year or so. Although he continued to have significant problems, the young man learned to use external aids that enabled him to compensate very efficiently. His anxiety and depression lessened as a result of attending a weekly memory group, he managed to pass a public examination, regain his driving licence, and obtain a place on a college course. His parents were convinced these changes took place because of the individual and group therapy he was offered outside the psychiatrist's province. Perhaps a more influential effect upon improvement in this case was the indirect therapy offered by the provision of information, explanations, problem-solving strategies and indeed hope for this traumatised family.

Listening, understanding, and providing information may be key factors in encouraging families to cope with difficulties they will face after one of their members becomes memory-impaired. This will remain true even in circumstances where memory impairment has not improved despite all the efforts of professional therapists. A useful reference on this topic, together with an important list of addresses of some of the support groups available to memory-impaired people, is provided by Wearing (1992).

Obviously we cannot rest back on any laurels awarded for a sympathetic ear. Emotional well-being in the patient and the family, however desirable and helpful, is an insufficient goal on its own for memory therapists whose brief is to design programmes suited to the individual needs of each patient. Patients are going to need rehabilitation that will enable them to bypass or compensate for the practical, everyday problems they will have to confront as a result of memory impairment.

When first seeing a patient who requires memory therapy, a good approach is to begin by interviewing the patient and one or more relatives. Ask about the precipitating accident or illness and question them about resultant problems as they are manifested in everyday life. Also ask them what they hope to achieve as a result of the referral. Questioning along these lines usually opens up an opportunity to explain that, although it may not be possible to restore or retrain memory functioning lost through certain accidents and illnesses, there may well be actions we can take that will help the patient manage his or her everyday life more successfully.

The nature of these actions will depend on a number of factors that include the nature and severity of the deficit (whether, for example, the memory impairment is due to a degenerative condition), the presence or absence of additional cognitive impairments, the current social and vocational situation of the patient, and the environmental demands of the patient's lifestyle.

A neuropsychological assessment will provide a picture of the patient's cognitive strengths and weakness (see Chapter 17 by Howieson and Lezak). This should be supplemented by a more direct assessment of everyday problems using procedures such as interviews, questionnaires, rating scales, checklists, memory diaries and direct observation (see Chapter 16 by Godfrey and Knight).

Combining information from different assessments will highlight problems that need tackling, thus enabling realistic treatment programmes to be designed in such a way that they are both relevant to the life of the patient and match the neuropsychological demands suggested by cognitive test results. Of course treatment programmes should be within the capabilities of the patient. We should not, for example, expect memory-impaired people to remember the arguments made in a previous session about the value of using external memory aids. Neither should we confuse patients having visuospatial difficulties by employing spatial terms when teaching routes. Those who are very ataxic will not be able to write quickly or even at all. People with deep dyslexia will have problems comprehending verbs, prepositions and abstract nouns. The message here is that our own treatment programmes should aim to bypass those areas that might rely on strengths or aptitudes that are themselves damaged in any particular patient.

Having identified particular problem areas and assessed cognitive functioning, a decision has to be made as to which of the problems should be tackled. Apart from the provisos listed immediately above, there is no right or wrong way of doing this. However, treatment planners will be influenced by the wishes of the patient, relatives and other staff members. Some patients are quite specific about the kind of help they want: for example, "I can't remember my partners' names when playing bridge" or "I always forget where I have parked the car". Others are more vague and might say something like "It's just everything, I can't remember a thing." Yet others will deny they have memory problems: "There's nothing wrong with my memory, it's people like you who are destroying my confidence." Relatives will also vary according to the clarity or vagueness of their descriptions of problems.

Future plans and placement will also influence the choice of problems to be tackled. For people planning to return to university the choice might involve teaching study techniques to improve verbal recall (see Wilson, 1987a) or teaching the use of one of the electronic personal organisers (see Chapter 22). For someone going into long-term care the focus might be on teaching how to transfer from a wheelchair to an ordinary chair, or teaching the location of the toilet.

Another question concerns the number of problems to be tackled at any one time. This will depend on factors such as the patient's general intellectual level, the level of insight into physical and mental status, degree of motivation, the amount of involvement of others in the programme, and of course time available. For a person with a pure amnesia, good intellectual functioning, good insight and high motivation, whose family is willing to assist, then it might be possible to work on four to six problems at any one time. With someone who is of poor intellectual functioning, with little insight or motivation and without family support, tackling one problem at a time is more appropriate.

When planning a treatment programme to overcome these problems, the present author usually follows a behavioural approach, using the steps involved in behaviour modification programmes (see Wilson, 1992, for a more detailed discussion). Working in this way provides a structure for the psychologist or therapist when attempting to get to grips with a difficult area: it enables them to measure the problem(s) and to determine whether goals have been achieved. There is a saying that "structure reduces anxiety", and this is true not only for brain-injured patients but also for those treating them.

The behavioural structure is adaptable to a wide range of patients, problems and settings, the goals are small and specific; treatment and assessment are inseparable, and there is continuous monitoring of results. Evidence that this approach is effective has been supplied by Wilson (1987a) and Moffat (1989). The number of steps in a behavioural programme may vary but can include as many as eleven:

1. Define the problem.
2. (An operational definition may be required).
3. Set goals (may need both short- and long-term).
4. Measure the problem (take baseline).
5. Consider reinforcers or motivators.
6. Plan treatment.
7. Begin treatment.
8. Monitor progress.
9. Evaluate.
10. Change if necessary.
11. Plan for generalisation.

Examples of successful treatment programmes using this structure can be found in Wilson (1987b, 1992).

GENERAL GUIDELINES FOR HELPING PEOPLE WITH MEMORY DISORDERS

As well as dealing directly with specific problems, there are more general guidelines to follow in the rehabilitation of people with disorders of memory.

When trying to rehabilitate memory-impaired people it may be wise to begin by sorting out indirect problems such as those connected with anxiety, depression and social isolation, all of which are relatively common (Wilson, 1991). Relaxation therapy such as that recommended by Butler (1985) may be useful in reducing anxiety in brain-injured people. Even if memory problems are severe enough to prevent the person remembering having completed the exercises, the beneficial effects of relaxation may remain. Relaxation audiocassette tapes can be bought or made for each patient so that the necessity to remember disappears. A word of caution is required when practising tense-and-release exercises (such as those advocated by Bernstein and Borkovec, 1973) with some brain-injured people, particularly those with motor difficulties. Tensing muscles may cause a spasm or increase spasticity. It is best to discuss the desirability of tense-and-release exercises with a physiotherapist treating the patient or, alternatively, look for another form of relaxation such as that recommended by Ost (1987) or those described by Clark (1989). Attendance at memory group sessions may also help to reduce anxiety (Evans and Wilson, 1992).

Depression can impair memory functioning in those without brain injury (see Chapter 12) and may well exacerbate memory difficulties in people with organic memory impairment. It is possible that cognitive behavioural therapy approaches such as those employed by Beck (1976) with non-brain-injured people would be appropriate for those with brain injury—although there do not appear to be any studies reporting this.

Psychotherapy, on the other hand, is a well-established intervention with brain-injured people. Prigatano et al. (1986) developed a detailed approach to group psychotherapy with brain-injured patients. They also advocate individual psychotherapy using principles from the school of Jung. Jackson and Gouvier (1992) provide descriptions and guidelines for group psychotherapy with brain-injured adults and their families.

Social isolation is common in memory-impaired people and their families (Talbot, 1989). Wearing (1992) describes some of the reasons for this. She points out:

> The social network of the family often falls away because a memory-impaired person may not be able to engage in normal chats, and in any case, forgets visits and perhaps forgets people. The individual may not be able to go out alone without getting lost or, with attendant behaviour problems, it may be impossible to go to social settings. So isolation is a very common complaint from individual and family. (p. 284)

Wearing recommends setting up a self-help group and provides suggestions and information on how to do this. Running memory group sessions as part of a general rehabilitation programme can achieve similar effects. Wilson and Moffat (1992) describe various groups for patients, and Moffat (1989) reports on a group for relatives of people with dementia. Psychotherapy groups can achieve the same ends. Jackson and Gouvier (1992) provide guidelines on running psychotherapy groups with brain-injured people.

Families will of course be affected more directly by the memory problems experienced by the impaired family member. Here they will need guidance as to how to encourage that member to encode, store and recall information. Such guidance is described in detail in Wilson (1992, 1993). A simple booklet is produced by the National Head Injuries Association entitled *Memory Problems After Head Injury* (Wilson, 1989). The main points to follow in these guidelines are as follows:

1. Simplify information you give to the person affected whose memory is impaired.
2. Reduce the amount of information supplied at any one time.
3. Ensure there is minimal distraction.
4. Make sure information is understood—by asking the person to repeat it in his or her own words.
5. Encourage the person to link or associate information with material that is already known.
6. Try to ensure processing at a deeper level—by encouraging the person to ask questions.
7. Use the "little and often" rule (Baddeley, 1992).
8. Make sure learning occurs in different contexts to avoid context specificity and enhance generalisation.

Kapur's (1991) manual *Managing Your Memory* provides further guidelines for relatives and patients, while Berg, Koning-Haanstra and Deelman (1991) describe guidelines they produced for a group of people referred for memory rehabilitation. They gave each patient an information book containing the following rules:

1. Use external aids whenever possible.
2. Pay more attention.
3. Spend more time.
4. Repeat information you wish to remember.
5. Make associations.
6. Organise material.
7. Link input and retrieval situations.

Berg and colleagues found a significantly greater improvement on objective memory tests 4 months after training in the experimental group than in a control group whose treatment consisted of drilling and repetition.

ERRORLESS LEARNING IN REHABILITATION

In the 1960s, Terrace taught pigeons to distinguish between a red and a green key (Terrace, 1963, 1966). For pigeons this is a difficult discrimination to make, yet during learning the pigeons made virtually no errors. This "errorless discrimination learning" was employed by Sidman and Stoddard (1967) who taught children with mental handicaps to make what was for them a difficult discrimination, namely to distinguish circles from ellipses. Again few or no errors were made during learning. Is it possible that this principle can be used in memory rehabilitation? We know that amnesic subjects show normal or almost normal learning on some tasks, even though they are unaware they have learned anything. This is, of course, known as "implicit learning" and has been the topic of much research (e.g. Brooks & Baddeley 1976; Graf & Schacter, 1985; Schacter, 1987). Glisky and Schacter (1987, 1989) tried to use the implicit learning abilities of amnesic subjects to teach them computer technology. Although some success was achieved it was at the expense of considerable time and effort. This and other attempts to build on the relatively intact skills of amnesic subjects have been disappointing so far. One reason for failures and anomalies could be that once amnesic subjects have made an error that error gets repeated. If procedural or implicit learning involves a simple incrementing of habit whenever a response is formed, then an erroneous response will strengthen the error, making trial-and-error learning a slow and laborious process.

Alan Baddeley and the present author posed the question: "Do amnesic subjects learn better when prevented from making errors during the learning process?" (Baddeley & Wilson, 1994). We tested 16 patients with severe memory disorders, 16 young and 16 elderly controls. We gave each subject two lists of five-letter words (five words in each list for patients and ten for controls). One list was presented in an errorful learning way and the other in an errorless way, with the order and condition counter balanced across subjects. In the *errorful* condition subjects were told, "I am thinking of a five-letter word beginning with 'br'. Can you guess what it might be?". After three incorrect responses (or 25 seconds), in which the subject might say "brain", "bread" and "brown", the tester said, "No, good guesses, but the word is 'bring'. Please write that down." This was repeated for the remaining words, after which two further trials were conducted. So altogether the subject wrote down each word three times; the incorrect guesses were not written down. In the *errorless* condition the subject was told, "I am thinking of a five-letter word beginning with 'br' and the word is 'bring'. Please write that down." Again there were three trials. Thus in one condition the subject was generating guesses while in the other only correct responses were produced. Words and conditions were counterbalanced across subjects. This was followed in both conditions by a further nine test trials over a 30-minute period. Each trial involved cueing with the first two letters and correcting any mistakes.

Of the 16 amnesic subjects, every single one of them recalled more words in the errorless condition than in the errorful. This suggests that learning is indeed better when the subject in not allowed to guess during the learning process. The young controls were almost at ceiling in both conditions while the elderly controls' scores fell between those of the young controls and the amnesic subjects. Looking at individual subjects, 10 of the 16 elderly controls did better under the errorless condition and 6 did better under the errorful.

Since then we have conducted several single-case studies with amnesic subjects, comparing errorful and errorless learning. These later studies included (a) teaching an agnosic man to recognise pictures, (b) helping a stroke patient to learn names of people, (c) assisting a Korsakoff patient to programme an electronic aid, and (d) teaching a head-injured man the names of his therapists, items of orientation, and general knowledge. In each case errorless learning resulted in superior performance to that of trial-and-error (Wilson, Baddeley, Evans & Shiel, 1994).

Our continuing work on errorless learning leads us to conclude that it is far from being a perfect tool for remembering. While it is true that results have been encouraging, they do not match those reported by Terrace in the 1960s. In order to achieve better results we have begun to incorporate other principles from learning theory and memory therapy into our programmes. These include strategies such as not teaching more than one piece of information at a time, and the method of expanding rehearsal. It remains to be seen whether other people such as children or those with progressive disorders such as Alzheimer's disease can benefit from errorless learning. Will they be able to learn names, practical skills, routes, vocabulary and so forth using errorless learning in combination with some of these other principles and strategies?

ENVIRONMENTAL ADAPTATIONS

One of the simplest ways to help people with memory impairment is to arrange the environment so that they rely less on memory. Examples include labelling doors for a person who cannot remember which room is which, or labelling cupboards in the kitchen or beds in a hospital ward. Other examples include drawing arrows or lines to indicate routes round a building, or positioning objects so they cannot be missed or forgotten (e.g. tying a front door key to a waist belt). Making rooms safer for confused, brain-injured people is also possible by altering the environment.

Sometimes it is possible to avoid irritating or problematic behaviours by identifying and then changing the environmental triggers of the behaviour. For example, people who constantly ask the same question may be responding to something said to them such as a greeting or request.

There are a few reports of environmental changes in the management of memory problems. Harris (1980), for example, describes a geriatric unit where the rate of incontinence was reduced by the simple strategy of painting all lavatory doors a different colour from other doors, thus making them easier to distinguish.

Lincoln (1989) reports how one woman was able to keep track of whether she had taken her medication by placing a chart next to the bottle of tablets rather than in another room. Lincoln also provides suggestions for further environmental adaptations. She notes that most hospital staff wear name badges that may be too small for elderly people to read, and contain surnames rather than the first names that are used more frequently on the ward.

The most densely amnesic person seen by the present author is C.W., a musician who developed herpes simplex encephalitis in 1985. The only strategies that seem to help this man are environmental adaptations. He has an unusual form of epilepsy that takes the form of jerking movements and belching. These occur with greater frequency when C.W. is under stress or agitated. A behavioural analysis undertaken by Avi Schmueli (personal communication) showed that the seizures were far more likely to occur when there was a change in activity (for example, when changing from one test to another during assessment), or when an additional person entered the room. Although it will not be possible or indeed ethical to prevent all such changes in activity or personnel, some changes could be introduced to minimise the frequency of this man's seizures.

Because C.W. was unable to remember any of the people involved in his care, he considered them all to be strangers and disliked being treated informally by them as though they were well known to him. Consequently, he was not called by his first name as was usual with long-stay patients. Demonstrations of affection also caused him fear and distress. One nurse, for example, who had known C.W. for four years, went on holiday for two weeks and on returning she approached C.W. to give him a hug. He saw what was for him a total stranger bear down upon him with open arms and panicked. Again, a more formal approach can reduce the number of occasions resulting in panic.

C.W. also repeats certain phrases hundreds of times in the course of each day, the most frequent stating that he has just that moment woken up. Every few minutes during a conversation or assessment he says something along the lines of, "This is the first time I've been awake, this is the first taste I've had, the first time I've seen anything or heard anything. It's like being dead. I don't remember you coming into the room but now for the first time, I can see." Sympathising with these statements or trying to offer explanations seems to increase his agitation and cause an escalation of the number of repetitions. Distracting him by introducing another topic of conversation results in calmer behaviour.

For people with severe intellectual deficits or progressive deterioration or very dense amnesia, environmental adaptations may be the best we can offer to enable them to cope and reduce some of their confusion and frustration. Few studies have discussed ways in which environments can be designed to help people with severe memory impairment, although it would seem to be a fruitful area for psychologists, engineers, architects and designers to join forces.

EXTERNAL MEMORY AIDS

As Kapur discusses external memory aids in some detail in Chapter 22 of this volume, and Glisky provides an account of the use of computers in memory rehabilitation in Chapter 23, only a brief account will be given in this section.

External aids help people to remember by using systems to access or record information. Harris (1992) points out that there are two major kinds of external memory aid. The first are those that enable us to access internally stored information, such as a timer to remind us to check something in the oven; and these are not very helpful for people with memory impairment who cannot remember what it is they should remember when the cue sounds. The second kind are those that record information externally, and are more useful for memory-impaired people.

All of us have used external aids at one time or another. They include diaries, notebooks, lists, alarm clocks, watches, wall charts, calendars and tape recorders. Some people with memory problems may resist external aids, claiming they do not wish to become dependent on them, or that they want their own memory to do the work. Such resistance should be discouraged because it is important to use anything that will aid memory. It should be pointed out that people with good memories use external aids and that in fact there is no evidence to suggest that using them prevents or slows down recovery of memory; the opposite is likely to be nearer the truth.

Use of a wide range of external aids should be encouraged until a selection that suits the individual is found. Examples of how such aids have helped people with memory impairment are cited below.

One woman who could not find her way round a rehabilitation centre dictated directions on to a mircocassette and would listen to this when she needed to find a ward or particular therapy department. A man with Alzheimer's disease who frequently wandered out of hospital was given a bleeper that was attached to his wrist. This sounded every time he left the ward and alerted hospital staff that he was leaving. Although introduced for the benefit of hospital staff, it began to act as a reminder to the man who would then turn back to the ward when he heard the bleep. In the third example a young man was given a timer as well as a notebook. Previously the man would forget to refer to his notebook but when combined with the alarm he checked his notes.

Davis and Binks (1983) used a small card the size of a credit card for a Korsakoff patient. On one side was the man's name and address and on the other was a written explanation as to how to interact with the man. When the Korsakoff patient met strangers he showed them the card, thus enabling them to understand his problems.

Wilson (1992) describes how an aphasic man used a visual symbol system to refer to the past and future, and she also provides an example of a pictorial external memory aid to help an aphasic woman remember how to transfer from her wheelchair to an ordinary chair.

Sometimes a very sophisticated system can be developed with memory aids. J.C. is a young man with pure amnesic syndrome following a haemorrhage when he was a university student. He lives alone and is self-employed making seats for cane chairs. He is able to function independently because he uses a number of external aids very efficiently. One of these is a Dictaphone on which he records ongoing information at frequent intervals during the day. In the evening he listens to the tape and transcribes information he considers to be important into a journal. He also uses a watch with an alarm, a personal nonelectronic organiser, a series of Post-It (sticky back) notes, a menu chart to ensure he does not eat the same thing several days running, and a number of other strategies.

J.C. is exceptionally adept at compensating for his severe memory difficulties. He says (personal communication) "I try to make the system foolproof. It's like a web, it's hard for anything to slip through the system. If I miss it with one thing, I'll pick it up with another. I've individualised the system, it's constantly developing and I'm constantly refining and correcting it."

Most people, of course, are not so well organised and proficient as J.C., and many of the aids alluded to above are too complicated for them to use. A recent development that looks promising for large numbers of memory-impaired people is the NeuroPage (Hersh and Treadgold, 1992). NeuroPage is a simple and portable paging system with a screen that can be attached to a belt. Larry Treadgold, the engineer father of a head-injured son, and Neil Hersh, a neuropsychologist, combined their skills to produce a programmable messaging system that utilises an arrangement of microcomputers linked to a conventional computer memory and, by telephone, to a paging company.

The scheduling of reminders or cues for each individual is entered into the computer and from then on no further human interfacing is necessary. On the appropriate date and time, "NeuroPage accesses the user's data files, determines the reminder to be delivered, transmits the information by modem to the terminal where the reminder is converted and transmitted as a wireless radio signal to only that receiver corresponding to the particular user. The user is alerted to an incoming reminder by a flashing light emitting diode and an audible 'chirp'. The reminder is graphically displayed on the screen of the receiver" (p. 7). Once the message appears, users are requested to telephone a person or an answer service to confirm the message. Without this confirmation, the message is repeated.

Users of NeuroPage can control everything with one rather large button, easy to press even for those having motor difficulties. It avoids most of the problems of existing aids. It is highly portable, unlike many computers. It has an audible alarm that can be adapted to vibrate if required, together with an accompanying explanatory message, unlike many watch alarms. It is not embarrassing for the majority of users and indeed may convey prestige. Perhaps the biggest advantage of the NeuroPage is that once it has been programmed it is easy to use. Most other systems require considerable time for memory-impaired people to learn how to handle them.

Remembering to use an external aid is, in itself, a memory task, so problems will arise for most people with impaired memory functioning. Those who seem best able to get round these difficulties and use the aids spontaneously are those with a pure amnesic syndrome, such as J.C. Unfortunately, most memory-impaired people have additional deficits and must be taught at some length how to use compensations.

In addition to the suggestions provided by Kapur and Glisky in this volume, Sohlberg and Mateer (1989), Wilson (1992) and Zencius, Wesolowski, Krankowski and Berke (1991) describe certain ways of teaching the use of such aids.

In the long-term follow-up study (Wilson, 1991) mentioned earlier, it was found that most subjects were using more aids, strategies and techniques to compensate for their difficulties, compared with the numbers they were using before and immediately at the end of rehabilitation. Of the 44 people for whom information was available, 38 of them were using compensations. The remaining six who were not using anything were all in long-term care. A further three people in long-term care were using memory compensations. Those using six or more aids, strategies or techniques were significantly more likely to be independent (i.e. in paid employment or living alone or in full-time education) than those using five or less ($\chi^2 = 10.87$, $p < 0.0001$).

Table 19.1 provides information on the use of memory compensations by these 44 people at follow-up. The list includes internal memory strategies which will be discussed in the next section.

INTERNAL MEMORY STRATEGIES

Harris (1992) identified two kinds of internal strategies, those that are learned naturally and those that can be defined as artificial mnemonics. The former include the tendency for adults to recall the last few items first when asked for free recall of a word list, and concentrating on items not recalled previously when attempting to learn a list of words. This may seem an obvious thing to do, after all people would not want to waste time and effort remembering things they had already learned. Children, however, although they show a recency effect, do not adopt the strategy of spending more time on previously failed items until they are between 7 and 9 years of age (Masur, McIntyre & Flavell, 1973). Harris (1992) suggests that we all use a multitude of natural memory strategies which are not normally thought of as memory *aids* because they are so much part of our normal memory skills.

Artificial mnemonics are verbal and visual aids employed to assist learning. They include sayings, rhymes or drawings that are employed by individuals when they want to remember certain things. For example, it is common for people to use an artificial mnemonic to help them remember the number of days in each calendar month. In Britain and America this is typically a rhyme ("Thirty days has September... etc"). In other parts of the world, knuckles of the hand are used to remind people of the longer months of the year and the dips between

Table 19.1 Memory Compensations (Wilson, 1991)

Compensation	Number of people reporting using this at follow-up	Compensation	Number of people reporting using this at follow-up
Notebooks/notes	29	Dictaphone or tape recorder	8
Mental retracing	28		
Wall calendars/ wall charts	25	Making associations	8
		First-letter mnemonics	3
Lists	25		
Alarm clocks	23	Personal organisers	2
Asking others to remind	22	Notes in special places	2
Watch with date	21	Rhymes	1
Appointments diary	19	Use of daily timetable	1
Leaving objects in unusual place	17		
		Pleasantness rating	1
Alphabetic searching	17	Chunking	1
Visual imagery	12	Tying knot in handkerchief	1
Writing on hand	9		

knuckles the shorter months. Rhymes can help us remember dates ("In 1492 Columbus sailed the ocean blue"). First-letter mnemonics can help us remember other information we might regard as important; for example, the first letters of each of the following words are the same as those of the cranial nerves: "On Old Olympus Towering Top, a Finn and German Dance and Hop". Such first-letter mnemonics are among the most widely used internal strategies by students (Gruneberg, 1973; Rawles, 1978).

Other verbal methods include turning numbers into words and the "story method". The latter involves creating a story incorporating information to be remembered. Crovitz (1979), who used this method with brain-injured people to improve their recall, provided a story that began something like the following: "The first word is 'airplane' and you can remember that anyway you like. The second word is 'giraffes' because the airplane was full of giraffes. The third word is 'bologna' because the giraffes were all eating bologna sausage". The story continued until there were ten words to remember. The present author has employed this method with control and memory-impaired subjects (Wilson 1987a) and found both groups remembered significantly more words using the story method than they did using three other mnemonic strategies or no strategy at all. One drawback with the story method, however, is that it is difficult to apply to everyday-life material. (A colleague who wanted to remember the way from St Paul's Cathedral to Liverpool Street Station in London had no map and nothing to write with, so when somebody gave him directions that involved going to Cannon Street, Victoria Street, Threadneedle Street and Broad Street, he made up the following: "A *cannon* was fired for *Queen Victoria's* birthday. She was *threading a needle* to do her mending before going *abroad*.")

Turning numbers into words in order to make the numbers more meaningful can make remembering them easier. Baddeley (1993) describes how this method can be used to remember the value of "pi" to the first 20 decimal places. Each number is converted into a word with the number of letters in each word representing the number itself. Words are arranged as a poem entitled *PIE*:

> *I wish I could determine pi*
> *Eureka cried the great inventor*
> *Christmas pudding, Christmas pie*
> *Is the problem's very centre*

This is decoded back into numbers, giving 3.14159265358979323846. Similarly, telephone or card numbers can be remembered, as the following illustrates: "Working with our small, elegant company" represents the telephone number 743577.

Visual mnemonics have been employed for many centuries (Yates, 1966), and have subsequently been adapted for use in memory therapy. One commonly used mnemonic is the simple procedure of turning a word or name into a picture. "Neil Kinnock", for example, can be drawn as a kneeling king knocking. Although you should not expect an amnesic person to use this method spontaneously, it is useful for teaching a few names of staff, neighbours and friends to even severely amnesic patients. Gruneberg, Sykes and Hammond (1991) used it with people who had developmental learning difficulties. The value in the method is that people learn quicker using it than they do when relying upon repetition or rote rehearsal. (See Wilson (1987a) for research findings concerning this procedure.)

It is important to ensure that drawings are not ambiguous. The author once tried to teach a memory-impaired man the name of his social worker, which was Mary Thorne, by drawing a picture of a merry thorn. The man looked at the picture carefully, understanding what was required of him. However, when next asked the name of the social worker he closed his eyes, thought about the drawing and replied confidently, "Gay Holly".

A more sophisticated version of visual imagery to learn names is to use the face–name association procedure. This involves four stages:

1. Selecting a distinctive feature of the person's face (e.g. large ears)
2. Transforming the name to one or more common nouns (e.g. "Mr Crosley" could be imagined as a cross leaf or a leaf on a cross)
3. Linking the distinctive feature with the transformed name (e.g. imagining the cross leaf sticking out from large ears)
4. When needing to remember the person's name, searching the face for the distinctive feature to be reminded of the image which should help recall of the name.

Although research with control subjects has shown this method works best when all stages are followed (McCarty, 1980), most memory-impaired people with whom the present author works find it too complicated.

One method which is useful for improving recall of written information is PQRST. This is an acronym for "Preview, Read, Question, State and Test" which comes from the field of study techniques. Robinson (1970) was probably the first person to write about it. A similar technique is known as SQR3 for "Survey, Question, Read, Recall, Review". In practice the stages followed are virtually identical. Wilson (1987a) describes a number of studies comparing rote rehearsal with PQRST. In each case PQRST was the superior method. However, none of the subjects in the 1991 long-term follow-up study were using the method spontaneously, although several had been taught the method during rehabilitation 5–12 years earlier.

Other mnemonic systems are described by Yates (1966), Wilson (1987a) and Moffat (1992).

Reasons for some degree of success when using mnemonics, particularly with people whose memory is not severely impaired, are probably due to the following:

- They encourage a deeper level of processing. Craik and Lockhart (1972) demonstrated that deeper processing resulted in better recall.
- Previously isolated items are integrated with one another (Bower, 1972).
- They provide inbuilt retrieval cues in the form of initial letters, locations or pegs.

There is considerable misunderstanding about the value of mnemonics in memory therapy. Some people think that memory-impaired people have been taught to use mnemonics and then apply them in novel situations, although there is in fact very little evidence that this occurs. To avoid misunderstanding, it needs to be stressed that mnemonics are useful for *teaching* new information and that they are used by relatives, teachers, psychologists and therapists to enable learning on the part of the memory-impaired person.

When using mnemonics only one thing at a time should be taught. It is of little use expecting memory-impaired people to learn several pieces of information at once. Individual styles and preferences should be taken into account, and, as with other techniques or aids, we must plan for generalisation if there is to be any chance of a particular subject using the strategy in situations other than the one in which it has been taught.

In the long-term follow-up study (Wilson, 1991) described above, many of the subjects interviewed were using mnemonics and other internal strategies. As can be seen in Table 19.1, 28 reported using mental retracing, 17 used alphabetic searching, 12 visual imagery, eight making associations, three reported using first-letter mnemonics, and one said he made up rhymes.

West (Chapter 20 this volume) also discusses the use of internal strategies and mnemonics, with elderly people.

GROUP TREATMENTS FOR MEMORY-IMPAIRED PEOPLE

As noted above, some of the emotional consequences of brain injury and memory impairment may be reduced by group treatment. Social relationships can develop within groups, and people may sometimes be more likely to imitate their peers who are using compensations.

Some memory-impaired people believe they are losing their sanity and this fear may be alleviated by observing that there are others with similar difficulties. Memory groups have face validity: participants (and their relatives) believe such treatment is effective and this may have indirect therapeutic value. Furthermore, it is possible to ensure that each member of the group succeeds at something, by adjusting the degree of task difficulty. For people used to failure it is no bad thing to provide some element of success. Memory groups are also educative for the therapists running them—it is possible to see which particular problems arise in a group setting, how different people cope in different ways, and which solutions are effective for which people.

There are, of course, disadvantages to memory groups. Participants can imitate bad habits as well as good. Some patients "play up" to an audience. Their behaviour may become more disruptive. Others, who are distractible, may become even more distractible in a group setting and some patients are just too shy or introverted to take part in the group. On the whole, however, the author has found that both brain-injured people and therapists enjoy memory groups which can be great fun.

Although greater numbers of patients can be treated in groups, it would be wrong to introduce them at the *expense* of essential individualised treatment, for it is only in the latter that strategies, use of aids, and certain problem-solving techniques can be taught adequately and specifically related to the needs of each individual. The best way forward would seem to lie in encouraging both individualised and group treatment.

Evans and Wilson (1992) found that anxiety and depression decreased in some brain-injured people following attendance at a weekly memory group. The group was also useful in developing social relationships. These were particularly in evidence in the 15-minute tea break which provided patients with an opportunity to talk informally about their experiences of memory difficulties, seeking and sharing advice on coping with specific problems, and exchanging telephone numbers. Also, group sessions enabled individuals to try out their own coping styles.

Two members of the group attended sessions at a day centre for head-injured people on the day before the memory group met. One of these was a 40-year-old woman with relatively mild problems and the other was an 18-year-old man with severe and wide-ranging cognitive problems. The woman assisted the young man in a number of ways, including a check to see that his homework for the memory group was completed the day before the group meeting. It is likely that the informal interaction that went on between the two of them in group situations benefited both of them socially and cognitively. In our memory group sessions we spent time discussing how we could solve individuals' problems, we role-played and practised explaining the nature of memory impairments and engaged in practising various aids and strategies. Each session ended with a memory game that proved to be the most popular if not the most important activity. We did not expect memory games or exercises to improve memory functioning but provided them because many of our memory-impaired subjects *believed* they had a beneficial effect on memory, and this in itself creates a positive attitude towards memory therapy. More importantly perhaps, these games were enjoyable and, with a little engineering, each member of the group achieved some success in front of peers.

Memory functioning *per se* does not seem to improve as a result of experiences in memory groups. However, as indicated above, this is not the main purpose of memory groups—or indeed any memory rehabilitation (although Steingass et al., 1994, found some improvement in the memory of alcoholic subjects undergoing training in groups). The purpose of a memory group is to increase the use of memory compensations and to decrease the emotional side-effects of memory impairment. The Evans and Wilson (1992) study found a significant increase in the overall use of memory aids and strategies as well as a reduction in clinical levels of anxiety and depression for some patients. In the words of one patient, "Being with people who understand and don't ask strange questions all the time is smashing."

Other memory groups have been reported. Wilson and Moffat (1992) describe inpatient and outpatient memory groups for people with head injuries, strokes, encephalitis and anoxia. Group membership consisted of four to six people of varying ages and aetiologies. Topics covered in sessions included work orientation, discussions of problem-solving strategies, and practice in using external and internal strategies.

Moffat (1989) also describes a support group he ran for relatives of confused elderly people for a period of ten weeks. Relatives in this group showed greater improvement in health as measured by the General Health Questionnaire than did relatives in a control group. In contrast, Zarit, Zarit and Reever (1982) found relatives involved in memory groups for confused elderly people became more distressed as a result of attending groups. Perhaps this was because they were too openly confronted by the extent of the problems of their elderly relatives. Moffat saw relatives separately and focused on providing information and compensatory strategies, so it is possible that these relatives were better prepared for the realisation of the magnitude of some of the problems.

Another kind of group treatment is "reality orientation" (RO). Designed originally for use with confused elderly people, some of its exercises are now used in groups consisting of younger brain-injured people. RO was initially designed to meet the sensory and emotional needs of long-stay patients by encouraging nursing assistants to spend more time with them, to change staff attitudes, and provide stimulating activities for patients (Folsom, 1968). Today most RO programmes are employed with confused elderly patients either in group work, known as "classroom RO", or on a more informal basis known as "24-hour RO". Holden and Woods (1982) and Moffat (1989, 1992) provide summaries of this treatment and evaluations of RO studies. Moffat believes that, in general, informal RO does not work because (a) staff do not incorporate the correct procedures in their contacts with patients, (b) staff remain unfamiliar with RO techniques, and (c) staff do not reinforce appropriate behaviour. The more formal "classroom RO", on the other hand, appears to lead to specific gains. Moffat (1992) gives examples of teaching routes round the ward and teaching orientation items.

Reminiscence therapy is another group treatment used primarily with elderly people, although it can be adapted for use with younger brain-injured people. It involves reminding memory-impaired people of times and incidents in their past. Old songs, photographs and clothes from earlier times in the twentieth century might be presented to the group and members encouraged to reminisce about old times. Although, as far as we know, this has not been tried with head-injured people, it might prove to be helpful for those with a memory gap of some years before an accident. Going through songs, scrapbooks and photographs of a time a person can remember is enjoyable and could perhaps be extended to reteach some information lost during the period of retrograde amnesia, a process that might also bring back other associated memories.

Brotchie and Thornton (1987) found little evidence to suggest reminiscence therapy enhanced any kind of memory functioning; but there is little doubt that elderly, memory-impaired people enjoy reminiscence groups, and for this reason they might be helpful in reducing some of the emotional consequences of memory impairment.

GENERALISATION ISSUES

Generalisation, in the sense of extending the application of principles, techniques and results used, learned or achieved in rehabilitation to situations outside rehabilitation, is of crucial importance. There are several kinds of generalisation, such as across subjects, across behaviours or across settings. Our concern here is with generalisation as it refers to transfer of training; i.e. generalisation across settings and generalisation across behaviours.

Generalisation across settings refers to a situation where a strategy taught in one setting is applied to other settings. An example would be where a patient is taught to use an electronic aid or a particular mnemonic in one setting (say in clinical psychology) and then uses the aid or the mnemonic at home or at school.

Generalisation across behaviours refers to situations in which a strategy taught to help with one problem is used to assist with another problem. An example would be teaching a patient to use the study method PQRST described earlier for remembering current events in the newspapers and finding the patient used the method for his school work. Once again there is little evidence that this occurs spontaneously in adults with acquired brain damage. If generalisation is considered desirable (as it usually is in treatment) then it should be built into the treatment programme in the same way as it is built into programmes with people with mental handicaps (Zarkowska 1987).

To promote generalisation across settings we can use a variety of settings as part of the treatment. For example, when teaching the use of a personal organiser, we might begin in clinical psychology. Once the patient is proficient at recording and referring to the organiser in this setting, the psychologist could see the patient in occupational therapy and, if necessary, reteach the use of the organiser there. The next step might be to repeat the procedure in physiotherapy, then speech therapy, on the ward, at home and so forth. The wider the range of settings the more likelihood there is of the strategy generalising to other settings (Zarkowska, 1987).

Similarly, to encourage generalisation across behaviours a patient could be taught how to use PQRST for newspaper articles, then encouraged or taught to use it for magazine stories, then chapters in books, and even studying for examinations.

Persuading patients to put into practice the strategies they have been taught may be more difficult. Again several options are open. It is possible to put some patients on a behaviour programme to reinforce the use of memory aids and mnemonics. Appropriate goals might include: "teaching Mrs X to refer to her notebook after each meal" or "increasing the number of times Mr Z uses the PQRST spontaneously when he is revising for examinations". The use of timers, together with prompting and fading, would perhaps be one way of achieving success. For example, a timer could be set to ring at the end of each meal. Initially when the timer sounds the therapists or psychologist may need to prompt (or remind) Mrs X to check her notebook. Gradually the verbal reminders could be abbreviated and eventually stopped. Later still, the timer could be omitted as the meal-time setting itself becomes the reminder to check the notebook. Alternatively, a chaining method could be used whereby a particular task is broken down into a series of smaller units and taught one at a time. With PQRST, for example, a beginning could be made by teaching patients to select key points in a passage of prose. Such a process might be spread over several weeks of treatment. The preview stage might be added next, when the patient spends a minute or two skimming through for the gist of the story. The P and Q stages could then be combined and other stages would follow one at a time. This procedure could be followed by some sessions spent teaching the patient when PQRST would be a suitable method to use and when it would not. Finally, sessions could be spent using PQRST in the way it was intended, that is, for remembering written material.

In other cases it might be necessary to allow more time before expecting strategies to be used spontaneously. Some patients are slow to start but when given sufficient time can sometimes begin to put into practice the skills they have been taught previously. One amnesic man frequently argued with his wife over whether or not he had taken a bath. Because of his amnesia he could not remember and therefore insisted he had bathed recently. His wife knew better but could not convince him. It was suggested that he kept a "bath diary" in which he recorded dates and times of baths. However, he kept forgetting to record times. With the help of his wife, frequent reminding and keeping the diary above the sink in the bathroom, he began to note his bath times and now he continues to bathe regularly.

It may be necessary to abandon a particular strategy in favour of another if a patient shows signs of distress when participating in therapy. One man, for example, hated visual imagery and his comment every time he worked with imagery was "Where's the logic in that?" Although he learned the names of staff by using imagery, he became angry whenever the method was presented. He was much happier using first-letter cueing and PQRST as he could see "the logic in it". In his case visual imagery was not recommended to his relatives when the time came for his discharge from the centre. At what point a therapist abandons a strategy in favour of another will usually be guided by observation, clinical experience, and intuition, but there is little doubt that a method that causes a patient some discomfort and even distress will be unlikely to produce a favourable outcome.

In ending this section on generalisation it should be emphasised again that generalisation must not be expected to occur automatically. When it does occur spontaneously it is a bonus, but to increase the chances of it happening more regularly we must ensure that planning for generalisation is always part of any treatment programme. If it is not possible to teach generalisation then relatives and staff can be taught to implement the procedure if necessary. For example, in the use of visual imagery for names, it can be explained to the relatives that if the memory-impaired person needs to learn the names of colleagues at work or neighbours, then they can teach these names by converting each name into a picture, drawing the picture and teaching one name at a time. The principles of errorless learning and expanding rehearsal can be explained too, so these can be incorporated. Finally, all explanations should be written down for the relatives as they, too, are likely to forget what has been said to them.

SUMMARY AND FUTURE DIRECTIONS

Although people with memory impairment and their families should not be led to believe that significant improvement in memory can occur once the period of natural recovery is over, they can nevertheless be helped to understand, manage, cope with or bypass problems arising from the impairment. Such help will normally be given to individual patients and their families by therapists and psychologists. They can also be put in touch with local and national self-help groups.

Indirect or emotional consequences of brain injury and cognitive deficit should be addressed by counsellors, psychologists and psychotherapists so that anxiety management and cognitive programmes can be introduced. When planning for a memory therapy programme, results from a neuropsychological assessment should be combined with more direct assessment of everyday problems obtained by observation, interviewing, rating scales and questionnaires. Neuropsychological assessment will identify cognitive strengths and weaknesses while direct assessment will highlight everyday problems requiring treatment.

In addition to treatment of specific problems revealed by neuropsychological assessment, more general guidelines are recommended to improve encoding, storage and retrieval. It is probably best to avoid trial-and-error learning as recent research studies suggest that memory-impaired people learn better when prevented from making errors during learning.

Specific problems can be dealt with in a number of ways, including environmental adaptations, teaching the use of external aids as compensatory strategies, and using mnemonics as a faster route to learning new information. Planning and imagination should be brought into play when teaching the use of external aids. Although mnemonics will not be used spontaneously by memory-impaired people, their teachers, therapists and psychologists can use them to enhance learning by the memory-impaired.

Memory groups have certain advantages. They are useful in reducing anxiety and depression, and in increasing social contacts. External aids can be introduced and practised. Memory-impaired group members may be more willing to imitate their peers than the non-impaired professionals running a group.

People with severe memory problems will probably need help in generalising from one setting to another, and from one problem to another. It is therefore recommended that the teaching of generalisation is an integral part of any rehabilitation programme.

At present drugs are of rather limited value in enhancing memory functioning (see Chapter 24). However, this disappointing situation may change in the future. If it does, a combination of pharmacological and psychological treatments is likely to enhance performance in everyday life. It is also possible in the future that neural transplants in people with Parkinson's or Huntington's disease may lead to better memory performance, although here again the recipients may need to be taught to use their memories to the best advantage by employing memory rehabilitation strategies.

In the immediate future advances are likely to be made in better design and implementation of external aids and better structuring of the environment, hence reducing the load on memory. Meanwhile, further development of the errorless learning technique described above, and perhaps other ways of improving learning, can be implemented to teach people to use their prosthetic memory more efficiently.

REFERENCES

Arkin, S.M. (1991). Memory training in early Alzheimer's disease: an optimistic look at the field. *American Journal of Alzheimer's Care and Related Disorders and Research*, July/August, 17–25.

Arkin, S.M. (1992). Audio-assisted memory training with early Alzheimer's patients: two single-subject experiments. *Clinical Gerontologist*, **12**, 77–96.

Baddeley, A.D. (1990). *Human Memory: Theory and Practice*. Erlbaum, London.

Baddeley, A.D. (1992). Memory theory and memory therapy. In B.A. Wilson & N. Moffat (eds), *Clinical Management of Memory Problems*, 2nd edn. Chapman & Hall, London, pp. 1–31.

Baddeley, A.D. (1993). *Your Memory: A User's Guide*, 2nd edn. Lifecycle Publications, London.

Baddeley, A.D. & Wilson, B.A. (1994). When implicit learning fails: amnesia and the problem of error elimination, *Neuropsychologia*, **32**, 53–68.

Beck, A.T. (1976). *Cognitive Therapy and Emotional Disorders*. International Universities Press, New York.

Berg, I.J., Koning-Haanstra, M. & Deelman, B.G. (1991). Long-term effects of memory rehabilitation: a controlled study. *Neuropsychological Rehabilitation*, **1**, 87–111.

Bernstein, D.A. & Borkovec, T.D. (1973). *Progressive Relaxation Training*. Illinois Research Press, Champaign.

Bower, G.H. (1972). A selective review of organizational factors in memory. In E. Tulving & W. Donaldson (eds), *Organization of Memory*. Academic Press, New York.

Brooks, D.N. (1984). *Closed Head Injury*. Oxford University Press, Oxford.

Brooks, D.N. & Baddeley, A.D. (1976). What can amnesic patients learn? *Neuropsychologia*, **14**, 111–122.

Brooks, D.N., Campsie, L., Symington, C. et al. (1987). The effects of severe head injury on patient and relative within seven years of injury. *Journal of Head Trauma Rehabilitation*, **2**, 1–13.

Brotchie, J. & Thornton, S. (1987). Reminiscence: a critical review of the empirical literature. *British Journal of Clinical Psychology*, **26**, 93–111.

Butler, G. (1985) *Managing Anxiety*. University of Oxford, Oxford.

Clark, D.M. (1989). Anxiety states: panic and generalized anxiety. In K. Hawton, P.M. Salkovskis, J. Kirk & D.M. Clark (eds), *Cognitive Behaviour Therapy for Psychiatric Problems: A Practical Guide*. Oxford Medical Publications, Oxford.

Craik, F.I.M. & Lockhart, R.S. (1972). Levels of processing: a framework for memory research. *Journal of Verbal Learning and Verbal Behavior*, **11**, 671–684.

Crovitz, H. (1979). Memory retraining in brain-damaged patients: the airplane list. *Cortex*, **15**, 131–134.

Davies, A.D.M. & Binks, M.G. (1983). Supporting the residual memory of a Korsakoff patient. *Behavioural Psychotherapy*, **11**, 62–74.

Evans, J.J. & Wilson, B.A. (1992). A memory group for individuals with brain injury. *Clinical Rehabilitation*, **6**, 75–81.

Folsom, J.C. (1968). Reality orientation for the elderly mental patient. *Journal of Geriatric Psychiatry*, **1**, 291–307.

Freed, D.M., Corkin, S. & Cohen, N. (1987). Forgetting in H.M.: a second look. *Neuropsychologia*, **25**, 461–472.

Glisky, E.L. & Schacter, D.L. (1987). Acquisition of domain-specific knowledge in organic amnesia: training for computer-related work. *Neuropsychologia*, **25**, 893–906.

Glisky, E.L. & Schacter, D.L. (1989). Extending the limits of complex learning in organic amnesia: computer training in a vocational domain. *Neuropsychologia*, **27**, 107–120.

Graf, P. & Schacter, D.L. (1985). Implicit and explicit memory for new associations in normal and amnesic subjects. *Journal of Experimental Psychology: Learning, Memory and Cognition*, **11**, 501–518.

Gruneberg, M.M. (1973). The role of memorization techniques in finals examination preparation—a study of psychology students. *Educational Research*, **15**, 134–139.

Gruneberg, M.M., Sykes, R.N. & Hammond, V. (1991). Face–name association in learning-disabled adults: the use of a visual associative strategy. *Neuropsychological Rehabilitation*, **1**, 113–116.

Harris, J.E. (1980). We have ways of helping you remember. *Concord: The Journal of the British Association for Service to the Elderly*, **17**, 21–27.

Harris, J. (1992). Ways to help memory. In B.A. Wilson & N. Moffat (eds), *Clinical Management of Memory Problems*, 2nd edn. Chapman & Hall, London, pp. 59–85.

Hersh, N.A. & Treadgold, L.G. (1992). *Prosthetic Memory and Cueing for Survivors of Traumatic Brain Injury*. Unpublished report, obtainable from Interactive Proactive Mnemonic Systems, 6657 Camelia Drive, San José, California.

Holden, U.P. & Woods, R.T. (1982). *Reality Orientation: Psychological Approaches to the Confused Elderly*. Churchill Livingstone, London.

Jackson, W.T. & Gouvier, W.D. (1992). Group psychotherapy with brain-damaged adults and their families. In C.J. Long and L.K. Ross (eds), *Handbook of Head Trauma: Acute Care to Recovery*. Plenum Press, New York, pp. 309–327.

Kapur, N. (1991). *Managing your Memory: A Self-Help Memory Manual for Improving Everyday Memory Skills*. Southampton General Hospital, Southampton.

Lezak, M.D. (1979). Recovery of memory and learning functions following traumatic brain injury. *Cortex*, **15**, 63–72.

Lincoln, N.B. (1989). Management of memory problems in a hospital setting. In L.W. Poon, D.C. Rubin & B.A. Wilson (eds), *Everyday Cognition in Adulthood and Late Life*. Cambridge University Press, Cambridge, pp. 639–658.

Luria, A.R. (1968). *The Mind of a Mnemonist*. Basic Books, New York.

McCarty, D. (1980). Investigation of a visual imagery mnemonic device for acquiring face–name associations. *Journal of Experimental Psychology: Human Learning and Memory*, **6**, 145–155.

Masur, E.F., McIntyre, C.W. & Flavell, J.H. (1973). Developmental changes in appointment of study time in a multi-trial free-recall task. *Journal of Experimental Child Psychology*, **15**, 237–246.

Moffat, N. (1989). Home-based cognitive rehabilitation with the elderly. In L.W. Poon, D.C. Rubin & B.A. Wilson (eds), *Everyday Cognition in Adulthood and Late Life*. Cambridge University Press, Cambridge, pp. 659–680.

Moffat, N. (1992). Strategies of memory therapy. In B.A. Wilson & N. Moffat (eds), *Clinical Management of Memory Problems*, 2nd edn. Chapman & Hall, London, pp. 86–119.

Oddy, M. (1984). Head injury and social adjustment. In N. Brooks (ed.), *Closed Head Injury: Psychological, Social and Family Consequences*. Oxford University Press, Oxford, pp. 108–122.

Ost, L.G. (1987). Applied relaxation: description of a coping technique and review of controlled studies. *Behavior Research and Therapy*, **25**, 397–410.

Prigatano, G.P., Fordyce, D.J., Zeiner, H.K., Roueche, J.R., Pepping, M., & Wood, B.C. (1986). *Neuropsychological Rehabilitation after Brain Injury*. Johns Hopkins University Press, Baltimore.

Rawles, R.E. (1978). The past and present of mnemotechny. In M.M. Gruneberg, P.E. Morris & R.N. Sykes (eds), *Practical Aspects of Memory*. Academic Press, London, pp. 164–171.

Robinson, F.B. (1970). *Effective Study*. Harper & Row, New York.

Schacter, D.L. (1987). Memory, amnesia and frontal lobe dysfunction. *Psychobiology*, **15**, 21–36.

Scoville, W.B. & Milner, B. (1957). Loss of recent memory after bilateral hippocampal lesions. *Journal of Neurology, Neurosurgery and Psychiatry*, **20**, 11–21.

Sidman, M. & Stoddard, L.T. (1967). The effectiveness of fading in programming simultaneous form discrimination for retarded children. *Journal of Experimental Analysis of Behavior*, **10**, 3–15.

Sohlberg, M. & Mateer, C. (1989). Training use of compensatory memory books: a three-stage behavioral approach. *Journal of Clinical and Experimental Neuropsychology*, **11**, 871–891.

Steingass, H.P., Bobring, K.H., Burgart, F., Sartori, G. & Schugens, M. (1994). Training of cognitive functions in alcoholics. *Neuropsychological Rehabilitation*, **4**, 49–62.

Sunderland, A., Harris, J.E. & Baddeley, A.D. (1984). Assessing everyday memory after severe head injury. In J.E. Harris & P.E. Morris (eds), *Everyday Memory, Actions and Absentmindedness*. Academic Press, London, pp. 191–206.

Talbot, R. (1989). The brain-injured person and the family. In R.L.I. Wood & P. Eames (eds), *Model of Brain Injury Rehabilitation*. Chapman & Hall, London, pp. 3–16.

Terrace, H.S. (1963). Discrimination learning with and without "errors". *Journal of Experimental Analysis of Behavior*, **6**, 1–27.

Terrace, H.S. (1966). Stimulus control. In W.K. Honig (ed.), *Operant Behaviour: Areas of Research and Application*. Appleton–Century–Crofts, New York, pp. 271–344.

Victor, M., Adams, R.A. & Collins, G.H. (1989). *The Wernicke–Korsakoff Syndrome and Related Neurologic Disorders due to Alcoholism and Malnutrition*, 2nd edn. F.A. Davis, Philadelphia.

Wearing, D. (1992). Self-help groups. In B.A. Wilson & N. Moffat (eds), *Clinical Management of Memory Problems*, 2nd edn. Chapman & Hall, London, pp. 271–301.

Wilson, B.A. (1987a). *Rehabilitation of Memory*. Guilford Press, New York.

Wilson, B.A. (1987b). Single-case experimental designs in neuropsychological rehabilitation. *Journal of Clinical and Experimental Neuropsychology*, **9**, 527–544.

Wilson, B.A. (1989). *Memory Problems After Head Injury*. National Head Injuries Association, Nottingham.

Wilson, B.A. (1991). Long-term prognosis of patients with severe memory disorders. *Neuropsychological Rehabilitation*, **1**, 117–134.

Wilson, B.A. (1992). Memory therapy in practice. In B.A. Wilson & N. Moffat (eds), *Clinical Management of Memory Problems*, 2nd edn. Chapman & Hall, London, pp. 120–153.

Wilson, B.A. (1993). Coping with memory impairment. In G.M. Davies & R.H. Logie (eds), *Memory in Everyday Life*. Elsevier Science Publishers, Amsterdam, pp. 461–495.

Wilson, B.A. & Baddeley, A.D. (1993). Spontaneous recovery of impaired memory span: does comprehension recover? *Cortex*, **29**, 153–159.

Wilson, B.A., Baddeley, A.D., Evans, J. & Shiel, A. (1994). Errorless learning in the rehabilitation of memory-impaired people. *Neuropsychological Rehabilitation*, **4**, 307–326.

Wilson, B., Cockburn, J. & Baddeley, A.D. (1985). *The Rivermead Behavioural Memory Test Manual*. Thames Valley Test Co., Flempton, Bury St Edmunds, Suffolk.

Wilson, B.A., Cockburn, J. & Baddeley, A.D. (1989). Assessment of everyday memory following brain injury. In M.E. Miner & K.A. Wagner (eds), *Neurotrauma: Treatment, Rehabilitation and Related Issues*, vol. 3. Butterworths, London, pp. 83–99.

Wilson, B.A. & Moffat, N. (1992). The development of group memory therapy. In B.A. Wilson & N. Moffat (eds), *Clinical Management of Memory Problems*, 2nd edn. Chapman & Hall, London, pp. 243–273.

Yates, F.A. (1966). *The Art of Memory*. Routledge & Kegan Paul, London.

Zarit, S.H., Zarit, J.M. & Reever, K.E. (1982). Memory training for severe memory loss: effects on senile dementia patients and their families. *Gerontologist*, **22**, 373–377.

Zarkowska, E. (1987). Discrimination and generalisation. In W. Yule & J. Carr (eds), *Behaviour Modification for People with Mental Handicaps*. Croom–Helm, London, pp. 79–94.

Zencius, A., Wesolowski, M.D., Krankowski, T. & Berke, W.H. (1991). Memory notebook training with traumatically brain injured clients. *Brain Injury*, **5**, 321–325.

Chapter 20

Compensatory Strategies for Age-Associated Memory Impairment

Robin Lea West
University of Florida, Gainesville, USA

INTRODUCTION

Although the aging process does not devastate memory functioning—it is still possible to learn new information, and to retain and recall previously learned material—clear deficits in memory efficiency and retrieval success are present in the older population (see Chapter 9). Because of these deficits, older adults often want memory experts to wave a magic wand "to make my memory better". There is no magic cure for age-related memory problems, but this chapter hopes to provide partial relief in the form of an outline of potential remedies. A recent meta-analysis of the aging literature on memory intervention has established the overall success of such programmes (Verhaeghen, Marcoen & Goossens, 1992). This chapter presents an explication of a variety of memory strategies that may be useful for some, if not all, older adults facing the normal changes in memory that accompany aging. In fact, much of this information would be valuable to anyone wanting to improve their memory skills. Strategic memory interventions have been developed, for example, for a variety of special populations such as mentally retarded or learning disabled children (see Pressley & Levin, 1983), Alzheimer's patients (e.g. Camp, 1989; McKitrick, Camp & Black, 1992), head injury, stroke and other amnesic patients (Poon, Rubin & Wilson, 1989; Wilson 1987; Wilson & Moffat, 1984a,b). Special populations are also discussed in several chapters in this volume.

Handbook of Memory Disorders. Edited by A.D. Baddeley, B.A. Wilson and F.N. Watts.
© 1995 John Wiley & Sons Ltd.

No known memory techniques are magical. And although some have demonstrated impact in memory training research, many require hard work and considerable effort before an individual reaches the requisite level of mastery and facility to achieve visible, real-world improvements in memory success. This is true, whether the individual has a memory disorder or has experienced normal age-related memory change. In any memory intervention programme it is critical for participants to understand the difficulty of maintaining the high levels of effort needed for long-term gains in remembering. Much of the research has focused on short-term gain, although long-term gain is possible after extensive intervention.

This chapter focuses on memory strategies or techniques, defined as any method used to enhance or improve memory. Most memory strategies share particular characteristics which make them helpful for learning and recall. First of all, most memory strategies cannot be executed without paying close attention to the material. Thus, the application of a memory strategy often forces a person to pay attention and careful attention, by itself, can enhance performance (Klatzky, 1984). Second, most strategies access stored semantic networks of meaningful information (Howard, 1988). Clearly, all association and organization strategies require the use of semantic memory, and most imaginal strategies also tap into semantic networks. There is considerable evidence to demonstrate that encoding of semantic meaning is a key to new learning (Cermak & Craik, 1979). Memory strategies are also useful when sets of items need to be remembered together, because they provide a means for connecting disparate items into one memory representation, facilitating the simultaneous recall of those items. Finally, the best strategies work because, in the process of encoding the material, the strategy requires us to establish a potential retrieval cue. This cue could be an image, a number, a word, a sentence, a face, an auditory signal —even smells can serve as memory cues. The most effective strategies are those which *practically guarantee* that the appropriate cue will be available to access memory when retrieval processes are initiated. It is clear, then, that memory strategies can serve more than one purpose and can have an impact on several aspects of the memory process. Nevertheless, the techniques presented here will be those that are used primarily for encoding, because evidence for the effectiveness of teaching retrieval strategies to older adults is scarce (see West, 1985; Storandt, 1991).

One interesting, and troublesome, feature of the extant memory intervention research is the scarcity of direct measures of strategy usage (Bellezza, 1983; West, 1989). The most common methodology is to train individuals to use a particular memory technique, spending as little as one hour to as much as 30 hours in a training programme that could span several weeks. The impact of training is assessed by comparing baseline (pretest) scores with scores obtained on a post-training assessment. If scores show improvement, the assumption is that this improvement is due to the training itself, and in particular, to the subjects' utilization of the trained strategy. This assumption is perhaps warranted, albeit unsubstantiated, in the case where there is measurable improvement for the training group over and above that of a control/placebo group. When no such control group exists, the assumption is not warranted—there is considerable evidence in the literature showing significant improvements in memory and cognitive test scores solely as a function of practice (e.g. Hultsch, 1974; Plemons, Willis & Baltes, 1978; Taub & Long, 1972). Thus, this review will emphasize those studies that included a control/placebo group.

IMAGERY

During the past twenty years, imagery has been treated as if it were the single most important learning strategy known to memory specialists. Most popular books on how to remember focus on imaginal mnemonics (Higbee, 1977; Lapp, 1987; Lorayne & Lucas, 1974). The cornerstone of all imagery methodology is the interactive image—an internal picture that is vivid and distinctive and that shows at least two objects interconnected in some way. For the image to work as an effective memory device, the two objects cannot simply be present in the same image, they must be interacting. To remember that the boots and umbrella were placed in the foyer, it is not sufficient to imagine the boots and the umbrella on the floor in the foyer. It would be better to imagine jazzy music playing and to visualize large, colorful boots dancing through the foyer using a brightly-painted umbrella as a fancy parasol in the dance. Such distinctive, interactive images are effective for remembering lists or word pairs (imaginal mediation) and these uses of imagery can be taught to older adults (Canestrari, 1968; Erber, Abello & Moninger, 1988; Hulicka & Grossman, 1967; Poon & Walsh-Sweeney, 1981; Treat, Poon & Fozard, 1981; Treat & Reese, 1976).

For instance, West & Crook (1992) developed a memory training programme on video to demonstrate the uses of imagery for recalling names (the *image–name match method*, explained below), lists (link system), and the locations of personal belongings (interactive imagery). The example with the boots and umbrella, above, illustrates the way in which interactive imagery can be employed to remember where personal articles have been placed. The link system represents a simple application of interactive imagery for list recall; lists of items are recalled through a series of connected images. The first item on the list (e.g. turkey) is connected to the second (e.g. tea) by imagery (i.e. a turkey is sipping from a cup of tea), then the second item is linked to the third (e.g. chips) with an image (i.e. tea being poured over chips), and the third is linked with the fourth (e.g. milk) in a mental picture (i.e. chips dipped in milk), and so on. Once the initial two-item interactive image is recalled, each subsequent item is connected to the previous item through imagery, creating a chain of images where each previous image cues the next one in the series. The link method has resulted in significant improvements in list memory for older adults (West & Crook, 1992).

The early memory training studies with older adults worked to teach older adults how to employ interactive images to remember lists of paired associates (reviewed by Poon, Walsh-Sweeney & Fozard, 1980), but much of the work in the 1980s focused on more complex strategies, based on interactive imagery, such as the image–name match method, and the method of loci.

Image–Name Match Method

This memory strategy applies solely to the learning of names and faces. The method involves several stages:

1. A distinguishing feature is identified for the individual's face (e.g. a prominent forehead, a crooked nose).
2. A keyword that represents a concrete, imageable object is identified for the name (e.g. Carson is *car-sun*).
3. The keyword is converted to a mental image (e.g. a car with the sun shining on it).
4. The face is visualized, with the prominent feature enlarged, and with the name image (created in steps 2 and 3) superimposed on top of the enlarged feature.

Steps 2 and 3 are relatively easy with meaningful last names like East, West or North (the names are pictured as the ends of a weather vane). In contrast, nonmeaningful names such as Blukowsky must be translated into something concrete like a *blue cow* in the *sky*. This process of converting nonconcrete words into a concrete image is similar to a keyword imagery system (Atkinson, 1975). To facilitate rapid completion of these steps, many individuals will memorize images that are invariably associated with a particular name. Gordon is pictured as a garden, and Smith as a blacksmith, etc.

Here is an example that relates all four steps. Arthur has a large nose. His name is similar to *artist*. Arthur is pictured mentally as an artist, painting a design on his own larger-than-life nose. This method is designed to aid memory for the name when the individual is seen again, because the prominent feature will again be noticed. When that feature is noticed in the context of the whole face, it serves as a cue. The name image which was attached to the face should then reappear in the mind's eye and, theoretically, serve as a reminder for the name. The method is not perfect. During recall, the imagery cue could be misinterpreted as *designer*, and the name recalled incorrectly as "Desi" instead of "Arthur" (Higbee, 1977). The method also breaks down when no prominent feature can easily be identified for an individual, and when there is insufficient time to establish a meaningful, concrete reference for a name. Nevertheless, once mastered, it can be a highly effective method for remembering names.

More importantly, there is evidence that older adults can be taught to use this technique in memory courses lasting 10–20 hours. This research has been carried out primarily by Yesavage and colleagues, with faces preselected for easy-to-identify prominent features. His research has demonstrated that older adults' recall for names significantly improves after training (Yesavage, 1984;

Yesavage, Rose & Bower, 1983; Yesavage, Sheikh, Friedman & Tanke, 1990). Furthermore, the immediate benefits of training are enhanced if older adults are also taught relaxation, concentration or attention strategies, or semantic evaluation (participants are asked to evaluate each name image—"Is it funny? Is it sad? Does it make you feel good?") or if they are given additional imagery training (Yesavage, Lapp & Sheikh, 1989). Although there is clear evidence that this technique can be learned and that it improves name recall at least one week after training, there are few studies showing long-lasting benefits (see Sheikh, Hill & Yesavage, 1986).

Method of Loci

According to Yates (1966), the method of loci was known as a memory technique even in Greek times. More recently, the method was popularized by Luria (1968) who described a young man who employed the method to remember hundreds of items at a time.

In the method of loci, a known series of locations is memorized in order, with a visual image for each location. Walking out of the house, one sees the door (1), the porch chair (2), the porch table (3), the sidewalk (4), the hedge (5), the apple tree (6), the gate (7), the azaleas (8), the fig tree (9), etc. These known locations become the cues for memory. Each item that needs to be remembered from a list is associated with each location, in order, by creating an interactive mental image of the list item in that location. For example, remembering to go to (1) the laundry, (2) the library and (3) the linen store is accomplished by imagining the laundry hanging from the door (1), library books stacked in the chair (2), and linen wrapped around the table legs (3). The proper use of this technique makes it possible to recall very long lists in order—the known locations are reviewed in memory, in order, and the most recent images "placed" in those locations then come to mind. Just as with interactive imagery, the most memorable images are "unique, vivid, and dynamic" (Kleigl, Smith & Baltes, 1986, p. 404).

This technique was used, with some success, by Anschutz and her colleagues (Anschutz, Camp, Markley & Kramer, 1985, 1987). They initially measured strategy usage and performance on a free recall test. The older adults were then taught to use the method of loci in a two-hour training programme. One week and four weeks later they were given the opportunity to employ this method to remember their grocery lists in a familiar grocery store. Similar, ceiling-level recall occurred on these two shopping tests. Four weeks after the second grocery shopping test, free recall was repeated and found to be significantly higher than at pretest. Although there was no control group, the researchers examined strategy usage to determine whether or not the improvements in recall were based on appropriate application of the method of loci strategy. The researchers discovered that about half of their subjects employed the method of loci, and these were the subjects who showed the highest free recall levels two months after training, suggesting that strategy maintenance has considerable benefits (Anschutz et al., 1985). Three years later, however, only one of ten subjects continued to use the strategy (Anschutz et al., 1987).

Yesavage and his colleagues have also reported significant improvements in list recall by subjects trained to use the method of loci (Hill, Sheikh & Yesavage, 1988; Yesavage & Rose, 1984; Yesavage, Sheikh, Friedman & Tanke, 1990). Other researchers have also used this technique with some success (Hill, Allen & McWhorter, 1991; Rebok & Balcerak, 1989; Robertson-Tchabo, Hausman & Arenberg, 1976). The most stunning achievement with this method is the work done with the testing-the-limits methodology (Kleigl, Smith & Baltes, 1986, 1989). The goal of this methodology is to determine the limits of memory improvement with repeated and extensive practice. Adults of all ages were taught to chunk digits into sets of three digits, and to associate a mental image with each set by connecting the three-digit set to an historical date (492 = 1492 = image of Columbus/Santa Maria). The method of loci was employed, with well-known locations in their city, to then learn long lists of digits by remembering the historical date images in sequence. With this technique, their older subjects were able to remember as many as 60 to 120 digits in sequence, demonstrating that the limits to memory capacity are much higher than previously known (Kleigl, Smith & Baltes, 1986).

Other Applications of Imagery

The other imagery-based methods that have been employed with older adults, albeit rarely, are the peg system and the keyword system. Pratt and Higbee (1983) reported some improvement in list recall and memory for aphorisms after training with the peg system, but Mason and Smith (1977) found no improvement. The method requires an individual first to memorize a set of mental images, called pegs, that are matched to numbers: 1 = bun, 2 = shoe, 3 = tree, and so forth. Once these mental image pegs are memorized, in order, they can be used to recall any ordered set of information—grocery lists, names, errands —as long as the to-be-remembered information can be stored in memory as a picture. The trick is to form an interactive image connecting the to-be-remembered item with the correct "number image"; that is, if the first errand is to pick up photographs, one imagines a bun filled to the brim with photos. If the second errand involves a visit to the green grocer, the second image is a shoe filled with salad, and so on. This method is not as complex as the image–name match method, and does not appear to be any more difficult to learn than the method of loci, but it has seldom been employed in older adult intervention research.

The same can be said for the keyword method, which allows one to connect two items in memory. The method is basically an extension of interactive imagery in which abstract words that are difficult to picture are translated into concrete, picturable items, before creating an interactive image. This method is recommended for foreign language learning (Atkinson, 1975). For example, the

French word for "horse"—*cheval*—would be recalled by picturing a horse kicking a "shovel" (similar in sound to *cheval*). In this way, an English word that sounds similar to the French word is used to aid in translation. To my knowledge, mnemonics based on the keyword system have been applied successfully in only one study with older adults (see Roberts, 1983).

Effectiveness of Imagery Mnemonics

Many of the early memory training studies with older adults worked to teach older adults how to employ interactive images to remember lists of paired associates (see Poon, Walsh-Sweeney & Fozard, 1980). This research was based largely on the fact that interactive imagery is highly effective with younger adults for paired associate learning (Kausler, 1991; Paivio, 1971). The short-term successes evident in this research encouraged geropsychologists to try the more complex mnemonic techniques with older adults. There is some question as to whether or not this approach has yielded sufficient benefits.

It is clear that imagery is very effective as a learning tool, especially for young people, but its overemphasis in the popular memory press has tended to make people forget the disadvantages of imagery as a strategy. First of all, its effective usage requires that the individual be able to rapidly create and retain vivid mental pictures. This may not be the case for some individuals whose memory functions better with the application of verbal techniques, and it may not be the case for older adults, in particular (Flynn & Storandt, 1990; Storandt, 1991; West & Tomer, 1989; Winograd & Simon, 1980). Second, many of the most effective imagery tools are highly complicated methods that are difficult to learn and even more difficult to master. There is evidence that older adults are reluctant to utilize highly effortful memory strategies (Pratt & Higbee, 1983) and that strategies are often abandoned immediately after training (West & Tomer, 1989). A better approach with older adults might be to teach them strategies that are based on verbal skills, which tend to remain intact with aging (Light & Burke, 1988), and may therefore represent a less effortful strategic approach.

VERBAL ASSOCIATION AND ELABORATION

A number of quite distinct methods of remembering will be considered in this section. Each uses semantic or linguistic relationships for memorization. Instead of mental pictures, this class of strategies requires the creation of a word or sentence to serve as a verbal mediator or verbal cue. "Robin West" is recalled as "The robin is headed west with her hair flying in the wind". The first and last names are meaningfully associated, in this case, with a physical feature of the individual (long hair). Sentences, such as the one used in this example, are often referred to as *elaborations*, whereas single-word cues are typically called *associations*.

Except for association, or verbal mediation, which was used extensively in early memory training studies to aid older adults' recall of paired associates, the verbal methods are generally not employed. This is surprising given the clear evidence that older adults retain their vocabulary skills and that semantic association networks are comparable for old and young adults (Kausler, 1991; Light & Burke, 1988). At the same time, older adults do not spontaneously employ association or verbal mediation in many memory situations in which younger adults do employ mediators (Poon, 1985), and when encouraged to use this encoding approach, older adults may not always spontaneously create associations or elaborations that are precise and distinctive (e.g. Rabinowitz & Ackerman, 1982; Rankin & Collins, 1985). Thus, the focus of this intervention method with older adults should be on teaching them to generate and retain distinctive, memorable associations.

The simplest type of verbal strategy is two-word association. Subjects are asked to develop verbal mediators that meaningfully connect the target word and its paired cue word in paired associate learning. For example, "elephant" and "giraffe" would both be associated by "jungle", and "off" and "clock" could be remembered together by thinking of an "alarm". This method can be employed to facilitate older adults' memory for lists or paired words (e.g. Catino, Taub & Borkowski, 1977; Hulicka & Grossman, 1967).

An extension of this technique, known as verbal elaboration, has more potential as a memory aid. This method requires one to formulate a sentence or expand a sentence in a meaningful way to aid recall. "George Wall" is remembered because "the side of a *gorge* is a *wall*". Verbal elaboration with sentences can also be used to remember where one has placed a common household object. The brush placed on the sofa can be remembered by thinking, "I've got a vacuum brush cleaning the sofa". Such elaborations are more effective if they are precise; that is, if the semantic connection between the target memory word and the elaboration represents a highly meaningful, strong association (Bransford, 1979). The sentence above connects George with Wall quite well but it is not a sufficient memory cue because it does not include any information about Mr Wall's appearance. If he were especially tall or short, reference to a tall or short wall could be added to make a more precise cue connecting his name to his appearance. Although this method has been shown to be effective in research with younger subjects (e.g. Bransford, 1979), there are no known research data on its effectiveness with older adults.

The final method under this heading is first-letter elaboration sometimes called first-letter mnemonics, which the present author uses extensively in speeches for older adults. Each topic is recalled by its first letter only, and the first letters are connected into a word. "REACH for a Better Memory" is the title of a speech in which the following topics are discussed: Relax (older people need to take more time to learn and more time to retrieve); Evaluate yourself (don't believe all the stereotypes about memory aging, know your strengths and build on them); Attention (work hard to focus attention and eliminate distractions); Cues (more cues are needed as aging occurs, use effective memory cues); and Health (maintain cardiovascular and mental health). It is important to note that this technique helps the speaker, as well as the audience, remember the topics! In a more typical usage, to remember lists or errands, it is common to emphasize the consonants (e.g. tea, grapes and sugar on the shopping list might be remembered as TaGS).

First-letter mnemonics are recommended for recalling the order of well-known information. For example, to recall the traditional order of the planets in terms of their distance from the sun—Mercury, Venus, Earth, Mars, Jupiter, Saturn, Uranus, Neptune, Pluto—use this elaboration: "My Very Earnest Mother Just Served Us Nine Pickles". At the same time, there is little evidence that first-letter mnemonics improve list learning (Morris, 1977). This method has been used with memory disordered patients (Moffat, 1984) and older adults. Hultsch (1969) taught older and middle-aged subjects to use a related method (alphabetic organization) to aid in list recall and found it to facilitate recall only for low verbal subjects. Perhaps the high verbal subjects were employing a comparable technique without training. This interpretation is plausible because of evidence showing that untrained middle-aged and older adults report using first letters as an encoding or retrieval cue (West, 1989).

With the exception of simple mediation as a strategy for paired associate learning, there is little evidence for the value of verbal association and elaboration for older adults. At the same time, it is wise for memory trainers to focus their interventions for older adults on techniques that are easily accepted and easily applied (West & Tomer, 1989). Because it is not unknown to older adults, first-letter mnemonics might have heuristic value as a memory intervention technique.

ORGANIZATION

Much of the author's recent research has been devoted to the use of organization as a memory aid. There are compelling reasons to believe that this approach to intervention will be successful:

1. The basic benefits of organization are known to older adults. They do not need to be convinced of its value, as is often the case for other techniques.
2. Like verbal mediation, it relies on their intact verbal/semantic systems.
3. In spite of intact semantic networks, there is considerable evidence that older adults are deficient in the spontaneous application of organization to memory tasks (Hultsch, 1971). Rankin and her colleagues, for instance, found that only 67% of their older adults reported spontaneous use of organization to remember a highly organized list, compared with 78% for the middle-aged adults and 83% for the young (Rankin, Karol & Tuten, 1984).

4. It is easy to draw an analogy in training between the organization of factual information in memory and household organization (e.g. in the kitchen, glasses are put in one place, plates in another, and pans in another location). This analogy both aids understanding of the purposes of organization and provides a vehicle for ensuring that participants know that organization is worthwhile and effective. Homework assignments requiring the use of organization *in vivo* can further the maintenance of organization skills once they are taught.

5. Organization can be applied to a variety of memory tasks (Bower, 1970) through the utilization of chunking (most often, for remembering numbers), taxonomic organization (for shopping lists and errands), hierarchical structure (for prose, organizational charts, or instructions), functional relationships, etc.

The most common use of organization in the training literature is to teach individuals to organize lists for recall, using taxonomic categories. This technique has been effective with older adults (Bäckman & Karlsson, 1986; Rankin, Karol & Tuten, 1984; Schmitt, Murphy & Sanders, 1981), although it does not always lead to positive results (e.g. Hultsch, 1969). In the author's laboratory, a recent Memory Improvement Program for older adults failed to find any improvements in immediate shopping list recall after a six-session training programme that included at least one hour of practice in list organization and recall. We attributed this result to the rapid pacing of our shopping list presentation (one word every 5 seconds) because older adults did show improvement on a self-paced task (see below) after training (West, Bramblett, Welch & Bellott, 1992). Similar results were found with undergraduate trainees after a 2-hour training programme; that is, improvements on a self-paced task and no change on a timed list learning task (Bellott, 1991). Self-paced study conditions should give the participants sufficient time mentally to reorder the to-be-remembered materials.

Another form of organization, which has been employed with some effectiveness in the author's laboratory, is *hierarchical* organization. Subjects are trained to use the PQRST method to identify and remember story structure. PQRST stands for Preview, Question, Read, Summarize, Test, and is similar to the SQ3R technique (Moffat , 1984). The basic PQRST method had been used with success with head injury patients (Wilson, 1987). In the author's laboratory, this technique is modified to emphasize the hierarchical organization of ideas in prose. Subjects are taught to preview a story for its main points and primary subpoints; then to restate these points in the form of questions which will guide their reading. The questions focus on the subordinate details. As they read the prose carefully, they look for the details in response to their questions, always keeping the main points and subpoints in mind. Finally, after reading, they perform a mental summary of the text before completing the oral recall test. This method was used in the Memory Improvement Program with older adults, and in a related study with undergraduates low in memory self-efficacy. Reading and recall were self-paced. In both studies, there were highly significant improvements in prose recall after training, compared with a control group (Bellott, 1991; West, Bramblett, Welch & Bellott, 1992). These results suggest that older adults can benefit from learning strategies that emphasize an organized approach to encoding, especially when self-pacing provides sufficient time for them to utilize new processing techniques.

EXTERNAL AIDS

Unlike the strategies discussed so far—imagery, verbal association and elaboration, and organization—which employ mental, internal manipulations of information as a memory aid, this approach emphasizes the application of cues and notes in the environment. An external memory aid is anything outside of the individual that serves to aid memory. This includes reminders from other people, lists, address books, alarms and timers, strings around the finger, calendars, and appointment books.

In addition to these well-known types of external aids, the author has also recommended that older adults employ memory places (West, 1985). A "daily memory place" is a location for personal articles used everyday, such as glasses, keys, money or watch. A special basket, box, desktop or counter can be used as the designated location for such items. Effort is required to establish the habit of placing personal articles in a singular location, but once the routine is established it becomes a very effective memory tool, and saves the time and worry involved in repeated searches for these items. A second memory place is needed for highly important items that are not used each day such as bills, tax receipts, train or airline tickets, business correspondence, and the like. Without referring to it as a "memory place", many people store such items in their desk, ensuring that they can easily be located when needed.

An essential extension of the memory place concept is to apply the method outside the home. It is often difficult to keep track of personal items when one is traveling or going to meetings or luncheons away from home. Hats and umbrellas are frequently misplaced. Upon arrival at a hotel or friend's home, it is recommended that a memory place be established, similar to the "daily memory place" mentioned above. In addition, it is valuable to identify a memory place in restaurants and meeting rooms (always on the right side of one's chair), or at parties (near a chair in sight of the front door). It is then necessary to establish a "checking" routine that ensures that the selected memory place is carefully inspected before leaving. These habits become ingrained more easily if comparable locations are used all the time. (Suggested locations that can be utilized across different settings are given in the parentheses above).

It is clear that older adults make use of external memory aids in their daily lives (Cavanaugh, Grady & Perlmutter, 1983; West, 1989). Furthermore, Harris

(1978) found that, in general, external aids are reported in everyday usage more often than any internal mnemonic methods, with lists and calendars being used most often. External aids are beneficial especially for prospective memory (e.g. remembering to make a phone call). Moscovitch (1982) reported that older adults were more successful than younger adults on a prospective memory task because they employed external aids, and the younger students relied on their internal memory systems. Evidence from my laboratory (West, 1988) also indicates that external strategies can often be more effective than internal strategies for prospective tasks.

Although external aids are often employed, they may not be employed as consistently and as effectively as possible. Harris (1978) argues that external cues vary in their effectiveness. He has suggested that cues must be active, timely and specific. Active cues are contrasted with passive ones. A calendar is a passive cue because the user has to take the initiative to consult it. Today's high-technology reminder systems are more active because they allow the user to set an alarm to remind him or her about important events on the calendar. External cues must also be timely, in two senses. Initially, when a person realizes that an external cue will be an effective memory aid, it is important that the external cue is put in place immediately to prevent forgetting (e.g. write the note or set the timer right away). The cue must also be timely with respect to retrieval; that is, the cue must come to one's attention at the critical time when remembering is needed. If the cue operates too early or too late, forgetting often occurs (Harris, 1978). Finally, cue specificity is important. A general note such as "Go to grocery store" is considerably less useful than a specific note which says "Buy chopped beef, string beans, and ice cream today". Similarly, placing a string on one's finger is a very general cue which may not be adequate unless the to-be-remembered information is highly significant for the individual.

These characteristics of effective usage of external aids could be taught in an intervention designed to facilitate proficient and successful employment of such aids. This, to the author's knowledge, has not been done with normal older adults, but there is research involving external aid training with Alzheimer's patients (see McKitrick, Camp & Black, 1992). In addition to teaching proficient usage of external aids, it would be valuable for older adults to know that external aids are both appropriate and beneficial. I am often asked by older adults if lists and cues are self-defeating, in the long run, because they reduce the extent to which individuals *challenge* their internal memory capacities. On the contrary, they increase total memory capacity. Furthermore, many external aids cannot be employed successfully by individuals with significant memory disorder because these individuals often forget to utilize potential cues, either at encoding or retrieval, unless the cueing system is active and is controlled by someone else in their environment (Wilson & Moffat, 1984a,b). Thus, external memory aids involve internal mental effort, albeit less than internal strategies require, and they can increase the total amount of information that can be retained in the memory system. The potential power of memory intervention programmes based on external aids remains to be explored.

RELATED ISSUES IN MEMORY INTERVENTION

Other Forms of Training

Because this review has focused on four particular strategic techniques, several very interesting memory training studies have not been considered. For example, manipulations of rehearsal strategies or study time were not explained (Murphy, Schmitt, Caruso & Sanders, 1987; Sanders, Murphy, Schmitt & Walsh (1980), nor were studies in which subjects were instructed to recall words by placing them in narrative (Hill, Allen & McWhorter, 1991). There are also a number of studies in which multiple techniques and strategies were taught, either in group training (e.g. Stigsdotter & Bäckman, 1989; Zarit, Cole & Guider, 1981; Zarit, Gallagher & Kramer, 1981) or with bibliotherapy (e.g. Scogin, Storandt & Lott, 1985; Flynn & Storandt, 1990). Most of the published studies using a multiple-strategy approach have yielded significant gains for the training group, but the research designs precluded an analysis of the impact of any single strategy.

Strategy Selection

A second issue concerns the selection of strategies to employ in an intervention programme. As is clear from this review, most of the extant research employed imagery-based encoding strategies. And when investigators taught more than one strategy, imagery was almost always included in the training programme. Although verbal encoding strategies could be very productive for older adults, they have not received sufficient attention. They have been used in most of the multiple-strategy training programmes described above, but their unique effects were not evaluated in those studies.

Even less attention has been given to methods that will enhance retrieval (see Storandt, 1991; West, 1985). A number of different retrieval techniques have been discussed in the literature—mental retracing, external aids, alphabetic cueing, and spaced retrieval—and there is some evidence that older adults spontaneously employ some of these techniques (West, 1989); but none, to the author's knowledge, has been employed in a training programme designed to improve the recall of normal, elderly adults.

Camp and his colleagues have developed an interesting intervention programme for teaching dementia patients, using the spaced retrieval technique (Camp, 1989; Camp & Schaller, 1989; McKitrick et al., 1992), and this method had also been employed with other memory disordered patients (Moffat, 1989). Spaced retrieval is clearly a highly effective technique and it would not be difficult to teach to a broader audience (West, 1991). In fact, many retrieval-based techniques could easily be incorporated into intervention programmes (see West, 1985, 1989).

Strategy selection, as well as selection of a particular task for practice, is quite important. There is considerable evidence suggesting that most training effects are specific to the task that is trained (West & Tomer, 1989). In other words, trainees improve their recall of the task and strategy they have learned and this rarely generalizes to related types of memory tasks that were not included in the training (for an exception, see West & Crook, 1992). Task and strategy selection is therefore critical to the long-term impact of training. Furthermore, this lack of generalization may explain why training programmes using a multiple-strategy approach have had quite a bit of success. With a multiple-strategy approach, participants are more likely to have an opportunity to improve their skills in an area that is personally relevant and to see that the strategic approach to memory can be applied to a wide range of memory activities.

Maintenance

It is clearly possible to enhance recall by teaching older adults to apply a particular strategy. It is even possible to achieve improved recall with very brief (less than 30 minutes) forms of training (e.g. Canestrari, 1968; Treat & Reese, 1976; Treat, Poon & Fozard, 1981). The challenge is to show that the impact of training lasts. If the effects of training are not maintained over time, its benefits are severely curtailed.

In memory intervention research, it has been difficult to establish maintenance of training effects for older adults (West & Tomer, 1989). The few exceptions are training programmes that have demonstrated at least one week (Zarit, Cole & Guider, 1981; Zarit, Gallagher & Kramer, 1981; West & Crook, 1992) to one month maintenance of a strategy, at least for some subjects (Anschutz, Camp, Markley & Kramer, 1985; Flynn & Storandt, 1990; Scogin, Storandt & Lott, 1985). Note that most of these training programmes were extensive, long-term interventions (with the exception of Anschutz et al., 1985, and West & Crook, 1992). To the author's knowledge only one investigation has successfully achieved more lengthy maintenance effects (Stigsdotter & Bäckman, 1989). Their intervention group focused on attention, relaxation and strategic encoding. Improvements of recall on a Buschke selective reminding task were significant following training and were maintained six months after training (Stigsdotter & Bäckman, 1989). Given the extensive knowledge that is now available about the positive *immediate* effects of memory training, it behooves investigators to focus more on *long-term* change in future research.

Individual Differences

It has become a catch-phrase in intervention research to mention the importance of individual difference factors that may interact with training effects (e.g. Treat, Poon, Fozard & Popkin, 1978). Clearly, there is evidence that some individuals benefit from training more than others (Anschutz et al., 1985, 1987; Kleigl et al., 1986; Schaffer & Poon, 1982) and that, before training, individuals vary in their usage of memory strategies (e.g. Camp, Markley & Kramer, 1987). At the same time, systematic investigations of the impact of specific individual differences are almost nonexistent because of the complexities involved in such an analysis.

Some investigators have begun to explore this area. Yesavage and colleagues (Yesavage, Sheikh, Friedman & Tanke, 1990) have established that individuals with a low mental status score were unable to learn more complex mnemonics. Hultsch (1969) reported a positive impact of training for low verbal subjects and not for high verbal subjects, but this effect was not explored as a predictor variable in later studies. Locus of control does not appear to predict training outcome (Erber, Abello & Moninger, 1988), but there is some indication that the MBTI personality measure may be related to training effectiveness (Yesavage, Lapp & Sheikh, 1989). This litany of individual studies represents the state of the art—very few investigations have explored individual difference effects.

Affective factors such as depression and anxiety have probably been considered more than any other individual difference variables. Training has often been associated with decreased subjective report of depression (e.g. Zarit, Gallagher & Kramer, 1981). At the same time, an intervention focused on alleviation of depression affected memory complaints but not recall (Popkin, Gallagher, Thompson & Moore, 1982). With respect to anxiety, Yesavage and his colleagues have addressed this issue in several training studies (Yesavage et al., 1989). They found that state anxiety reduction was more evident with subjects trained in relaxation plus a memory strategy than with subjects exposed only to strategy training. The latter group showed higher state anxiety before post-testing (Yesavage, 1984). They have also shown that individuals with high anxiety performed better on cognitive tests after using a trained relaxation technique (Yesavage, Rose & Spiegel, 1982), and that reduced levels of state anxiety just prior to testing were associated with higher recall levels after training (Yesavage & Jacob, 1984; Yesavage, Sheikh, Tanke & Hill, 1988).

Although its application to memory intervention in older adults has been limited, memory self-efficacy may be an important individual difference factor to evaluate in future studies. Efficacy is defined as a person's assessment of their own potential skill level in a testing situation in which one's own performance level is not well known (Bandura, 1986). Certainly, there is considerable evidence that level of self-efficacy is strongly related to outcome in clinical phobia interventions (Bandura, 1986) and in cognitive interventions with children (Schunk, 1989), and Bandura's theory of self-efficacy clearly explicates the importance of raising levels of efficacy during any intervention (Bandura, 1986). Without increased efficacy, individuals are likely to experience only momentary changes in skills, because they have not changed their beliefs about their memory potential. Lower self-efficacy is associated with reduced effort and failure to persist in the face of difficulty (Bandura, 1986). Thus, subjects who have been taught to use a strategy, but have not changed their view of their potential—that is, have not raised their level of memory self-efficacy—may quickly abandon newly learned skills when faced with real-world memory problems.

In the one published intervention study with older adults in which efficacy was measured directly, improvements in efficacy were not evident after training even though recall improved (Rebok & Balcerak, 1989). It may not be possible, however, to raise efficacy simply by training. It may be necessary for the training to emphasize change in efficacy beliefs, as has been the case in the efficacy-related intervention literature (Schunk, 1989). Two studies, mentioned earlier, have been carried out in the author's laboratory using this approach. In the first, younger adults, preselected for low levels of memory self-efficacy compared with their peers, were given organization training which was based on efficacy intervention principles; that is, the training was designed to provide successful mastery experiences for the participants and to change their beliefs about their memory potential. The results were positive in showing increased memory self-efficacy after training, along with improvements on one of the two criterion memory tests (Bellott, 1991). In a similar study with older adults, self-efficacy was raised after training (West, Bramblett, Welch & Bellott, 1992). In addition, the observed improvements on one of the two criterion tests, as well as increased levels of memory self-efficacy were maintained by older adult trainees at a one-month follow-up assessment. This preliminary evidence supports the notion that interventions focusing on changes in memory efficacy beliefs may be related to maintenance of training effects, at least for one month.

CONCLUSIONS

The purpose of this chapter has been to review and evaluate memory intervention programmes for older adults, with an emphasis on particular types of strategy training that have proven effective. Clinicians who wish to apply this knowledge need to be aware of the potential pitfalls. Maintenance of memory intervention effects requires strong motivation, effort, and positive beliefs on the part of the learner. In designing an intervention, it may be best to use a multiple-strategy, multiple-task approach so that subjects see the potential for widespread application of new learning. Success has been greater for memory programmes that are lengthy (5–20 hours). Such programs give older adults the time and experience needed to become facile with memory strategies that may be unfamiliar or difficult to learn. Finally, individual difference factors that affect training have not been sufficiently studied but they should be considered in designing an intervention because there is some evidence that they may have an effect on outcome.

REFERENCES

Anschutz, L., Camp, C.J., Markley, R.P. & Kramer, J.J. (1985). Maintenance and generalization of mnemonics for grocery shopping by older adults. *Experimental Aging Research*, **11**, 157–160.

Anschutz, L., Camp, C., Markley, R.P. & Kramer, J.J. (1987). Remembering mnemonics: a three-year follow-up on the effects of mnemonics training in elderly adults. *Experimental Aging Research*, **13**, 141–144.

Atkinson, R.C. (1975). Mnemotechnics in second-language learning. *American Psychologist*, **30**, 821–828.

Bäckman, L. & Karlsson, T. (1986). Episodic remembering in young adults, 73-year-olds, and 82-year-olds. *Scandinavian Journal of Psychology*, **27**, 320–325.

Bandura, A. (1986). *Social Foundations of Thought and Action: A Social Cognitive Theory*. Prentice-Hall, Englewood Cliffs.

Bellezza, F.S. (1983). Mnemonic-device instruction with adults. In M. Pressley & J.R. Levin (eds), *Cognitive Strategy Research*. Springer-Verlag, New York, pp. 51–73.

Bellott, B.D. (1991). *Achievement Efficacy and Attributions: Effects of Memory Intervention on College Undergraduates with Low Self-efficacy*. Unpublished master's thesis, University of Florida, Gainesville.

Bower, G.H. (1970). Organizational factors in memory. *Cognitive Psychology*, **1**, 18–46.

Bransford, J.D. (1979). *Human Cognition*. Wadsworth, Belmont, CA.

Camp, C.J. (1989). Facilitation of new learning in Alzheimer's disease. In G.C. Gilmore, P.J. Whitehouse & M.L. Wykle (eds), *Memory, Aging and Dementia: Theory, Assessment and Treatment*. Springer, New York, pp. 212—225.

Camp, C.J., Markley, R.P. & Kramer, J.J. (1987). Spontaneous use of mnemonics by elderly individuals. *Educational Gerontology*, **9**, 57–71.

Camp, C.J. & Schaller, J.R. (1989). Epilogue: spaced retrieval memory training in an adult day-care center. *Educational Gerontology*, **15**, 641–648.

Canestrari, R.E. (1968). Age changes in acquisition. In G.A. Talland (ed.), *Human Aging and Behavior*. Academic Press, New York, pp. 169–188.

Catino, C., Taub, S.I. & Borkowski, J.G. (1977). Mediation in children and the elderly as a function of memory capabilities. *Journal of Genetic Psychology*, **130**, 35–47.

Cavanaugh, J.C., Grady, J.G. & Perlmutter, M. (1983). Forgetting and use of memory aids in 20- to 70-year-olds' everyday life. *International Journal of Aging and Human Development*, **17**, 113–122.

Cermak, L.S. & Craik, F.I.M. (1979). *Levels of Processing in Human Memory*. Erlbaum, Hillsdale, NJ.

Erber, J.T., Abello, S. & Moninger, C. (1988). Age and individual differences in immediate and delayed effectiveness of mnemonic instructions. *Experimental Aging Research*, **14**, 119–124.

Flynn, T.M. & Storandt, M. (1990). Supplemental group discussions in memory training of older adults. *Psychology and Aging*, **5**, 178–181.

Harris, J.E. (1978). External memory aids. In M.M. Gruneberg, P.E. Morris & R.N. Sykes (eds), *Practical Aspects of Memory*. Academic Press, London, pp. 172–179.

Higbee, K.L. (1977). *Your Memory: How It Works and How to Improve It*. Prentice Hall, Englewood Cliffs.

Hill, R.D., Allen, C. & McWhorter, P. (1991). Stories as a mnemonic aid for older learners. *Psychology and Aging*, **6**, 484–486.

Hill, R.D., Sheikh, J.I. & Yesavage, J.A. (1988). Pretraining enhances mnemonic training in elderly adults. *Experimental Aging Research*, **14**, 207–211.

Howard, D.J. (1988). Aging and memory activation: the priming of semantic and episodic memories. In L.L. Light & D.M. Burke (eds), *Language, Memory and Aging*. Cambridge University Press, Cambridge, pp. 77–99.

Hulicka, I.M. & Grossman, J.L. (1967). Age group comparisons for the use of mediators in paired-associate learning. *Journal of Gerontology*, **22**, 46–51.

Hultsch, D.F. (1969). Adult age differences in the organization of free recall. *Developmental Psychology*, **1**, 673–678.

Hultsch, D.F. (1971). Organization and memory in adulthood. *Human Development*, **14**, 16–29.

Hultsch, D.F. (1974). Learning to learn in adulthood. *Journal of Gerontology*, **29**, 302–308.

Kausler, D.H. (1991). *Experimental Psychology, Cognition and Human Aging*, 2nd edn. Springer-Verlag, New York.

Klatzky, R.L. (1984). *Memory and Awareness*. W.H. Freeman, New York.

Kliegl, R., Smith, J. & Baltes, P.B. (1986). Testing-the-limits, expertise, and memory in adulthood and old age. In F. Klix & H. Hagendorf (eds), *Human Memory and Cognitive Capabilities*. Elsevier Science Publishers, Amsterdam, pp. 395–407.

Kliegl, R., Smith, J. & Baltes, P.B. (1989). Testing-the-limits and the study of adult age differences in cognitive plasticity of a mnemonic skill. *Developmental Psychology*, **25**, 247–256.

Lapp, D.C. (1987). *Don't Forget*. McGraw-Hill, New York.

Light, L.L. & Burke, D.M. (1988). *Language, Memory and Aging*. Cambridge University Press, Cambridge.

Lorayne, H. & Lucas, J. (1974). *The Memory Book*. Ballantine Books, New York.

Luria, A.R. (1968). *The Mind of a Mnemonist*. Basic Books, New York.

Mason, S.E. & Smith, A.D. (1977). Imagery in the aged. *Experimental Aging Research*, **3**, 17–32.

McKitrick, L.A., Camp, C.J. & Black, F.W. (1992). Prospective memory intervention in Alzheimer's disease. *Journal of Gerontology*, **47**, 337–343.

Moffat, N. (1984). Strategies of memory therapy. In B.A. Wilson & N. Moffat (eds), *Clinical Management of Memory Problems*. Aspen, Rockville, MD, pp. 63–88.

Moffat, N. (1989). Home-based cognitive rehabilitation with the elderly. In L.W. Poon, D. Rubin & B. Wilson (eds), *Everyday Cognition in Adulthood and Late Life*. Cambridge University Press, Cambridge, pp. 659–680.

Morris, P. (1977). Practical strategies for human learning and remembering. In M.J.A. Howe (ed.), *Adult Learning*. John Wiley, London, pp. 125–144.

Moscovitch, M.C. (1982). A neuropsychological approach to perception and memory in normal and pathological aging. In F.I.M. Craik & S. Trehub (eds), *Aging and Cognitive Processes*. Plenum Press, New York, pp. 55–178.

Paivio, A. (1971). *Imagery and Verbal Processes*. Academic Press, New York.

Plemons, J.K., Willis, S.L. & Baltes, P.B. (1978). Modifiability of fluid intelligence in aging: a short-term longitudinal training approach. *Journal of Gerontology*, **33**, 224–231.

Poon, L.W. (1985). Differences in human memory with aging: nature, causes and clinical implications. In J.E. Birren & K.W. Schaie (eds), *Handbook of the Psychology of Aging*, 2nd edn. Van Nostrand Reinhold, New York, pp. 427–462.

Poon, L.W., Rubin, D. & Wilson, B. (eds) (1989). *Everyday Cognition in Adulthood and Late Life*. Cambridge University Press, Cambridge.

Poon, L.W. & Walsh-Sweeney, L. (1981). Effects of bizarre and interacting imagery on learning and retrieval of the aged. *Experimental Aging Research*, **7**, 65–70.

Poon, L.W., Walsh-Sweeney, L. & Fozard, J.L. (1980). Memory skill training for the elderly: salient issues on the use of imagery mnemonics. In L.W. Poon, J.L. Fozard, L.S. Cermak, D. Arenberg & L.W. Thompson (eds), *New Directions in Memory and Aging*: *Proceedings of the George A. Talland Memorial Conference*. Erlbaum, Hillsdale, NJ, pp. 461–484.

Popkin, S.J., Gallagher, D., Thompson, L.W. & Moore, M. (1982). Memory complaint and performance in normal and depressed older adults. *Experimental Aging Research*, **8**, 141–145.

Pratt, J.D. & Higbee, K.L. (1983). Use of an imagery mnemonic by the elderly in natural settings. *Human Learning*, **2**, 227–235.

Pressley, M. & Levin, J.R. (1983). *Cognitive Strategy Research*: *Psychological Foundations*. Springer-Verlag, New York.

Rabinowitz, J.C. & Ackerman, B.P. (1982). General encoding of episodic events by elderly adults. In F.I.M. Craik & S. Trehub (eds), *Aging and Cognitive Processes*. Plenum, New York, pp. 145–154.

Rankin, J.L. & Collins, M. (1985). Adult age differences in memory elaboration. *Journal of Gerontology*, **40**, 451–458.

Rankin, J.L., Karol, R. & Tuten, C. (1984). Strategy use, recall, and recall organization in young, middle-aged, and elderly adults. *Experimental Aging Research*, **10**, 193–196.

Rebok, G.W. & Balcerak, L.J. (1989). Memory self-efficacy and performance differences in young and old adults: the effect of mnemonic training. *Developmental Psychology*, **25**, 714–721.

Roberts, P. (1983). Memory strategy instruction with the elderly: what *should* memory training be the training of? In M. Pressley & J.R. Levin (eds), *Cognitive Strategy Research*. Springer-Verlag, New York, pp. 75–100.

Robertson-Tchabo, E.A., Hausman, C.P. & Arenberg, D. (1976). A classical mnemonic for older learners: a trip that works. *Educational Gerontology*, **1**, 215–226.

Sanders, R.E., Murphy, M.D., Schmitt, F.A. & Walsh, K.K. (1980). Age differences in free recall rehearsal strategies. *Journal of Gerontology*, **35**, 550–558.

Schaffer, G. & Poon, L.W. (1982). Individual variability in memory training with the elderly. *Educational Gerontology*, **8**, 217–229.

Schmitt, F.A., Murphy, M.D. & Sanders, R.E. (1981). Training older adult free recall rehearsal strategies. *Journal of Gerontology*, **36**, 329–337.

Schunk, D.H. (1989). Social cognitive theory and self-regulated learning. In B.J. Zimmerman & D.H. Schunk (eds), *Self-regulated Learning and Academic Achievement*. Springer-Verlag, New York.

Scogin, F., Storandt, M. & Lott, L.A. (1985). Memory-skills training, memory complaints, and depression in older adults. *Journal of Gerontology*, **40**, 562–568.

Sheikh, J.I., Hill, R.D. & Yesavage, J.A. (1986). Long-term efficacy of cognitive training for Age-Associated Memory Impairment: a six-month follow-up study. *Developmental Neuropsychology*, **2**, 413–421.

Stigsdotter, A. & Bäckman, L. (1989). Multifactorial memory training with older adults: how to foster maintenance of improved performance. *Gerontology*, **35**, 260–267.

Storandt, M. (1991). Memory-skills training for older adults. *Nebraska Symposium on Motivation*, **39**, 39–62.

Taub, H.A. & Long, M. (1972). The effects of practice on short-term memory of young and old subjects. *Journal of Gerontology*, **27**, 494–499.

Treat, N.J., Poon, L.W. & Fozard, J.L. (1981). Age, imagery, and practice in paired-associate learning. *Experimental Aging Research*, **7**, 337–342.

Treat, N.J., Poon, L.W., Fozard, J.L. & Popkin, S.J. (1978). Toward applying cognitive skill training to memory problems. *Experimental Aging Research*, **4**, 305–319.

Treat, N.J. & Reese, H.W. (1976). Age, pacing and imagery in paired-associate learning. *Developmental Psychology*, **12**, 119–124.

Verhaeghen, P., Marcoen, A. & Goossens, L. (1992). Improving memory performance in the aged through mnemonic training: a meta-analytic study. *Psychology and Aging*, **7**, 242–251.

West, R.L. (1985). *Memory Fitness Over 40*. Triad, Gainesville, FL.

West, R.L. (1989). Planning practical memory training for the aged. In L.W. Poon, D. Rubin & B. Wilson (eds), *Everyday Cognition in Adulthood and Late Life*. Cambridge University Press, Cambridge, pp. 573–597.

West, R.L. (1991). The adaptive memory: maintaining skill in the older years. *Outlook on Aging*, Series 3. Center for Gerontological Studies, Gainesville, FL.

West, R.L., Bramblett, J.P., Welch, D.C. & Bellott, B. (1992). Memory training for the elderly: an intervention designed to improve memory skills and memory self-evaluation. Paper presented at the Cognitive Aging Conference, Atlanta, April 1992.

West, R.L. & Crook, T.H. (1992). Video training of imagery for mature adults. *Applied Cognitive Psychology*, **6**, 307–320.

West, R.L. & Tomer, A. (1989). Everyday memory problems of healthy older adults:

characteristics of a successful intervention. In G.C. Gilmore, P.J. Whitehouse & M.L. Wykle (eds), *Memory, Aging and Dementia: Theory, Assessment and Treatment*. Springer, New York, pp. 74–98.

Wilson, B.A. (ed.) (1987). *Rehabilitation of Memory*. Guilford Press, New York.

Wilson, B.A. & Moffat, N. (1984a). *Clinical Management of Memory Problems*. Aspen Systems, Rockville, MD.

Wilson, B. & Moffat, N. (1984b). Rehabilitation of memory for everyday life. In. J.E. Harris & P.E. Morris (eds), *Everyday Memory, Actions and Absentmindedness*. Academic Press, London, pp. 207–233.

Winograd, E. & Simon, E.W. (1980). Visual memory and imagery in the aged. In L.W. Poon, J.L. Fozard, L.S. Cermak, D. Arenberg & L.W. Thompson (eds), *New Directions in Memory and Aging: Proceedings of the George A. Talland Memorial Conference*. Erlbaum, Hillsdale, NJ, pp. 485–506.

Yates, F.A. (1966). *The Art of Memory*. Routledge & Kegan Paul, London.

Yesavage, J.A. (1984). Relaxation and memory training in 39 elderly patients. *American Journal of Psychiatry*, **141**, 778–781.

Yesavage, J.A. & Jacob, R. (1984). Effects of relaxation and mnemonics on memory, attention and anxiety in the elderly. *Experimental Aging Research*, **10**, 211–214.

Yesavage, J.A., Lapp, D. & Sheikh, J.I. (1989). Mnemonics as modified for use by the elderly. In L.W. Poon, D. Rubin & B. Wilson (eds), *Everyday Cognition in Adulthood and Late Life*. Cambridge University Press, Cambridge.

Yesavage, J.A. & Rose, T.L. (1984). Semantic elaboration and the method of loci: a new trip for older learners. *Experimental Aging Research*, **10**, 155–159.

Yesavage, J.A., Rose, T.L. & Bower, G.H. (1983). Interactive imagery and affective judgements improve face-name learning in the elderly. *Journal of Gerontology*, **38**, 197–203.

Yesavage, J.A., Rose, T.L. & Spiegel, D. (1982). Relaxation training and memory improvement in elderly normals: correlation of anxiety ratings and recall improvement. *Experimental Aging Research*, **8**, 195–198.

Yesavage, J.A., Sheikh, J.I., Friedman, L. & Tanke, E. (1990). Learning mnemonics: roles of aging and subtle cognitive impairment. *Psychology and Aging*, **5**, 133–137.

Yesavage, J.A., Sheikh, J.I., Tanke, E.D. & Hill, R. (1988). Response to memory training and individual differences in verbal intelligence and state anxiety. *American Journal of Psychiatry*, **145**, 636–639.

Zarit, S.H., Cole, K.D. & Guider, R.L. (1981). Memory training strategies and subjective complaints of memory in the aged. *Gerontologist*, **21**, 158–164.

Zarit, S.H., Gallagher, D. & Kramer, N. (1981). Memory training in the community aged: effects on depression, memory complaint, and memory performance. *Educational Gerontology*, **6**, 11–27.

Chapter 21

Memory Disturbances of Children with Learning Disabilities: A Neuropsychological Analysis of Two Academic Achievement Subtypes

Byron P. Rourke
University of Windsor, Ontario, Canada and
Yale University, New Haven, USA
and
Katherine D. Tsatsanis
University of Windsor, Ontario, Canada

INTRODUCTION

In our society, children are expected to go to school from roughly the age of 5 years until well into late adolescence. Indeed, attendance at, and benefiting substantially from, school constitute what most consider to be the principal developmental demands for children of these ages. While in school, children are expected to learn a large number of skills and remember a large amount of material. They are expected to emerge from this experience as literate young adults who are capable of comporting themselves in an adaptive manner in the world of work and in the social pursuits that are common to our society.

Handbook of Memory Disorders. Edited by A.D. Baddeley, B.A. Wilson and F.N. Watts.
© 1995 John Wiley & Sons Ltd.

For many—as a result of the burgeoning academic requirements of our increasingly sophisticated technological society, or out of a love of learning, or because of parental expectations, or for any number of other reasons—"school" will continue well past this point. Indeed, for most young persons in our society, post-secondary education or formal training of some sort is now the norm rather than the rule, and we can expect this to continue to be the case.

Whether in school or not, the capacity to benefit from experience and to fashion one's responses to meet the demands of such experience in an adaptive fashion (i.e. to learn and to remember what one has learned) lies at the very core of what it is to be human. Hence, it should come as no surprise that significant difficulties in learning and memory are thought to eventuate in much more than simple failure in school or failure to learn or hold a job. Indeed, it is a commonly held notion that persons who experience significant difficulties in learning and memory—especially when these are thought to be "learning disabilities" (LD)—are most definitely prone to disorders in other areas of human existence, such as the "emotional" and "social" dimensions of life. It is in this sense that some characterize LD as "life" or "lifetime" disabilities.

At this point, it would be well to define what we mean by the term "learning disabilities". The following constitutes what we consider to be a "generic" definition of this term (Rourke, 1989):

> LD is a generic term that refers to a heterogeneous group of disorders manifested by significant difficulties in the mastery of one or more of the following: listening, speaking, reading, writing, reasoning, mathematical, and other skills and abilities that are traditionally referred to as "academic." The term LD is also appropriately applied in instances where persons exhibit significant difficulties in mastering social and other adaptive skills and abilities. In some cases, investigations of LD have yielded evidence that would be consistent with hypotheses relating central nervous system dysfunction to the disabilities in question. Even though learning disabilities may occur concomitantly with other handicapping conditions (e.g. sensory impairment, mental retardation, social and emotional disturbance) or environmental influences (e.g. cultural differences, insufficient/inappropriate instruction, psychogenic factors), they are not the direct result of those conditions or influences. However, it is possible that emotional disturbances and other adaptive deficiencies may arise from the same patterns of central processing assets and deficits that generate the manifestations of academic and social LD. LD may arise from genetic variations, biochemical factors, events in the pre- to perinatal period, or any other subsequent events resulting in neurological impairment. (pp. 214–215)

It would take us too far afield to discuss the *specific* definitions of various subtypes of LD, although some statements regarding the issues surrounding subtypes and the specific definitions implied thereby will be discussed below. For a fuller discussion of specific definitions of subtypes of LD, the interested reader is referred to Rourke (1989, especially Chapter 8).

This presentation was designed to address the mnestic deficiencies of two major subtypes of children with LD within the context of recent developmental neuropsychological models emanating from our laboratory. These models (Rourke, 1975, 1976a,b, 1978b, 1982, 1983, 1987, 1988b, 1989; Rourke & Fisk,

1988) were designed to encompass aspects of learning and its disabilities within the principal spectrums of the academic and social milieux to which children and adolescents are expected to adapt. Various dimensions of mnestic performance afford a particularly fruitful avenue for testing the principal tenets of these models. This is especially the case for children with nonverbal LD (NLD) and those whose LD appear to arise primarily from deficits in auditory perceptual deficits.

We begin with a summary of our work with respect to subtypes of children with "academic" LD. In this section, a series of investigations that have differentiated two subtypes of children with LD is described. The principal features found to characterize each of these two subtypes are summarized in the ensuing two sections. In accord with the aims of this chapter, particular attention is paid to the different dimensions of memory and its perturbations as these pertain to the two subtypes of children with LD herein examined. Where appropriate to do so, the investigations of other researchers are also included. Our primary aim in this exercise—to consider the implications of these findings for habilitational/interventive strategy planning—is presented in the final section.

PATTERNS OF READING, SPELLING AND ARITHMETIC

A series of studies carried out in our laboratory over the past few years was designed to determine the neuropsychological significance of patterns of academic achievement in children with LD. These investigations were stimulated by the unexpected patterns of Wide Range Achievement Test (WRAT; Jastak & Jastak, 1965) Reading, Spelling, and Arithmetic performances that turned up in our examination of the relevance of Verbal IQ (VIQ)–Performance IQ (PIQ) discrepancies in children with LD (Rourke, Dietrich & Young, 1973; Rourke & Telegdy, 1971; Rourke, Young & Flewelling, 1971). (The WRAT is designed to provide a convenient measure of basic academic learning. It comprises three subtests: Reading, Spelling, and Arithmetic. The Reading subtest provides a measure of oral single-word reading. The Spelling subtest is a measure of written single-word spelling to dictation. The Arithmetic subtest is a timed test that consists of both basic mechanical arithmetic operations and more advanced mathematical reasoning and problem-solving questions.) Specifically, we were interested in determining whether children who exhibit particular patterns of WRAT Reading, Spelling, and Arithmetic performances would also exhibit predictable patterns of neuropsychological assets and deficits.

Study 1

In the first of these investigations (Rourke & Finlayson, 1978), children with LD (defined in a fairly traditional manner: see Rourke, 1975) between the ages of 9 and 14 years were divided into three groups (15 subjects in each group) on the basis of their patterns of performance on reading and spelling tasks relative to their level of performance in arithmetic. The three groups were equated for age and Wechsler Intelligence Scale for Children (WISC; Wechsler, 1949) Full Scale IQ. The subjects in Group 1 were uniformly deficient in reading, spelling, and arithmetic. Group 2 was composed of subjects whose arithmetic performance, although clearly below age expectation, was significantly better than their performances in reading and spelling. The subjects in Group 3 exhibited normal reading and spelling and markedly impaired arithmetic performance. Although *all three groups performed well below age-expectation in arithmetic*, the performances of Groups 2 and 3 were superior to that of Group 1; *Groups 2 and 3 did not differ from one another in their impaired levels of arithmetic performance*. (It should be noted in this context that, in the traditional "contrasting-groups" (Doehring, 1978; Rourke, 1978a) type of study of arithmetic disability, children from Groups 1, 2, and 3 would have "qualified" for admission to the "disabled arithmetic" group. The alarming shortcomings of such a research design are well illustrated by the results of the studies under consideration.)

The three groups' performances on 16 dependent measures, chosen in the light of the results of previous studies in this series (e.g. Rourke, Young & Flewelling, 1971), were compared. The results of this investigation may be summarized as follows:

1. The performances of Groups 1 and 2 were superior to those of Group 3 on measures of visual–perceptual and visual-spatial abilities (e.g. WISC Block Design, Target Test).
2. Group 3 performed at superior levels to Groups 1 and 2 on measures of verbal and auditory–perceptual abilities (e.g. WISC Vocabulary, Speech-Sounds Perception Test).

In the context of the results of the previous studies in this series, it was notable that all subjects in Group 1 had a lower VIQ than PIQ, that 14 of the 15 subjects in Group 2 had a lower VIQ than PIQ (one subject had equivalent VIQ and PIQ), and that all subjects in Group 3 had a higher VIQ than PIQ.

It is clear that Groups 1 and 2 performed in a fashion very similar to that expected of groups of older children with LD who exhibit the WISC High Performance IQ (HP)–Low Verbal IQ (LV) pattern, and that Group 3 performed in a manner expected of older children with LD who exhibit the WISC High Verbal IQ (HV)–Low Performance IQ (LP) pattern (Rourke et al., 1971). It is also important to emphasize that *individual subjects* within the three groups exhibited results on the WISC that were all but indistinguishable from the *group* results reported above. Thus, this type of nomothetic research tack did not do violence to any idiosyncratic (ideographic) imperatives, at least in terms of WISC VIQ–PIQ discrepancies.

If there is a reason to believe that WISC VIQ–PIQ discrepancies may be associated with or reflect the differential integrity of information-processing systems within the two cerebral hemispheres in older children with LD, as has been suggested (e.g. Rourke, 1982), then it would appear that the basis on which the groups were chosen in the Rourke and Finlayson (1978) study may also reflect this difference. At the very least, the results of the latter investigation would be consistent with the view that the subjects in Group 3 may be limited in their performance because of compromised functional integrity of systems within the right cerebral hemisphere, and that the subjects in Groups 1 and 2 were suffering from the adverse effects of relatively dysfunctional left-hemi-spheric systems. These inferences were felt to be reasonable because the subjects in Group 3 did particularly poorly *only* in those skills and abilities ordinarily thought to be subserved primarily by systems within the right cerebral hemisphere, whereas the subjects in Groups 1 and 2 were markedly deficient *only* in those skills and abilities ordinarily thought to be subserved primarily by systems within the left cerebral hemisphere.

Also of importance in the present context was the fact that the two groups of subjects who had been equated for deficient arithmetic performance (Groups 2 and 3) exhibited vastly different performances on verbal and visual–spatial tasks. These differences were clearly related to their *patterns* of reading, spelling, and arithmetic rather than to their *levels of performance* in arithmetic *per se*. Indeed, although the WRAT Reading, Spelling, and Arithmetic subtest scores of Group 2 were in no case significantly superior to that of Group 3, the performance of Group 2 was significantly superior to that of Group 3 on all of the measures of visual–perceptual and visual–spatial skills employed in this investigation (WISC Picture Completion, Picture Arrangement, Block Design, and Object Assembly; Target Test). More generally, it seemed reasonable to infer that the neuropsy-chological bases for the impaired arithmetic performances of Groups 2 and 3 differed markedly: whereas subjects in the Group 2 subtype would appear to experience difficulty in mechanical arithmetic because of "verbal" deficiencies, subjects of the Group 3 subtype would be expected to encounter difficulties with mechanical arithmetic as a direct result of deficiencies in "visual–spatial" abilities. Indeed, a qualitative analysis of the errors made by these two subtypes of youngsters with LD suggested very strongly that this is, in fact, the case (see Strang & Rourke, 1985b).

Within the present context, the principal import of these results is that Groups 2 and 3 appeared to differ markedly in their mnestic skills. At the risk of oversimplifying these differences at this point, it was apparent that Group 2 exhibited deficiencies in "verbal" memory whereas children in Group 3 ap-peared to experience their principal mnestic difficulties within the area of "visual" memory.

Study 2

Following the Rourke and Finlayson (1978) study, we decided to determine whether these same three groups of 9- to 14-year-old subjects with LD would differ in predictable ways on tests from a very different neuropsychological domain: namely, those designed to measure motor, psychomotor, and tactile–perceptual skills. In this investigation (Rourke & Strang, 1978), we were particularly interested to determine if any evidence might be adduced to support a view that these groups of children with LD were suffering from differential impairment of functional systems thought to be subserved primarily by structures and systems within the left or the right cerebral hemisphere. We hoped to accomplish this through an analysis of the right- and left-hand performances of these groups of right-handed children with LD on selected motor, psychomotor, and tactile–perceptual measures.

The results of this study demonstrated that children with LD in Group 3 have marked deficiencies relative to Groups 1 and 2 in some psychomotor and tactile–perceptual skills. In addition, comparisons of these results with the norms available for these tests (Knights & Norwood, 1980) indicated that the performances of Group 3 fell well below age-expectation on these measures, whereas the performances of Groups 1 and 2 were well within normal limits.

Confining our discussion to the performances of Groups 2 and 3 in the two studies under consideration, it is clear that Group 2 scored lower than expected on measures of abilities ordinarily thought to be subserved primarily by systems within the left cerebral hemisphere, and much better (in an age-appropriate fashion) on measures of abilities ordinarily thought to be subserved primarily by right-hemispheric systems. The opposite state of affairs obtained in the case of children with LD of the Group 3 subtype.

Comparison of the results of the Rourke and Strang (1978) study with those of Rourke and Finlayson (1978) is especially important in the case of Group 3. The particular pattern that emerged for this group is one that is somewhat analogous to that seen in the Gerstmann syndrome (Benson & Geschwind, 1970; Kinsbourne & Warrington, 1963). That is, the children in Group 3 exhibited the following: outstanding deficiencies in arithmetic (within a context of normal reading and spelling); visual–spatial orientation difficulties, including right–left orientation problems; general psychomotor incoordination, including problems that would fall under the rubric of "dysgraphia"; and impaired tactile-discrimination abilities, including finger agnosia. At the same time, it must be emphasized that the pattern of assets and deficits exhibited by children in Group 3 would appear to be most compatible with relatively deficient *right*-hemispheric systems rather than with deficient *left*-hemispheric systems as advanced by Benson and Geschwind (1970).

The results of the Rourke and Finlayson (1978) and the Rourke and Strang (1978) investigations would appear to have significant and widespread import for the determination of subtypes of youngsters with LD. Indeed, several groups of investigators have carried out studies that have attested to the reliability and validity of this classification system (e.g. Fletcher, 1985; Loveland, Fletcher & Bailey, 1990; Mattson, Sheer & Fletcher, 1992; Share, Moffit & Silva, 1988; Siegel & Heaven, 1986; White, Moffitt & Silva, 1992). Rather than deal with these implications at this juncture, however, it would be instructive to consider the results of the last studies in this series—one dealing with the concept-formation and problem-solving abilities of 9- to 14-year-old Group 2 and 3 children (Strang & Rourke, 1983); two others, with the determination of the verbal, visual–spatial, psychomotor, and tactile–perceptual capacities of 7- to 8-year-old Group 1, 2, and 3 children (Ozols & Rourke, 1988, 1991).

Before proceeding to a discussion of the next investigation in this series, it would be well to point out the reasons for excluding children with Group 1 characteristics from an in-depth analysis in conjunction with this and other studies. Reasons for this exclusion relate to the fact that Group 1 appears to be made up of several discrete subtypes of children with LD (Fisk & Rourke, 1979; Petrauskas & Rourke, 1979). For the purposes of this presentation, we will continue with a description of the findings of an investigation of the nonverbal problem-solving and concept-formation abilities of Groups 2 and 3.

Study 3

In this investigation (Strang & Rourke, 1983), 9- to 14-year-old Group 2 and 3 children (15 in each group) were chosen in a fashion virtually identical to that employed in Study 1 and Study 2 just reviewed; that is, the primary criteria for group selection were their patterns of academic performance in reading, spelling, and arithmetic. These groups were equated for age and WISC Full Scale IQ (range: 86–114). The dependent measure employed in this study included the number of errors on the six subtests of the Halstead Category Test (Reitan & Davison, 1974) and the total number of errors exhibited on the entire test. The form of the Category Test used for children 9–15 years of age includes six subtests and 168 items. The sixth subtest includes only review items from subtests 2, 3, 4, and 5, presented in a randomly ordered fashion. The Category Test is a relatively complex concept-formation measure involving nonverbal abstract reasoning, hypothesis-testing, and the ability to benefit from positive and negative informational feedback. The most important results of this study were the following.

As predicted, Group 3 children scored significantly higher on the Category Test total errors score than did children in Group 2. Furthermore, the level of performance of Group 3 children on this measure was approximately one standard deviation below age expectation (Knights & Norwood, 1980), whereas Group 2 children performed in an age-appropriate manner. An analysis of performances on the subtests of the Category Test revealed that the performance of Group 2 was significantly superior to that of Group 3 on the final three subtests (4, 5, and 6). It is notable that subtests 4 and 5 of the Category Test are those that are most complex in terms of their requirements for visual–spatial analysis, and that subtest 6 requires *incidental memory* for the previously correct solutions. As such, subtest 6 is one measure of the child's capacity to benefit from experience with the task.

These results were expected in view of those previously documented deficits exhibited by Group 3 children that we thought would have interfered with the normal development of the higher-order cognitive skills presumably tapped by the Category Test. Our reasoning for this assertion was as follows. It would seem highly likely that the majority of children in Group 3 have suffered since birth from the ill-effects of their neuropsychological deficiencies (i.e. bilateral tactile–perceptual impairment; bilateral psychomotor impairment; and poorly developed visual–perceptual–organizational abilities). In terms of the theory regarding the development of intellectual functions formulated by Piaget (1954), one would expect that these deficiencies would have a negative effect on the successful acquisition of cognitive skills at later stages. Piaget's description of what he considered to be significant sensorimotor activities serves to high-light the importance of tactile–perceptual, psychomotor, and visual–perceptual–organizational functions for the infant and young child. Since Group 3 children are particularly deficient in these neuropsychological functions (and probably have been so since birth), it would seem highly probable that they have not benefited as much as have most children from the sensorimotor period of development. Furthermore, their cognitive operations, particularly those that are not regulated easily by language functions (e.g. higher-order analysis, organization, and synthesis), would also be expected to be deficient.

The essentially intact Category Test performance of Group 2 would suggest strongly that language and thought, as Piaget suggested, are quite distinct. Group 2 youngsters, although deficient in many aspects of linguistic and auditory–perceptual functioning, performed at normal levels on this very complex test of nonverbal concept formation and problem-solving. Apart from some difficulties exhibited on subtest 1 (which involves the *reading* of Roman numerals), they performed well within age-expectations on the other subtests. They also exhibited a much better developed capacity to benefit from experience with this task than did the Group 3 children. Finally, they showed considerable capacity to deal effectively and adaptively with the novel problem-solving, hypothesis-testing and cognitive flexibility requirements of the Category Test.

The fact that there is absolutely no evidence of impairment in tactile–perceptual, visual–spatial–organizational, and psychomotor skills in Group 2 children would suggest that their course through the sensorimotor period of intellectual development described by Piaget (1954) would be expected to have been normal. Even though afflicted with fairly obvious difficulties in the development and elaboration of some important psycholinguistic skills, their development of higher-order cognitive processes seems to have proceeded without complication. On the other hand, Group 3 children exhibit signs of significant impairment in tactile–perceptual, visual–spatial–organizational, and psychomotor skills. It may be the case that these constitute the conceptual underpinnings or "building blocks" for the development of skills involving reasoning (such as mathematics), and that deficiencies in them are responsible for the fact that these children have failed to develop higher-order concept-formation and problem-solving abilities to a normal degree. Whether and to what extent the relative failures in conceptual reasoning and related abilities are a direct function of inadequate sensorimotor experience must wait upon the results of further research.

Study 4

Finally, the results of recent studies that employed almost all of the aforementioned measures in the investigation of Group 1 (R–S–A), 2 (R–S), and 3 (A) children with LD between the ages of 7 and 8 years (Ozols & Rourke, 1988, 1991) yielded results in the case of verbal, auditory–perceptual, and visual–spatial skills and abilities that were quite comparable with those obtained in the studies of 9- to 14-year-old children (Rourke & Finlayson, 1978). However, as in the Rourke et al. (1973) study of 6- to 8-year-old children who were assigned to groups on the basis of their patterns of WISC VIQ–PIQ discrepancies, the results were not as clear-cut as were those evident for older children with LD, especially in the areas of motor, psychomotor and tactile–perceptual skills (Rourke & Strang, 1978). In addition, it was not possible to measure higher-order (formal) reasoning and concept-formation abilities in an adequate fashion in these younger children, who are, in Piaget's terms, still functioning within the stage of concrete operational thought.

This completes our survey of the levels and configurations of neuropsychological assets and deficits exhibited by subtypes of children with LD who have been classified on the basis of their patterns of academic performances in reading, spelling, and arithmetic. For a summary of validation studies of these subtype comparisons from other laboratories, the interested reader is referred to Fletcher (1985) and Rourke (1991).

Summary of Major Findings for Group 2 (R–S) and Group 3 (A)

The major findings of the three studies of 9- to 14-year-old children in Groups 2 and 3 (hereafter referred to as Group R–S and Group A(NLD), respectively; Group 1 will be referred to as Group R–S–A; see Table 21.1) with respect to the topic under consideration are as follows.

The deficiencies, relative to age-based norms, exhibited by Group R–S children are virtually confined to the "verbal" and especially the "auditory–perceptual" areas. On the other hand, Group A children exhibit deficiencies in a wide variety of visual–perceptual–organizational, psychomotor, tactile–perceptual, and conceptual areas. Their relative problems with the Auditory Closure Test and the Sentence Memory Test may be a reflection of their difficulties in dealing with novel tasks (Auditory Closure) and their problems in understanding and utilizing semantic/meaningful content as a memory aid (Sentence Memory), as would be expected in terms of the Rourke (1982) model. Some dimensions of the relative discriminant validity of the assets and deficits that distinguish these

Table 21.1 A comparison of the designations of LD subtypes used in various studies

Studies:

Rourke et al. (1971)	Rourke & Finlayson (1978)	
Rourke & Telegdy (1971)	Rourke & Strang (1978)	Rourke (1982, 1987)
Rourke et al. (1973)	Strang & Rourke (1983)	

Designations:

Group V = P	Group 1	Group R–S–A
Group HP–LV	Group 2	Group R–S
Group HV–LP	Group 3	Group A

Abbreviations: H = high; L = low; V = Verbal IQ; P = Performance IQ.
The group designations in each column are those used in the studies at the head of the column.
There is a rather close comparability between the pairs of designations in the rows of the middle and
last columns (i.e. between Group 1 and Group R–S–A and so on). With regard to the designations in
the first and middle columns, Group HP–LV is most like Groups 1 and 2, and Group HV–LP is most
like Group 3.

two subtypes of children with LD have been the subject of recent investigations
in our laboratory (e.g. Harnadek & Rourke, 1994).

Upon examination of the WRAT arithmetic performances of Group R–S, it is
typically found that they make fewer mistakes than is generally the case for
children who are deficient in this area. They exhibit a tendency to avoid
unfamiliar arithmetic operations or those about which they are uncertain. An
exception to this state of affairs is sometimes seen in younger (9- to 10-year-old)
children who seem to find ways to calculate correctly without being entirely
familiar with the standard procedures (e.g. they may count on their fingers
because they do not remember the multiplication tables). The errors made by
these children usually reflect some difficulty in *remembering* mathematical
tables or remembering a particular step in the correct procedure for solving a
problem. They also tend to avoid problems that require the reading of printed
words. It is clear that problems in exact memory for verbal material (e.g.
calculation facts; multiplication tables) play a large role in the arithmetic
calculation deficiencies of children in Group R–S.

It should be clear that the problems that Group R–S children exhibit in the
studies described above (i.e. primarily "verbal" in nature) are reflected in a
qualitative analysis of their mechanical arithmetic errors. Also reflected in such
analyses is their capacity for understanding when problems are too difficult for
them and other forms of adaptive behaviour that one would expect to see
in children whose nonverbal problem-solving, strategy-generating, hypothesis-
testing, and feedback processing skills are intact.

A qualitative analysis of the mechanical arithmetic errors of Group A reveals
a far different picture from that obtaining for Group R–S children. However, as

is the case for Group R–S children, the quality of the errors made by Group A children is predictable in terms of their pattern of neuropsychological assets and deficits. Such an analysis reveals that they tend to make a large number and a wide range of types of errors on the WRAT Arithmetic subtest. As would be expected, the type and, in some cases, the quality of errors varies somewhat with age. Nevertheless, it is found that some of the oldest children in Group A persist in making the same types of errors as are found in the WRAT profiles of the younger (9-year-old) children in this group.

One type of mechanical arithmetic error found in the WRAT Arithmetic performance of Group A children involves "memory". For example, in some cases, the Group A child's errors appear to result from his or her failure to remember a particular number fact. It should be noted that this type of error is not predominant in the profiles of Group A children. Often it is clear that the child has the rule available in memory, but fails to access the remembered rule at the point at which it is needed in the arithmetic calculation process. In a sense, they seem to "forget" that a particular rule should be invoked—or a particular fact retrieved—at a particular point in the calculation process. This appears to be a function of their problems in judgement and reasoning rather than a reflection of their mnestic capacities *per se*.

Indeed, children in this group typically attempt questions that are clearly beyond their current realm of expertise. In these cases, they produce solutions that are completely unreasonable in view of the task demands. Unreasonable solutions are also exhibited on questions for which there is some evidence that the child understands the procedure. In other instances, such children fail to generate a reasonable plan of action when the requirements of a particular mechanical arithmetic question are only slightly different from procedures that the child has obviously mastered. This failure to generalize (remember?) a particular skill so that it can be adapted to a new, slightly different situation is a predominant feature of the general adaptational characteristics of Group A children.

These aspects of the mechanical arithmetic performance of Group A would appear to be qualitative reflections of (a) their difficulties in visual–spatial–organizational and psychomotor skills and concept-formation and hy-pothesis-testing abilities, and (b) their adequate verbal memory skills (but with shortcomings in their capacity to deploy such skills adaptively due to difficulties in understanding when particular bits of stored information are needed during the course of a calculation procedure). Some of these types of mechanical arithmetic errors can be found in the profiles of other children with arithmetic impairment who exhibit types and degrees of neuropsychological deficiencies that are somewhat different from those of children in Group A (DeLuca, Rourke & Del Dotto, 1991). However, many of the foregoing characteristics (especially as regards errors that result from deficient judgment and reasoning) distinguish Group A children from their peers with LD whose levels of psycho-metric intelligence fall within the average range.

Comparisons of Group R–S and Group A

Based upon the foregoing analyses, there are several specific conclusions that apply to these two subtypes with respect to their mnestic and related skills and abilities. (In the following, "older" refers to 9- to 14-year-old children, "younger" to 7- and 8-year-old children.)

1. Older Group R–S children exhibit some (often no more than mild) deficiencies in the more rote aspects of psycholinguistic skills, such as the recall of information and word definitions. Group A exhibits average to superior skills in these areas. (It is clear that children in Group A exhibit good memory for the straightforward, rote verbal dimensions of such material.)
2. Older Group R–S children exhibit outstanding deficiencies in the more complex semantic–acoustic aspects of psycholinguistic skills such as sentence memory and auditory analysis of common words. (Often, these deficiencies are characterized as problems in "memory" for the material in question.) Group A children exhibit less than average performances in these areas, but their levels of performance are superior to those of group R–S children. Group A children tend to perform least well on those tests of semantic–acoustic processing that place an emphasis upon the processing of novel, complex, and/or meaningful material. (Once again, these deficiencies are often thought of as mnestic problems.)
3. Older Group R–S children exhibit normal levels of performance on visual–spatial–organizational, psychomotor and tactile–perceptual tasks. Group A children have outstanding difficulties on such tasks. In general, the more novel the visual–spatial, psychomotor and tactile–perceptual task, the more impairment, relative to age-based norms, is evident in the Group A child's performance. (Often the impairment on such tests is interpreted as a failure to "remember" aspects of the material presented.)
4. Older Group R–S children perform normally on nonverbal problem-solving tasks. They have no difficulty in benefiting from experience with such tasks. They are particularly adept at utilizing nonverbal informational feedback in order to modify their performance to meet the demands of such tasks. (It is clear that these children have no difficulty in "remembering" the informational feedback provided on this task.) Group A children exhibit profound problems on nonverbal problem-solving tasks. They give little or no evidence of benefiting from informational feedback and continued experience with such tasks, even when the information provided would be expected to be well within estimates based upon their rote verbal learning and mnestic capacities (e.g. Verbal IQ).
5. Younger Group R–S children and Group A children exhibit inter- and intra-group patterns of relative assets and deficits on automatic (rote) verbal, semantic–acoustic, and visual–spatial–organizational tasks that are similar to those exhibited by older children in these two groups. The exception is that

the more rote aspects of verbal skills tend to be more deficient relative to age-based norms in younger than in older Group R–S children.

These conclusions and generalizations should be sufficient to make the desired point: children with LD who are chosen solely on the basis of specific variations in patterns of academic performance (with adequate controls for age, Full Scale IQ, and other important attributes) can be shown to exhibit very different patterns of neuropsychological assets and deficits, including those in various mnestic functions. In this connection, it should be noted that both of the subtypes under consideration exhibited deficient mechanical arithmetic performance. Thus, members of each of these groups could have been included in the "learning-disabled" sample of a contrasting-groups type of study that is designed to compare "arithmetic-disabled" and "normal" children. It should be clear, from the above conclusions and generalizations, that such an "arithmetic-disabled" group could be made up of at least two very distinct arithmetic-disabled subtypes. It is also the case that:

- These subtypes of children share virtually nothing in common, from a neuropsychological standpoint, with each other
- Their similarly deficient levels of performance in mechanical arithmetic reflect these quite different "etiologies"
- Their needs for academic habilitation/rehabilitation with respect to mechanical arithmetic differ markedly from one another.

For a discussion of these issues, see Rourke (1983, 1989), Rourke, Bakker, Fisk & Strang (1983), Rourke, Fisk & Strang (1986), Rourke & Strang (1983) and Strang & Rourke (1985a,b). Below we discuss the quite different modes of intervention that appear necessary to deal with the various dimensions of their mnestic deficiencies.

An examination of Figures 21.1 and 21.2 will elucidate the models that we have used in our attempts to explain the developmental dynamics of the neuropsychological and adaptive dimensions of these two subtypes of LD. For example, the summaries of the assets and deficits of the NLD (Group A) subtype should be viewed within a specific context of cause–effect relationships; that is, the Primary neuropsychological assets and deficits are thought to lead to the Secondary neuropsychological assets and deficits, and so on within the four categories of neuropsychological dimensions, and the foregoing are seen as causative *vis-à-vis* the academic and socioemotional/adaptive aspects of this subtype. In this sense, the latter dimensions are, essentially, *dependent* variables (i.e. effects rather than causes) in the NLD subtype. The same applies, *mutatis mutandis*, to the summary of the assets and deficits of the R–S subtype. Note particularly the primary and secondary causes of the (tertiary) assets and deficits in memory of these two subtypes.

For both theoretical and clinical reasons (Rourke, 1982, 1987, 1988b, 1989), it is important to note that the adaptive implications of the relative assets and

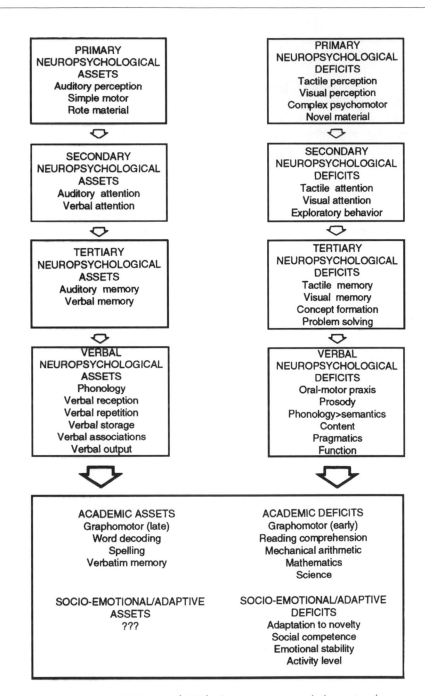

Figure 21.1 Summary of Group A(NLD) characteristics and dynamics (see text for a description of the dynamics)

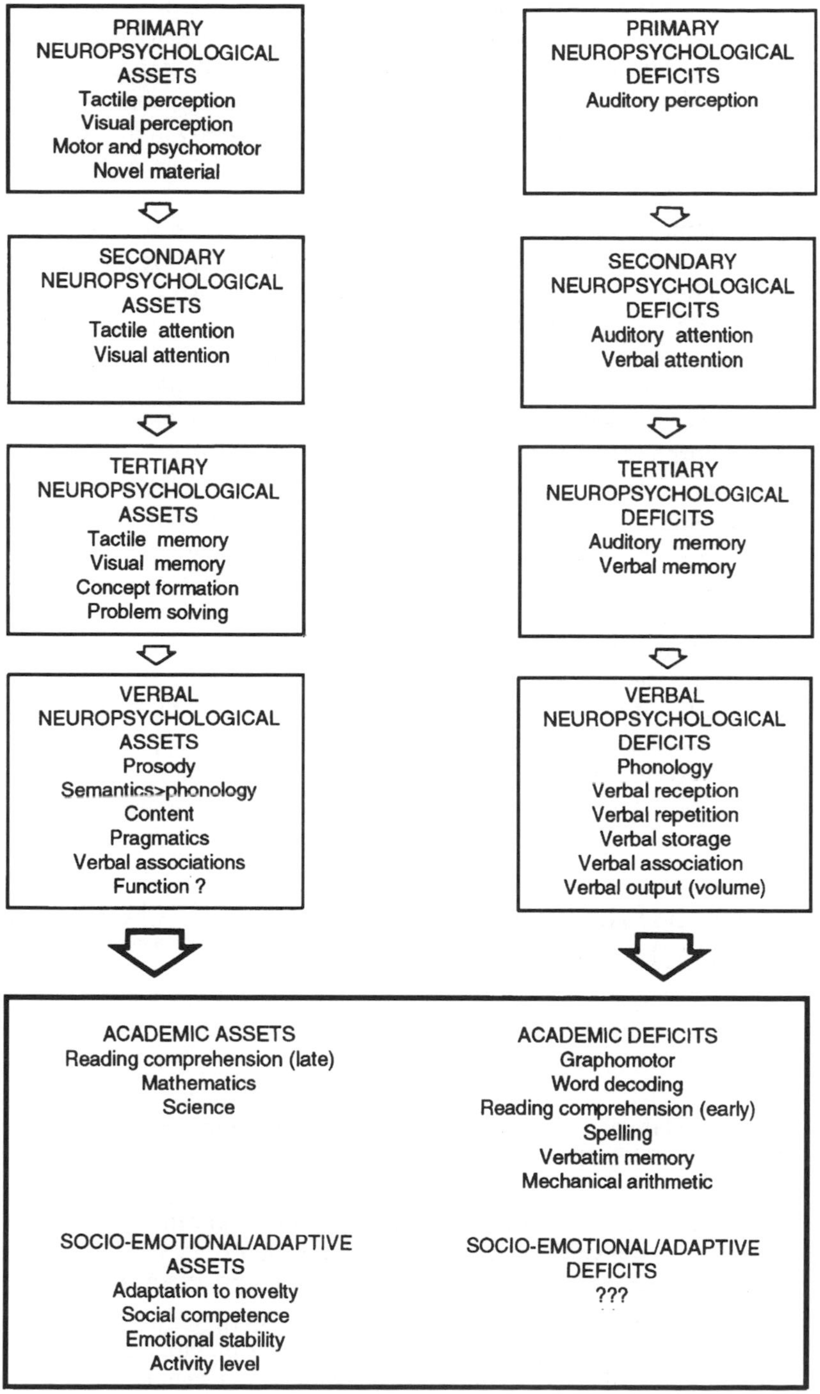

PRIMARY NEUROPSYCHOLOGICAL ASSETS Tactile perception Visual perception Motor and psychomotor Novel material	PRIMARY NEUROPSYCHOLOGICAL DEFICITS Auditory perception
SECONDARY NEUROPSYCHOLOGICAL ASSETS Tactile attention Visual attention	SECONDARY NEUROPSYCHOLOGICAL DEFICITS Auditory attention Verbal attention
TERTIARY NEUROPSYCHOLOGICAL ASSETS Tactile memory Visual memory Concept formation Problem solving	TERTIARY NEUROPSYCHOLOGICAL DEFICITS Auditory memory Verbal memory
VERBAL NEUROPSYCHOLOGICAL ASSETS Prosody Semantics>phonology Content Pragmatics Verbal associations Function ?	VERBAL NEUROPSYCHOLOGICAL DEFICITS Phonology Verbal reception Verbal repetition Verbal storage Verbal association Verbal output (volume)

ACADEMIC ASSETS Reading comprehension (late) Mathematics Science	ACADEMIC DEFICITS Graphomotor Word decoding Reading comprehension (early) Spelling Verbatim memory Mechanical arithmetic
SOCIO-EMOTIONAL/ADAPTIVE ASSETS Adaptation to novelty Social competence Emotional stability Activity level	SOCIO-EMOTIONAL/ADAPTIVE DEFICITS ???

Figure 21.2 Summary of Group R–S characteristics and dynamics (see text for a description of the dynamics)

deficits of older Group R–S and children with NLD extend well beyond the confines of the academic setting. For example, it is quite clear that Group R–S children tend to fare far better in social situations than do children with NLD. More precise delineations of these psychosocial learning considerations are contained in Rourke (1988a, 1989), Rourke & Fuerst (1991) and in other recent investigations (e.g. Loveland, Fletcher & Bailey, 1990; Ozols & Rourke, 1985, 1991; Rourke & Fisk, 1992; White, Moffitt & Silva, 1992).

One very important implication of these views relates to the qualitative analysis of the arithmetic performance of children who exhibit the NLD profile that was explained above. When a similar qualitative analysis of the *psychosocial* behaviour of children with NLD is carried out, we find that the neuropsychological assets and deficits that appear to lie at the root of their social adaptation deficiencies are virtually identical to those that have a negative impact on their performance in mechanical arithmetic. In a word, the maladaptive social behaviour of children with NLD is seen as stemming from the very same neuropsychological deficits as do their problems in arithmetic calculation (e.g. those in visual–perceptual–organizational, psychomotor, and concept-formation skills, and difficulties in dealing with novel problem-solving situations).

Subtypes of children with patterns virtually identical to those focused on herein (i.e. subtypes R–S–A, R–S, and A) have been found by other investigators in North America (Fletcher & Satz, 1985; Morris, Blachfield & Satz, 1986), the Netherlands (van der Vlugt, 1991; van der Vlugt & Satz, 1985), and Finland (Korhonen, 1991). It is especially important to note that children with outstandingly impaired arithmetic (relative to reading and spelling) appear in these large samples of children whose neuropsychological performances have been subjected to statistical subtyping algorithms (primarily cluster analysis).

VALIDITY STUDIES OF MEMORY IN GROUPS R–S AND A(NLD)

Many investigators in a variety of different laboratories have contributed to the validation of this academic achievement subtype system. These would include investigations by the following: Siegal & Heaven (1986), Loveland, Fletcher & Bailey (1990), Mattson, Sheer & Fletcher (1992), Miles & Stelmack (1994), Share, Moffitt & Silva (1988), Stelmack & Miles (1990), and White, Moffitt & Silva (1992).

Recently, short-term memory has been examined as another dimension upon which to validate subtypes of learning disabled children. Within the present context, the studies of Siegal and her colleagues (see below), Fletcher (1985), and Brandys & Rourke (1991) are especially important.

Siegel and Linder (1984) compared the short-term memory processes of two groups of children with LD, ranging in age from 7 to 13 years, on a variety of memory tasks. The groups consisted of children with a specific arithmetic deficit (similar to Group A) and children who displayed a concurrent deficit in reading and arithmetic performance on the WRAT (similar to Groups R–S–A and R–S). The tasks in this study varied in terms of presentation (visual versus oral), content (rhyming versus nonrhyming), and response modality (oral versus written). The stimuli consisted of letters of the alphabet. Whereas the children with reading disabilities (Group R–S) experienced difficulties in the recall of both auditory and visual stimuli, the children with "specific" arithmetic LD (Group A) displayed poor recall only for the visually presented material. In the younger age groups, both subtypes exhibited an insensitivity to the phonological aspects (e.g., rhyming versus nonrhyming) of the stimuli.

This latter result was also found in a second study conducted by Siegel and Ryan (1988). The children with LD in this study were again between the ages of 7 and 14 years and were divided into similar groups. In addition, however, the researchers examined the development of grammatical and phonological as well as short-term memory skills in the children. The items in the short-term memory task consisted of alphabet letters (rhyming and nonrhyming) that were presented visually. The reading disabled (but not arithmetic disabled) children were found to demonstrate significant difficulty on tasks involving the grammatical and syntactic aspects of language, phonics, and phonological processing. Compared with control subjects, both reading disabled and arithmetic disabled children displayed below-average short-term memory skills. It is noteworthy, however, that while the children with arithmetic disabilities were found to be insensitive to the phonological aspects of the stimuli in the memory task, they were also shown to be efficient phonological processors. Thus, it is possible that, in fact, the children with "specific" arithmetic disabilities (Group A) were processing the letters as visual stimuli, independent of a connection to language.

Together, these two studies appear to suggest that children with reading disabilities (Group R–S) display short-term memory deficits for verbal stimuli, whereas children with "specific" arithmetic disabilities (Group A) experience difficulty remembering visual material. Of course, these results correspond quite precisely with our own findings with respect to "memory" (see above).

The development of working memory has also been examined by Siegel and Ryan (1988) in children achieving at an average level in school and children with LD. Working memory was defined as the temporary storage of information whilst other cognitive tasks are being performed. The nature of the tasks administered to the children reflected this definition. Two types of tasks were employed—one involved sentence completion and the other involved counting. Briefly, the children with reading disabilities were found to perform poorly on both tasks whereas the children with "specific" arithmetic disabilities obtained significantly lower scores only on the counting task. The latter result was interpreted to suggest that such children have a working memory deficit specifically for processing numerical information.

It can be argued, however, that the results of this study reflect the findings of the previous studies. That is, in the first instance, the group with reading disabilities displayed a generalized deficit in working memory because both tasks relied heavily on the use of language. In addition, the counting task involved a complex visual display consisting of patterns of dots of different colours. Siegel and Ryan (1988) comment that working memory requires both simultaneous processing of incoming information and the retrieval of other information. If this be the case, it is likely that the deficient performance of the children with arithmetic disabilities (Group A) on this memory task reflected an inability to process the complex and novel visual stimuli. This inference is bolstered by the findings of two other studies (Brandys & Rourke, 1991; Fletcher, 1985).

Fletcher (1985) conducted a study comparing four groups of disabled learners on a verbal and nonverbal selective reminding task. The children were placed into four groups on the basis of their pattern of WRAT scores: (1) reading–spelling disabled (similar to Group R–S); (2) reading–spelling–arithmetic disabled (similar to Groups R–S–A; (3) spelling–arithmetic disabled; and (4) arithmetic disabled (similar to Group A). The results of the study showed that the LD subgroups displayed distinct patterns of memory deficits. Specifically, the children with reading problems exhibited retrieval difficulties on verbal tasks, whereas the children similar to Group A exhibited both storage and retrieval problems on nonverbal tasks.

In addition to indicating a memory deficit for verbal material, the findings for the group with reading disabilities may reflect inadequate rehearsal strategies leading to poor retrieval scores. Furthermore, the verbal selective reminding task in this instance consisted of animal names that were semantically related in a fairly straightforward manner. Therefore, it is possible that the group with reading disabilities was able to make use of this semantic information for encoding purposes. The findings for the group with arithmetic disabilities (similar to Group A) may reflect (a) a difficulty in the encoding of nonverbal (visually-presented) material, and/or (b) an inability to encode novel material that is neither easily organized nor readily mediated through verbal strategies. It is clear that these findings are consistent with our own, and are in accord with expectations deducible from the Rourke (1982, 1989) models.

Brandys and Rourke (1991) examined the performances of reading disabled (Group R–S) and arithmetic disabled (Group A) children, between the ages of 10 and 14 years, on verbal and nonverbal memory tasks. The nonverbal task consisted of both the copy and delayed recall aspects of the Rey–Osterrieth Complex Figure Task. The children similar to Group A were found to exhibit significantly deficient encoding and recall on this task. Moreover, when the memory bias against poor encoders was removed, no significant difference was found between the groups of children. This finding suggests that Group A children experience particular difficulty in organizing complex visual information and developing an effective encoding strategy.

Overall, the results of these studies indicate that children who display an arithmetic-specific deficit (Group A) experience difficulty encoding visually presented material. In addition, however, the visual stimuli in these studies were typically complex, not easily encoded using verbal strategies, and novel. Therefore, it is not completely clear whether these children are exhibiting a modality-specific (visual) memory deficit and/or a difficulty encoding complex novel material. One way to investigate this question would be to present the children with verbal tasks that consist of complex and/or novel stimuli (compared with the relatively straightforward list-learning tasks administered in the aforementioned studies). It is suggested, however, that evidence from the performance of these children on other neuropsychological measures would certainly seem to suggest a deficit in both areas.

Finally, the results of these studies indicate a memory deficit that is specific to verbal stimuli in the instance of children who perform poorly in both arithmetic and reading (Group R–S). In addition, there is evidence to suggest that their deficient language skills affect their ability to remember complex nonverbal stimuli that might otherwise be encoded with the assistance of verbal mediation.

RELATED STUDIES WITH IMPLICATIONS FOR MEMORY IN CHILDREN WITH NLD

There is evidence that the evoked potentials of children who manifest impaired arithmetic performance in addition to impaired reading and spelling differ markedly from those whose impaired arithmetic performance is seen within the context of well-developed single-word reading and spelling (Mattson, Sheer & Fletcher, 1992; Miles & Stelmack, 1994; Stelmack & Miles, 1990). The results are in accord with the Rourke models (1982, 1989), and reinforce the external validity of the typology under review.

Different patterns of impaired arithmetic performance *vis-à-vis* reading and spelling performance are associated with predictable patterns of neuropsychological assets and deficits as well as predictable patterns of socioemotional assets and deficits. Evidence in support of this view is found in the following: DeLuca, Rourke & Del Dotto (1991), Casey, Rourke & Picard (1991), Fletcher (1985), Fuerst & Rourke (1993), Fuerst, Fisk & Rourke (1989, 1990), Loveland, Fletcher & Bailey, (1990), White, Moffitt & Silva (1992), Ozols & Rourke (1985, 1991), Rourke & Fuerst (1991), Rourke, Young & Leenaars (1989), and Strang & Rourke (1985a,b).

Methods for the neuropsychological assessment of and intervention with children who exhibit the NLD syndrome as well as other subtypes of children with LD have been developed (Rourke, 1976a, 1981; Rourke, Bakker, Fisk & Strang, 1983; Rourke, Del Dotto, Rourke & Casey, 1990; Rourke, Fisk & Strang, 1986). Some of these have been subjected to empirical test (e.g. Williams, Richman & Yarbrough, 1994). A précis of our suggested methods is presented in the final section of this chapter.

Finally, there is considerable evidence to suggest that outstandingly poor arithmetic performance relative to performance in single-word reading and spelling is a characteristic of children who exhibit a number of neurological diseases of childhood and a wide variety of developmental disabilities wherein brain impairment is thought to be a principal feature. Examples of this include hydrocephalus (Fletcher, Francis et al., 1992); myelomeningocele (Wills, Holmbeck, Dillon & McLone, 1990); traumatic brain injury (Fletcher & Levin, 1988); metachromatic leukodystrophy (Shapiro, Lipton & Krivit, 1992); callosal agenesis (Casey, Del Dotto & Rourke, 1990); Williams syndrome (Udwin & Yule, 1991); fetal alcohol syndrome (Streissguth & LaDue, 1987); congenital hypothyroidism (Rovet, 1990); Turner's syndrome (Rovet & Netley, 1982); velocardiofacial syndrome (Golding-Kushner, Weller & Shprintzen, 1985); insulin dependent diabetes mellitus (Rovet, Ehrlich, Czuchta & Akler, 1993); adrenal hyperplasia (Nass et al., 1990); Asperger's syndrome (Stevens & Moffitt, 1988); and autism (Szatmari, Tuff, Finlayson & Bartolucci, 1990). It is also the case that children who have been exposed to very high doses of cranial irradiation for treatment of various forms of cancer exhibit many elements of the NLD syndrome (Fletcher & Copeland, 1988).

What is of crucial importance in this connection is that there are thought to be significant perturbations of white matter development and/or functioning in most of the aforementioned diseases and disabilities. And it is disordered myelinization and/or myelin functioning that has been hypothesized to be the "final common pathway" that eventuates in the NLD syndrome (Rourke, 1987, 1988b, 1989); current and future research will indicate whether and to what extent this is the case. For an example of such efforts, see Fletcher, Bohan et al. (1992). In the present context, it is important to note the incidence of the NLD syndrome in these neurological diseases because of the potential generalizability of research findings to these patient groups, both in terms of presenting symptoms and in terms of commonality of mnestic disturbances.

SUMMARY OF MEMORY DIFFICULTIES ENCOUNTERED BY GROUPS R–S AND A

In order to summarize some dimensions of the mnestic tribulations and needs of the two subtypes of children with LD under consideration, we offer the outline in Table 21.2. This is not meant to be exhaustive. Rather, we present it to suggest to the reader the type of summarical scheme that can be devised for quick reference in the clinic, classroom, or home. It should be clear that a finer differentiation could be made in the list for a particular child, and that the scheme can be modified slightly to accommodate the treatment recommendations that we offer below.

We turn now to a consideration of the implications of the aforementioned findings and models for habilitative intervention *vis-à-vis* the memory disorders associated with them.

Table 21.2 Examples of interactions between type of memory task and expected response of children of the NLD and R–S subtypes

Memory task	NLD	R–S
Rote-verbal	+	−
Visual–spatial	−	+
Auditory–verbal input only	+	−
Visual–spatial input only	−	+
Sequential (verbalizable)	+	?
Sequential (rational)	−	+
Sequential (visual–spatial; not easily verbalized)	−	?
Visual demonstrations not accompanied by words	−	+
Verbal demonstrations not accompanied by visual demonstrations	?	−

+ = average to above-average probability of remembering;
− = below-average to very low probability of remembering;
? = varies as a function of level of difficulty and other factors

IMPLICATIONS FOR HABILITATIVE/INTERVENTIVE STRATEGY PLANNING

The delineation of subtypes of children with LD provides a potential basis for the development of effective remedial intervention strategies. Yet, research concerning remedial efforts for such children has typically followed a paradigm in which a single treatment intervention is tested on a single group of undifferentiated children with LD. This approach assumes that such children constitute a homogeneous group and that they do not vary with respect to academic performance, neuropsychological assets and deficits, or other factors such as personality functioning (Fletcher & Satz, 1985). (Fortunately, there are exceptions to this tack, as exemplified by the studies of Lyon and his colleagues; see e.g. Lyon & Flynn (1991).) The abovementioned subtyping studies have demonstrated clearly that this is not the case and, thus, remedial efforts cannot be expected to bear a simple relationship to the diagnosis of learning disability. Moreover, it is clear from the above discussion on memory that, although children with LD may perform at similar levels on various tasks, they may do so for very different reasons.

In the following section, an outline of some of the common features of an intervention programme for children and adolescents who exhibit patterns of neuropsychological assets and deficits corresponding to the R–S subtype and NLD syndrome is presented. These suggestions are adapted from material previously presented by Brandys and Rourke (1991), Rourke (1989), and Strang and Rourke (1985). For more general considerations concerning the care and treatment of brain-impaired children and adolescents, the reader is referred to Rourke, Bakker, Fisk and Strang (1983) and Rourke, Fisk and Strang (1986).

R–S Subtype

Encoding "short-cuts". For the most part, R–S children display poor verbal skills (particularly with respect to phonetic processing) and difficulty encoding verbal material. Their strengths lie in their comprehension of verbal material and their visual–perceptual, visual–spatial, and nonverbal problem-solving skills.

These children, then, are likely to benefit from specific training in short-cuts to encoding linguistic information. That is, the use of techniques such as "chunking", conceptual and semantic encoding, and elaborative rehearsal should be encouraged. Younger children, who are in the early stages of learning to read, may benefit from encoding chunks consisting of vowel digraphs (e.g. *oo*, *oi*) and word affixes (e.g. *re*, *ment*, *ing*). In this instance, an attempt is made to promote a "holistic" approach to learning, thereby reducing the demands of remembering each individual grapheme–phoneme correspondence.

Visual and tactile aids. In a similar vein, it may be beneficial to promote the strengths of these children in the visual–perceptual domain. In general, visual imagery mnemonics may be preferred to verbal encoding for remembering specific types of material. In younger children, the visual aspects of words and letters can be emphasized and paired with memorable pictures and/or textures. For example, letters may be incorporated with an item that represents the letter sound (e.g. an "a" is drawn to resemble an apple). The use of personal computers and computer games in the school system and at home may further afford teachers and students the opportunity to design visual presentations of material and lessons.

Reading. In general, the use of whole-word multi-sensory approaches to reading are likely to be more effective than are emphases on phonemic decoding and sequencing tasks. In fact, these children tend to experience difficulty with stimuli that are serial in nature (such as verbal material). Thus, training in recalling the temporal and/or spatial order of sequentially presented stimuli may provide a useful approach to overcome this deficit.

Cognitive strategies with older children. Older (i.e. roughly 9–14 years) children of this subtype usually benefit from being encouraged to recode complex verbal concepts and material in visual terms; for example, by drawing pictures or diagrams. These children are also likely to benefit from the development of metacognitive awareness as it applies to reading. Thus, training them to distinguish relevant from irrelevant text, rate the difficulty of a passage, or draw upon prior knowledge to manage present material would be expected to aid in their memory for text that is read. These children tend to demonstrate well-developed problem-solving skills and thus it is not unlikely that they will generate their own adaptive strategies as they grow older. It would be worthwhile then to inquire about these strategies and further promote their use and refine their development, as needed.

The whole-language approach. The use of a "whole language" approach to learning (in which speaking, reading, and writing are united around one theme or topic of interest) usually enhances the verbal skills of these children. Thus, before the child embarks upon reading a paragraph aloud, the subject material in the text is discussed, general facts presented, and words that may not be in the child's lexicon are broached. The child is then asked to read through the text, skipping over words with which she/he experiences difficulty. The child is asked to summarize what has been read, the material is further discussed, and the process repeated and elaborated as necessary.

Remembering reading material. The results of studies described by Russell and Rourke (1991) and Sweeney and Rourke (1985) suggest further that level of phonetic accuracy of mispellings in children with reading and spelling disabilities is a significant variable to consider in remedial planning. For example, children with reading disabilities who tend to overuse phonetic analysis in their approach to reading and spelling may especially benefit from remedial strategies that emphasize visual analysis. These children probably experience difficulty remembering the content of what they have read because they expend too much time and effort stumbling over words that they attempt to read with painstaking phonetic accuracy. In these instances, the child should be encouraged to focus on the general meaning of the text (see whole-language approach above), and speed should be emphasized over accuracy.

In addition, techniques that focus on the visual–spatial aspects of words should be emphasized. These include the following: sight–word strategies; increasing the salience of the visual–spatial features of word configurations; encouraging "visualization" of the graphic features of the words to be spelled or read; assessing whether the word produced graphically "looks right"; using "flashcard" exercises; and employing multisensory (e.g. kinaesthetic, tactile) methods of teaching in conjunction with dramatization. These techniques should lead to the enhancement of memory for the meaning of material that is read and memory for the visual dimensions of words. In time, this should be beneficial with respect to learning to read and to spell individual words (Russell & Rourke, 1991; Sweeney & Rourke, 1985).

NLD syndrome

In contrast to children of the R–S subtype, children with NLD demonstrate assets in verbal skills and rote memory for simple verbal material, and deficits in nonverbal problem-solving, visual–spatial–organizational skills, and memory for visual material. Moreover, these children present with particular difficulties in processing complex and novel information whether it be verbal or visual in nature.

A frequent shortcoming of remedial intervention programmes involving the child with NLD is that remedial instructors appear to be unaware of the extent and significance of the child's deficits. In part, this misperception arises because of a failure to appreciate the fact that children who read and spell well can have other academic and psychosocial difficulties. Therefore, it is particularly important to observe the children's behaviour closely, especially in novel or complex situations. The following rule of thumb may be considered: focus intently on what they do, despite what they say. When teachers and other caregivers do so in a systematic fashion, the child's deficits become quite salient.

A general teaching strategy. A significant and pervasive difficulty demonstrated by these children concerns learning new strategies and knowing when and how to apply them to changing task demands. A parts-to-whole verbal teaching approach is recommended to overcome these difficulties. That is, these children appear to learn best when material is presented to them in a systematic, step-by-step fashion. Children with NLD tend to benefit from an approach that is slow, repetitive, and highly redundant.

Moreover, if the idea, concept, or procedure can be put into words and described in a straightforward manner, these children are likely to grasp at least some aspects of the material-to-be-learned. It is important to note that these children will need to be provided with the structure of the material. That is, each of the verbal "steps" must be placed in the appropriate sequence for them and the overall structure (concept, theme...) of the subject matter provided. Furthermore, children with NLD usually benefit from child-therapist interactions in terms of generating the steps or rules, since this activity encourages a more active role on their part.

Verbal mediation. In this way, concepts of procedures to-be-learned by these children should be broken down into steps or rules that are described verbally. There are two readily observable benefits of this approach. First, the children are provided with a set of verbal rules or steps that can be written out and then reapplied as needed in other situations. Second, reducing the to-be-learned material to smaller chunks that are verbal in nature affords them the opportunity to make use of their other neuropsychological asset—rote memory for relatively simple verbal material. Furthermore, once these verbal mediation skills are learned sufficiently well, they can be used by the child to monitor, plan, and execute their behaviour more effectively in a wide domain of tasks (DeLuca, Rourke & Del Dotto, 1991).

Although this step-by-step verbal mediation approach may appear to be rather slow and tedious, it is important to keep in mind that, because of their well-developed verbal memory skills, these children often appear to be more advanced than is actually the case. In order to "absorb" material, they require much more structure and careful assistance than would, at first blush, appear necessary.

Establishing interrelationships and context. As noted, these children typically exhibit particular difficulty processing complex, nonverbal, and novel material. Thus, they usually benefit from being permitted more time to encode the information and recode it through verbally mediated strategies (as outlined above). Similarly, it is useful to present new material cumulatively, in small units, while drawing parallels/outlining relationships to facts and concepts already encoded or learned. In the first instance, this approach allows for a kind of gradual stimulus desensitization that usually reduces anxiety and stimulus overload. Second, relations between the component and the whole and between known and unknown information are drawn out for the child who is unlikely to make these necessary connections in a spontaneous manner. In a similar vein, novel verbal material should be approached by relating words to superordinate and subordinate examples within the child's lexicon. These procedures tend to enhance memory for the material learned thereby.

Elaborative rehearsal strategies. Specific training in elaborative rehearsal techniques is also beneficial for children with NLD. In particular, encouraging the child to rehearse orally is helpful, since these children seem to benefit most from auditory–verbal feedback. Another useful technique is to invite the children to "reteach" the therapist, teacher, or even another child the procedure or concept that they have just learned. In this way, understanding, analysis, and integration of the material are increased and are more likely to be remembered and applied in other situations.

Teaching generalization. The issue of generalization of learned strategies and concepts is particularly relevant with respect to children with NLD. In contrast to most normally achieving children, children with NLD typically exhibit difficulties perceiving (a) how a particular strategy or procedure may apply to several different situations, and/or (b) how a particular concept may apply to a range of topics. Thus, such children must not only be taught in a step-by-step fashion, but this procedure must be applied both within the therapeutic setting and in everyday settings. Otherwise, they appear to "forget" how to apply the procedures in question.

Encoding visual material. Dealing effectively with and remembering visual nonverbal material is a second pervasive area of difficulty for these children.

Children with NLD typically present with deficits in visual–spatial–organizational skills and their memory for visual material tends to be deficient. Based on the research conducted by Brandys and Rourke (1991), it was noted that this deficit consists of inefficient encoding strategies rather than deficient storage mechanisms. Thus, in order to enhance memory for visual nonverbal material, these children usually benefit from being trained to encode such material by means of verbally mediated strategies. That is, visual material may be recoded verbally, reinforced by specific training in labelling, followed by a listing of the visual material in highly redundant sequential steps. Younger children may be taught to name visual details in pictures as a means of encouraging them to pay attention to and record these details. In addition, it is usually beneficial to ask these children to talk about the relationships between various details in a picture in order to draw attention to the importance and complexity of the features in a visual stimulus presentation. These techniques should also encourage the child to organize the material to be encoded, thereby increasing the probability of mnestic storage and eventual recall.

Applications in social learning. In older children, this approach may take on a more functional role. That is, since children with NLD are also observed to display deficient social skills, this approach could also be employed with respect to the decoding and accurate interpretation of nonverbal behaviours. Their problems in the perception of, and memory for, significant social discriminanda (facial features, gestures, and the like) are amenable to positive change through the sorts of intervention strategies described thus far.

Applications in academic study and testing. In terms of testing course content, these children appear to benefit from multiple-choice or oral examinations. Typically, they demonstrate deficient writing skills and benefit from extra time on written assignments or tests. These writing difficulties (especially apparent among younger children with NLD) may be further circumvented by using a tape recorder in class to supplement verbal memory. For study purposes, material that requires visual organization is more salient for them if recoded into its oral form. In addition, using graph paper or colour-coded paper helps to overcome their crowding and spatial orientation difficulties. In all of this, memory is thought to be enhanced through changes in the ordinary mode of stimulus presentation in the direction of modes that "fit" the information-processing assets and deficits of the child with NLD.

CONCLUDING REMARKS

Finally, we should emphasize that a consideration of each child's individual strengths and weaknesses is essential to the design of remedial programmes aimed at enhancing memory. Just as children with LD do not constitute a homogenous group, it is also the case that not all children within a particular subtype are completely identical.

The recommendations outlined above are based on a theory of LD that is necessarily limited. Thus far, however, the following has been established: the existence of subtypes of children with LD; the reliability and external validation of these subtypes; a comprehensive description of two subtypes in particular; the specification of promising memory-enhancing strategies for two of these subtypes; and the development of tentative predictions regarding their response to treatment.

Lyon and Flynn (1991) suggest the following:

> From a clinical standpoint, it is our view that the descriptive and predictive validity of the LD diagnosis depends on the facility by which it generates testable hypotheses about instructional methodologies that have the highest probability of success with a given LD individual. (p. 223)

We are very much inclined to expand this task to include extra-academic performance. Nevertheless, a final goal remains: to conduct research examining the efficacy of these different remedial strategies for different subtypes of children with LD. This would appear to be especially efficacious for those dimensions of memory that are crucial for the successful adaptation of different subtypes of children with LD in both their academic and extra-academic pursuits.

REFERENCES

Benson, D.F. & Geschwind, N. (1970). Developmental Gerstmann syndrome. *Neurology*, **20**, 293–298.

Brandys, C.F. & Rourke, B.P. (1991). Differential memory capacities in reading- and arithmetic-disabled children. In B.P. Rourke (ed.), *Neuropsychological Validation of Learning Disability Subtypes*. Guilford Press, New York, pp. 73–96.

Casey, J.E., Del Dotto, J.E. & Rourke, B.P. (1990). An empirical investigation of the NLD syndrome in a case of agenesis of the corpus callosum. *Journal of Clinical and Experimental Neuropsychology*, **12**, 29.

Casey, J.E., Rourke, B.P. & Picard, E.M. (1991). Syndrome of nonverbal learning disabilities: age differences in neuropsychological, academic, and socioemotional functioning. *Development and Psychopathology*, **3**, 329–345.

DeLuca, J.W., Rourke, B.P. & Del Dotto, J.E. (1991). Subtypes of arithmetic-disabled children: cognitive and personality dimensions. In B.P. Rourke (ed.), *Neuropsychological Validation of Learning Disability Subtypes*. Guilford Press, New York, pp. 180–219.

Doehring, D.G. (1978). The tangled web of behavioural research on developmental dyslexia. In A.L. Benton & D. Pearl (eds), *Dyslexia: An Appraisal of Current Knowledge*. Oxford University Press, New York, pp. 125–135.

Fisk, J.L. & Rourke, B.P. (1979). Identification of subtypes of learning-disabled children at three age levels: a neuropsychological, multivariate approach. *Journal of Clinical Neuropsychology*, **1**, 289–310.

Fletcher, J.M. (1985). External validation of learning disability typologies. In B.P. Rourke (ed.), *Neuropsychology of Learning Disabilities: Essentials of Subtype Analysis*. Guilford Press, New York, pp. 187–211.

Fletcher, J.M., Bohan, T.P., Brandt, M.E., Brookshire, B.L., Beaver, S.R., Francis, D.J., Davidson, K.C., Thompson, N.M. & Miner, M.E. (1992). Cerebral white matter and cognition in hydrocephalic children. *Archives of Neurology*, **49**, 818–825.

Fletcher, J.M. & Copeland, D.R. (1988). Neurobehavioural effects of central nervous system prophylactic treatment of cancer in children. *Journal of Clinical and Experimental Neuropsychology*, **10**, 495–537.

Fletcher, J.M., Francis, D.J., Thompson, N.M., Brookshire, B.L., Bohan, T.P., Landry, S.H., Davidson, K.C. & Miner, M.E. (1992). Verbal and nonverbal skill discrepancies in hydrocephalic children. *Journal of Clinical Experimental Neuropsychology*, **14**, 593–609.

Fletcher, J.M. & Levin, H. (1988). Neurobehavioural effects of brain injury in children. In D.K. Routh (ed.), *Handbook of Pediatric Psychology*. Guilford Press, New York, pp. 258–295.

Fletcher, J.M. & Satz, P. (1985). Cluster analysis and the search for learning disability subtypes. In B.P. Rourke (ed.), *Neuropsychology of Learning Disabilities: Essentials of Subtype Analysis*. Guilford Press, New York, pp. 40–64.

Fuerst, D.R., Fisk, J.L. & Rourke, B.P. (1989). Psychosocial functioning of learning-disabled children: replicability of statistically derived subtypes. *Journal of Consulting and Clinical Psychology*, **57**, 275–280.

Fuerst, D.R., Fisk, J.L. & Rourke, B.P. (1990). Psychosocial functioning of learning-disabled children: relations between WISC Verbal IQ–Performance IQ discrepancies and personality subtypes. *Journal of Consulting and Clinical Psychology*, **58**, 657–660.

Fuerst, D.R. & Rourke, B.P. (1993). Psychosocial functioning of children: relations between personality subtypes and academic achievement. *Journal of Abnormal Child Psychology*, **21**, 597–607.

Golding-Kushner, K.J., Weller, G. & Shprintzen, R.J. (1985). Velo-cardio-facial syndrome: language and psychological profiles. *Journal of Craniofacial Genetics and Developmental Biology*, **5**, 259–266.

Harnadek, M.C.S. & Rourke, B.P. (1994). Discriminant validity of the NLD syndrome in children. *Journal of Learning Disabilities*, **27**, 144–154.

Jastak, J.F. & Jastak, S.R. (1965). *The Wide Range Achievement Test*. Guidance Associates, Wilmington, DL.

Kinsbourne, M. & Warrington, E.K. (1963). The developmental Gerstmann syndrome. *Archives of Neurology*, **8**, 490–501.

Knights, R.M. & Norwood, J.A. (1980). *Revised Smoothed Normative Data on the Neuropsychological Test Battery for Children*. The authors, Ottawa.

Korhonen, T.T. (1991). An empirical subgrouping of Finnish learning-disabled children. *Journal of Clinical and Experimental Neuropsychology*, **13**, 259–277.

Loveland, K.A., Fletcher, J.M. & Bailey, V. (1990). Nonverbal communication of events in learning-disability subtypes. *Journal of Clinical and Experimental Neuropsychology*, **12**, 433–447.

Lyon, G.R. & Flynn, J.M. (1991). Educational validation studies with subtypes of learning-disabled readers. In B.P. Rourke (ed.), *Neuropsychological Validation of Learning Disability Subtypes*. Guilford Press, New York, pp. 223–242.

Mattson, A.J., Sheer, D.E. & Fletcher, J.M. (1992). Electrophysiological evidence of lateralized disturbances in children with LD. *Journal of Clinical and Experimental Neuropsychology*, **14**, 707–716.

Miles, J.E. & Stelmack, R.M. (1994). Reading disability subtypes and the effects of auditory and visual priming on event-related potentials. *Journal of Clinical and Experimental Neuropsychology*, **16**, 43–64.

Morris, R., Blashfield, R. & Satz, P. (1986). Developmental classification of reading-disabled children. *Journal of Clinical and Experimental Neuropsychology*, **8**, 371–392.

Nass, R., Speiser, P., Heier, L., Haimes, A. & New, M. (1990). White matter abnormalities in congenital adrenal hyperplasia. *Annals of Neurology*, **28**, 470.

Ozols, R.J. & Rourke, B.P. (1985). Dimensions of social sensitivity in two types of learning-disabled children. In B.P. Rourke (ed.), *Neuropsychology of Learning Disabilities: Essentials of Subtype Analysis*. Guilford Press, New York, pp. 281–301.

Ozols, R.J. & Rourke, B.P. (1988). Characteristics of young learning-disabled children classified according to patterns of academic achievement: auditory–perceptual and visual–perceptual disabilities. *Journal of Clinical Child Psychology*, **17**, 44–52.

Ozols, R.J. & Rourke, B.P. (1991). Classification of young learning-disabled children according to patterns of academic achievement: validity studies. In B.P. Rourke (ed.), *Neuropsychological Validation of Learning Disability Subtypes*. Guilford Press, New York, pp. 97–123.

Petrauskas, R.J. & Rourke, B.P. (1979). Identification of subtypes of retarded readers: a neuropsychological, multivariate approach. *Journal of Clinical Neuropsychology*, **1**, 17–37.

Piaget, J. (1954). *The Construction of Reality in the Child*. Basic Books, New York.

Reitan, R.M. & Davidson, L.A. (eds) (1974). *Clinical Neuropsychology: Current Status and Applications*. Wiley, New York.

Rourke, B.P. (1975). Brain–behaviour relationships in children with learning disabilities. *American Psychologist*, **30**, 911–920.

Rourke, B.P. (1976a). Issues in the neuropsychological assessment of children with learning disabilities. *Canadian Psychological Review*, **17**, 89–102.

Rourke, B.P. (1976b). Reading retardation in children: developmental lag or deficit? In R.M. Knights & D.J. Bakker (eds), *Neuropsychology of Learning Disorders: Theoretical Approaches*. University Park Press, Baltimore, pp. 125–137.

Rourke, B.P. (1978a). Neuropsychological research in reading retardation: a review. In A.L. Benton & D. Pearl (eds), *Dyslexia: An Appraisal of Current Knowledge*. University Press, New York, pp. 141–171.

Rourke, B.P. (1978b). Reading, spelling, arithmetic disabilities: a neuropsychologic perspective. In H.R. Myklebust (ed.), *Progress in Learning Disabilities*, vol 4. Grune & Stratton, New York, pp. 97–120.

Rourke, B.P. (1981). Neuropsychological assessment of children with LD. In S.B. Filskov & T.J. Boll (eds), *Handbook of Clinical Neuropsychology*. Wiley-Interscience, New York, pp. 453–478.

Rourke, B.P. (1982). Central processing deficiencies in children: toward a developmental neuropsychological model. *Journal of Clinical Neuropsychology*, **4**, 1–18.

Rourke, B.P. (1983). Reading and spelling disabilities: a developmental neuropsychological perspective. In U. Kirk (ed.), *Neuropsychology of Language, Reading and Spelling*. Academic Press, New York, pp. 209–234.

Rourke, B.P. (1987). Syndrome of nonverbal learning disabilities: the final common pathway of white-matter disease/dysfunction? *Clinical Neuropsychologist*, **1**, 209–234.

Rourke, B.P. (1988a). Socioemotional disturbances of learning disabled children. *Journal of Consulting and Clinical Psychology*, **56**, 801–810.

Rourke, B.P. (1988b). The syndrome of nonverbal learning disabilities: developmental manifestations in neurological disease, disorder, and dysfunction. *The Clinical Neuropsychologist*, **2**, 293–330.

Rourke, B.P. (1989). *Nonverbal Learning Disabilities: The Syndrome and the Model*. Guilford Press, New York.

Rourke, B.P. (ed.) (1991). *Neuropsychological Validation of Learning Disability Subtypes*. Guilford Press, New York.

Rourke, B.P., Bakker, D.J., Fisk, J.L & Strang, J.D. (1983). *Child Neuropsychology: An Introduction to Theory, Research and Clinical Practice*. Guilford Press, New York.

Rourke, B.P., Del Dotto, J.E., Rourke, S.B. & Casey, J.E. (1990). Nonverbal LD: the syndrome and a case study. *Journal of School Psychology*, **28**, 361–385.

Rourke, B.P., Dietrich, D.M. & Young, G.C. (1973). Significance of WISC verbal-performance discrepancies for younger children with LD. *Perceptual and Motor Skills*, **36**, 275–282.

Rourke, B.P. & Finlayson, M.A.J. (1978). Neuropsychological significance of variations in patterns of academic performance: verbal and visual–spatial abilities. *Journal of Abnormal Child Psychology*, **6**, 121–133.

Rourke, B.P. & Fisk, J.L. (1988). Subtypes of learning-disabled children: implications for a neurodevelopmental model of differential hemispheric processing. In D.L. Molfese & S.J. Segalowitz (eds), *Developmental Implications of Brain Lateralization*. Guilford Press, New York, pp. 547–565.

Rourke, B.P. & Fisk, J.L. (1992). Adult presentations of learning disabilities. In R.F. White (ed.), *Clinical Syndromes in Adult Neuropsychology: The Practitioner's Handbook*. Elsevier, Amsterdam, pp. 451–473.

Rourke, B.P., Fisk, J.L. & Strang, J.D. (1986). *Neuropsychological Assessment of Children: A Treatment-Oriented Approach*. Guilford Press, New York.

Rourke, B.P. & Fuerst, D.R. (1991). *Learning Disabilities and Psychosocial Functioning*. Guilford Press, New York.

Rourke, B.P. & Strang, J.D. (1978). Neuropsychological significance of variations in patterns of academic performance: motor, psychomotor, and tactile–perceptual abilities. *Journal of Pediatric Psychology*, **3**, 62–66.

Rourke, B.P. & Strang, J.D. (1983). Subtypes of reading and arithmetical disabilities: a neuropsychological analysis. In M. Rutter (ed.), *Developmental Neuropsychiatry*. Guilford Press, New York, pp. 473–488.

Rourke, B.P. & Telegdy, G.A. (1971). Lateralizing significance of WISC verbal-performance discrepancies for older children with learning disabilities. *Perceptual and Motor Skills*, **33**, 875–883.

Rourke, B.P., Young, G.C. & Flewelling, R.W. (1971). The relationships between WISC verbal-performance discrepancies and selected verbal, auditory–perceptual, visual–perceptual, and problem-solving abilities in children with learning disabilities. *Journal of Clinical Psychology*, **27**, 475–479.

Rourke, B.P., Young, C.G. & Leenaars, A. (1989). A childhood learning disability that predisposes those afflicted to adolescent and adult depression and suicide risk. *Journal of Learning Disabilities*, **21**, 169–175.

Rourke, B.P., Young, G.C., Strang, J.D. & Russell, D.L. (1986). Adult outcomes of central processing deficiencies in childhood. In I. Grant & K.M. Adams (eds), *Neuropsychological Assessment in Neuropsychiatric Disorders: Clinical Methods and Empirical Findings*. Oxford University Press, New York, pp. 244–267.

Rovet, J.F. (1990). Congenital hypothyroidism: intellectual and neuropsychological functioning. In C.S. Holmes (ed.), *Psychoneuroendocrinology: Brain, Behaviour, and Hormonal Interactions*. Springer Verlag, New York, pp. 273–322.

Rovet, J.F., Ehrlich, R.M., Czuchta, D. & Akler, M. (1993). Psychoeducational characteristics of children and adolescents with insulin dependent diabetes mellitus. *Journal of Learning Disabilities*, **26**, 7–22.

Rovet, J. & Netley, C. (1982). Processing deficits in Turner's syndrome. *Developmental Psychology*, **18**, 77–94.

Russell, D.L. & Rourke, B.P. (1991). Concurrent and predictive validity of phonetic accuracy of misspellings in normal and disabled readers and spellers. In B.P. Rourke (ed.), *Neuropsychological Validation of Learning Disability Subtypes*. Guilford Press, New York, pp. 57–72.

Shapiro, E.G., Lipton, M.E. & Krivit, W. (1992). White matter dysfunction and its neuropsychological correlates: a longitudinal study of a case of metachromatic leukodystrophy. *Journal of Clinical and Experimental Neuropsychology*, **14**, 610–624.

Share, D.L., Moffitt, T.E. & Silva, P.A. (1988). Factors associated with arithmetic-and-reading disability and specific arithmetic disability. *Journal of Learning Disabilities*, **21**, 313–320.

Siegel, L.S. & Heaven, R.K. (1986). Categorization of learning disabilities. In S.J. Ceci (ed.), *Handbook of Cognitive, Social and Neuropsychological Aspects of Learning Disabilities*, vol 1. Erlbaum, Hillsdale, NJ, pp. 95–121.

Siegel, L.S. & Linder, B.A. (1984). Short-term memory processes in children with reading and arithmetic learning disabilities. *Developmental Psychology*, **20**, 200–207.

Siegel, L.S. & Ryan, E.B. (1988). Development of grammatical sensitivity, phonological, and short-term memory skills in normally achieving and learning disabled children. *Developmental Psychology*, **24**, 28–37.

Stelmack, R.M. & Miles, J. (1990). The effect of picture priming on event-related potentials of normal and disabled readers during a word recognition memory task. *Journal of Clinical and Experimental Neuropsychology*, **12**, 887–903.

Stevens, D.E. & Moffitt, T.E. (1988). Neuropsychological profile of an Asperger's syndrome case with exceptional calculating ability. *The Clinical Neuropsychologist*, **2**, 228–238.

Strang, J.D. & Rourke, B.P. (1983). Concept-formation/non-verbal reasoning abilities of children who exhibit specific academic problems with arithmetic. *Journal of Clinical Child Psychology*, **12**, 33–39.

Strang, J.D. & Rourke, B.P. (1985a). Adaptive behaviour of children with specific arithmetic disabilities and associated neuropsychological abilities and deficits. In B.P. Rourke (ed.), *Neuropsychology of LD: Essentials of Subtype Analysis*. Guilford Press, New York, pp. 302–328.

Strang, J.D. & Rourke, B.P. (1985b). Arithmetic disability subtypes: the neuropsychological significance of specific arithmetical impairment in childhood. In B.P. Rourke (ed.), *Neuropsychology of LD: Essentials of Subtype Analysis*. Guilford Press, New York, pp. 167–183.

Streissguth, A.P. & LaDue, R.A. (1987). Fetal alcohol syndrome: teratogenic causes of developmental disabilities. In S.R. Schroeder (ed.), *Toxic Substances and Mental Retardation: Neurobehavioural Toxicology and Teratology*. American Association on Mental Deficiency, Washington, DC, pp. 1–32.

Sweeney, J.E. & Rourke, B.P. (1985). Spelling disability subtypes. In B.P. Rourke (ed.), *Neuropsychology of Learning Disabilities: Essentials of Subtype Analysis*. Guilford Press, New York, pp. 147–166.

Szatmari, P., Tuff, L., Finlayson, M.A.J. & Bartolucci, G. (1990). Asperger's syndrome and autism: neurocognitive aspects. *Journal of the American Academy of Child and Adolescent Psychiatry*, **29**, 130–136.

Udwin, O. & Yule, W. (1991). A cognitive and behavioural phenotype in Williams syndrome. *Journal of Clinical and Experimental Neuropsychology*, **13**, 232–244.

van der Vlugt, H. (1991). Neuropsychological validation studies of learning disability subtypes: verbal, visual–spatial, and psychomotor abilities. In B.P. Rourke (ed.), *Neuropsychological Validation of Learning Disability Subtypes*. Guilford Press, New York, pp. 140–159.

van der Vlugt, H. & Satz, P. (1985). Subgroups and subtypes of learning-disabled and normal children: a cross-cultural replication. In B.P. Rourke (ed.), *Neuropsychology of Learning Disabilities: Essentials of Subtype Analysis*. Guilford Press, New York, pp. 212–227.

Wechsler, D. (1949). *Wechsler Intelligence Scale for Children*. Psychological Corporation, New York.

White, J.L., Moffitt, T.E. & Silva, P.A. (1992). Neuropsychological and socio-emotional correlates of specific arithmetic disability. *Archives of Clinical Neuropsychology*, **7**, 1–16.

Williams, J.K., Richman, L. & Yarbrough, D. (1994). Comparison of visual–spatial performance strategy training in children with Turner syndrome and learning disabilities. *Journal of Learning Disabilities*, **25**, 658–664.

Wills, K.E., Holmbeck, G.N., Dillon, K. & McLone, D.G. (1990). Intelligence and achievement in children with myelomeningocele. *Journal of Pediatric Psychology*, **15**, 161–176.

Chapter 22

Memory Aids in the Rehabilitation of Memory Disordered Patients

Narinder Kapur
Wessex Neurological Centre, Southampton, UK

The use of techniques to improve memory dates back thousands of years (Herrmann & Chaffin, 1987). Mnemonic *strategies* intended to improve memory functioning have been well documented (Patten, 1990; McGlynn, 1990), but less attention has been paid to what has been termed "external memory aids". These act as a form of "prosthesis" for everyday memory functioning. Unlike novel mnemonic strategies, they are not intended to result in any change in learning ability as such, but they may sometimes be as valuable or more valuable than conventional techniques in improving memory. Their main benefit is often seen in preventing everyday memory lapses from occurring in the first place rather than in improving memory test scores.

Although cognitive-based memory strategies have a role to play in some aspects of memory rehabilitation, many memory-disordered patients may not have the motivation or prerequisite concentration/learning skills to acquire some of the mnemonic strategies which are advocated (certainly those which are put forward in popular books on memory improvement). In a recent long-term follow-up of memory-disordered patients, Wilson (1991) found that when patients used techniques to improve their memory functioning they tended to rely on written lists, calendars or wall-charts rather than internal cognitive strategies. Even psychologists involved in memory research thought that simple external memory aids, such as writing things down on a notepad, were amongst the

Handbook of Memory Disorders. Edited by A.D. Baddeley, B.A. Wilson and F.N. Watts.
© 1995 John Wiley & Sons Ltd.

techniques they themselves most commonly used for improving their memory (Park, Smith & Cavanaugh, 1990).

The purpose of this chapter is to review the external memory aids currently available, and to assess their suitability for use in clinical settings. More general reviews of memory rehabilitation, which include some discussion of memory aids, are available elsewhere (Wilson & Moffat, 1992; Herrmann, Weingartner, Searleman & McEvoy, 1992; Harrell, Parenté, Bellingrath & Lisicia, 1992; Harris, 1992). This chapter classifies external memory aids into two broad types: those which are part of a person's environment, and those which take the form of portable items.

ENVIRONMENTAL MEMORY AIDS

Personal Environmental Cues

A form of memory aid commonly used is to introduce a novel aspect to one's attire or personal appearance as a reminder to do something. Examples include putting one's ring or watch on the wrong hand, putting a wallet in a different pocket, putting an elastic band around a finger, writing a message on the palm/back of a hand, tying a knot to the inside of one's tie, etc. As effective memory aids, they have the limitation that some form of sensory habituation may set in, with the result that the memory aid may simply be ignored. In addition, the cue may fulfil its "alerting role", but the person may then forget what the particular memory cue was for.

Proximal Environmental Cues

"Proximal environment" means the layout within a room or vehicle, and the design of machines with which the patient interacts in everyday domestic or work settings. This has been a rather neglected area of scientific inquiry in relation to memory aids. Norman's (1988) excellent book focuses on some of the practical manifestations of poor ergonomic design, and more research needs to be carried out on the design of our environment as it relates to everyday memory functioning.

A proximal environment which is well structured and tidy can lead to fewer memory lapses, such as forgetting where something has been put. "Be more organized" is a piece of advice one often gives to a friend or colleague who keeps losing things—but how can one make such advice more concrete? As a basic principle, the items to be stored for later retrieval should be categorized, and separate storage units should be allocated to each category. Categories should, of course, be meaningful to the individual, and may have a number of subcategories, which also may be reflected in the structure of the storage unit. Distinctive storage units should differ in features such as size, shape, colour and/or spatial position. They should be clearly labelled, and bottles and containers within the storage units should also be labelled. The writing on the labels should be in large, upper-case print and may be of different colours, though black against white is often best for populations such as the elderly or neurologically impaired. If the storage units have to be retrieved according to a sequence, then some form of alphanumeric labelling is of value.

Factors which determine how prominently a storage unit may be located in a room, compared with other units, include—how frequently the items stored within it are used, how important they are and how often they tend to be forgotten. If possible, there should be some relationship between the contents of a storage unit and the visual features of the unit—for example, a brown container for storing coffee and a white one for storing sugar. Transparent storage boxes are preferable.

Machines ranging from photocopiers and ovens to cars and computers may have inbuilt alarm systems which remind the user to do something or other. In such situations, auditory cues, or combined auditory and visual cues, are particularly useful. Some cars even have spoken commands to remind the user to do things such as close a door or put on a seat belt. In such contexts, there may be some overlap between what one might call "knowledge aids" and "memory awareness aids". If you only partly close your car door thinking that it is fully closed, and have a "door-open" alarm, then this will appear as a visual or an auditory cue. You may not have had any knowledge that your door was in fact open, so this then would classify as a knowledge aid rather than a memory aid—if you did have the knowledge, you would probably not have forgotten to close the door. If, however, you completely forgot to close the car door, and went along with the door flung wide open, then the door-open alarm signal would constitute an external memory aid. Alarms such as these help to bring information into current awareness, as an individual's sensory system may become habituated to other sources of awareness or perhaps ignore them due to being distracted. The relevant signals then act as a memory aid because they bring facts into your current awareness.

In some circumstances, tactile memory aids may be useful to help locate a particular item. For example, when one is driving a car it is often not possible to glance in the direction where various switches are located. As Norman (1988) has pointed out, the layout of such switches often pays little respect to how and when they are used as part of driving behaviour. If, as is often the case, switches of a similar design are in close proximity, or are particularly important to locate, then it is useful to attach a distinctive tactile cue, such as a Velcro pad, onto one of the switches. Similar applications may well arise for settings other than driving a car, such as when finding switches in a room in the dark, or where the individual is visually impaired.

Changes to a workplace or home environment can also be engineered to minimize another form of memory lapse—forgetting to do something. Commonly used techniques include leaving something beside the front door, writing a message on a mirror in the hallway, leaving around an empty carton of something that needs to be replaced, etc. Simple changes to the design of an environment may be effective. For example, for items one has to take when leaving a room or house it is important to locate an appropriate shelf near the exit itself. The location of such a shelf (which should be clearly labelled) is critical—it should be within the horizontal and vertical limits of the person's visual field. In addition, putting together two items in an environment helps to act as a visual cue to trigger one's memory; e.g. if a pill-bottle is next to a toothbrush one is more likely to take one's medicine.

Distal Environmental Cues

"Distal environment" means the features (including people) of the home or work building, streets and transportation networks.

Effective distal environmental cues help with the prevention of two types of memory lapse: finding the location of something, and remembering to do something. In this context, remembering to do something may relate to the retrieval of a well-established rule or piece of knowledge that is already in long-term storage, rather than remembering to act on information which has been recently acquired. The use of simple labels to help with this form of memory lapse is often ignored in the design of everyday settings—as Norman (1988) has pointed out, we all know of doors where there is no indication whether to Pull or to Push.

The carefully planned use of signs can clearly be of benefit as preventative measures: e.g. warning signs near stairs in homes for the elderly and road-traffic warning signs. Other visual cues may be of similar value: e.g. having distinctive visual cues on steps to remind someone who is visually impaired or absent-minded that the step actually exists, and large windows at ground level to allow individuals to see the trees and therefore enable them to have cues to indicate the time of year.

In residential homes or hospitals where memory-impaired subjects may reside, having direction markers on the floor or walls and having rooms clearly labelled is important. The therapist should carry out a "site visit" to a patient's residence in order to obtain a first-hand perspective of both distal and proximal environmental cues, how they might best be used and/or changed, and how new ones might be introduced. Moffat (1989) has described the use of a simple flowchart of likely places to search which may benefit individuals who frequently lose items around the home and who may easily get into a panic about this.

Outside the home, if there are easily understood maps, which are located at critical points, these also represent useful environmental cues. These same principles should apply to the layout of sites such as factories, shopping centres, transport terminals, etc. The design of road networks, and visual and orthographic features of road signs, also contribute to the prevention of memory difficulties in finding a location. Unfortunately, with most distal environmental cues the scope for change lies not in the hands of the therapist or the patient but with government and other agencies.

A final form of distal environmental memory aid which one should never forget is a carer/family member who can act as a storage device and as a reminder for the memory-disabled person.

PORTABLE EXTERNAL MEMORY AIDS

A portable external memory aid is probably best defined as an external device that may improve everyday memory, and which in theory could be used by someone else or taken elsewhere. The device is external to the individual, but it may often be manipulated or adjusted in some way. There may often be some overlap between good environmental design and a portable external memory aid —a simple way of distinguishing the two is to note whether the item can be sent in the mail, or whether it is integral to the particular environment of the subject —if the former is the case, it would qualify as a portable external memory aid.

A range of commercial portable memory aids has been reviewed by Herrmann and Petro (1990). Here I shall concentrate on those which may be of particular benefit in rehabilitation settings. A selection of electronic memory aids which may be useful in clinical work is described briefly in the Appendix to this chapter.

Stationery, Mechanical and Related Memory Aids

Stationery aids are perhaps the most widely used form of memory prosthesis, both amongst the lay public and amongst professionals. Examples are notepads (which may be self-adhesive Post-it pads), diaries, calendars/wall-charts, address tags/labels that help items to be identified, and wallet-type organizers that include diaries, notebooks, etc. Such aids should not only be readily visible and accessible, but should also be in close proximity to the to-be-remembered activity. Thus, a notepad with a list of people to phone should be near the telephone, one that deals with groceries to buy could be somewhere such as on the refrigerator door, a checklist relating to how to operate a piece of equipment should be kept near that equipment. Pencils/pens should form an integral part of the stationery memory aid. "Personal organizers" vary in the extent to which they incorporate "reminder" sections, and in some cases it may be appropriate to create distinctive sections dealing with separate categories such as things to buy, people to meet, phone calls to make, etc.

Memory notebooks and related items such as diaries and organizers have been available for some time. Although they may seem fairly straightforward to use, using them successfully with patients who have marked memory difficulties requires some thought. Where notebooks are designed specially for patients, features such as colour coding and size of print need to be considered. In addition, the patient should be involved at an early stage in the design of the notebook, and care-staff or family members also need to be made familiar with the memory aid.

One of the few systematic attempts to develop a coherent method for doing this has been described by Sohlberg and Mateer (1989). They made up purpose-built notebooks with different sections and emphasized that these can be reduced or increased in number according to the patient. Their list of possible sections included Orientation, Memory Log, Diary, Things to Do, Transportation, Feeling Log, Names, and Today at Work. In the case of the head-injury patient reported by Sohlberg and Mateer, they used a memory notebook with five sections: Orientation, Memory Log, Calendar, Things to Do and Transportation.

Whereas Sohlberg and Mateer divided their patients' training into "acquisition", "application" and "adaptation", the present author prefers to think in terms of two stages: (a) learning about the item and understanding its features, and (b) using it in everyday situations. Learning about the item involves going through the various parts of the notebook, understanding what they are for and when they should be used, how to make and change entries, etc. One can test the subject's retention of particular items by usual question-and-answer techniques, but it is also useful to include role rehearsal that involves practice of real-life examples while still in the clinic. Use of direct feedback in such role-rehearsal settings, perhaps also with video feedback, is important.

Sohlberg and Mateer suggested that before patients can go on to use the item in real-life settings they should have "explicit knowledge" of features of the notebook. In this author's experience, as long as there is accurate and successful use of the various notebook features, it does not really matter if the patient can provide explicit recall of particular features of the notebook.

Training in the use of a memory notebook in real-life settings entails giving the patient homework tasks to do, and having some way of noting how successfully these are done; this is where a carer may come in especially useful. The homework activities can be tried initially in a hospital setting, where there may be a shop to which the person can travel and come back within a short time.

A few *mechanical* memory aids are still available, though in general they have been overtaken by electronic equivalents. Mechanical alarm clocks and countdown timers are available as, for example, kitchen memory aids. These may simply involve turning a dial to set a time period, after which the alarm will go off to indicate that something is cooked; for some patients they are easier to understand and to use than electronic timers.

Rotating pill boxes and wallets are available which are designed around the days of the week. A set number of pills can be placed in each compartment that relates to a day of the week or time of the day. These compartments have to be filled at weekly or other intervals, but they have the convenience of being simple to use and letting the patient know whether he or she has taken necessary tablets.

Clocks should be positioned in places where they are readily seen by patients, and ideally should have day and (less importantly) date built-in.

Electronic Memory Aids

Electronic Organizers / Reminders

General-purpose electronic count-down timers—as found on a number of watches and clocks—may be useful in certain contexts. In the past, they have been limited in the number of alarms which can be set, but some timers are now available that can be programmed for different times on different days of the week. A number of such timers are now built into the design of electric plugs, so that they can be used with any appliance that is plugged into mains electricity.

Commercially available electronic organizers/reminders have in recent years become more compact, more sophisticated and less expensive. Such a device can act as an electronic diary to help keep appointments and as a general prospective memory aid. It can also store shopping lists, messages and names/telephone numbers. Situations where the device may be of particular benefit include:

- Instances where events may occur between thinking about doing something and remembering to do it, e.g. deciding in the morning that one needs to buy something in the evening—this is particularly important when the intervening activities preoccupy the individual to a significant degree.
- Situations where a long interval separates thinking about doing something and having to do it (e.g. making an appointment for several months in the future).
- When there is a high premium on very accurate, precise recall and where internal memory aids may be fallible (e.g. remembering to take a cake from an oven at a specific time).
- Where multiple alarm reminders are required (e.g. having to take tablets several times a day).

Electronic organizers range from those that are truly pocket-sized to those the size of a small book. Alarms can be set to go off at the same time as a stored message is displayed, and some models have multiple or weekly alarms. Most electronic organizers can be interfaced to enable them to transfer data to computers, and for the more expensive models electronic insert cards can be bought for specific applications. Most models now have back-up batteries to safeguard against loss of stored memory. Electronic organizers vary greatly in features which may or may not be "user-friendly" for neurologically impaired patients. The following features need to be borne in mind when selecting an organizer.

General Features

Size. The organizer should be compact enough to fit into a shirt pocket or other place which is handy for the patient. Some of the more elaborate organizers may be rather too bulky to be carried around all the time, though they could still be kept in a coat pocket or a briefcase

Databank watches are available with many of the functions of electronic organizers. While they are obviously more compact and easier to carry around, they have more limited clinical application owing to the fine motor control and fine visual acuity needed to operate them.

Folding/wallet cover. It is useful to have some form of cover to guard against keys being accidentally pressed and to save the device from damage.

Power supply. Batteries may need to be changed only once every few years, depending on the extent of use of features such as the auditory alarm, but both the motor dexterity involved, and the simplicity of the instructions, are of importance. The life of the battery, and whether there is a backup are worth noting. The latter is useful especially where there is a large amount of stored data which needs to be retained in the device's memory.

Transfer of data to personal computer/printer. This is useful mainly for those who are using the organizer as a data-gathering device in settings remote from their workplace. For patients, the feature may be useful to download information on the sorts of activities in which the patient has been engaged over the previous few weeks.

Price. Electronic memory aids are not yet routinely available in publicly funded healthcare systems, so in the present author's department we have tended to restrict ourselves to items costing less than £50 or $75. The more expensive ones fall into two categories: organizers with a QWERTY keyboard, such as the Sharp IQ9000 and the Psion Organizer and "personal digital assistants" such as those marketed by Sharp (ExpertPad), Apple (MessagePad) and Amstrad (PenPad). These dispense with a keyboard and have touch-screen input that involves the user touching a screen icon that controls a particular function. They accept script, which can if necessary be transcribed by the device into typed text, but the script usually has to be written slowly and carefully. These "top-of-the-market" devices cost between £200 and £700 ($350–$1050). They obviously have many more features than simple organizers, including in some cases programming capability, though many of these may not be relevant to the types of memory difficulties displayed by patients. They are too expensive for routine clinical use.

Manufacturers. It is best to choose items from a reputable manufacturer or supplier. Be wary of lesser known manufacturers.

Screen display. The length and number of lines which can be displayed is important. Obviously the larger the screen the better, though the cost will rise for larger screens. At least 10 characters are needed on a single line for the minimum sorts of cue words to remind patients about particular things they have to do. In some cases, especially if there is a limited amount of screen space, it is necessary to train the patient to use keywords or abbreviations—fortunately, it is a feature of human memory that even a single cue word or an abbreviation will often suffice at the time of retrieval to cue the patient into remembering what has to be done.

The clarity/resolution of the screen display is also important. Some of the cheaper organizers have quite poor displays despite being useful in other ways. Clarity is critical for many neurologically impaired patients, especially those with reduced visual acuity.

Keyboard. Since electronic organizers were designed originally for professionals or executives rather than for disabled people, there are usually keys which are superfluous for use of the device as a memory aid. For some patients, these may well serve as a distraction, especially if the patient has problems in visual search or in handling information overload. The keys themselves should be clearly labelled and well laid out, and if possible operations should be executed by a single key press rather than by a sequence of keys.

Keyboards with raised keys are much to be preferred to "membrane" keyboards with flat keys. There should be the facility to have tone feedback when a key is pressed. A few organizers still have multiple letters per single key, or joint letter/number keys: these are usually less satisfactory than a single-letter-per-key design. Most patients are happier with the ABC layout than the QWERTY layout.

It may sometimes be desirable to mask redundant keys, especially if the patient is being distracted by visually similar keys. Some rubber or plastic surfaces do not respond well to marking with waterbased felt pens, and so it is worth keeping this point in mind. Paint-based pens are quite good for writing over organizer keyboards. It may be necessary to write additional legends, or write over existing legends, so it is useful to ensure that the legend will remain clearly visible after several weeks of use.

Memory capacity. Some of the smaller and earlier organizers have only around 2K bytes of memory, and this may be insufficient for patients with lots of memos or diary entries. Anything over 5K bytes is probably sufficient for most uses.

Ease of learning of particular operations. This is obviously a critical feature. Important variables include the number of key presses for an operation, and any cues given by the legend on the key.

There are three basic operations which patients will have to learn: *entering* information, *reviewing* stored information from time to time, and *deleting* information from storage. One needs to discover how simple or complicated these basic operations are for the patient to learn. Depending on how much information a particular patient is going to enter, word-processing features may be useful—such as having abbreviated glossary codes so that if a particular phrase is being entered frequently a code only need be entered.

Size and clarity of the manual. Patients should not have to consult the manual, but it still helps if it is clear and not too intimidating in its length. Summarized forms of information such as "help cards" provide a quick reference to which patients can turn.

Alarm Features

With/without message. There are essentially two types of alarms, those that come with a message and those without any message. The major virtue of electronic organizers is their ability to display text when an   alarm goes off. Therefore, having an alarm with a simultaneous message display is a critical feature. This facility can be used for two main purposes: in those prospective memory situations where something has to be done on a particular day and at a specific time; and in those situations where it is very important that certain things are done which are not necessarily tied to a particular time, thus avoiding the risk of forgetting to look up the memo directory.

Pre-alarm time reminder. Some organizers will emit an alarm several minutes before the actual alarm. For some types of activities, such as having to go to a meeting which requires some initial preparation, this can be quite useful.

Distinctive alarm tones. It goes without saying, but is worth remembering, that the alarm should be loud enough to be clearly heard, and should continue sounding for a reasonable period of time. It is also useful if the alarm for one type of cued reminder is different, say in the pattern or sequence of tone, from that for other types of cued reminders.

Hourly chime. Hourly chimes are quite important, and are available on most, though not all, organizers. They are also available on many watches. Their value is that they can be used as a reminder for the person to carry out a regular activity such as consult a diary/notebook. This linked use of two memory aids in itself involves a form of "paired-associate" learning, but since the response is a motor act rather than production of a verbal response it may be relatively easy for most patients to acquire.

Daily alarm. Daily alarm features are available on most electronic organizers. It can be used as a means of reminding the person to ensure the organizer is in his or her pocket or to look at the organizer at the beginning of the day. Multiple alarms during the day are invaluable where a patient has, for example, to take medicine several times a day, but there are relatively few organizers in the less expensive range which have this feature.

Weekly alarm. Having a weekly alarm can be useful for weekly meetings or where it is decided to set aside a fixed day per week to review things that are written down in the aid.

Monthly alarm. This is seldom important in a clinical context, but may be of relevance in business or professional settings.

Annual anniversary alarm. Some organizers (such as the Sharp and Casio) have an anniversary alarm as a feature. An alarm is rung at regular intervals throughout the particular date that has been programmed. This is not a particularly critical feature for disabled people.

Text Storage Features

In addition to having a prospective memory feature which gives an alarm with or without an associated message, it is useful to have a general memo facility in which one can write those things which need to be done at some time, but not necessarily at a particular day and time. The less expensive organizers may not have a Memo facility as such, but the telephone storage facility—which most have—can be used to store such memos.

Text entry. Ease of text entry relates in part to keyboard and screen features described earlier. The particular operations for entering text into memory should be simple and few in number. Some of the more expensive organizers allow one to have letter codes for frequently used phrases or sentences, so that these need not be typed in full on each occasion.

Text review and deletion. One of two main types of search feature may be present. Some units scan through alarm or memo entries in chronological or alphabetical order, while with others it is possible to search by a particular feature—name of memo entry, word or part of word contained in the alarm message, etc. For most therapeutic applications, where there may not be a particularly large number of text entries at any one time, an alphabetical search facility should suffice. The procedures for review and deletion of stored text should be reasonably simple. Inserting or deleting characters within a sample of text should also be easy for the patient to learn.

Other Electronic Aids

Pocket Dictating Machines

Dictating machines which use microcassettes have, of course, been around for some time, but they are now becoming more compact and more sophisticated. Features on some current models include voice-activated onset (though this can sometimes be translated to mean "noise-activated onset"), digital tape counting facility, and the ability to use an electronic "marker" to index parts of the tape. As memory aids these features are useful when long messages need to be stored, or for memory-disordered patients who may be limited in their ability to use an electronic organizer, possibly owing to additional motor or visual impairment. They could, for example, be handy for a head-injured student who finds that he or she cannot readily take notes or absorb material during lectures.

Location Devices

The domestic location device, usually attached to a key ring, operates in response to a loud noise such as hand-clapping, which provides a sonic pulse to activate an acoustic alarm. However, some versions of these devices tend to be rather temperamental, being activated by any extraneous noise or sometimes failing to activate when an appropriate sound is made. Other location devices employ an infrared beam in a similar manner to remote control car-locking devices.

Telephone Memory Aids

Many telephones now have the facility to store and easily retrieve frequently used numbers: the storage capacity is generally in the range of 10 to 40 numbers. Various other features are available, such as a visual display of a number while it is being dialled, ample space for the names associated with coded numbers, and "hands-free" dialling. Some phones will remember to ring back an engaged number automatically a few minutes later. For patients living alone who may suddenly become disabled at some distance from the phone, a unit is available which can automatically dial a prerecorded number as the result of a remote control switch (carried by the patient) being activated.

As a complement to telephones with inbuilt memories, portable diallers are available. These may take the form of calculators/organizers that have an automatic dialling facility, or a databank watch having this feature. They cater for both local and long-distance calls, and allow for the name to be stored along with the number. The user generally keys in the first letter(s) of the name to retrieve the telephone number, and this can then be dialled automatically by holding the device next to the phone handset and pressing a button. These diallers are useful as a portable memory aid. As in the case of memory phones, they may be of value for situations/individuals where pressing lots of keys on a telephone is either difficult or too time-consuming.

Computer Software

The electronic diary/alarm functions that are found on organizers are also available in the form of software for personal computers, both for IBM-compatible PCs and for the Apple Macintosh range. At the clinical level this software is potentially valuable in certain situations, because a number of memory-disordered patients may find keyboard skills to be within their repertoire but still have poor memory (e.g. Glisky, Schacter & Tulving, 1986). This software may enable them to have a memory aid quite close at hand. Telephone-dialling software, with features similar to those of portable diallers, is available for most microcomputers.

APPLYING MEMORY AIDS IN REHABILITATION SETTINGS

Relatively few systematic studies have been carried out on the value of electronic aids for memory rehabilitation, and most take the form of preliminary case studies. Fowler, Hart and Sheehan (1972) used a timer combined with a schedule card to help their patient stick to a daily routine in his rehabilitation programme. Naugle, Naugle, Prevey and Delaney (1988) used an "alarm-display" Casio watch to help their patient to remember to attend activities in his rehabilitation programme, because he consistently forgot to use stationery memory aids such as diaries and log books. They found this aid of benefit, but the patient sometimes ignored the alarm, and sometimes turned it off without reading the message first; further training in the use of the aid was then given. Giles and Shore (1989) used a Psion organizer to help their patient remember to do weekend domestic chores: it was found to be more beneficial than a pocket diary, although sometimes the alarm was not loud enough to be heard.

Factors which need to be taken into account when considering the use of memory aids include *general* factors that are applicable to most forms of neuropsychological intervention and memory rehabilitation, and *specific* factors that relate to the particular use of memory aids to help overcome memory difficulties.

General Factors

General factors include age, educational level, and premorbid knowledge and skills of the patient; any physical disability, such as sensory or motor loss; the intactness or otherwise of cognitive functions other than memory; supportive and possible negative influences that the patient's family/carer may bring to bear on the therapeutic programme; the patient's current daily routine and the demands which this places on his or her memory; and any behavioural or motivational problems that the patient may have.

The severity and pattern of memory loss is obviously a major factor, so it is important to pay particular attention to a number of areas:

• Everyday memory symptoms as reported by the patient and by informed observers, noting the patient's insight and concern about memory difficulties.

- The severity and pattern of anterograde memory loss.
- The severity and pattern of retrograde memory loss, in particular the extent to which past knowledge and skills have been lost.
- The extent to which new skill learning and implicit memory are preserved.

Adequate baseline measures should be obtained before memory therapy is introduced, to allow a post-intervention assessment to be carried out on the effectiveness of the programme. As with any therapy, intervention must be cost-effective both in financial terms and in terms of the amount of time spent by the therapist, the patient and his/her family.

Specific Factors

A number of specific factors need to be borne in mind when considering whether to encourage and train a patient in the use of memory aids to help everyday memory.

First, how often has the patient used memory aids in the past, and which types have been used? Many elderly subjects have become accustomed to using simple diaries and are quite reluctant to change over to electronic diaries, no matter how much more effective they may be (cf. Petro, Herrmann, Burrows & Moore, 1991). Some patients may need to be reassured that using memory aids will not lead to their becoming lazy or their brain wasting away through lack of use. They also need to be reassured that using memory aids with other people around is nothing to be ashamed of, since such aids are increasingly being used by the normal population.

Second, although it is the principal duty of the clinician to find a memory aid that will help a specific form of memory lapse that the patient suffers, and one that is simple to use, the patient should if possible be given a choice of memory aids and be involved in deciding what is best for him or her.

Third, a carer/spouse needs to be closely involved in the process from the beginning, to encourage the use of the memory aid in domestic settings. In particular, where the aid is in any way complicated to use, this person also needs to be taught how to use the device in case any problem arises.

Fourth, there is a fallacy that memory aids may simply be given to patients to use, and little further intervention is required from the therapist. If only this were the case! As Intons-Peterson and Newsome (1992) have pointed out, there are a number of cognitive processes involved in the use of even simple external memory aids. Thus, the patient needs to be trained to recognize situations where a memory aid of the appropriate kind will be of particular use, and must develop motivation to set about using it effectively. For the more complex aids such as electronic organizers, a specific training programme must be designed. This should incorporate:

- Learning a particular procedure by breaking it down into steps

- Principles such as spaced rehearsal, graded reduction of support/vanishing cues and error-free learning (Wilson, Baddeley, Evans & Shiel, 1994)
- Feedback and encouragement throughout the training programme
- Help-cards which summarize the steps involved in a particular operation and which can be a backup if problems arise outside the therapy setting.

The training programme in the Clinic should mimic as closely as is feasible everyday uses of the memory aid, with concrete examples being drawn from the patient's daily routine. Training a patient to use something like an electronic organizer requires at least 4–6 sessions, and if these are spaced apart weekly it is advisable to set homework for the patient and to use the beginning of a therapy session to test long-term retention of what was taught a week earlier.

PILOT STUDY OF THE USEFULNESS OF ELECTRONIC ORGANIZERS

The aim of this study conducted at the Wessex Neurological Centre was to obtain preliminary experience of a fairly simple electronic organizer with a range of patients suffering from memory disorders. The device was tried with a range of severity and types of memory loss, so as to give us a good feel for the potential of electronic organizers. In two of the five cases there was a close observer available who could gather a week-long baseline rating of prospective memory followed by around 4 weeks use of the organizer, followed in turn by a repeat measure of prospective memory. Each of the patients was seen individually.

Patient A with Herpes Simplex Encephalitis

This was a 59-year-old man who was densely amnesic following his encephalitis. His case has been reported in more detail elsewhere (Kapur, 1988). We gave him a Tandy electronic organizer. However, we had great problems in teaching him to use even the memo facility of the device, and so we ended up simply trying to teach him to use it to look up the time and day of the week whenever the hourly chime went off. Regrettably, he completely failed to learn how to use the organizer for this simple task. Our lack of success with this patient was probably due not only to his very poor memory, but also to his marked lack of initiative, lack of insight and lack of concern for his memory loss.

Patient B with Parkinson's Disease

This was a 67-year-old man who had a prorated WAIS–R Verbal IQ of 80, Performance IQ of 90 and Full Scale IQ of 83. His estimated premorbid IQ was

105. He showed a moderate impairment on the Wechsler Memory Scale–Revised paired-associate learning subtests (4/24 and 2/18 on the initial trials of the verbal and pattern–colour subtests respectively), and a significant impairment on words (31/50) and faces (30/50) recognition memory tests (Warrington, 1984). We initially had doubts as to whether to try the organizer with this patient, but decided it was worth having a go.

We started with the Tandy organizer, using cue cards to explain the various operations, but then went on to the Sharp MemoMaster because the Tandy keyboard was too cumbersome for him. We included three cue cards inside the casing of the organizer–one giving guidance on general use of the device, one indicating how to enter information into the Memo Directory, and a third indicating how to review and delete information. One of the limitations of the Sharp MemoMaster organizer is that it does not have an hourly chime, so we "piggy-backed" on to the back of the MemoMaster a thin card-clock with a chime facility, to cue the patient every hour to look up his memos that he had stored in the organizer's memory.

On the basis of around 6 weeks' experience of using the organizer, the patient's wife was very enthusiastic and claimed that he was able to use the aid to enhance his everyday prospective memory. However, when he arrived in our clinic he would invariably have great difficulty in operating the basic entry, review and delete functions, though his wife thought that he was particularly anxious when he came to the clinic and that he was much better when using the device at home. In the clinic he could not reliably enter an item into the memo directory, and had to be told regularly to look at the instructions on the card. He also had a lot of difficulty reviewing and deleting information from the organizer's memory without any assistance, though when he was guided through the instructions on the cards he could manage this.

His difficulties in using the organizer were due partly to limitations in learning, in visual search, in motor control and in simple problem-solving ability. He also tended to give up easily when he encountered a problem. It is of note that there is evidence for procedural learning impairments in some Parkinson's disease patients (Heindel et al., 1989), and this type of learning may have been similar to that attempted by our patient.

Although we failed to train this patient to use the organizer fluently as a general memo device, it did turn out to be useful, simply as a means for telling the time and the day of the week. He would repeatedly ask his wife what day it was, and she found the device to be of value if only because she could reply—"Look at your organizer!"

Patient C with Epilepsy

This was a 27-year-old woman who had suffered epilepsy for the previous five years. She had a prorated WAIS–R verbal IQ of 87, a Performance IQ of 96 and a Full Scale IQ of 89. Her estimated premorbid IQ was around 109. She showed a mild impairment on the Wechsler Memory Scale–Revised pattern–colour paired-associate learning subtests (5/18) but close to normal on the verbal subtest (17/24). Her everyday memory difficulties were, however, significant enough to interfere with her performance as a bank clerk.

She used the Tandy organizer and managed well even with having to use single keys for multiple letters. We trained her to use the organizer in two sessions, one for detailed use of the memo facility, and one to use the text–alarm facility. We went over the three basic steps: entering information, reviewing stored information, and deleting information. We also discussed the use of abbreviated entries for the memo facility, since a maximum of 12 characters can be displayed. She was rapidly able to learn both the memo and alarm–diary types of operations. In her daily work routine, she had the organizer on her desk. At the beginning of her day at work, she would enter into the memo store the various job-related activities that she would need to do, and at 5 o'clock, when she finished work, she would delete those things which she had done during the day. Whenever the hourly chime went off she would review her memo directory, and carry out any of the things which remained to be done. She did not find the text–alarm feature of much use, as she said she did not have many appointments which were tied down to a particular time or day. She did not use the device very much in the evening, apart from the important function of checking the memo and seeing that she had to take her anticonvulsant medication, as she entered the word "tablets" permanently into her memo directory. She tended not to take the organizer with her when she went out on social occasions.

In summary, then, this patient found the electronic organizer very helpful and considered that it greatly improved her adjustment at work, and she incorporated the device into many aspects of her daily routine.

Patient D with Head Injury, and Patient E with Multiple Sclerosis

Patient D was a 44-year-old man who, prior to his head injury, was a self-employed builder, painter and decorator. He was seen two years after his injury. He had a prorated WAIS–R Verbal IQ of 105. Performance IQ of 107 and Full Scale IQ of 106. His estimated premorbid IQ was 106. He showed a mild impairment on the Wechsler Memory Scale–Revised paired-associate learning subtests (14/24 and 9/18 on the initial trials of the verbal and pattern–colour subtests respectively), and a moderate impairment on words (37/50) but not faces (42/50) recognition memory test (Warrington, 1984). This patient will be considered alongside another patient who suffered from multiple sclerosis (MS).

Patient E was a 56-year-old man who had been suffering from MS for the past 22 years. He was a senior planning assistant with a bus company, and had been retired a couple of years earlier owing to his memory problems. He had a prorated WAIS–R Verbal IQ of 109, Performance IQ of 109 and Full Scale IQ of 110. His estimated premorbid IQ was 110. He showed a mild impairment on the Wechsler Memory Scale–Revised pattern–colour paired-associate learning subtests (12/18) but was close to normal on the verbal subtest (12/24). He had a moderate impairment on words (30/50) and faces (34/50) recognition memory tests (Warrington, 1984).

With both patients, we were able to get formal data before therapy started using a prospective memory questionnaire that covered a range of 14 categories of everyday memory symptoms, mainly prospective memory activities such as remembering to keep appointments, to take tablets, etc. This was completed for a week before therapy and then for a week after therapy. Both patients were trained to use the Tandy organizer.

Prior to training in the use of the organizer, the MS patient had 23 memory lapses (12/14 categories). After four weeks using the electronic organizer, this had reduced to 17 lapses (9/14 categories). He found the diary–alarm particularly useful, but the memo less useful. He said he did not always hear the hourly chime, and did not use this a lot. He used the memo facility more for permanent information such as telephone numbers. Both he and his wife were pleased with the impact that the organizer had on his everyday memory functioning.

The head-injury patient, on pre-therapy testing, had 26 occasions of lapses in prospective memory (over 7/14 categories) as observed by his wife on the questionnaire. Four weeks later, after he had been using the organizer during this period, this questionnaire was repeated and there were now 14 memory lapses (3/14 categories). The patient also found it useful for passing on phone messages and keeping appointments. Although he used both memo and diary–alarm entry, he found the diary alarm more useful and found the memo of less benefit. He also used the diary alarm for daily routines such as putting out the cat!

Compared with the first two patients (A and B), these two were a success story in terms of an electronic organizer improving everyday memory.

CONCLUSIONS

In many cases, external memory aids may represent a more appropriate means of overcoming everyday memory difficulties than mnemonic strategies, although both cognitive strategies and external aids may each have their own specific value in particular settings (Intons-Peterson & Fourner, 1986). The contribution of aids to memory rehabilitation holds considerable promise, but many questions remain unanswered. We need to know which memory aids benefit which memory problems in which memory-disordered patients. Memory aids may often best be used in combination, and we need to know the optimal combinations for particular clinical needs. We also need to know if the magnitude of any benefit to patients is significant and makes a meaningful difference to their everyday adjustment, if the change is permanent and if it is cost-effective in money and in therapists' time.

Advances in technology mean that electronic memory aids should become more "user-friendly", more useful for a range of memory situations, more purpose-built with memory-disordered patients in mind, and (last but not least) cheaper. In parallel with these developments, we need more creative application of learning and behavioural-change principles in the training of patients to use memory aids, and we also need more research into environmental memory aids.

ACKNOWLEDGEMENTS

The author is grateful to the Nuffield Foundation for financial support, to Keith Scholey, Michelle Smith and Barbara Wilson for their assistance in the preparation of this chapter, and to Amstrad, Casio, Memory Aids, Micronta, Sharp, and Tandy for making available the memory-aid models displayed in the Appendix to this chapter.

REFERENCES

Fowler, R.S., Hart, J. & Sheehan, M. (1972). A prosthetic memory: an application of the prosthetic environment concept. *Rehabilitation Counselling Bulletin*, **16**, 80–85.

Giles, G.M. & Shore, M. (1989). The effectiveness of an electronic memory aid for a memory-impaired adult of normal intelligence. *American Journal of Occupational Therapy*, **43**, 409–411.

Glisky, E., Schacter, D.L. & Tulving E. (1986). Computer learning by memory-impaired patients: acquisition and retention of complex knowledge. *Neuropsychologia*, **24**, 313–328.

Harrell, M., Parenté, F., Bellingrath, E.G. & Lisicia K.A, (1992). *Cognitive Rehabilitation of Memory*. Aspen Publishers, Gaithersburg.

Harris, J.E. (1992). Ways to improve memory. In B.A. Wilson & N. Moffat (eds), *Clinical Management of Memory Problems*, 2nd edn. Croom Helm, London.

Heindel W.C., Salmon D.P., Shults C.W., Walicke P.A. & Butters, N. (1989). Neuropsychological evidence for multiple memory systems: a comparison of Alzheimer's, Huntington's and Parkinson's disease patients. *Journal of Neuroscience*, **9**, 582–587.

Herman, D.J. & Chaffin, R. (1987). Memory before Ebbinghaus. In R. Hoffman and D. Gorfein (eds), *Memory and Learning*. Erlbaum, Hillsdale, NJ.

Herrman, D.J. & Petro, S.J. (1990). Commercial memory aids. *Applied Cognitive Psychology*, **4**, 439–450.

Herrmann, D.J., Weingartner, H., Searleman, A. & McEvoy, C. (1992). *Memory Improvement: Implications for Memory Theory*. Springer Verlag, New York.

Intons-Peterson, M.J. & Fourner, J. (1986). External and internal memory aids: when and how often do we use them? *Journal of Experimental Psychology: General*, **115**, 267–280.

Intons-Peterson, M.J. & Newsome, G.L. (1992). External memory aids: effects and effectiveness. In D.J. Herrmann, H. Weingartner, A. Searleman & C. McEvoy (eds), *Memory Improvement: Implications for Memory Theory*. Springer-Verlag, New York, pp. 101–121.

Kapur, N. (1988). Selective sparing of memory functioning in a patient with amnesia following herpes encephalitis. *Brain and Cognition*, **8**, 77–90.

McGlynn S.M. (1990). Behavioural approaches to neuropsychological rehabilitation. *Psychological Bulletin*, **108**, 420–441.

Moffat, N.J. (1989). Home-based cognitive rehabilitation with the elderly. In L.W. Poon, D.C. Rubin & B.A. Wilson (eds), *Everyday Cognition in Adulthood and Late Life*. Cambridge University Press, Cambridge.

Naugle, R., Naugle, C., Prevey, M. & Delaney, R. (1988). New digital watch as a compensatory device for memory dysfunction. *Cognitive Rehabilitation*, **6**, 22–23.

Norman, D.A. (1988). *The Psychology of Everyday Things*. Basic Press, New York.

Park, D.C., Smith, A.D. & Cavanaugh, J.C. (1990). Metamemories of memory researchers. *Memory and Cognition*, **18**, 321–327.

Patten, B.M. (1990). The history of memory arts. *Neurology*, **40**, 346–352.

Petro, S.J., Herrmann, D., Burrows, D. & Moore, C.M. (1991). Usefulness of commercial memory aids as a function of age. *International Journal of Aging and Human Development*, **33**, 295–309.

Sohlberg, M.M. & Mateer, C.A. (1989). Training use of compensatory memory books: a three-stage behavioural approach. *Journal of Clinical and Experimental Neuropsychology*, **11**, 871–891.

Warrington, E.K. (1984). *Recognition Memory Test*. NFER–Nelson, Windsor.

Wilson, B.A. (1991). Long-term prognosis of patients with severe memory disorders. *Neuropsychological Rehabilitation*, **1**, 117–134.

Wilson, B.A., Baddeley, A., Evans, J. & Shiel, A. (1994). Errorless learning in the rehabilitation of memory-impaired people. *Neuropsychological Rehabilitation*, **4**, 307–326.

Wilson, B.A. & Moffat, N. (eds) (1992). *Clinical Management of Memory Problems*, 2nd edn. Croom Helm, London.

APPENDIX:
SELECTION OF ELECTRONIC MEMORY AIDS

This selection of electronic memory aids is representative rather than exhaustive. The range of commercially available aids changes every few months, and readers should note that some aids are not marketed in all countries.

Tandy EC323 Electronic Organizer

This has memo storage and message–alarm facilities. It also has an hourly chime. While it is compact and has a relatively clear two-line display, it has multiple letters for a single keypress, rather than a key for each letter. It measures 110 mm by 75 mm. It costs around £25 ($38) and is available from Tandy retail outlets.

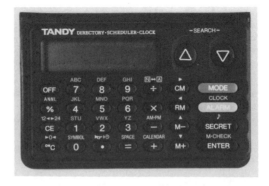

Figure 22.1   Tandy EC323 electronic organizer

Figure 22.2 Sharp EL6190 MemoMaster electronic organizer

Sharp EL6190 MemoMaster Electronic Organizer

This has memo/telephone storage and message-alarm facilities. Thus, text up to 10 characters in length can be entered which will be displayed at a certain date and specific time. It measures 130 mm by 80 mm. It normally costs around £29 ($44) in the shops. It is available in most commercial outlets.

Amstrad PenPad

This device is one of the first purpose-built "personal digital assistants" with a touch-screen as its major entry mode. It is similar to the Apple "Newton" MessagePad, the

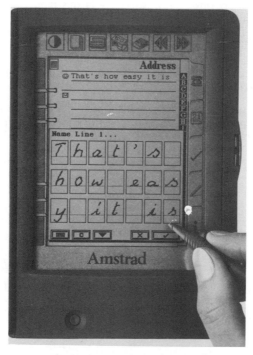

Figure 22.3 Amstrad PenPad

Figure 22.4   Talking day planner

Sharp ExpertPad and the Tandy Zoomer. None of these "personal digital assistants" is yet suitable or inexpensive enough for routine clinical use, but one device is listed here to give an idea of the direction in which some electronic memory aids may be moving.

The PenPad has standard organizer features, such as alarm–diary and storage of text, and also has communication features for information transmission. Its touchscreen feature includes a capacity for character recognition, so that this information can be recalled in standard typewritten mode. As with most touchscreen devices, there is less than perfect correspondence between intended and actual script when one writes at normal speed, and writing therefore has to be slow and consistent. In addition, translation of user's script into typed text requires the machine to go through a trial-and-error learning process, and this inevitably slows down text entry in this mode. The PenPad is 115 mm wide by 160 mm high by 27 mm deep, and is rather more bulky than most standard electronic organizers. This item is available from most commercial outlets and at the time of writing costs around £300 ($450).

Talking Day Planner

This device is one of the few currently available that can generate a previously entered spoken message at a preprogrammed time. The message can be up to eight seconds in length, and four separate messages/alarms can be set. It measures 120 mm by 70 mm by

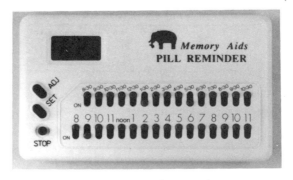

Figure 22.5   Daily reminder

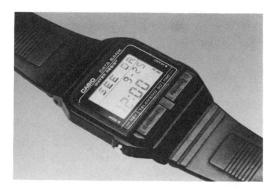

Figure 22.6   Casio Telememo watch

25 mm and costs around £25 ($38). However, at the time of writing it is available only in the USA from Radio Shack outlets.

Daily Reminder

This is a very simple-to-operate electronic reminder, where an alarm time is set by moving one of the switches in the horizontal rows. The alarm will then come on for up to 10 minutes at the set time, and at the same time every day. As many alarms as necessary can be set from 8.30 am to 11 pm. Time is displayed on a small panel. When the alarm is put off by pressing the STOP key, an indicator increments by one, thus giving an index of how many times the alarm has been switched off. This index resets to zero at midnight. The device has therefore been found to be useful as a pill reminder, in that it can indicate indirectly how many times the individual took his or her tablets. It measures 90

Figure 22.7   Casio watch/dialler

Figure 22.8   Calculator/dialler

mm by 52 mm. It costs around £15 ($23) and is available from MemoryAids, 6 Redward Road, Rownhams, Southampton SO16 8JE, England.

Casio Telememo Watch

In addition to usual features such as stopwatch, countdown alarm and hourly chime, this "databank watch" has two other features of value in memory rehabilitation settings: a storage facility for names/telephone numbers and, more importantly, a text–alarm feature whereby up to five alarms may be set, each with a text of up to eight characters. Thus, the text is displayed whenever the alarm goes off. The alarm can be set to go off at a set time every day, on a particular date each month (e.g. the second day of every month), every day in a particular month (e.g. every day in September), and on a particular date and time (e.g. 4.30 pm on 3 March). The watch costs around £30 ($45) and is available in usual commercial outlets.

Casio Watch / Dialler

This has many of the features of the Casio Telememo watch, but differs in two main ways. First, it can store up to 50 text–alarms, but these can only be set for a specific date and time. It does not have the multiple daily alarm capability of the Telememo model. Second, it has a feature whereby the numbers stored in the telephone memory can be dialled automatically by activating a tone generator next to the handpiece of a pushbutton phone. It costs around £50 ($75) and is available in usual commercial outlets.

Calculator Diallers

These devices have the same dialling capacity as the Casio Watch/Dialler, but are of the size and in the format of a calculator. It is therefore easier to key in and to retrieve numbers, and most diallers have a rapid-search facility by which numbers can be retrieved easily by keying in the first letters of the person's name. Items similar to this cost around £30–40 ($45–55) and are available in a few selected high-street stores.

Chapter 23

Computers in Memory Rehabilitation

Elizabeth L. Glisky
University of Arizona, Tucson, USA

INTRODUCTION

At the same time as the demand for rehabilitation services for neurologically impaired patients has intensified during the past decade, advances in technology have raised expectations concerning the role that computers might play in remedial interventions. Earliest applications focused on sensory and motor handicaps, but by the early 1980s (see Vanderheiden, 1982) possibilities for the use of computers as intelligent prostheses were being considered (e.g. Furst, 1984; Jones & Adam, 1979; Skilbeck, 1984) and "cognitive retraining" software began to emerge (e.g. Bracy, 1983; Gianutsos & Klitzner, 1981). By 1985, 73% of rehabilitation centers surveyed in the United States (Bracy, Lynch, Sbordone & Berrol, 1985) reported the use of microcomputers in the rehabilitation of closed head injury patients; yet little research documented the efficacy of remedial software, and serious doubts concerning its benefits had begun to be raised (Schacter & Glisky, 1986). As failures to achieve positive outcomes were recounted, many clinicians became disenchanted with computer interventions and discontinued their use altogether; others continued to use computer-delivered service primarily as a convenience, although "real" rehabilitative value was no longer assumed. More recently, however, promising new methodologies have been developed and it has become evident that computer interventions, like other forms of cognitive rehabilitation, can provide benefits, given that they are based on solid psychological principles.

This chapter reviews the various uses of computers in the rehabilitation of patients with memory disorders. The advantages and disadvantages of computer-

Handbook of Memory Disorders. Edited by A.D. Baddeley, B.A. Wilson and F.N. Watts.
© 1995 John Wiley & Sons Ltd.

ized neuropsychological assessment are not discussed here, nor will space be given to enumerating the obvious general benefits of computer presentation —flexibility, time-saving, consistency of timing and feedback, ease of data collection and analysis, and so forth (see Bradley, Welch & Skilbeck, 1993; Skilbeck & Robertson, 1992). Rather, the focus will be on treatment methods and their efficacy with respect to improved memory functioning. There is nothing inherently therapeutic about a microcomputer (Matthews, Harley, & Malec, 1991; O'Connor & Cermak, 1987), but nevertheless the microcomputer offers some distinct advantages over noncomputerized memory rehabilitation techniques. No attempt is made here to describe and evaluate all the individual pieces of memory retraining software that are available (see Skilbeck & Robertson, 1992, for more detailed descriptions). Instead, this review considers more broadly the ways in which computers have been incorporated into the rehabilitation process, the goals and theories of rehabilitation that have supported this integration, and the extent to which different computer interventions have satisfied these goals.

GOALS AND THEORIES OF REHABILITATION

Memory rehabilitation has generally focused on one of two goals: (a) the repair of damaged memory processes, or (b) the alleviation of functional disabilities associated with memory deficit (Goldstein, 1987; Harris, 1984; Kurlychek & Levin, 1987; Miller, 1978; Schacter & Glisky, 1986). The first goal assumes that mnemonic *ability* can be re-established and that, if such a goal is attained, problems arising from impaired memory will thereby be eliminated. The second goal attacks memory problems directly in an attempt to alter *performance* on memory-dependent tasks. The assumption here is that general memory ability or skill cannot be easily retrained and so the appropriate targets for intervention are specific tasks, which if mastered could improve an individual's functioning in everyday life. The effectiveness of any particular rehabilitation technique can then be assessed in terms of the extent to which it has satisfied one of these goals.

The distinction between memory ability and memory performance was articulated more than 100 years ago by William James (1890) as a difference between "general physiological retentiveness" and the "retention of particular things", and by Lashley almost 50 years later (1938) as a contrast between "general capacities" and "specific associations". Both James and Lashley believed that general memory ability was a given and could not be altered, whereas improvements in performance on specific tasks could be achieved (Prigatano, Glisky & Klonoff, in press). Some 50 years later, the issue is still being debated and comprehensive theories of rehabilitation have still not been well formulated (Caramazza, 1989). Many rehabilitation professionals continue to approach their task, at least initially, with a goal towards restoration of ability (e.g. Gianutsos,

1992; Sohlberg & Mateer, 1989a). Others have adopted a more purely functional approach (e.g. Mayer, Keating & Rapp, 1986). Underlying these different approaches are implicit assumptions concerning the cognitive and neural mechanisms that might be affected by particular interventions although, in general, theories of rehabilitation remain somewhat vague and poorly specified. Three classes of rehabilitation theories are summarized below:

- Those that are directed towards restoration of function
- Those that focus on ways to compensate for lost function
- Those that propose the substitution of intact functions for damaged ones.

For a similar classification, see Wilson (1989).

Restoration of Function

The notion of restoration of function is consistent with a rehabilitation program that focuses on treatment of general or basic memory ability. Typically, rehabilitation techniques developed within this framework involve activation or stimulation of damaged memory processes through extensive exercise and practice or through a relearning of general memory skills and strategies (Sohlberg & Mateer, 1989a). This approach assumes that stimulation of affected memory mechanisms will promote neural changes that may speed spontaneous recovery (Kurlychek & Levin, 1987; Rothi & Horner, 1983) or otherwise restore memory function to premorbid levels. Although recovery of temporarily deactivated brain functions usually occurs within six months following trauma, there is as yet little empirical evidence to suggest that such recovery can be enhanced by stimulation (e.g. Dombovy, Sandok & Basford, 1986). Nor is there evidence to support significant neural regeneration beyond the stage of spontaneous recovery (Meier, Strauman & Thompson, 1987). Nevertheless, many clinicians persist in attempts to restore memory function long beyond the time that natural recovery would have occurred and justify such rehabilitation efforts on the basis of face validity. Gianutsos (1992), for example, suggests that "restoration as a goal" should be pursued "even when that goal might be remote", because patients view it as appropriate (p. 29).

Compensation for Lost Function

Other approaches to memory rehabilitation are based on the assumption that damaged neural and cognitive mechanisms cannot be restored and that the focus of treatment should be on finding ways to bypass or alleviate problems resulting from impaired mnemonic function. The emphasis here is on improved performance of functional tasks through the use of alternative means such as environmental aids or assistive devices that reduce or eliminate the need for memory ability. According to this theory, behavioral outcomes can be accomplished in the absence of any neural or cognitive changes. This approach is often adopted when brain damage is extensive and the memory impairment is severe (Kirsch, Levine, Fallon-Krueger & Jaros, 1987).

Substitution of Intact Function

A third theory of rehabilitation assumes that the neural and cognitive mechanisms that have been damaged by brain injury cannot be restored but that alternative mechanisms may be recruited to perform memory tasks (Franzen & Haut, 1991; Luria, 1963; Miller, 1978; Rothi & Horner, 1983). This approach focuses on performance as the goal of rehabilitation but attempts to achieve improved functioning through the use of unimpaired cognitive and neural structures, rather than through external means.

Associated with each of these theories of rehabilitation are several different remedial techniques, many of which are now delivered by means of computer. These will be reviewed in the next section with particular emphasis on computerized methods. (For a review of noncomputerized methods, see Glisky and Schacter (1989b).)

METHODS OF REHABILITATION

Exercises and Drills

The method most commonly used in an attempt to restore general memory ability is repetitive practice. Clinically, this method probably derives from a basic medical model of physical rehabilitation, whereby various parts of the body that have been impaired or weakened as a result of damage or disuse are exercised in order to restore them to normal levels of functioning. Psychologically, the method may represent a misinterpretation of one of the oldest ideas in cognitive psychology—that practice improves memory (Ebbinghaus, 1885). Such a practice effect has been demonstrated numerous times (e.g. Newell & Rosenbloom, 1981); but although memory for the material practised improves, there is no evidence that memory ability is affected in any general sense. For example, Chase and Ericsson (1981) showed that a college student, after months of practice, was able to increase his digit span from 7 to 80 digits, but his ability to remember letters remained unchanged. Practice had enabled him to develop a complex coding system for the memory of numbers, but the strategy did not generalize to other materials. Failure to find any general mnemonic benefits from repetitive practice is consistent with James' and Lashley's views that "general physiological retentiveness" or "general capacities" cannot be altered although performance on specific tasks can be improved.

Despite evidence to the contrary, the notion that memory ability can be augmented through exercise has persisted in clinical settings (Harris & Sunderland, 1981), perhaps because of an expectation that damaged memories might respond differently from intact ones. Neuropsychological evidence, however, indicates that general improvements in memory, as a result of practice or exercise, are no more likely in memory-impaired individuals than in normal persons. For example, the well-known amnesic patient H.M. has been tested repeatedly for more than 30 years, but his basic memory ability has not improved during that time (Corkin, 1984). Similarly, Glisky, Schacter and Tulving (1986b) taught a number of memory-impaired patients new vocabulary items over a period of several weeks. Although patients were able to learn the specific new items, their memory scores on the Wechsler Memory Scale did not improve. Finally, Godfrey and Knight (1985) failed to find any differences in memory function between amnesic patients who participated in 32 hours of memory skill training and a control group who engaged in nonspecific social activities for the same period of time (also see Berg, Koning-Haanstra & Deelman, 1991).

Although evidence for restoration of function using exercise and drill therapies has generally not been positive, advances in computer technology and the ready availability of relatively inexpensive hardware have revived interest in such methods. The computer represents an ideal medium for presentation of repetitive exercises, and therapists have been attracted by the time-saving features of computer-delivered services. Proponents of the restoration approach to rehabilitation have eagerly adopted computers as "the ultimate drillmasters" (Gianutsos, 1992, p. 34) and have urged others to continue their use "...whatever the outcome" (Gianutsos, 1992, p. 29). Still, evidence of beneficial effects of memory exercises has not been forthcoming, whether they are delivered by computer or in the more traditional pencil-and-paper format (Skilbeck & Robertson, 1992). A study by Middleton, Lambert and Seggar (1991), for example, found no specific effects of 32 hours of drill-oriented computer training of cognitive skills, including memory. And Skilbeck and Robertson (1992), in their review of computer techniques for the management of memory impairment, concluded that when appropriate controls are included in empirical studies, there is little evidence of positive outcome following computer drills.

Some investigators (e.g. Sohlberg & Mateer, 1989a) have suggested that *attention* may be more amenable to computer training than memory and that improvements in attentional processing might secondarily benefit memory performance. Although the evidence for restoration of function in the attentional domain is somewhat more promising than in the memory domain (Matthews, Harley & Malec, 1991; Robertson, 1990), it is, as yet, far from persuasive. For example, Sohlberg and Mateer (1987), in four single-case studies with brain-injured patients, demonstrated improved performance on the Paced Auditory Serial Addition Task (Gronwall, 1977) following computerized practice on other attention-demanding tasks. They also reported improved memory performance on the Randt Memory Test. Ben-Yishay, Piasetsky and Rattok (1987) similarly found that improved performance on computer training tasks (for attentional deficits) was associated with small gains on relevant neuropsychological tests. And Gray, Robertson, Pentland and Anderson (1992) have recently reported long-term improvements in untrained attentional tasks as a result of computerized training (see also Sturm & Willmes, 1992). On the other hand, Wood & Fussey (1987) found no generalized improvements in attention after 20 hours of computer practice although performance on the specific training tasks did improve; Ponsford and Kinsella (1988) also reported negative results. No benefits for real-life functioning were indicated in any of these studies. Given the paucity and inconsistency of findings with respect to attention, no firm conclusions concerning computerized training of attentional deficits nor of its possible impact on memory seem warranted (see Wood, 1992).

Exercise and drill therapy has not proved useful for restoring general memory ability. Although repetitive practice is probably essential for memory-impaired patients to improve on any specific task or to learn any specific information, there is no evidence that such gains generalize beyond the training task or yield any benefits in everyday life. Repetitive practice at remembering meaningless lists of numbers, letters, shapes, or locations thus plays no beneficial role in memory rehabilitation, whether the materials are presented in paper-and-pencil format or on computer (Glisky & Schacter, 1989b; Wilson, 1991).

Mnemonic Strategies

Another method commonly used for the rehabilitation of memory-impaired patients has been the teaching of mnemonic strategies. Much of the work in this area has been associated with attempts to restore memory function by providing patients with proven strategies for remembering information. Results in general, however, have been variable and for the most part disappointing. Although some mildly-impaired patients have been able to learn how to form distinctive visual images or make use of verbal mnemonics such as first-letter cueing (Wilson, 1987), there is little evidence that patients use such strategies spontaneously either in the clinic or in everyday life (Cermak, 1975; Crovitz, Harvey & Horn, 1979; Wilson, 1981; but see Berg, Koning-Haanstra & Deelman, 1991). Thus, although the strategies may facilitate learning of particular information, they are rarely incorporated into a patient's daily activities, and so memory functioning is not improved in any general sense.

Although restoration of memory ability appears not to be attainable through the learning of mnemonic strategies, mnemonic techniques may nevertheless be useful in helping memory-impaired patients acquire new information that is important for their everyday functioning. For example, a number of investigators have reported case studies of patients who could learn the names of people in their environment through the use of visual imagery mnemonics (Glasgow, Zeiss, Barrera & Lewinsohn, 1977; Wilson, 1982, 1987). The same patients, however, never employed the strategy on their own to learn the names of new people that they met. Thus the interventions were not restorative, but rather served to alleviate a specific problem in these patients' everyday lives.

There have been only a few reported attempts to test the effectiveness of computers with respect to the teaching of mnemonic strategies. In one study, Skilbeck (1984) used a microcomputer to teach a head-injured patient the pegword technique for learning short lists of items, such as shopping lists. The patient, who had sustained primarily left-hemisphere damage, learned the ten pegs (i.e. one is a bun, two is a shoe, etc.) and was then provided with computer instructions concerning the interactive images that were to be formed for each to-be-remembered item and the pegword. The patient was able to use the visual imagery strategy to improve her verbal recall performance relative to a straight-forward repetition condition. However, there was no indication that she employed the strategy on her own. The technique thus enabled her to learn specific information relevant to her everyday functioning but did not improve her memory ability in any general sense.

A somewhat different use of a microcomputer for teaching mnemonic strategies was employed by Johnson (1990). In this study, a relatively high functioning patient with a mild verbal memory impairment was allowed to experiment on the computer with different strategies for learning word lists. Although the patient did not adopt any of the presented strategies, he subsequently generated his own techniques after coming to realize the memorial benefits of strategy use. This study implies that some form of generalized benefits of strategy learning may be possible, at least with mildly-impaired patients.

The finding that mnemonic strategies are most useful for patients with relatively mild memory deficits (Benedict, 1989; Wilson, 1987) is consistent with the notion that the strategies rely on the use of residual memory processes. To the extent that memory is damaged rather than lost, residual skills may be tapped to facilitate the acquisition of new information. Such strategies, however, may not be as advantageous for patients with severe memory disorders, who lack the residual memory processes needed for their efficient use.

Evidence with respect to the teaching and use of mnemonic strategies in rehabilitation suggests that the strategies may be beneficially employed by patients with mild-to-moderate disorders for the purposes of learning specific information important in their everyday lives. There is little indication, however, that strategy use generalizes beyond the training situation or that general improvements in memory functioning can be obtained. Repetitive use of strategies with meaningless laboratory materials therefore appears to be of little value (Wilson, 1991).

External Aids

Because of the failure of rehabilitation techniques aimed at restoring memory and the difficulty encountered by severely-impaired patients in using mnemonic strategies, a number of investigators have turned to the development and use of external means for enhancing the functioning of memory-impaired patients (Harris, 1992; Wilson & Moffat, 1984). These have included relatively simple environmental re-structurings such as labels on cupboards and instructions on appliances, as well as aids requiring more active participation of the individual such as notebooks and diaries to keep track of information, and alarm watches or timers to use as reminders. For the most part, patients have been able to take advantage of these aids to improve their everyday functioning, although in many cases—for example, in the use of a notebook—extensive training and role-playing is required if the aids are to be beneficial (Sohlberg & Mateer, 1989b). In addition, some of the devices such as bell timers and alarm watches (Gouvier, 1982; Kurlychek, 1983) have only limited utility because they lack specificity; that is, they do not provide information concerning the course of action to be followed when the alarm sounds.

The external aid that has the greatest potential for beneficial use by memory-impaired patients is the microcomputer, although as yet its capabilities have not been fully exploited (Ager, 1985; Harris, 1992). As an external aid, the computer has the power to act as a memory prosthesis, storing and producing on demand all kinds of information relevant to an individual's functioning in everyday life. It may also have the ability to assist directly in the performance of tasks of daily living (see Cole & Dehdashti, 1990).

Progress in this area, however, has been slow for at least two reasons:

1. Early attempts to teach memory-impaired patients how to use even simple computing devices were not successful. Patients simply could not remember the commands needed to operate them (Wilson, Baddeley & Cockburn, 1989; Wilson & Moffat, 1984).
2. Until recently computers have been too cumbersome to carry around and so their utility in everyday life has been somewhat limited (Harris, 1991; Vanderheiden, 1982).

Both of these problems, however, have been largely solved in the past few years and so, although there are as yet few demonstrations of effective use of computers as external aids, there is reason for some optimism concerning the future use of computers by memory-impaired patients.

A series of studies that has been successful in employing the microcomputer to assist patients with tasks of daily living has been conducted by Kirsch and his colleagues (Kirsch, Levine, Fallon-Krueger & Jaros, 1987; Kirsch, Levine, Lajiness-O'Neill & Schnyder, 1992). These investigators have used the computer as an "interactive task guidance system" that provides a series of cues to guide patients through the sequential steps of real-world tasks such as cookie baking and janitorial activities. In these studies, the computer acts solely as a compensatory device providing the patient with step-by-step instructions for the performance of a task. Little knowledge of computer operation is required on the part of the subject who merely responds with a single key-press to indicate that he has followed the instruction.

Another promising line of research has been conducted by Cole and colleagues (Cole & Dehdashti, 1990; Cole, Dehdashti, Petti & Angert, 1993), who have designed highly customized computer interventions for brain-injured patients with a variety of cognitive deficits (see also Chute, Conn, Dipasquale & Hoag, 1988). Each intervention is directed towards helping patients perform some activity of daily living that they were able to accomplish prior to trauma but can no longer perform without assistance. For example, a patient with severe memory and attentional deficits was able to use a customized text editor and software to construct things-to-do lists, to take notes during telephone conversations, and to carry out home financial transactions (check writing, deposits, withdrawals, mailings, etc.)—all activities that had become impossible since her injury. In this case, the computer was modified to simplify these tasks and to bypass the particular cognitive deficits that were problematic for the patient.

Memory-impaired patients have also been able to learn how to use computers as word-processors. For example, Batt & Lounsbury (1990) constructed a simple flowchart with colored symbols and simple wording that enabled a memory-impaired patient to use a word-processing package. The bypassing of confusing menus and the reduction of memory load enabled the patient to carry out the appropriate word-processing steps without difficulty and to operate the computer by himself (see also Glisky, in press).

In all of these studies, patients used the computer to support some important activity of daily life. Hardware and software were modified in accordance with a patient's deficits so that problems were eliminated or reduced and only a few simple responses needed to be learned. The computer essentially served a prosthetic function, allowing brain-injured patients to perform activities that were otherwise impossible. These kinds of interventions require no assumptions concerning adaptation of the neural or cognitive mechanisms involved in memory, and in general they make no claims concerning restoration or changes in underlying mnemonic ability. Frequently, however, increases in self-confidence and self-esteem are observed in patients following successful computer experience (Batt & Lounsbury, 1990; Cole et al., 1993; Glisky & Schacter, 1987; Johnston, 1990), although whether these psychosocial changes are specifically attributable to computer use, as opposed to other non-specific features of training, has not been empirically documented.

The one negative feature of these kinds of interventions, from a clinical perspective, is their high cost and limited applicability. Design of customized systems requires time, money and expertise and each design may be useful only for a single patient. With continued development in this area, however, prototypical systems may become available that might serve a broader range of patients and be easily administered in the clinic.

Acquisition of Domain-Specific Knowledge

An alternative way to circumvent problems associated with memory impairment is to teach patients knowledge and skills relevant to specific domains of everyday life (Glisky & Schacter, 1989b; Mayer, Keating & Rapp, 1986; Wilson, 1987). For example, patients have been taught the names of people in their environments (Dolan & Norton, 1977; Wilson, 1982), activities of daily living (Cermak, 1976), information concerning characteristics of their deficits (Wilson, 1987), and orientation information relevant to person, place and time (Moffat, 1992; Wilson & Moffat, 1992). Although the goal of these studies was primarily functional and no assumptions concerning the contribution of underlying cognitive and neural mechanisms were indicated, one might nevertheless assume that learning was achieved either through the use of damaged residual memory processes or through the use of other intact cognitive processes not normally involved in memory.

That patients with severe memory disorders might have some preserved memory functions has become increasingly evident in recent years. For example, it has been demonstrated that amnesic patients can acquire a variety of motor, perceptual and cognitive skills—what is often referred to as procedural knowledge (Squire, 1987)—in a near-normal fashion (e.g. Brooks & Baddeley, 1976; Charness, Milberg & Alexander, 1988; Cohen & Squire, 1980; Milner, Corkin & Teuber, 1968). Memory-impaired patients also exhibit normal repetition priming effects; that is, they are as likely as normal subjects to produce recently encountered information in response to partial cues, even though they fail to recollect the prior encounter (Warrington & Weiskrantz, 1968, 1974). Performance on the priming task is thought to reflect what Graf and Schacter (1985) have called "implicit memory", a form of memory that is preserved in amnesic patients and does not require conscious retrieval of the past.

In an effort to capitalize on the preserved memory abilities of amnesic patients, Glisky, Schacter and Tulving (1986b) devised a faded cueing technique, called the *method of vanishing cues*, which was designed to take advantage of patients' normal responses to partial cues to teach them complex knowledge and skills that might be used in everyday life. The training technique provides as much cue information as patients need to make a correct response and then gradually withdraws it across learning trials. The microcomputer serves essentially the role of teacher, presenting information and feedback in a consistent fashion, controlling the amount of cue information in accordance with patients' needs and prior responses, and allowing people to work independently at their own pace. Unlike interventions in which the computer is provided as a continuing prosthetic support, the goal of these interventions is to teach people the information that they need in order to function without external support (see Glisky, 1992b).

Using the method of vanishing cues, Glisky and colleagues successfully taught memory-impaired patients information associated with the operation of a microcomputer (Glisky, Schacter & Tulving, 1986a,b; Glisky, & Schacter, 1988b), the names of various business-related documents (Butters, Glisky & Schacter, 1993), and a number of vocational tasks including computer data-entry (Glisky, 1992a; Glisky & Schacter, 1987, 1989a), microfilming (Glisky & Schacter, 1988a), database management (Glisky, 1993) and word-processing (Glisky, in press). Other researchers have demonstrated successful learning of a daily schedule (Heinrichs et al., 1992), basic items of orientation (Moffat, 1992), information pertaining to treatment goals, sections of a college course in sociology, and instructions for behavior modification (Cotgageorge, personal communication). With the recent completion of a simple authoring system that allows easy access to the vanishing-cues methodology (Glisky, Olsen & Kessler, 1992), rehabilitation professionals can now easily customize the program for individual patients and can teach any information that may be relevant to treatment goals.

There are, however, some caveats concerning the domain-specific learning approach. Although memory-impaired patients are able to learn considerable amounts of complex information, their learning may be exceedingly slow and may result in knowledge representations that are different from those of normal subjects. In particular, patients cannot always access newly acquired knowledge on demand or use it flexibly in novel situations. In other words, transfer beyond the training context cannot be assumed (Wilson, 1992), although it has been demonstrated under some conditions (Glisky & Schacter, 1989a; Glisky, in press). It is therefore essential that all information relevant to the performance of a particular functional task be taught directly so that the need for generalization is minimal (Glisky, Schacter & Butters, 1994).

The problems of transfer and generalization are well known to rehabilitation specialists, and seem to plague all rehabilitation methodologies to some degree. The domain-specific learning approach assumes that transfer to new contexts is not automatic, and so the focus of the approach is on teaching information that is useful to patients. Approaches directed towards the restoration of general memory ability assume that generalization can occur and that exercising memory is the key to that outcome. The material to be practised is viewed as irrelevant and consists generally of useless information such as random digits, locations, words and so forth. To the extent that exercising memory does not improve basic memory ability, the procedure thus provides no benefits to patients whatsoever. The method of vanishing cues also requires extensive practice and repetition, but the technique has been found to be significantly more effective than simple repetition (Glisky, Schacter & Tulving, 1986b; Leng, Copello & Sayegh, 1991) and has enabled the learning of more complex knowledge than was previously thought possible.

The vanishing cues methodology was designed to capitalize on preserved abilities of amnesic patients in order to teach them knowledge and skills relevant in everyday life. Use of intact memory processes to compensate for those that have been disrupted or lost has often been suggested as an appropriate strategy for rehabilitation (Baddeley, 1992; Salmon & Butters, 1987); yet, as Baddeley has pointed out, few interventions of this type, other than the one used by Glisky and colleagues, have been attempted. It is likely that we still lack sufficient knowledge concerning the nature of the processes preserved in amnesia to take optimal advantage of them in rehabilitation. Nevertheless, this approach seems to be a promising one that may gain momentum as basic research provides additional information concerning processes and structures involved in normal memory.

REAL-WORLD APPLICATIONS OF COMPUTER LEARNING

The primary use for computers in memory rehabilitation, as described in the preceding sections, has been as a tool for the presentation of practice drills and mnemonic strategies, for use as an external aid, or for teaching patients domain-specific knowledge. Learning how to operate a computer in a real-world context, however, may constitute a rehabilitation goal in itself. As noted earlier, for example, ability to use a computer may be associated with an increase in self-esteem (e.g. Johnson, 1990). Yet because of the difficulties encountered in teaching patients how to use computers (Wilson & Moffat, 1984), the opportunity to do so has generally been available only to a small number of relatively high functioning individuals. More recently, however, it has been demonstrated that, given appropriate training, even patients with severe memory deficits can learn computer operating procedures (Glisky, Schacter & Tulving, 1986a). This finding suggests that computers might play a greater role in the everyday lives of memory-impaired individuals than was heretofore thought possible.

Vocational Tasks

One area in which computers might serve a potentially important function is the workplace. Glisky (1992a,b) has suggested that some vocational tasks that require the use of a computer may present particularly good opportunities for employment for memory-impaired patients for a number of reasons. First, patients are capable of procedural learning; they can acquire a fixed set of procedures such as those required for data-entry or word-processing, and apply them in a consistent fashion over time. Second, computers in general require rather rigid adherence to a set of rules and can be counted on to be highly consistent, unlike their human counterparts. Once patients have learned the rules and their applications, they are less likely to be called upon to make online decisions or respond to novel circumstances. Third, many computer tasks lend themselves rather well to laboratory simulations so that job training can be accomplished before patients enter the workplace. Glisky and colleagues have found that careful step-by-step training in the laboratory of all components of a task facilitates transfer to the real-world environment and allows the patient to enter the workplace with a high degree of confidence and skill (Glisky & Schacter, 1989a).

In general, computer jobs have been overlooked by rehabilitation and vocational specialists perhaps because they seem too high-tech and complex and, therefore, beyond the capabilities of brain-injured patients. Yet, even patients with quite severe memory impairments have been able to acquire the knowledge and skills needed to perform computer data-entry and word-processing tasks (Glisky, 1992a, in press). It is worth keeping in mind, however, that all aspects of a task need to be taught explicitly and directly in order to minimize any problems in generalization. Although transfer of work skills across changes in materials (Glisky, 1992a) and from a training to a work or home environment has been demonstrated (Glisky, in press; Glisky & Schacter, 1989a), changes in the actual procedures may present serious difficulties.

Home Use of a Computer

Most of the computerized external aids described earlier in the chapter require special adaptation of hardware or software and are applicable in a relatively limited domain. A recent entry into the computer market with great potential for broad application by memory-impaired patients is the pocket computer, variously referred to as an electronic scheduler, organizer, or diary (Harris, 1992). These devices, which are easily portable and inexpensive, have the capability to perform a number of functions useful in everyday life. For example most are able to keep track of appointments via a calendar, and store telephone numbers, addresses and memos. Some of them also signal the user when a scheduled activity is to be carried out and display a message indicating the particulars of the activity. These electronic schedulers thus provide greater specificity than alarm watches and potentially allow the memory-impaired patient much greater independence than was previously possible.

Realization of that potential requires that patients be able to learn to operate these devices on their own. At the time of writing, no empirical demonstrations of this capability have been reported in the literature. Our laboratory, however, is beginning investigations into the possibility of using the method of vanishing cues to train patients how to operate a pocket electronic scheduler. Given previous success with other kinds of computer training, we anticipate that patients will be able to learn the procedures, although the extent to which they can later make use of the device to increase their independence in everyday life is less certain.

CONCLUSIONS AND FUTURE DIRECTIONS

Evidence seems to support a direction for rehabilitation that focuses on functional outcomes—on achieving real-world gains, whether they are accomplished by the use of mnemonic strategies, external aids, or the acquisition of domain-specific knowledge. Which method is adopted depends on one's theory of rehabilitation and the kind of patient that is being treated. If deficits are relatively mild, mnemonic strategies are often successful presumably because the memory processes needed for strategy use have been at least partly retained. When deficits are severe and involve many cognitive and neural structures, external aids that require little in the way of initiating activity or memory are often employed. Domain-specific learning approaches are used with patients who have deficits of varying severity, although procedures such as the method of vanishing cues may be most beneficial for patients with little residual memory function who must rely on the use of alternative preserved mechanisms.

The nature of the material to be learned may also determine the most appropriate method of rehabilitation. Recent studies in our laboratory (Thoene & Glisky, 1995) suggest that learning to associate names with faces may be accomplished more readily through the use of mnemonic strategies than by the method of vanishing cues. Further research is needed to explore the relations between training method and the properties of the learning task.

The past decade has taught us that computerized interventions are not all good or bad just because they involve computers. New applications need to be tested rigorously and evaluated critically in terms of the extent to which they satisfy treatment goals and are based on established psychological principles. Computers will likely play an increasingly important role in rehabilitation as further technologies are developed and the interface between computer and patient is improved. Opportunities for employment and for greater independence at home may also expand as more patients become able to operate computers either as tools of a trade or as external supports for everyday activities. Finally, continued basic research may enable us to discover other preserved cognitive processes that may be used beneficially in the development of rehabilitation methodologies and to solve some of the most intractable problems such as those relating to transfer and generalization.

ACKNOWLEDGEMENTS

Preparation of this manuscript was supported by grant AG09195 from the National Institute on Aging. The author is grateful to Michael Polster for comments on the manuscript.

REFERENCES

Ager, A. (1985). Recent developments in the use of microcomputers in the field of mental handicap: implications for psychological practice. *Bulletin of the British Psychological Society*, **38**, 142–145.

Baddeley, A.D. (1992). Implicit memory and errorless learning: a link between cognitive theory and neuropsychological rehabilitation? In L.R. Squire & N. Butters (eds), *Neuropsychology of Memory*, 2nd edn. Guilford Press, New York, pp. 309–314.

Batt, R.C. & Lounsbury, P.A. (1990). Teaching the patient with cognitive deficits to use a computer. *American Journal of Occupational Therapy*, **44**(4), 364–367.

Benedict, R.B.H. (1989). The effectiveness of cognitive remediation strategies for victims of traumatic head injury: a review of the literature. *Clinical Psychology Review*, **9**, 605–626.

Ben-Yishay, Y., Piasetsky, E.B. & Rattok, J. (1987). A systematic method for ameliorating disorders in basic attention. In M.J. Meier, A.L. Benton & L. Diller (eds), *Neuropsychological Rehabilitation*. Guilford, Press, New York, pp. 165–181.

Berg, I.J., Koning-Haanstra, M. & Deelman, B.G. (1991). Long-term effects of memory rehabilitation: a controlled study. *Neuropsychological Rehabilitation*, **1**, 97–111.

Bracy, O. (1983). Computer-based cognitive rehabilitation. *Cognitive Rehabilitation*, **1**, 7–8, 18.

Bracy, O., Lynch, W., Sbordone, R. & Berrol, S. (1985). Cognitive retraining through computers; Fact or fad? *Cognitive Rehabilitation*, **3**, 10–25.

Bradley, V.A., Welch, J.L. & Skilbeck, C.E. (1993). *Cognitive Retraining Using Microcomputers*. Erlbaum, Hove.

Brooks, D.N. & Baddeley, A.D. (1976). What can amnesic patients learn? *Neuropsychologia*, **14**, 111–122.

Butters, M.A., Glisky, E.L. & Schacter, D.L. (1993). Transfer of learning in memory-impaired patients. *Journal of Clinical and Experimental Neuropsychology*, **15**, 219–230.

Caramazza, A. (1989). Cognitive neuropsychology and rehabilitation: an unfulfilled promise? In X. Seron & G. Deloche (eds), *Cognitive Approaches in Neuropsychological Rehabilitation*. Erlbaum, Hillsdale, NJ, pp. 383–398.

Chute, D.L., Conn, G., Dipasquale, M.C. & Hoag, M. (1988). Prosthesis Ware: a new class of software supporting the activities of daily living. *Neuropsychology*, **2**, 41–57.

Cermak, L.S. (1975). Imagery as an aid to retrieval for Korsakoff patients, *Cortex*, **11**, 163–169.

Cermak, L.S. (1976). The encoding capacity of a patient with amnesia due to encephalitis. *Neuropsychologia*, **14**, 311–322.

Charness, N., Milberg, W. & Alexander, M.P. (1988). Teaching an amnesic a complex cognitive skill. *Brain and Cognition*, **8**, 253–272.

Chase, W.G. & Ericcson, K.A. (1981). Skilled memory. In J.R. Anderson (ed.), *Cognitive Skills and their Acquisition*. Erlbaum, Hillsdale, NJ, pp. 141–190.

Cohen, N.J. & Squire, L.R. (1980). Preserved learning and retention of pattern-analyzing skill in amnesia: dissociation of "knowing how" and "knowing that". *Science*, **210**, 207–209.

Cole, E. & Dehdashti, P. (1990). Interface design as a prosthesis for an individual with a brain injury. *SIGCHI Bulletin*, **22**(1), 28–32.

Cole, E., Dehdashti, P., Petti, L. & Angert, M. (1993). Design parameters and outcomes for cognitive prosthetic software with brain injury patients. *Proceedings of the RESNA International '93 Conference*, **13**.

Corkin, S. (1984). Lasting consequences of bilateral medial temporal lobectomy: clinical course and experimental findings in H.M. *Seminars in Neurology*, **4**, 249–259.

Crovitz, H.F., Harvey, M.T. & Horn, R.W. (1979). Problems in the acquisition of imagery mnemonics: three brain-damaged cases. *Cortex*, **15**, 225–234.

Dolan, M.P. & Norton, J.C. (1977). A programmed training technique that uses reinforcement to facilitate acquisition and retention in brain-damaged patients. *Journal of Clinical Psychology*, **33**, 495–501.

Dombovy, M.L., Sandok, B.A. & Basford, J.R. (1986). Rehabilitation for stroke: a review. *Stroke*, **17**(3), 363–369.

Ebbinghaus, H. (1885). *Uber das gedachtnis*. Duncker & Humblot, Leipzig.

Franzen, M.D. & Haut, M.W. (1991). The psychological treatment of memory impairment: a review of empirical studies. *Neuropsychology Review*, **2**(1), 29–63.

Furst, C.J. (1984). Utility of a computer prosthesis for impaired intention memory. Paper presented to the American Psychological Association, Toronto, Canada, 1984.

Gianutsos, R. (1992). The computer in cognitive rehabilitation: it's not just a tool anymore. *Journal of Head Trauma Rehabilitation*, 7(3), 26–35.

Gianutsos, R. & Kiltzner, C. (1981). *Computer Programs for Cognitive Rehabilitation*. Life Science Associates, Bayport, NY.

Glasgow, R.E. & Zeiss, R.A., Barrera, M. & Lewinsohn, P.M. (1977). Case studies in remediating memory deficits in brain-damaged individuals. *Journal of Clinical Psychology*, **33**, 1049–1054.

Glisky, E.L. (1992a). Acquisition and transfer of declarative and procedural knowledge by memory-impaired patients: a computer data-entry task. *Neuropsychologia*, **30**, 899–910.

Glisky, E.L. (1992b). Computer-assisted instruction for patients with traumatic brain injury: teaching of domain-specific knowledge. *Journal of Head Trauma Rehabilitation*, 7(3), 1–12.

Glisky, E.L. (1993). Training persons with traumatic brain injury for complex computer jobs: the domain-specific learning approach. In D.F. Thomas, F.E. Menz & D.C. McAlees (eds), *Community-Based Employment Following Traumatic Brain Injury*. University of Wisconsin, Menomonie, WI, pp. 3–27.

Glisky, E.L. (in press). Acquisition and transfer of word processing skill by an amnesic patient. *Neuropsychological Rehabilitation*.

Glisky, E.L., Olsen, D.R. & Kessler, M. (1992). *The Multi-Domain Programmable Teacher*, 2.0. Department of Psychology, University of Arizona, Tucson.

Glisky, E.L. & Schacter, D.L. (1987). Acquisition of domain-specific knowledge in organic amnesia: training for computer-related work. *Neuropsychologia*, **25**, 893–906.

Glisky, E.L. & Schacter, D.L. (1988a). Acquisition of domain-specific knowledge in patients with organic memory disorders. *Journal of Learning Disabilities*, **21**, 333–339.

Glisky, E.L. & Schacter, D.L. (1988b). Long-term retention of computer learning by patients with memory disorders. *Neuropsychologia*, **26**, 173–178.

Glisky, E.L. & Schacter, D.L. (1989a). Extending the limits of complex learning in organic amnesia: computer training in a vocational domain. *Neuropsychologia*, **27**, 107–120.

Glisky, E.L. & Schacter, D.L. (1989b). Models and methods of memory rehabilitation. In F. Boller & J. Grafman (eds), *Handbook of Neuropsychology*. Elsevier, Amsterdam.

Glisky, E.L., Schacter, D.L. & Butters, M.A. (1994). Domain-specific learning and memory remediation. In M.J. Riddoch & G.W. Humphreys (eds), *Cognitive Neuropsychology and Cognitive Rehabilitation*. Erlbaum, London, pp. 527–548.

Glisky, E.L., Schacter, D.L. & Tulving, E. (1986a). Computer learning by memory-impaired patients: acquisition and retention of complex knowledge. *Neuropsychologia*, **24**, 313–328.

Glisky, E.L., Schacter, D.L. & Tulving, E. (1986b). Learning and retention of computer-related vocabulary in amnesic patients: method of vanishing cues. *Journal of Clinical and Experimental Neuropsychology*, **8**, 292–312.

Godfrey, H.P.D. & Knight, R.G. (1985). Cognitive rehabilitation of memory functioning in amnesiac alcoholics. *Journal of Consulting and Clinical Psychology*, **53**, 555–557.

Goldstein, G. (1987). Neuropsychological assessment for rehabilitation: fixed batteries, automated systems, and non-psychometric methods. In M.J. Meier, A.L. Benton & L. Diller (eds), *Neuropsychological Rehabilitation*. Guilford Press, New York, pp. 18–40.

Gouvier, W. (1982). Using the digital alarm chronograph in memory retraining. *Behavioral Engineering*, **7**, 134.

Graf, P. & Schacter, D.L. (1985). Implicit and explicit memory for new associations in normal and amnesic patients. *Journal of Experimental Psychology*: *Learning, Memory and Cognition*, **11**, 501–518.

Gray, J.M., Robertson, I., Pentland, B. & Anderson, S. (1992). Microcomputer-based attentional retraining after brain damage: a randomised group controlled trial. *Neuropsychological Rehabilitation*, **2**(2), 97–115.

Gronwall, D. (1977). Paced auditory serial addition task: a measure of recovery from concussion. *Perceptual Motor Skills*, **44**, 367–373.

Harris, J.E. (1984). Methods of improving memory. In B. Wilson & N. Moffat (eds), *Clinical Management of Memory Problems*, 1st edn. Aspen, London, pp. 46–62.

Harris, J.E. (1992). Ways to help memory. In B.A. Wilson & N. Moffat (eds), *Clinical Management of Memory Problems*, 2nd edn. Chapman & Hall, London, pp. 59–85.

Harris, J.E. & Sunderland, A. (1981). A brief survey of the management of memory disorders in rehabilitation units in Britain. *International Rehabilitation Medicine*, **3**, 206–209.

Heinrichs, R.W., Levitt, H., Arthurs, A., Gallardo, C., Hirscheimer, K., MacNeil, M., Olshansky, E. & Richards, K. (1992). Learning and retention of a daily activity schedule in a patient with alcoholic Korsakoff's syndrome. *Neuropsychological Rehabilitation*, **2**(1), 43–58.

James, W. (1890). *The Principles of Psychology*, vol. 1. Dover, New York.

Johnson, R. (1990). Modifying memory function: use of a computer to train mnemonic skill. *British Journal of Clinical Psychology*, **29**, 437–438.

Jones, G.H. & Adam, J.H. (1979). Towards a prosthetic memory. *Bulletin of the British Psychological Society*, **32**, 165–167.

Kirsch, N.L., Levine, S.P., Fallon-Krueger, M. & Jaros, L.A. (1987). The microcomputer as an "orthotic" device for patients with cognitive deficits. *Journal of Head Trauma Rehabilitation*, **2**(4), 77–86.

Kirsch, N.L., Levine, S.P., Lajiness-O'Neill & Schnyder, M. (1992). Computer-assisted interactive task guidance: facilitating the performance of a simulated vocational task. *Journal of Head Trauma Rehabilitation*, **7**(3), 13–25.

Kurlychek, R.T. (1983). Use of a digital alarm chronograph as a memory aid in early dementia. *Clinical Gerontology*, **1**, 93–94.

Kurlychek, R.T. & Levin, W. (1987). Computers in the cognitive rehabilitation of brain-injured persons. *CRC Critical Reviews in Medical Informatics*, **1**(3), 241–257.

Lashley, K.S. (1938). Factors limiting recovery after central nervous lesions. *Journal of Nervous and Mental Diseases*, **88**, 733–755.

Leng, N.R.C., Copello, A.G. & Sayegh, A. (1991). Learning after brain injury by the method of vanishing cues: a case study. *Behavioural Psychotherapy*, **19**, 173–181.

Luria, A.R. (1963). *Restoration of Function after Brain Injury*. Macmillan, New York.

Matthews, C.G., Harley, J.P. & Malec, J.F. (1991). Guidelines for computer-assisted neuropsychological rehabilitation and cognitive remediation. *Clinical Neuropsychologist*, **5**(1), 3–19.

Mayer, N.H., Keating, D.J. & Rapp, D. (1986). Skills, routines, and activity patterns of daily living: a functional nested approach. In B. Uzzell & Y. Gross (eds), *Clinical Neuropsychology of Intervention*. Nijhoff, Boston, pp. 205–222.

Meier, M.J., Strauman, S. & Thompson, W.G. (1987). Individual differences in neuropsychological recovery: an overview. In M.J. Meier, A.L. Benton & D. Diller (eds), *Neuropsychological Rehabilitation*. Guilford Press, London, pp. 71–100.

Middleton, D.K., Lambert, M.J. & Seggar, L.B. (1991). Neuropsychological rehabilitation: microcomputer-assisted treatment of brain-injured adults. *Perceptual and Motor Skills*, **72**, 527–530.

Miller, E. (1978). Is amnesia remediable? In M.M. Gruneberg, P.E. Morris & R.N. Sykes (eds), *Practical Aspects of Memory*. Academic Press, London, pp. 705–711.

Milner, B., Corkin, S. & Teuber, H.L. (1968). Further analysis of the hippocampal amnesic syndrome: 14-year follow-up study of H.M. *Neuropsychologia*, **6**, 215–234.

Moffat, N. (1992). Strategies of memory therapy. In B.A. Wilson & N. Moffat (eds), *Clinical Management of Memory Problems*. Chapman & Hall, London, pp. 86–119.

Newell, A. & Rosenbloom, P.S. (1981). Mechanisms of skill acquisition and the law of practice. In J.R. Anderson (ed.), *Cognitive Skills and their Acquisition*. Erlbaum, Hillsdale, NJ, pp. 1–56.

O'Connor, M. & Cermak, L.S. (1987). Rehabilitation of organic memory disorders. In M.J. Meier, A.L. Benton & L. Diller (eds), *Neuropsychological Rehabilitation*. Guilford, New York, pp. 260–279.

Ponsford, J.L. & Kinsella, G. (1988). Evaluation of a remedial programme for attentional deficits following closed head injury. *Journal of Clinical and Experimental Neuropsychology*, **10**(6), 693–708.

Prigatano, G.P., Glisky, E.L. & Klonoff, P. (in press). Cognitive rehabilitation after traumatic brain injury. In P.W. Corrigan & S.C. Yudofsky (eds), *Cognitive Rehabilitation and Neuropsychiatric Disorders*. American Psychiatric Press.

Robertson, I. (1990). Does computerized cognitive rehabilitation work? A review. *Aphasiology*, **4**(4), 381–405.

Rothi, L.J. & Horner, J. (1983). Restitution and substitution: Two theories of recovery with application to neurobehavioral treatment. *Journal of Clinical Neuropsychology*, **5**, 73–81.

Salmon, D.P. & Butters, N. (1987). Recent developments in learning and memory: implications for the rehabilitation of the amnesic patient. In M.J. Meier, A.L. Benton & L. Diller (eds), *Neuropsychological Rehabilitation*. Guilford, New York, pp. 280–293.

Schacter, D.L. & Glisky, E.L. (1986). Memory remediation: restoration, alleviation, and the acquisition of domain-specific knowledge. In B. Uzzell & Y. Gross (eds), *Clinical Neuropsychology of Intervention*. Nujhoff, Boston, pp. 257–282.

Skilbeck, C. (1984). Computer assistance in the management of memory and cognitive impairment. In B. Wilson & N. Moffat (eds), *Clinical Management of Memory Problems*, 1st edn. Aspen, Rockville, MD, pp. 112–133.

Skilbeck, C. & Robertson, I. (1992). Computer assistance in the management of memory and cognitive impairment. In B.A. Wilson & N. Moffat (eds), *Clinical Management of Memory Problems*, 2nd edn. Chapman & Hall, London, pp. 154–188.

Sohlberg, M.M. & Mateer, C.A. (1987). Effectiveness of an attention training program. *Journal of Clinical and Experimental Neuropsychology*, **9**(2), 117–130.

Sohlberg, M.M. & Mateer, C.A. (1989a). *Introduction to Cognitive Rehabilitation*. Guilford, New York.

Sohlberg, M.M. & Mateer, C.A. (1989b). Training use of compensatory memory books: a three-stage behavioral approach. *Journal of Clinical and Experimental Neuropsychology*, **11**(6), 871–891.

Squire, L.R. (1987). *Memory and Brain*. Oxford University Press, New York.

Sturm, W. & Willmes, K. (1991). Efficacy of a reaction training on various attentional and cognitive functions in stroke patients. *Neuropsychological Rehabilitation*, **1**(4), 259–280.

Thoene, A.I.T. & Glisky, E.L. (1995). Learning of name–face associations in memory-impaired patients: A comparison of different training procedures. *Journal of the International Neuropsychological Society*, **1**(1).

Vanderheiden, G.C. (1982). The practical use of microcomputers in rehabilitation. *Bulletin of Prosthetic Research*, **19**, 1–5.

Warrington, E.K. & Weiskrantz, L. (1968). New method of testing long-term retention with special reference to amnesic patients. *Nature*, **217**, 972–974.

Warrington, E.K. & Weiskrantz, L. (1974). The effect of prior learning on subsequent retention in amnesic patients. *Neuropsychologia*, **12**, 419–428.

Wilson, B.A. (1981). Teaching a patient to remember people's names after removal of a left temporal tumor. *Behavioral Psychotherapy*, **9**, 338–344.

Wilson, B. (1982). Success and failure in memory training following a cerebral vascular accident. *Cortex*, **18**, 581–594.

Wilson, B. (1987). *Rehabilitation of Memory*. Guilford, New York.

Wilson, B.A. (1989). Models of cognitive rehabilitation. In R.Ll. Wood & P. Eames (eds), *Models of Brain Injury Rehabilitation*. Chapman & Hall, London, pp. 117–141.

Wilson, B.A. (1991). Theory, assessment, and treatment in neuropsychological rehabilitation. *Neuropsychology*, **5**(4), 281–291.

Wilson, B.A. (1992). Memory therapy in practice. In B.A. Wilson & N. Moffat (eds), *Clinical Management of Memory Problems*, 2nd edn. Chapman & Hall, London, pp. 120–153.

Wilson, B.A., Baddeley, A.D. & Cockburn, J.M. (1989). How do old dogs learn new tricks: teaching a technological skill to brain injured people. *Cortex*, **25**, 115–119.

Wilson, B. & Moffat, N. (1984). Rehabilitation of memory for everyday life. In J.E. Harris & P.E. Morris (eds), *Everyday Memory: Actions and Absentmindedness*. Academic Press, London, pp. 207–233.

Wilson, B.A. & Moffat, N. (1992). The development of group memory therapy. In B.A. Wilson & N. Moffat (eds), *Clinical Management of Memory Problems*, 2nd edn. Chapman & Hall, London, pp. 243–273.

Wood, R. Ll. (1992). Disorders of attention: their effect on behaviour, cognition and rehabilitation. In B.A. Wilson & N. Moffat (eds), *Clinical Management of Memory Problems*, 2nd edn. Chapman & Hall, London, pp. 216–242.

Wood, R. Ll. & Fussey, I. (1987). Computer-based cognitive retraining: a controlled study. *International Disability Studies*, **9**, 149–153.

Chapter 24

Pharmacological Treatment of Impaired Memory Function

Wendy J. Lombardi
and
Herbert Weingartner
Cognitive Neurosciences Section, LCS, NIAAA, Bethesda, USA

INTRODUCTION

This chapter focuses on several theoretical and practical issues which are important at the current stage of development of treatments for memory disorders. We will not attempt to provide a thorough review of the literature on memory-enhancing drugs in this chapter. Such reviews can be found in Squire & Davis (1981) and Thal (1992). Nor will we provide an outline of practical recommendations for the treatment of memory disorders with pharmacological agents. Such conclusions would be premature. Instead, we will take a step back and attempt to examine the search for pharmacological treatments of memory impairments from a new perspective.

A theoretical issue we will consider in detail is the specificity of the memory impairments that are targets for treatment. In particular we will discuss the importance of specificity of deficits and of treatments, and the various ways in which such specificity can be defined. We will develop the view that most memory-enhancing drugs are likely to produce distinctive effects on a limited set of individual memory processes rather than general changes in memory functions. We will argue that knowledge of the precise nature of memory impairments and of drug effects should be used to match particular deficits to particular drug treatments.

Handbook of Memory Disorders. Edited by A.D. Baddeley, B.A. Wilson and F.N. Watts.
© 1995 John Wiley & Sons Ltd.

In the first section of the chapter, specificity will be defined and discussed in general terms. We will define two types of specificity, neurobiological and behavioral, in the context of memory-inhibiting drugs. More is known about the precise effects of memory-inhibiting drugs than of memory-enhancing drugs. Specificity of memory-inhibiting drugs can therefore serve as a model for the development of greater precision in characterizing the effects of memory-enhancing drugs. In the second section of the chapter, both neurobiological and behavioral specificity are discussed in relation to developing treatments for memory deficits. We describe the ways in which specificity plays a role in the pharmacological treatment of diseases and disorders of all types, and argue that drug treatment of memory impairments should be dealt with in a similar way.

The final section of the chapter discusses research methods in the investigation of drug treatments for memory disorders. We use current research on the use of tacrine in the treatment of Alzheimer's disease as an example of the problems and challenges that face us in developing memory therapies. Rather than a detailed review of this literature, we present instead a critical review of some selected aspects of this research which we hope will be useful to both those planning research in this area and those attempting to evaluate such research.

NEUROBIOLOGICAL AND BEHAVIORAL SPECIFICITY

For the purposes of the discussion in this chapter, we will define memory processes to be all cognitive processes which contribute to performance on a memory measure. We will therefore not consider whether a particular drug or disease state has an intrinsic effect on memory, affecting the pathways in which memory representations are actually stored, or an extrinsic effect, affecting those systems which influence encoding, consolidation, and use of information stored in intrinsic systems, but which do not themselves store memory representations (Kranse, 1978; Squire & Davis, 1981). Instead, we will discuss specificity in terms of the types of memory processes which are influenced by a drug or a disorder. A major focus of this discussion will be on the need to match drug treatments to memory disorders on the basis of both the pathological characteristics of the disorder and the types of memory processes which are affected. We turn first to a discussion of memory-inhibiting drugs to illustrate both types of specificity.

Specificity of Memory-Inhibiting Drugs

Neurobiological Specificity

A number of drugs have been shown to interfere with memory functioning. These drugs are grouped into classes according to the neural mechanisms by which they exert their effects. Benzodiazepines, including diazepam and tria-zolam, have been demonstrated to induce robust impairments in performance on many types of memory tests, such as recall and recognition tests (e.g. Brown et al., 1982; Clarke, Eccersley, Frisby & Thornton, 1970; Curren et al., 1988; Ghoneim, Hinrichs & Mewaldt, 1984; Ghoneim & Mewaldt, 1975, 1977; Hinrichs, Mewaldt, Ghoneim & Berie, 1982; Hommer, Weingartner & Breir, 1993; Lister & File, 1984; Weingartner et al., 1992c; see also Curran, 1991 and Lister, 1985, for reviews). This class of drugs acts primarily by facilitating the activity of the neurotransmitter GABA, although the activities of other types of neurotransmitters are also altered.

Drugs with anticholinergic action have also been demonstrated to interfere with performance on some types of memory test. Anticholinergic drugs interfere with the action of the neurotransmitter acetylcholine. Those drugs which act at muscarinic-type receptors have received the most attention. Scopolamine, a muscarinic cholinergic receptor antagonist, has been shown to interfere with both recall and recognition performance (Beatty, Butters & Janowsky, 1986; Cain et al., 1981; Drachman, 1977; Drachman & Leavitt, 1974; Ghoneim & Mewaldt, 1975, 1977; Kopelman & Corn, 1988; Molchan et al., 1992; Nissen, Knopman & Schacter, 1987; Peterson, 1977; Safer & Allen, 1971; Sitaram, Weingartner & Gillin, 1978).

Alcohol has also been shown to produce deficits in memory performance (Birnbaum, Parker, Hartley & Noble, 1978; Hastroudi et al., 1984; Lister et al., 1991; Maylor & Rabbit, 1987; Nelson, McSpadden, Fromme & Marlatt, 1986; Petrol et al., 1985; Williams & Rundell, 1984). The effects of alcohol on neural activity are not completely understood. It appears that alcohol has an effect on a number of areas in the central nervous system, resulting from its action on a number of neural transmitters. At present, it seems to be the case that on a neurophysiological level, the effects of alcohol are less selective than are the effects of scopolamine and benzodiazepines.

Thus far, the discussion of memory-inhibiting drugs has emphasized one aspect of specificity, the distinctive effects of a particular drug on neural activity. The effects of benzodiazepines and anticholinergics are both relatively precise, mostly involving a single type of transmitter, whereas the effects of alcohol do not appear to specifically involve a particular neural transmitter.

Behavioral Specificity

A second type of specificity, behavioral specificity, has also been demonstrated in the literature on drug effects on memory. In general, the drugs which impair memory affect certain types of memory processes and spare others (Lister & Weingartner, 1987). The distinction between declarative memory, which underlies the retention of facts and events, and procedural memory, which underlies the retention of skills, is an important one in this regard (Cohen & Squire, 1980; Squire, 1992). Benzodiazepines affect declarative memory processes, as measured by tests of recall and recognition, but spare procedural learning processes, as measured by reading transformed text (Lister & File, 1984) and solving anagrams (Weingartner & Wolkowitz, 1988). Scopolamine has also been found to impair performance on tests of declarative memory (Ghoneim & Mewaldt, 1975, 1977; Nissen et al., 1987; Peterson, 1977). The effects of scopolamine on tests of procedural memory are less clear, however, with some investigators finding no effect on such tests (Kopelman & Corn, 1988; Nissen et al., 1987), and others finding an effect (Curran, Schifano & Lader, 1991; Frith, McGinty, Gergel & Crow, 1989).

Declarative memory can be further subdivided into episodic and semantic memory (Tulving, 1972, 1983, 1985). Studies of the memory-impairing effects of drugs have tended either to lump these two forms of declarative memory together, or to confound the type of memory tapped with whether encoding or retrieval processes exert the primary influence on performance. It is therefore difficult to determine if any drugs can be found which selectively affect one type of declarative memory and not the other. The distinction between episodic and semantic memory will become important in the discussion of the selective memory impairments found in disease states, however.

The distinction between explicit and implicit memory has proven useful in examining the effects of drugs on learning memory. Implicit memory facilitates performance on a task in the absence of conscious recollection, whereas explicit memory involves conscious recollection of previous experiences (Graf & Schacter, 1985; Schacter, 1987, 1992; see also Richardson-Klavehn & Bjork, 1988, Roediger & McDermott, 1993, and Tulving & Schacter, 1990, for reviews and discussion of this literature). Alcohol impairs performance on explicit tests of memory, while leaving performance on implicit tests of memory intact (Hastroudi et al., 1984; Lister et al., 1991). Both benzodiazepines and scopolamine also produce impairments in explicit memory (Beatty et al., 1986; Brown et al., 1982; Cain et al., 1981; Clarke et al., 1970; Curran et al., 1988; Drachman, 1977; Drachman & Leavitt, 1974; Ghoneim et al., 1984; Ghoneim & Mewaldt, 1975, 1977; Hinrichs et al., 1982; Hommer et al., 1993; Kopelman & Corn, 1988; Lister & File, 1984; Nissen et al., 1987; Peterson, 1977; Safer & Allen, 1971; Sitaram et al., 1978; Weingartner et al., 1992b), but their effects on implicit memory are less clear. One group of investigators has found an effect of scopolamine on implicit memory performance (Nissen et al., 1987), whereas other investigators have failed to do so (Knopman, 1991; Kopelman & Corn, 1988). Several investigators have found an effect of a benzodiazepine on implicit memory (Brown, Brown & Bowes, 1989; Curran, 1991), whereas other investigators have found implicit memory to be unaffected by a drug of this class (Danion et al., 1989, 1990; Fang, Hinrichs & Ghoneim, 1987).

A third dichotomy, the distinction between encoding and retrieval processes, has also been useful in examining drug effects on memory performance. Benzodiazepines and scopolamine appear to interfere with encoding of new material, but not with the retrieval of previously learned material. Following benzodiazepine administration, subjects are able to generate category exemplars, access general knowledge, and recall and recognize previously learned information as well as under placebo conditions (Hommer et al., 1986; Weingartner et al., 1992c). File, Skelly and Girdler (1992), however, have recently reported finding midazolam to interfere with retrieval of semantic knowledge on a word-completion task. Following scopolamine administration, subjects have been found to recall and recognize previously learned information normally while showing a deficit on tests of material learned following administration (Ghoneim & Mewaldt, 1975, 1977; Peterson, 1977). Unlike benzodiazepines and scopolamine, alcohol does appear to interfere with retrieval processes, as measured by performance on general-information questions requiring subjects to access their long-term semantic knowledge base (Nelson et al., 1986).

The above discussion of distinctions among memory processes by no means exhausts the list of such varieties that may prove useful in analyzing the effects of drugs on memory. There is also a great deal more to be learned about the effects of scopolamine, benzodiazepines, and alcohol on learning and memory. Nevertheless, this brief review of drug-inhibiting effects on memory serves to emphasize the importance of considering behavioral specificity. All three classes of drugs show behavioral specificity in that they interfere selectively with some types of memory processes and spare others. In addition, each of the three classes of drugs produces a pattern of effects on memory tests which is different from the pattern produced by each of the other two types. It is not enough simply to know that a drug influences performance on memory tasks. It is also necessary to discover which types of memory tasks are affected and which are not. The issue of behavioral specificity will be of central importance in the following discussion of the drug therapy of memory disorders.

THE ROLE OF SPECIFICITY IN TREATING MEMORY DISORDERS

In treating any disease process with pharmacological agents, a drug therapy is matched to the particular disorder on the basis of two types of specificity: specificity based on pathology and specificity based on symptoms. In many cases, a drug treatment can be designed which is based directly on the pathology of the disease itself. The drug will at least partially reverse the physiological basis of the disease. Successful examples of this approach include the treatment of diabetes with insulin and the treatment of Parkinson's disease with levodopa.

Although treatment of a disease with a drug which will address its basic pathology is obviously desirable, in many cases it is not yet possible to design a drug treatment which will specifically correct the underlying pathology of the disease. Two examples of such diseases are depression and multiple sclerosis. In the case of depression, the underlying pathology of the disease is poorly understood. It has not therefore been possible to use the pathology of the disease to develop pharmacological interventions. Medications used to treat depression are those which are successful at ameliorating the behavioral symptoms of depression. In fact, much of what is believed about the possible causes of depression is based on the physiological actions of antidepressant medications. In the case of multiple sclerosis, the underlying pathology, demyelination of neurons in the central nervous system, is known. It is not possible to base pharmacological interventions on this pathology, however, because no medications exist which will reverse demyelination of neurons. In this case, as in the case of depression, medications are chosen based on their ability to ameliorate the symptoms of multiple sclerosis. In cases such as multiple sclerosis and depression, drug therapies are designed on the basis of their symptomologic characteristics. Drugs are chosen to alleviate the specific symptoms of the disease, whether or not they reverse its basic pathology.

Treating a memory disorder with a pharmacological intervention should involve the same matching process that is fundamental to the treatment of any disorder with a drug. As with any disease state, both types of specificity, pathologic and symptomologic, must be taken into account when matching a drug treatment to a deficit. The neurobiological and behavioral aspects of memory disorders should first be identified. Then, drug treatments can be matched to specific disorders on the basis of both neurobiological and behavioral specificity.

Neurobiological Specificity

Memory deficits stem from a wide variety of causes, including some which are acute and reversible, and some which are chronic and progressive. Common causes of memory disorders include closed-head injury, herpes simplex encephalitis, surgery involving medial temporal and diencephalic structures, Wernicke–Korsakoff syndrome, vascular accidents such as ruptured aneurysms and stroke, Alzheimer's disease, Parkinson's disease, and depression. A complete list of the known etiologies of memory disorders would be considerably longer. The etiology of the memory disorder can provide information about the type of drug treatment that is likely to be effective.

In the case of some of these disorders, the underlying pathology suggests a pharmacological intervention. Memory deficits stemming from diseases which involve neurotransmitter imbalances are likely to be reversed, at least partially, by drug therapy which corrects the imbalance. Such diseases include Alzheimer's disease, Parkinson's disease and depression. In Alzheimer's disease, for example, cortical levels of choline acetyltransferase and acetylcholine are reduced (Bowen, Smith, White & Davidson, 1976; Davies & Maloney, 1976; Op Den Velde & Stam, 1976; White et al., 1977), possibly due to the degeneration of neurons in the nucleus basalis, which comprise the major cholinergic input to the cortex (Whitehouse et al., 1982). Furthermore, the reduction in choline acetyltransferase has been correlated with both the number of senile plaques and the severity of the dementia in Alzheimer's disease patients (Perry et al.,

1978). Patients with Alzheimer's disease also appear to be more sensitive to the cognitive-impairing effects of scopolamine than are age-matched controls (Sunderland et al., 1987). Loss of acetylcholine is therefore an important component of Alzheimer's disease (Coyle, Price & Delong, 1983), although it should be kept in mind that the levels of other neurotransmitters are affected as well. In Parkinson's disease, the primary pathology includes a loss of dopaminergic cells in the substantia nigra, locus ceruleus, and the dorsal motor nucleus of the vagus, as well as the formation of Lewy bodies in cells of these nuclei, although loss of cells occurs in other locations (Adams & Victor, 1989). Furthermore, the motor deficits characteristic of Parkinson's disease are ameliorated to at least some extent by dopaminergic drugs in virtually all patients with the disease (Adams & Victor, 1989; Young, 1977). As is the case with Alzheimer's disease, however, it must be kept in mind that levels of other neurotransmitters are affected by Parkinson's disease.

There are at least two problems with relying solely on pathologic specificity in the development of drug treatments for memory disorders. The first is that there are many instances in which matching on the basis of pathologic specificity is not possible The underlying pathology which leads to a memory deficit is not always known. In the case of Wernicke–Korsakoff syndrome, for example, the sites of the lesions which result in a chronic amnesic syndrome appear to include diencephalic structures, although the exact location of critical damage within the diencephalon is currently the subject of controversy (see Langlais, 1992, for a review). The cause of these lesions is not known however. Most aspects of the Wernicke–Korsakoff syndrome appear to result from thiamine deficiency, and most of the accompanying symptoms respond to treatment with thiamine. Amnesia, however, does not respond completely to thiamine treatment, and the role of thiamine in causing the chronic memory impairment is therefore unclear (Adams & Victor, 1989; Langlais, 1992). In cases such as Korsakoff's disease, in which the underlying pathology is unknown, it is currently impossible to match the deficit to a treatment on the basis of pathology.

In the case of other etiologies of memory deficit, the underlying pathology may be known, but it is not amenable to pathologic matching with a pharmacological intervention. Such etiologies include deficits which result from either severe damage or surgical removal of structures known to be important components of memory circuits. A well-known example is the memory disorder that resulted from the removal of medial temporal structures in the famous amnesic patient H.M. (Scoville & Milner, 1975). No specific drug therapy can be designed which will correct the physiological disorder in these cases.

The second problem with relying solely on pathological specificity to treat memory disorders is that this strategy has thus far led to very limited success. Given the pathology of Alzheimer's disease, for example, treatment of the memory disorder with drugs which enhance cholinergic activity appears to be an obvious choice. Attempts to treat the memory deficit with cholinergic drugs have met with limited success however. Treatment with the acetylcholine precursors choline and lecithin, drugs which increase release of acetylcholine, or cholinergic agonists such as arecoline, has generally failed to produce effects on memory performance in Alzheimer's disease patients (Dysken et al., 1982; Little, Levy, Chuaqui-Kidd & Hand, 1985; Renvoize & Jerram, 1979; Smith et al., 1978; Weintraub et al., 1983; but see Fovall et al., 1980, and Signoret, Whiteley & Lhermitte, 1978, for exceptions).

Acetylcholinesterase inhibitors have received the most experimental attention. Drugs of this class inhibit acetylcholinesterase, the enzyme which breaks down acetylcholine in the synapse, thereby prolonging the activity of acetylcholine at the postsynaptic receptor. Physostigmine inhibits acetylcholinesterase at muscarinic synapses. This drug has been demonstrated to improve performance on memory tests in normals (e.g. Davis et al., 1978). A number of experiments have examined the effects of physostigmine in Alzheimer's disease. Most of these studies have found some degree of improvement in memory performance when physostigmine is administered alone or in combination with lecithin, a cholinergic precursor (Beller, Overall & Swann, 1985; Christie, Shering, Ferguson & Glen, 1981; Davis & Mohs, 1982; Harrell et al., 1986; Peters & Levin, 1979; Schwartz & Kohlstaedt, 1986; Stern, Sano, & Mayeux, 1988; Thal et al., 1986, 1989). These effects are generally modest, however, and are not found in patients with severe dementia. A second cholinesterase inhibitor, tetrahydroaminoacridine (tacrine), has also been tested in Alzheimer's disease patients. One such study, that of Summers et al. (1986), reported substantial improvement in Alzheimer's disease patients following treatment with tacrine, as measured by a global assessment rating and several tests of cognitive function. This study, however, has been widely criticized for its methodology. Other studies using tacrine, either alone or in combination with lecithin, have reported modest improvement in memory performance (Kay et al., 1982) or in cognitive performance (Davis et al., 1992; Eagger, Levy & Sahakian, 1991; Farlow et al., 1992). Both the Davis et al. (1992) and the Farlow et al. (1992) are large-scale trials of tacrine, with the Davis et al. (1992) study including data obtained from multiple centers throughout the USA. Other studies have failed to find any effects of anticholinergic treatment on memory performance in Alzheimer's disease patients (Gauthier et al., 1990; Mitchell, Drachman, O'Donnell & Glasser, 1986; Schmechel et al., 1984).

The evidence reviewed above makes it clear that the effects of treatment with drugs which enhance cholinergic activity on the memory deficits found in Alzheimer's disease patients are disappointing. The studies which do find effects find a very modest improvement in memory in some Alzheimer's disease patients. (See Thal (1992) for a more complete review of this research.) It therefore appears that even when the pathology of a disease suggests an obvious drug therapy for the treatment of a memory deficit, choosing a drug to treat the memory disorder on the basis of disease pathology alone is no guarantee of success. Matching a memory disorder to a drug therapy on the basis of behavioral specificity as well as pathologic specificity may provide a means of increasing the success of pharmacological interventions.

Behavioral Specificity

A great deal has been learned by psychologists in the last two decades about the varieties of memory systems and processes that exist, as well as the different ways in which memory can fail. In fact, most types of memory deficit which have received careful study have been found to be specific, affecting some types of memory processes while sparing others. The amnesias which result from a variety of etiologies (e.g. Wernicke–Korsakoff Syndrome, encephalitis, or surgery, as in H.M.) have been demonstrated to result in a deficit in explicit memory, while leaving implicit memory and procedural memory intact (Cohen & Squire, 1980; Schacter, 1987; Shimamura, 1986; Squire, 1992). Aging appears to affect performance on explicit memory tests more than implicit memory tests. Elderly subjects are consistently found to have deficits on explicit memory tests (see Craik, 1977; Light, 1991; Poon, 1985, for reviews), whereas several studies have found their performance on implicit memory tests to be intact (Light & Singh, 1987; Light, Singh & Capps, 1986; Moscovitch, 1982). The memory disorder which accompanies depression may be the result of a deficit in effortful processing, while automatic processes remain intact (Cohen et al., 1982; Weingartner et al., 1992a, b). Both Parkinson's disease and multiple sclerosis also appear to interfere with effortful memory processes (e.g. free recall), while leaving automatic processes intact (e.g. monitoring of frequency and modality) (Appollonio et al., 1994; Grafman, Rao, Bernardin & Leo, 1991). Patients with Alzheimer's disease appear to have deficits in explicit episodic memory (see Albert & Moss, 1992, and Huppert, in press, for recent reviews), implicit memory (Salmon & Heindel, 1992; Salmon, Shimamura, Butters & Smith, 1988; Shimamura, Salmon, Squire & Butters, 1987), and semantic memory (see Martin, 1992; Nebes, 1989, 1992, for recent discussions of the semantic memory deficit in Alzheimer's disease).

Two studies from the authors' laboratory illustrate the specificity of memory impairments evident in cognitively-impaired patients. We have chosen examples that include patients with Alzheimer's disease, since pharmacological treatment of the memory impairment in this patient population has received the most attention. We have also attempted to select examples which are readily applicable in evaluating cognitively-impaired patients in the context of a clinical setting. Weingartner et al. (1993) compared the effects of repetition on recall performance in patients with a diagnosis of Alzheimer's disease, depression or alcoholic amnesia, as well as in a group of normal volunteers. Free-recall performance in the three patient groups was impaired relative to the performance of controls. Repetition enhanced performance on both a single-trial free-recall test and a selective-reminding task in depressed patients, alcoholic amnesia patients and controls. The recall performance of Alzheimer's disease patients, however, did not benefit from repetition in either task (see Figure 24.1). Alzheimer's disease patients, therefore, appear to have a selective deficit in the ability to benefit from multiple presentations of stimuli which is not found uniformly in all types of memory impairment. It should be pointed out, however, that while

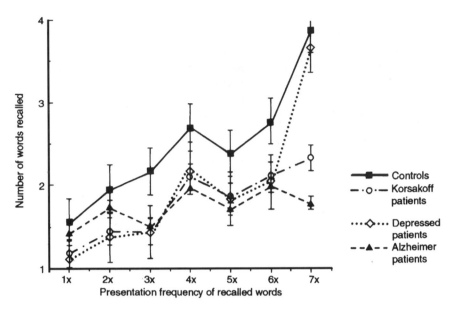

Figure 24.1 Repetition effects on recall of words in elderly normal controls, depressed patients, Alzheimer's disease patients, and Korsakoff amnesics.

Alzheimer's disease patients may be relatively insensitive to repetition effects in remembering explicitly, they do benefit from "practice effects" in implicit memory. This difference highlights the specificity of memory impairments that can be seen in cognitively-impaired patients.

Patients with Alzheimer's disease also appear to have a specific deficit in semantic memory that is not found in many other types of memory-impaired patients. Weingartner et al. (1983) compared explicit episodic and semantic memory functions in Alzheimer's disease patients, patients with Korsakoff amnesia, and elderly normal controls. On tests of explicit episodic memory, the performances of the two groups of patients were similar to one other, and impaired relative to the performance of the controls. On tests of semantic memory, however, the performance of the Alzheimer's disease patients was impaired relative to that of both the amnesics and the controls. There was no difference between the performance of the amnesics and the controls on tests of semantic memory. For example, although both amnesic patients and controls performed almost errorlessly on a task requiring the completion of simple sentence frames, patients with Alzheimer's disease appeared to have difficulty with this task (see Figure 24.2). Alzheimer's disease patients also had more difficulty than either controls or amnesics in sequencing activities that were part of a more complex activity and in generating answers in response to the questions, "What are things you would do after getting up in the morning?" This brief survey of some of the memory disorders which have received attention from cognitive scientists makes it clear that such deficits can be specific,

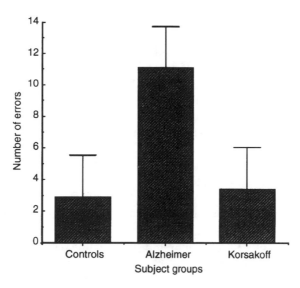

Figure 24.2   Errors in sentence completion made by elderly normal controls, Alzheimer's disease patients, and Korsakoff amnesics.

interfering selectively with some memory stores and processes, while sparing others. What is known about the functional specificity of a memory disorder can be used in conjunction with what is known about its pathology in designing drug treatments. When the pathology of a disease which causes memory impairment is known, and a number of potential drug treatments exist which have some basis in disease pathology, behavioral specificity can be used to select one drug treatment from among the other equally neurobiologically compelling candidates. For example, both the pathology of the disease and the behavioral specificity of its cognitive effects suggest the possibility that L-deprenyl might be useful in ameliorating the memory deficit found in patients with Alzheimer's disease. L-deprenyl is a monoamine oxidase inhibitor, and disturbances of central monoamine systems can be found in at least some patients with this disease (Adolfsson, Gottfries, Roos & Winblad, 1979; Arai, Kosaka & Iizuka, 1984; Bondareff, Mountjoy & Roth, 1982; Cross et al., 1981; Mann et al., 1980; Yates et al., 1983). Tariot et al. (1987) studied the effects of L-deprenyl on memory performance in a group of patients with Alzheimer's disease using the selective-reminding task (Buschke, 1973). L-Deprenyl had no effect on recall performance on the early trials of this task. Performance on later trials was improved relative to placebo conditions, however. It appears, therefore, that L-deprenyl does not generally facilitate memory performance, but may have a very selective effect. L-Deprenyl appears to enhance the effects of repetition on recall performance in patients with Alzheimer's disease. This specific effect of L-deprenyl matches the specific deficit in repetition effects found in Alzheimer's disease by Weingartner et al. (1993).

Behavioral specificity can also be used on its own in designing a drug treatment for a memory deficit. In many cases, we currently know more about the behavioral specificity of a disorder than we do about its pathology. For example, as discussed above, a substantial literature exists on the characteristics of the cognitive deficit in Korsakoff amnesia (Janowsky, Shimamura, Kritchevsky & Squire, 1989; Mayes, 1992; Parkin, 1992; Squire, 1982), whereas relatively little is known about the pathology which underlies this disorder. Functional specificity might also be used in cases in which the pathology is known but is not amenable to pathologic matching for drug selection. Surgical lesions to the hippocampus or thalamus would fit into this category. Although no obvious drug candidate is suggested by the pathology of the deficit in such cases, it is still possible that a drug treatment might augment whatever residual memory capacities remain. All but the most severe memory deficits can be expected to respond in some degree to any pharmacological agent which improves memory in normal populations.

D-amphetamine, for example, may improve memory performance in normal subjects, possibly by increasing arousal and attention. At least one study has found an improvement in memory performance in neurologically intact subjects following administration of this drug (Hurst, Radlow, Chubb & Bagley, 1969), although another study has found it to produce an impairment in memory performance (Burns, House, Fensch & Miller, 1967). It is therefore possible that D-amphetamine will improve memory performance in many patient populations whose deficit is of mild to moderate degree, even if the deficit is caused by structural damage. Residual memory capacities should be improved by increased arousal and attention, just as they are in normals. Cholinergic drugs such as physostigmine might also improve memory performance in such patients, just as they do in normals, by improving residual memory capacities.

Although the degree of facilitation these drugs have on memory performance in normal populations is small, it is possible that effects would be larger in a patient population with memory deficit. In memory-disordered patients, augmenting undamaged processes, even those which do not benefit from facilitation when the entire system is operating normally, might have unexpectedly substantial effects. Knowledge of the specific memory processes which are spared and impaired in a given patient population is just as critical in designing drug therapies in cases in which the aim is to augment undamaged processes as it is in cases in which the aim is to repair damaged processes. Augmenting undamaged processes would involve selecting a drug which is known to affect those processes which are not severely disrupted by disease or damage, rather than one which affects the processes which are disrupted. Unfortunately, the side effects of many memory-enhancing drugs limit their clinical usefulness to some extent. Future development of a drug which has significant memory-enhancing properties in normals without causing side effects that limit its potential usefulness would be of significant benefit in treating these memory deficits.

It should be pointed out that the experimental analysis of individual memory disorders is still in an early stage. For example, while we know something about the specificity of the amnesic syndrome, we know relatively little about the possible differences that might exist between amnesias of different etiologies.

This is not an argument for neglecting behavioral specificity when matching drug treatments to memory disorders. What is already known about the specificity of memory deficits can be usefully applied. Furthermore, our understanding of the specificity of the memory deficits found in a variety of disorders has begun to accumulate at a rapid rate. Increasing knowledge of specific memory deficits will make a behavioral matching strategy even more useful in the near future.

Behavioral specificity of memory-enhancing drugs might also lead to clues about the underlying pathology of a memory disorder. As pointed out above, most current theories about the physiology of depression are based upon the actions of antidepressant medication. Drugs which ameliorate the symptoms of depression have led to theories about the pathology of depression. In the same way, drugs which ameliorate the specific behavioral symptoms of a particular memory disorder might lead to developments in uncovering the pathology of the deficit. For example, the match of the specific memory effects of L-deprenyl to one specific aspect of the memory deficit in Alzheimer's disease might lead us to speculate that the memory impairment in Alzheimer's disease is partially caused by disturbances in catecholamine neurotransmitters.

Unfortunately, little is known about the behavioral specificity of drugs which facilitate learning and memory. Without this knowledge, matching drug therapies to specific deficits on the basis of behavior is impossible. Most of the work with humans has been motivated by attempts to demonstrate the efficacy of a memory-enhancing drug for the purpose of a clinical application rather than for the purpose of theoretical development. Few carefully controlled experiments using theoretically useful measures of retention have been conducted. Furthermore, work with animals may tell us little about the specific processes which are enhanced by a drug in humans, even when some specificity appears in its effects on animals. The tasks used to measure memory in humans and animals are often quite different. Extrapolating from the performance of one animal species on one type of task to the performance of another animal species on a different type of task, or to the performance of humans on tasks typically used to measure human memory, is not a straightforward matter. It is difficult to generalize findings from the experimental memory tasks performed by animals to the processes which are impaired in a human memory deficit such as Alzheimer's disease or Parkinson's disease. There is obviously a need for more carefully controlled drug experiments in humans. We use the rest of this chapter to discuss issues which will be important in designing future research on memory-enhancing drugs.

ISSUES IN THE DEVELOPMENT OF FUTURE RESEARCH

The issues that arise in research on memory-enhancing drugs can be illustrated by the history of research on the cholinergic drug tetrahydroaminoacridine (THA, or tacrine) for treatment of the cognitive symptoms of Alzheimer's disease. Tacrine appeared to be an excellent candidate for an antidementia drug. Research has established a role for the cholinergic system in memory functions (Deutsch, 1971), and for cholinergic-dysfunction in Alzheimer's disease (Bartus, Dean, Beer & Lipa, 1982; Coyle, Price & DeLong, 1983). Furthermore, a preliminary study of tacrine treatment in Alzheimer's disease appeared to demonstrate dramatic effects of this drug (Summers et al., 1986).

A large-scale collaborative research project, involving a partnership between several government agencies, private industry, and nearly two dozen university based research–clinical centers, was established to study the efficacy of tacrine in Alzheimer's disease (Davis et al., 1992). The double-blind crossover design was agreed upon by all of the participants and included the uniform application of methods and procedures for evaluating the clinical (cognitive) status of patients with both laboratory and clinical instruments. The design also included a first stage in which patients were tested for a positive response to an acute dose of tacrine. Only those patients who demonstrated a positive response to the drug were included in the crossover stage of the study. Three years later, the available findings were reviewed. The research community was divided as to the effectiveness of tacrine. All agreed that the effects that were apparent were not robust and that clearly many patients did not respond to the drug. Nevertheless, earlier this year the Scientific Advisory panel of the Food and Drug Administration (FDA) voted to recommend to the FDA that tacrine be approved as the first antidementia drug. Tacrine had been rejected by the same review panel on several previous occasions.

Whatever the ultimate fate of tacrine as a memory-enhancing drug, the research designed to evaluate this drug has been far from ideal. Despite the commitment of a large amount of resources to the evaluation of tacrine, the results have been inconclusive. It is not known how many patients benefit, which patients are likely to benefit, what the range of possible effects of tacrine is, or whether the drug actually harms some patients. Furthermore, nothing theoretical was learned about the effects of tacrine which might guide the development of future research.

Why were the results available to the FDA, the scientific community, and clinicians so difficult to interpret? Many potentially important issues were not considered adequately in the multicenter study of tacrine, and some of these issues may be responsible for the ambiguity of the results. We will briefly consider a few problems and issues we believe may be important in the study of drugs which affect cognitive processes. The research on tacrine will be used for illustrative purposes.

Patient Heterogeneity

A great deal of discussion in this chapter has been devoted to the specificity of the memory deficits found when different types of patient populations are compared. Differences also exist in the memory disorders found within a given patient population, however. The presentation of the memory impairment in syndromes such as Korsakoff's disease, Alzheimer's disease, Parkinson's disease, stroke, or closed-head injury is extraordinarily varied.

The diversity of cognitive symptoms within a population is not surprising, given that the neuropathological nature of any of these syndromes is also varied. For example, Korsakoff's disease can occur with or without frontal lobe pathology (Bowden, 1990; Joyce & Robbins, 1991). The pattern of progression of the pathology in Alzheimer's disease is also quite different from patient to patient (Jorm, 1985). Furthermore, diseases and injuries occur to individuals with personal histories that can modulate and interact with the effects of the insult to the brain (Martin, 1990). Premorbid intelligence or education, for example, may be an important factor in determining the way in which cognitive symptoms are expressed in a condition such as Alzheimer's disease (Boller et al., 1992).

A study must address the problems created by this intrasyndrome heterogeneity. It is therefore essential that patients be characterized as precisely and thoroughly as possible in studies of potentially memory-enhancing drugs. Patients within a syndrome may be differentially sensitive to treatment. Cognitive, pathological and other characteristics of patients can be used as a covariant measure in evaluating whether a patient population responds to a drug treatment. For example, the presence or absence of frontal pathology in patients with Korsakoff's disease might help to predict whether a particular patient with this disease will respond to a potential treatment. The relative severities of language and memory deficits in Alzheimer's disease patients might also be a useful predictor of whether a patient will respond to a drug treatment. The criterion for successful treatment may also vary as a function of the pathological and cognitive characteristics of a disorder in individual patients.

In research on the effects of tacrine on cognition in Alzheimer's disease, patient heterogeneity may well have obscured the potential value of this drug treatment. Based upon group effects, tacrine produced a weak facilitory effect on memory in patients with Alzheimer's disease. Positive effects were seen in some but not all, or even most of the patients studied. Given that individual variation clearly exists in responsiveness to tacrine, some patients would have been found to benefit more than is apparent in the group data had individual patients been examined. Other patients would have been found to benefit less than is suggested by the group data. A wide range of responses probably existed even though all subjects included in the crossover stage of the study were selected as responders to tacrine.

No systematic strategy for explaining individual differences in response to tacrine was included in the studies reported thus far. Group data do not provide information about the range of responses found in individuals. Group data also do not provide information about the distinguishing characteristics of those subjects who do and do not show an effect of the drug. The issue of patient heterogeneity is thus important in evaluating the cognitive effects of a drug.

Experimental Design

Two broad types of design are generally used in studies of the efficacy of cognitive enhancers:

- Between-subjects randomized designs, in which different patients are randomly assigned to different treatment conditions
- Within-subject repeated-measures designs, in which the same subject is treated with drug and placebo in double-blind crossover designs.

Both of these designs are useful, but careful consideration must be given to the best choice of design at a given stage of drug evaluation.

A comparison of the Davis et al. (1992) study to another study of tacrine effects in Alzheimer's patients, that of Farlow et al. (1992), provides an example of the importance of choosing a design which can provide unambiguous information given the current state of knowledge. The repeated-measures experimental design used to test the effectiveness of tacrine in the Davis et al. (1992) study was complex, with multiple stages in which drug and placebo were introduced for a period of weeks in a double-blind randomized crossover design. That design made the statistical analysis of findings far from straightforward, and was the source of considerable controversy at the time findings were open for review. Patterns of memory performance which created interpretive problems included a positive response during the first leg of the design, followed by accelerated impairment during a period when the patient was treated with placebo, a decreased rate of deterioration, and a positive response that was not apparent during active drug treatment but appeared when the patient was shifted to the placebo leg of the design. The design and analysis of results was further complicated by the fact that different subjects were treated with different doses of tacrine. In addition, the effects of tacrine in this repeated-measures design were superimposed upon the steady deterioration of cognitive functioning typically found in Alzheimer's disease patients. Given the complexity of the design, it is not surprising that this study did not provide clear and interpretable results.

The repeated-measures design used in the Davis et al. (1992) study had the potential to provide a great deal of information. Furthermore, a within-subject design is inherently powerful, thus decreasing the possibility of failing to find an effect which actually exists (see below). Unfortunately, at the current stage of research, information necessary to the interpretation of the results is missing. The length of time necessary to completely wash out the effects of tacrine is not established. Nor is it known whether cessation of treatment with tacrine can accelerate cognitive decline in some patients. Under the circumstances, a simpler, randomized, between-subjects design would have provided less ambiguous results.

Farlow et al. (1992) also reported the results of a multicenter study of the effects of tacrine in Alzheimer's disease. In contrast to the crossover design used by Davis et al. (1992), Farlow et al. (1992) used a randomized, parallel-group design. Patients were assigned to placebo, or to one of two doses of tacrine. Midway through the study, 50% of the subjects in each group were given a larger dose of tacrine, while the other 50% continued to receive the same dose. Subjects were not pretested for a response to tacrine, as they were in the Davis et al. (1992) study. Tacrine was found to have significant effects on cognition in this study. This design, while not as powerful as that of the Davis et al. study, is simpler. Given the current state of our knowledge a simpler design with more clearly interpretable results may ultimately add more to our knowledge of tacrine effects than a more powerful, crossover design. When more is known about the effects of tacrine, the more powerful within-subjects design might become more useful.

Carefully controlled single-case studies, or studies with small numbers of subjects, might be particularly valuable in the early stages of drug development research. Gathering a great deal of data about a few subjects under each treatment condition can provide important information about the range of possible responses that might be produced by a drug. This type of design is not always possible, however, particularly when testing drug treatments that require long "washout" periods before another treatment condition can be introduced. Variation among patients within a syndrome such as Alzheimer's disease must also be kept in mind when generalizing results from small numbers of patients to the population as a whole.

Finally, evaluation of possible Type I and Type II statistical errors must be considered in choosing a design. The impact of both types of errors cannot be overestimated, although they clearly have different implications. An apparent positive response that turns out to be an error may result in the commitment of enormous resources to the investigation of the potential drug treatment, resources which could have been allocated to other possible candidate treatments. A false rejection of a drug with a positive effect on a memory deficit can interrupt further development of a potentially useful treatment.

The Dependent Measure

Laboratory and clinical methods chosen as indices of cognitive change should take into account the way in which memory is impaired in the patient population being studied. Given that memory deficits can usually be demonstrated to be specific, with some memory processes affected while others are spared, it is necessary to choose target measures which tap the deficient process. For example, if the memory deficit in Parkinson's disease is limited to processes which require effort, it would be useless to test the effects of a drug on this cognitive impairment by using a measure which largely taps more automatic processes. In addition, at least some of the measures used should ideally be valid indicators of the patients' functioning in their daily lives, thereby allowing the clinical, functional status of patients to be assessed. To be clinically useful, a drug treatment should improve patients' ability to function normally in their daily lives. Finally, laboratory and clinical findings should provide convergent but not redundant evidence that a drug treatment enhances cognitive functioning.

Nature of the Target Response

A facilitory cognitive effect of a drug can take many forms. A positive response can be an acute change in symptoms following drug administration, a lasting change in symptoms when treatment is discontinued, a slowing of the progression of symptoms in the course of a disease, or an increase in the delay of onset of symptoms in individuals at risk. The criteria for demonstrating drug efficacy must be stated clearly, and must be testable given the study design that is being used. This includes a precise formulation of the target responses that serve as the key indices of improvement or decline in cognitive functioning. For example, in the Davis et al. (1992) study of tacrine, the criterion used was an absolute change in symptoms during drug treatment. It would also have been possible to assess whether the drug might be slowing the progression of the cognitive symptoms, or whether there was an attenuation or potentiation of symptoms after drug treatment was discontinued. Use of either of these two criteria might have led to different conclusions about the effects of tacrine on cognitive function in Alzheimer's disease.

CONCLUSIONS

The development of a drug treatment for a memory disorder can be approached in much the same way that the drug treatment of any disease is approached. First, the specific pathologic and symptomologic characteristics of a disease must be specified. In cases in which the pathology is unknown, or the pathology cannot be treated with a pharmacological agent, or treatment based on pathology alone proves inadequate, treatment must be aimed at the symptoms of the disease. In the case of memory disorder, the specific memory processes affected by the disease or injury must be specified. A drug treatment can then be sought which will either reverse the specific deficit which exists or augment those processes which are spared.

Finally, research which tests a drug treatment for a particular memory disorder should be designed with several issues in mind. These issues include patient heterogeneity within a syndrome, the usefulness of a potential design at a given stage of research, the importance of choosing a dependent variable which taps the specific deficit which is present, and the types of responses which may occur to treatment. Designing research with both theoretical and clinical considerations in mind may result in more successful allocation of drug development resources in the future.

REFERENCES

Adams, R.D. & Victor, M. (1989) *Principles of Neurology*. McGraw-Hill, New York.
Adolfsson, R., Gottfries, C.G., Roos, B.E. & Winblad, B. (1979). Changes in brain

catecholamines in patients with dementia of Alzheimer type. *British Journal of Psychiatry*, **135**, 261–223.

Albert, M.S. & Moss, M.B. (1992). The assessment of memory disorders in patients with Alzheimer's disease. In L.R. Squire & N. Butters (eds), *Neuropsychology of Memory*. Guilford Press, New York.

Apollonio, I., Grafman, J., Clark, K., Nichelli, P., Zeffiro, T. & Hallet, M. (1994). Implicit and explicit memory in Parkinson's disease with and without dementia. *Archives of Neurology*, **51**, 359–367.

Arai, H., Kosaka, K. & Iizuka, R. (1984). Changes of biogenic amines and their metabolites in postmortem brains from patients with Alzheimer-type dementia. *Journal of Neurochemistry*, **43**, 388–393.

Bartus, R.T., Dean, R.L., Beer, B. & Lippa, A.S. (1982). The cholinergic hypothesis of geriatric memory dysfunction. *Science*, **217**, 401–417.

Beatty, W.W., Butters, N. & Janowsky, D.S. (1986). Patterns of memory failure after scopolamine treatment: implications for cholinergic hypotheses of dementia. *Behavioral and Neural Biology*, **45**, 196–211.

Beller, S.A., Overall, J.E. & Swann, A.C. (1985). Efficacy of oral physostigmine in primary degenerative dementia. *Psychopharmacology*, **87**, 147–151.

Birnbaum, I.M., Parker, E.S., Hartley, J.T. & Noble, E.P. (1978). Alcohol and memory: retrieval processes. *Journal of Verbal Learning and Verbal Behavior*, **17**, 325–335.

Boller, F., Forette, F., Khachaturian, Z., Poncet, M. & Christen, Y. (eds) (1992). *Heterogeneity of Alzheimer's Disease*. Springer-Verlag, New York.

Bondareff, W., Mountjoy, C.Q. & Roth, M. (1982). Loss of neurons of origin of the adrenergic projection to cerebral cortex (nucleus locus ceruleus) in senile dementia. *Neurology*, **32**, 164–168.

Bowden, S.C. (1990). Separating cognitive impairment in neurologically asymptomatic alcoholism from Wernicke–Korsakoff syndrome: Is the neuropsychological distinction justified? *Psychological Bulletin*, **107**, 355–366.

Bowen, D.M., Smith, C.G., White, P. & Davidson, A.N. (1976). Neurotransmitter-related enzymes and indices of hypoxia in senile dementia and other abnormalities. *Brain*, **99**, 459–496.

Brown, M.W., Brown, J. & Bowes, J.B. (1989). Absence of priming coupled with substantially preserved recognition in lorazepam-induced amnesia. *Quarterly Journal of Experimental Psychology*, **41A**, 599–618.

Brown, J., Lewis, V., Brown, M., Horn, G. & Bowes, J.B. (1982). A comparison between transient amnesias induced by two drugs (diazepam or lorazepam) and amnesia of organic origin. *Neuropsychologia*, **20**, 55–70.

Burns, J.T., House, R.F., Fensch, F.C. & Miller, J.G. (1967). Effects of magnesium pemoline and dextroamphetamine on human learning. *Science*, **155**, 849–851.

Buschke, H. (1973). Selective reminding for the analysis of memory and learning. *Journal of Verbal Learning and Verbal Behavior*, **12**, 543–550.

Caine, E.D., Weingartner, H., Ludlow, D.L., Cudahy, E.A. & Wehry, S. (1981). Qualitative analysis of scopolamine-induced amnesia. *Psychopharmacology*, **74**, 74–80.

Christie, J.E., Shering, A., Ferguson, J. & Glen, A.I.M. (1981). Physostigmine and arecoline: effects of intravenous infusions in Alzheimer presenile dementia. *British Journal of Psychiatry*, **138**, 46–50.

Clarke, P.R.F., Eccersley, P.S., Frisby, J.P. & Thornton, J.A. (1970). The amnesic effect of diazepam (Valium). *British Journal of Anaesthesiology*, **42**, 690.

Cohen, N.J. & Squire, L.R. (1980). Preserved learning and retention of pattern-analyzing skill in amnesia: dissociation of "knowing how" and "knowing that." *Science*, **210**, 207–209.

Cohen, R.M., Weingartner, H., Smallberg, S.A., Pickar, D. & Murphy, D.L. (1982). Effort and cognition in depression. *Archives of General Psychiatry*, **39**, 593–597.

Coyle, J.T., Price, D.L. & DeLong, M.R. (1983). Alzheimer's disease: a disorder of cholinergic innervation. *Science*, **219**, 1184–1190.

Craik, F.I.M. (1977). Age differences in human memory. In J.E. Birren & K.W. Schaie (eds), *Handbook of the Psychology of Aging*. Van Nostrand Reinhold, New York.

Cross, A.J., Crow, T.J., Perry, E.K., Perry, R.H., Blessed, G. & Tomlinson, B.E. (1981). Reduced dopamine-beta-hydroxylase activity in Alzheimer's disease. *British Medical Journal*, **282**, 93–94.

Curran, H.V. (1991). Benzodiazepines, memory and mood: a review. *Psychopharmacology*, **105**, 1–8.

Curran, H.V., Schifano, F. & Lader, M. (1991). Models of memory dysfunction? A comparison of the effects of scopolamine and lorazepam on memory, psychomotor performance and mood. *Psychopharmacology*, **103**, 83–90.

Curran, H.V., Schiwy, W., Eves, F., Shine, P. & Lader, M. (1988). A "levels of processing" study of the effects of benzodiazepines on human memory. *Human Psychopharmacology*, **3**, 21–25.

Danion, J.-M., Zimmermann, M.-A., Willard-Schroeder, D., Grange, D. & Singer, L. (1989). Diazepam induces a dissociation between explicit and implicit memory. *Psychopharmacology*, **99**, 238–243.

Danion, J.-M., Zimmermann, M.-A., Willard-Schroeder, D., Grange, D., Welsch, M., Imbs, J.-L. & Singer, L. (1990). Effects of scopolamine, trimipramine and diazepam on explicit memory and repetition priming in healthy volunteers. *Psychopharmacology*, **102**, 422–424.

Davies, P. & Maloney, A.J. (1976). Selective loss of central cholinergic neurons in Alzheimer's disease. *Lancet*, **2**, 1403.

Davis, K.L. & Mohs, R. (1982). Enhancement of memory processes in Alzheimer's disease with multiple-dose intravenous physostigmine. *American Journal of Psychiatry*, **139**, 1421–1424.

Davis, K.L., Mohs, R.C., Tinklenberg, J.R., Pfefferbaum, A., Hollister, L.E. & Kopell, B. S. (1978). Physostigmine: improvement of long-term memory processes in normal humans. *Science*, **201**, 272–274.

Davis, K., Thal, L., Gamzu, E., et al. (1992). A double-blind, placebo-controlled multicenter study of tacrine for Alzheimer's disease. *New England Journal of Medicine*, **327**, 1253–1259.

Deutch, J.A. (1971). The cholinergic synapse and the site of memory. *Science*, **174**, 783–794.

Drachman, D.A. (1977). Memory and cognitive function in man: does the cholinergic system have a specific role? *Neurology*, **27**, 783–790.

Drachman, D.A. & Leavitt, J. (1974). Human memory and the cholinergic system. *Archives of Neurology*, **30**, 113–121.

Dysken, M.W., Fovall, P., Harris, C.M., Davis, J.M. & Noronha, A. (1982). Lecithin administration in Alzheimer dementia. *Neurology*, **32**, 1203–1204.

Eagger, S.A., Levy, R. & Sahakian, B.J. (1991). Tacrine in Alzheimer's disease. *Lancet*, **337**, 989–992.

Fang, J.C., Hinrichs, J.R. & Ghoneim, M.M. (1987). Diazepam and memory: evidence for spared memory function. *Pharmacology, Biochemistry and Behavior*, **28**, 347–352.

Farlow, M., Gracon, S.I., Hershey, L.A., Lewis, K.W., Sadowsky, C.H. & Dolan-Ureno, J. (1992). A controlled trial of tacrine in Alzheimer's disease. *Journal of the American Medical Association*, **268**, 2523–2529.

File, S.E., Skelly, A.M. & Girdler, N.M. (1992). Midazolam-induced retrieval impairments revealed by the use of flumazenil: a study in surgical dental patients. *Journal of Psychopharmacology*, **6**, 81–87.

Fovall, P., Dysken, M.W., Lazarus, L.W., Davis, J.M., Kahn, R.J., Jope, R., Rinkel, S. & Rattan, P. (1980). Choline bitartrate treatment of Alzheimer-type dementias. *Communications in Psychopharmacology*, **4**, 141–145.

Frith, C.D., McGinty, M.A., Gergel, I. & Crow, T.J. (1989). The effects of scopolamine and clonidine upon the performance and learning of a motor skill. *Psychopharmacology*, **98**, 120–125.

Gauthier, S., et al. (1990). Tetrahydroaminoacridine–lecithin combination treatment in patients with intermediate-stage Alzheimer's disease. *New England Journal of Medicine*, **322**, 1272–1276.

Ghoneim, M.M., Hinrichs, J.V. & Mewaldt, S.P. (1984). Dose–response analysis of the behavioral effects of diazepam. I: Learning and memory. *Psychopharmacology*, **82**, 291–295.

Ghoneim, M.M. & Mewaldt, S.P. (1975). Effects of diazepam and scopolamine on storage, retrieval and organization processes in memory. *Psychopharmacologia*, **44**, 257–262.

Ghoneim, M.M. & Mewaldt, S.P. (1977). Studies on human memory: the interactions of diazepam, scopolamine and physostigmine. *Psychopharmacology*, **52**, 1–6.

Graf, P. & Schacter, D.L. (1985). Implicit and explicit memory for new associations in normal and amnesic subjects. *Journal of Experimental Psychology: Learning, Memory and Cognition*, **11**, 501–518.

Grafman, J., Rao, S., Bernardin, L. & Leo, G.J. (1991). Automatic memory processes in patients with multiple sclerosis. *Archives of Neurology*, **48**, 1072–1075.

Harrell, L., Galfout, J., Leli, D., Jope, R., McClain, C., Spiers, M., Callaway, R. & Halsey, J. (1986). Behavioral effects of oral physostigmine in Alzheimer's disease patients. *Neurology*, **36** (suppl 1), 269.

Hashtroudi, S., Parker, E.S., DeLisi, L.E., Wyatt, R.J. & Mutter, S.A. (1984). Intact retention in acute alcohol amnesia. *Journal of Experimental Psychology: Learning, Memory and Cognition*, **10**, 156–163.

Hinrichs, J.V., Mewaldt, S.P., Ghoneim, M.M. & Berie, J.L. (1982). Diazepam and learning: assessment of acquisition deficits. *Pharmacology, Biochemistry and Behavior*, **17**, 165–170.

Hommer, D., Matsuo, Wolkowitz, Chrousos, Greenblatt, Weingartner & Thompson (1986). Benzodiazepine sensitivity in normal human subjects. *Archives of General Psychiatry*, **43**, 542–551.

Hommer, D., Weingartner, H.J. & Breier, A. (1993). Dissociation of benzodiazepine induced amnesia from sedation by flumazenil pretreatment. *Psychopharmacology*, **112**, 455–460.

Huppert, F.A. (in press). Memory function in dementia and normal ageing—dimension or dichotomy? In F.A. Huppert, C. Brayne & D. O'Connor (eds), *Dementia and Normal Ageing*. Cambridge University Press, Cambridge.

Hurst, P.M., Radlow, R., Chubb, N.C. & Bagley, S.K. (1969). Effects of D-amphetamine on acquisition, persistence and recall. *American Journal of Psychology*, **82**, 307–319.

Janowsky, J.S., Shimamura, A.P., Kritchevsky, M. & Squire, L.R. (1989). Cognitive impairment following frontal lobe damage and its relevance to human amnesia. *Behavioral Neuroscience*, **103**, 548–560.

Jorm, A.F. (1985). Subtypes of Alzheimer's dementia: a conceptual analysis and critical review. *Psychological Medicine*, **15**, 543–553.

Joyce, A. & Robbins, T.W. (1991). Frontal lobe functions in Korsakoff and non-Korsakoff alcoholics: planning and spatial memory. *Neuropsychologia*, **29**, 709–723.

Kaye, W.H., Sitaram, H., Weingartner, H., Ebert, M.H., Smallberg, S. & Gillin, J.C. (1982). Modest facilitation of memory in dementia with combined lecithin and anticholinesterase treatment. *Biological Psychiatry*, **17**, 275–280.

Knopman, D. (1991). Unaware learning versus preserved learning in pharmacologic amnesia: similarities and differences. *Journal of Experimental Psychology*, **17**, 1017–1029.

Kopelman, M.D. & Corn, T.H. (1988). Cholinergic "blockade" as a model for cholinergic depletion. *Brain*, **111**, 1079–1110.

Krasne, F.B. (1978). Extrinsic control of intrinsic neuronal plasticity: an hypothesis from work on simple systems. *Brain Research*, **14**, 197–216.

Langlais, P.J. (1992). Role of diencephalic lesions and thiamine deficiency in Korsakoff's amnesia: insights from animal models. In L.R. Squire & N. Butters (eds), *Neuropsychology of Memory*. Guilford Press, New York.

Light, L.L. (1991). Memory and aging: four hypotheses in search of data. *Annual Review of Psychology*, **42**, 333–376.

Light, L.L. & Singh, A. (1987). Implicit and explicit memory in young and older adults. *Journal of Experimental Psychology: Learning, Memory and Cognition*, **13**, 531–541.

Light, L.L., Singh, A. & Capps, J.L. (1986). Dissociation of memory and awareness in young and older adults. *Journal of Clinical and Experimental Neuropsychology*, **8**, 62–74.

Lister, R.G. (1985). The amnesic action of benzodiazepines in man. *Neuroscience and Biobehavioral Reviews*, **9**, 87–94.

Lister, R.G. & File, S.E. (1984). The nature of lorazepam-induced amnesia. *Psychopharmacology*, **83**, 183–187.

Lister, R.G., Gorenstein, C., Risher-Flowers, D., Weingartner, H.J. & Eckardt, M.J. (1991). Dissociation of the acute effects of alcohol on implicit and explicit memory processes. *Neuropsychologia*, **29**, 1205–1212.

Lister, R.G. & Weingartner, H.J. (1987). Neuropharmacological strategies for understanding psychobiological determinants of cognition. *Human Neurobiology*, **6**, 119–127.

Little, A., Levy, R., Chuaqui-Kidd, P. & Hand, D. (1985). A double-blind, placebo controlled trial of high-dose lecithin in Alzheimer's disease. *Journal of Neurology, Neurosurgery and Psychiatry*, **48**, 736–742.

Mann, D.A., Lincoln, J., Yates. P.O., Stamp, J.E. & Toper, S. (1980). Changes in the monoamine containing neurons of the human CNS in senile dementia. *British Journal of Psychiatry*, **136**, 533–541.

Martin, A. (1990). Neuropsychology of Alzheimer's disease: the case for subgroups. In M. F. Schwartz (ed.), *Modular Deficits in Alzheimer-Type Dementia*. MIT Press, Cambridge, MA.

Martin, A. (1992). Degraded knowledge representations in patients with Alzheimer's disease: implications for models of semantic and repetition priming. In L.R. Squire & N. Butters (eds), *Neuropsychology of Memory*. Guilford Press, New York.

Mayes, A.R. (1992). What are the functional deficits that underlie amnesia? In L.R. Squire & N. Butters (eds), *Neuropsychology of Memory*. Guilford Press, New York.

Maylor, E.A. & Rabbit, P.M.A. (1987). Effect of alcohol on rate of forgetting. *Psychopharmacology*, **91**, 230–235.

Mitchell, A., Drachman, D., O'Donnell, B. & Glasser, G. (1986). Oral physostigmine in Alzheimer's disease. *Neurology*, **36**, 295.

Molchan, S.E., Martinez, R.A., Hill, J.L., Weingartner, H.J., Thompson, K., Vitiello, B. & Sunderland, T. (1992). Increased cognitive sensitivity to scopolamine with age and a perspective on the scopolamine model. *Brain Research Reviews*, **17**, 215–226.

Moscovitch, M. (1982). A neuropsychological approach to perception and memory in normal and pathological aging. In F.I.M. Craik & S. Trehub (eds) *Aging and Cognitive Processes*. Plenum Press, New York.

Nebes, R.D. (1989). Semantic memory in Alzheimer's disease. *Psychological Bulletin*, **106**, 377–394.

Nebes, R.D. (1992). Semantic memory dysfunction in Alzheimer's disease: disruption of semantic knowledge or information-processing limitation? In L.R. Squire & N. Butters (eds), *Neuropsychology of Memory*. Guilford Press, New York.

Nelson, T.O., McSpadden, M., Fromme, K. & Marlatt, G.A. (1986). Effects of alcohol intoxication on metamemory and on retrieval from long-term memory. *Journal of Experimental Psychology: General*, **115**, 247–254.

Nissen, M.J., Knopman, D.S. & Schacter, D.L. (1987). Neurochemical dissociation of memory systems. *Neurology*, **37**, 789–794.

Op Den Velde, W. & Stam, F.C. (1976). Some cerebral proteins and enzyme systems in Alzheimer's pre-senile and senile dementia. *Journal of the American Geriatrics Society*, **24**, 12–16.

Parkin, A.J. (1992). Functional significance of etiological factors in human amnesia. In L.R. Squire & N. Butters (eds), *Neuropsychology of Memory*. Guilford Press, New York.

Perry, E.D., Tomlinson, B.E., Blessed, G., Bergmann, K., Gibson, P. & Perry, R.H. (1978). Correlation of cholinergic abnormalities with senile plaques and mental test scores in senile dementia. *British Medical Journal*, **2**, 1457–1459.

Peters, B. & Levin, H.S. (1979). Effects of physostigmine and lecithin on memory in Alzheimer's disease. *Annals of Neurology*, **6**, 219–221.

Peterson, R.C. (1977). Scopolamine-induced learning failures in man. *Psychopharmacology*, **52**, 283–289.

Petros, T.V., Kerbel, N., Beckwith, B.E., Sacks, G. & Sarafolean, M. (1985). The effects of alcohol on prose memory. *Physiology and Behavior*, **35**, 43–46.

Poon, L.W. (1985). Differences in human memory with aging: nature, causes and clinical implications. In J.E. Birren & K.W. Schaie (eds), *Handbook of Psychology of Aging*. Van Nostrand Reinhold, New York.

Renvoize, E.B. & Jerram, T. (1979). Choline in Alzheimer's disease. *New England Journal of Medicine*, **301**, 330.

Richardson-Klavehn, A. & Bjork, R.A. (1988). Measures of memory. *Annual Review of Psychology*, **39**, 475–543.

Roediger, H.L. & McDermott, K.B. (1993). Implicit memory in normal human subjects. In H. Spinnler & F. Boller (eds), *Handbook of Neuropsychology*, vol. 8. Elsevier, Amsterdam.

Safer, D.J. & Allen, R.P. (1971). The central effects of scopolamine in man. *Biological Psychiatry*, **3**, 347–355.

Salmon, D.P. & Heindel, W.C. (1992). Impaired priming in Alzheimer's disease: neuropsychological implications. In L.R. Squire & N. Butters (ed), *Neuropsychology of Memory*. Guilford Press, New York.

Salmon, D.C., Shimamura, A.P., Butters, N. & Smith, S. (1988). Lexical and semantic priming deficits in patients with Alzheimer's disease. *Journal of Clinical and Experimental Neuropsychology*, **10**, 477–494.

Schacter, D.L. (1987). Implicit memory: history and current status. *Journal of Experimental Psychology: Learning, Memory and Cognition*, **13**, 501–518.

Schacter, D.L. (1992). Understanding implicit memory: a cognitive neuroscience approach. *American Psychologist*, **47**, 559–569.

Schmechel, D.E., Schmitt, F., Horner, J., Wilkinson, W.E., Hurwitz, B.J. & Heyman, A. (1984). Lack of effect of oral physostigmine and lecithin in patients with probable Alzheimer's disease. *Neurology*, **34**, 280.

Schwartz, A.S. & Kohlstaedt, E.V. (1986). Physostigmine effects in Alzheimer's disease: relationship to dementia severity. *Life Sciences*, **38**, 1021–1028.

Scoville, W.B. & Milner, B. (1957). Loss of recent memory after bilateral hippocampal lesions. *Journal of Neurology, Neurosurgery and Psychiatry*, **20**, 11–21.

Shimamura, A.P. (1986). Priming effects in amnesia: evidence for a dissociable memory function. *Quarterly Journal of Experimental Psychology*, **38A**, 619–644.

Shimamura, A.P., Salmon, D.P., Squire, L.R. & Butters, N. (1987). Memory dysfunction and word priming in dementia and amnesia. *Behavioral Neuroscience*, **101**, 347–351.

Signoret, J.L., Whiteley, A. & Lhermitte, F. (1978). Influence of choline on amnesia in early Alzheimer's disease. *Lancet*, **2**, 837.

Sitaram, N., Weingartner, H. & Gillin, J.C. (1978). Human serial learning: enhancement with arecoline and choline and impairment with scopolamine. *Science*, **201**, 274–277.

Smith, C.M., Swase, M., Exton-Smith, A.N., Phillips, M.J., Oversall, P.W., Piper, M.E. & Bailey, M.R. (1978). Choline therapy in Alzheimer's disease. *Lancet*, **2**, 318.

Squire, L.R. (1982). Comparisons between forms of amnesia: some deficits are unique to Korsakoff's syndrome. *Journal of Experimental Psychology: Learning, Memory and Cognition*, **8**, 560–571.

Squire, L.R. (1992). Memory and the hippocampus: a synthesis from findings with rats, monkeys, and humans. *Psychological Review*, **99**, 195–231.

Squire, L.R. & Davis, H.R. (1981). The pharmacology of memory: a neurobiological perspective. *Annual Review of Pharmacology and Toxicology*, **21**, 323–356.

Stern, Y., Sano, M. & Mayeux, R. (1988). Long-term administration of oral physostigmine in Alzheimer's disease. *Neurology*, **38**, 1837–1841.

Summers, W.K., Majovski, L.V., Marsh, G.M., Tachiki, K. & Kling, A. (1986). Oral tetrahydroaminoacridine in long-term treatment of senile dementia, Alzheimer type. *New England Journal of Medicine*, **315**, 1241–1245.

Sunderland, T., Tariot, P.N., Cohen, R.M., Weingartner, H., Mueller, E.A. & Murphy, D.L. (1987). Anticholinergic sensitivity in patients with dementia of the Alzheimer type and age-matched controls: a dose–response study. *Archives of General Psychiatry*, **44**, 418–426.

Tariot, P.N., Sunderland, T., Weingartner, H., Murphy, D.L., Welkowitz, J.A., Thompson, K. & Cohen, R.M. (1987). Cognitive effects of L-deprenyl in Alzheimer's disease. *Psychopharmacology*, **91**, 489–495.

Thal, L.J. (1992). Cholinomimetic therapy in Alzheimer's disease. In L.R. Squire & N. Butters (eds), *Neuropsychology of Memory*. Guilford Press, New York, pp. 277–284.

Thal, L.J., Masur, D.M., Blau, A.D., Fuld, P.A. & Klauber, M.R. (1989). Chronic oral physostigmine without lecithin improves memory in Alzheimer's disease. *Journal of American Geriatric Society*, **37**, 42–48.

Thal, L.J., Masur, D.M., Sharpless, N.S., Fuld, P.A. & Davies, P. (1986). Acute and chronic effects of oral physostigmine and lecithin in Alzheimer's disease. *Progress in Neuropsychopharmacological and Biological Psychiatry*, **10**, 627–636.

Tulving, E. (1972). Episodic and semantic memory. In E. Tulving & W. Donaldson (eds), *Organization of Memory*, Academic Press, New York.

Tulving, E. (1983). *Elements of Episodic Memory*. Clarendon Press, Oxford.

Tulving, E. (1985). How many memory systems are there? *American Psychologist*, **40**, 385–398.

Tulving, E. & Schacter, D.L. (1990). Priming and human memory systems. *Science*, **247**, 301–306.

Weingartner, H., Eckardt, M., Molchan, S., Sunderland, T. & Wolkowitz, O. (1992a). Neuropsychological factors in mental disorders and their treatments. *Psychopharmacology Bulletin*, **28**, 331–340.

Weingartner, H.J., Eckardt, M., Grafman, J., Molchan, S., Putnam, K., Rawlings, R., Sunderland, T. (1993). The effects of repetition on memory performance in cognitively impaired patients. *Neuropsychology*, **7**, 385–395.

Weingartner, H., Grafman, J., Boutelle, W., Kaye, W. & Martin, P.R. (1983). Forms of memory failure, *Science*, **221**, 380–382.

Weingartner, H., Grafman, J., Herrmann, D., Molchan, S., Sunderland, T., Thompson, K. & Wolkowitz, O. (1992b). Neuropharmacological modeling of memory disorders. In R.M. Coe & R. Strong (eds), *Memory Function in Aging and Age-Related Disorders*. Springer, New York.

Weingartner, H.J., Hommer, D., Lister, R.G., Thompson, K. & Wolkowitz, O. (1992c). Selective effects of triazolam on memory. *Psychopharmacology*, **106**, 341–345.

Weingartner, H. & Wolkowitz, O.M. (1988). Pharmacological strategies for exploring psychobiologically distinct cognitive systems. *Psychopharmacology, Suppl*, S125.

Weintraub, S., Mesulam, M.-M., Auty, R., Baratz, R., Cholakos, B.N., Ransil, B., Tellers, J.G., Albert, M.S., LoCastro, S. & Moss, M. (1983). Lecithin in the treatment of Alzheimer's disease. *Archives of Neurology*, **40**, 527–528.

White, P., Goodhart, M.J., Keet, J.P., Carrasco, L.H., Williams, I.E. & Bowen, D.M. (1977). Neocortical cholinergic neurons in elderly people. *Lancet*, **2**, 668–671.

Whitehouse, P.J., Price, D.L., Struble, R.G., Clark, A.W., Coyle, J.T. & DeLong, M.R. (1982). Alzheimer's disease and senile dementia: loss of neurons in the basal fore-brain. *Science*, **215**, 1237–1239.

Williams, H.L. & Rundell, O.H. (1984). Effect of alcohol on recall and recognition as functions of processing levels. *Journal of Studies on Alcohol*, **45**, 10–15.

Yates, C.M., Simpson, J., Gordon, A., Maloney, A.F.J., Allison, Y., Ritchie, I.M. & Urquhart, A. (1983). Catecholamines and cholinergic enzymes in pre-senile and senile Alzheimer-type dementia and Down's syndrome. *Brain Research*, **280**, 119–126.

Young, R.R. (1977). The differential diagnosis of Parkinson's disease. *International Journal of Neurology*, **12**, 210.

Chapter 25

Personality and Social Aspects of Memory Rehabilitation

George P. Prigatano
St Joseph's Hospital and Medical Center, Phoenix, USA

INTRODUCTION

In the early and late 1940s, Kurt Goldstein (1942), Oliver Zangwill (1947) and Alexander Romanovich Luria (1948) discussed issues and methods surrounding attempts to rehabilitate soldiers who had suffered gunshot wounds to the head. Each of these seminal thinkers recognized the importance of personality factors not only in shaping the symptom picture, but in potentially influencing adaptation to the permanent effects of brain damage. Sheppard Ivory Franz (1924) and Karl Lashley (1938) had even earlier discussed the important role motivation played in the long-term outcome after brain injury. Yet, modern methods of memory rehabilitation often emphasize cognitive strategies or mnemonic devices to aid the patient, with only passing recognition of how emotional or motivational variables may influence treatment strategies and outcome. In fact, the entire field of cognitive neuropsychology seems to perpetuate this bias.

Clinicians working in the field of brain injury rehabilitation encounter a wide variety of memory disorders in people who have equally variable personality characteristics. The relationship between personality variables with memory disorders and the implications for rehabilitation have not been explored adequately. Yet, there have been some discussions of the theoretical relationship of affect to memory (Blaney, 1986; Bower, 1981; Rapaport, 1971).

The psychosocial impact of a memory disorder is not easily revealed by reviewing the scientific literature on this topic (Lezak, 1987; Lezak & O'Brien, 1990). Reports of surveys or summaries of questionnaire findings often fail to

Handbook of Memory Disorders. Edited by A.D. Baddeley, B.A. Wilson and F.N. Watts.
© 1995 John Wiley & Sons Ltd.

capture the realities of what happens to patients and their families when a severe memory disorder persists. These reports typically rely on a cross-sectional group research design. To collect, however, adequate information concerning the personal impact of memory impairment, individual patients must be followed longitudinally for extended periods (Thomsen, 1984, 1989).

This chapter illustrates that personality variables can influence the process of "memory" rehabilitation and explores the psychosocial consequences of memory disorder in young adults who have suffered traumatic brain injury (TBI). The clinical experiences reported emanate from working with brain dysfunctional patients within the context of a neuropsychologically oriented rehabilitation programme. Consequently, the discussion first attempts to place memory rehabilitation activities within that context.

MEMORY REHABILITATION IN THE CONTEXT OF NEUROPSYCHOLOGICAL REHABILITATION

Memory disorders can and do occur in the presence of a vast array of other cognitive impairments and can be related directly or indirectly to a number of complex personality characteristics (Levin, Benton & Grossman, 1982; Prigatano, 1992a). The process of rehabilitating patients with a memory disorder therefore inevitably requires an appreciation of their overall neuropsychological status and their capacity to participate in rehabilitation activities that have the potential to help them. Although disorders of memory might be approached in isolation or independently, memory rehabilitation is often embedded in a social milieu that emphasizes either a holistic or, at least, an interdisciplinary approach to the patient's problems and care. It may be useful, therefore, to place "memory rehabilitation" into the broader schema of what has been previously termed "neuropsychological rehabilitation".

Neuropsychological rehabilitation consists of five interconnected activities (see Prigatano et al., 1986; Prigatano, 1991a; Prigatano et al., 1994):

- Cognitive retraining and rehabilitation
- Psychotherapy
- Establishment of a therapeutic milieu
- Protected work trials
- Family education/consultation.

Memory rehabilitation is one form of cognitive rehabilitation. Cognitive rehabilitation has been defined somewhat differently by different authors (see Ben-Yishay & Prigatano, 1990; Kreutzer & Wehman, 1991; Sohlberg & Mateer, 1987) and can be cast in "broad" or "specific" terms (Prigatano, Glisky & Klonoff, in press). As Zangwill (1947) noted years ago, however, cognitive rehabilitation basically refers to teaching or training activities aimed at ameliorating higher cerebral deficits by direct retraining, substitution training, or compensation training. For recent reviews dealing directly with memory retraining, see Franzen and Haut (1991) and Prigatano, Glisky and Klonoff (in press). For a recent example of excellent research on the long-term effects of memory rehabilitation that utilizes controls, see Berg, Koning-Haanstra and Deelman (1991).

While working with patients who present with memory impairments, it has been the present author's experience that personality characteristics determine the direction in which rehabilitation activities proceed and ultimately develop. The personality characteristics of certain patients enable them to enter a neuropsychological rehabilitation programme and to be actively engaged in various therapeutic activities, some of which are directed at managing their memory problems. The personality characteristics of other patients, however, make it difficult for them to engage in the rehabilitation programme.

For example, a 53-year-old school teacher suffered a severe TBI three years before entering a neuropsychological rehabilitation programme. During the first few years after his brain injury, he demonstrated severe memory impairment and the expected problems of reduced speed of information processing (Levin et al., 1990). He also demonstrated intense emotional lability that included angry outbursts. Before he could be helped to use a "memory notebook" to aid his daily performance, his angry outbursts had to be controlled. With the aid of time, psychotropic medications, and psychotherapy, this goal was eventually achieved and he can now use mnemonic devices successfully.

A 47-year-old school teacher with a history of epilepsy had a less favourable, but not uncommon, outcome. A left temporal lobectomy "cured" his seizure disorder but severely impaired his verbal memory. He did not recognize and/or accept the seriousness of his memory disorder and insisted that others exaggerated the degree of his impairment. He uniformly accused rehabilitation therapists of attempting to undermine his self-confidence. He only learned to use mnemonics partially because he often became angry over how he was approached with rehabilitation. His affective reactions progressively discouraged therapists who became emotionally depleted by their inability to establish a therapeutic alliance with him (a scenario that we repeatedly find important to the outcome of such patients; see Prigatano et al., 1994). He was never able to use mnemonic techniques adequately because his emotional/motivational disturbances were not managed adequately.

A university student who suffered cerebral anoxia secondary to cardiac arrest provides another example. He had undergone a comprehensive neuropsychological rehabilitation programme but was convinced that his memory problem was "not as bad" as the therapists indicated. Unlike the former patient, however, he was less vocal in his complaints and exhibited no angry outbursts. As is common, he continued in his rehabilitation programme without therapists working towards his active discharge. After completing the rehabilitation programme he returned to the university despite being cautioned against it. Although his course load was less demanding than before his hospitalization, it still exceeded his capacities given his impairment. As he failed academically, he began to experience headaches but did not connect his academic failures with his somatic complaints.

With time and supportive long-term psychotherapy, he eventually agreed to enter a less ambitious course of study at another university. With considerable effort he was able to identify himself as a "disabled student" and thereby obtain extra help to meet the course requirements of another field of study. He then enjoyed the first true academic success he had had in several years. With this sense of achievement, he adjusted to his altered neuropsychological and social status. After a year of academic success, he independently decided to stop using the various memory compensations that he had learned to determine if he could "handle it on his own". He again failed. He spontaneously resumed the use of his memory compensations noting that even though he disliked using them he now recognized his need to use them.

These clinical vignettes highlight classic examples of how personality characteristics of the individual interact with their willingness to engage in rehabilitation activities and their use of various methods of memory compensation. Only when personality characteristics are understood and managed does the long-term adjustment of these patients go well. Unfortunately, few investigations have studied the interactions between personality characteristics and an individual's ability to engage in and benefit from various forms of memory rehabilitation. As noted, some psychologists even believe that attention to emotional and motivational factors is relatively unimportant. Cognitive strategies are often emphasized in theoretical discussions of rehabilitation with only passing recognition of how emotional and motivational characteristics actually influence the course of treatment. This shortcoming has created a gap between what is discussed as theoretically relevant in cognitive rehabilitation and what is done practically for a given patient.

THE PATIENT'S EXPERIENCE: PERSONALITY AND SOCIAL CHANGES FOLLOWING TBI

Any rehabilitation effort must begin with some understanding of what the patient experiences. In the case of memory impairment, patients report three common experiences.

First, while many TBI patients recognize their memory difficulties, they tend to underestimate the extent of these problems (Oddy, Coughlan, Tyerman & Jenkins, 1985). They also often fail to perceive the extent that their memory problems affect their daily life (Prigatano et al., 1986).

Second, they resent using memory compensations and believe that if they just try harder they may in fact improve their functional memory. This misperception leads to a natural resistance in performing compensation activities (Prigatano, Amin & Jaramillo, 1993).

Third, it is socially acceptable for individuals from an Anglo-Saxon culture to admit to memory problems while simultaneously affirming that their intelligence is unaffected. This problem clearly relates to the symbol of intelligence in our culture as an indication of personal worth (Prigatano, 1991b). Patients may thus approach memory rehabilitation with mixed feelings and experiences. The therapist who attempts memory rehabilitation must have some insight into the common personality and social changes that follow different types of brain injuries.

Common social and vocational problems in TBI patients can be summarized under four headings. For a detailed description, however, see Prigatano (1991c). TBI patients with severe memory impairments often:

- Underestimate the extent of their memory impairment and other cognitive problems and therefore pursue unreasonable vocational or employment goals
- Alienate friends and family members because their control of negative emotional reactions is poor (Elsass & Kinsella, 1987)
- Report that they have achieved greater social adjustment than their relatives report (Newton & Johnson, 1985)
- Experience progressive social isolation with time (Kozloff, 1987).

In this latter regard, Kozloff points out that the symmetry of relationships ("the degree to which affective and instrumental aids are given and received across network relationships") seriously suffers, particularly between husbands and wives.

Therapists involved in neuropsychological rehabilitation and its subcomponent of memory rehabilitation must keep these long-term social consequences in mind. If a memory compensation helps the patient to be more realistic and independent in daily activities, and fosters greater social integration, then it can be credited as a success even if the underlying memory function remains impaired.

Families, as well as rehabilitation therapists who work with patients with severe memory impairments, can also experience a considerable emotional distress (Florian & Katz, 1991; Brooks et al., 1987; Livingston & Brooks, 1988; Wearing, 1992). There has been a growing recognition that the emotional/motivational reactions of these individuals must also be managed within the context of neuropsychological rehabilitation. A further discussion of this topic, however, is beyond the scope of this chapter (see Gans 1983; Prigatano et al., 1986; Prigatano, 1989; Jackson & Gouvier, 1992; Novack, Bergquist & Bennett, 1992).

THE ROLE OF AWARENESS AND MOTIVATION IN MEMORY REHABILITATION

Engaging patients in memory rehabilitation as well as in the broader effort of neuropsychological rehabilitation requires that they achieve some insight into their difficulties and why they need various rehabilitation activities. If patients are reasonably aware of their deficits, they may be more motivated to compensate for them. However, this is not always the case. The problems of motivation and awareness are complex and may interact with each other in various ways (Prigatano & Schacter, 1991). These two dimensions should be studied more systematically to determine how to engage a patient in memory rehabilitation. Figure 25.1 illustrates a simple model of interaction between motivation and awareness. A patient may be high in awareness and high in motivation, or low in both. Some patients have good awareness of some deficits, but low motivation to do anything about them. Conversely, patients can be "high" in motivation to achieve a certain goal (e.g. return to work) but low in awareness of how their neuropsychological deficits actually affect their functioning. The following clinical case examples illustrate the interactions.

Case Examples

Perhaps the ideal situation for memory rehabilitation is a cooperative, highly motivated patient who demonstrates focal neuropsychological deficits. If a patient's premorbid psychosocial adjustment is also good, this situation is favourable for determining the efficacy of memory rehabilitation training.

Several years ago, the present author described one such patient ("G.B." in Figure 25.1) and a subsequent follow-up (Prigatano, 1983; Prigatano et al., 1986, pp. 61–62). This patient had suffered a ruptured arteriovenous malformation (AVM) in the splenium of the corpus callosum. Primarily, he showed a memory disturbance and underwent various forms of mnemonic training. Although his performance on memory tests improved, his daily functioning in the real world was not improved by this memory retraining. At the time this lack of generalization was not anticipated, and the patient assumed job responsibilities that he was ill-prepared to handle. He subsequently became depressed and suicidal.

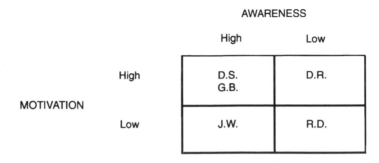

Figure 25.1 Simple model of interaction between motivation and awareness in memory rehabilitation

Evaluation of the patient several years after training showed that he could use the techniques spontaneously to remember information but could not apply them flexibly in the real world. This patient exemplifies high awareness and high motivation; yet, the memory retraining had little impact on his day-to-day functioning.

A second, more favorable outcome example was achieved by a young man who suffered a craniocerebral trauma when he was 18 months old ("D.S."). This patient, who is also discussed in more detail elsewhere (Prigatano, O'Brien & Klonoff, 1993), had focal encephalomalacia in the left frontal region. Approximately 30 years after the onset of his brain injury, he was referred for neuropsychological evaluation when he had difficulty performing his work as a technician. The examination revealed a decreased capacity to remember information after any interfering activity. By using the compensation of completing one set of job responsibilities before moving to the next, he adequately compensated for his memory impairment at work. He once decided to forego the compensation to see if he needed it. When he recognized that his performance was again deteriorating, he returned to using the compensatory technique. This is the type of patient who is most successful with current memory therapies. He was highly motivated and became aware, through neuropsychological consultation, of his need to compensate. Although he briefly deviated from the treatment plan, his awareness of his need to use the compensation resulted in his reliable use of a technique that substantially improved his day-to-day functioning.

Clearly, individuals who are high in both awareness and motivation may or may not be able to apply mnemonic techniques to their real-world responsibilities. The psychosocial situations that determine success or failure for this highly desirable subgroup need to be explored further.

Another scenario is that of the patient who lacks awareness but is highly motivated. For example, "D.R." suffered a severe craniocerebral trauma at the age of 27. A computed tomography (CT) scan revealed a bilateral cerebral injury that primarily involved the right cerebral hemisphere and he exhibited residual left hemiparesis. The patient was enrolled in a neuropsychological rehabilitation programme but was eventually discharged because the therapists were frustrated by their inability to help him achieve a realistic perception of his abilities and limitations. After his discharge, the present author worked with D.R. individually to see whether he could be helped to appreciate his lack of insight. D.R. was extremely motivated and, on his own, had sought and obtained at least 20 jobs within five years. Nonetheless, he was unable to maintain any of these positions. He continued to lack insight into how his higher cerebral deficits affected his job performance and social interactions. For example, when he behaved inappropriately, he attributed his misbehavior to other people's mistreatment of him rather than to his own difficulties. Despite many attempts at cognitive rehabilitation, this patient was unable to recognize his need to use compensatory methods. He is an example of an individual who is highly motivated but shows poor awareness of deficits and does not benefit from therapy.

Another possible interaction occurs when patients are reasonably aware of their higher cerebral deficits, but their motivation to work at rehabilitation activities is low. For example, "J.W." was a 49-year-old executive who suffered bilateral thalamic infarctions after a cardiac arrest. On neuropsychological examination, his capacity for abstract reasoning was restricted (i.e. he made 72 errors on the Halstead Category Test) despite normal IQ values (Verbal IQ, 111; Performance IQ, 115). Most notable, however, was his poor memory. For example, on the Wechsler Memory Scale–Revised (WMS–R), his delayed recall for visuospatial designs was at the 20th percentile. On the Rey–Osterrieth Complex Figure Test, both his immediate and delayed recall were at the 10th percentile. In day-to-day functioning, he had notable trouble remembering important events. However, he was undisturbed by his impairment.

J.W.'s wife, in contrast, was highly distressed over her husband's poor memory, lack of attention to detail, failure to keep up his physical appearance, and total lack of interest in returning to a productive lifestyle. Verbally, this man could identify his memory problems but stated that he liked the changes in his personality and enjoyed being more "laid back". He has not yet been enrolled in memory rehabilitation, but he would be expected to have a difficult time participating because of his lack of motivation to do so.

The most common scenario after severe craniocerebral trauma and the one most difficult to handle involves individuals with both low motivation to work at rehabilitation and low awareness of their neuropsychological deficits. Typically, these individuals do not perceive the need for postacute rehabilitation and often resent those who recommend it. A recent example is a 31-year-old man who had experienced a craniocerebral trauma five years earlier ("R.D."). A CT scan showed bilateral cerebral injury, with evidence of greater injury to the right hemisphere than to the left. Five years after injury, his Verbal IQ was in the mid-80s, and his Performance IQ was in the 70s. His index scores for verbal and visual recall on the Wechsler Memory Scale–Revised (WMS–R) were 65 and 64, respectively. Delayed recall was 60.

He insisted that he could function independently in the home and needed no rehabilitation. This type of patient poses the most formidable challenge. Often, the major goal in rehabilitation is to establish gradually a therapeutic alliance, so that the patient can recognize the need to begin working on memory compensation techniques. This issue is discussed in further detail elsewhere (Prigatano et al., 1986; Ben-Yishay & Prigatano, 1990).

MEMORY IMPAIRMENT AND REHABILITATION OUTCOME

An initial outcome study (Prigatano et al., 1984) on the efficacy of a neuropsychologically oriented rehabilitation programme documented that memory and personality characteristics were associated with psychosocial outcome. In that study, the performance of treated patients on a variety of cognitive tests, including the Paired Associate Learning of the WMS, improved. These patients were also described by their relatives as less socially withdrawn and more responsible. Treated patients who were not working at the time of follow-up tended to exhibit more impaired personality functioning before their treatment began. Clinically, patients who performed better on a variety of memory tests and who were perceived by their families as more emotionally stable tended to be productive at discharge and follow-up.

Brooks et al., (1987) further documented the role of memory and personality problems as these factors relate to gainful employment. TBI patients who were working were described by relatives as having fewer memory problems than TBI patients who were not working. Working patients also performed better on a number of "objective" memory tests than did nonworking patients. Of six cognitive variables, the best predictor that a patient would not return to work was poor verbal memory. Emotional variables were also examined. Patients described as more "mature" were more likely to be working. Similar findings had been reported earlier (Prigatano et al., 1984; Prigatano et al., 1986).

Recently, Rattok et al. (1992) demonstrated that memory performance is related to rehabilitation outcome. Interestingly, however, the various rehabilitation regimes developed for cognitive deficits in TBI patients did not differentially affect memory performance. This finding is consistent with previous reports. To date, no treatment programme appears to make a "bad memory good". Nevertheless, the various rehabilitation programmes may affect emotional and motivational dimensions differently. For example, in the Rattok et al. study, patients who received a combination of group-oriented and cognitive therapies often showed enhanced self-esteem and more realistic self-appraisals than did patients who had mainly experienced cognitive retraining activities but no therapies that dealt with interpersonal or personality disturbances.

Interestingly, Wilson (1991) noted that patients with severe memory disorders who functioned independently used substantially more compensatory techniques than did patients who were not independent. Reflecting on why some patients used memory aids and others did not, Wilson commented as follows:

> It would appear that despite being introduced to a variety of memory aids during memory therapy, subjects did not use these aids immediately, but began doing so after some time had elapsed. A possible explanation for this might have something to do with subjects themselves recognizing [possibly under the influence of relatives] the need for such aids as they were confronted by problems associated with the actuality of daily living. (p.131)

This observation highlights the important role of awareness and motivation in treatment and outcome.

SUMMARY AND CONCLUSIONS

Memory rehabilitation does not occur in a vacuum. Social factors influence whether memory rehabilitation is attempted and what methods of treatment are considered appropriate. Also, the patients' personality—their complex feelings

—influence how they approach rehabilitation activities and may ultimately affect how they attempt to acquire or learn new information. In the course of neuropsychologically oriented rehabilitation, the problems of motivation and awareness are especially important. Patients with low motivation and low awareness after their brain injury present the most formidable cases. Furthermore, various combinations of these two dimensions interact and their impact on memory rehabilitation has not been assessed adequately.

This chapter presents clinical vignettes to highlight the interaction of these variables and their impact on rehabilitation. Further studies might explore how these variables interact and influence efforts on the part of the patient (as well as the therapists) to engage various memory therapies. Clinicians attempting this work must consider how personality and social variables influence the patient's engagement of the rehabilitation process and affect long-term outcome. Although various cognitive strategies can provide practical steps for coping with problems, patients will not use such strategies unless they recognize their value or at least find them appealing in some way. Thus, the role of social and personality factors in memory rehabilitation needs to be considered more systematically in future clinical and research efforts.

ACKNOWLEDGEMENTS

The author would like to thank Dennis Chiapello, Ivan Smason and Shelley Kick for their comments on early drafts of this chapter.

REFERENCES

Ben-Yishay, Y. & Prigatano, G.P. (1990). Cognitive remediation. In E. Griffith, M. Rosenthal, M.R. Bond & J.D. Miller (eds), *Rehabilitation of the Adult and Child with Traumatic Brain Injury*. F.W. Davis, Philadelphia, pp. 393–409.

Berg, I.J., Koning-Haanstra, M. & Deelman, B.G. (1991). Long-term effects of memory rehabilitation: a controlled study. *Neuropsychological Rehabilitation*, 1, 97–11.

Blaney, P.H. (1986). Affect and memory: a review. *Psychological Bulletin*, 99, 229–246.

Bower, G.H. (1981). Mood and memory. *American Psychologist*, 36, 129–146.

Brooks, N., Campsie, L., Symington, C., Beattie, A. & McKinlay, W. (1987). The effects of severe head injury on patient and relatives within seven years of injury. *Journal of Head Trauma Rehabilitation*, 2(3), 1–13.

Brooks, N., McKinlay, W., Symington, C., Beattie, A. & Campsie, L. (1987). Return to work within the first seven years of severe head injury. *Brain Injury*, 1(1), 5–19.

Elsass, L. & Kinsella, G. (1987). Social interaction following severe closed head injury. *Psychological Medicine*, 17, 67–78.

Florian, V. & Katz, S. (1991). The other victims of traumatic brain injury: consequences for family members. *Neuropsychology*, 5, 267–279.

Franz, S.I. (1924). Studies in re-education: the aphasias. *Comparative Psychology*, IV, 349–429.

Franzen, M.D. & Haut, M.W. (1991). The psychological treatment of memory impairment: a review of empirical studies. *Neuropsychology Review*, 2, 29–63.

Gans, J.S. (1983). Hate in the rehabilitation setting. *Archives of Physical Medicine Rehabilitation*, **64**, 176–179.

Goldstein, K. (1942). *Aftereffects of Brain Injury in War*. Grune & Stratton, New York.

Jackson, W.T. & Gouvier, W.D. (1992). Group psychotherapy with brain-damaged adults and their families. In C.J. Long & K.K. Ross (eds), *Handbook of Head Trauma: Acute Care to Recovery*. Plenum Press, New York, pp. 309–327.

Kozloff, R. (1987). Networks of social support and the outcome from severe head injury. *Journal of Head Trauma Rehabilitation*, **2**, 14–23.

Kreutzer, J.S. & Wehman, P.H. (1991). *Cognitive Rehabilitation for Persons with Traumatic Brain Injury: A Functional Approach*. Paul H. Brookes, Baltimore.

Lashley, K.S. (1938). Factors limiting recovery after central nervous lesions. *Journal of Nervous and Mental Diseases*, **88**, 733–755.

Levin, H.S., Benton, A.L. & Grossman, R.G. (1982). *Neurobehavioral Consequences of Closed Head Injury*. Oxford University Press, New York.

Levin, H.S., Gary, H.E., Eisenberg, H.M., Ruff, R.M., Barth, J.T., Kreutzer, J., High, W., Portman, S., Foulkes, M.A., Jane, J., Marmarou, A. & Marshall, L.F. (1990). Neurobehavioral outcome 1 year after severe head injury: experience of the Traumatic Coma Data Bank. *Journal of Neurosurgery*, **73**, 699–709.

Lezak, M.D. (1987). Relationships between personality disorders, social disturbance, and physical disability following traumatic brain injury. *Journal of Head Trauma Rehabilitation*, **2**(1), 57–69.

Lezak, M.D. & O'Brien, K.P. (1990). Chronic emotional, social, and physical changes after traumatic brain injury. In E.D. Bigler (ed.), *Traumatic Brain Injury*, Pro-ed, Austin, pp. 365–380.

Livingston, M.G. & Brooks, D.N. (1988). The burden on families of the brain injured: a review. *Journal of Head Trauma Rehabilitation*, **3**(4), 6–15.

Luria, A.L. (1948). *Restoration of Functions After Brain Trauma* (in Russian). Academy of Medical Science Press, Moscow. Translation published by Pergamon Press, Oxford, 1963.

Newton, A. & Johnson, D.A. (1985). Social adjustment and interaction after severe head injury. *British Journal of Clinical Psychology*, **24**, 225–234.

Novack, T.A., Bergguist, T.F. & Bennett G. (1992). Family involvement in cognitive recovery following traumatic brain injury. In C.J. Long & L. K. Ross (eds), *Handbook of Head Trauma: Acute Care to Recovery*. Plenum Press, New York, pp. 329–353.

Oddy, M., Coughlan, T., Tyerman, A. & Jenkins, D. (1985). Social adjustment after closed head injury: a further follow-up seven years after injury. *Journal of Neurology, Neurosurgery and Psychiatry*, **48**, 564–568.

Prigatano, G.P. (1983). Visual imagery and the corpus callosum: a theoretical note. *Perceptual and Motor Skills*, **56**, 296–298.

Prigatano, G.P. (1989). Bring it up in milieu: toward effective traumatic brain injury rehabilitation interaction. *Rehabilitation Psychology*, **34**(2), 135–144.

Prigatano, G.P. (1991a). Science and symbolism in neuropsychological rehabilitation after brain injury. The Tenth Annual James C. Hemphill Lecture. Rehabilitation Institute of Chicago, Chicago.

Prigatano, G.P. (1991b). Disordered mind, wounded soul: the emerging role of psychotherapy in rehabilitation after brain injury. *Journal of Head Trauma Rehabilitation*, **6**(4), 1–10.

Prigatano, G.P. (1991c). Deficits in social and vocational functioning after traumatic brain injury. *BNI Quarterly*, **7**(1), 32–40.

Prigatano, G.P. (1992a). Personality disturbances associated with traumatic brain injury. *Journal of Consulting and Clinical Psychology*, **60**, 360–368.

Prigatano, G.P. (1992b). Neuropsychological rehabilitation and the problem of altered self-awareness. In N. von Steinbuchel, D.Y. von Cramon & E. Poppel (eds), *Neuropsychological Rehabilitation*. Springer-Verlag, New York, pp. 55–65.

Prigatano, G.P., Amin, K. & Jaramillo (1993). Memory performance and use of a compensation after traumatic brain injury. *Neuropsychological Rehabilitation*, **3**(1), 53–62.

Prigatano, G.P., Fordyce, D.J., Zeiner, H.K., Roueche, J.R., Pepping, M. & Wood, B. (1984). Neuropsychological rehabilitation after closed head injury in young adults. *Journal of Neurology, Neurosurgery and Psychiatry*, **47**, 505–513.

Prigatano, G.P., Glisky, E. & Klonoff, P. (in press). Cognitive rehabilitation after traumatic brain injury. In P.W. Corrigan & S.C. Yudofsky (eds), *Cognitive Rehabilitation of Neuropsychiatric Disorders*.

Prigatano, G.P., Klonoff, P.S., O'Brien, K.P., Altman, I., Amin, K., Chiapello, D.A., Shepherd, J., Cunningham, M. & Mora, M. (1994). Productivity after neuropsychologically oriented, milieu rehabilitation. *Journal of Head Trauma Rehabilitation*, **9**(1), 91–102.

Prigatano, G.P., O'Brien, K.P. & Klonoff, P.S. (1993). Neuropsychological rehabilitation of young adults who suffered brain injury in childhood: clinical observations. *Neuropsychological Rehabilitation*, **3**, 411–421.

Prigatano, G.P., et al. (1986). *Neuropsychological Rehabilitation After Brain Injury*. Johns Hopkins University Press, Baltimore.

Prigatano, G.P. & Schacter, D.L. (1991). *Awareness of Deficit After Brain Injury: Clinical and Theoretical Issues*. Oxford University Press, New York.

Rapaport, D. (1971). *Emotions and Memory*. International Universities Press, New York.

Rattok, J., Ben-Yishay, D., Lakin, P., Piasetsky, E., Ross, B., Silver, S., Vakil, E., Zide, E. & Diller. L. (1992). Outcome of different treatment mixes in a multidimensional neuropsychological rehabilitation program. *Neuropsychology*, **6**, 395–415.

Sohlberg, M.D. & Mateer, C.A. (1987). Training use of compensatory memory books: a three-stage behavioral approach. *Journal of Clinical Experimental Neuropsychology*, **11**, 395–415.

Thomsen, I.V. (1984). Late outcome of very severe blunt head trauma: a 10–15 year second follow up. *Journal of Neurology, Neurosurgery and Psychiatry*, **47**, 260–268.

Thomsen, I.V. (1989). Do young patients have worse outcomes after severe blunt head trauma? *Brain Injury*, **3**(2), 157–162.

Wearing, D. (1992). Self-help groups. In B.A. Wilson & N. Moffat (eds), *Clinical Management of Memory Problems*, 2nd edn. Chapman & Hall, London, pp. 274–302.

Wilson, B. (1991). Long-term prognosis of patients with severe memory disorders. *Neuropsychological Rehabilitation*, **1**, 117–134.

Zangwill, O.L. (1947). Psychological aspects of rehabilitation, in cases of brain injury. *British Journal of Psychology*, **37**, 60–69.

Chapter 26

Accessibility, Reconstruction, and the Treatment of Functional Memory Problems

George A. Bonanno
The Catholic University of America, Washington DC, USA

INTRODUCTION

Historical developments in the treatment of functional memory problems are to some extent a reflection of the larger history of modern psychology. Functional amnesias and conversion disorders were among the most salient problems presented to practitioners of the nineteenth century. Indeed, the intriguing nature of such problems instigated many early therapeutic approaches, including the clinical application of hypnosis by Charcot, Janet, Bernheim and others, as well as Breuer and Freud's inaugural psychoanalytic techniques (Breuer & Freud, 1895/1955). Treatment of such difficulties remained somewhat of a curiosity and was examined primarily within the psychoanalytic domain until the advent of the Second World War. A significant feature of the treatment of "war neurosis" or "shell shock" at that time was the re-enactment of trauma through hypnosis or drug-altered states. The goals of such treatments were, however, relatively short-term and centered primarily around returning soldiers to active combat. Consequently, in the prosperity that followed the war, the notion of functional, trauma-induced disorders was almost completely absent from the literature (Peterson, Prout & Schwarz, 1991).

Two subsequent sets of events instigated a renewed and, in fact, unprecedented interest in functional memory problems that has continued to the present. One precursor was the Vietnam war. The unusual combination of

Handbook of Memory Disorders. Edited by A.D. Baddeley, B.A. Wilson and F.N. Watts.

extreme combat stressors and volatile social climate produced a disquieting array of psychological casualties clearly pointing to the role of functional memory disturbances. The incorporation in 1980 of PTSD as an officially recognized disorder in DSM-III has fostered an empirical and theoretical ferment. Another important set of events was the revolution in cognitive psychology and the return of the notion of unconscious processes as a valid scientific endeavour (Bowers & Meichenbaum, 1984). These latter developments, in particular, produced a rapid advance in our understanding of normal dissociative memory processes and distortions, as well as memory dysfunctions related to actual physical injury and trauma.

The literature on the treatment of functional memory problems, however, has lagged somewhat behind. The sheer magnitude of relevant empirical information has slowed assimilation into the clinical literature. Clinicians almost unavoidably tend to rely most heavily on personal experiences and shared assumptions (Turk & Salovey, 1988). As a consequence, treatment descriptions vary greatly and are not as consistent as they might be with the larger scope of psychological knowledge. This chapter is in part motivated by the need for a more consistent body of clinical theory. With this aim in mind, the chapter first reviews some of the basic assumptions underlying earlier treatment approaches, then some of the literature from the experimental study of normal memory processes. Specifically, it addresses the class of repression-like processes so often attributed to the human response to traumatic events and continually evoked in explanation of apparent stress-related memory disturbances. In follow-up to earlier work (Bonanno, 1990a,b), the chapter discusses the inefficacy of repression-based treatment models and elucidates, instead, a view based on the notions of memory accessibility and reconstruction. The final part of this chapter is devoted to considering the implications of this distinction for a number of treatment issues.

THE REPRESSION MODEL

The original and to some extent still dominant view of functional memory disturbances is based on the notion of repression. In simplified terms, this view holds that disturbing experiences are stored in memory in a fully intact form. Because of the powerful and troubling affects associated with such memories, the mechanism of repression is believed to keep these contents from reaching conscious awareness (Freud, 1915/1957). Repression functions by blocking normal retrieval processes and producing an amnesia-like inability to recall the details, and in extreme cases, the occurrence of distressing events (Kaszniak, Nussbaum, Berren & Santiago, 1988). Unconscious memories find their expression, instead, in the form of conversion disorders and somatic symptoms (Freud, 1926/1966).

Treatment in the context of a repression model inevitably requires that the patient re-experience the antecedent distressing event and consciously accept its occurrence. This was originally achieved through hypnotic induction (Breuer & Freud, 1985/1955), free-association, transference interpretation, and other techniques of the classic psychoanalytic approach (Freud, 1917/1966). Once the repressed memories could be made conscious, the patient's symptoms were expected to abate.

The repression model is still evident in contemporary psychoanalytic approaches to functional memory problems (cf. Lindy, 1986; van der Kolk & Kadish, 1987). Importantly, a number of treatment approaches that are not directly aligned with the psychoanalytic school also appear to utilize techniques based on the repression model. Perhaps the most common evocation of the repression explanation in the literature is the emphasis on the importance of re-experiencing traumatic events (Peterson, Prout & Schwarz, 1991; Williams, 1988). Yet, while it may be effective in many instances to have patients re-experience the original traumatic events, this does not always appear to be a necessary (Bard, Arnone & Nemiroff, 1986) or even an advisable (Ehrlich, 1988; Kinzie, 1988) treatment component.

How, then, might clinicians understand these different circumstances and make informed decisions regarding the most efficacious use of the original trauma in the treatment of functional memory disturbances? The answer to this question lies, at least partially, in a broader understanding of the role of memory representation in ongoing conscious experience and, particularly, in response to traumatic events. Much of the literature from the experimental study of memory processes, for example, clearly indicates that the classic repression model should no longer be considered viable. The general theoretical and clinical implications of this problem have been discussed elsewhere (Bonanno, 1990a,b). The next section briefly reviews some of this evidence and suggests an alternative framework for understanding the treatment of functional memory problems.

THE ACCESSIBILITY MODEL

As noted earlier, the repression view of functional memory problems is based on the notion that a relatively full memory of the antecedent traumatic event is stored in memory but blocked from retrieval and expressed, instead, in the form of symptoms. An overwhelming body of evidence now exists, however, which portrays human encoding, representational and retrieval processes in quite a different light. To begin with, how and what we perceive in any given situation is selective and, thus, incomplete. What and how much might be perceived varies greatly across individuals and situations (Johnson & Dark, 1986). The partial representation of any event, the selected details, is dependent upon these encoding processes and also upon additional cognitive activity, such as the degree that the features of an event are remembered and rehearsed on subsequent occasions, associated with the same event in time, or connected or associated with other events, ideas and categories (Craik & Lockhart, 1972). Factors that influence the encoding and representation of an event over time also influence the degree that the details of the event are *accessible* to retrieval (Crowder, 1985). The accessibility of memory representation is further influenced by, among other things, the compatibility of the encoding and retrieval context (Tulving & Thomson, 1973).

Despite these many influences, we seem to remember in a coherent and fluid narrative. This phenomenon is a product of the fact that autobiographical remembering is a reconstructive process (Barclay, 1986; Bonanno, 1990a; Erdelyi, 1990; Rosenfield, 1988). The capacity limits of the human mind (Fehling, Baars & Fisher, 1990) necessitate that we effectively organize what we experience at each stage of information processing. When we remember something, in essence we are reconstructing an event based on whatever information is *accessible* at that time.

The reconstruction view of human memory does not exclude the *possibility* of repression, or the motivated avoidance of specific contents, at retrieval. Rather, this broader view of memory indicates that repression may be one of several possible explanations for the failure to remember. Yet, there are a growing number of investigators who question even the existence of a specific unconscious repression mechanism at retrieval and, instead, suggest that repression-like phenomena are more likely the result of *conscious* suppression (Erdelyi, 1990) or distraction mechanisms (Bonanno, 1990b; Bonanno, Davis, Singer & Schwartz, 1991). This notion will be explored further in the following pages. Readers wishing a more elaborate review of the literature are directed to Erdelyi (1990), Rubin (1986), Davis (1990), or Hintzman (1990).

ENCODING TRAUMATIC EXPERIENCES AND THE MYTH OF REMEMBRANCE

One implication that the concept of memory accessibility holds for the treatment of functional memory disorders is that sometimes it is not possible to remember the details of a traumatic event, not because they were repressed but because they were never adequately encoded. For example, Williams (1988) describes two types of emotional response that comprise shock reactions to trauma. One type of response is characterized by confusion, disorganization, and an immobilization or inability to perform even simple or routine tasks. This is illustrated, for instance, when robbery victims become so frozen with fear that they are unable to open a cash register drawer. In a second type of response, however, the trauma appears surreal and as if it is not really happening or is occurring in slow motion. The experience of trauma is sometimes associated also with a speeded-up sense of time, or a distortion of the actual sequence of events (Peterson, Prout & Schwarz, 1991). Perceptual experiences in this type of response are described as sometimes having a derealized "out-of-body" quality or as a hysteria-like tunnel vision (Williams, 1980) in which selective aspects of the event are perceived at all. Williams (1988) cites the example of robbery victims who are so transfixed by the assaulter's weapon that they cannot recall the assaulter's face or whether or not others were present. Empirical demonstrations of the phenomenon of "weapon focus" (cf. Kramer, Buckhout & Eugenio, 1990) have also pointed up the attention-narrowing aspect of traumatic events. Other investigators have noted that traumatic events tend to be "remembered" primarily in the "form" of images and bodily sensations, as opposed to conceptual or lexical representations that typically characterize episodic remembrance (Bonanno, 1990a; Horowitz, 1983). Individuals who experience traumatic events may, thus, encode very few details of the actual event or may encode only specific perceptual features of the event and may do so in a distorted manner.

The treatment implication here is that it is potentially harmful for any clinician treating a patient with functional memory difficulties to assume that a full memory of the antecedent trauma is, or will eventually become, available for remembrance. If a clinician presses too strongly for a re-experiencing of the traumatic event, as in the case when the patient is presented with memory cues and asked to relive the event in the context of a therapy group, the patient may become understandably resistant, angered, or may even oblige the clinician by producing a fictitious, distorted remembrance, or a story pieced together from "facts" supplied by others (Silver, 1986).

A sizeable number of empirical investigations of eyewitness testimony have demonstrated, for example, that it is quite easy to bias an individual's recall of an event (Loftus, 1979; Smith & Ellsworth, 1987). The memory for personal history is readily distorted when an individual is motivated to match implicit expectations of what that history should be (Conway & Ross, 1984; Ross, 1989). In a similar vein, a number of factors have been shown to foster confusion quite easily between the memory for imagined events versus those that actually occurred (Johnson & Raye, 1981; Johnson, 1985, 1988). The limited validity of autobiographical recall is compounded further by common findings that personal memories seem quite real phenomenologically even when they are proven false (Brewer, 1986; Johnson, 1985). Memory distortions and augmentations of this nature tend to occur without conscious awareness. Thus, a patient may recall details and events that had never actually taken place, or had not taken place as remembered, and may do so on the basis of implicit cues from the clinician without having any awareness of these cues.

Another potential treatment danger is that patients with functional memory problems may develop their own myths about hidden or repressed memories. My own observations regarding this point suggest that patient's myths can sometimes reflect the theoretical assumptions of clinicians with whom they have worked. Consider the case of a patient "Randy". He served in Vietnam and later evidenced acute anxiety, the inability to concentrate, and intrusive combat memories. While in Vietnam, Randy frequently traveled in and out of combat in the same helicopter with the small circle of men with whom he worked. On one occasion, near the end of his tour of duty, a twist of fate necessitated that Randy board a different helicopter. Tragically, however, the helicopter in which Randy was normally carried was downed in combat and all aboard were killed. The death of his closest companions on a flight he was somehow excused from was the metaphorical straw that broke Randy's back. From that point on, he could no longer keep the distress of war out of his thoughts.

Randy sought respite in a long-overdue leave at a transport station on the Vietnam coast. Yet, several days after his arrival he experienced a fugue-type state and seemed to lose awareness of his current situation. He spent his days wandering the beaches. He had lost track of time. Somehow Randy had also managed to slip through the wartime bureaucracy and, interestingly, had failed to notice that his tour of duty had expired. When he was finally discovered, Randy was immediately flown back to the United States. He had almost no memory of his last days in Vietnam and, with the aid of substance abuse, was able to put the experience out of his mind for a number of years.

The present author's work with Randy began almost 18 years later, just after his first inpatient treatment for PTSD. He felt that he had learned some remarkable "facts" about the workings of his own memory and described the image of specific traumatic memories that had been locked away, as if "walled up in brick" in his mind. He reported that he had uncovered a number of difficult memories during the inpatient treatment and that this had allowed him to feel a little bit better. He also related that he could "sense" that "there are still a few big memories that I haven't got to yet", and felt that these memories would be a source of his dysfunction until he could recall them. It was clear that this expectation was also the belief of Randy's previous treating clinicians.

Unfortunately, the belief in hidden and powerful memories also caused Randy a great deal of anxiety. Because he assumed that these memories must have been quite powerful to require such strong repressions on his part, Randy also assumed that he would be overwhelmed by their magnitude when they were finally retrieved from memory. He tormented himself by seeking out reminders of his past, with the aim of finally freeing himself, but would then become so overwhelmed with anxiety that he doggedly avoided the same reminders.

Clearly, for Randy there was an undeniable draw to uncover the forgotten past. The myth of powerful repressed traumatic memories colored this urge in what seemed to be an unproductive pattern of approach–avoidance anxiety. A more useful technique involved a de-emphasis on the power of unrecovered, seemingly "lost" experiences and, instead, a more explicit focus on the meaning of *remembered* events both currently and across time. The next section reviews the relationship of this procedure and an alternative view of the continuity of human memory related to the organizing principle of narrative construction.

EVOKING THE INITIAL NARRATIVE RECONSTRUCTION

Williams (1988) summarizes his experiences with over 2000 victims of many different types of traumas by stressing that "for a therapeutic intervention to be successful, one must get the story of the trauma in precise detail . . . as clearly and vividly as possible" (p. 324). We have already reviewed the historical notion of repressed memories and seen that this is neither consistent with empirical evidence nor entirely viable as a treatment assumption. The question to ask here is, given the limited validity of autobiographic recall, especially in the case of traumatic memories, why would re-experiencing such memories prove efficacious?

An answer to this question is suggested by the organized and *organizing* nature of reconstructed experience. Narrative reconstructions integrate the past, present and anticipated future and are intimately bound up with our personal sense of identity and purpose (McAdams, 1985, 1991). For this reason, the act of telling and retelling a past experience serves a number of potentially valuable treatment functions. Describing a traumatic event helps patients to structure and organize their often fragmented recollections and various associated emotional responses into somewhat of a coherent narrative picture. The telling and retelling of the antecedent trauma is also highly informative for the treating clinician and serves to guide treatment planning. The traumatic story not only provides whatever details and context that are available to the patient but also indicates in a profound manner the patient's reconstructed experience and the implicit pathogenic meaning.

This is subtle and artful work. The identification and communication of narrative representations requires emotional effort on the patient's part and a consistent measure of self-reflection. Organized representations that are developed over a long period of time become increasingly automated and, thus, operate outside of conscious awareness (Hayes-Roth, 1977; Langer, 1978). Even under normal circumstances, we often remain unaware of the organized "schematic" nature of our beliefs (Greenwald, 1980; Singer & Salovey, 1991) and of our narrative memory reconstructions (Johnson, 1985; Ross, 1989). We tend to cling to these condensed knowledge structures out of the human need to maintain a sense of safety and predictability in a complex world (Kelly, 1955).

An individual who is already traumatized and suffering from the disorganizing effects of functional memory difficulties would be even less able to present a coherent narrative account of the past. One manner in which repressive or dissociative mechanisms at retrieval may operate is to prohibit the simultaneous consideration of various fragmented representations of the same event (Bonanno, 1990b). As noted earlier, traumatic memories may exist in various isolated fragments—fleeting images, a vague but powerful sense of helplessness, a bodily memory of a frantic movement or gesture. The reluctance to re-experience the event leaves these fragments as isolated representations that may intrude "unbidden" (Horowitz, 1983) into conscious experience. Each piece of information related to the traumatic event may capture some feature or form of the experience but, in isolation, lacks a cohesive, narrative element. The "translation" of these various fragments into a unified and integrated representation of a single moment in time also requires that the patient confront the inherent meaning of that moment in time. Clearly, the treatment situation must provide the patient with a sense of safety and trust (Silver, 1986; van der Kolk & Kadish, 1987) to ensure the readiness to make such connections.

Clinicians working in this area often assist patients in reconstructing antecedent events by providing provocative cues, such as historical facts or actual fragments of a patient's history garnered from the treatment records, and if possible audio visual materials related to the event. In the safety of the proper treatment atmosphere, techniques of this sort stimulate retrieval and associative processing.

As a caution, consider a poignant illustration of how such techniques might fail. This example occurred in the context of a research study of conjugal bereavement. Each participant in the study first underwent a structured clinical interview which included a lengthy section on the death event and the grief response. This provided an opportunity for the participant to describe events related to the loss and to communicate some of their more distressing feelings to a clinician perceived as an expert in this area. Each participant then returned for a second, less structured interview in which they were asked to recount narrative memories of the deceased. The present author conducted one of the latter narrative interviews with a severely bereaved woman, Mrs M. Because of a chance confusion in scheduling, Mrs M's narrative interview was conducted before the clinical interview. Thus, she did not have the usual opportunity first to discuss the death of her spouse and to "normalize" some of her responses by describing them to a perceived expert. The result was that Mrs M was virtually unable to recall narrative memories involving herself and her deceased husband. Interestingly, however, when she returned one week later she described her inability to remember during the previous interview but also revealed that she was "flooded with memories" involving her deceased spouse almost immediately upon leaving the interview. The request for memories without first establishing a safe context had evidently made retrieval almost impossible. This example also underscores the importance of gradually building up the narrative reconstruction over a number of sessions.

THE PATHOGENIC MEANING

The essence of any reconstructed story is that it can vary depending upon the elements involved. Each story will hold some form of implicit or explicit meaning. The reconstructions evoked from patients with functional memory difficulties are likely to be the first fully realized narrative versions of the antecedent or dissociated events. The first glimpse of the meaning that these events hold for the patient is also likely to emerge at this time (Lifton, 1988). The perceived randomness or cruelty of traumatic and distressing events is, by its very nature, difficult to understand. Furthermore, experiences that have been dissociated, fragmented or avoided are very likely to be associated with very primitive and frightening meanings. I will refer to this emergent element as the *pathogenic meaning* of the event.

Functional memory disturbances and dissociative states are often character-ized by a sense of depersonalization and derealization (Carlson, 1992). This seems to be at least partially related to the difficulty in sharing the traumatic nature of such events. Such is often the case, for example, with Vietnam veterans who have found it difficult upon their return to the USA to reconcile their combat experiences with the anti-war sentiment of the time.

As another example, severely grieved individuals consistently report that, while family and friends are sympathetic to their loss, they do not feel that they can share some of their deeper and seemingly bizarre reactions, such as pseudo-hallucinations of the deceased. The simple act of organizing and telling the story of the loss, including some of the more distressing subjective reactions, to another who is perceived as an expert and capable of understanding such experiences may be in itself enough to foster assimilation and to reduce dissociative symptoms. Similarly, Williams (1988) emphasizes the importance of telling and retelling the story as a means of reducing survivor guilt.

In many cases, traumatic experiences include violations or disastrous conse-quences which challenge an individual's fundamental sense of safety and well-being in the world (Harber & Pennebaker, 1992; Horowitz, 1986). The pathogenic meaning of the trauma will often color this basic challenge to the self with pre-existing, personal dysfunctional meaning structures; e.g. core conflicted themes (Luborsky, 1984), nuclear scripts (Tomkins, 1979), or negative schemas of the self, world and future (Greenberg & Beck, 1990). The clinician's task here is to help the patient untangle these meanings and to move towards the beginnings of an emotional understanding of the dissociated event(s) in relation to the larger patterns of their life. The adaptive nature of a dissociative response (van der Kolk & Kadish, 1987) must not be underestimated. The association of the pathogenic meaning with larger core issues is likely to be highly volatile for the patient. The therapeutic importance of building a sense of trust is again emphasized. Indeed, for those who have endured extreme traumatic stress and deprivation, such as holocaust survivors and the more recent victims of auto-genocide in Cambodia, exploratory work may be next to impossible (Ehrlich, 1988; Kinzie, 1988). In these cases, merely establishing a safe bond and address-ing general social supports and adaptive issues has proven efficacious (Van Boemel & Rozee, 1992). Such interventions, while not directly addressing dissociated experiences, may nonetheless interact with the patient's more en-compassing narrative understanding of life and to some extent serve to lessen the pathogenic meaning of the traumatic events.

HYPNOSIS AND FUNCTIONAL RETROGRADE AMNESIA

A rare but startling manifestation of psychological trauma is the functional loss of memory for events *prior* to the traumatic occurrence. The many potential avenues for confabulation and distortion that we have already reviewed strongly suggest, however, that such phenomena be considered with great caution. Until recently, reports of functional retrograde amnesia were garnered exclusively from clinical case studies and had not been subject to rigorous quantitative methods. A large number of deliberately falsified amnesias have been reported (e.g. Price & Terhune, 1919), while rigorous empirically-based methods for assessing malingering are only just becoming available (cf. Horton, Smith, Barghout & Connolly, 1992). Yet, sporadic cases of apparently genuine functional retrograde amnesia continue to appear in the literature (cf. Kaszniak, Nussbaum, Berren & Santiago, 1988; Schacter, Wang, Tulving & Freedman, 1982) and, thus, some discussion of their treatment is warranted.

Functional amnesia appears to abate most quickly when poignant reminders of past events are provided. Schacter et al. (1992) describe a carefully studied case of a man so traumatized by the death of his grandfather that he temporarily lost all sense of personal identity, including recall of his own name. A visit by the patient's cousin could not trigger retrieval. The patient's memory returned, however, following the chance viewing of a funeral ceremony during a television programme. The television scene triggered the recent memory of the grandfather's funeral. Within several hours most of the amnesia abated.

One feature of functional retrograde amnesia that distinguishes it from the simple dissociation of trauma is that the unremembered information had been encoded prior to the trauma and is, thus, clearly *available* but rendered temporarily *inaccessible*. We must assume, then, that a retrieval failure has occurred. In explanation of this failure, we might further assume that the patient's dissociated state following the trauma is so different from their state prior to the trauma that ordinary retrieval cues are not effective. Further deduction would suggest that memory for the past would return with the re-emergence of a normal state of consciousness. Thus, functional retrograde amnesia would not be likely to endure for long periods of time. Readers wishing a more detailed discussion of "state-dependent" memory effects are directed to Eich (1980), Matt, Vazquez and Campbell (1992), and Singer and Salovey (1988).

A common clinical approach to functional amnesia involves hypnosis. Yet, a considerable body of data has demonstrated that hypnotized individuals are even more accepting of misleading information and show greater distortion of memory for actual events than do control subjects (McCann & Sheehan, 1988; Murray, Cross & Whipple, 1992; Sheehan, Grigg & McCann, 1984). Of particular relevance are the findings of Sheehan and Statham (1989) which demonstrated that the strongest tendency in hypnotized subjects to distort memories occurred during free recall, a procedure that most closely resembles the clinical situation in functional amnesia. A thorough review of the extensive literature on clinical hypnosis is beyond the scope of this chapter. We might conclude, however, that, given the scope of reconstructive memory processes and the inconclusiveness of hypnotic recall, hypnosis may be best employed to stimulate the retrieval of fragmented or isolated information. This procedure would serve as a means of fostering the gradual associative priming of temporarily inaccessible elements.

An even more cautious approach is suggested in cases of purported "lost" traumatic memories that cannot be easily verified. Kingsbury (1992), for example, reports the case of an adult patient suffering from panic attacks. Both the patient and her previous therapist, it is reported, "had been convinced that the patient had been sexually abused as a child by her father despite the absence of any specific memories" (p. 91). The patient then sought hypnotherapy as a means of uncovering the assumed repressed memory of the trauma. Kingsbury describes a useful approach to hypnosis that embraces the broader functions of the technique and lessens the emphasis on uncovering specific historical events. Hypnosis is described as a method for "self-soothing" and for providing a safe atmosphere to explore dissociated or fragmented meanings. Reframing the past and exploration of meaning are also seen as an important aspect of hypnotic technique. Such an approach should prove quite useful in revealing the pathogenic meaning of past events and in fostering the development, in the patient, of new and more efficacious meaning structures.

PSYCHOSOMATIC MANIFESTATIONS

Another intriguing but also elusive aspect of functional memory problems is their manifestation as psychosomatic dysfunction. The "classic" instances of dissociated memories are found in the abundance of psychosomatic maladies observed in the nineteenth and early twentieth centuries. Numerous reports from this period document first the existence of physical problems (e.g. pain, paralyses) in the absence of an observable physical cause and, then, the apparent alleviation of these symptoms through psychological treatments. The most widely recognized examples from this period are, of course, Freud's poignant case reports, in which the patient's symptoms disappeared virtually immediately following the conscious identification of a traumatic and previously repressed memory (cf. Breuer & Freud, 1985; Freud, 1917/1966).

As psychotherapy advanced in the twentieth century, the notion of psychosomatic manifestation of dissociated memories seems to have taken a back seat to a more subtle and varied array of psychological difficulties. Given the inadequacies of the repression-based view of functional memory problems, we might conclude at this point that the earlier prevalence of such problems might be best attributed to the particular social factors of that historical epoch. This would be a simple enough conclusion were it not for the recent and quite prevalent occurrence of psychosomatic dysfunction in PTSD and, in particular, the recent reports of functional blindness in survivors of the Cambodian holocaust (Rozee & Van Boemel, 1989; Van Boemel & Rozee, 1992).

During the late 1970s, the almost unimaginable autogenocide instigated by the Khmer Rouge government of Cambodia resulted in the death of approximately three million of the country's seven million people. News of these events first received broad public attention in the west through the film "The Killing Fields". While language and cultural barriers made initial study of the refugee survivors extremely difficult, it now seems quite apparent that mass torture and slaughter had occurred on a scale unparalleled since the Nazi holocaust of the Second World War (Kinzie, 1988; Rozee & Van Boemel, 1989). The refugee survivors of this experience were primarily women since most of Cambodia's male population had been killed. The women were taken from their homes, separated from their children, and forced to work in labour camps, often for several years and without adequate food.

Virtually all of the survivors were forced to witness the apparently random torture and execution of family and friends. The graphic nature of this violence dominates each of the survivor's stories. They witnessed others being forced to the edge of mass graves and clubbed from behind. They witnessed others being buried alive or tortured and impaled on bamboo trees. They witnessed infants being beaten to death against trees. Most strikingly, almost all of the survivors reported having been forced to watch the brutal executions of the members of their own families.

A number of Cambodians managed to slip away, sometimes living many months in the jungle, and to cross the Thai border. There they were placed into over-crowded refugee camps when they commonly experienced starvation, disease, and often rape or sexual assault at the hands of the Thai guards. Finally, a relatively small number of these survivors managed to relocate to safer lives in other countries. (For more detailed accounts of the Cambodian holocaust, see Kinzie (1988) and Rozee & Van Boemel (1989).)

Among the female refugees living in Southern California in the USA, it was noted that an inordinate number had lost their sight. Ophthalmological examinations revealed the startling fact that most of these women showed no physical impairments. Thus they exhibited "psychosomatic blindness", as well as a number of other somatic complaints, such as leg pain or dizziness, in the absence of verifiable organic pathology (Rozee & Van Boemel, 1989). The visual acuity in these women was worse the longer they had been held in the labour camps. Those with the poorest visual acuity also tended to have trauma-related nightmares (Rozee & Van Boemel, 1989).

Perhaps the most important treatment consideration related to psychosomatic difficulties is that they seem to represent symbolically the pathogenic meaning of the underlying antecedent events. The almost unimaginable experience of such events, coupled with the perceptual omissions and distortions that often accompany psychological trauma, typically leave survivors more or less unable to comprehend what has happened to them. In the terms of multiple forms or modes of representation (Bonanno, 1990a,b; Bruner, 1964; Bruner et al., 1966; Horowitz, 1983; Johnson, 1992; Leventhal, 1984; Pope & Singer, 1978), only a minimal and primitive conceptual representation of the traumatic event is encoded. The event is represented in memory primarily in the *enactive* (Bruner, 1964; Loewald, 1979) or *imagistic* modes as sensory experiences, motor representations, and crude action sequences. Gestures and other motoric actions, in particular, often represent "separate manifestations of meaning" from those contained in speech and conceptual representations (McNeill, 1989) and may portray the patient's only true, albeit minimal, understanding of the event.

In the case of psychosomatic blindness in Cambodian refugees, the dysfunction symbolizes the "need not to see" (Rozee & Van Boemel, 1989). For these individuals, the representation of the holocaust may consist simply of horrific images and actions or muscular representations of the act of wanting or trying not to see. One survivor stated, for example, "My family was killed in 1975 and I cried for 4 years. When I stopped crying, I was blind" (Rozee & Van Boemel, 1989). Such experiences approximate what Geller (1987) has called "lexically inexpressible" representations, or fleeting glimpses of the past which "stand in closer proximity to actual, immediate physical experience".

Given these conditions, the clinician's task is not to uncover the lost or repressed memories of the antecedent event, which as we have seen may be markedly incomplete, but to provide a conceptual framework from which the patient can begin to develop some understanding of the trauma. The gradual development of comprehension will enable a "translation" of meaning from the enactive and imagistic modes to the lexical/conceptual mode of knowing (Bonanno, 1990b). The association of conceptual understanding will, in turn, alter the entire network of representations of the traumatic event. A broader understanding will produce a richer set of associative connections between representations of the trauma and instigate links with conceptual representations in memory related to similar but less distressing events, including those in which the patients may see themselves as safer or more efficacious human beings (Harber & Pennebaker, 1992). Importantly, understanding also produces an association of the traumatic event with the safety and efficacy of the treatment context (Kingsbury, 1992; Silver, 1986).

These changes render the representations of a traumatic past more accessible and more amenable to conscious control (Bonanno, 1990a,b), thus making their expression in the form of somatic symptoms no longer necessary. Indeed, the research of Pennebaker and colleagues has demonstrated an empirical association between the disclosure of feelings and thoughts related to traumatic memories and a decrease in illness (Pennebaker & Beall, 1986; Pennebaker, Colder & Sharp, 1990; Pennebaker, Kiecolt-Glaser & Glaser, 1988) and an increase in immune functioning (Pennebaker, Kiecolt-Glaser & Glaser, 1988).

Obviously, in some cases this may not be a simple task. The somatic expression in the absence of conceptual understanding indicates that patients might not be able immediately to "talk" about their experiences. In most cases, it is advantageous for therapists to familiarize themselves with the general background information, and cultural and social norms, relevant to the patient's experience (Kinzie, 1988; Van Boemel & Rozee, 1992). Sometimes interventions designed to bolster social skills and community supports are efficacious in that they provide the patient with a firmer base from which to attempt an understanding of their recent experiences (Van Boemel & Rozee, 1992).

THE CLINICAL USEFULNESS OF INTRUSIVE EXPERIENCES

The pathogenic meaning of dissociated experiences may also be assuaged over time. One method for achieving this aim is provided naturally to the clinician in the form of intrusive experiences. Intrusions of dissociated or split-off fragments seem to be to some extent phasic. Horowitz (1986, 1989) has proposed a number of normal sequential stages of stress responding in which the more distressing aspects or memory fragments of traumatic events are first avoided or denied. This allows for an adaptive period of recovery. When the individual has to some extent recovered from the initial stress, the dissociated contents may then intrude into awareness. Nightmares related to the trauma are also quite common (Wood et al., 1992).

A similar process seems to occur following the initial reconstruction of dissociated events. The act of integrating various dissociated memory fragments into a narrative whole naturally enriches—in a sense "primes"—the associative structure of all related information in memory. Any associated memory fragments, such as images, words or body movements, would then be rendered more accessible and, consequently, more likely to intrude into conscious awareness. This is evidenced in normal memory processes as the phenomenon of hypermnesia (Erdelyi, 1990). When distressing or emotionally-charged memory fragments have been dissociated, however, one may anticipate that their intrusion will be accompanied by considerable apprehension.

Clinicians need to help such patients manage this continued emergence of new material. The author has found that it is best to communicate to the patient that, given the nature of human memory, his or her intrusive experiences are natural and perhaps even adaptive. Yet, rather than suggest to the patient that powerful, walled-off memories are waiting to spring out when least expected, it is more helpful to emphasize the emergent understanding that accompanies the intrusive material. Similarly, it may be comforting to remind patients that they have already managed to re-experience significant portions of the past. In essence, the anxiety and fear over what may be uncovered is far more distressing than the actual process of recovery.

Reversal Techniques and the Empty Chair

Another means of collecting associative fragments and fostering the development of a new, emergent meaning is found in Gestalt-like reversal techniques. The patient is first persuaded to imagine that a specific distressing or traumatic event is "reversed" and that what was can be temporarily undone and re-experienced from the vantage point of the present. The patient is then often asked to speak to the past. An empty chair serves as a useful focal point when a specific person is involved. This technique is particularly useful, for example, in cases of severe grief. The survivor may be asked to imagine that the deceased has returned for one final conversation and encouraged to say the things that had been left unsaid. The empty chair has also proven useful in cases of survivor guilt (Williams, 1988).

Writing About the Traumatic Experience

The research of Pennebaker and colleagues (Pennebaker & Beall, 1986; Pennebaker, Colder & Sharp 1990; Pennebaker, Kiecolt-Glaser & Glaser, 1988) has pointed up the usefulness of writing as a therapeutic tool for assimilating traumatic experiences. As noted earlier, their work has demonstrated an association between such disclosure and decreased illness and increased immune function. Recently, Harber and Pennebaker (1992) have emphasized the active, structuring features of writing about traumatic experiences. They note that writing allows an individual to explore traumatic memories under psychologically safe conditions. A therapist might set a time limit for such an exercise to allow for "tolerable limits" of emotional exposure. More importantly, writing about traumatic experience provides an inherent narrative coherence that fosters assimilation into existing knowledge structures.

Cognitive and Cognitive–Behavioral Interventions

Many additional techniques offered by cognitive and cognitive–behavioral theorists may be useful in helping patients access and assimilate dissociated memory contents. For example, Foa and Kozak (1986, 1991) describe exposure treatments for anxiety and phobia problems which involve identifying and then modifying the structure of fear-related memories. This is achieved by first identifying the components of the fear structure: the ideas or situations that provoke fear, the patterns of response, including rituals and avoidant behavior, and the meaning patients ascribe to their own responses, which may include "pathological inferences". The structure of the fear-related memories is then altered and augmented through the benign experience of controlled exposure.

The features of this treatment model may be quite appropriate with functional memory problems which are accompanied by anxiety and fear. The exposure component of Foa and Kozak's model, while perhaps most explicit with specific phobic stimuli, may be broadened to include trauma-related expectations of harm or disaster. The measured exposure to the ideas and situations associated with the traumatic memories will help illuminate patients' response patterns as well as their pathogenic meaning structures. In particular, Foa and Kozak note that response structures which serve the function of helping an individual avoid or escape harm become less necessary as patients habituate during continued exposure. This feature suggests that gradual exposure to ideas and situations related to the antecedent trauma will likewise lessen the propensity toward dissociation or towards the avoidance of rehearsal and elaborative consideration of the trauma. Once dissociated memory fragments and pathogenic meanings associated with traumatic experience are illuminated, treatment may be augmented by a number of other standard cognitive techniques designed to foster the revision of dysfunctional knowledge structures; e.g. helping the patient test the validity of their automatic thoughts (Beck & Emery, 1985) or emphasizing the contrast of the traumatic episode with other more benign or successful episodes (Goldfried & Robins, 1983).

NARRATIVE REVISION AND THE SEARCH FOR ADAPTIVE MEANING

The initial narrative reconstruction and the gradual emergence of dissociated material produces a continually evolving story. In the therapeutic situation, this is also influenced by the feedback of the clinician and the insight gained from the act of telling. The representational network for the dissociated event is gradually "restructured" (Peterson, Prout & Schwarz, 1991; Williams, 1988) and fitted into a larger narrative understanding. The author has elsewhere termed this overall process *narrative revision* (Bonanno, 1990a) and suggested that such a process is, in essence, "the re-evaluation and re-experiencing of the past in the context of a new conceptual framework" (p. 176).

The later stages of therapy are characterized by this emphasis on the broader-based understanding of the trauma. This is not to say that the trauma itself always needs to be understood—some traumatic events may seem so random or cruel that an adequate explanation cannot be provided. Rather, it is the patient's own reaction to the trauma that must be understood. We might even conclude ultimately that such understanding is the only real goal of the treatment. Indeed, Kinzie (1988) has suggested that "explorative or dynamic approaches should be used only to the extent that they provide clarification or meaning of the trauma to the patient" (p. 316).

HYSTERIA, BORDERLINE PERSONALITY, AND THE DISPOSITION TOWARDS PERCEPTUAL COGNITION

Prior to the diagnostic recognition of PTSD in the 1980s, a major portion of the literature on functional memory problems concerned amnesia and dissociation as features of hysteria (Freud, 1917; Sullivan, 1953). As suggested at the beginning of this chapter, much of this earlier literature is dated by its reliance on an outmoded repression model and failure to account for the reconstructive nature of human remembering. More recent proposals of hysterical cognitive styles (Chodoff, 1982; Horowitz, 1977; Horowitz et al., 1984; Shapiro, 1965), borderline disorders (Adler, 1985; Kernberg, 1975), and anaclitic configurations of psychopathology (Blatt & Shichman, 1983) have also included the broader notions of selective attention and characterologic patterns of information processing. While these concepts provide a greater explanatory range, they nonetheless continue to maintain a somewhat ambiguous alliance to the classic repression model.

It has been suggested elsewhere (Bonanno, 1990b) that many of the repression-like memory lapses attributed to hysterical or borderline patients may be more parsimoniously understood as a product of characterological patterns of attention and reconstruction. Consider, for instance, Shapiro's (1965) astute observation that "it is possible that the mode of cognition of hysterical people is, by its nature, particularly conducive to forgetting and the operation of repression" (p. 111). In the same manner as we considered the experience and reconstruction of traumatic events, however, we must consider the characterologic disposition towards repression-like processes as a disposition toward (a) the selective and superficial encoding of the details of events, and (b) the later reluctance or inability to reconstruct the fragmented information into a coherent whole. In this way, the various pieces of information from the same event may be accessible to retrieval but, because they are only minimally associated with each other as an episodic whole, relatively inaccessible. Thus, distressing events are typically experienced in a fragmented, dissociated manner.

Bonanno and Singer (1993) have proposed that such patterns may be viewed as relatively severe manifestations of a more general attentional mode, termed *perceptual cognition*. The defining features of everyday perceptual cognition are a global and superficial focus of attention and a minimization of the experience of the self. Individuals engaged in perceptual processing are less self-conscious and either frequently fail to notice or fail to understand their own personal responses to situations. Consequently, external events tend to be experienced in isolation, divorced from their subjective interpretation, and less well remembered.

Perceptual cognition is contrasted with the greater level of self-focus characteristic of *reflective cognition*. In reflective cognition, it is not the self but the external environment that is minimized. Individuals actively engaged in reflective processing often fail to notice what is going on around them or to selectively process and distort information from the external environment on the basis of an internal frame of reference (Bonanno & Singer, 1993).

A crucial feature of perceptual and reflective processing is that they are "normal" processes that regulate everyday, ongoing conscious experience. Yet, some situations tend to pull more for one type of processing over the other. A range of clinical and empirical evidence suggests that the habitual emphasis of one of these types of processing over the other also typifies a number of personality dispositions. Individuals categorized by questionnaire as repressors (Weinberger, Schwartz & Davidson, 1979), for example, are less self-conscious (Bonanno & Horowitz, 1993), appear to dissociate physiological arousal (Asendorpf & Scherer, 1983; Newton & Contrada, 1992), show a greater ability to ignore specified information (Bonanno, Davis, Singer & Schwartz, 1991), and evidence poorer memory for emotional events (Davis, 1987; Davis & Schwartz, 1986; Hansen & Hansen, 1988). This same pattern is also suggested in specific categories of psychological dysfunction (Bonanno & Singer, 1990). In the case of borderline patients, for example, the tendency towards perceptual cognitive habits produces frequent instances of dissociated experience.

A specific point to consider here is that the cognitive habits of repressors or borderline patients, and others showing a disposition toward perceptual cognition, have served and may continue to serve an adaptive function. Thus, the treating clinician must be cautious in confronting such patients with dissociated and otherwise only superficially experienced memories so as not to threaten too fully this adaptive mechanism. Evidence from a number of sources, for example, suggests that patients with perceptual cognitive habits are best suited by exploratory and evocative approaches which allow a gradual immersion into autobiographical material (Bonanno & Castonguay, 1994).

Similarly, many of the same concerns reviewed earlier in this chapter in relation to traumatic memories may also be applied to patients exhibiting propensities towards perceptual cognition. The limited self-awareness characteristic of perceptual processing suggests that such patients will not be able to articulate a well-developed narrative understanding of specific distressing aspects or events from their lives. After patients are carefully guided towards a more clear, consciously realized narrative, what had previously been only a global pathogenic meaning will also emerge in a more pronounced form. Again, the gradual emergence of fragmented and dissociated memories will foster the processes of narrative revision and the emergence of a new and more adaptive meaning structure.

Patients with memory problems related to their cognitive dispositions may also show improved functioning following interventions aimed at "balancing" reflective and perceptual cognition (Bonanno & Castonguay, 1994). For example, Horowitz (1977) has described encouraging patients with an hysterical cognitive style to pay closer attention to the specific details of events and situations rather than to global perceptions. Similarly, Orne (cited in Chodoff, 1982) has suggested having such patients review audio tapes of themselves in psychotherapy so that they may develop a greater capacity for self-reflection.

SUMMARY

This chapter began by discussing the limitations of treatment approaches based on the repression model (motivated blockage of retrieval) and, as an alternative, described a view of memory based on the concepts of accessibility and narrative reconstruction. Applying this approach to functional memory problems de-emphasizes the importance of remembering and recounting the details of antecedent traumatic events and places crucial emphasis, instead, on the subjective meaning of the antecedent events in the context of a gradually emerging narrative understanding. This distinction was elaborated upon through discussion of specific features of functional memory problems, such as intrusive experiences, psychosomatic manifestations, and the distinction between pathogenic and adaptive meaning, and specific issues of clinical technique, such as memory falsification and distortion, the uses of hypnosis, and the consideration of individual differences.

REFERENCES

Adler, G. (1985). *Borderline Psychopathology and its Treatment*. Basic Books, New York.

Asendorpf, J.B. & Scherer, K.R. (1983). The discrepant repressor: differentiation between low anxiety, high anxiety, and repression of anxiety by autonomic–facial–verbal patterns of behavior. *Journal of Personality and Social Psychology*, **45**, 1334–1346.

Barclay, C.B. (1986). Schematization of autobiographical memory. In D.S. Rubin (ed.), *Autobiographical Memory*. Cambridge University Press, Cambridge, pp. 82-99.

Beck, A.T. & Emery, G. (1985). *Anxiety Disorders and Phobias: A Cognitive Perspective*. Basic Books, New York.

Blatt, S.J. & Shichman, S. (1983). Two primary configurations of psychopathology. *Psychoanalysis and Contemporary Thought*, **6**, 187–254.

Bonanno, G.A. (1990a). Remembering and psychotherapy. *Psychotherapy*, **27**, 175–186.

Bonanno, G.A. (1990b). Repression, accessibility, and the translation of private experience. *Psychoanalytic Psychology*, **7**, 453–474.

Bonanno, G.A. & Castonguay, L. (1994). On balancing approaches to psychotherapy: prescriptive patterns of attention, motivation, and personality. *Psychotherapy*, in press.

Bonanno, G.A., Davis, P.J., Singer, J.L. & Schwartz, G.E. (1991). The repressor personality and avoidant information processing: a dichotic listening study. *Journal of Research in Personality*, **25**, 386–401.

Bonanno, G.A. & Horowitz, M.J. (1993). Dispositional threat avoidance: a comparison of repressors, blunters, and self-deceivers in a normative and a bereaved sample. Unpublished manuscript, University of California, San Francisco.

Bonanno, G.A. & Singer, J.L. (1990). Repressor personality style: theoretical and methodological implications for health and pathology. In J.L. Singer (ed.), *Repression and Dissociation*. University of Chicago Press, Chicago pp. 435-470.

Bonanno, G.A. & Singer, J.L. (1993). Controlling one's stream of thought through perceptual and reflective processing. In D. Wegner & J. Pennebaker (eds), *Handbook of Mental Control*. Prentice Hall, New York.

Bowers, K.S. & Meichenbaum, D. (1984). *The Unconscious Reconsidered*. Wiley, New York.

Breuer, J. & Freud, S. (1895/1955). Studies on hysteria. In J. Strachey (ed.), *The Standard Edition of the Complete Psychological Works of Sigmund Freud*, vols 4&5. Hogarth, London.

Brewer, W.F. (1986). What is autobiographical memory? In D.S. Rubin (ed.), *Autobiographical Memory*. Cambridge University Press, Cambridge, pp. 25–49.

Bruner, J.S. (1964). The course of cognitive growth. *American Psychologist*, **19**, 1–15.

Bruner, J.S., Oliver, R.R., Greenfield, F.M., et al. (1966). *Studies in Cognitive Growth*. John Wiley, New York.

Carlson, E.B. (1992). Studying the interaction between physical and psychological states with the Dissociative Experiences Scale. In D.A. Spiegel (ed.), *Dissociation: Mind and Body*. American Psychiatric Press, Washington, DC.

Chodoff, P. (1982). The hysterical personality disorder: a psychotherapeutic approach. In A. Roy (ed.), *Hysteria*. John Wiley, New York, pp. 277–285.

Conway, M. & Ross, M. (1984). Getting what you want by revising what you had. *Journal of Personality and Social Psychology*, **47**, 738–748.

Craik, F.I.M. & Lockhart, R.S. (1972). Levels of processing: a framework for memory research. *Journal of Verbal Learning and Verbal Behavior*, **11**, 671–684.

Crowder, R.G. (1985). On access and the forms of memory. In N.M. Weinberger, J.L. McGaugh & G. Lynch (eds), *Memory Systems of the Brain*. Guilford, New York, pp. 433–441

Davis, P.J. (1987). Repression and the inaccessibility of affective memories. *Journal of Personality and Social Psychology*, **53**, 585–593.

Davis, P.J. (1990). Repression and the inaccessibility of emotional memories. In J.L. Singer (ed.), *Repression and Dissociation*. University of Chicago Press, Chicago.

Davis, P.J. & Schwartz, G.E. (1987). Repression and the inaccessibility of emotional memories. *Journal of Personality and Social Psychology*, **52**, 155–163.

Eich, J.E. (1980). The cue-dependent nature of state-dependent retrieval. *Memory and Cognition*, **8**, 157–173.

Ehlich, P. (1988). Treatment issues in the psychotherapy of holocaust survivors. In J.P. Wilson, Z. Harel & B. Kahana (eds), *Human Adaptation to Extreme Stress*. Plenum, New York, pp. 285-304.

Erdelyi, M. (1990). Repression, reconstruction, and defense: history and integration of psychoanalytic and experimental frameworks. In J.L. Singer (ed.), *Repression and Dissociation*. University of Chicago Press, Chicago, pp. 1–32.

Fehling, M., Baars, B. & Fisher, C. (1990). A functional role for repression in an autonomous, resource-constrained agent. *Program of the XII Annual Conference of the Cognitive Science Society*. Erlbaum, Hillsdale, NJ.

Foa, E.B. & Kozak, M.J. (1986). Emotional processing of fear: exposure to corrective information. *Psychological Bulletin*, **99**, 20–35.

Foa, E.B. & Kozak, M.J. (1991). Emotional processing: theory, research and clinical implications for anxiety disorders. In J.D. Safran & L.S. Greenberg (eds), *Emotion, Psychotherapy and Change*. Guilford, New York, pp. 21–49.

Freud. S. (1915/1957). Repression. In J. Strachey (ed.), *The Standard Edition of the Complete Psychological Works of Sigmund Freud*, vol. 14. Hogarth, London, pp. 146-158.

Freud, S. (1917/1966). Introductory lectures on psychoanalysis. In J. Strachey (ed.), *The Standard Edition of the Complete Psychological Works of Sigmund Freud*, vols 15 & 16. Hogarth, London.

Freud, S. (1926/1966). Inhibition, symptoms and anxiety. In J. Strachey (ed.), *The Standard Edition of the Complete Psychological Works of Sigmund Freud*, vol 20. Hogarth, London, pp. 87-172.

Geller, J.D. (1987). The process of psychotherapy: separation and the complex interplay among empathy, insight and internalization. In J. Bloom-Feshback & S. Bloom-Feshback (eds), *The Psychology of Separation and Loss*. Jossey-Bass, San Francisco.

Goldfried, M.R. & Robins, C. (1983). Self-schema, cognitive bias, and the processing of therapeutic experiences. In P.C. Kendal (ed.), *Advances in Cognitive–Behavioral Research and Therapy*, vol. 2. Academic Press, New York, pp. 35-80.

Greenberg, M.S. & Beck, A.T. (1990). Cognitive approaches to psychotherapy: theory and therapy. In R. Plutchik & H. Kellerman (eds), *Emotion: Theory, Research and Experience*, vol. 5. Academic Press, New York, pp. 177-194.

Greenwald, A.G. (1980). The totalitarian ego: fabrication and revision of personal history. *American Psychologist*, **35**, 603–618.

Hansen, R.D. & Hansen, C.H. (1988). Repression of emotionally tagged memories: the architecture of less complex emotions. *Journal of Personality and Social Psychology*, **55**, 811–818.

Harber, K.D. & Pennebaker, J.W. (1992). Overcoming traumatic memories. In S.-A. Christianson (ed.), *The Handbook of Emotion and Memory: Research and Theory*. Erlbaum, Hillsdale, NJ, pp. 359-387.

Hayes-Roth, B. (1977). Evolution of cognitive structures and processes. *Psychological Review*, **84**, 260-278.

Hintzman, D.L. (1990). Human learning and memory: connections and dissociations. *Annual Review of Psychology*, **41**, 109-139.

Horton, K.D., Smith, S.A., Barghout, N.K. & Connolly, D. (1992). The use of indirect memory tests to assess malingered amnesia: a study of metamemory. *Journal of Experimental Psychology: General*, **121**, 326-351.

Horowitz, M.J. (1977). *Hysterical Personality*. Aronson, New York.

Horowitz, M.J. (1983). *Image Formation and Psychotherapy*. Aronson, New York.

Horowitz, M.J. (1986). *Stress Response Syndromes*, 2nd edn. Aronson, Northvale, NJ.

Horowitz, M.J. (1989). A model of mourning: changes in schemas of self and other. *Journal of the American Psychoanalytic Association*, **38**, 297-324.

Horowitz, M.J., Marmar, C., Krupnick, J., Wlner, N., Kalteider, N. & Wallerstein, R. (1984). *Personality Styles and Brief Psychotherapy*. Basic Books, New York.

Johnson, M.K. (1985). The origin of memories. In P.C. Kendall (ed.), *Advances in Cognitive-Behavioral Research and Therapy*, vol. 4. Academic Press, New York.

Johnson, M.K. (1988). Reality monitoring: an experimental phenomenological approach. *Journal of Experimental Psychology: General*, **117**, 390-394.

Johnson, M.K. (1992). MEM: mechanisms of recollection. *Journal of Cognitive Neuroscience*, **4**, 268-280.

Johnson, M.K. & Raye, C.L. (1981). Reality monitoring. *Psychological Review*, **88**, 67-85.

Johnson, W.A. & Dark, V.J. (1986). Selective attention. *Annual Review of Psychology*, **37**, 43-75.

Kaszniak, A.W., Nussbaum, P.D., Berren, M.R. & Santiago, J. (1988). Amnesia as a consequence of male rape: a case report. *Journal of Abnormal Psychology*, **97**, 100-104.

Kelly, G.A. (1955). *The Psychology of Personal Constructs. Vol. 1, A Theory of Personality*. Norton, New York.

Kernberg, O. (1975). *Borderline Conditions and Pathological Narcissism*. Aronson, New York.

Kingsbury, S.J. (1992). Strategic psychotherapy for trauma: hypnosis and trauma in context. *Journal of Traumatic Stress*, **5**, 85-95.

Kinzie, J.D. (1988). The psychiatric effects of massive trauma on Cambodian refugees. In J.P. Wilson, Z. Harel & B. Kahana (eds), *Human Adaptation to Extreme Stress*. Plenum, New York, pp. 305-318.

Kramer, T.H., Buckhout, R. & Eugenio, P. (1990). Weapon focus, arousal, and eyewitness memory: attention must be paid. *Law and Human Behavior*, **14**, 167-184.

Langer, E.J. (1978). Rethinking the role of thought in social interactions. In J. Harvey, W. Ickes & R. Kidd (eds), *New Directions in Attribution Research*, vol 2. Erlbaum, Hillsdale, NJ.

Leowald, H. (1979). Reflections on the psychoanalytic process and its therapeutic potential. *Psychoanalytic Study of the Child*, **34**, 155-167.

Leventhal, H. (1984). A perceptual-motor theory of emotion. *Advances in Experimental Social Psychology*, **17**, 117-182.

Lifton, R.J. (1988). Understanding the traumatized self. In J.P. Wilson, Z. Harel & B. Kahana (eds), *Human Adaptation to Extreme Stress*. Plenum, New York, pp. 7-31.

Lindy, J.D. (1986). An outline for the psychoanalytic psychotherapy of Post-Traumatic Stress Disorder. In C.R. Figley (ed.), *Trauma and Its Wake, Vol. II: Traumatic Stress Theory, Research, and Intervention*. Brunner/Mazel, New York, pp. 195-212.

Loftus, E.F. (1979). *Eyewitness Testimony*. Harvard University Press, Cambridge, MA.

Luborsky, L. (1984). *Principles of Psychoanalytic Psychotherapy: A Manual for Supportive-Expressive (SE) Treatment*. Basic Books, New York.

Matt, G.E., Vazquez, C. & Campbell, W.K. (1992). Mood-congruent recall of affectively toned stimuli: a meta-analytic review. *Clinical Psychology Review*, **12**, 227–255.

McAdams, D.P. (1985). *Power, Intimacy, and the Life Story: Personological Inquiries into Identity*. Guilford, New York.

McAdams, D.P. (1991). The development of a narrative identity. In D.M. Buss & N. Cantor (eds), *Personality Psychology: Recent Trends and Emerging Directions*. Springer-Verlag, New York.

McCann, T. & Sheehan, P. (1988). Hypnotically induced pseudomemories—sampling conditions among hypnotizable subjects. *Journal of Personality and Social Psychology*, **54**, 339–346.

McNeill, D. (1989). A straight path—to where? A reply to Butterworth and Hadar. *Psychological Review*, **94**, 175–179.

Murray, G.J., Cross, H.J. & Whipple, J. (1992). Hypnotically created pseudomemories: further investigation into the "Memory distortion or response bias" question. *Journal of Abnormal Psychology*, **101**, 75–77.

Newton, T.L. & Contrada, R.J. (1992). Repressive coping and verbal–autonomic response dissociation: the influence of social context. *Journal of Personality and Social Psychology*, **62**, 159–167.

Pennebaker, J.W. & Beall, S.K. (1986). Confronting a traumatic event: toward an understanding of inhibition and disease. *Journal of Abnormal Psychology*, **85**, 274–281.

Pennebaker, J.W., Colder, M. & Sharp, L. (1990). Accelerating the coping process. *Journal of Personality and Social Psychology*, **58**, 528–537.

Pennebaker, J.W., Kiecolt-Glaser, J. & Glaser, R. (1988). Disclosure of traumas and immune function: health implications for psychotherapy. *Journal of Consulting and Clinical Psychology*, **56**, 239–245.

Peterson, K.C., Prout, M.F. & Schwarz, R.A. (1991). *Post-Traumatic Stress Disorder: A Clinician's Guide*. Plenum, New York.

Pope, K.E. & Singer, J.L. (1978). Regulation of the stream of consciousness: toward a theory of ongoing thought. In G.E. Schwartz & D. Shapiro (eds), *Consciousness and Self-Regulation*, vol. 2. Plenum, New York.

Price, G.E. & Terhune, W.B. (1919). Feigned amnesia as a defense reaction. *Journal of the American Medical Association*, **72**, 565–567.

Rosenfield, I. (1988). *The Invention of Memory*. Basic Books, New York.

Ross, M. (1989). Relation of implicit theories to the construction of personal histories. *Psychological Review*, **96**, 341–357.

Rozee, P. & Van Boemel, G. (1989). The psychological effects of war trauma and abuse on older Cambodian refugee women. *Women and Therapy*, **8**, 23–50.

Rubin, D.C. (1986). *Autobiographical Memory*. Cambridge University Press, Cambridge.

Schacter, D.L., Wang, P., Tulving, E. & Freedman, M. (1982). Functional retrograde amnesia: a qualitative case study. *Neuropsychologia*, **20**, 523–532.

Shapiro, D. (1965). *Neurotic Style*. Basic Books, New York.

Sheehan, P.W., Grigg L. & McCann, T. (1984). Memory distortion following exposure to false information in hypnosis. *Journal of Abnormal Psychology*, **93**, 259–265.

Sheehan, P.W., & Statham, D. (1989). Hypnosis, the timing of its introduction, and acceptance of misleading information. *Journal of Abnormal Psychology*, **98**, 170–176.

Silver, S.M. (1986). An inpatient program for Post-Traumatic Stress Disorder: content as treatment. In C.R. Figley (ed.), *Trauma and its Wake. Vol. II: Traumatic Stress Theory, Research and Intervention*. Brunner/Mazel, New York, pp. 213–231.

Singer, J.A. & Salovey, P. (1988). Mood and memory: evaluating the network theory of affect. *Clinical Psychology Review*, **2**, 211–251.

Singer, J.L. & Salovey, P. (1991). Organized knowledge structures and personality. In M.J. Horowitz (ed.), *Person Schemas and Maladaptive Interpersonal Patterns*. University of Chicago Press, Chicago, pp. 33-80.

Smith, V.L. & Ellsworth, P.C. (1987). The social psychology of eyewitness accuracy: misleading questions and communicator expertise. *Journal of Applied Psychology*, **72**, 294–300.

Sullivan, H.S. (1940). *Conception of Modern Psychiatry*. Norton, New York.

Sullivan, H.S. (1953). *The Interpersonal Theory of Psychiatry*. Norton, New York.

Tomkins, S.S. (1979). Script theory: differential magnification of affects. In H. E. Howe (ed.), *Nebraska Symposium on Motivation*, vol. 26. University of Nebraska Press, Lincoln NB.

Tulving, E. & Thomson, D.M. (1973). Encoding specificity and retrieval processes in episodic memory. *Psychological Review*, **80**, 352–373.

Turk, D.C. & Salovey, P. (1988). *Reasoning, Inference and Judgment in Clinical Psychology*. Free Press, New York.

Van Boemel, G.B. & Rozee, P.D. (1992). Treatment for psychosomatic blindness among Cambodian refugee women. *Women and Therapy*, **13**, 239–266.

Van der Kolk, B.A. & Kadish, W. (1987). Amnesia, dissociation, and the return of the repressed. In B.A. van der Kolk (ed.), *Psychological Trauma*. American Psychiatric Press, Washington, DC.

Weinberger, D.A., Schwartz, G.E. & Davidson, J.R. (1979). Low-anxious and repressive coping styles: psychometric patterns of behavioral and physiological responses to stress. *Journal of Abnormal Psychology*, **88**, 369–380.

Williams, T. (1988). Diagnosis and treatment of survivor guilt: the bad penny syndrome. In J.P. Wilson, Z. Harel & B. Kahana (eds), *Human Adaptation to Extreme Stress*. Plenum, New York, pp. 319-336.

Wood, J.M., Bootzin, R.R., Rosenham, D., Nolen-Hoeksema, S. & Jourdan, F. (1992). Effects of the 1989 San Francisco earthquake on frequency and content of nightmares. *Journal of Abnormal Psychology*, **101**, 219–224.

Index

Index compiled by Caroline Sheard

Wiley Titles of related interest

HANDBOOK OF SPELLING
THEORY, PROCESS AND INTERVENTION
Edited by Gordon D.A. Brown *and* Nick C. Ellis

Brings together international and interdisciplinary research to provide an edited collection on theoretical advances of normal and disturbed spelling over the last decade, and examines the implications for rehabilitation and interventions.
0-471-94342-8 560pp 1994

WORRYING
PERSPECTIVES ON THEORY, ASSESSMENT AND TREATMENT
Edited by Graham Davey *and* Frank Tallis

Places the experience and function of worry in the context of the latest developments in cognitive and behavioural therapy. The book outlines how worry may be assessed; how it may affect people throughout the lifespan—in children, adults and the elderly; and shows what new developments exist in the treatment of worrying.
0-471-94114-X 328pp 1994

THE PSYCHOLOGY OF DEMENTIA
Edgar Miller *and* Robin Morris

Provides a valuable contribution to the literature on this debilitating condition. Including an up-to-date discussion of recent developments, practical aspects of assessment and management, the book also considers the impact on the sufferer's family.
0-471-92776-7 216pp 1993

THE PSYCHOLOGY OF INTERROGATIONS, CONFESSIONS AND TESTIMONY
Gisli H. Gudjonsson

Brings together knowledge of the vulnerabilities of witnesses and integrates this with research on interviewing skills and practice in a way which is both academically innovative and practically useful.
0-471-92663-9 376pp 1992

COGNITIVE PSYCHOLOGY AND EMOTIONAL DISORDERS
J. Mark G. Williams, Fraser N. Watts, Colin Macleod *and* Andrew Mathews

"... a psychological landmark."

British Journal of Psychology

0-471-92966-2 236pp 1990